THE ASHGATE RESEARCH COMPANION
TO THEOLOGICAL ANTHROPOLOGY

An invigoratingly diverse collection of essays focused on the Christian understanding of human nature in general and its bearing the image of God in particular; it would serve as an excellent introduction to the developing interest shown by analytic theology in these and related topics.

T.J. Mawson, University of Oxford, UK

This Ashgate volume, brilliantly crafted by first-rate scholars from multiple disciplines, is a paragon of excellence for research companions. Rigorous, well informed, and refreshingly insightful, it is a tour de force of theological anthropology!

Chad Meister, Bethel College, USA

Excellent in breadth and depth of treatment of relevant topics, with an international group of contributors, senior scholars and scholars newer to their fields but already published therein, this is a superb contribution to the fresh interest in theological anthropology, which it expands, develops, and encourages.

Keith E. Yandell, University of Wisconsin–Madison, USA

ASHGATE
RESEARCH
COMPANION

The *Ashgate Research Companions* are designed to offer scholars and graduate students a comprehensive and authoritative state-of-the-art review of current research in a particular area. The companions' editors bring together a team of respected and experienced experts to write chapters on the key issues in their speciality, providing a comprehensive reference to the field.

The Ashgate Research Companion to Theological Anthropology

Edited by

JOSHUA R. FARRIS

Houston Baptist University and Trinity School of Theology, USA

CHARLES TALIAFERRO

St Olaf College, USA

Routledge
Taylor & Francis Group

LONDON AND NEW YORK

First published 2015 by Ashgate Publishing

Published 2016 by Routledge
2 Park Square, Milton Park, Abingdon, Oxfordshire OX14 4RN
711 Third Avenue, New York, NY 10017, USA

First issued in paperback 2017

Routledge is an imprint of the Taylor & Francis Group, an informa business

British Library Cataloguing in Publication Data
A catalogue record for this book is available from the British Library

Library of Congress Cataloging-in-Publication Data
The Ashgate research companion to theological anthropology / Edited by Joshua Ryan Farris and Charles Taliaferro.
    pages cm
  Includes index.
  ISBN 978-1-4724-1093-1 (hardcover)
1. Theological anthropology. I. Farris, Joshua Ryan, editor. II. Taliaferro, Charles, editor.
  BL256.A84 2015
  233—dc23

                                                                                    2014033445

ISBN 13: 978-1-138-05156-0 (pbk)
ISBN 13: 978-1-4724-1093-1 (hbk)

Contents

List of Contributors   *ix*
Foreword   *xiii*
Preface   *xvii*
Acknowledgments   *xix*

Introduction   1
Joshua R. Farris and Charles Taliaferro

PART I   METHODOLOGY IN THEOLOGICAL ANTHROPOLOGY

1   The Madness in Our Method: Christology as the Necessary Starting Point
     for Theological Anthropology   15
     Marc Cortez

2   Scripture and Philosophy on the Unity of Body and Soul:
     An Integrative Method for Theological Anthropology   27
     John W. Cooper

PART II   THEOLOGICAL ANTHROPOLOGY, THE BRAIN, THE BODY, AND THE SCIENCES

3   Evolutionary Biology and Theological Anthropology   45
     Joshua M. Moritz

4   Theological Anthropology and the Cognitive Sciences   57
     Aku Visala

5   Theological Anthropology and the Brain Sciences   73
     Daniel N. Robinson

6   Feminism and Theological Anthropology   81
     Emilie Judge-Becker and Charles Taliaferro

PART III   MODELS FOR THEOLOGICAL ANTHROPOLOGY

7   Self-Organizing Personhood: Complex Emergent Developmental Linguistic
     Relational Neurophysiologicalism   91
     Warren S. Brown and Brad D. Strawn

8   Physicalism, Bodily Resurrection, and the Constitution Account   103
    Omar Fakhri

9   Anthropological Hylomorphism   113
    Bruno Niederbacher, S.J.

10 Substance Dualism   125
    Stewart Goetz

11 The Human Person as Communicative Event: Jonathan Edwards on the
    Mind/Body Relationship   139
    Marc Cortez

12 Why Emergence?   151
    William Hasker

PART IV   THEOLOGICAL MODELS OF THE *IMAGO DEI*

13 A Substantive (Soul) Model of the *Imago Dei*: A Rich Property View   165
    Joshua R. Farris

14 Why the *Imago Dei* Should Not Be Identified with the Soul   179
    Joel B. Green

15 The Dual-Functionality of the *Imago Dei* as Human Flourishing in the
    Church Fathers   191
    Fr. David Vincent Meconi, S.J.

16 Ecclesial-Narratival Model of the *Imago Dei*   207
    Dominic Robinson, S.J.

17 A Christological Model of the *Imago Dei*   217
    Oliver Crisp

PART V   HUMAN NATURE, FREEDOM, AND SALVATION

18 Free Will and the Stages of Theological Anthropology   233
    Kevin Timpe and Audra Jenson

19 Human Beings, Compatibilist Freedom, and Salvation   245
    Paul Helm

PART VI   HUMAN BEINGS IN SIN AND SALVATION

20 Created Corruptible, Raised Incorruptible: The Importance of
    Hylomorphic Creationism to the Free Will Defense   261
    Nathan A. Jacobs

21   Redemption of the Human Body   277
     Adam G. Cooper

22   Redemption, the Resurrected Body, and Human Nature   293
     Stephen T. Davis

23   Theosis and Theological Anthropology   303
     Ben C. Blackwell and Kris A. Miller

24   Glory and Human Nature   319
     Charles Taliaferro

PART VII   CHRISTOLOGICAL THEOLOGICAL ANTHROPOLOGY

25   The Mortal God: Materialism and Christology   331
     Glenn Andrew Peoples

26   Hylomorphic Christology   345
     Josef Quitterer

27   A Cartesian Approach to the Incarnation   355
     J.H.W. Chan

Index   *369*
Index of Scripture References   *381*

From Joshua, to Jenna for teaching me what it means to be human.

From Charles, to my students with gratitude and love.

List of Contributors

William Abraham is Albert Cook Outler Professor of Wesley Studies at SMU Perkins School of Theology.

Ben C. Blackwell is Assistant Professor and Chair in the Theology Department at Houston Baptist University. Blackwell has contributed a few pieces at the intersection of patristic theology and New Testament studies.

Warren S. Brown is Professor of Psychology and Director of the Lee Travis Research Institute at the Fuller Graduate School of Psychology.

J.H.W. Chan has completed a postdoctoral fellowship in philosophy at Heythrop College, University of London. He is currently a consultant in theology and contemporary religious issues in Kuala Lumpur, Malaysia.

Adam G. Cooper, STD, PhD, STL, is a senior lecturer and permanent fellow at the John Paul II Institute for Marriage and Family, Melbourne. His research and teaching areas cover Greek patristics and theological anthropology, with special focus on deification and the theology of the body.

John W. Cooper is Professor of Philosophical Theology at Calvin Theological Seminary. He has been at the forefront of the monism and dualism debate in Christian thought (*Body, Soul and Life Everlasting*).

Marc Cortez is Associate Professor of Theology at Wheaton College. He is the author of *Embodied Souls, Ensouled Bodies: An Exercise in Christological Anthropology and Its Significance for the Mind/Body Debate* and *Theological Anthropology: A Guide for the Perplexed*.

Oliver Crisp is Professor of Systematic Theology at Fuller Theological Seminary. He is the senior editor of the *Journal of Analytic Theology* and has contributed to several journals in philosophy of religion and theology.

Stephen T. Davis is the Russell K. Pitzer Professor of Philosophy at Claremont McKenna College. He has published works in philosophy of religion, resurrection, Christology, and the mind-body problem.

Omar Fakhri is currently completing his PhD in philosophy at the University of California, Berkeley. His main areas of research are metaphysics, epistemology, and philosophical theology.

Joshua R. Farris is currently finishing his doctoral research on substance dualism and theological anthropology. He is Assistant Professor of Theology, Houston Baptist University. He is also founder and director of Trinity School of Theology.

Stewart Goetz is the Ross Frederick Wicks Distinguished Professor in Philosophy and Religion at Ursinus College. Goetz is the senior editor of the Bloomsbury book series *Bloomsbury Studies in Philosophy and Religion*.

Joel B. Green is Professor of New Testament Interpretation and Associate Dean for the Center for Advanced Theological Studies, Fuller Theological Seminary.

William Hasker is Professor Emeritus of Philosophy at Huntington University, where he taught from 1966 until 2000. He was the editor of *Christian Scholar's Review* from 1985 to 1994, and the editor of *Faith and Philosophy* from 2000 until 2007.

Paul Helm was Professor of the History and Philosophy of Religion at King's College, London, 1993–2000.

Nathan A. Jacobs is Lecturer in Philosophy at the University of Kentucky.

Audra Jenson is a philosophy student at Northwest Nazarene University, as well as a Visiting Student at Wycliffe Hall, Oxford University.

Emilie Judge-Becker is an author and musician currently living in Minneapolis; she has studied philosophy, film, and music at St Olaf College, Smith College, and the University of Florence.

David Vincent Meconi, S.J., is Assistant Professor of Theology in the Department of Theological Studies at Saint Louis University; he is also the editor of *Homiletic and Pastoral Review*. He holds the pontifical license in Patrology from the University of Innsbruck and the DPhil in Ecclesiastical History from Oxford University.

Kris A. Miller recently completed research on the religious epistemology of Thomas Torrance at Durham University, and works for the national office of the Vineyard church.

Joshua M. Moritz is Lecturer of Philosophical Theology and the Natural Sciences at the Graduate Theological Union in Berkeley, Adjunct Professor of Philosophy at the University of San Francisco, and Academic Editor of the journal *Theology and Science*.

Bruno Niederbacher, S.J., is Associate Professor of Philosophy in the Department of Christian Philosophy at the University of Innsbruck.

Glenn Andrew Peoples graduated in theology (MTheol, distinction) and philosophy (PhD) from the University of Otago in Dunedin, New Zealand. He is a scholar at the forefront of the Rethinking Hell organization and a published defender of Christian materialism.

Josef Quitterer studied philosophy and theology at the University of Regensburg and the Gregorian University in Rome; has visiting professorships in Frankfurt, Rome, and New Orleans; and since 2001 is Associate Professor for Philosophy at the Theological Faculty of the University of Innsbruck.

Daniel N. Robinson is Distinguished Professor Emeritus, Georgetown University and Fellow of the Faculty of Philosophy, Oxford University.

Dominic Robinson is currently a lecturer in Dogmatic and Pastoral Theology at Heythrop College, University of London, while also working in adult religious education in the Archdiocese of Westminster, in parish ministry and as assistant superior of the Mount Street Jesuit Community in central London.

Brad D. Strawn received his graduate degrees from Fuller Theological Seminary where he now serves as the Evelyn and Frank Freed Professor for the Integration of Psychology and Theology.

Charles Taliaferro is Professor and Chair of the Philosophy department at St Olaf College. He has given public lectures in several universities including Yale, Princeton, NYU, Oxford, Cambridge, University of St Andrews to name just a few.

Kevin Timpe is Professor of Philosophy at Northwest Nazarene University, and formally a Research Fellow at St Peter's College, University of Oxford, UK.

Aku Visala works at the intersection of cognitive science, philosophy, and theology. He has held research positions in the Ian Ramsey Centre for Science and Religion at the University of Oxford and the Center of Theological Inquiry in Princeton. He was a postdoctoral researcher in the Department of Anthropology at the University of Notre Dame, USA. Presently, he is Senior Researcher of Theology, University of Helsinki.

Lummie Robinson is currently a lecturer in Dogmatic and Pastoral Theology at Heythrop College, University of London, while also working in adult religious education, in the Archdiocese of Westminster, in parish ministry and as assistant superior of the Mount Street Jesuit Community in central London.

Brad D. Strawn received his graduate degrees from Fuller Theological Seminary where he now serves as the Evelyn and Frank Freed Professor for the Integration of Psychology and Theology.

Charles Taliaferro is Professor and Chair of the Philosophy department at Olaf College. He has given public lectures in several universities including Yale, Princeton, NYU, Oxford, Cambridge, University of St Andrews to name just a few.

Kevin Timpe is Professor of Philosophy at Northwest Nazarene University, and formerly a Research Fellow at St Peter's College, University of Oxford, UK.

Aku Visala works at the intersection of cognitive science, philosophy, and theology. He has held research positions in the Ian Ramsey Centre for Science and Religion at the University of Oxford and the Center of Theological Inquiry in Princeton. He was a postdoctoral researcher in the Department of Anthropology at the University of Notre Dame, USA. Presently, he is Senior Researcher of Theology, University of Helsinki.

Foreword

There is a quiet, virtually invisible revolution underway in the academy and this volume gives splendid access to it.

The revolution is the revitalization of theology as a serious discipline; its agents once lived on and identified with enemy territory. It even has a name: it is called analytic theology. It lives in the cracks between and within philosophy and theology, so it does not need the patronage of holy departments and buildings. It is spreading like a fragrance across the world from North America, back to Europe, into the Middle East, and all the way to China. Changing the metaphors, it is providing bread where there once were stones; it is turning philosophical water into wine.

To speak of revolution is, of course, to invite disbelief; to speak of the revitalization of theology is to invite disbelief twice over. When I trained in analytic philosophy a generation ago I could find no one to teach me philosophy of religion; I had to seek out a tutor in moral philosophy who was hostile to religion but was wonderfully generous as a teacher; so we read and discussed what texts we could find. This bizarre situation arose because at the time, even though positivism was on its last legs, the dismissal of theology as a bankrupt species of metaphysics was commonplace. Things had eased up during the period of linguistic analysis, but the positivist afterglow was still in place. To be sure, there were philosophers who stood against the stream but they were a minority; happily, they were not intimidated by the repetition of philosophical dogma and error. They even made forays into theology itself, providing seeds for later growth and harvesting. Similar shifts were happening when philosophers of science came to terms, say, with the more exact findings of physics or biology. There was a radical turn to the particular without abandoning the standard preoccupation with the general and universal.

Things changed in earnest in the 1970s when there were significant changes in epistemology and metaphysics that created intellectual space for the revival of philosophy of religion. Debates about the existence and attributes of God, the problem of evil, miracles, the nature of religious discourse, and the like, took off and show no signs of abating. Philosophy of religion still has to be incorporated into the curricula of our universities. Once they are given their rightful place in the guild, philosophy will flourish even more abundantly because religion is more often than not the backdoor into the profession. Despite the bizarre marginal status of the field, before long philosophers of the first rank published an array of texts in philosophy of religion in which the philosophical skill and content was clearly as good as it gets in philosophy. In time they began to deal with topics that were internal to Christian theology, say, trinity, incarnation, and atonement.

Theologians for the most part ignored these developments. Long ago they had turned for help to the Continental tradition as a resource; alternatively, they dug in behind the ramparts of divine revelation and dismissed philosophy as a lure into idolatry. These options still have legs, as they should have in any field where following the evidence wherever it leads matters. However, philosophers in the analytic tradition interested in theological topics were not persuaded by these options; in some cases they rejected them vehemently without expending much effort to understand them. For these philosophers it was natural to follow through on the initial forays into theology proper. So they named this enterprise and set to work. It certainly helped that they had the political savvy and drive to proceed with caution even as they moved with haste. Like secret agents quietly moving into new territory they have now developed outposts, as noted earlier, as far away as China. Their work has also provoked a younger generation of Jewish and Islamic philosophers to see the potential for their traditions.

Philosophers in the analytic tradition, at least, in Britain and North America tend to assume that their take on method—a method devoted to a certain kind of formalism and precision—is the only way forward for analytic philosophy. Thus it is no surprise that work in analytic theology can reflect this vision. The merit of this angle of vision is that there are crucial theological topics that lend themselves to this kind of work; indeed precise, formal investigation is exactly what is needed. However, philosophical method is itself a philosophical issue. Moreover, in both analytic philosophy proper and the philosophy of religion, there have always been those who insisted that philosophy should not be confined to such a procrustean bed. Precisionists could vilify or ignore the alternatives; but one could not excommunicate them. In analytic theology there is in fact a wonderfully inclusive orientation, even though nobody is going to surrender their cherished methodological aspirations without a fight.

Given the prevalence of the precisionist vision, it was only natural that the first round of analytic theology in its new self-conscious phase should cherry pick its topics to fit their expertise and go to work. Thus the logical and metaphysical issues evoked, say, by the doctrine of the trinity, cried out for intensive and precise analysis. However, theology has its own subject matter and terrain; while it can be constrained and tamed by philosophers to suit their prior commitments, it has its own constraints and requirements. In any case, once one recognizes the contested and limiting character of precisionism, a host of other theological themes readily open up for attention. In reality, of course, philosophy has always had to reckon with messy concepts and topics, as one finds, say, in political philosophy or aesthetics; so the expansion of method and subject matter has always been in play. Topics less amenable to precisionism are now under investigation, even though formal and logically precise methods may always be needed no matter what the debate. No-one is going to abandon clarity and rigor; the issue is what kind of clarity and rigor are appropriate for the full round of questions taken up within theology.

Aside from the philosophical sophistication on display in this volume, the important point to register is that analytic theology has already expanded to include the issues thrown up by theological anthropology. Within theology proper, two distinct kinds of claims have always been on show in this arena: metaphysical proposals about what constitutes human nature and soteriological proposals about sin and alienation from God. It is a delight to see these themes now being taken with such seriousness and care. The revolution is taking hold; there is no stopping it; so stay tuned as the whole range of theological topics from creation to eschatology come into view over the next generation. Things are developing much faster than a prophet might have predicted a decade ago.

These developments are by no means the end of the matter. I mentioned earlier that things began to change dramatically in part because of changes in epistemology. The study of such important concepts as justification, warrant, and knowledge has been pivotal in modern philosophy. Yet the debate about these, like the debate about meaning among positivists, was also hopelessly bound by the repetition of dogma and error. There is now a healthy debate about the desiderata of epistemology that rightly focuses on a wider set of concepts, like wisdom, intellectual virtue, character formation, and understanding. Add to this the following epistemic platitude that is as old as Aristotle: our methods of inquiry should be appropriate to the subject matter under consideration. Theology has its own subject matter: God and everything else insofar as it relates to God will do as an initial description. So we are now watching the development of a new sub-discipline, the epistemology of theology, which will open up new vistas in the borders between philosophy and theology.

We are indeed in the midst of a quiet revolution and its methods, content, and fruit are becoming more and more visible by the decade.

William J. Abraham

Preface

All great stories lived out in the world of human affairs entail metaphysical commitments. For example, the well-known twelfth-century *The Ladder of Divine Ascent* icon portrays the Christian story of the journey toward God as a treacherous ladder that must be climbed to come to Jesus and God the Father. Monks are making their way up the ladder, aided by saints and angels, while demons terrorize them with weapons.

Given the role of this icon, at first in the life of the monasteries in Egypt and then throughout much of the world, it displays a Christian narrative with metaphysical significance. While the story of salvation, damnation, and grace in the Christian tradition does not require a metaphysics in which there is an actual ladder to ascend, anymore than it requires believing that the icon accurately depicts God's hand, philosophy and theology that engages the Christian tradition must come to terms with how the concepts of human nature relate to the philosophy of God. To what extent are humans akin to the divine, if at all? What does it mean to claim that human persons are made in the image of God?

Theological anthropology is the ongoing, multi-disciplinary study of human nature in light of the philosophy of God and theistic tradition. While there are rich contributions to theological anthropology in Judaism, Islam, and other religious traditions, *The Ashgate Research Companion to Theological Anthropology* is dedicated to philosophical and theological work on the metaphysics of human nature and God in light of Christian tradition. The focus on Christianity should not, however, be thought of as a limitation in terms of homogeneity. There is, instead, such an extraordinary, rich, diversity of theological anthropologies in Christian tradition that a companion dedicated to Christian as well as multiple non-Christian traditions could not begin to do justice to the theological anthropology in Christianity, Judaism, Islam, theistic Hinduism, and so on.

The *Companion* consists of original chapters commissioned for this work on theological anthropology with the intention of displaying a variety of methods and positions. At the level of methodology, Christian anthropology has been developed using different concepts and assessments of the philosophical significance and use of scripture, the theological implications of modern science, the importance of contemporary philosophy of mind, Catholic or Reformed traditional views on human agency, and so on. On the level of detailed positions, topics that are distinctively theological (such as the belief that human beings are made in the image of God) are developed with more references to theologians such as Karl Barth, Hans Urs von Balthasar, Karol Jozef Wojtyla (Pope John Paul II), Rudolf Bultmann, Oscar Cullman among others. Topics that are more philosophical—for example, an investigation into whether a belief in resurrection is compatible with some form of materialism—will have more references to philosophers. This inclusion of theology and philosophy is intended to overcome what is sometimes seen as two disciplines that are not on speaking terms.

The *Companion* may be likened to a companion who gets readers oriented to this multi-disciplinary field as well as to make original contributions to the field, much as someone might help you get started exploring a garden by getting you through the door and planting some trees, but not a companion who will explore with you every plant in every detail. Even limiting our scope to Christian theological anthropology has not allowed us, in a single volume, to cover all the themes we would like without becoming a dictionary, rather than a companion.

Acknowledgments

We owe a great debt to many individuals who offered comments, suggestions, or some thoughtful contribution on parts of the *Companion*. To the following individuals we are grateful for their help and support: Craig Thompson, Jeffrey Schloss, William Wainwright, Richard Swinburne, Scott Prather, Ross Inman, Jason Maston, Carl Mosser, Jason McMartin, Ian McFarland, Thomas Carroll Lambert, Jordan Wessling, Douglas Hoffman, Ryan Mullins, Thomas Churchill, James Arcadi, J.H.W. Chan, Joel Green, Ben Arbour, Kevin Timpe, Ben Blackwell, Daniel Robinson, Mark Hamilton, Eleonore Stump, Lynne Rudder Baker, Kathryn Tanner, Marc Cortez, Mellissa Flynn Hager, Yujin Nagasawa, Keith Hess, Trenton Merricks, Matthew Richy, Christophe Marc Porot, and Oliver Crisp. We also thank Vera Lochtefeld, Meredith Varie, and Glenn Gordon for their expert editorial assistance. A special thank you to Sarah Lloyd at Ashgate for her patience and help through the process. We would also like to thank Katie McDonald, David Shervington and Sadie Copley-May for their help on administrative, technical and editorial matters related to production of the book, and Caroline Jones for preparing the index. We are also grateful to all the authors for their time and contribution, which made the book the success that it is.

Introduction

Joshua R. Farris and Charles Taliaferro

Theological anthropology involves theological and philosophical reflection on what it is to be human, exploring the religious significance of our understanding of human nature in light of the sciences, history, theology, and philosophy. Presently, there is a burgeoning literature devoted to the question of what it means to be a person, and, more specifically, what it means to be a human being. Diverse portraits of human beings have emerged from the sciences, theology, and philosophy. Developments in the areas of theological anthropology are present from a variety of angles. To date, there is no comprehensive treatment of theological anthropology that draws from philosophy, science, and theology. Furthermore, there is not a resource that provides the foundation for further construction in the area of theological anthropology. As such, *The Ashgate Research Companion to Theological Anthropology* offers both the student and the scholar new writings from scholars from a variety of disciplinary backgrounds that will motivate and inform academic debate. In this way, we hope to make a positive contribution to the literature as well as remedy a deficiency in the literature.

Scope of the *Companion*

While the *Companion* does not seek to address every topic concerning theological anthropology in detail, it does provide a ground for addressing the variety of doctrinal loci traditionally categorized as falling under theological anthropology. By doctrine, we mean to convey theological categories and concepts generally accepted within a particular tradition, namely the Christian tradition. The *Companion* focuses on Christian theological anthropology rather than theological anthropology in other religious contexts. However, the content will overlap with other religious views on anthropology.

The *Companion*'s unique contribution concerns the topic of human constitution (specifically in a Christian context) and the *imago Dei*. Almost every chapter zeros in on one of these two loci from a broader perspective (i.e. scientific, philosophical, or doctrinal). Many treatments of the person in modern western philosophy may seem indifferent to theological anthropology, but Descartes, Hobbes, Spinoza, Locke, Berkeley, Hume, Leibniz, Kant, Bentham, J.S. Mill, and others, were keenly aware of the religious implications of their philosophy of human nature. Finally, a couple of chapters only address the metaphysical and theological foundations for anthropology, making this *Companion* both comprehensive and specific in different ways.

Virtues of the *Companion*

Analytic Literature

The *Companion* bears the marks of analytic theology. What we mean by this is that the general approach to theology is analytic in nature. Having said this, the analytic approach is subtle. By *analytic*, we the editors mean to convey the approach to theology that draws from analytic philosophy that is characteristically interested in clarity, logical rigor, and detail. Michael Rea has rightly defined the task of analytic theology as follows, "it seems to me the right theoretical task for Christian philosophers and theologians to pursue is in fact one that involves clarifying, systematizing, and model-building—precisely the sort of project that analytic philosophers are engaged in."[1] In this way, we, as well as many of the authors, are Christians interested in tying the doctrinal matters (traditionally construed as God, creation, fall, redemption, and glory laid out in the Christian scriptures and the first four ecumenical councils) to what we think is the most convincing metaphysics and epistemology. Our interest is in conceptual clarity through analysis of central concepts within a theology of human beings. Thus, analytic theology is not merely the task of the philosopher, but of the theologian working within a boundary of topics that comprise the study of theology. In line with this assessment, William J. Abraham claims, "It is systematic theology attuned to the deployment of the skills, resources, and virtues of analytic philosophy."[2] Representative examples of analytic theology are seen in *Analytic Theology* edited by Michael Rea and Oliver Crisp, *Theology as Epistemology: In Search of the Foundations* by Randall Rauser, and *God Incarnate* by Oliver Crisp. More specifically, as of late, there have been three representative examples of analytic approaches to human nature. They include *Persons: Human and Divine* edited by Peter van Inwagen and Dean Zimmerman; *Soul, Body, and Survival* edited by Kevin Corcoran; and *Personal Identity and the Resurrection* edited by Georg Gasser. While the *Companion* is motivated by these works, it is distinct in important ways. Concerning *Persons: Human and Divine* and *Soul, Body, and Survival*, these two are by design analytic pieces of philosophy of religion intersecting with the philosophy of mind. As such, the aim of the authors is to provide a philosophically satisfying analysis and exploration of various different ontologies (e.g. idealism, substance dualism, emergentism, materialism, and the constitution view) as they overlap with religious topics. The authors within the *Companion* address the overlap of different ontology and religious topics, but it moves beyond this to offer a comprehensive look at humans in a theological context. Where the two edited works are philosophically heavy and theologically light, the *Companion* is theologically heavy and situated in the historical, biblical, and dogmatic literature within the Christian tradition. *Personal Identity and the Resurrection* advances analytic work on persons and the physical resurrection along with a few other related topics (e.g. the afterlife, purgatory, and time). The *Companion* touches upon these topics, but offers a more comprehensive look at persons and provides a foundation for further constructive work. It is important to note that while the *Companion* is by design analytic, not all of the authors assume an analytic method in their approach to theology. Some of the authors are sympathetic to and willing to explore analytic theology (e.g. Cortez, Cooper, Meconi, Blackwell) and others are explicitly not analytic in their perspective (e.g. Brown and Strawn, Green). This is intentional for two reasons. First, we believe that other approaches have something to contribute to the discussion. It is clear that current analytic theology is not alone sufficient in theological inquiry and requires

---

[1]   Oliver D. Crisp and Michael C. Rea (eds), *Analytic Theology: New Essays in the Philosophy of Theology* (Oxford: Oxford University Press, 2008), 19.

[2]   Ibid., 59.

interaction with other theological methods. Second, this allows for a useful comparison between analytic approaches and other well represented approaches.

Multi-Disciplinary

Another virtue of the *Companion* is the variety of disciplinary perspectives at work throughout the book. Unique to this collection is its inclusion of philosophers and theologians alongside those trained in the sciences. For example, some of the chapters are written by authors trained in psychology, biology, cognitive science, and neuroscience. By way of contrast, in one chapter the authors address the topics of feminism and gender studies as they intersect and inform theological anthropology. In addition to this, there are theologians trained in biblical studies (e.g. Joel Green, Ben Blackwell) and historical theology (e.g. Meconi, Adam Cooper, Crisp, Dominic Robinson), making this volume a well-rounded theologically constructive treatment of human beings.

Doctrinal Loci

The organization of the chapters align with traditional categorizations of doctrine, thus highlighting the theological nature of the *Companion*. The first section includes two chapters on method and provides a broad sweeping perspective on theological anthropology. The second and third sections address foundational terrain to be used in theology: science, gender, ontology. The fourth section, specifically, addresses models of the *imago Dei*. The fifth section concerns human nature and "free will" in the context of soteriology. Authors in the sixth section address human nature, specifically, in the context of "harmatiology" and "soteriology." The authors of the seventh section concern themselves with Christological anthropology as a way to study humans theologically. The idea is that one can study human nature in light of the doctrine of Christ and the incarnation. Models of anthropology inform the doctrine of the incarnation. Another way to approach Christological anthropology is to begin with the doctrine of Christ by analyzing how it impacts our thinking on human nature. In all, the *Companion* provides a comprehensive, systematic overview and set of contributions to theological anthropology.

Novelty

All of the chapters included here are newly commissioned writings by authors in their areas of expertise. In addition to this, each chapter provides the reader with an introduction, as well as makes a contribution to different dimensions of theological anthropology.

Part I: Methodology in Theological Anthropology

Part I addresses and defends the different methodologies used in theological anthropology. In this Part, we see two forms of theological anthropology, one which is built on a high view of revelation in the tradition of Karl Barth, and the other that employs Christian tradition but with a wider use of concepts and methods that can be brought to bear in elucidating and assessing scriptural teachings.

3

Chapter 1: The Madness in Our Method: Christology as the Necessary Starting Point for Theological Anthropology (Marc Cortez)

Herein, Cortez advances a methodology inspired by the theologian Karl Barth with stress on the normative role of revelation. For Cortez, anthropology should be practiced as a part of the tradition's emphasis upon humans as made in the *imago Dei*. Cortez begins with Christology as the starting point for anthropology.

Chapter 2: Scripture and Philosophy on the Unity of Body and Soul: An Integrative Method for Theological Anthropology (John Cooper)

The methodology employed in this chapter does not presume a Christological starting point for anthropology, but, instead, considers what models of anthropology account for the scriptural teaching on the afterlife. Cooper offers a big picture on the contemporary debate concerning theology and human composition. The chapter provides the reader with how one philosophical and historical theologian approaches anthropology. Additionally, Cooper encourages a grammatical-historical-theological approach to human beings. What he means by this is that we should engage the subject of humans on the basis of the historical and grammatical meaning of Christian scriptures by drawing from contemporary philosophical models of anthropology (e.g. monism and dualism) in order to describe a position accounting for the scriptural teaching about humans. With this, he suggests that all the texts of scripture must be taken together in an overarching theological framework, and when this is done it will yield a theological anthropology that distinguishes the person (soul or mind) from body. Although the term *dualism* was not a part of the vocabulary of scripture or first century philosophy, Cooper defends what is normally referred to as dualism as an essential tenant of Christian theological anthropology.

Part II: Theological Anthropology, the Brain, the Body, and the Sciences

As of late, the theology of human beings has evolved to incorporate the insights of the physical/natural sciences and social sciences. These terms should be expected given the extraordinary success in the particular scientific disciplines. Chapters in this section involve theological anthropology in light of different scientific points of view.

Chapter 3: Evolutionary Biology and Theological Anthropology (Joshua Moritz)

Joshua Moritz integrates theology with insights from recent research within evolutionary biology. Moritz employs evolutionary biology to challenge theological anthropologies that exaggerate the uniqueness of human nature. Additionally, he is critical of traditional anthropologies, namely, variations of substance dualism.

Chapter 4: Theological Anthropology and the Cognitive Sciences (Aku Visala)

Aku Visala, trained in cognitive science, philosophy, and theology, contributes an overview of research on the implications cognitive science has for theological anthropology. He highlights several areas in which cognitive science has import to the study of theological anthropology. Visala extends the debate by addressing the necessity for further work on the topic of cognitive science and theological anthropology. For example, Visala argues that recent findings in cognitive science from mind-brain correlation in religious experience seem to be in tension with variations of dualism on offer.

Chapter 5: Theological Anthropology and the Brain Sciences (Daniel N. Robinson)

Daniel Robinson advances the debate on anthropology. His chapter explores the intersection between psychology, neuroscience, philosophy of religion, and the philosophy of mind. He addresses the theological nature of human personhood, arguing in favor of the soul as a reality that is evident in experience and should be treated more as a datum than something posited by a theory. Robinson contends that the brain sciences have done nothing to show that the mental and physical are identical. In a unique and appealing manner, Robinson also raises the question of the possibility that scientists would find something like a physical particle of the God-belief in the brain. Some scientists might suggest that this disproves the need for God's existence to account for belief or experience of God, but it is difficult to see how the scientist would begin to justify this claim. The role of the particle may correlate with mental states, but to claim an identity-relation or a causal-relation exists between the mental-state and the brain is unclear given what we seem to know about neural states and mental states.

Chapter 6: Feminism and Theological Anthropology (Emilie Judge-Becker and Charles Taliaferro)

Recent feminist philosophy charges analytic conceptions of God and persons with male domination and oppression of women. In fact, there are several notable feminist philosophers (e.g. Pamela Susan Anderson among others) who argue that the Christian tradition is hopelessly linked to patriarchy. Emilie Judge-Becker and Charles Taliaferro argue that an Anselmian philosophy of God and human nature is not at all intrinsically the result of, or essentially in alliance with, patriarchy. Such an Anselmian theological anthropology rightly condemns patriarchy and the historical domination of women by men in all religious traditions. By upholding an ideal, God's eye point of view, Judge-Becker and Taliaferro propose that Christian theism provides a foundation and supports a methodology that exposes cases of wrongful domination whether in matters of gender, sexual orientation, ethnicity, and so on.[3]

---

[3] For a further development of the view that a theistic vantage point provides a desirable, regulative ideal of seeking to be impartial, affectively apprised of the points of view of all involved parties—including those who are socially marginalized—see Charles Taliaferro's contribution "A God's Eye Point of View: The Divine Ethic," in *Faith and Philosophical Analysis: The Impact of Analytical Philosophy on the Philosophy of Religion*, H. Harris and C.J. Insole (eds) (Aldershot: Ashgate, 2005), pp. 76–84.

Part III: Models for Theological Anthropology

Recent work in philosophy of mind has seen a wider scope of live options from the 1960s through the 1990s as materialism of different stripes seemed "the only game in town," but now, in addition to fruitful new efforts on behalf of materialism, there are defenses of substance dualism, hylomorphism, emergent dualism among others. These models are mostly explored in the philosophical literature in terms of their coherence and compatibility with the sciences, but a vital area to consider is the theological implications of these different models. For Christian philosophers and theologians there are three central questions: First, can materialism be thoughtfully integrated with a Christian view of persons? Second, should we reject the notion of the soul given its predominance throughout Ecclesiastical history? Third, can substance dualism accommodate a Christian view of the body—especially as it concerns the doctrine of the incarnation and the physical resurrection?

Chapter 7: Self-Organizing Personhood: Complex Emergent Developmental Linguistic Relational Neurophysiologicalism (Warren S. Brown and Brad Strawn)

Warren S. Brown and Brad Strawn are trained psychologists with training in theology. Both Brown and Strawn propose a model of anthropology informed by developmental psychology, anthropological studies, neuroscience, and relational ontology. They propose that humans are monistic in nature not dualistic. In fact, Brown and Strawn are convinced that there is not a need for the soul given the evidence from the sciences. Persons are products of culture, biology, physiology, and heredity. Although Brown and Strawn resist using the term, *non-reductive materialism* is the term that is used in the literature for their position.

Chapter 8: Physicalism, Bodily Resurrection, and the Constitution Account (Omar Fakhri)

Fakhri advances an argument for the coherence and compatibility of the constitution view of persons and the doctrine of physical resurrection. In a unique and appealing way, Fakhri contrasts constitutionalism with what he calls mainline materialism and concludes that constitutionalism is consistent with the doctrine of the resurrection, but mainline materialism is not. Thus, constitutionalism has the resources to handle one of the most challenging doctrinal problems within theological anthropology making constitutionalism a viable option.

Chapter 9: Anthropological Hylomorphism (Bruno Niederbacher, S.J.)

Bruno Niederbacher argues in favor of the plausibility of hylomorphism and for its virtues as a model in theological anthropology. Additionally, Niederbacher applies hylomorphism to relevant theological issues, namely the creation of individual human beings, moral responsibility, and the resurrection. Niederbacher argues that a consideration of anthropological hylomorphism accounts for both Christian teaching and human experience.

Chapter 10: Substance Dualism (Stewart Goetz)

Goetz defends a form of substance dualism as distinct from Platonic dualism. Goetz argues that the substance dualism model is the common sense position and that, in the absence of compelling reasons for rejecting it, the model should be accepted and used in theological anthropology.

Chapter 11: The Human Person as Communicative Event: Jonathan Edwards on the Mind/Body Relationship (Marc Cortez)

Cortez develops a model of anthropology inspired by the theology of Jonathan Edwards. Herein, Cortez argues that Edwards affirms a view in the spirit of Berkeley in that humans are immaterial substances that instantiate mental and physical properties (where physical properties are mental products). The conclusion of this chapter is that we humans are substantial individuals, but not, technically, substances in the full, classical sense in that none of us can exist without some other thing our substance. In Christian theism, human beings, like all other finite substantial individuals, cannot exist without the sustaining creative power of God. In this metaphysics, God is the sole substantial reality, and yet God can create beings that have powers that are not themselves fully fixed by divine power or fiat. In this way, theologians refer to ways in which God can communicate some of God's attributes—such as divine freedom—whereas other divine attributes are incommunicable—for example, God cannot make multiple Gods.

Chapter 12: Why Emergence? (William Hasker)

Hasker advances a form of emergent dualism that is distinct from the substance dualism found in traditional Christian anthropology and defended in the *Companion* by Goetz and Farris. Hasker contends that emergent dualism better coheres with contemporary science and it provides all the advantages of a non-materialist account of persons, without the liabilities facing substance dualism.

Part IV: Theological Models of the *Imago Dei*

The belief that humans are made in the *imago Dei* is more than an important theme throughout the Christian scriptures and Ecclesiastical history. While the most prominent position throughout Ecclesiastical history has been a substantive/structural model of the *imago Dei*, as of late, there has been a shift among systematic theologians and philosophers of religion toward a relational model. This is due in part to the influence of Karl Barth. Alternatively, biblical scholars have generally affirmed some version of the functional model of the *imago Dei*. Each chapter in this section includes the notion of "image" in the context of the philosophical, theological and biblical literature and affirm a particular model they wish to defend.

Chapter 13: A Substantive (Soul) Model of the *Imago Dei*: A Rich Property View (Joshua Farris)

Farris articulates a substantive view of the image of God in contrast to Tanner's Christological and participatory view. Farris seeks to revitalize a conception of humans as made in God's image in the spirit of Augustine and proposing that it better accommodates the scriptural narration of human beings and the image than do participatory and relational views, yet it is also able to incorporate some of the insights of Tanner's sophisticated view. While he argues that under ordinary conditions the image-bearing nature of human life is apparent, its full manifold expression is only seen under extraordinary conditions (eschatologically).

Chapter 14: Why the *Imago Dei* Should Not Be Identified with the Soul (Joel Green)

Biblical scholar and theologian, Joel Green, raises an objection against treating the image of God as a matter of both God and humans being incorporeal. He argues that the image is not identical to soul. While he does not claim to refute the view that souls could undergird or be a part of what supports the image, he argues that there are no good reasons on the grounds of biblical scholarship to identify the soul as the "image."

Chapter 15: The Dual-Functionality of the *Imago Dei* as Human Flourishing in the Church Fathers (David Vincent Meconi)

David Meconi draws from Catholic thought and western conceptions of the image of God and advances a structural view. In a unique way, Meconi draws from hylomorphism as the model of anthropology undergirding a theological view of persons and the image. Interestingly, he argues from hylomorphism that humans are unique in that they are comprised of an immaterial and intellectual part in addition to a material part that correspond to human nature as a heavenly and earthly reality.

Chapter 16: Ecclesial-Narratival Model of the *Imago Dei* (Dominic Robinson)

Robinson surveys the history of thought making note of significant themes within the tradition (including Rome, Protestantism, and the East) and constructively suggests an ecclesial or narratival view of persons and the image whereby humans relationally receive the Divine and participate in the Divine.

Chapter 17: A Christological Model of the *Imago Dei* (Oliver Crisp)

Oliver Crisp advances Christology as a promising route for developing a doctrinal model of the *imago Dei*. He argues that there are two distinctive options on the "image" in contrast to a Christological view, namely, a substantive model and a relational model, where Crisp subsumes a functional view under a relational model. He suggests that both of these models have their problems, but that a Christological model is superior.

Part V: Human Nature, Freedom, and Salvation

As of late, the theological debate concerning the will of humans has reached an impasse. Both theological libertarians and theological compatibilists must move beyond arguments of the past into fresh areas of thought to make progress in the debate. This section is a survey of the basic issues concerning freedom of the will. It offers new avenues for thinking about libertarianism or compatibilism, and ties the notion of the will to a comprehensive Christian view of human persons.

Chapter 18: Free Will and the Stages of Theological Anthropology (Kevin Timpe and Audra Jenson)

Timpe and Jenson outline three stages of theological anthropology specifically focusing on human agency. These stages include *status integritatis* (Garden of Eden), *status corruptionis* (fall), and *status gloriae* (glorification in the afterlife). Throughout, the authors argue that both compatibilists and libertarians are able to account for personal actions at each one of the stages. Additionally, they note the liabilities with libertarianism concerning the state of glory.

Chapter 19: Human Beings, Compatibilist Freedom, and Salvation (Paul Helm)

As a Christian philosopher and historian, Paul Helm gives a cost-benefit analysis of compatibilism as a theological view of human freedom. He argues that there are several benefits for affirming compatibilism within a Christian framework. It is able to affirm a robust doctrine of God's sovereignty, a traditional account of the Fall, and the efficaciousness of Divine grace. On compatibilism, God seems to be the author of sin. Helm suggests that while it may seem this way, the evidence is underwhelming and libertarians encounter similar problems when offering a moral response to God's relationship to evil in the world.

Part VI: Human Beings in Sin and Salvation

The authors in this Part focus on the nature and constitution of human persons in the context of sin and salvation. The authors are able to navigate the particular loci of doctrine and integrate it with the literature on human persons. The authors provide insight into the contemporary dialogue on human persons by integrating the contemporary work in theology and philosophy for the purpose of constructive systematic theology.

Chapter 20: Created Corruptible, Raised Incorruptible: The Importance of Hylomorphic Creationism to the Free Will Defense (Nathan A. Jacobs)

Jacobs constructively draws from a variation of hylomorphism within the Patristic tradition of Christian thought to provide a metaphysical explanation for the problem of evil. He suggests that hylomorphic entities begin in a state of corruption, and, that moral evil comes about through free will (e.g. the free will defense for the problem of evil). Furthermore, Jacobs suggests that hylomorphism provides a metaphysical explanation distinguishing

God and humans. Finally, hylomorphic beings are dependent upon Divine energy forever. Thus, he offers a novel defense of corruption that is richly situated in the hylomorphic tradition of Christian thought.

Chapter 21: Redemption of the Human Body (Adam Cooper)

Cooper explores the doctrine of the soul and its relation to the body. He constructively reflects on the body as an object of deification by retrieving from the tradition. He addresses the debated question over whether redemption is primarily a concern of the incarnation or, more specifically, the cross. In the end, he persuasively unites these two concerns and shows how they are intimately related.

Chapter 22: Redemption, the Resurrected Body, and Human Nature (Stephen T. Davis)

Davis explores a Christian doctrine of redemption as it is situated in a variation of substance dualism. In the course of exploring redemption, Davis explicates the notion of guilt, forgiveness, love, incarnation, Christ's life and death, and, finally, somatic resurrection. In contrast to hylomorphism, Davis works with a model that humans are either a compound or composite of soul and body. Davis explores that the doctrine of redemption is inclusive of both the soul and the body. Finally, he offers that forgiveness and resurrection make it possible for humans to see God (i.e. the beatific vision), which is the final goal for all of humanity.

Chapter 23: Theosis and Theological Anthropology (Ben Blackwell and Kris Miller)

Blackwell and Miller put forward an account of theosis as a holistic and integrative account of redemption by drawing from the work of St Maximus and T.F. Torrance. Interestingly, Blackwell and Miller offer a unique approach to constructive theology by providing a lens in which to read the scriptures on the notion of soteriology (primarily as a matter of theosis) that is richly situated in two historical thinkers (Maximus and Torrance). They conclude with an account of human nature that is participatory in nature, teleological, and they argue that salvation is primarily a union with Christ. Interspersed within, the authors draw from recent analytic literature on human constitution and suggest that their account best fits with a hylomorphic view of human beings, yet they prefer to speak of humanity in terms of relational ontology. They are critical of earlier variations of substance dualism often associated with Gnosticism and Origenism, but remain open to contemporary variations of substance dualism as plausible accounts of human beings and theosis.

Chapter 24: Glory and Human Nature (Charles Taliaferro)

Taliaferro constructively contrasts a Christian view of glory with a Greek view of glory. On the basis of this contrast, he offers a new argument in favor of substance ontology as the metaphysical ground and explanation for Christian glory. He also discusses the inter-relationship between glory, substance, and dignity.

Part VII: Christological Theological Anthropology

Theological anthropology would be incomplete without considering Christology. A particularly Christian anthropology depends upon Christology—a Barthian inspired method. By reflecting on Christologically informed anthropology, the contributors seek to constructively account for a traditional Christology by drawing from a model of philosophical anthropology. This proves invaluable in several ways. It provides concrete material deserving further attention from philosophers and theologians, it motivates fresh and insightful thought, and it provides an explanatory ground beyond abstract philosophical reasoning for thinking about human persons.

Chapter 25: The Mortal God: Materialism and Christology (Glenn Andrew Peoples)

Peoples explores a relatively underdeveloped topic in the literature on anthropology, namely materialist Christology. To date, there have been two noteworthy contributions to the subject of materialist Christology (e.g. Trenton Merricks' "The Word made Flesh," and Oliver Crisp's "Materialist Christology"). In this chapter, Peoples challenges a common assumption, namely, the idea that dualism provides a better explanation than materialism concerning the incarnation. Toward the end of his chapter, Peoples offers reasons for thinking that materialism is a coherent anthropology worth developing in relation to Christology. While Peoples does not put forward a positive account of materialist Christology, he seeks to dispel the notion that dualism is an easy solution and sets the stage for further constructive work in materialist Christology.

Chapter 26: Hylomorphic Christology (Josef Quitterer)

Quitterer distinguishes himself from Swinburne's account that the soul of Jesus is not identical to the subject. Instead, he suggests that the soul is a fundamental power for human cognitive and non-cognitive operations, which is a distinctive contribution from a hylomorphic articulation of Christianity. In the end, Quitterer's view begins to resemble Rea's hylomorphic Christology. However, there is a distinction and this is Quitterer's contribution to the literature. By way of contrast, Rea claims that human nature is a fundamental power that unites other powers whereas Quitterer posits that the human soul is the fundamental power of the living body. This means that the human soul has these basic capacities not as an immaterial substance but as the form of body (where matter is essentially a part of form).

Chapter 27: A Cartesian Approach to the Incarnation (Jonathan Chan)

Chan tests the viability of a Cartesian model of anthropology for Christology. He criticizes recent concrete Cartesian accounts of Christology as necessarily yielding nestorianism, namely, the heresy that the Logos took on a human person at the incarnation. Chan rejects a three-part Cartesian Christology, he contends that an abstract Cartesian Christology is theologically and philosophically defensible and aligned with traditional Chalcedonian Christology.

PART I
Methodology in
Theological Anthropology

The Madness in Our Method: Christology as the Necessary Starting Point for Theological Anthropology

Marc Cortez

Many theological anthropologies claim that Jesus Christ is in some way the revelation of true humanity. He is "the mystery of man,"[1] "true humanity,"[2] the "archetype" of humanity,[3] and the revelation of "what human nature is intended to be."[4] Thus, Ray Anderson argues that only "the humanity of Christ ... discloses the radical form of true humanity,"[5] exemplifying what may be described as a widespread consensus among theologians that Jesus Christ lies at the heart of theological anthropology.[6]

At first glance, such claims seem intuitively obvious. Given the long-standing conviction that Jesus Christ is both fully and truly human—fully human as the complete union of deity and humanity in the incarnation and truly human as the sole postlapsarian example of a human life lived without sin—the theological intuition that a proper understanding of the human person must begin with Christology seems almost self-evident.

However, such claims do not go unchallenged. Indeed, for some contemporary thinkers such a Christologically-centred anthropology is necessarily doomed, offering a sadly limited and isolating perspective for understanding something as beautiful and complex as the human person. While they often recognize Christology as a significant point of departure for theological anthropology, they typically stop short of claiming that he alone provides the proper vantage point for understanding humanity.

Nonetheless, I argue in this chapter that we can still maintain the long-standing intuition that Christology alone provides the proper ground for theological anthropology, provided that we offer a more robust methodological account of how Christology and anthropology should be related. To that end, we will need to consider first some of the more significant

---

[1] John D. Zizioulas, "Human Capacity and Human Incapacity: A Theological Exploration of Personhood," *Scottish Journal of Theology* 28.5 (1975): 433.

[2] Charles Sherlock, *The Doctrine of Humanity* (Downers Grove, Ill: Intervarsity Press, 1996), 18.

[3] Panayiotis Nellas, *Deification in Christ: The Nature of the Human Person* (Crestwood, NY: St. Vladimir's Seminary Press, 1987), 33.

[4] Millard J. Erickson, *Christian Theology* (Grand Rapids: Baker, 1998), 532.

[5] Ray Sherman Anderson, *On Being Human: Essays in Theological Anthropology* (Grand Rapids: Eerdmans, 1982), 19.

[6] E.g., Ian A. McFarland, *Difference & Identity* (Cleveland, Ohio: Pilgrim, 2001) and Alan J. Torrance, "What Is a Person?," in *From Cells to Souls—and Beyond: Changing Portraits of Human Nature*, ed. Malcom Jeeves (Grand Rapids: Eerdmans, 2004), 199–222.

objections. Having identified the primary challenges facing a Christological anthropology, we will then consider Karl Barth's anthropology as one of the more robustly Christological anthropologies available. There we will see that Barth's approach offers resources for responding to the major concerns about Christological anthropology. Nonetheless, in the final section, we argue that although Barth may serve as a useful dialogue partner, pointing the way toward a more adequate Christological anthropology, more work needs to be done in addressing the theological and methodological issues involved.

Confronting the Madness: Key Criticisms for Christological Anthropology

We can summarize most of the concerns about Christological anthropology by asking three key questions, each challenging the extent to which a Christological starting point is really adequate for understand the human person.

First, why exactly does Jesus deserve this prominent location in theological anthropology? Few things could be more startling than claiming that a single human individual has revelatory significance for the entirety of human life. And this is particularly the case given the limited biblical justification for such a claim. While the Bible certainly describes Jesus as a true human and offers his life as an example for the rest of us to follow,[7] suggesting that Jesus may play a central role in understanding human moral and/or religious action, it never explicitly states that Jesus in any way functions as the ground for understanding the human person in general. Thus, any theologian making such a robust anthropological claim owes some explanation of the biblical justification for this move.

Some also balk at any attempt to ground an understanding of universal humanity in the particular humanity of a single individual. Consider yourself, for example. Unless you are an extraordinary person who has somehow managed to live in virtually every human culture, experienced life from the standpoint of multiple ethnicities, genders, economic circumstances and all the states of ability and disability, your identity has been shaped by certain particularities—like the rest of us—that will not allow us simply to move from your case to the human experience of people in general.

This becomes problematic for many modern Christologies precisely because they tend to emphasize Christ's particular humanity.[8] He was a Jewish male raised in first-century Galilee, among other things. Like me, his humanity is marked and limited by these distinguishing characteristics, making it difficult to see how his humanity could reveal universal humanity any more than mine could.

Probably the most significant concerns developed along these lines have come from feminist theologians who point out the difficulty of developing a general anthropology from a single, male individual.[9] In what sense can we say that he reveals what it means to be

---

[7]   E.g., 1 Cor. 11:1; 1 Pet. 2:21.

[8]   Scholars involved in the various "quests" for the historical Jesus have played a particularly important role in emphasizing historical existence, even if they routinely disagree on how to interpret the various details.

[9]   E.g., Rosemary Radford Ruether, *Sexism and God-Talk* (London: SCM, 1983); Elizabeth A. Johnson, "The Maleness of Christ," in *The Special Nature of Women?*, eds Anne Carr and Elisabeth Schüssler Fiorenza (London: SCM, 1991), 108–16; Elisabeth Schüssler Fiorenza, *Jesus: Miriam's Child, Sophia's Prophet : Critical Issues in Feminist Christology* (New York: Continuum, 1995); L. Susan Bond, *Trouble with Jesus: Women, Christology, and Preaching* (St. Louis, Mo.: Chalice Press, 1999); and Halvor Moxnes, "Jesus in Gender Trouble," *Cross Currents* 54.3 (2004): 31–46.

human? In taking this approach, do we not run the risk of associating the human with being male? Or, at the very least, do we not marginalize what it means to be female if we say that all of humanity can be adequately revealed through the male form of humanity?[1] After all, as a junior high student once pointed out, "Jesus was never a teenage girl."

Although feminist theologians have expressed these concerns most clearly, similar questions could be raised about every aspect of Christ's particularized human experience (e.g. class, race, geographical location).[10] How do we privilege Christ's humanity without, at the same time, privileging these particular expressions, and, consequently, marginalizing other particular expressions of being human?

Second, how exactly do you draw anthropological conclusions from a Christological starting point? In other words, what are the methodological principles by which we derive anthropological insights from our Christological starting point? Do you simply read the gospels, look at your situation, and ask, "What would Jesus do?" Surely it is more complicated than that, but in what ways? Unfortunately, few theologians have given explicit attention to this question, affirming the Christological starting point without discussing the precise how involved. Although we do not want to become so burdened by methodological issues that we never get around to dealing with substantive anthropological questions, we must give some attention to the appropriate steps that must be considered when relating Christology and anthropology in this way.

This question becomes even more significant when we turn to unique aspects of the life of Jesus like his sinlessness and deity. Regardless of how you answer the question of whether Jesus was born with a "sin nature,"[11] most orthodox[12] Christologies affirm that Jesus lived a truly sinless life. Since that is true of no other human, it becomes difficult to see how the humanity that Jesus reveals could be related to the humanity that we experience in our everyday lives. Many have argued that it is precisely in virtue of his sinlessness that Jesus can reveal what it means to be truly human—i.e. humanity untainted by sin. So Jesus reveals humanity as God intended it and toward which he is redeeming it. While that may be true, however, such an approach raises significant questions for the applicability of such a Christologically grounded theological anthropology. At the very least, it runs the risk of only revealing a "true" humanity so removed from our everyday existence as to be a useless abstraction.

Questions also stem from the uniqueness of the incarnation. Orthodox Christologies affirm that Jesus was truly human but not merely human. As the unique and inseparable

---

[10]   See esp. Andrea M. Ng'weshemi, *Rediscovering the Human: The Quest for a Christo-Theological in Africa* (New York: Peter Lang, 2002).

[11]   Historically, most theologians have argued that Jesus' true humanity is best safeguarded by affirming that he assumed a sinless human nature at the incarnation (for a more recent defense of this position, see Oliver Crisp, "Did Christ Have a Fallen Human Nature?" *International Journal of Systematic Theology* 6.3 [2004]: 270–88). On this account, Jesus' humanity is clearly distinct from our own fallen nature. Others contend that to truly become one with a sinful humanity and heal that which was broken, Jesus assumed a sinful human nature, even though he himself did not perform acts of personal sin (e.g., Edward Irving, *The Orthodox and Catholic Doctrine of Our Lord's Human Nature* [London: Baldwin & Craddock, 1830]; Karl Barth, *Church Dogmatics* I/2, ed. G.W. Bromiley and T.F. Torrance [Edinburgh: T. & T. Clark, 1957], 147–59; Thomas Weinandy, *In the Likeness of Sinful Flesh: An Essay on the Humanity of Christ* [Edinburgh: T. & T. Clark, 1993]). Although this suggests greater commonality with our own sinful condition, even this account affirms Jesus' perfect expression of covenantal faithfulness throughout Jesus' life, markedly different from our own faithlessness. Thus, both perspectives need to offer some account of how Jesus' sinlessness, and the corresponding differences this creates between him and other humans, impacts the development of a Christological anthropology.

[12]   I use "orthodox" throughout this chapter to describe those theologies shaped by the theological consensus of the early ecumenical councils and not a particular Christian tradition (e.g. Eastern Orthodoxy).

union of deity and humanity in a single individual, how do we discern which aspects of Jesus' life that are applicable to other humans and which might be unique to the incarnate God-man? And if we make such distinctions, on what basis? The concern here is that we might end up using a pre-established understanding of what it means to be human—i.e. one developed independently of Christology—to determine that which is truly human about Jesus in the incarnation.[13] Such an approach, however, would mean that we are actually developing an anthropocentric Christology rather than a Christocentric anthropology. Surely there will always be a dynamic relationship between those two fields of inquiry, but for a Christological anthropology to succeed, there must be a way to identify what is truly human about Jesus without appealing to a definition of "human" developed independently of Christology.

Third, how should a Christological anthropology relate to other anthropological disciplines? Even a theological anthropology thoroughly shaped by Christology must acknowledge the wealth of information about the human person produced by disciplines like biology, sociology, psychology, and the neurosciences, among many others. What does it mean to say that Jesus reveals true humanity with respect to the humanity revealed by these non-Christological approaches?

Even if a Christological anthropology acknowledges that other disciplines might be able to generate meaningful insight into humanity, it still claims a privileged perspective on humanity, one that stands outside the reach of any other discipline. For many, the inevitable result of prioritizing Christology in this way is to instantiate a theological ghetto, isolating theology from the other anthropological disciplines by its totalizing claims.[14] It would seem that any adequate approach to anthropology must account for the data produced by such disciplines. But can a Christological anthropology do so with integrity? Or does the claim that only Jesus reveals true humanity create a situation in which Christological anthropology can only accept as true data that agrees with its predetermined starting point? If so, can there be any meaningful dialogue?

We could certainly identify other significant questions, but these seem the most pressing for developing a Christological anthropology today. And it is questions like these that might leave some wondering about the apparent madness of trying to develop a comprehensive understanding of humanity from the limited perspective of a single human individual.

The Only Proper Vantage Point: Karl Barth as a Case Study for Christological Anthropology[15]

Few would question that Karl Barth offered one of the most thoroughly Christological approaches to theological anthropology. Indeed, T.F. Torrance considered it "in some ways the most arresting aspect of Barth's theology."[16] And Barth himself thought it was more

---

13   As Wolfhart Pannenberg argues, though, this is precisely the error of "most contributions to modern anthropology" (*Anthropology in Theological Perspective* [Edinburgh: T. & T. Clark, 1985], 19).

14   E.g. Roger Trigg, *Rationality and Religion: Does Faith Need Reason?* (Oxford: Blackwell, 1998).

15   This section summarizes material that I dealt with in more depth in *Embodied Souls, Besouled Bodies: An Exercise in Christological Anthropology and Its Significance for the Mind/Body Debate*, T. & T. Clark Studies in Systematic Theology (London: T. & T. Clark, 2008), chs. 2–3.

16   Thomas F. Torrance, *Karl Barth, Biblical and Evangelical Theologian* (Edinburgh: T. & T. Clark, 1990), 22. Herbert Hartwell similarly described it as "revolutionary in content" (Herbert Hartwell, *The Theology of Karl Barth* [London: Gerald Duckworth & Co., 1964], 123).

revolutionary than his famous Christological reorientation of the doctrine of election.[17] Essentially it involves the conviction that "The nature of the man Jesus alone is the key to the problem of human nature."[18] Thus, according to Ray Anderson, "Karl Barth, more than any other theologian of the church, including the Reformers, has developed a comprehensive theological anthropology by beginning with the humanity of Jesus Christ as both crucified and resurrected."[19]

Clearly, then, Barth falls in the ranks of those who follow the theological intuition that Jesus Christ reveals humanity in some significant way. So the question becomes whether Barth has managed to do so in a way that addresses the concerns raised above.

The Why of Christological Anthropology

For Barth, Christological anthropology finds its theological ground in the doctrine of election. As Barth famously declared, the doctrine of election is "the whole of the Gospel, the Gospel in nuce."[20] This is because it is in the doctrine of election that we find God's eternal self-determination to be God-for-us in the person of Jesus Christ, his free and gracious decision that "the goal and meaning of all His dealings with the as-yet non-existent universe should be the fact that in His Son He would be gracious towards man, uniting Himself with them."[21] This means that ultimately and eternally, Jesus is the human. All others are human insofar as they are included within the scope of God's eternal decision to be God-for-us-in-Christ, which fortunately includes all of us.[22]

Jesus' unique status as the revealer of true humanity, then, ultimately has an eternal ground in the doctrine of election. But he does not stop here. In a second move, Barth argues that Jesus also grounds our humanity through his covenantal (sinless) faithfulness. Although all humans have fallen into sin and thus stand in contradiction to their own Christologically-determined nature, God's gracious love ensures that humans are and always will remain human. And this is specifically because Jesus remains the one human who has not fallen into the self-contradiction of sin and thus continues to be rightly related to God as his covenantal partner (i.e., human).[23] This means that Jesus' humanity is ontologically decisive for our humanity because it is his faithful humanity that maintains and redeems our own.[24] But it

---

[17]   CD III/2, ix. We will see, though, that the substantial departure evidenced in his anthropology is grounded in his unique understanding of election and, thus, the two departures cannot be so neatly distinguished.

[18]   CD II/2, 136.

[19]   Anderson, *On Being Human: Essays in Theological Anthropology*, 18.

[20]   CD III/2, 3.

[21]   CD II/2, 101.

[22]   Thus, "all who are elected" includes all human persons. Thus, we cannot regard non-Christians "as if they were not elect" (CD II/2, 416). But should approach every person with the assurance that "he, too, is an elect man" (CD II/2, 318). There is no limit to God's gracious decision to be God-for-us.

[23]   As mentioned earlier, Barth argues that Jesus took on our sinful human nature, and, consequently, there is no ontological difference between his humanity and our own (CD I/2, 151ff.). Nevertheless, Jesus lived a truly sinless life in his covenantal faithfulness.

[24]   According to Hans Urs von Balthasar, then, the sinlessness of Jesus is that which "guarantees human nature an unbroken continuity" (*The Theology of Karl Barth*, trans. Edward T. Oakes [San Francisco: Communio, 1992], 116.). Thus, the continuity of human nature established by Christ's covenantal faithfulness ensures the continued availability of real human nature for theological consideration.

is also epistemologically decisive because Jesus is the one in whom we see true humanity unspoiled by sin.[25]

In a third move, Barth argues that we also need to take into account the "divine summons" that we all receive in Christ, one that calls us into our own true humanity. Because the Son has entered creation through the incarnation, "To be a man is to be in the particular sphere of the created world in which the Word of God is spoken and sounded."[26] Jesus' very existence summons all humans as the sphere within which they are encountered by the divine Other. For Barth, then, being truly human is not a static concept. Instead, we find true humanity insofar as we respond to the summons we all receive in Christ, a summons that we may not even be consciously aware of, but one that grasps all humans as creatures who live in the sphere in which God became one of us.

Almost uniquely among theologians, then, Barth offers a robust theological explanation for the Christological determination of theological anthropology. Jesus alone determines what it means to be human because (1) His humanity grounds ours eternally through God's eternal decision to be God-for-us-in-Jesus (election); (2) His humanity grounds ours redemptively through the covenantal faithfulness that both maintains our humanity and reveals true humanity; and (3) His humanity grounds ours existentially through the divine summons that we all receive to likewise enact covenantal faithfulness in the world.

The How of a Christological Methodology

If Barth is in limited company in laying out a theological framework for Christological anthropology, he is virtually alone in explicitly addressing the key methodological issues involved. And he does so by first arguing that we need to recognize the two distinct "moments" in a Christological anthropology. Then, when he begins modeling his methodology, we see that each moment can itself be divided into two distinct stages, leaving us with a Christological methodology that comprises four steps.

First, consistent with his Christological starting point, Barth argues first that we can and must affirm the revelatory significance of Christ's humanity, which remains constitutionally identical with ours, even though it also has a status that differs for the reasons identified above.[27] This means that theologians must focus on this unique individual, seeking to understand human nature in the light of his distinct reality. Anything incompatible with this picture is "ipso facto non-human."[28] This emphasis is on clear display throughout volume III/2 of the Church Dogmatics where Barth seeks to orient each anthropological issue by looking first at Jesus Christ.

Barth balances this first methodological principle, however, with the conviction that the differences between Jesus and the rest of humanity entail that there can be no direct move from Christology to anthropology. "There can be no question, therefore, of a direct knowledge of the nature of man in general from that of the man Jesus."[29] This means that a Christological anthropology is an anthropology of inference. Instead of simplistically

---

[25] CD III/2, 41–2.

[26] CD III/2, 149.

[27] CD III/2, 53; IV/1, 131.

[28] CD III/2, 226.

[29] CD III/2, 71.

drawing general anthropological truths directly from what we observe about Jesus, we must "infer from His human nature the character of our own."[30]

Methodologically, then, Barth's Christological anthropology comprises two distinct moments:

> *in our exposition of the doctrine of man we must always look in the first instance at the nature of man as it confronts us in the person of Jesus, and only secondarily—asking and answering from this place of light—at the nature of man as that of every man and all other men.*[31]

So Barth argues that theological anthropology must begin with the particularity of the person of Christ; only here do we see true humanity on display in a fallen world.[32] And here the scandal of particularity identified in the concerns mentioned above is on full display. Barth argues, however, that we cannot move directly from those particularities to truths about humanity in general. They serve as the starting point for theological anthropology, not its actual content.

Such an approach, of course, immediately raises the question of precisely how one moves from Christology to anthropology inferentially. However, this is a question that Barth rightly does not try to "answer," recognizing that there may be many legitimate approaches to such a complex task. Instead, he models one way of moving between the two moments, and in the process demonstrates a four-step anthropological method.

First, focus on Christ's soteriological work. For Barth, Christ's soteriological work is the right place to start any Christological considerations because everything about Jesus is soteriological. He is the Savior.[33] And the biblical testimony focuses almost exclusively on the soteriological significance of his life. This does not mean that we can or should exclude more apparently mundane aspects of his existence (e.g. personal relationships, the "inner life" of the mind, physical experiences like eating and sleeping), indeed, for Barth, such things comprise the "field" on which humanity takes place.[34] So these may be important sources for anthropological reflection,[35] but even they must be understood in the broader context of Jesus' soteriological work since they are only disclosed through his public work as Savior.[36]

Second, discern appropriate Christological criteria. From this consideration of Jesus as Savior and the manifold ways in which this shapes his particular existence, we can begin to discern Christological criteria. For Barth, these are the fundamental assertions that must be made in light of the truths revealed through Jesus' historical existence in step one. In other

---

[30]   CD III/2, 54. Because of the two movements in Barth's Christological anthropology, John Gibbs argues that his approach should be viewed as having two foci: Christology and anthropology (John G. Gibbs, "Secondary Point of Reference in Barth's Anthropology," *Scottish Journal of Theology* 16 [1963], 132–5). But Gibbs' argument downplays the fact that the two moments in Barth's methodology are sequential and hierarchical. The Christological move holds ontological, epistemological, and methodological primacy over the anthropological move and we should, therefore, be very cautious about picturing them as two foci in the same elliptical system.

[31]   CD III/2, 46.

[32]   For Barth, this is less interpretation than revelation: "It is not that we interpret Him, but that He discloses and explains Himself to us, that through and in Himself He manifests His nature to us as our own true nature" (CD III/2, 53).

[33]   CD III/2, 58.

[34]   CD III/2, 249.

[35]   CD III/2, 328–31.

[36]   CD III/2, 209.

words, you move from "X is how Jesus revealed Himself to be" (step one) to "Y is what we must affirm to be true of Jesus in light of X" (step two). Thus, for example, Barth concludes that any analysis of Jesus' life and ministry must affirm that God's action toward humanity in Jesus is a manifestation of his own sovereignty rather than an infringement upon it.[37] In other words, in Jesus we see a God who acts graciously toward us, not through obligation, but through sovereign self-determination. This then serves as a fundamental Christological affirmation, something we must believe if we are to make sense of Jesus as he has revealed himself to us.

Third, draw inferences for humanity in general. This third step marks the critical move from the Christological moment to the anthropological one. So here we need to keep in mind Barth's warning against trying to move directly from Christology to anthropology, as though affirmations about Christ could be adopted straightforwardly as statements about humanity in general. So the Christological criteria identified in step two do not serve as the content of a theological anthropology, but as the framework within which a Christologically adequate anthropology must function. Thus, these criteria are "the limits within which we shall always have to move in our search for a theological concept of man."[38] For example, then, when moving from the Christological criterion mentioned above to its anthropological significance, Barth reasons as follows:

> If it is the case in relation to the man Jesus that in the divine action in favour of each and every man in Him it is also a matter of the freedom, the sovereignty and the glory of God, then necessarily ... the being of every man ... is not an end in itself, but has its true determination in the glory of God.[39]

Fourth, develop specific anthropological conclusions. From the Christological criteria, then, Barth discerns a set of anthropological criteria, which in turn serve as the basis for dealing with more material concerns in theological anthropology. Stopping short of this step would leave us with an abstract anthropology filled with general criteria that lack sufficient specificity to deal with real issues like gender, embodiment, free will, and personhood, among others. But Barth contends that his Christological approach "gives rise to a definite anthropology" specifically because it can and must turn its attention to the content of anthropology as the final step in considering the human person Christologically.[40]

It would take far too long to summarize how Barth develops this in his Church Dogmatics, but after summarizing the anthropological criteria in step three, he uses them as the basis for discussing issues as complex as gender, embodiment, free will, and relationality. In each case, the specific content of his theological anthropology develops from his anthropological criteria, which were in turn generated from his Christological considerations.

This, then, is how Barth develops a theological anthropology that is thoroughly Christological without naïvely trying to reduce anthropology to Christology.

---

[37] CD III/2, 69.
[38] CD III/2, 74.
[39] CD III/2, 73–4.
[40] CD III/2, 552.

The Who of Interdisciplinary Dialogue

One final issue remains before we can turn our attention to the adequacy of Barth's project, and that is the extent to which Barth's Christological anthropology remains open to dialogue with other anthropological disciplines. And it is precisely here that many think Barth's project fails, emphasizing so strongly the Christological determination of the human person that it seems to be just the kind of totalizing theological discourse that prevents meaningful engagement with other voices.[41] If these criticisms are correct, then Barth's anthropology will fail to satisfy in at least one important respect.[42]

The first thing that needs to be taken into account here is that Barth regularly engages in precisely the kind of interdisciplinary dialogue that such criticisms think are impossible given his rigorous Christocentrism. [43] In volume III/2 alone, Barth demonstrates his interest in philosophical, psychological, and scientific dialogue partners, as he engages what he refers to as the "phenomena of the human," that is, those aspects of human nature and existence that are susceptible to scientific inquiry.[44] As long as science remains content to be science and limit its inquiry to those things within its purview, Barth places high value on its results and emphasizes the importance of theology interacting meaningfully with

---

[41] E.g., Daniel D. Williams, "Brunner and Barth on Philosophy," *Journal of Religion* 27 (1947), 243; Albert Ebneter, *Der Mensch in Der Theologie Karl Barths* (Zurich oJ, 1952), 36; Robert S. Crawford, "Theological Method of Karl Barth," *Scottish Journal of Theology* 25 (1972), 327; Stephen H. Webb, *Re-Figuring Theology: The Rhetoric of Karl Barth* (Albany, N.Y.: State University of New York Press, 1991), 504; and Richard H. Roberts, "The Ideal and the Real in the Theology of Karl Barth" in *A Theology on Its Way? Essays on Karl Barth* (London: T. & T. Clark, 1991), 59–79. According to Bruce Marshall, then, the most common complaint against Barth's theology is its apparent isolationism (Bruce D. Marshall, "Book Review," *Journal of Theological Studies* 44 [1993], 445). And even the term *Christocentric* itself is often associated with anti-intellectualism and isolationism (J.K. Riches, "What Is 'Christocentric' Theology," in *Christ, Faith and History: Cambridge Studies in Christology*, ed. S.W. Sykes and J.P. Clayton [Cambridge: CUP, 1972], 223–4). And to be fair, Barth does occasionally make comments that seem to indicate a real reticence to engage in any such dialogue. As early as CD I/1, Barth cautions that theology should restrict itself to "its own relevant concerns" (CD I/1, xvi) and refuse to learn anything methodologically from other disciplines (CD I/1, 8). And then there is Barth's famous statements regarding the practical non-existence of a *philosophia christiana* (CD I/1, 6) and the incompatibility of theology with any world-view (cf. CD III/1, 340–44; III/2, 4–11; and IV/3.1, 255–6). Such statements, however, need to be read in the broader context of Barth's theology. For example, Barth's comments in I/1 must be read in conjunction with his extensive discussions regarding the close relationship that exists between theology and the non-theological disciplines (CD I/1, 5–6, 84, 284), the possibility of revelation coming through any medium (CD I/1, 55), his rejection of anti-intellectualism (CD I/1, 200–201), and his assertion of the "dignity" of other disciplines as they seek to carry out their own task (CD I/1, 256). Therefore, while Barth regularly expresses some reservation regarding such interdisciplinary dialogue, it is not that he thinks impossible or even invaluable, but only that he is well aware of the temptation to bend theology to the rules and frameworks of non-theological disciplines.

[42] Thus, Barth is often regarded as having little or no interest in the natural sciences and what they have to say about humanity (Pannenberg, *Anthropology in Theological Perspective*, 16; Alister E. McGrath, *A Scientific Theology*, Vol. 1 [Grand Rapids: Eerdmans, 2001], 176; and Wolf Krötke, "The Humanity of the Human Person in Karl Barth's Anthropology" in *The Cambridge Companion to Karl Barth*, ed. John B. Webster [Cambridge: CUP, 2000], 159).

[43] See esp. Torrance, *Karl Barth, Biblical and Evangelical Theologian*; Daniel J. Price, *Karl Barth's Anthropology in Light of Modern Thought* (Grand Rapids: Eerdmans, 2002); John C. McDowell, "Theology as Conversational Event: Karl Barth, the Ending of 'Dialogue' and the Beginning of 'Conversation,'" *Modern Theology* 19.4 (2003), 483–510; Daniel Migliore, "Response to 'The Barth-Brunner Correspondence,'" in *For the Sake of the World: Karl Barth and the Future of Ecclesial Theology*, ed. George H. Hunsinger (Grand Rapids: Eerdmans, 2004), 44–51; and Cortez, *Embodied Souls, Besouled Bodies: An Exercise in Christological Anthropology and Its Significance for the Mind/Body Debate*.

[44] See CD III/2 §43.2.

those results. True humanity, however, is only discerned in its relationship to God, which is something that no non-theological science can possibly hope to study. Whenever science tries to transcend its own limits and develop abstract and speculative "axiomatic principles" about true humanity, it ceases to be science and warrants condemnation.[45]

Given Barth's appreciation for the scientific study of the "phenomena of the human," it cannot be the case that Barth's Christological methodology prevents interdisciplinary dialogue of any kind. But it may still be possible to critique Barth's approach for precluding meaningful dialogue. With his predetermined Christological starting point, Barth seems to engage in dialogue having already determined what we must and must not believe, which would suggest that Barth is only interested in the kind of "dialogue" where people only say things that confirm what he already knows to be true.

Such a conclusion, however, misunderstands the nature of Barth's Christological approach. When dealing with anthropological phenomena, Christology does not provide a definitive "answer" to how those should be understood; instead, it is more rightly understood as a way of thinking about and interpreting that data. This certainly means that Barth's Christological starting point will render certain interpretations inadequate from the beginning—e.g. any "scientific" study that determines the incarnation to be impossible. But even these will prove fruitful in thinking through the data and understanding it from a Christological perspective. Much more often, though, the non-theological interpretations of the phenomena will not be Christologically invalid from the beginning, and will instead offer important perspectives on being human that theological anthropology can and must engage. Rather than irrationally isolated from other forms of discourse, Barth's theology, then, remains critically open to other approaches, though always in such a way that the conversation is guided on his side by his Christological starting point, which is the only vantage point from which we can integrate all sources of knowledge about humanity into a perspective on true humanity—i.e. humanity in relationship to God.[46]

No Free Rides: Assessing the Adequacy of Barth's Christological Anthropology

From the above summary, it would seem that Barth's Christological anthropology has resources for addressing the three major concerns that we have raised. First, and most clearly, Barth offers a robust biblical justification for his Christological anthropology grounded primarily in his doctrine of election. So, unlike many theologians, Barth does not simply assume that theological anthropology should begin with Jesus; he makes a strong biblical argument for why this must be the case. Second, although Barth's anthropological approach explicitly embraces the particularity of Christ's humanity as the necessary starting point for understanding humanity in general, his refusal to allow any direct move from Christology to anthropology seems sufficient to block any concerns about those particulars becoming unwarranted generalizations. Finally, Barth's approach demonstrates that theological anthropology can remain strongly committed to a Christological starting point and still engage in meaningful interdisciplinary dialogue.

Nonetheless, at least two significant issues remain. First, and most importantly, Barth's Christological anthropology rises and falls on his understanding of election, and many

[45] CD III/2, 22.
[46] CD III/2, 132.

continue to have serious reservations on precisely this point. Although many find his Christological reorientation of election to be a worthy contribution to our understanding of election, they remain concerned with the exegetical basis for his claim that Jesus alone is the Elect,[47] and they are also concerned that including all humans within the scope of election necessarily entails some form of universalism,[48] despite Barth's objections to the contrary.[49]

This creates a problem for using Barth as a paradigm for Christological anthropology because his doctrine of election is what provides the ground on which it makes sense to affirm that Jesus is the revelation of true humanity. If you alter Barth's doctrine of election so that it no longer revolves exclusively around Jesus Christ, his Christological anthropology has no basis.

Unfortunately few other theologians have developed the theological ground for a Christological anthropology as thoroughly and vigorously as Barth, leaving the anthropologist with limited resources if she remains unsatisfied with grounding it in Barth's doctrine of election. Granted, she could follow the lead of other theologians and develop a Christological anthropology on the basis of Jesus as the "recapitulation" of human life (Irenaeus), the one who begins the transformative journey of human nature toward its ultimately mysterious telos (Gregory of Nyssa), the eternal Logos who was the archetype for humanity (Maximus the Confessor), or even Jesus as the uniquely God-conscious individual who opens the door for the rest of us to follow into absolute dependence (Schleiermacher). Theologians have suggested a variety of ways in which Christology and anthropology might be related, each offering possibilities for developing a Christological anthropology, but to my knowledge, no one has developed any of these proposals with the methodological rigor and theological consistency as Barth. Thus, anyone seeking a different theological basis for a Christological anthropology has some work to do.

A second area of concern surrounding Barth's Christological anthropology involves the application of his methodological framework. Barth does an excellent job explaining that there can be no direct or simplistic move from Christology to anthropology. He is less clear,

---

[47]   E.g. D.F. Ford, "Barth's Interpretation of the Bible" in *Karl Barth, Studies of His Theological Method*, ed. S.W. Sykes (Oxford: Clarendon, 1979), 55–87; Michael O'Neill, "Karl Barth's Doctrine of Election," *Evangelical Quarterly* 76.4 (2004): 311–26; Sung Wook Chung, "A Bold Innovator: Barth on God and Election," in *Karl Barth and Evangelical Theology*, ed. Sung Wook Chung (Grand Rapids; Milton Keynes, UK: Baker Academic Paternoster, 2006), 60–76; and David Gibson, "The Day of God's Mercy: Romans 9–11 in Barth's Doctrine of Election" in *Engaging with Barth: Contemporary Evangelical Critiques*, ed. David Gibson and Daniel Strange (New York: T. & T. Clark, 2008), 136–7. Such concerns remain despite a number of recent studies pointing out the importance of exegesis in Barth's theology (see Richard E. Burnett, *Karl Barth's Theological Exegesis: The Hermeneutical Principles of the Romerbrief Period* (Grand Rapids: Eerdmans, 2004); Donald Wood, *Barth's Theology of Interpretation*, ed. John Webster, George Hunsinger and Hans-Anton Drewes, *Barth Studies* (Aldershot: Ashgate, 2007); George Hunsinger, ed., *Thy Word Is Truth: Barth on Scripture* (Grand Rapids: Eerdmans, 2012). For good studies of Barth's exegetical method as it relates specifically to his doctrine of election see Mary Kathleen Cunningham, *What Is Theological Exegesis? Interpretation and Use of Scripture in Barth's Doctrine of Election* (Valley Forge, Pa.: Trinity Press International, 1995) and Paul Dafyyd Jones, "The Heart of the Matter: Karl Barth's Christological Exegesis" in *Thy Word Is Truth: Barth on Scripture*, ed. George Hunsinger (Grand Rapids: Eerdmans, 2012), 173–95.

[48]   E.g. Emil Brunner, *The Christian Doctrine of God: Dogmatics*, vol. I (London: Lutterworth, 1949), 314; G.C. Berkouwer, *The Triumph of Grace in the Theology of Karl Barth* (London: Paternoster, 1956); Colin Brown, *Karl Barth and the Christian Message* (London: Tyndale, 1967), 130–33; Bruce Demarest, *The Cross and Salvation* (Wheaton: Crossway, 1997), 112; Oliver D. Crisp, "On Barth's Denial of Universalism," *Themelios* 29.1 (2003): 18–29; idem, "The Letter and the Spirit of Barth's Doctrine of Election: A Response to Michael O'Neil," *Evangelical Quarterly* 79.11 (2007): 53–67.

[49]   According to Lewis Smedes, Barth explicitly denied in person being a universalist, saying flatly "Ich bin keine universalist" (My God and I: A Spiritual Memoir [Grand Rapids: Eerdmans, 2003], 99), something Barth continued to maintain throughout his career (e.g. CD II.2, 417ff; IV.3, 461ff).

however, when it comes to discerning what qualifies as a valid move from Christology to anthropology. For example, in his discussion of the *imago Dei*, Barth argues that humans image God as male and female, grounding the imago in humanity's sexual nature[50] and drawing the further conclusion that the genders exist in an ordered relationship in which the male leads and the female follows.[51] And it does not seem like too much of a stretch to say that the reality of Jesus' gendered nature would lead us to conclude that sexuality has fundamental significance for being human. But what makes Barth's particular interpretation of the meaning of our gendered existence the appropriate anthropological conclusion to draw from the Christological starting point? Why not conclude instead, as some have done, that Jesus' maleness warrants viewing masculinity as somehow more amenable to imaging God than femininity?[52] Or why not argue that Jesus' way of living should have primacy over his physical body, drawing egalitarian conclusions from the way he treated women as vital partners in his life and ministry?[53] Each of these could legitimately claim to be drawing anthropological insights from a Christological starting point. They may lack the robust theological framework for doing Christological anthropology that Barth developed, but we still need some way of assessing the Christological validity of anthropological claims. Otherwise, as might be the case here, we run the risk of wrapping a pre-existing understanding of the human person in the comforting folds of an ostensibly "Christological" anthropology.

Conclusion

Theologians have long held to the intuition that Jesus Christ in some way reveals what it means to be truly human. But few have worked through the significant objections that can be raised against that presupposition, as well as the methodological issues involved in moving from Christology to anthropology. Karl Barth's theological anthropology stands as a marked exception, developing his Christological proposal with marked rigor and consistency. Nonetheless, many will find the theological basis of his proposal unsatisfying, and questions remain about how to assess the adequacy of various anthropological claims, raising the specter of an anthropology that only pretends to be Christological. Thus it would seem that more work remains for those who would like to continue affirming that Jesus reveals what it means to be truly human, either building off the work of Karl Barth and strengthening the methodological framework that he left us, or building a Christological anthropology off an as-yet-underdeveloped basis.

---

[50]   CD III/1, 195.

[51]   CD III/4, 169.

[52]   Augustine, for example, seems to have held that women do not image God in their femininity but only in their shared humanity, even though men image God through both their masculinity and their humanity (*De Trinitate*, 12.7.10).

[53]   E.g. Aida Besancon Spencer, "Jesus' Treatment of Women in the Gospels," in *Discovering Biblical Equality: Complementarity without Hierarchy*, ed. Ronald W. Pierce, Rebecca Merrill Groothuis, and Gordon D. Fee (Downers Grove, IL: InterVarsity Press, 2005), 126–41.

Scripture and Philosophy on the Unity of Body and Soul: An Integrative Method for Theological Anthropology

John W. Cooper

Overview

The goal of Christian theological anthropology as an academic discipline is daunting: a comprehensive account of scripture's teaching about humanity in relation to God. In principle it addresses all the characteristics, capacities, relationships, and ends of human life as presented in the Bible, from our creation in God's image and fall into sin, through redemption in Jesus Christ, to our future in God's everlasting kingdom.

This chapter, like the others in this volume, does not address theological anthropology as a whole; its focus is on the body–soul relation as an essential part. My goal is to survey how philosophy can help to clarify, elaborate, and integrate what scripture teaches about the unity of body and soul into a comprehensive theological anthropology.

A major reason for this focus is the current debate among Christian scholars whether body-soul dualism or some kind of monism best represents the teaching of scripture.[1] Historically and existentially, the body–soul relation is primarily a religious issue that has to do with death and the afterlife. But it is also a perennial question in philosophy, where the problem is to explain the unity and diversity of human life—how single beings possess irreducibly different physical, mental, and spiritual properties and capacities—as well as the possibility of post-mortem existence. Dualists hold that humans consist of two basic parts or ingredients—soul and body, or spirit and matter—and many affirm the metaphysical possibility of the soul or person existing without the body after death. Monists counter that humans consist of only one basic ingredient which constitutes or generates the whole person—body and soul. But monists disagree about the basic ingredient—whether it is immaterial (idealist, spiritualist, and personalist monism), material (physicalism and emergentism), or neither purely immaterial nor material but generating both soul and body (neutral and psychophysical monism). With respect to the afterlife, immaterialism is the only kind of monism which can readily affirm disembodied existence. These kinds of dualism and monism are the main options in philosophical anthropology. Most of them

---

[1]   Diverse positions are stated in *Faith and Philosophy* 12(4) (October 1995), on "Christian Philosophy and the Mind-Body Problem"; *Soul, Body, and Survival: Essays on the Metaphysics of Human Persons*, ed. Kevin Corcoran (Cornell 2001); and *In Search of the Soul: Four Views of the Mind-Body Problem*, ed. Joel Green and Stuart Palmer (InterVarsity 2005).

are currently endorsed by Christian academics, but versions of dualism, psychophysical monism, and non-reductive materialism are the main contenders.

Philosophical disagreement is not the only reason for the debate among Christians, however. Different views of scripture, its enduring truth-content, and its relation to philosophy and science are more basic. Philosophy cannot resolve these differences, but it can help clarify and elaborate biblical hermeneutics, doctrine, and the relation of revelation and reason. Its role in theological anthropology is extensive.

Given these issues, this chapter first summarizes the biblical presentation of the body–soul relation in this life and the life to come. It then presents the historical background of the current diversity of Christian views, contrasting the historic and modern views of scripture, the relation of revelation and reason, and the body–soul relation. The final section summarizes the strengths and challenges of the competing positions in Christian anthropology and eschatology. My primary intention is to describe the debate fairly rather than to promote a position. But it is clear why I affirm historic Christianity's two-stage eschatology—that persons exist between death and resurrection—and the dualistic-holistic anthropology it entails.[2]

The Unity of Body and Soul in Scripture

Biblical Hermeneutics[3]

The historic Christian approach to interpreting scripture is the grammatical-historical-theological method. It consists of three interrelated phases or operations: exegesis, theological or canonical interpretation, and application. Exegesis aims to understand the meaning and purpose of the original text by considering its vocabulary, syntax, genre, literary devices, related biblical texts, and its extra-biblical, cultural-religious context. Theological or canonical interpretation collates and synthesizes the teaching of all texts to formulate the doctrine of scripture as a whole on specific topics and into a coherent synthesis of all doctrines. Application relates biblical doctrine to current issues of faith, life, and learning.

The genre of biblical doctrine is a key hermeneutical issue. Are scripture's teachings about body, soul, life, death, and resurrection precise philosophical or scientific concepts? Or are they ancient near-eastern religious imagery that is irrelevant to science and philosophy? In my judgment the right view is between these extremes—ordinary-language realism. Scripture teaches universally intelligible truths expressed in historically-situated, common-

---

[2]   John Cooper, *Body, Soul and Life Everlasting: Biblical Anthropology and the Monism-Dualism Debate* (Eerdmans 1989; Eerdmans and Apollos, 2000); "Biblical Anthropology and the Body-Soul Problem," *Soul, Body and Survival: Essays on the Metaphysics of Human Persons*, ed. Kevin Corcoran (Cornell 2001), 218–28; "The Current Body-Soul Debate: A Case for Dualistic Holism," *Southern Baptist Journal of Theology* 13/2 (2009): 32–50.

[3]   Mark Bowald, *Rendering the Word in Theological Hermeneutics* (Ashgate 2007), Werner Jeanrond, *Theological Hermeneutics: Development and Significance* (Crossroad 1991); William Klein, Craig Blomberg, and Robert Hubbard, Jr., *Introduction to Biblical Interpretation, Revised and Updated* (Thomas Nelson, 1993, 2004); Manfred Oeming, *Contemporary Biblical Hermeneutics*, trans J. Vette (Ashgate 2006); Grant Osborne, *The Hermeneutical Spiral: A Comprehensive Introduction to Biblical Interpretation* (IVP Academic 1991, 2004); and Daniel Treier, *Introducing Theological Interpretation of Scripture: Recovering a Christian Practice* (Baker Academic 2008).

sense, ordinary (sometimes figurative) language.[4] It is realistic but not always literal or precise in what it teaches about God, angels, miracles, body, soul, life, death, resurrection, and the world to come. Thus biblical anthropology (if it takes a position) is monistic or dualistic in a generic, religious worldview sense. Philosophical and scientific conclusions may or may not be consistent with the view of humanity presented in scripture, which raises the question of ultimate authority.

The following sections apply the grammatical-historical-theological method to ascertain what scripture teaches about the unity of body and soul in this life and the life to come. The number of relevant texts is massive, so we focus on three key issues: God's composition of human beings, the unity of human beings, and the disintegration and reintegration of death and resurrection. These are central issues in the narrative from Genesis to Revelation.

Philosophy can assist with the methodological and epistemological aspects of interpreting these texts, formulating doctrine from them, and applying the biblical view of human nature to contemporary scientific, philosophical, and practical discussions of persons, minds, and organisms. Thus it can be an important bridge between scripture and theological anthropology.

God's Composition of Human Beings

Two Old Testament texts depict God composing human beings. Genesis 2:7 narrates God's creation of the first man by forming his body from soil and breathing into it *neshama*, the breath or spirit of life, so that he becomes a *nephesh chayah*, a living being.[5] (The King James translation, "living soul," understood dualistically, has caused much confusion.) Ezekiel 37:1–10 prophesies the future resurrection of God's people. The Spirit of God reassembles their bones and tissue into bodies and infuses them with *ruach*—breath or spirit—which brings them to life.

In both texts, God makes living humans by infusing spirit or life-breath into a formed body. One being is constituted of two different components. The body is a non-living entity derived from the earth. *Ruach* and *neshama* are synonyms in ancient near-eastern animism. They refer not only to wind and breath but to the whole range of animal powers—self-movement, sentience, emotions—as well as the powers of angels and gods and the distinctive abilities of humans, who interact with the gods and earthly creatures.[6] Each kind of being has its own *ruach*. These powers are not derived from the earth but are bestowed and withdrawn by God (cf. Ps. 104:29–30).

It is currently popular to assert that *ruach* and *neshama* are not substances but non-subsistent physical or biological powers—wind and breath. But that claim is too hasty. Evidence suggests that powers imply spiritual entities. *Ruach* refers to God, the gods, angels, and evil spirits—spiritual beings, not mere powers. Further, animist worldviews typically hold that visible powers manifest unseen beings—wind is the breath of God; an epileptic fit is the work of an evil spirit. By that logic, human *ruach* is substantive in the Old Testament because humans have the ability to interact with God and spiritual beings, a power which animals lack even though they are animated by (their kinds of) *ruach*. Spiritual power must come from the (subsistent) spirit in humans. In the Old Testament worldview, humans are

---

[4]   Kevin Vanhoozer, "The Semantics of Biblical Literature: Truth and Scripture's Diverse Literary Forms," in *Hermeneutics, Authority, and Canon*, ed. D. Carson and J. Woodbridge (Zondervan 1986).

[5]   John Walton, *Ancient Near Eastern Thought and the Old Testament* (Baker Academic 2006), Ch. 9.

[6]   Hans Walter Wolff, *Anthropology of the Old Testament*, trans. M. Kohl (Fortress 1974), Ch. 4 on *ruach*.

unique creatures in that we are both earthly and spiritual beings—both rulers of nature and a little lower than the angels (Psalm 8)—and composed of both. But it is not clear that human *ruach* is a substance that survives death. Ecclesiastes 12:7 is traditionally regarded as proof that the spirit ascends and exists with God after death. But Ecclesiastes also expresses agnosticism about human destiny (3:19–20) and considers the dead in Sheol as unaware and inactive (9:1–10). Its anthropology is not clear. *Ruach* could simply be an impersonal component withdrawn by God, leaving the dead powerless. All things considered, whether human spirit is substantive or merely functional cannot be determined with certainty from these texts.

What is the doctrinal import of the composition texts, and what might they imply for philosophy? Throughout the history of Christianity, both texts are taken to support dualism: God created humans and will resurrect them by conjoining two irreducible elements— a material body and a spiritual entity, a soul. But monists claim that the texts depict God endowing bodily beings with the whole range of human capacities.

Scoring this debate is a sobering exercise in the complexities of relating scripture and philosophy. A key issue, noted above in the introduction, is genre—how precise and realistic the components and divine actions are meant to be. Assuming contextualized ordinary-language realism as stated above, bones, flesh, life-breath, and divine inspiration in Genesis 2 and Ezekiel 37 are not scientific terms or metaphysical categories that stand for substances, ingredients, powers, or their combination. But they do express a realistic worldview using the terms of animistic Hebrew anthropology. They do claim that God constitutes living humans by animating their bodies with spirit. But doctrinal content is another matter—what does the text teach us or require us to believe? Perhaps it teaches that God fused two disparate ingredients. But perhaps the doctrinal point is only that God created human nature as a spiritual-physical duality-in-unity, which is a non-philosophical generalization that most philosophical models of the body–soul relation claim to represent.

As noted, sound biblical hermeneutics forbids drawing conclusions until these texts are related to others that are relevant. We consider two other kinds of texts: those that present humans as integral unities with diverse capacities; and those that envision what happens to humans after death. The same terms and themes expressed in Genesis 2 and Ezekiel 37 are present in these other texts. Taken all together, they present a much clearer picture of the anthropology and eschatology that emerge from the Old Testament and are affirmed in the New Testament.

The Unity of Body and Soul

There is virtual consensus among biblical scholars, theologians, and philosophers that scripture affirms the unity and integration of human life. Monists and dualists agree that body, soul, spirit, heart, mind, and will—whatever their metaphysical nature and relation—are diverse but interdependent, interactive, and integrated aspects or parts of living, active humans. No one in the monism-dualism debate thinks that body and soul are separate, independent, antithetical, or merely juxtaposed in human life, or that bodies are not essential to human life as God intends it. These are popular caricatures that do not fit historic Christian or philosophical substance dualism. Biblical anthropology assumes and confirms universal human experience and belief that our bodies, minds, emotions, relationships, values, hopes, fears, beliefs, choices, and actions are interrelated and affect each other in countless ways.

The most important feature of the biblical emphasis on the unity of human nature is spiritual—that all of life images God, is a gift from him, and should be lived for God according to his will. All of life is religious or spiritual. No part is purely secular or religiously indifferent; natural life is not separate from spirituality or public life from private faith.

Two iterations of the love command exemplify the diversity and spiritual unity of human nature, Deuteronomy 6:5, "Love the Lord your God with all your heart and with all your soul and with all your strength"; and Jesus' quotation in Mark 12:30, "Love the Lord your God with all your heart, and with all your soul, and with all your mind, and with all your strength."[7] Loving God [and neighbour] is the unifying meaning and purpose of human life.

Pre-modern commentators often understood these anthropological terms as separable parts, echoing Plato's philosophy. But modern scholars largely agree instead that they pick out distinct but overlapping and interdependent aspects, powers, and functions that constitute an integral existential unity. *Nephesh*, for example, which is frequently rendered as soul in older translations, also refers to the throat and diaphragm, to living (and dead) humans and animals, and to life-breath, as well as to the person—the self or "I"—who know, acts, and relates to God and other humans. *Ruach* shares with *nephesh* the meanings of life-breath and the person as self, subject, or agent.[8] The terms are synonyms in the Song of Mary: "My soul magnifies the Lord, and my spirit rejoices in God my Saviour" (Lk. 1:46–7). But unlike *nephesh*, *ruach* does not refer to living organisms or parts of them. In both Testaments, the semantic ranges of *nephesh* and *ruach*, and their Greek equivalents, *psuche* and *pneuma*, are distinct but overlapping when referring to humans. The same is true of "heart"—*leb* or *kardia*. Both Testaments refer to the physical organ that beats in the chest, but they speak of it almost exclusively as the seat of emotions, thoughts, choices, actions, and responses to God. The terms for flesh (*basar*, *sarx*) and body or organism (*soma*) are likewise used in distinct but overlapping ways that have personal-spiritual as well as physical functions: "my heart and my flesh cry out" (Ps. 84:2, KJV).

The cumulative result of studying these words in hundreds of texts of various genres from Old and New Testament books is massive and consistent. Human life is a fundamental God-related unity of diverse aspects, capacities, and parts which may have distinct roles and functions but are not self-sufficient or isolated from other parts and aspects within life as a whole. Perhaps phrases like "diversity in God-related unity" or "parts of an integral God-related whole" are adequate. This conclusion is consistent with and enriches the picture of humans as created and resurrected by God in Genesis 2 and Ezekiel 37.

Does this outcome preference a particular philosophical anthropology? All contenders claim to express diversity-in-unity. Dualists hold that God has integrated metaphysically distinct ingredients. (Trichotomists view body, soul, and spirit as distinct components.) Monists counter that God has elicited the interconnected diversity from a single primordial ingredient. But neither group can declare victory or disqualify the other on the basis of the biblical data.

Dualists can account for the diversity more readily than basic unity. Monists can explain basic unity more easily than how diversity arises. Neither side is able to explain fully the interaction between body and soul/spirit. Dualists and psychophysical monists acknowledge the integrity of both the spiritual and physical dimensions better than materialists or idealists, who view one as more basic than the other.

The diversity of aspects or parts does not require dualism. Soul, spirit, and body could be dimensions of an irreducible whole, or parallel terms that refer to the whole person. Thus texts which conjoin the terms, such as Deuteronomy 6 and Mark 12, discussed above, and others like Paul's expression "your whole spirit, soul, and body" in 1 Thessalonians 5:23,

---

7   Matthew and Luke repeat Deuteronomy 6. Mark uses a Septuagint version which adds mind.
8   Wolff, Chs. 2, 4, and 5 on *nephesh*, *ruach*, and *leb* (heart).

provide no basis for metaphysical dualism or trichotomy. Traditional commentaries which appeal to these texts as proofs are on shaky ground. But it is equally true that such texts do not exclude dualism or trichotomy. It is possible that the integrity of human life does consist of different ingredients or parts woven seamlessly together by God, and that texts about the afterlife provide the evidence that soul and spirit are separable.

In the same way, the unity and integrity of existence do not require monism—the view that all of human nature consists of or derives from one basic stuff. What unity and integrity do entail is holism—that human life involves an operational part–whole relation. Whatever its composition and decomposition at death, the divinely-designed state of humanity in this life and the life to come is integrally spiritual, mental, affective, and bodily. This point is crucial, because some monists fail to distinguish monism from holism and fallaciously argue that monism is the biblical position from the evidence for holism.[9] Although Deuteronomy 6, Mark 12, and 1 Thessalonians 5 do not entail dualism, it does not follow that they imply monism. They are certainly not direct evidence of monism.

In sum, analysis of the biblical texts about human composition and the unity of human nature yields no definitive resolution to the monism-dualism debate. *Prima facie*, dualism and psychophysical monism are closer to the biblical view of diversity-in-unity because they accord spirit and body as parallel components whereas idealism and materialism derive one from the other. But psychophysical monism fits only if the texts do not imply that we are constituted of two components. Dualism is consistent with two components, but it remains unclear whether soul or spirit can exist disembodied until we consider death and resurrection.

Disintegration and Reintegration: Death and Resurrection

Failure to resolve the debate thus far brings us to biblical eschatology—death, resurrection, and everlasting life. This move is not due to a morbid attempt to define life in terms of death, but because it may be decisive for monism or dualism. If not, the issue may be irresolvable. Most monists who hold that embodiment is essential for personal existence propose two alternative eschatologies: immediate resurrection or non-existence between death and future resurrection (discussed below). Thus if scripture implies a division or split in the psychophysical unity of human nature—especially if souls, spirits, or persons are said to exist apart from their flesh or bodies—then generic dualism is established. Monism cannot be proven by eschatology because the unity of human nature merely entails holism, not monism, as argued above. Dualism could be true even if immediate resurrection or a gap in existence occurred—the soul immediately switches bodies, or both body and soul are annihilated and recreated instantly or after a temporal gap. But monism is a reasonable account of biblical anthropology if biblical eschatology involves no separation of body and soul.

So we consider what scripture says about death and what follows. In spite of claims that the Old Testament is monistic and does not envision an afterlife, there is much evidence that it does. Like the other religions around the Mediterranean from Egypt to Greece, the Israelites held that the dead descend into the Underworld—Sheol, Abaddon, or Hades (Septuagint).[10]

---

[9]   Joel Green, *Body, Soul, and Human Life: The Nature of Humanity in the Bible* (Baker Academic 2008), 34: "my analysis will demonstrate how the Bible can portray the human person as a single whole or unified being (some sort of monism)"; also Warren Brown and Brad Strawn, *The Physical Nature of the Christian Life: Neuroscience, Psychology, and the Church* (Cambridge 2012), esp. Chs 1 and 2.

[10]   Alan Bernstein, *The Formation of Hell: Death and Retribution in the Ancient and Early Christian Worlds* (Cornell 1996), Part Two, Ch. 5; Walton, Ch. 14, esp. 320–21; Wright, *The Resurrection of the Son of God* (Fortress 2003), Ch. 2.

Existence there is apparently lethargic, ghost-like, perhaps even comatose—the allusions are figurative—but it pales in comparison with a good life on earth, blessed by God. Jacob hopes to be with his son, Joseph, in Sheol (Gen. 37:35). Isaiah 14 depicts the proud king of Babylon there, and the prophets warn against consorting with the dead. The clearest historical text is 1 Samuel 28, where Samuel returns from Sheol to prophesy the doom of Saul and his sons. The ultimate destiny of the faithful dead is not clear. The Psalmist hopes to "dwell in the house of the Lord forever" (23:6). Only Isaiah 26:19, Ezekiel 37, Daniel 12:2, and possibly Job 19:26 speak explicitly about resurrection. Almost all of these references involve figurative language, but there is ample evidence that the Israelites were realists about an afterlife for human individuals.

Post-mortem existence entails some sort of generic dualism in the Old Testament. The dead body is buried, and what is left of the person endures in the realm of the dead. It seems to be ghost-like—the person is in ethereal bodily form without the flesh, bones, and energy of living humans. *Ruach* departs—taken by God (Eccl.12:7), but not necessarily an enduring entity. *Nephesh* occasionally refers to the dead in Sheol (e.g. Ps. 16:10, 49:15) but *rephaim* (the cognate term for deified ancestors in Ugaritic) is more common. The Old Testament does not have a well-developed eschatology, but the combination of Sheol with future resurrection anticipates Second Temple and New Testament affirmations of two-stage eschatology. If monism precludes discarnate existence, it does not fit the Old Testament anthropology of death and resurrection.

It is important to consider Second Temple Judaism because it bridges the Old and New Testaments. The eschatological writings of the period are varied and diverse, but three important positions are relevant. The Sadducees held that Sheol symbolizes annihilation, appreciated Greek materialism, and did not believe in an afterlife. Philo of Alexandria used Plato to articulate the immortality of the soul and spiritual resurrection. The Pharisees and rabbis developed the Old Testament teachings about Sheol and future resurrection into a two-stage view—a conscious intermediate state until the resurrection and final judgment at the coming of the Messiah. A number of texts from this period refer to the dead awaiting resurrection as souls or spirits, an elaboration of their Old Testament meanings. Like the Old Testament, the anthropology of the Pharisees valued the body and emphasized resurrection. Its dualistic holism is a third option between Platonism and materialism.[11] There is no precedent for immediate bodily resurrection or non-existence until future resurrection, the two monist eschatologies.

The New Testament adapts the view of the Pharisees and rabbis.[12] In Acts 23:6–8, Paul identifies with the Pharisees against the Sadducees regarding the existence of angels, the spirits of the dead, and the resurrection. This is a key to understanding Paul's letters. When all his assertions are combined into a coherent whole, they present a two-stage eschatology of fellowship with Christ until future resurrection. In 2 Corinthians 5:6–8 (Philippians 1:20–22 is parallel), remaining alive is "at home in the body and away from the Lord," whereas death is "to be away from the body and at home with the Lord." In 1 Thessalonians 4:16 and 1 Corinthians 15:52, he dates the resurrection at the future return of Christ. Together these texts envision continuing fellowship with Christ between bodily death and future bodily resurrection. There is no gap in fellowship with Christ and no immediate resurrection. With respect to anthropological terminology, Paul does not write that his soul or spirit will be with Christ but I—the first person pronoun—"I … in the body or apart from the body," a meaning which soul and spirit sometimes share. He also uses the first person in 2 Corinthians 12:2–4,

---

[11] Wright, 190–200.
[12] Wright, 327, 424, 448, and 475–9.

where he wonders whether he left his body to visit Paradise in the Third Heaven while still alive. Surely Paul believed that persons can exist without their bodies.[13]

More fundamental than Paul is Jesus. Luke 23:43 makes clear that Jesus was with the thief in Paradise between his death and resurrection. Jesus is truly human as well as true God. He enacted a two-stage eschatology in which there is neither an existential gap nor an immediate resurrection. His disembodied human spirit existed between his death and resurrection, not just his divinity. His journey through death to resurrection blazes the trail for all who find salvation in him to follow (1 Cor. 15:20). Meanwhile, the gift of eternal life in him means that, although we die physically, we never die spiritually [cease to exist] as we await final resurrection (Jn. 11:25–6). Not even death can separate us from the love of God in Christ (Romans 8:38–9). All these texts promise continuous existence in God's plan of salvation.

With respect to terminology, the spirits of the existent dead are mentioned in Acts 23:8, Hebrews 12:26, and 1 Peter 3:19. The disciples thought that Jesus was a spirit—a ghost, a dead human—when they saw him walking on water (Matt. 14:26, Mk. 6:49). He assured them he was not a ghost when he appeared on Easter evening (Luke 24:37–9). Jesus warns his hearers to fear God, who can destroy body and soul (psyche) in hell, and not humans, who can kill the body but not the soul (Matt. 10:28).[14] The souls of the martyrs in Revelation 6:9–11 await resurrection and final justice at the end of history, as well as the 144,000 saints of the church triumphant who surround God's throne in Revelation 7. Soul and spirit do sometimes refer realistically to the not yet resurrected dead.

Given the texts and context, the most natural and reasonable conclusion is that the New Testament, like prominent strands of Second Temple Judaism, speaks of body, soul, and spirit dualistically in connection with death and the afterlife.

It is unnecessary to survey the numerous references to resurrection in the New Testament to establish it as the central teaching about life after death. Two issues are relevant to the current body-soul debate, however: the time of the resurrection and the nature of the resurrection.

With respect to timing, the resurrection occurs at the return of Christ, according to Paul, noted above. In Romans 8:18–23 he also correlates "the redemption of our bodies" with "the renewal of all things," which Christ will bring about at the end of this age. John correlates the resurrection with the return of Christ and the final judgment in Revelation 20. John 6:54 and 11:24 place the resurrection "on the last day." Every text that indicates when resurrection is to occur puts it at the end of the world.

The nature of the resurrection is most clearly described by Paul in 1 Corinthians 15:35–54. He states that the body raised is the same body that died. He also makes clear that our earthly bodies, which are like Adam's "soulish" body (soma psuchikos), will be transformed into spiritual bodies (soma pneumatikos) like Jesus' resurrected body. This does not mean that a material entity will become immaterial, but what was mortal, weak, and dishonorable will be made immortal, powerful, and glorious by God's Spirit.

In sum, the most natural and coherent reading of the New Testament is a two-stage eschatology of discarnate existence and final resurrection. It affirms personal existence between death and resurrection but provides little description of it. Its major emphasis is bodily resurrection, which completes and perfects the salvation of humans as created by God. In God's everlasting kingdom, humans will worship God, fellowship with him, and

---

[13] Joel Green, *Body, Soul, and Human Life*, 170–78, argues that Paul is a monist. George Van Kooten, *Paul's Anthropology in Context: The Image of God, Assimilation to God, and Tripartite Man in Ancient Judaism, Ancient Philosophy and Early Christianity* (Mohr Siebeck 2008), argues that Paul blends Jewish and Platonic anthropology.

[14] It is possible to read Matthew 10:28 non-dualistically, but spirit is certainly dualistic in 14:26.

rule with Christ in the new creation as bodily beings, just as we were created to do. In teaching that persons, souls, or spirits temporarily exist apart from their bodies, scripture implies that human beings disintegrate or "come apart" at death—a dichotomy that entails a dualism of some sort. But the language of the New Testament is the vernacular of its Jewish and Greco-Roman context, not philosophy.

Conclusion: Body and Soul in Scripture

We have considered the composition, unity, and destiny of humans in scripture. Its presentation of the composition and unity of humans during life affirms duality within a basic unity but does not clearly imply monism or dualism. However, the most natural and coherent exegesis of the eschatological texts does require some sort of generic dualism to account for disembodied personal existence between death and future resurrection. Both monistic alternatives—immediate resurrection and temporary non-existence—conflict with some texts. The most coherent conclusion from all three topics is the following: God created body and soul/spirit as an existential-functional holistic unity. But they are sufficiently distinct that the soul and/or spirit—the individual person—by God's power can exist and respond to God temporarily apart from the body. Thus biblical anthropology is a generic, non-philosophical holistic dualism or dualistic holism.

The Historical Development of the Christian Dualism-Monism Debate

This conclusion is the same one that the vast majority of Christians have reached for almost two millennia. Since earliest times the church and Christian scholars have interpreted the Bible as teaching body-soul dualism and two-stage eschatology. There was no real challenge to these doctrines until the seventeenth century, when some Christians re-ordered the relationship between revelation and reason and affirmed theistic naturalism. This reversal allowed for a variety of conclusions about the Christian doctrine of the life to come and the body–soul relation.

The Historic Ecumenical Position

The historic consensus and current doctrine of Orthodox, Roman Catholic, and confessional Protestant churches is that holy scripture is divinely inspired, true, and authoritative in all that it teaches. God is the primary author of the biblical canon, has meticulously superintended its formation and content through human authors and traditions, and continues to speak through it. Christian doctrine, formulated by the church as led by the Holy Spirit, summarizes the truth of God's enduring revelation in scripture.[15] Sometimes

---

[15] Website of the Greek Orthodox Archdiocese of American, Our Faith, "The Basic Sources of the Teachings of the Eastern Orthodox Church," http://www.goarch.org/ourfaith/ourfaith7064/, accessed 7/3/13; Catechism of the Catholic Church, Pt I., Ch. 2, Art. 3, "Sacred Scripture"; *Belgic Confession*, Arts. 3, 5, and 7. Orthodox, Roman Catholic, and Protestant churches disagree over the relation of the church's authority and the authority of scripture, but not over the nature, inspiration, and authority of scripture or the church's responsibility for true interpretation.

extra-biblical knowledge properly challenges received interpretations of scripture. But ultimately, truth-claims about nature, history, morality, God, and the body–soul relation which are based on experience and reason should be compatible with and understood in terms of the truth taught in scripture.

Historic Christianity affirms God's transcendence and supernatural action in the world, as well as his immanent action within the natural order. It holds that created reality consists of physical and spiritual dimensions, and that humans participate in both. By and large, historic Christianity has (sometimes reluctantly) incorporated modern scientific conclusions about the age, structure, processes, and development of the universe and life on earth into this theological-philosophical worldview.[16] It remains the official doctrine of most churches and is embraced by respected scientists, philosophers, theologians, and thoughtful non-academics.

The anthropology of historic ecumenical Christianity is holistic in emphasizing the unity of body and soul as created for earthly life, redeemed by Christ, and consummated in everlasting life. It is dualistic in affirming that God created humans from material and immaterial ingredients and that souls or persons exist between death and resurrection.[17] To elaborate these biblical doctrines, the church fathers reformulated Plato's substance dualism—the view that soul and body are distinct entities or substances so conjoined that the body is "in" the soul and the soul permeates every part of the body. This position has been held by Christians ever since. It was revised as dualistic interactionism by Descartes in the seventeenth century. World-class Christian philosophers currently defend substance dualism (A. Plantinga, R. Swinburne). A recent addition is emergent dualism (W. Hasker, D. Zimmerman), which holds that persons develop from physical organisms but are sufficiently distinct beings that God can sustain them without their organisms after death.[18]

In the thirteenth century, Thomas Aquinas modified substance dualism with Aristotle's metaphysics of form and matter. He taught that the soul is the form of the body. It not only thinks and wills but also organizes and animates matter to be a living, sensing body. Thus a human is one integral being or substance consisting of two basic ingredients, not two substances conjoined. Unlike Aristotle, Thomas considered the soul to be subsistent, so it can exist and function intellectually in the unnatural disembodied state between death and resurrection. His view is neither substance dualism nor standard monism but has features of both. It is a variation of the historic Christian position and is still widely held (John Paul II, E. Stump, J.P. Moreland).

The holistic-dualistic anthropology of historic Christianity remains the teaching of most churches and presumably is believed by most Christians, including some leading scholars.

---

[16] For example, B.B. Warfield, "Calvin's Doctrine of Creation," *The Princeton Theological Review*, xiii (1915), 190–255; John Paul II, "Message to the Pontifical Academy of Sciences: On Evolution" (1996), Catholic Information Network website, http://www.cin.org/jp2evolu.html; and Francis Collins, *The Language of God: A Scientist Presents Evidence for Belief* (Free Press 2006).

[17] Catechism of the Catholic Church (1994), exposition of Articles 11 and 12 of the Apostles' Creed; website of The Greek Orthodox Archdiocese of America, Our Faith: "Death: The Threshold to Everlasting Life" (http://www.goarch.org/ourfaith/ourfaith7076), July 2013; *The Heidelberg Catechism*, Question/Answers 1 and 57 on the unity of body and soul in life, their separation at death, and their reunion at the resurrection.

[18] Stewart Goetz and Charles Taliaferro, *A Brief History of the Soul* (Wiley-Blackwell 2011) is an excellent overview of the various dualist and monist positions.

Modern Christianity

A significant change occurred during the Enlightenment, when Deists and Christian rationalists, tired of interdenominational bickering, progressively adopted the rules and conclusions of reason as basic criteria for determining the truth of scripture.[19] Reversing the historic order of revelation and reason, they engaged in biblical interpretation and theological construction within the framework of the philosophy and science that developed after Galileo and Newton. Modern criteria of rationality trumped traditional doctrines when they conflicted. Rationalists agreed that the uniformity of nature—an operative assumption of science—is a universal principle. An implication for religion and theology is theistic naturalism, the view that all of God's action in nature and history is immanent in and in complete conformity to the order and states of nature.[20] Supernatural action is relegated beyond the universe to the afterlife.

Theistic naturalism has implications for the nature of scripture and what it teaches.[21] First, revelation and inspiration are entirely natural and historical. The Bible is a divinely guided collection of human responses to historically situated experiences of God. Its doctrinal content is much less coherent and detailed than historic orthodoxy supposes. Second, theistic naturalism eliminates supernatural miracles and, when coupled with scientific materialism or psychophysical monism, it denies that human beings have a metaphysically distinct spiritual component. Theistic naturalism has been widely assumed in historical-critical biblical scholarship and mainstream theology since the Enlightenment. It has nurtured the development of theological anthropologies and eschatologies consistent with scientific naturalism and physicalism.

The first major departure from ecumenical Christian doctrine pertained to the afterlife, not body-soul dualism. Most Christian rationalists and Deists in the seventeenth and eighteenth centuries were dualists who believed in personal immortality but, committed to naturalism, no longer affirmed the resurrection of the earthly body. In the nineteenth century, some liberal Christians—influenced by Kant, Hegel, and Schleiermacher—adopted idealism, which allows for personal existence beyond earthly life but considers the earthly body incidental. These dualist and idealist eschatologies have more in common with Socrates and Plato than with historic Christianity. They were the target of Cullmann's famous essay, "Immortality of the Soul or Resurrection of the Dead."[22]

Currently the main challenges to historic Christian anthropology and eschatology are from materialism and psychophysical monism. They have not been widely held until recently but also have roots in the seventeenth century. Thomas Hobbes was the first

---

[19] James Livingston, *Modern Christian Thought*, Vol. 1 (Fortress 1997, 2006), Chs 1 and 2. Locke in *The Reasonableness of Christianity* still accepted biblical miracles as "beyond reason" but not "contrary to reason." But Hume's "On Miracles" argues that belief in supernatural miracles is always contrary to reason. Hume's contemporary, Hermann Reimarus, the father of modern biblical scholarship, interpreted scripture according to Hume's principle in his Wolfenbuettel Fragments, published posthumously by Lessing.

[20] Arthur Peacock, *All That Is: A Naturalistic Faith for the Twenty-First Century*, ed. P. Clayton (Fortress 2007), especially "Emergent Monism" and "Theistic Naturalism."

[21] C. Stephen Evans, *The Historical Christ and the Jesus of Faith: The Incarnational Narrative as History* (Oxford 1996) for an elaboration and critique of the assumptions of critical biblical scholarship; also Alvin Plantinga, *Warranted Christian Belief* (Oxford 2000), Ch. 12, "Two (or More) Kinds of Scripture Scholarship."

[22] Oscar Cullmann, "Immortality of the Soul or Resurrection of the Dead?," *Theologische Zeitschrift* (1956), *Immortality and Resurrection* (London: Macmillan, reprint 1965). Cullman famously argued that the dominant teaching within the Christian scriptures is the physical resurrection of the body not the immortality of the soul, thus undermining dualist readings of scripture.

Christian to interpret scripture and explain the body–soul relation in terms of materialism. Not many Christians followed him until recently, because materialism was long regarded as antithetical to theism. Spinoza held that mind and body are two aspects of one substance. In his wake, nineteenth-century panpsychism regarded mind and body as distinct but correlative configurations of primordial vital or psychic energy. This perspective was adapted by William James, Teilhard de Chardin, and A.N. Whitehead early in the twentieth century. The synthesis of theology with Big Bang cosmology since the 1960s for the first time made materialism and psychophysical monism tenable and attractive to Christians from a range of theological outlooks. They could now propose that God has progressively generated everything in the universe, including human souls, from primordial (physical) energy by natural evolutionary processes. It is noteworthy that this synthesis of theology and the scientific worldview is embraced by adherents of traditional and evangelical Christianity (P. van Inwagen, J. Green, N. Murphy) as well as those in the theological mainstream (W. Pannenberg, J. Moltmann, A. Peacocke).

Most who adopt this theistic-naturalist perspective understand the body–soul relation in terms of materialism, emergentism, or psychophysical monism. All these alternatives to dualism attempt to avoid the reductionism and determinism of classical materialism and to defend human agency and spirituality. Non-reductive physicalism (N. Murphy) affirms that souls or persons are generated by organisms but not explainable by biological categories. They "supervene" on organisms and interact with them. Material constitution (L. Baker, K. Corcoran) is the view that persons are constituted by their bodies but are distinct beings with distinct capacities. Emergentism (A. Peacocke, P. Clayton, T. O'Connor) holds that souls are individual persons who possess ontologically distinct and irreducible properties and capacities generated by physical and biological processes of their bodies. Psychophysical monism holds that souls and bodies or persons and organisms are correlative aspects of human beings who are constituted of primal energy or events that are neither purely material nor immaterial but generate both (J. Polkinghorne, W. Pannenberg, D. Griffin). I refer to these views collectively as monism.

Christians who hold monism typically deny disembodied interim existence because they regard the soul as essentially embodied. They propose two alternative scenarios. One is immediate resurrection at the moment of death (J. Hick, W. Pannenberg). The other is non-existence until the final resurrection (J. Polkinghorne, J. Green, N. Murphy). Persons cease to exist until their bodies are resurrected—a gap in existence but not in experience.

A few monists have hypothesized a bodily intermediate state (L. Baker, K. Corcoran, T. O'Connor). At death God splits the matter of the earthly body into a corpse and a body that constitutes or generates the person until resurrection.[23] This scenario does account for interim existence and continuing personal identity.

Summary

The diversity of positions in the current Christian body-soul debate has developed since the seventeenth century from different beliefs about the Bible, different understandings of how it portrays human beings and the afterlife, and different ways of relating its perspective to science and philosophy. Currently, holistic dualism and two-stage eschatology remain the doctrines of most Christian churches and many Christian scholars. But theologically

---

23   T. O'Connor and J. Jacobs, "Emergent Individuals and the Resurrection," *European Journal for Philosophy of Religion* 2 (2010), 69–88.

conservative and progressive Christians alike promote several kinds of non-reductive monism as well.

Scripture, Philosophy, and the Unity of Body and Soul

This historical survey of approaches to scripture, theology, and theological anthropology identifies three general positions in the current body-soul debate: historic Christian dualism, modern theistic naturalist monism, and historic Christian monism. This section summarizes the strengths and challenges of each position's philosophical mediation of scripture to theological anthropology.

Historic Christian Dualism-in-Unity

The historic position seems to be the most natural interpretation of the biblical text in its historical context. Scripture has been understood that way in ecumenical Christianity since the early church. It not only affirms the biblical emphasis on the unity of human life, but also accounts for its two-stage eschatology—personal existence between death and resurrection. It takes the biblical perspective as the framework for philosophical and scientific reflection on the human constitution. Its holistic dualism remains the doctrine of Orthodox, Roman Catholic, and most historic and evangelical Protestant churches, and thus it is likely the faith of a large majority of the world's Christians. In addition, this anthropology shares with most of the world's religions the belief that embodiment is not necessary for the soul or consciousness—Islam, Hinduism, Buddhism, animism, and popular deism.

Dualism is also important for three other major topics in theological anthropology I can only mention—the image of God, freedom of the will, and the two natures of Christ.

Dualism provides a substantial and not merely functional view of the image of God. Because God is Spirit and does not have a body, traditional orthodoxy locates the image of God in the human spirit understood as a substance that expresses its God-imaging powers bodily.

Dualism supports libertarian free will (if humans possess it—an old Christian debate) because it holds that persons as agents transcend and can engage the causal chains of physical-organic processes upon which they also partially depend. Monisms which completely correlate mental events with bodily events have difficulty avoid determinism or compatibilism (of freedom and determinism).

Dualism supports Chalcedonian Christology, which asserts that the divine and human natures of Christ are neither mixed nor separated. If Jesus' human life depended on his embodiment, as monism holds, then he ceased to exist when he died, which would have separated his humanity and divinity. His resurrection would have been God the Son taking on flesh a second time. Dualism allows that the humanity of Jesus existed disembodied but united to his divinity until his resurrection on Easter.

These are some strengths of dualism-in-unity philosophies for theological anthropology. The main weakness of dualism is that it seems false and old-fashioned to people partial to scientific naturalism.

Theological anthropology requires sound philosophy as well as faithfulness to scripture. Space does not permit a summary of the philosophical strengths and criticisms of dualism in relation to various monisms or the merits and challenges of different kinds of dualism.[24] Theologians who are convinced that scripture teaches dualistic anthropology must decide which kind of philosophical dualism is most compatible with the nuances of the biblical perspective, earns the highest score in philosophical debate, and best comports with the evidence of ordinary experience and the sciences that study humans.

Theistic Naturalism and Monism

Christians who accept theistic naturalism and the current scientific worldview are entirely consistent in adopting a monistic anthropology and reading scripture accordingly. They can take either of two approaches toward the biblical perspective on humanity. One is to acknowledge that the traditional interpretation is correct—a dualistic anthropology and two-stage eschatology—but not regard these beliefs as enduring doctrines, just as other pre-scientific views, such as a flat earth and a recent creation, are not counted as doctrines. The other conclusion is that the tradition is mistaken and scripture does present a monistic anthropology and embodied eschatology. They can point to the biblical emphasis on the unity of human life and bodily resurrection. They can reinterpret the relatively few texts that seem to support dualism as figurative references to embodied persons and embodied eschatology. They can even affirm two-stage eschatology and adopt a monistic account of embodied interim existence. In these ways monists can claim to agree with biblical doctrine.

Theistic naturalism and monistic anthropology may not be the doctrines of most churches, most Christians, or most world religions. But Christians who affirm them believe they will gain increasing acceptance as scientific research and education progress. They wish to show that the Christian faith is not tied to outdated philosophy and science.

Monists are eager to reformulate theological anthropology, including the image of God, freedom of the will, and even the deity and humanity of Jesus Christ.

The image of God in humans is functional—those abilities that embodied humans have which are analogous to God's abilities to love, know, do justice, care for creation, and the like. The fact that God is Spirit and humans are physical is not important to God's image in humans.

Most monists hold that human choice and action are not simply effects of brain functions but are irreducible and exercise "top-down" causality on brain functions. Even if this explanation implies compatibilism (freedom and determinism are compatible), it agrees with traditional theologians, such as Jonathan Edwards. Emergentism can allow for libertarian free will if emergent personal agency sufficiently transcends the causal nexus of its organism. The psychophysical monism of process theology does affirm libertarian free will because process metaphysics holds that all entities self-actualize from genuine options.

Jesus' death and resurrection can be understood as an immediate resurrection followed by a series of appearances to his disciples, or as a temporary ethereal embodiment followed by resurrection. Only the non-existence/future resurrection view separates Christ's divine and human nature.

These examples illustrate how monism can approach other topics of theological anthropology.

The monist eschatologies of immediate resurrection and non-existence/future resurrection face a philosophical problem, however: the identity of the person before and

---

[24] *Soul, Body, and Survival: Essay on the Metaphysics of Human Persons*, ed. Kevin Corcoran (Cornell 2001) and *In Search of the Soul: Four Views of the Mind-Body Problem*, ed. Joel Green and Stuart Palmer (InterVarsity 2005) are anthologies of various dualisms and monisms.

after resurrection.[25] Immediate resurrection seems to imply two different persons because it posits two different bodies—a corpse and a resurrection body—and holds that persons are essentially tied to their bodies. Exact similarity is not numerical identity. Identity would be preserved if a soul switched bodies, but that requires dualism. If resurrection follows a gap in existence, then the identity of the person has no metaphysical basis, no continuity between embodiments. It is as possible that the resurrected person is a copy of the earthly person as that they are identical. Multiple copies of the earthly person are hypothetically possible, and all would have equally valid claims to being that person, which is impossible. Monists respond that personal identity is guaranteed if this is how God brings about everlasting life. But this view commits God to a weak and arbitrary ontology of identity.

The third monist eschatology—survival of an embodied person—does account for personal identity in immediate or future resurrection. God supernaturally causes an ontological dichotomy in which the person survives the dissolution of the whole. She is an ethereal bodily being—a ghost, a spirit. This scenario does account for two-stage eschatology and the souls and spirits of the dead. But it looks suspiciously like emergent dualism. It is most similar to a dualism which hold that persons, souls, or spirits are immaterial bodily beings—humans are always bodily beings but not always material.[26]

Monist anthropologies, like dualisms, have philosophical assets and liabilities which are constantly debated. Non-reductive physicalism, material constitution, and emergent monism offer non-reductive, multi-dimensional, functionally integral accounts of the unity of body and soul. Psychophysical monism might be more appealing theologically because it accords the soul and body correlative status, as scripture does, whereas physicalism and emergentism view the body as basic and the soul as derivative.

Biblical Monism

Unless it can account for two-stage eschatology, biblical monism in my view is the most difficult position to hold in the body-soul debate because of the tension between its view of scripture and its anthropology. It affirms the historic ecumenical view of the nature and authority of scripture but holds that current monism is correct about body and soul. Its greatest challenge is to show that scripture teaches monism instead of dualism. Given their view that scripture is the ultimate authority, biblical monists may not evaluate the scripture's truth-claims and construe its doctrine in conformity with science and philosophy. They must interpret scripture on its own terms by the most reliable methods and then see how its doctrines comport with current science and philosophy. Unless they can demonstrate that the Bible teaches monism, or at least that it does not teach dualism, biblical monists hold an anthropology which is at odds with their professed view of scripture and which sides with scientific naturalism.

A sound case requires an alternative monistic exegesis of the texts about death and the life to come because, as argued above, the texts about the composition and unity of human life are not decisively dualist or monist. (Duality does not entail dualism; holism does not warrant monism.) Biblical monism must make its case using hermeneutics (exegesis and theological interpretation) consistent with the historic doctrine of the inspiration and

---

[25] K. Corcoran, ed., *Soul, Body, and Survival*, and Georg Gasser, *Personal Identity and Resurrection: How Do We Survive our Death?* (Ashgate 2010), are recent anthologies on this topic.

[26] Thomas Schaertel, "Bodily Resurrection: When Metaphysics Needs Phenomenology," in *Personal Identity and Resurrection*, ed. G. Gasser, 103–25, proposes something like this. Aquinas held that the soul is the subsistent form of the body.

authority of scripture, which regards all texts as parts that contribute to a coherent whole. It must re-exegete all the texts that refer to the souls or spirits of the dead, existence apart from the body, and most crucially the texts about Jesus' death and resurrection. It must show that all are figurative references to embodied persons—that historic Christian realism has misinterpreted them. It must show that monist exegeses of the texts in context are as strong as the best case for dualist exegeses. (Simply proposing an alternative interpretation does not justify it.) Further, biblical monism must present an alternative theological interpretation, which synthesizes all the particular texts into a coherent biblical monism with the same breadth and depth as the case for dualism.

In my judgment, biblical monism has not made this case.[27] Most monists only address a few selected texts. Granted that modern biblical studies have shown that some traditional interpretations of anthropological terms are not sufficiently nuanced and overly Platonic, they have not shown that the texts imply monism. In fact current scholarship strengthens the case for a two-stage view of the life to come and a non-Platonic dualistic-holistic anthropology.[28]

It might be possible to develop a complete case for biblical monism. Two-stage monist eschatology might be a way. Monists have been at it only a few decades, whereas dualists have had two millennia. But if sufficient time and effort fail to produce an adequate case, it will be reasonable to conclude that scripture cannot be interpreted monistically using historic hermeneutics. Then biblical monists will have to choose between what follows from the historic doctrine of scripture and what follows from scientific naturalism. The choice will not be between revelation and reason, however, because generic holistic dualism will still be the most reasonable interpretation of scripture, and dualism will still be an ample metaphysical framework for physics, biology, and psychology.

Conclusion: Scripture, Philosophy, Theological Anthropology, and the Gospel

Philosophy has played an important historical role in interpreting scripture, relating it to extra-biblical knowledge, and elaborating theological anthropology. It continues to do so. Depending on their readings of scripture and its relation to extra-biblical knowledge, theologians employ philosophical dualism, idealism, psychophysical monism, emergentism, and non-reductive physicalism to formulate what they regard as the most faithful and reasonable articulations of the Bible's teaching about the unity of body and soul.

The debate remains vigorous, rigorous, and sometimes tedious. Important issues are at stake, but not the Gospel. All participants agree that God created us—body and soul—and that through the life, death, and resurrection of Jesus Christ, he graciously gives us everlasting life—body and soul.

---

[27] Joel Green is the leading Bible scholar who is a biblical monist. See his *Body, Soul, and Human Life*; and "What about ...? Three Exegetical Forays into the Body-Soul Discussion," *Criswell Theological Review* 7 (2010), 3–18. I challenge his exegesis in "The Bible and Dualism Once Again: Reply to Joel B. Green and Nancey Murphy," *Philosophia Christi* 9/2 (2007), 459–69; and "Exaggerated Rumors of Dualism's Demise: A Review Essay on [Joel Green's] *Body, Soul and Human Life*," *Philosophia Christi* 11/2 (2009), 453–64.

[28] N.T. Wright, *Resurrection*, is the most extensive study to date.

PART II
Theological Anthropology, the Brain, the Body, and the Sciences

PART II

Evolutionary Biology and Theological Anthropology

Joshua M. Moritz

Within the field of theology and science, discussions regarding the relationship between evolutionary biology and theological anthropology have tended to focus on the themes of "human nature" and "human uniqueness." The way these concepts have traditionally been formulated, however, has been rendered problematic in light of evolutionary biology and paleoanthropology. Even while divisions between the human and non-human, and between species, intuitively appear to be real, the common ancestry and evolutionary continuity of all life entails that there are no sharp and unambiguous dividing lines between various species, or between humans and other animals. Moreover, taking into account an evolutionary perspective, there appears to be no philosophically consistent or theoretically unproblematic way to establish biological essences or empirical natures. Consequently, the task of scientifically demarcating an unequivocal concept of human nature through which one might assert the essential biological uniqueness of *homo sapiens* would seem perennially elusive. It is precisely through an affirmation of an essential human uniqueness, though, that many projects in theological anthropology have proceeded, and many traditional and contemporary theological anthropological models have sought a scientifically discernible human nature that can be distinguished from that of other creatures. This chapter will discuss the empirical and methodological dimensions of various approaches to theological anthropology as they relate to evolutionary biology.[1]

Taking the Christian Doctrine of Creation Seriously

The natural sciences are in the business of discovering and describing material reality. Within the Christian theological tradition this same physical reality has been viewed as a cosmic window unto the divine nature, declaring God's glory, and "proclaiming the work of God's hands" (Psalm 19). To take the Christian doctrine of creation and understanding of God's work seriously entails taking the cosmic narrative reported by the natural sciences seriously. This, in turn, demands that theologians pay close attention to what practicing scientists and philosophers of science are saying. Regarding the origin and history of all terrestrial biological life, there are presently a variety of theories pertaining to the details of

[1]   I would like to express my deep gratitude to Oliver Putz for his critical engagement with various drafts of this chapter and for his many perceptive suggestions and constructive comments.

the mechanism (or mechanisms) that are thought to drive evolutionary change over time.[2] This scientific and philosophical deliberation over evolutionary mechanisms, however, must not be confused with the broader scientific fact that all varieties of organisms have indeed evolved. Biologists agree that "the facts of evolution are clear and are not disputed by any serious scientific worker."[3] The National Academy of Science in summarizing the scientific status of evolution affirms that "it is no longer possible to sustain scientifically the view that living things did not evolve from earlier forms or that the human species was not produced by the same evolutionary mechanisms that apply to the rest of the living world."[4]

Because the vast majority of scientists have accepted the basic facts of human evolution, systematic theologians who have accepted the theological challenge to take the Christian doctrine of creation seriously have likewise embraced evolution as the way God creates life.[5] This theological acceptance of the facts of evolution by both prominent individuals and by entire church traditions is reflected in Pope John Paul II's statement on evolution, which reads: "Today, more than a half century after the appearance of the encyclical [*Humani Generis*], new knowledge has led us to realize that the theory of evolution is no longer a mere hypothesis."[6] Lutheran theologian Wolfhart Pannenberg echoes the Pope's conclusion as he writes, "Darwinian theory has been victorious … . For all its difficulties, the theory of evolution still provides the most plausible interpretation of what is known about the history of organic life on this planet."[7] Similarly, Eastern Orthodox theologian and metropolitan, John Zizioulas, refers to Darwinian evolution as "a blessing in disguise." Darwin, Zizioulas continues, "pointed out that the human being is by no means the only intelligent being in creation … and that consciousness, even self-consciousness, is to be found in animals, too, the difference between them and man being one of the degree, not of kind. Thus man was thrown back to his organic place in nature." Since the idea of evolutionary continuity has "virtually won the science of biology," concludes Zizioulas, "theology has to make the best use of it."[8]

The Reality of Evolutionary Continuity and the Nature of Species

Having theologically accepted the reality of biological evolution one might still wonder where to draw the dividing line between humans and the rest of nature. In both popular and academic discourse it is common to speak of the essential distinction between "humans and animals." The axiomatic character of this presumed fundamental dichotomy can be seen,

2   See David Depew and Bruce Weber, *Darwinism Evolving: Systems Dynamics and the Genealogy of Natural Selection* (Cambridge, MA: MIT Press, 1995).

3   Richard C. Lewontin, quoted in Laurie Godfrey, ed. *Scientists Confront Creationism* (New York: Norton & Co., 1983), xxiii.

4   Kenneth R. Miller, *Finding Darwin's God: A Scientist's Search for Common Ground Between God and Evolution* (New York, NY: Harper Collins, 1999), 166.

5   See *Voices for Evolution*, ed. Molleen Matsumura (Berkeley, CA: The National Center for Science Education, 1995).

6   Pope John Paul II, quoted in Peter Hess and Paul Allen, *Catholicism and Science* (Westport, CT: Greenwood Press, 2008), 122.

7   Wolfhart Pannenberg, "Human Life: Creation versus Evolution?" in *The Historicity of Nature: Essays on Science and Theology*, ed. Niels Gregersen (West Conshohocken, PA: Templeton Foundation Press, 2008), 88.

8   John Zizioulas, "Preserving God's Creation: Three Lectures on Theology and Ecology," *King's Theological Review*, 12 (1989), 4.

for example, in assertions "that animals are not human" and that one "makes a crippling category mistake by failing to recognize the insuperable barrier that separates humans from all other creatures."[9] Many theologians and philosophers have upheld humans as radically discontinuous from animals and would agree with Martin Heidegger that "the animal is separated from man by an abyss."[10]

However, are such cultural and philosophical assertions positing a fundamental qualitative dichotomy between humans and other animals empirically untenable? A straightforward reflection upon the century and a half of scientific research substantiating Charles Darwin's understanding of the evolution of species would certainly lead one to seriously question the assumption of a sharp dividing line between humans and animals. While there is some debate over the question of the predominant mechanisms of evolution and how abruptly evolution can occur, among biologists there is no doubt that evolution has occurred and that the history of life on earth is characterized by common ancestry and phylogenetic continuity. Regardless of a variety of views regarding the means and tempo of evolution, Neo-Darwinists, process structuralists, symbiogenesists, saltationists, quantum evolutionists, and evolutionary gradualists alike agree that common ancestry and continuity are the norm.

According to philosopher of biology Elliot Sober, the unbroken nature of evolutionary transformations along with "the fact that species evolve gradually, entails that the boundaries of species are vague."[11] A century and a half ago Darwin referred to the problem of determining the correct theoretical definition of "species" as "that mystery of mysteries" and today evolutionary biologists acknowledge over 20 different definitions of the term "species."[12] Currently there is no consensus among biologists on the proper definition of "species," and some have questioned whether species actually exist in nature, whether an inclusive definition of the term "species" is possible, and even whether the category of "species" itself is conceptually incoherent and thus fatally flawed.[13] While evolutionary biologists have developed several working definitions of species there is general acknowledgment that no single understanding adequately encompasses both the empirically observed dynamic of historical continuity and the present discontinuity between life forms.[14] This conundrum concerning where to draw dividing lines between species while, at the same time, taking into account evolutionary continuity between such groups is called "the species problem" in evolutionary biology.

One of the most profound implications of the theory of common ancestry, combined with the realization that the process of the evolutionary transformation of life is characterized by continuity, is that "it is only with '20/20 hindsight,' the perspective of time, that we designate

---

[9]   Robert Nozick's dismissal of ethicist Tom Regan's Case for Animal Rights quoted in James J. Sheehan and Morton Sosna, eds, *The Boundaries of Humanity: Humans, Animals, Machines* (Berkeley, CA: University of California Press, 1991), 70.

[10]   Martin Heidegger, *The Fundamental Concepts of Metaphysics: World, Finitude, Solitude*, trans. William McNeill and Nicholas Walker (Bloomington: Indiana UP, 1995), 264.

[11]   Elliot Sober, "Evolution, Population Thinking, and Essentialism," in *Conceptual Issues in Evolutionary Biology*, 3rd edition, ed. Elliott Sober (Cambridge, MA: MIT Press, 2006), 334.

[12]   Charles Darwin (1859[1964]) *On the Origin of Species: A Facsimile of the First Edition* (Cambridge, MA: Harvard University Press), 1; Hey, J., 2001, "The mind of the species problem," *Trends in Ecology and Evolution*, 16:326–9.

[13]   Marc Ereshefsky, "Microbiology and the species problem," *Biology and Philosophy* (4 May 2010).

[14]   Jody Hey, *Genes, Categories, and Species: The Evolutionary and Cognitive Causes of the Species Problem* (Oxford: Oxford University Press, 2001), 20.

the breaks between ancestor and descendant species at a particular point."[15] In this way evolutionary continuity is like a spectrum of colors and the various forms of life are akin to the various color shades with no clear divisions that define and differentiate the various species from each other. While the colors themselves can be seen as real in a certain sense (thus justifying the use of the plural "colors," rather than speaking of the spectrum as a single "color") the exact boundaries between the various shades are eternally elusive.

The evolutionary and biological problem of defining species has been seen as having a direct bearing on the question of the ontological status of species. As we have noted, species, like colors in a spectrum, have fuzzy boundaries, and such vagueness is difficult to reconcile with understanding species as having specific biological essences or existing as empirically discernible natural kinds. As philosopher of biology Marc Ereshefsky explains, "no qualitative feature—morphological, genetic, or behavioral—is considered essential for membership in a species."[16] In order to be an essential trait (or assemblage of traits) which defines a given species as such (by being paradigmatic or typical for that particular species), consider the conditions that such a trait would need to satisfy: 1) A species' essential trait (or assemblage of traits) would have to occur in all the members of a species, without exception, for the entire life of that species, and 2) If that defining trait (or assemblage of traits) is to be unique to that species, it cannot occur in any other species for the entire existence of life on this planet—otherwise the other species would have the same defining traits.[17] While the dynamics of natural history do not in principle rule out the possibility of a trait occurring in all and only the members of a species, the possibility is highly unlikely. Moreover, in light of the historical contingency ubiquitous in Darwinian evolution and the sort of wide-ranging variability which is standard in biological species, it is hard to imagine how one characteristic or specimen "could possibly be 'typical' in even a statistical sense."[18] The "received view" in the philosophy of biology, then, is that biological taxa (species and higher taxa) do not have biological essences (where essences are defined as some empirically discernible "attribute or set of attributes which make the individual the kind of individual it is").[19] This view has been championed by David Hull, Elliot Sober, John Dupré, Ernst Mayr, Michael Ghiselin, and many others.[20]

---

[15] John Pojeta, Jr. and Dale A. Springer, *Evolution and The Fossil Record* (Alexandria, Virginia American Geological Institute, 2001).

[16] Marc Ereshefsky, "Species," in *The Stanford Encyclopedia of Philosophy*, ed. Edward N. Zalta (2010) http://plato.stanford.edu/entries/species/.

[17] Hey, 20.

[18] David Hull, "A Matter of Individuality," *Philosophy of Science* 45:3 (September 1978), 351.

[19] David Hull, "Are Species Really Individuals?" *Systematic Zoology* 25:2 (June 1976), 176.

[20] Marc Ereshefsky, "What's Wrong with the New Biological Essentialism," *Philosophy of Science*, vol. 77, no. 5 (December 2010), 674–85. This is not to say that these thinkers all deny the reality of species. Rather, the problem is one of demarcation. Mayr, for example, argued that species exist as populations with the potential to interbreed and produce fertile offspring. Ghiselin argues for the ontological status of species. "The reason that both Mayr and Ghiselin have argued against essentialism is that essentialism in their understanding would not allow for macroevolutionary changes (if there were essences which clearly defined species, then evolution would have to be saltationist rather than gradual)." Oliver Putz, personal communication.

The Nature of Species and the Problem of 'Human Nature'

Many evolutionary biologists who have rejected species essentialism have interpreted "species" as historical entities such that "particular organisms belong in a particular species because they are part of that genealogical nexus" and "not because they possess any essential traits."[21] In this understanding an organism is a member of a certain species because it is part of a lineage and not because it has a particular or essential morphological characteristic, a unique capacity, or a distinctive, empirically discernible qualitative feature. Consequently, no species, including *homo sapiens*, is seen as having an atemporal essence or any type of generic nature that lends itself to a scientific description. According to the "received view" of species in evolutionary biology, insofar as one wishes to identify or define human beings as the biological species *homo sapiens* he or she is forced to acknowledge that from an evolutionary perspective, there is no such thing as an empirical human nature and no biological essence to being a human.

Evolutionarily speaking "there is no essential feature that all and only humans must have to be part of *homo sapiens*. Humans are not essentially rational beings or social animals or ethical agents. An organism can be born without any of these features and still be a human. From a biological perspective, being part of the lineage *homo sapiens* is both necessary and sufficient for being a human."[22] While there may be certain characteristics which all and only living human beings possess, "this state of affairs is contingent, depending on the current evolutionary state of *homo sapiens*. Just as not all crows are black (even potentially), it may well be the case that not all humans are rational (even potentially)."[23] Some persons may—due to a number of genetic or developmental reasons (such as Autism or Rett syndrome)—lack the ability to speak or to comprehend a genuine language. If it is scientifically shown that bees do have this ability, it makes no difference with regard to including bees in the species *homo sapiens*. Regardless of their capacity for language, bees and people remain biologically distinct species because inclusion is determined by ancestry and not by essential traits or characteristics. Considering, then, the great degree of variation within humans, along with the evolutionary continuity between humans and other animals (and non-human hominins) it would appear that "the very ideas of human nature and 'normal' behavior sit very uneasily in a Darwinian world."[24]

The Quest for Human Nature and Theological Anthropology

It appears, then, that the biological essentialist approach to defining human nature stands in contrast to what has become the consensus view of evolutionary biology. However, it is precisely this essentialist understanding of human nature that is operative in a number of understandings of theological anthropology. To this end much theological work has been done attempting to substantiate the empirical uniqueness of human beings and to verify human distinction from animals in an effort to establish the anthropological locus of the tzelem Elohim (צֶלֶם אֱלֹהִים), the image of God, or *imago Dei*. This type of endeavor to demarcate and define the human being and the *imago Dei* in terms of uniqueness, by contrasting the

---

[21]   Hull, "A Matter of Individuality," in *Conceptual Issues*, 382.
[22]   Ereshefsky, "Species."
[23]   Hull, "A Matter of Individuality," *Philosophy of Biology*, 358.
[24]   Paul E. Griffiths, "David Hull's Natural Philosophy of Science," *Biology and Philosophy*, 5:3 (June 2000), 302; Horvath, 321.

human with the non-human, has been called the comparative approach to theological anthropology. This comparative approach has been described as "a quest for ways in which the human is different from other entities."[25] The comparative approach assumes that if animals and humans share some characteristic in common then that mutually held quality cannot be part of what defines the image of God.

Establishing Human Uniqueness as the *Imago Dei*

The association between human uniqueness and theological anthropology is quite widespread. Within the contemporary theological discussion this perspective is exemplified by Roman Catholic theologian Karl Rahner, Lutheran theologian Wolfhart Pannenberg, and Reformed theologian J. Wentzel van Huyssteen. Using the comparative approach to theological anthropology, Rahner offers an understanding of the personal relationship between God and spiritual being (that being capable of the transcendental experience by means of the Vorgriff or pre-apprehension of being as such) as it relates to human uniqueness. For Rahner, the human person is the unique point in evolutionary history where matter becomes aware and is able to transcend itself through consciousness and freedom. In this way humanity is the ultimate point of God's self-communication within history—a process of the emergence of spirit from matter, which Rahner calls Hominization. Rahner explains, "the history of nature and of spirit form an intrinsic and stratified unity in which the history of nature develops towards man, continues on in him as his history, is preserved and surpassed in him, and therefore reaches its own goal with and in the history of man's spirit."[26] Furthermore, humans as a species are uniquely defined by a supernatural existence—a type of graced nature or transcendental orientation.[27]

Pannenberg develops the doctrine of the *imago Dei* in light of the unique capacities of the human species. Approaching the matter of human distinctiveness, Pannenberg explains that, "modern anthropology no longer follows Christian tradition in defining the uniqueness of humanity explicitly in terms of God; rather, it defines this uniqueness through reflection on the place of humanity in nature and specifically through a comparison of human existence with that of the higher animals."[28] For Pannenberg, the *imago Dei* resides in the human being's unique Spirit-driven quality of being open to the world through freedom, imagination, and reason, and human openness to the world (Weltoffenheit) or

---

[25]   Colin Gunton, "Trinity, Ontology, and Anthropology: Towards a Renewal of the Doctrine of the Imago Dei," in *Persons, Divine and Human: King's College Essays in Theological Anthropology*, ed. Christoph Schwöbel and Colin Gunton (Edinburgh: T. & T. Clark, 1991), 47. Gunton describes the two primary approaches towards anthropology as 1) the ontological enquiry and 2) the comparative enquiry.

[26]   Karl Rahner, *Foundations of Christian Faith: An Introduction to the Idea of Christianity* (New York: Crossroad, 1978), 187–8.

[27]   See Karl Rahner, "Concerning the Relationship between Nature and Grace," in *Theological Investigations*, vol. 1 (London: Darton, Longman & Todd, 1961), 297–317. See also Karl Rahner, *Hominization: The Evolutionary Origin of Man as a Theological Problem*, trans. W.J. O'Hara (New York: Herder and Herder, 1965). It is important to note that Rahner at other places speculates about the possibility of Extraterrestrial Intelligence and comes to the conclusion that, given the notion of the active self-transcendence of matter toward spirit (one really should say of spirit-matter) ETI should be expected to exist elsewhere and that, if they do, they are equally oriented toward God as we are. In other words, in his discussion of ETI Rahner abandoned a human-centric view of evolution. Oliver Putz, personal communication.

[28]   Wolfhart Pannenberg, *Anthropology in Theological Perspective*, trans. Matthew J. O'Connell (Edinburgh: T. & T. Clark, 1999), 27.

exocentricity reveals a fundamental disposition within human nature itself. This human disposition towards openness to the world is "in distinction from the dependence of the animals on their environment," and such behavior "gives the human being a special place in the animal world."[29] Unlike animals, says Pannenberg, "human beings are no longer limited by a set of drives and instincts."[30] The human being "is open to constantly new things and fresh experiences, while animals are open only to a limited, fixed number of environmental features that are typical of the species."[31] Thus, human exocentricity far transcends the openness of all other animals to their environment, and is indeed the key characteristic that distinguishes humans from other living creatures. In this way there is a "profound distinction between man and all animals" as "the openness to the world that modern anthropology has in view [for humans] differs not only in degree but also in kind from the animal's bondage to its environment."[32] Consequently, humans are understood to be qualitatively different from animals and this difference lies within the dissimilar natures of humans and animals as these natures are empirically discerned. For Pannenberg, then, there is not so much an ontological difference between humans and nonhumans as much as there is a scientific or behavioral difference owing to the distinctive natures or essences of humans as compared with non-humans.

Like Pannenberg, van Huyssteen in his Gifford Lectures engages in a project where he explores "scientific notions of human distinctiveness" in order to ground "theological notions of human uniqueness" as they mutually inform the doctrine of the *imago Dei*.[33] To this end he surveys the data of paleoanthropology in order to rediscover the evolutionary origins of human rationality and "the meaning of embodiment for theological anthropology." Recovering a biological basis underpinning the uniquely human capacities for consciousness, self-awareness, and rationality—capacities that are grounded in the distinctive cognitive fluidity and linguistic aptitude of pre-historic behaviorally modern humans—van Huyssteen hopes to avoid "baroque theological abstractions" about the image of God, and to re-envision "notions of human uniqueness and the imago Dei that resonate powerfully with the embodied, flesh-and-blood humans we encounter in the Genesis texts."[34] For van Huyssteen, if theologians take science "seriously on the issue of human uniqueness," then "the notion of the imago Dei finally is strikingly revisioned as emerging from nature itself."[35] The reality of human uniqueness as surmised from the findings of paleoanthropology and the neurosciences, explains van Huyssteen, is of crucial importance for defining the *imago Dei* in theology. It is the entire ensemble and constitution of our unique biological and spiritual human nature that delineates the *imago Dei*, and science can assist in providing anthropological content for this theological doctrine. Furthermore, for van Huyssteen the *imago Dei* was only achieved around 35–40 kya when, he argues, anatomically modern human beings achieved "behavioral modernity"—a cognitive capacity that allowed for religious thought and behavior—in a cultural and cognitive "big bang" called the Upper Paleolithic Revolution. According to van Huyssteen, until that point in time anatomically

---

29   Pannenberg, *Anthropology in Theological Perspective*, 34–5.

30   Ibid., 35.

31   Wolfhart Pannenberg, *What is Man? Contemporary Anthropology in Theological Perspectives*, trans. Duane A. Priebe (Philadelphia: Fortress, 1970), 7ff.

32   Pannenberg, *What is Man?*, 8.

33   J. Wentzel van Huyssteen, *Alone In the World?: Human Uniqueness in Science and Theology* (Grand Rapids, MI: Eerdmans, 2006), 113.

34   Van Huyssteen, *Alone in the World*, 113.

35   J. Wentzel van Huyssteen, "Human Origins and Religious Awareness," *Studia Theologica—Nordic Journal of Theology*, 59:2 (2005): 124; Van Huyssteen, *Alone in the World*, xviii.

modern humans were incapable of religion (which goes along with language evolution and artistic expression) and thus did not possess the *imago Dei*.

Questioning Human Uniqueness, Extending the *Imago Dei*, or Rejecting the *Imago Dei*

What appears to be implied by the term "uniqueness" within many current theological discussions is a certain evaluative measure that is really saying "our human capacities count" in a way that is more important or valuable than the unique capacities of other animals. However, current research has tended to undermine normative biological understandings of human nature and the scientific search for human uniqueness has come up empty handed. In the last 20 years it has become increasingly clear that modern humans cannot be held up as possessing a more valuable or significant type of biological or behavioral uniqueness than that of earlier humans or non-human hominins. For decades, paleoanthropologists starkly contrasted earlier "archaic" humans and non-human hominins with their "behaviorally-modern" Upper Paleolithic counterparts, and they explained the differences between them in terms of a single "Human Revolution" or cognitive big bang about 40,000 years ago that dramatically transformed human biology and behavior. However, there is now a growing consensus among researchers that the behavior of the earliest *homo sapiens* was not significantly different from that of more-recent "modern" humans.[36] Forcefully making this point, paleoanthropologist John Shea "tests and falsifies the core assumption of the behavioral modernity concept—the belief that there were significant differences in behavioral variability between the oldest H. sapiens and populations younger than 50 kya." He concludes that from an empirical perspective the notion of an Upper Paleolithic Revolution is highly problematic and that the corresponding "analytical construct, 'behavioral modernity' is deeply flawed at all epistemological levels." Consequently, says Shea, "behavioral modernity and allied concepts have no further value to human origins research."[37]

Beyond the empirical and philosophical difficulties associated with making distinctions between archaic and behaviorally modern humans are those related to distinguishing between the traits and behaviors of humans and those of non-human hominins who equally possessed the capacity for complex language, culture, and symbolic representation. For example, it now appears that the faculty for complex language was possessed by several non-human hominins such as Neanderthals, the Denisovans, the Flores hominins, and at least one African hominin that can be inferred from genetic admixture.[38] Reviewing the available data, Dan Dediu and Stephen C. Levinson maintain that modern language and speech can be traced back to the last common ancestor we shared with a number of non-human hominins roughly half a million years ago.[39] Other studies point to the presence

---

[36] Christopher Henshilwood, "Late Pleistocene Techno-traditions in Southern Africa: A Review of the Still Bay and Howiesons Poort, c. 75 ka," *Journal of World Prehistory*, Nov. 6, 2012.

[37] John Shea, "Homo sapiens Is as Homo sapiens Was: Behavioral Variability versus 'Behavioral Modernity' in Paleolithic Archaeology," *Current Anthropology*, 52:1 (February 2011), 1.

[38] Michael Hammer et al, "Genetic Evidence for Archaic Admixture in Africa," *PNAS* 108(37), September 13, 2011; Karl C. Diller and Rebecca L. Cann, "Evidence against a genetic-based revolution in language 50,000 years ago," in *The Cradle of Language*, ed. Rudolf Botha and Chris Knight (New York: Oxford UP, 2009), 136; J. Krause et al., "The derived FOXP2 variant of modern humans was shared with Neanderthals," *Current Biology*, 17: (2007): 1908–12.

[39] Dan Dediu, Stephen Levinson. "On the antiquity of language: the reinterpretation of Neandertal linguistic capacities and its consequences." *Frontiers in Psychology*, July 2013.

of symbolic art in non-human hominins,[40] and investigators have shown that non-human hominins were even as technologically innovative as their human counterparts. For instance, studies on the development of specialized bone tools among Neanderthals (called *lissoirs* or burnishers) indicate that a number of such advanced tool types found among these hominins predate the arrival of *homo sapiens*. This shows that Neanderthals developed such tools independently of humans and some researchers have even argued that it is likely that humans learned about certain tools from Neanderthals. [41]

A number of current thinkers at the interface of theology and the natural sciences, such as Gregory Peterson and Celia Deane-Drummond, have accepted this challenge from evolution and paleoanthropology and have recommended extending the *imago Dei* to non-human hominins and to certain cognitively sophisticated animals. Peterson, utilizing the comparative-substantive approach to theological anthropology, recommends that we significantly rethink our understanding of the *imago Dei*. He concludes that we "change the locus of the image of God from human beings to nature" and that we consider the *imago Dei* within human beings as a smaller part of the much more broadly bestowed divine image. Peterson specifically raises the question of non-human hominins and asks, "were they, too, in the image of God, and at what point, assuming that one can be specified, did they cross the threshold to being human in the morally and theologically relevant sense of the word?"[42] Deane-Drummond points to the recent discovery of *homo floresiensis* who lived contemporaneously with humans and asks if these findings "undermine the meaning of humans as made in the image of God, imago Dei?" In a similar vein as Peterson, Deane-Drummond argues, "there is certainly support for the idea that all animals share in the likeness of the divine nature, even non-rational animals."[43]

Still other theologians, such as David Cunningham suggest moving away from the *imago Dei* as a doctrinal focus or dispensing with the category altogether.[44] Cunningham raises "some critical questions about the traditional interpretation of the Christian doctrine of the imago Dei as describing human beings, and human beings alone, as created in the image and likeness of God." He explains that previous theological conclusions were based on the "assumption that rational thought and language-use are exclusively human faculties." However, says Cunningham, this understanding is no longer possible. Employing the comparative-substantive approach to theological anthropology, he points out that "a great deal of recent scientific evidence has brought our assumptions about rationality and language-use into question, particularly with respect to other animals." As a result, if Christian theology continues to maintain a distinction between humans and animals with regard to the divine image, then "it must do so with specifically theological arguments—rather than relying on a scientific distinction that has long since fallen out of favour." Cunningham doubts whether the image of God is a useful theological category. Even "if we were to grant that the language of the imago Dei could be applied, at least in a

---

[40]   Joao Zilhao, "The Emergence of Ornaments and Art: An Archaeological Perspective on the Origins of 'Behavioral Modernity,'" *Journal of Archaeological Research,* 15 (2007), 1–54.

[41]   Marie Soressi et al. "Neandertals made the first specialized bone tools in Europe," *Proc. Natl Acad. Sci.,* vol 110:35 (Aug 27, 2013).

[42]   See Gregory Peterson, "The Evolution of Consciousness and the Theology of Nature," *Zygon,* 34:2 (June 1999): 299; Gregory Peterson, "Uniqueness, the Image of God and the Problem of Method: Engaging Van Huyssteen," *Zygon,* 43:2 (2008), 473.

[43]   See Celia Deane-Drummond, "Are Animals Moral? Taking Soundings through Vice, Virtue, Conscience and Imago Dei," in *Creaturely Theology: On God, Humans and Other Animals,* ed. Celia Deane-Drummond and David Clough (London: SCM Press, 2009), 209.

[44]   A similar position is held by Oliver Putz. See Oliver Putz, "Moral Apes, Human Uniqueness, and the Image of God," *Zygon,* 44:3 (2009), 613–24.

limited sense, to all human beings and to them alone," he says, "we are unlikely to settle on any clear understanding of what this actually means." In light of this lack of consensus on the theological definition of the image of God, Cunningham recommends "moving away from a central focus on humanity as the image of God."[45]

Transcending Human Uniqueness and Electing the *Imago Dei*

Others, such as philosophical theologian Joshua Moritz, have pointed out that within scripture the bestowal of the image of God is not based on any particular traits or unique capacities which humans possess to the exclusion of non-human creatures; in light of this have focused on theologically reframing the *imago Dei* category in light of biblical or historical election. Moritz points out that in scripture the "image and likeness of God" is never said to be about exceptional capacities or traits that humans alone have which automatically qualify them (and disqualify other creatures) for inclusion in the *imago Dei* category. In fact, assertions of human uniqueness based on certain characteristics and "claims for a 'special creation' of humanity in comparison with animals and the material world conflict with the strong assertion in Genesis 2 that, physically (organically), Adam does not differ from the 'beasts of the field.'"[46] The theological language of anthropology in Genesis 1 and 2 "underscores Adam's linkage with the animal creation, not his difference from it."[47] The terms "'image' and 'likeness' ... make no statements about the nature of human beings."[48] To properly understand the meaning of the *imago Dei* texts, then, Moritz recommends that theologians heed the words of Bible scholar Claus Westermann and strive to resist "the tendency to see the image and likeness of God as a something, a quality."[49]

For Moritz, the historical concept of election, the central interpretive framework in Hebrew thought, illuminates the meaning of how humans are designated and created as the image and likeness of God. As is well known, the concept of the "image" as used in Genesis "has a deep ancient Near Eastern background."[50] From a comparison of the Hebrew text with ancient Near Eastern parallels it is clear that the phrase "image of God" emerges from a common royal ideology where individual Mesopotamian, Hittite, Assyrian, Babylonian,

---

[45]   David S. Cunningham, "The Way of all Flesh: Rethinking the Imago Dei," in *Creaturely Theology: On God, Humans and Other Animals*, ed. Celia Deane-Drummond and David Clough (London: SCM, 2009): 100.

[46]   Lawson Stone, "The Soul: Possession, Part, or Person? The Genesis of Human Nature in Genesis 2:7" in *What About the Soul? Neuroscience and Christian Anthropology*, ed. Joel B. Green, Murphy and Maloney (Nashville: Abingdon, 2004), 50.

[47]   Ibid., 57. There is no reason, explains James Barr, to believe that the author of Genesis chapter one "had in his mind any definite idea about the content or location of the image of God." James Barr, "The Image of God in the Book of Genesis: A Study of Terminology", *Bulletin of the John. Rylands Library*, 51 (1968–69), 13.

[48]   Horst Dietrich Preuss, *Old Testament Theology*, vol 2, trans. Leo G. Perdue (Edinburgh: T. & T. Clark, 1996), 115.

[49]   Claus Westermann, *Creation*, trans. John H. Scullion, S.J. (Philadelphia: Fortress Press, 1974), 57–8.

[50]   W. Randall Garr, "The Nouns תומד and צלם," in *In His Own Image and Likeness: Humanity, Divinity, and Monotheism* (Leiden: Brill, 2003), 136.

and Egyptian priest-kings are referred to as the image and likeness of particular gods.[51] In this ancient Near Eastern conception, the king—more accurately understood as a priest-king—was seen as "the gods' authorized deputy or viceroy on earth."[52] Within this same ancient Near Eastern royal ideology (Königsideologie), Moritz explains, we find that the very kings predicated as the image and likeness of a god are simultaneously chosen or elected as king by the god whom they image.[53] Beyond this, says Moritz, each of the structural elements describing historical election within the Hebrew textual tradition—including divine blessing, the multiplication of progeny, the giving of commandments and the promise of the land—are also present in the early chapters of Genesis as they describe the first humans who are created as the image and likeness of God (Gen 1:28 and Gen 2:15–16). As a consequence, human beings, acting as vice-regents or kings on God's behalf, are the brethren of the non-human creatures that are under their dominion. As the elected high priests of creation, *homo sapiens* are called to intercede before God for the sake of the entire created realm with the ultimate aim that all creatures should live in God's presence.

According to Moritz, then, the *imago Dei* stands for God's historical choosing or election of human beings from among the animals and setting them apart as God's representatives for the sake and fulfillment of God's purposes. He maintains that both the functional and relational understandings of the *imago Dei* can be seen as emerging from—and can be unified through—viewing the "image and likeness of God" as God's historical choosing or election of human beings from among the created creatures.[54] Moritz maintains that the relationship between God and human beings is precisely one of election, and points out that election within the ancient Near Eastern context specifically entails dominion. Moreover, he holds, viewing the *imago Dei* as election provides a central place for the substantive or structural interpretation of the *imago Dei* in that one may understand such substantive capacities or traits (e.g. rationality and language) as providing the content of what Moritz calls the necessary—but not sufficient—prerequisites or preconditions for divine election.[55]

Considering the *imago Dei* in light of the Jewish theological framework of historical election, Moritz has argued that within scripture the primary (and perhaps only) defining locus of human uniqueness and the content of the *imago Dei* is the fact that humans were chosen by God from among creatures to accomplish God's particular purposes for creation.

---

[51] The Hebrew phrase, "image of God," (selem elohîm) used in Genesis 1:26–7 is the exact counterpart of the Akkadian expression (salam [God's name]: "image of Enlil [Marduk, etc.]"), an expression which often appears as an epithet of Mesopotamian priest-kings. See Bird, "Theological Anthropology in the Hebrew Bible," 260–61. See A.R. Millard and P. Bordreuil, "A Statue from Syria with Assyrian and Aramaic Inscriptions," *The Biblical Archaeologist*, 45:3 (Summer, 1982), 135–41. "References to the king as the image (salmu) of God abound in the Neo-Assyrian royal correspondence." See Simo Parpola, "The Assyrian Tree of Life: Tracing the Origins of Jewish Monotheism and Greek Philosophy," *Journal of Near Eastern Studies*, 52:3 (July 1993) 168. One Neo-Babylonian text declares "The king of the world is the very image of Marduk," see J. Richard Middelton, *The Liberating Image: The Imago Dei in Genesis 1* (Grand Rapids: Brazos, 2005), 113. An ancient Assyrian text reads, "the father of the king my lord was the very image of Bel, and the king my lord is likewise the very image of Bel." Simo Parpola, *Letters from Assyrian Scholars to the Kings Esarhaddon and Ashurbanipal* (Eisenbrauns, 2007), 99.

[52] Middelton, 119.

[53] Preuss, *Old Testament Theology*, vol. 1, 29. For example Thutmose IV of Egypt, "son of Atum, living image of the All-Lord, sovereign, begotten of Re" inscribed on a stele "that in a dream at the foot of the great Sphinx of Giza he had the experience of being elected king by the sun god Re"—the god of whom he is the living image.

[54] Joshua M. Moritz, "Evolution, the End of Human Uniqueness, and the Election of the Imago Dei," *Theology and Science*, 9:3 (Aug 2011).

[55] See Joshua M. Moritz and Ralph Stearley, "The Elusive Horizon of Behavioral Modernity, the Boundaries of Cultural Humanity, and the Elected Image of God," *Science and Christian Belief* (forthcoming).

Human beings are elected as the *imago Dei* to exercise an office within the family of fellow creatures, and their election is not the result of any biologically or behaviorally discernible uniqueness.[56] The image and likeness of God in humans is not dependent upon any morphological features, behaviors, or cognitive capacities that *homo sapiens* might possess in distinction from animals or other non-human creatures, but rather on the historical act of God's sovereign and mysterious choice.

Conclusion

This chapter has explored how a variety of theologians understand theological anthropology in light of human nature and human uniqueness. While one sense of human nature is uncontroversial (i.e. human nature as an intuitive idea about what human beings are like), the scientific sense of human nature, as "something that causes us to have certain human characteristics," needs to be substantially rethought in the light of current understandings of biology.[57] Beyond the empirical fact that "there is no special part, such as our blood or our genes, where human nature resides," is the fact that in the last few decades evolutionary biologists and philosophers of biology have raised a number of concerns about any discussion of generic biological natures as they correspond to individual species. The developments within evolutionary biology, concerned with the problems related to defining "natures," directly impact theological conceptions of the human being that depend upon such scientifically elusive definitions. Traditional understandings of theological anthropology that are delineated according to biological concepts of human nature and human uniqueness will likewise be susceptible to the empirical challenges facing those concepts. Viable alternatives are 1) to extend the categories of theological anthropology (such as the *imago Dei* and the incarnation) into a more inclusive theological zoology, 2) to dispense with such categories altogether and perhaps focus on purely metaphysical or ontological aspects of human nature (such as the soul), or 3) to shift the theological anthropological locus of human uniqueness to an understanding of historical election where the basic model assumes a certain equivalency of humans and non-humans in terms of both value and biological characteristics.

---

[56] Jon D. Levenson, "The Universal Horizon of Biblical Particularism" in *Ethnicity and the Bible*, ed. Mark G. Brett (Leiden: Brill, 2002), 155.

[57] Paul E. Griffiths, "Our Plastic Nature," in *Transformations of Lamarckism*, edited by Snait Gissis and Eva Jablonka (Cambridge, MA: MIT Press, 2011).

Theological Anthropology and the Cognitive Sciences

Aku Visala

The last 50 years have seen an explosion of scientific research into the nature of information processing in humans, animals, and machines. Most of this research has been conducted under the rubric of the cognitive sciences and their sub-disciplines. Roughly put, cognitive science is the study of the information processing systems of the human mind.[1] This chapter provides an overview of the cognitive sciences and discusses several areas where theological anthropology and the cognitive sciences overlap. Along the way, it will also introduce some theological and philosophical engagements with the theories of this multidisciplinary field.

The chapter is organized in the following way. First, it will provide a brief overview of the cognitive sciences and currently hot areas of research and theorizing. It will then discuss some of the reasons why the cognitive sciences might be relevant for theological anthropology. This section will provide several brief explorations of topics where theological anthropology and cognitive science share mutual concerns. The rest of the chapter examines two specific topics where cognitive science research is relevant for theological anthropology. The first has to do with what the cognitive sciences tell us about consciousness and how that might affect our views of what persons are. The second is the recent surge of research into religious cognition, the so-called cognitive science of religion.

The Cognitive Sciences as a Field of Research

There is no such thing as *the* cognitive science. Instead, it would be more accurate to talk about the cognitive sciences as a multidisciplinary field of research that is loosely connected by assumptions about how minds works and how minds should be studied. As such, it consists of several sub-disciplines that include cognitive psychology, philosophy of mind and cognition, artificial intelligence, cognitive linguistics, cognitive anthropology, and cognitive neuroscience. Topics that cognitive scientists study include the following: mechanisms of perception and attention, development and acquisition of concepts as well as language in

---

[1]   Accessible introductions to contemporary cognitive science include P. Thagard, *Mind: Introduction to Cognitive Science* 2nd edn (Cambridge: MIT Press, 2005); and A. Clark, *Mindware: an Introduction to the Philosophy of Cognitive Science* (New York: Oxford University Press, 2001). This chapter draws heavily from essays in Frankish and Ramsey (eds), *The Cambridge Handbook of Cognitive Science* (Cambridge: Cambridge University Press, 2012). G. Peterson, *Minding God: Theology and Cognitive Science* (Minneapolis: Fortress Press, 2003) is a good introduction to cognitive science from a theological point of view.

general, implicit and explicit reasoning, decision-making, and memory. Although some of these topics have to do with humans only, the cognitive sciences are not restricted to human cognition. Cognitive scientists work with artificial intelligence and animal cognition as well.

Very roughly, all cognitive approaches can be characterized by a specific take on what it means to have a mind. For the cognitive scientist, to have a mind is to *process information*. To be more specific, to have a mind is to have internal states that carry information or mental content. These *mental representations* are then processed according to certain rules. Finally, mental representations are taken to have genuine causal effects so they can be invoked to explain the behavior of the organism in question.

The assumption of mental representations as internal states distinguishes cognitive science from those approaches to the mind that do not admit internal content or hold that such content and its processing are not important in explaining behavior. According to *psychological behaviorists*, human behavior can be explained without any reference to internal psychological mechanisms or content. Human behavior, according to this view, is an outcome of environmental stimuli only. Early cognitive psychologists and linguists opposed behaviorism and argued, among other things, that even basic linguistic behavior requires internal rules and representations. Since there can be an almost infinite number of ways an individual can react to a given stimuli, there must be internal processes that constrain various responses. With respect to language learning, for example, the basic idea is that there are innate rules of grammar that constrain the structure of natural languages.

This *computational* or *representational theory of mind* has it roots in the development of computers and linguistics from the 1950s onwards. Early cognitive scientists thought that minds are more or less like computers, namely, systems that process symbols according to certain rules. The influence of the mind as computer metaphor in cognitive science cannot be overstated. On this view, the mind is related to the brain as software of a computer is related to its hardware. The brain is the hardware (or wetware) that runs the program (or various programs) that constitutes the mind.

A typical feature of the early computational theory of mind was that the physical basis of representations and their processing was thought to be rather unimportant. On this view, mental content and processing is *multiply realizable*. That is to say, various physical bases can carry the same mental content by virtue of their organization: silicon chips, brains or even large enough collections of empty cans of beer can carry out the same functions, if organized the same way. This basic stance led early cognitive scientists to think that given enough processing power, an artificial intelligence program could be created and it could, in principle, perform the same tasks as human cognition.

Given computationalism and multiple realizability, the preferred method of early cognitive science was a strategy known as *functional decomposition* or what Daniel Dennett calls the "homunculus approach." The idea is to break a complex cognitive process, like perception, down into smaller and simpler processes until one would arrive at processes so simple they can be performed by basic physical systems. This method has proven rather effective in analyzing and understanding basic cognitive capacities like perception and memory.[2]

Despite the early success of computationalism, it came under severe criticism in the 1980s. First, some argued that the computational approach could not account for the most interesting and important aspect of human cognition, consciousness. John Searle and Thomas Nagel, for example, contended that the functionalist approach to mental states neglects their conscious aspect, "what they feel like." The claim was that the qualitative aspects of

---

[2] Psychologist David Marr's work on vision in the 1970s is often mentioned as a successful example of this explanatory strategy. See David Marr, *Vision: a Computational Investigation into the Human Representation and Processing of Visual Information* (San Francisco: W.H. Freeman, 1982).

our mental life (qualia) are left out. Eventually in the 1990s, these criticisms grew into a multidisciplinary field we now know as consciousness studies. The issue of consciousness will be discussed at length below.

Second, the computational approach faced other difficult challenges, such as the frame (or the framing) problem. Computers excel at tasks that require complex calculations—tasks that humans are not naturally very good at. However, computational models have difficulties dealing with even the most basic everyday human tasks that require motor skills, social interaction or flexible learning and modification of behavior. This is because, computationally, these tasks include millions and millions of options that would quickly clutter even the most capable calculator. So, instead of calculating all the possibilities, it seems that human cognition includes various speedy heuristics and cognitive frameworks that allow it to radically reduce the calculations needed. Computational models lack knowledge of these relevant frames.

Third, there was the scientific critique coming from neuroscience and related disciplines. If one looks at how brains actually work, they look nothing like computers: there seems to be no central processor or easily observable component parts that would house functionally specialized processes like memory. This suggests, among other things, that if brains compute, they do not compute linearly, but in parallel. Pushing this argument further, various parallel processing and neural network models were formed to replace the classical lineal processing models. This development is usually known as the rise of *connectionism* against standard computationalism.

In the beginning of the twenty-first century, the cognitive sciences are best characterized by a plurality of theories and approaches. Both computationalist and connectionist approaches have their advocates and there are numerous attempts to combine them. Philosophy of mind and psychology has become increasingly integrated with empirical approaches in cognitive psychology, cognitive neuroscience and linguistics. Cognitive approaches have been applied (with good results) to subject matters from economics to literary criticism. This has resulted in claims about a *cognitive revolution* sweeping the academia.

In contemporary cognitive science, there are three movements that seek to challenge the standard computational paradigm or at least modify or expand it significantly: extended cognition, cognitive neuroscience and evolutionary psychology.

There has been a lot of debate about *extended, situated,* or *embodied cognition.* After the classic paper "The extended mind" (1998) by David Chalmers and Andy Clark, there has been an explosion of theoretical treatises and empirical research into the extended mind hypothesis.[3] This notion challenges one of the basic assumptions of standard computationalism, namely, that mental processes are largely independent of bodies and their environment. Esther Thelen writes,

> to say that cognition is embodied means that it arises from bodily interactions with the world. From this point of view, cognition depends on the kinds of experiences that come from having a body with particular perceptual and motor capacities ... The contemporary notion of embodied cognition stands in contrast to the prevailing cognitivist stance which sees the mind as a device to manipulate symbols.[4]

---

[3] The original paper with the most important responses can be found in D. Menary (ed.), *The Extended Mind* (Cambridge: The MIT Press, 2010). Andy Clark, *Supersizing the Mind: Embodiment, Action and Cognitive Extension* (New York: Oxford University Press, 2008) is a classic. See also M. Rowlands, *The New Science of the Mind: From Extended Mind to Embodied Phenomenology* (Cambridge: The MIT Press, 2010).

[4] Quoted in Andy Clark, "Embodied, Embedded, and Extended Cognition," in K. Frankish and W. Ramsey (eds), *The Cambridge Handbook of Cognitive Science* (Cambridge: Cambridge University Press, 2013), 275.

In addition to emphasizing the embodied nature of cognitive functions and their development, defenders of extended cognition maintain that cognitive processes are "spread out" in the environment: one of the most typical features of human cognition is that it tends to create an environment that externalizes many of its basic processes. Our cognitive system seems geared to function in a certain kind of information-embedded environment only. Finally, many defenders of the extended mind hypothesis adopt a non-standard view of how mental representations and their meaning are understood. On this view, mental content crucially depends on the environment for its meaning. Brain states themselves do not really code information at all; instead mental content is realized in our brains, bodies and our interactions with the world as a whole.[5] If extended cognition is correct, the standard computational and representational view of the mind needs to be radically rethought.

Second, *cognitive neuroscience* seeks to remedy some of the problems of standard computationalism by linking neural and cognitive explanations together. The aim of cognitive neuroscience is to bridge the gap between cognitive mechanisms, their behavioral outcomes and the physical mechanisms of the brain. Cognitive neuroscience received a significant boost in the late 1980s when increasingly accurate brain-imaging techniques (fMRI, PET) were developed. For the first time, it became possible to study the living brain in action. Since then, a wide variety of theories linking, for example, computational models of memory and perception to specific brain mechanisms have been put forward.[6] Cognitive neuroscience reasserts the more general question of the boundary between neuroscience and the cognitive sciences.

Finally, there is *evolutionary psychology*. If cognitive neuroscience is an attempt to link the neuronal and cognitive explanations together more closely, evolutionary psychology seeks to add a new, evolutionary, level of explanation: an explanation of how human cognition came to be in the first place. The standard model of evolutionary psychology, advocated by Steven Pinker and David Buss, for instance, holds that human cognition consists in functionally specialized modules (modularity) that were individually selected in our ancestral environment (adaptationism).[7] We often use our cognition for various tasks and in different environments than it was originally designed for. Evolutionary psychologists offer explanations of various recurrent cultural and behavioral patterns, such as morality, jealousy and gossip. The simplified slogan "we have stone age minds in our modern heads" captures something important about evolutionary psychology.

The basic assumptions of evolutionary psychology (modularity, adaptationism, and the fixity of brain development) have been challenged. David Buller, for instance, argues that natural selection would not produce functionally separate modules, but rather a generally flexible learning mechanism.[8] Buller and others also maintain that developmental

---

5   This is known as the thesis of wide content (versus narrow content).

6   One of the reasons for the increased prominence of cognitive neuroscience is that successful theories show great clinical promise: the more we know about the physical mechanisms of the brain the better drugs we can design and treat brain based diseases.

7   Canonical accounts of the standard model of evolutionary psychology include Stephen Pinker, *How the Mind Works* (London: Penguin, 1999); D. Buss, *Evolutionary Psychology: The New Science of the Mind* 3rd edn (Boston: Pearson/Allyn and Bacon, 2008); and Barkow, Cosmides, and Tooby, *The Adapted Mind: Evolutionary Psychology and the Generation of Culture* (Oxford: Oxford University Press, 1992).

8   Kim Sterelny, *The Evolved Apprentice: How Evolution Made Humans Unique* (Cambridge: The MIT Press, 2012), has also argued along these lines.

neurobiology provides evidence against the fixity of brain development and the modularity thesis.[9]

In sum, contemporary cognitive science points towards a closer integration of the brain, mind and their environment. In artificial intelligence research, for example, researchers no longer think that disembodied programs can model human cognitive performance. Instead, they focus on building machines that learn through bodily actions in their environment. Similarly, research in cognitive psychology has sought to better understand the way in which human cognition is shaped by its natural and cultural environment. It is also becoming clear that human cognition is essentially dependent on the kinds of brains and bodies we have. Instead of treating the mind, brain, body, and the environment in isolation, it seems that the boundaries between, for example, the mind and the active body, are more porous than previously assumed and that more holistic and situated models of cognition and culture should be developed.

Theological Anthropology and the Cognitive Sciences

So far, there has been surprisingly little interaction between theology and the cognitive sciences. There have been numerous publications discussing some challenges and overlapping issues between theology and psychology in general and some of this work discusses topics that originate from cognitive science research. Nevertheless, apart from a few exceptions, systematic attempts to discuss the relationship of theology and cognitive science have been few and far between.[10] Such a state of affairs is problematic for theology in general and theological anthropology in particular.

Even if one believes that theological anthropology should begin from an explicitly theological account of humanity being created by God, there is room for a contribution from the cognitive sciences. A Christian theological anthropology likely includes at least the three following components. First, the Christian narrative of the creation of humans in the image of God, their subsequent fall into sin, and their eventual salvation and the fulfillment of the image of God through Christ. Second, theological anthropologies make metaphysical assumptions about the nature of human persons (for example, human beings have been seen as identical to or essentially constituted by non-natural souls). Third, theological claims also include assumptions about psychological capacities, including the intellect, will, and emotion. Even if the Christian theologian believes the Christian narrative is immune to the cognitive sciences, the other two aspects, the metaphysics of persons and human psychology, still remain open for dialogue and possible revision. Consider, for example, the following topics:[11]

---

[9]   Buller's criticisms are outlined in Buller, *Adapting Minds: Evolutionary Psychology and the Persistent Quest for Human Nature* (Cambridge: The MIT Press, 2005). Other criticisms of evolutionary psychology include R. Richardson, *Evolutionary Psychology as Maladapted Psychology* (Cambridge: The MIT Press, 2007), and J. Dupré, *Human Nature and the Limits of Science* (Oxford: Clarendon Press, 2001). For an overview of a wide variety of hypotheses in the area, see A. Fuentes, *Evolution of Human Behavior* (New York: Oxford University Press, 2008).

[10]   See Peterson, *Minding God*, and Jeeves and Brown, *Neuroscience, Psychology and Religion* (West Conshohocken: Templeton Foundation Press, 2009).

[11]   The motivation behind such claims has mostly been soteriological and ethical. On the Augustinian view, for example, sanctification involves supernatural repairing of damaged psychological and moral capacities (the will and emotions linked to loving God and others). Furthermore, assumptions are often being made about the development of virtues through practice and supernatural assistance as well as about the conditions of human flourishing.

Reason and Intellect. Theological anthropology has often made assumptions about what human reason is and how it works. Even theologians who acknowledge that theological anthropology should start from deeply theological premises cannot avoid dealing with reason and intellect. Robert Jenson, for example, argues that one part of our sinful state is our tendency towards irrationality.[12] Our fallen reason and intellect are not functioning properly. The fragility of reason may be illuminated by research in both cognitive psychology and neuroscience. Various cognitive scientists have pointed out that our reasoning capacities and decision-making processes rely on quick and dirty heuristics, information-processing biases and context-based models. The term of the trade is *bounded rationality*.[13] Neuroscientists, such as Antonio Damasio, have produced evidence of the close link between our emotions and our capacity for reasoning. Without properly functioning emotions, humans tend to lose their abilities to reason and act on the basis of their reasoning.[14] Such results further highlight the fact that our reason and intellect might not be singular or isolated mechanisms, but depend for their operation on various lower-level cognitive and neuronal mechanisms.[15]

Human Uniqueness. Theologians have historically postulated a variety of psychological capacities that make humans unique. These include at least symbolic language, higher-order intellect and the capacities required for complex sociality. Although contemporary theologians have been skeptical of some traditional notions of human uniqueness, they have offered accounts of their own. Wolfhart Pannenberg and Karl Rahner, for instance, argued that humans are unique in their openness to transcendence.[16] The cognitive sciences give us a new perspective on such claims. Comparative studies and the study of animal cognition suggest that the gap between human and non-human cognitive capacities is smaller than previously assumed.[17] This is not to say that such a gap does not exist: indeed, humans are still the only animals that can write books, build computers and speak Klingon. Nevertheless, some of the basic cognitive capacities that allow humans to perform these tasks are present, at least in some rudimentary form, in our non-human ancestors. All attempts to argue for human uniqueness must engage with the cognitive sciences and their results.

Emotions. Shaping the emotions is a central part of one's spiritual and religious life, eliciting theological reflection on the emotions. There has also been an extensive debate on emotion in the cognitive sciences. One aspect of this debate concerns the origins of emotion. Many evolutionary psychologists have argued that emotions are adaptations produced by natural selection to guide human behavior in various contexts, such as finding food, mating, and navigating the social environment. On this view, emotions are biological programs that help our survival by turning us away from polluted food and toward potential mates, for instance. Such a view of emotions implies that they are relatively fixed and involuntary.[18] Opposing such nativist views of emotions are those who argue that emotions have their

---

[12] R. Jenson, *Systematic Theology, vol. II: The Works of God* (New York: Oxford University Press, 2001), chapter 22.

[13] D. Kahneman, *Thinking, Fast and Slow* (London: Allen Lane, 2011) summarizes the literature on cognitive biases. Among others, Gerd Gigerenzer, *Rationality for Morals: How People Cope with Uncertainty* (New York: Oxford University Press, 2008), has argued for bounded rationality.

[14] A. Damasio, *Descartes' Error: Emotion, Reason, and the Human Brain* (London: Vintage, 2005).

[15] Murphy and Brown, *Did My Neurons Make Me Do It? Philosophical and Neurobiological Perspectives on Moral Responsibility and Free Will* (Oxford: Oxford University Press, 2007), includes an attempt to understand reason and intellect from a cognitive neuroscience perspective.

[16] See, e.g., Wolfhart Pannenberg, *Anthropology in Theological Perspective*, trans. Matthew O'Connell (Edinburgh: T. & T. Clark, 1999).

[17] For an overview, see S. Shettleworth, "Animal Cognition," in K. Frankish and W. Ramsey (eds), *The Cambridge Handbook of Cognitive Science* (Cambridge: Cambridge University Press, 2012).

[18] For nativist views of emotions, see, e.g., Pinker 1999, chapter 6.

origin in our cultural environment rather than our evolutionary heritage. If this is the case, emotions may be more sensitive to our actions and surroundings.[19]

Moral Cognition. Theological anthropology has long wrestled with the doctrine of sin, a topic discussed under different names in cognitive science. Given standard theological anthropology, humans are fallen creatures and although theologians disagree about the effects of sin, it is clear that our moral capacities have somehow been damaged or impaired. Theologian Gregory Peterson, for example, argues that the study of moral cognition fits together well with some accounts of original sin. On the one hand, we have a tendency towards morality and altruistic behavior, but that is mostly restricted to our kin and our own culturally defined group. On the other hand, humans are capable of immense cruelty and selfishness, especially towards those who are seen as outsiders.[20]

Cognitive scientists have also debated the origins of our moral cognition extensively. A prevalent view is that our moral judgments are largely grounded in our moral emotions.[21] In the contemporary study of moral cognition, the view of morality as emotionally driven inspired by David Hume (1711–76) has prevailed against that of Immanuel Kant (1724–1804), who insisted that moral judgments are products of reflective reason, or the intellect.[22] What is more controversial is the origin of our moral emotions. Some cognitive scientists hold that our moral emotions are simply products of natural selection: they are hardwired responses to adaptive challenges in our social and natural environments. Such constraints would make the possible set of human moral norms rather limited.[23] Others emphasize how culturally sensitive our moral emotions are. They claim that human moral norms have no innate or biological grounding and can, therefore, vary significantly from culture to culture.[24] Natural law ethicists might find inspiration in the former view, because it entails a kind of "natural morality" for everyone, whereas those emphasizing the need for divine guidance in formulating moral norms might find common ground with the latter.

Character and Virtue. Traditional theological anthropologies have emphasized the close connection between moral life and character development. Shaping of one's character towards virtue and away from vice has been seen as a crucial task of Christian spirituality. The extent to which the development of character and virtue is considered a natural (as opposed to supernatural) process varies among theological traditions. Thomas Aquinas, for example, made a distinction between natural virtues that can be developed via reflection and training and infused or supernatural virtues that are given by God. In any case, theologians have mostly maintained that human beings can at least partly contribute to the work of the Spirit in reforming their moral life.

One area of contemporary psychology that has dealt with empirical issues related to character and virtue is 'the positive psychology' movement.[25] For positive psychologists

---

[19] J. Prinz, *The Emotional Construction of Morals* (Oxford: Oxford University Press, 2007), summarizes the most of the recent research on emotions and defends a strong anti-nativist view.

[20] Peterson's account of sin and the evolution of morality can be found in Peterson, *Minding God*, chapter 7.

[21] For recent research into moral cognition and its philosophical reflection, see, e.g., Sinnott-Armstrong (ed.), *Moral Psychology*, vol. I–III (Cambridge: The MIT Press, 2008).

[22] See Prinz 2007 chapters 1–3 for discussion.

[23] See, e.g., R. Joyce, *The Evolution of Morality* (Cambridge: The MIT Press, 2006). Jonathan Haidt, *The Righteous Mind: Why Good People are Divided by Politics and Religion* (London: Allen Lane, 2012), has defended a theory of moral judgments inspired by evolutionary psychology.

[24] See, e.g., Jesse Prinz's (2007) defense of this view.

[25] For an overview of the research, see Peterson and Seligman, *Character Strengths and Virtues: A Handbook and Classification* (New York: Oxford University Press, 2004). See also J. Haidt, *The Happiness Hypothesis: Putting Ancient Wisdom to the Test of Modern Science* (London: Arrow Books, 2006).

however, the central task is to identify the factors that contribute, both negatively and positively, to human flourishing. The last few years have also seen psychological studies that aim to address the issue of character formation and virtues directly. Christian Miller, for instance, argues that the relationship between an individual's character and possible virtues and vices is much more complex than previously thought. Our characters are inclined to both virtue and vice and a highly moral character does not make moral failure impossible. Miller presents research which points towards the fact that barring conscious attention and training most of us lack many basic virtues, such as compassion for strangers.[26]

Artificial Intelligence and the Future of Human Intellect. One could say that nineteenth- and twentieth-century theological anthropology had to face the Darwinian challenge of acknowledging our close relationship to our non-human ancestors. One challenge of twenty-first century theological anthropology is to understand the relationship of human intelligence and increasingly more sophisticated artificial intelligences, robots and computers. Should theologians maintain that morally valuable intelligent life must be biologically based, or is it the case that if artificially created beings had the same cognitive and affective capacities as we have, they would be intrinsically valuable too? Is dignity tied to biology? In addition to such ethical and political issues, there are deeply philosophical and metaphysical issues involved. How might such beings fit into the narrative of theological salvation history? Are such beings conscious?[27]

Freedom. Despite disagreement among Christian theologians about what free will means, theologians across traditions affirm human freedom at least in the sense of moral responsibility. Some cognitive scientists and neuroscientists, however, have been rather skeptical about all notions of freedom. Inspired by the classic studies of Benjamin Libet in the 1980s and more contemporary research by Daniel Wegner, for instance, they argue that free will is an illusion.[28] Their main claim is that conscious decisions are not involved in the production of our actions. Instead, underlying neural mechanisms cause both our actions and our feeling of conscious decision making. In other words, our conscious "decisions" are more like rationalizations that attempt to retroactively make rational the actions caused by subconscious mechanisms.[29] Such claims have sparked an enormous philosophical and scientific debate. Critics have pointed out, among other things, that both Libet and Wegner assume a curiously limited notion of free will: both assume that an action must be preceded by a conscious decision in order for that action to be free. Philosopher Alfred Mele, for instance, has pointed out that free decisions need not have such proximate conscious decisions among their causes and even if they did, the studies of Libet and others do not rule the possibility out.[30]

---

[26] See Miller 2013, and Miller, *Moral Character: An Empirical Theory* (New York: Oxford University Press, 2014).

[27] These issues are also connected to the ethical concerns surrounding new technologies of human cognitive and bodily enhancement. See, e.g., N. Herzfeld, *In Our Image: Artificial Intelligence and the Human Spirit* (Minneapolis: Fortress Press, 2002), for one theological treatment.

[28] See, e.g., Pockett, Banks and Gallagher (eds), *Does Consciousness Cause Behavior* (Cambridge: The MIT Press, 2006). See also Robert Kane (ed.), *The Oxford Handbook of Free Will*, 2nd edn (Oxford: Oxford University Press, 2011).

[29] For a comprehensive argument along these lines, see D. Wegner, *The Illusion of Conscious Will* (Cambridge: The MIT Press, 2002).

[30] See A. Mele, *Effective Intentions: The Power of Conscious Will* (New York: Oxford University Press, 2009); and S. Horst, *Laws, Mind and Free Will* (Cambridge: The MIT Press, 2011).

Consciousness, the Nature of the Self and Theological Accounts of Persons

Traditionally, theologians and philosophers in the West have thought that human persons are either identical to or constituted partly by souls. The idea has been that souls are what make bodies persons and provide them with the psychological capacities that distinguish them from other beings (animals and angels). Oftentimes, the soul was also seen as the seat of the image of God.

Contemporary cognitive scientists typically reject the soul as metaphysically unnecessary. Instead, they refer to the mind, the self, and consciousness. On the cognitive view, the mind consists of various lower-level information-processing mechanisms that give rise to basic human cognitive capacities, like memory, perception, reasoning, decision making, and so on. To have a mind is not the same thing as having a self: to have a self is to be able to refer to oneself and represent oneself to oneself. To have a self requires a capacity to form higher-level mental representations. Definitions of consciousness vary significantly, but generally speaking consciousness refers to the peculiar capacity to have a certain point of view. Since cognitive accounts of the mind were explored above, this section will focus on the notions of consciousness and selves.

Results of the cognitive sciences are problematic for a non-natural soul. One of the historically most powerful arguments for the existence of the soul was that a non-natural, non-material entity was the best explanation for our higher-level mental capacities. It was inconceivable that a material thing could give rise to or have thoughts, feelings and desires. The cognitive scientist's materialist story of the human cognitive ability to perform such tasks as intelligence and reasoning, diminishes this traditional case for the existence of the soul.

However, dualism has not been refuted: most contemporary dualists concede that non-natural souls are not involved in explanations of our basic cognitive capacities. Instead, souls account for phenomena that are outside the purview of the cognitive sciences, like consciousness. Thus, contemporary dualists do not usually present their metaphysical account of persons as souls as competitors to cognitive science, but simply maintain that cognitive science leaves something out.[31]

Is consciousness (and self-consciousness) outside the domain of the cognitive sciences? We have already seen that philosophers like Searle and Nagel argued against prevailing functionalist and computationalist approaches to the mind in the 1980s. In the 1990s, Searle went on to present his more biologically inspired account of consciousness,[32] whereas Nagel has remained skeptical as to whether a materialistic theory of consciousness is even possible.[33] Nevertheless, the emergence of consciousness studies in philosophy and the cognitive sciences from the 1990s onwards, has produced a plethora of theories about consciousness.

Representational theories of consciousness attempt to refute Searle's and Nagel's arguments and maintain that the phenomenal properties of conscious experiences can be fully explained in terms of representations. In other words, qualitative aspects of experience are nothing more than mental representations of certain qualities of objects, like color. The problem with representational theories is that they seem to fall prey to the problem identified by David Chalmers: why would a representation of some quality make that representation

---

[31]   Karl Popper and John Eccles, *The Self and Its Brain* (London: Routledge Press, 1990), is a classical defense of dualism in the context of neuroscience.

[32]   John Searle, *The Rediscovery of the Mind* (Cambridge: The MIT Press, 1992).

[33]   Thomas Nagel, *Mind and Cosmos: Why the Materialist Neo-Darwinian Conception of Nature is Almost Certainly False* (New York: Oxford University Press, 2012).

conscious instead of some other representation? Something extra is needed, but there is no consensus about what that might be. Higher-order representation theories attempt to solve the problem by maintaining that mental states become conscious only when they are represented by other mental states. What is doing the second-order representing varies from perceptions to higher-order thoughts.[34]

Debates over representational theories are mostly philosophical in nature. On the science side, the general strategy has been consonant with the functionalist stance described above. *Functionalistic accounts* have attempted to break consciousness down into more specific mechanisms and then to offer explanations of these lower-level mechanisms. This approach has been popular among scientists. On Bernard Baar's global workspace model, for example, mental states become conscious when they are made accessible to short-term memory. The short-term memory functions as a kind of workspace, where multiple psychological mechanisms, like imagination, perception, and motivation can have access to the same mental content simultaneously.[35] Other functionalist theories include neuroscientist Antonio Damasio's account of consciousness as a kind of perception of one's own bodily reactions.[36] On Damasio's view, consciousness appears when perceptual information, especially feelings and perceptions of one's own body, are linked with self-representation.[37]

The issue of the existence and nature of the *self* has to be distinguished from the issue of consciousness. One may deny the existence of robust selves but still maintain that we are conscious. Also, it is possible that some animals are conscious but do not possess a sense of self. The capacity for having a self has to do with being able to represent oneself to oneself. In other words, to be a self requires that one is able to form mental representations about oneself.

It is difficult to imagine a theological anthropology that does not hold onto the commonsense view that we retain our identities over time, even through changes in our minds and bodily conditions. While our self-understanding and body can change, there is something constant behind the changes we endure, a self or a person that tries to understand herself. Moreover, theological anthropology usually maintains that our existence persists even after the death of our current physical bodies.

Recent cognitive and neuroscientific literature has been rather skeptical of the notion of a self. Cognitive and neuroscientific research suggests that not only is our sense of self based on the workings of various unconscious mechanisms, our introspection is far from infallible: we often make mistakes about our own mental states, beliefs, and emotions. It seems that our self-understanding is much more fragile and dependent upon unconscious cognitive processes than previously believed. Such conclusions could, perhaps, be incorporated into theological anthropology by maintaining, alongside Augustine, for instance, that we are ultimately unknowable and mysterious even to ourselves.

---

[34] One representational theory is Michael Tye, *Ten Problems of Consciousness: A Representational Theory of the Phenomenal Mind* (Cambridge: The MIT Press, 1995).

[35] J. Baars, *In the Theater of Consciousness: The Workspace of the Mind* (New York: Oxford University Press, 1997).

[36] See Damasio, *The Feeling of What Happens: Body and Emotion in the Making of Consciousness* (New York: Harcourt Brace, 1999).

[37] The representational and functional theories of consciousness mentioned here do not exhaust the pool of theories of consciousness. Empirical research continues and the philosophical debate rages on without any consensus in sight. The literature on consciousness is vast. Prominent theories not mentioned here include: the multiple drafts model of Daniel Dennett, *Consciousness Explained* (London: Penguin, 1993). See the quantum consciousness model of Roger Penrose, *The Emperor's New Mind: Concerning Computers, Minds and the Laws of Physics*, 2nd edn (Oxford: Oxford University Press, 1999) and Douglas Hofstadter's *I am a Strange Loop* (New York: Basic Books, 2007).

There is, however, a deeper problem: for many cognitive scientists, the self is not just fragile, it might not exist at all. Thomas Metzinger, for example, has famously argued that there is nothing beyond our continuously changing representations of ourselves.[38] To be a self requires that one is able to represent oneself to oneself, a kind of self-representation. For Metzinger, however, there is no person or agent doing the self-representing: the conscious being is nothing more than what Metzinger calls a "self-model," the self-representation itself. He puts his claim rather bluntly: "no such things as selves exist in the world: Nobody ever was or ever had a self. All that ever existed were conscious self-models that could not be recognized as models."[39] It appears to us as if there were a subject of experience. In reality, nothing exists beyond the self-representation.

Lynne Rudder Baker has argued against Metzinger's theory and defended the existence of objective selves and persons. Baker also outlines a broadly speaking anti-naturalist stance on consciousness and the self. On her view, the cognitive sciences can study the underlying mechanisms of self-consciousness and other such personal phenomena, but they cannot eliminate or reduce self-consciousness or persons to such mechanisms.[40]

Theologians have rather large stakes in the game of consciousness and selves. Christian theological anthropology has tended to affirm a set of common-sense assumptions about the nature of human persons. These assumptions include the claim that we are self-conscious agents who are morally responsible and who retain an identity over the course of their earthly lives and even in bodily death and resurrection. Similarly, conscious agency is implied in various ways in which the image of God in humans has been understood. If consciousness were purely epiphenomenal (that is, conscious thinking is not the cause of actions but instead is a product of brains causing our actions), holding onto any traditional notion of moral responsibility would be extremely difficult. Similarly, if there were no personal identity over time, the Christian view of persons surviving death and maintaining some level of agency would be undermined.

There are two basic approaches that Christian theologians and philosophers might adopt to deal with such problems. One might abandon the traditional metaphysical understanding of persons and develop a modified notion of persons, selves, and consciousness inside a framework of something like non-reductive physicalism (or emergent materialism). Alternatively, one might defend the traditional view and maintain that there are limits to cognitive science's explanations.

If the first route is taken, the challenge is to account for moral responsibility, freedom, personality, reason, and the image of God in terms that both retain the theological significance and are compatible with essentially a scientific account of the human mind and its evolution. Theologians like Nancey Murphy, Philip Clayton, and Gregory Peterson as well as psychologists like Malcolm Jeeves and Warren Brown have argued along these lines.[41] Murphy, for instance, argues that while theologians should reject dualism and a nonnatural origin of the mind, they should not eliminate persons, consciousness, and agency. Although consciousness and personal agency are based on underlying physical mechanisms, they

---

[38] T. Metzinger, *Being No One: The Self-Model of Subjectivity* (Cambridge: The MIT Press, 2003), and his *The Ego Tunnel* (New York: Basic Books, 2009). Galen Strawson, *An Essay on Revisionary Metaphysics* (Oxford: Oxford University Press, 2007).

[39] Metzinger, *Being No One*, 1.

[40] See Lynne Rudder Baker, *Naturalism and the First-Person Perspective* (Oxford: Oxford University Press, 2013), for counter arguments to Metzinger's view.

[41] Philip Clayton, *Mind and Emergence: From Quantum to Consciousness* (Oxford: Oxford University Pres, 2004). See Malcolm Jeeves, *Human Nature: Reflection on the Integration of Psychology and Christianity* (Wesk Conshohocken: Templeton Foundation Press, 2006).

cannot be reduced to or explained away by them. Nonetheless, Murphy maintains that the biblical view of persons is closer to the embodied view of the contemporary cognitive sciences than to metaphysical dualism. In collaboration with Brown, Murphy has developed this emergent materialist perspective further to account for higher-order reason and personal agency.[42]

J. Wentzel van Huyssteen defends human uniqueness in the context of the cognitive sciences and evolutionary psychology. For van Huyssteen, both science and theology point away from the traditional picture of humans as the image of God because of their supernaturally created souls. Instead, human uniqueness is something that evolves gradually out of physical nature and involves the capacity for symbolic representation. This capacity is the ground from which art, culture, human society, and religion arise. For van Huyssteen, dualism is problematic because it introduces a strong distinction between mental and physical capacities. The symbolic capacity that he argues for is more embodied and contextual than any traditionally conceived mental capacity.[43] Finally, many Christian philosophers, like Kevin Corcoran, have argued that materialist views of persons are not in conflict with an enduring personal identity and survival after death.[44]

Although many theologians have given up on dualism, many Christian philosophers still defend it.[45] Their argument is mostly of a negative nature: the personal or human world of values, norms, consciousness, reason, and freedom cannot be accounted for under materialism or physicalism. Conversely, they claim that a purely physicalist view of consciousness leaves out something important and leads to an impoverished view of the human person. If we do not accept the metaphysical framework for persons provided by theology, we risk losing the personal realm of agency, responsibility, reason, and freedom completely. Such arguments turn on the truth of our commonsense view of persons as conscious, free agents with moral dignity and value. Only non-naturalist worldviews, like theism, are able to incorporate the commonsense view (or so the argument goes).[46]

Notice that both the physicalist and the dualist make assumptions about the limits of the cognitive sciences. The non-reductive physicalist maintains that a scientific account of higher cognitive functions, like consciousness and reason, is in principle possible. The idea that a naturalist theory of the self might emerge from the cognitive sciences should not be unexpected or unwelcome for similar reasons. Against this, the dualist (or other anti-naturalists, like Baker) maintains that the metaphysical question at stake in the case of consciousness is one the sciences cannot address.

---

[42]   See Nancy Murphy, *Bodies and Souls, or Spirited Bodies?* (Cambridge: Cambridge University Press, 2006), and Murphy and Brown in *Did My Neurons Make Me Do it?*

[43]   J.W. Van Huyssteen, *Alone in the World? Human Uniqueness in Science and Theology* (Grand Rapids: Eerdmans, 2006).

[44]   Kevin Corcoran, *Rethinking Human Nature: A Christian Materialist Alternative to the Soul* (Grand Rapids: Eerdmans, 2006). For discussion, see essays in Corcoran, *Soul, Body and Survival* (Ithaca: Cornell University Press, 2001). Also see Peter van Inwagen and Dean Zimmerman, *Persons: Human and Divine* (Oxford: Oxford University Press, 2007).

[45]   See, e.g., Richard Swinburne, *Mind, Brain and Free Will* (Oxford: Oxford University Press, 2013). See J.P. Moreland, *The Recalcitrant Imago Dei* (London: SCM Press, 2009). Additionally see William Hasker, *The Emergent Self* (Ithaca: Cornell University Press, 1999).

[46]   Thomas Nagel, *Mind and Cosmos*.

The Cognitive Science of Religion and the Naturalness of Religion

Adopting a scientific approach to religion was not very popular in twentieth-century anthropology and social sciences. By the 1990s however, the emerging fields of cognitive anthropology, developmental psychology and evolutionary psychology inspired a movement we now know as the *cognitive science of religion* (CSR). Representatives of the standard model of CSR, like Pascal Boyer, Scott Atran, E. Thomas Lawson, Robert McCauley, and Justin Barrett, have attempted to explain the prevalence of religious ideas and behavior by the underlying cognitive mechanisms that make them easy to learn and adopt.[47] The cognitive science of religion is a part of a larger family of scientific approaches to religion that include the neuroscientific study of religion (sometimes called neurotheology) and the biology and evolution of religion. Oftentimes, cognitive accounts of religion overlap and interact with biological accounts, but for the purposes of our chapter, we can keep cognitive science of religion and evolution of religion distinct. The following discussion only focuses on the cognitive aspects.

Most representatives of CSR assume that very ordinary, natural cognitive mechanisms underlie the diversity of religious ideas and behaviors.[48] Religion, according to the standard view, is a *by-product* of everyday cognition in the sense that it employs cognitive mechanisms that ordinarily have non-religious functions. Reasoning about supernatural entities, like gods and spirits, for instance, employs the same cognitive mechanisms that are used to represent and predict the behavior of mundane agents, like animals and other humans. To understand how people think about gods and spirits, we can examine our capacity to represent the mental states of how other agents (theory of mind and social cognition) works.

CSR maintains that *religious ideas and behavior are natural for humans*. This claim does not mean that all humans are born with religious ideas or mechanisms, but instead it emphasizes how easy it is for humans to adopt religious ideas and behaviors. This combination of the by-product and the naturalness of religion theses has proven fruitful for empirical research. The Minimal Counterintuitiveness theory of Pascal Boyer is among the most discussed hypotheses in the field.[49] Boyer maintains that all humans have cognitive systems that create intuitive ontologies, that is, assumptions about the different characteristics and causal properties of things in the world (such as physical objects, living things, and intentional agents). He further claims that ideas closely corresponding to intuitive ontologies are easier to adopt and transmit and thus become a part of the prevailing culture easier than ideas that deviate strongly from our intuitive assumptions. However, if an idea includes a small deviation from intuitive ontology but is otherwise concurrent with it, it is more likely to be attention-grabbing and memorable than highly counterintuitive ideas or ideas that agree completely with intuitive ontologies. Boyer has coined the term *minimally counterintuitive* to refer to such ideas and claims that ideas of non-natural agents, like gods, spirits, and

---

[47] See, e.g., P. Boyer, *Religion Explained: The Human Instinct that Fashion God, Spirits, and Ancestors* (London: Vintage, 2001). S. Atran, *In Gods We Trust: The Evolutionary Landscape of Religion* (New York: Oxford University Press, 2002). For more contemporary introductions, see Barrett, *Born Believers: The Science of Children's Religious Belief* (New York: Free Press, 2012). Also, R. McCauley, *Why Religion is Natural and Science is Not* (New York: Oxford University Press, 2012).

[48] For some representatives of CSR, like Pascal Boyer and Scott Atran, the by-product thesis also entails a certain view of the evolution of religious thought. Rather than being an adaptation to, say, handling increased group sizes or policing cheaters, religion is more of a by-product of mechanisms and behaviors that were themselves adaptations for some non-religious purpose. Religion is like a cultural contraption built upon universal human psychology.

[49] Boyer, *Religion Explained*.

ancestors, are minimally counterintuitive in this sense. Therefore, we might expect such ideas become widely spread.

Boyer's theory of minimally counterintuitive ideas has subsequently been developed further and other theories using the same framework have emerged. Scott Atran, for instance, has emphasized the role of rituals in signaling commitment to the group's religious beliefs.[50] Justin Barrett and other developmental psychologists have conducted studies about the cognitive foundation of religion in early childhood. Deborah Kelemen's research points towards children having a natural tendency to see purposes and designs in the natural world and take them as expressions of the intentions of god-like beings. Finally, Paul Bloom and Jesse Bering have, among other things, studied how children and adults represent and understand death and afterlife. They have argued that belief in souls and afterlife might include only a minor tweak on intuitive ontologies about persons, minds, and bodies.[51]

Most philosophical and theological engagements with CSR have so far been motivated by the concern that CSR might prove theological claims false or make them irrational. This work is interesting and sophisticated but it is not strictly relevant for the present topic.[52] What is more relevant is the way in which CSR seems to point to religion being rather deep in human nature: instead of being a product of very specific religious experiences, cultural contexts, or some underlying pathology, the propensity for religion might be a fixed feature of human cognition.

Most theological anthropologies have maintained that humans are naturally and essentially open to non-natural realities, revelation, or the experience of God. Traditionally, John Calvin and Thomas Aquinas, for instance, maintained that humans have something like a basic, natural ability to know God. Paul Tillich, Karl Rahner and Wolhart Pannenberg attempted to flesh out the implication of this with tools they often derived from European philosophies of their time. Similarly, late nineteenth century and early twentieth century theories in religious studies and sociology of religion emphasized universal religious experience and the fundamental social nature of religion, respectively. Some contemporary theologians, such as Robert Jenson and J. Wentzel van Huyssteen, have emphasized the close links between the emergence of religion, humanity, and ritual behavior.[53] All these converging threads seem to point in the direction of religion and religiousness being deeply ingrained into human nature and human beings.

Van Huyssteen holds that this conclusion leads to a far more complex and deep notion of human religion than simply believing or not believing in God. If religion is informed and caused by our basic cognitive mechanisms, religious belief, behavior, and ritual are deeply embedded in our brains, biology, and our relationship to the natural world around us. Here theologians should, according to van Huyssteen, follow the contemporary cognitive sciences and move away from the idea of disembodied intelligences and non-natural persons of

---

[50] Atran, *In Gods We Trust*.

[51] Barrett, *Born Believers* provides a good overview.

[52] See, e.g., Leech and Visala, "How the Cognitive System of Religion Might Be Relevant for Philosophy of Religion?" in Nagasawa, Yujin (ed.), *Scientific Approaches to Philosophy of Religion* (London: Palgrave Macmillan, 2012); and Aku Visala, *Theism, Naturalism, and the Cognitive Study of Religion: Religion Explained?* (Farnham, Ashgate, 2011). See J. van Slyke, *The Cognitive Science of Religion* (Farnham: Ashgate, 2011); K.J. Clark and Barrett, "Reformed Epistemology and the cognitive science of Religion," *Faith and Philosophy*, 27 (2010), 174–89; Clark and Rabinowitz, "Knowledge and the Objection to Religious Belief from Cognitive Science," *European Journal for Philosophy of Religion*, 3.1 (2011), 67–82. Scloss and Murray (eds), *The Believing Primate: Scientific, Philosophical, and Theological Reflections on the Origin of Religion* (New York: Oxford University Press, 2009).

[53] Van Huyssteen 2006; Jenson 2001.

dualism and marvel at how deeply humans are embedded in the physical world via their biology, cognition and evolutionary heritage.

According to Barrett, the results of CSR might be viewed as supporting a theological account of humans. Although being products of biology and psychology, our propensity for religion could at the same time be seen as God-given: "God created people with the capacity to know and love him but with the free will to reject him. Consequently, our God-endowed nature leads us to believe, but human endeavours apart from God's design may result in disbelief."[54] According to Barrett, therefore, God has set up our cognitive system in such a way that given a normal human environment, we acquire correct beliefs about God.[55]

Against the explicitly theistic interpretation of Barrett and van Huyssteen, Wesley Wildman has argued that the emerging scientific view of humans challenges supernaturalist interpretations of the human condition.[56] Drawing from CSR and the biological study of religion, Wildman maintains that humans are indeed naturally religious. At the same time, however, he claims that a naturalistic explanation of this fact is more plausible than a supernaturalist one. On Wildman's view, we should be *religious naturalists* who see religion as an important part of being human, but independent of non-natural realities (such as God). Nevertheless, religious claims, he contends, can be understood as referring to value and meaning in the natural world. In this way, a religious way of life could and should be maintained without the metaphysical baggage of the supernatural.[57]

---

[54]   Barrett 2004, 123.

[55]   Barrett, "Cognitive Science, Religion, and Theology" in *Believing Primate: Scientific, Philosophical, and Theological Reflection on the Origin of Religion*, ed. Jeffrey Schloss and Michael Murray (New York: Oxford University Press, 2009), 97–8. He proceeds to suggest that the perceived plurality of god-concepts today is due to the "sinful, fallen world" in which we live: in the ideal condition, he speculates, humans might develop a unified theistic concept of God automatically

[56]   Wildman 2009.

[57]   The author would like to thank the *Human Nature(s)* project at the University of Notre Dame and the John Templeton Foundation for financial support. Special thanks go to Agustín Fuentes and Kelly James Clark for comments and suggestions.

Theological Anthropology and the Brain Sciences

Daniel N. Robinson

In his celebrated Gifford Lectures, published as *The Varieties of Religious Experience*,[1] William James titled his first lecture "Religion and Neurology" and expressed disdain for attempts to absorb religious experience into the framework of what he called "medical materialism." He wrote,

> *To plead the organic causation of a religious state of mind, then, in refutation of its claim to possess superior spiritual value, is quite illogical and arbitrary, unless one has already worked out in advance some psycho-physical theory connecting spiritual values in general with determinate sorts of physiological change. Otherwise none of our thoughts and feelings, not even our scientific doctrines, not even our dis-beliefs, could retain any value as revelations of the truth, for every one of them without exception flows from the state of its possessor's body at the time. (p. 16)*

James insisted that one "play fair in this whole matter" and admit that the states of mind regarded as significant do not derive that status from their real or assumed organic substrates.

Nonetheless, despite James's *caveat*, the neurologist, Kevin Nelson, surely speaks for many when contending that,

> *... our spiritual experiences depend ... upon the operations of our brain. Whether we're believers or nonbelievers; whether we believe ... that we have actually witnessed Christ and Satan battling for our soul or think that it was merely a hallucination; whether we think the brain creates an illusion of God or believe it is a receptacle for something untouchable and absolute, we should be able to agree the brain is the seat of spiritual experience.*[2]

Agreement on this point is but agreement on the more general claim that the mind/ body problem is settled and that the solution is that the "seat" of mental life is the brain. However, "seat" is one of those metaphysically cautious and finally useless bits of furniture or (pick your metaphor) locations. One seeks to learn about the battle of Waterloo and is

---

1 Available online at: http://web.archive.org/web/20110221111229/http://etext.lib.virginia.edu/ etcbin/toccer-new2?id=JamVari.sgm&images=images/modeng&data=/texts/english/modeng/parsed&t ag=public&part=1&division=div1.

2 Kevin Nelson, *The God Impulse: Is Religion Hardwired into the Brain?* (New York: Simon & Schuster, 2011).

told its locus was Earth or, more precisely, Belgium. Agreed! Waterloo is in Belgium. In a sense, Napoleon's battle there was, accordingly, "in" Belgium. Is (the illusion of) God "in" the brain? As an icon? A protein? A pattern of neuronal discharges? But to one who thinks of God, the content of thought is neither icon nor protein nor a discharge pattern. Whatever is "in" the brain is not the end of an explanation but the beginning of one, if that.

In some respects, the difficulty facing brain-based accounts of convictions and beliefs is the reverse side of the *mental causation* coin. In just the way there is difficulty in treating reasons and beliefs as having *physical* (behavioral) consequences, it is far from clear how physical events in the nervous system generate reasons and beliefs. For most, an acceptable explanation of Jane's making mortgage payments is that she has committed herself legally to this obligation and she feels duty-bound to honor it. It would not only be odd but eerie, to most at any rate, to be told that her sense of obligation is a brain-state or a response to a particular pattern of neural events. Such a pattern explains the hand movements involved in writing the check and addressing the envelope, but here the behavior is merely the outward sign of an inwardly felt obligation. Entirely different hand movements would be engaged if Jane were to make payment by direct deposit, by credit card or with gold bullion carried in a woolen sock. In a word, then, the agreement asserted in the passage from *The God Impulse* seems more confident than the conceptual traffic will bear.

Perhaps a more measured position from which to examine briefly the complex issue of theology within the context of brain science is a specific conception of human nature. This, at least, might offer a manageable profile of just what brain function is supposed to explain or ground or enable. What features establish the human person as warranting *theological* consideration?

Of the many sources that might be considered, the *Catechism* of the Roman Catholic Church is specific and economical.[3] In Part I, in the first chapter of Sec. II, it is stated that,

> Man occupies a unique place in creation: (I) he is "in the image of God"; (II) in his own nature he unites the spiritual and material worlds ...

Further,

> Being in the image of God the human individual possesses the dignity of a person, who is not just something, but someone. He is capable of self-knowledge, of self-possession and of freely giving himself and entering into communion with other persons.

Expressed in these passages is an *essentialist* position on the nature of human nature. The properties in question are taken to be not merely contingent features of some or even many persons but properties that constitute the human person. To speak of something having an essential nature delineates what it is to be a certain kind of thing. On this understanding, to be "man" is to be a specific "kind" of creature, possessed of self-awareness, naturally disposed toward a rational and social form of life, and imbued with a spiritual dimension distinct from corporeality. As this unique set of essential properties mark man off from the balance of the (merely) natural world, the bearer of such properties is worthy (*dignus*) of a special form of respect, often even legally protected by "rights."

Clearly, if all this were taken to be an incorrigibly accurate account of human nature, the methods and findings of the brain sciences would be reduced to summaries of the functional anatomy of a primate nervous system—one with unusually great brain mass.

---

[3]   Available online at: http://www.vatican.va/archive/ENG0015/_INDEX.HTM.

The dignity of the human person is not a reward for having a large brain nor are the moral and civic dimensions of life intelligible at the level of excitable tissue. Thus, if the brain sciences are to inform or be informed by theological anthropology, one or more of the following assumptions would seem to be necessary:

1. The theological depiction of human persons refers to unique features but, properly understood, these are natural features ultimately accessible to scientific modes of observation and explanation;
2. The theological depiction of human nature is but superstition raised to the level of an implausible theory grounded in an even more implausible theory;
3. If the properties are real—that is, part of the very ontology of all that qualifies as *real*—their expression is by way of the corporeal assets of the human person and are thus inextricably bound to the functions of the nervous system.

The first assumption calls for some sort of translation algorithm rendering such terms as "dignity," "self-consciousness," "spiritual," "image of God," etc. meaningful without assuming the validity of the theological presuppositions. However, attempts to relate, e.g., self-awareness to events in the nervous system have been fragmentary and of arguable relevance to the question. One strategy makes use of so-called lucid dreams; those during which the dreamer is (or seems to be) not only aware but able to shape the events taking place in the dream. Comparing brain measures during lucid with those during non-lucid intervals points to the dorsolateral prefrontal cortex.[4] But on July 7 of the same year neuroscientists meeting at Cambridge University issued "The Cambridge Declaration on Consciousness in Non-Human Animals," concluding that all mammals and birds, and many other creatures, including octopuses, possess consciousness. As this variety of animal life reveals very great differences in the complexity and organization of nervous systems, it seems unlikely that the human capacity for conscious and self-conscious life is related to the mere size of the human brain or some specific region within it. As of now, then, the desired "translation" would seem to be the useless "self-consciousness is a brain state" with little precision qualifying either "consciousness" or "brain state."

The second assumption is just skepticism regarding the claims of theology and a denial of the stated theologically conferred properties. If the very notion of "God" is mere superstition, then *imago Dei* is a conceit, even a sign of a clinically significant grandiosity! This gambit moves the issue directly into the thickets of metaphysics. There is an unavoidable interdependence between ontology and epistemology. To take a position on what really exists requires one to take a position on the proper methods and the relevant findings regarding the ontological question. Thus, to contend ontologically that nothing exists, except insofar as it is physical, is to limit one's methods of investigation and verification to physical modes. If reality consists solely of nails, then the right instrument for every job is a hammer.

Of course, to contend that there is something in human nature that reflects, however poorly, a mark of the maker on His works—summarized in the phrase *imago Dei*—is to offer an account of something incontestably real, even if the account is doubtful or wanting. Human beings possess and exercise the capacity for abstract thought, for lives conducted under the rule of law, for interpersonal relations grounded in fundamental moral precepts, for aspirations that are irreducibly aesthetic, and for powers of the imagination capable of framing extraordinary possibilities that are marvelously realized in the course of time. Every attempt to absorb this record into an evolutionary framework becomes ever more strained,

---

[4]   Martin Dresler et al., "Neural Correlates of Dream Lucidity Obtained from Contrasting Lucid versus Non-Lucid REM Sleep: A Combined EEG/fMRI Case Study," *SLEEP* (2012) 35(7): 1017–20.

even incredible, the more closely it is examined. If the theological account is incredible, the evolutionary account is absurd. The great advantage of the former is that it neither depreciates nor denies the facts. Whatever the fate of these two accounts may prove to be, it will never be sufficient to defeat the theological account on the grounds that scientific methods are incapable of addressing it. Indeed, that is part of the very theological account under consideration.

The third option has the advantage of a realistic inventory of the defining features of human nature. Granting these features, scientists might productively inquire into various physiological correlates, particularly those occurring in the nervous system. An especially enlightened statement of this perspective is given by Saver and Rabin:

> Religious experience is brain-based. This should be taken as an unexceptional claim. All human experience is brain based including scientific reasoning, mathematical deduction, moral judgment, and artistic creation, as well as religious states of mind. Determining the neural substrates of any of these states does not automatically lessen or demean their spiritual significance. The external reality of religious percepts is neither confirmed nor disconfirmed by establishing brain correlates of religious experience. (p. 498)[5]

The envisaged project began as early as medicine in Egypt's First Kingdom and had already become somewhat sophisticated by the time of the Hippocratic physicians. The book of clinical neurology is vast and various, and leaves no doubt about the relationship between the functions of the nervous system and the perceptual, intellectual, and social functions of human and nonhuman animal life. This is a worthy project, already highly developed, and surely capable of expansion to include what we recognize to be the spiritual elements in life. That there may be reliable relationships is an empirical question but one that presupposes the reality of just those elements at the level of experience.

Efforts along these lines are well under way.[6] Systematic studies routinely disclose reliable correlates between reported states of a religious character and events in specific regions of the brain.[7] Following Saver and Rabin, progress in this area would not, for it could not demean or depreciate religious experience. Indeed, to deny the reality of the very phenomenology of that experience is to have nothing with which to correlate measures of brain activity.

Saver and Rabin[8] relate aspects of religious experience to a wide range of neurological and neuropsychiatric conditions, including epilepsy and other disorders associated with aberrant electrical activity in the brain. Their general conclusion is that religious experiences are typically similar to ordinary experiences but with what might be called a spiritual overlay. They put it this way:

---

[5]   Jeffrey Saver and John Rabin, The Journal of Neuropsychiatry and Clinical Neurosciences (1997) 9: 498–510.

[6]   Mario Beauregard, The Spiritual Brain: A Neuroscientist's Case for the Existence of the Soul (New York: Harper Collins, 2008).

[7]   See, e.g., Dimitrios Kapogiannis et al. "Cognitive and neural foundations of religious belief," Proc. Nat. Acad. Sci. (2009) 106(12); P. Boyer, "Religion: Bound to believe?" Nature (2008) 455: 1038–9; O. Devinsky "Religious experiences and epilepsy," Epilepsy Behav (2003) 4: 76–7; H. Naito and N. Matsui, "Temporal lobe epilepsy with ictal ecstatic state and interictal behavior of hypergraphia," Journal of Nervous and Mental Disease (1988) 176(2): 123–4; V.S. Ramachandran et al., "The neural basis of religious experiences," Society for Neuroscience Conference Abstracts (1997), p. 1316; R. Joseph "The limbic system and the soul: Evolution and neuroanatomy of religious experience," Zygon (2001) 36: 105.

[8]   Op. cit.

The core qualities of religious and mystical experience ... are the noetic and the ineffable—the sense of having touched the ultimate ground of reality ... We suggest that the primary substrate for this experience is the limbic system ... the perceptual and cognitive contents of numinous experience are seen as similar to those of ordinary experience, except that they are tagged by the limbic system as of profound importance, as detached, as united into a whole, and/or as joyous. (p. 507)

Needless to say, such findings lend themselves to a variety of interpretations. To say that the nouminous experience is "tagged" by the limbic system is quite different from suggesting that it is somehow caused by the limbic system. Whatever it is that might confer profundity on an experience is likely to be augmented by any number of corporeal correlates; heart rate, blood pressure, pupillary diameter, even white blood cell counts. Then, too, many experiences are coextensive with such physiological events without ever giving rise to a sense of transcendence. One can be overcome by the thrill of victory or the agony of defeat without having any sense whatever of the divine presence!

There is no reliable evidence to suggest that persons who suffer from epilepsy do not have profound religious experiences independently of any sign of seizures or aberrant EEG activity. Epilepsy refers to a pattern of symptoms rather than a specific disease. It varies in frequency and intensity. It is more or less manageable pharmacologically. It is episodic, generally triggered by stress, sometimes related even to allergies. It is facile to suggest that the best understanding of the nearly universal sense of the transcendent reality beyond the plane of ordinary experience is in terms of neural discharges in the brain. A serious person is under no obligation to take such a proposal seriously.

Apart from these considerations is the veritable legion of saints and scholars whose religious faith is grounded in sustained study and contemplation. Surely the *Summa Theologiae* of Thomas Aquinas is not the product of ictal discharges in temporal cortex, nor must one be in the throes of such neurological storms to weigh and even accept the conclusions offered in that estimable work. There is a tendency among those interested in the neural substrates of religious belief to restrict the evidence for the latter to unusual states bordering on pathology! This is not the result of sloth or mere habit. As the primary modes of measurement on the brain-side of the equation are restricted to relatively transient events, the "religious" side must be fit into temporal containers of comparable size.

Such brain states are, however, neither necessary nor sufficient grounds on which religious belief depends. In relation to the varieties of religious experience, these states are rather monotonous and predictable, even when alarming to behold. Viewed over time and across cultures—or even over the course of a single life—religious consciousness is dynamic, contextual, given to whole epochs of doubt and deep conviction, rendered alternately true and false through the work of faith and hope.

There is no one "religious experience." Consider in this connection the large-scale study by Ogata and Miyakawa.[9] The major findings are based on a sample of 234 epileptic patients examined for ictus-related religious experiences. Of these, only three reported religious experiences. Evidence indicated the influence of the religions long adopted by the patients. The authors note that the reported experiences were associated with certain personality features characteristic of temporal lobe epilepsy. They also note a general lack of religious conviction and activity in Japan. Thus, interpreting correlations between religious experience and brain activity calls for an awareness of those cultural and personal factors

---

[9]   Akira Ogata and Taihei Miyakawa. "Religious experiences in epileptic patients with a focus on ictus-related episodes," *Psychiatry and Clinical Neurosciences* (1998) 52(3): 321–5.

that have contributed to a person's religious (or non-religious) attitudes and perspective over the course of years.

An additional consideration, surely controversial, pertains to the epistemic status of religious experiences. Do they reach a level of knowledge otherwise not accessible through conventional forms of experience? To illustrate this point with an actual case (of which a great many could be presented) one might ponder the achievements of Daniel Temmet. He suffered from epileptic seizures in childhood and was diagnosed as autistic. It was soon recognized that he had unusual powers, especially that of memorization. In 2004 he set the European record for reciting values of pi to more than 22,500 places after the decimal.[10] There is no question but that unusual features of Temmet's brain are directly related to his abilities. For argument's sake, one might insist that the early seizures and the continuing autism reflect a *diseased* brain. However, what bearing would this fact have, if it is a fact, on the question of whether Temmet's recitation of the value of pi is correct? Of course, the answer is *None*.

Scientific inquiries into the nature of religious experience and factors associated with it require no special justification. Religion has been perhaps the greatest source of motivation in human history in every arena of human activity. Such inquiries are unlikely to teach much, however, if confined to but a few highly stereotypical instances of religious experience somehow to be "explained" by way of simplistic correlational paradigms. It is hazardous enough attempting to explain the phenomenology of after-images in terms of brain processes. It should be assumed that the phenomenology of religious experiences will be less tractable.

Acknowledging the enduring and powerful source of motivation arising from religious convictions, one is hard pressed to establish just what the foundational motives are. Experimental approaches appear with increasing frequency but are hampered by the narrowness of the adopted understanding of "motivation" and by research strategies requiring rather gross correlational data of arguable relevance.

One such study fairly represents the aims and methods now dominant in this field of inquiry.[11] The hypothesis entertained by the investigators is that there is a strong general motive to impose meaning on an otherwise complex and disordered world. Thus, persons are moved to create meaning, now understood by the investigators as, "a sense of coherency between beliefs, goals, and perceptions of the environment (providing) individuals with the feeling that the world is an orderly place." Given this, it is a short step to identify the anterior cingulate cortex which, as a source of "distress signals," should be activated by conflict or "expectancy violation." Religion, then, should attenuate activity in the anterior cingulate cortex, which, in this research, it seems to have done.

As it happens, the functions of this area of the brain are various. The species of "conflict" typically associated with its increased activity involves rather routine cognitive and perceptual task. Summarizing a substantial body of relevant literature, Critchley has concluded,

> The cognitive consequences of anterior cingulate lesions remain rather equivocal, with a number of case reports of intact general neuropsychological and executive function in the presence of large anterior dorsal cingulate lesions.[12]

---

[10] See the Wikipedia entry at: http://en.wikipedia.org/wiki/Daniel_Tammet.

[11] Michael Inzlicht, Alexa M. Tullett, and Marie Good, "The need to believe: a neuroscience account of religion as a motivated process," *Religion, Brain & Behavior* (2011) 1: 192–212.

[12] H.D. Critchley, "Neural mechanisms of autonomic, affective, and cognitive integration," *J Comp Neurol.* (2005) 493(1): 154–66.

The picture, of course, is more cluttered than any given study might suggest. Moreover, the biographical facts gleaned from the lives of persons of faith scarcely support the generalization that religion yields a calm and comforting perspective on oneself and one's world. Even expressing such a qualification grants too much explanatory power to what are finally neurochemical and neuroelectrical events in brain tissue. The brain has no motives and seeks no solace. That actual persons—possessed of brains and other anatomical structures—are, indeed, motivated and do, indeed, strive to find deeper meaning in an otherwise indifferent cosmos is beyond dispute. That such motives and longings are somehow enabled by the brain should be readily granted but not as a fact that would give the motives and longings *to* the brain or locate them *in* the brain. Such inferences might well trigger activity in the anterior cingulate cortex in any creature expecting propositions to be meaningful.

Feminism and Theological Anthropology

Emilie Judge-Becker and Charles Taliaferro

"Feminism" has many strands, some of which are compatible with traditional Christian theological anthropology. Victoria Harrison and Janet Soskice, for example, have made important contributions to philosophy of religion, without taking leave of Christian tradition. But a common, forceful component of much feminist philosophical and theological work today is profoundly opposed to traditional, especially Christian, theological anthropology. If Mary Daly, Pamela Sue Anderson, Grace Jantzen, and Nancy Frankenberry are correct, Christian theism is irremediably patriarchal, a religion built upon and supportive of a male bias. Because of the importance of this critique to the present volume dedicated to theological anthropology, we concentrate chiefly on reasons for thinking that Christian anthropology and theism support (historically and today) a damaging oppositional dualism of mind and body, God and world. Our concern is with the feminist critique of Christian anthropology both in terms of content and method. We highlight the charge by Anderson and others that the supposedly impartial, disinterested philosophical literature that appeals to "reason" and a "God's eye point of view" by leading philosophers of religion (Richard Swinburne, Alvin Plantinga, William Alston) involve the promotion of a disembodied, male point of view that has been used in the past and today to overshadow our bodily life, our sexuality, and the passion of those who are currently still marginalized in western culture.

Three important notes before launching the feminist critique of traditional theological anthropology: First, it is vital to stress that this critique is not the one and only important contribution of feminists to account for human nature and God. Space does not permit us to canvas the many alternative feminist positions. We highlight below one very important feminist re-conception of persons and the God–world relationship as a representative of a creative, novel case of feminist theological anthropology. Second, there are significant differences between the representative feminist philosophers we cite (for example, Jantzen and Anderson disagree about epistemology), but our concern here is more with what Anderson et al. have in common than what distinguishes them from each other. Third, in a final section of this chapter we offer reasons for thinking that a *rejection of historical and contemporary uses of theism and anthropology in the service of patriarchy and male domination* is compatible with affirming a Christian theistic theological anthropology. We also challenge some feminist accounts of recent philosophy of religion. We believe that a Christian theist *should* adhere to an ethic and anthropology that is profoundly opposed to injustice and sexism. We consider ourselves to be feminists as well as Christians, but because we do not wish to draw attention to our own views, the way we refer to feminists in what follows might make it appear that we are "outsiders" or not feminists, whereas this is not the case.

Part of what makes this chapter different from others in the *Companion* is that our focus is solely on the ethical, cultural, and personal implications of theological anthropology, more so than on metaphysics, epistemology, hermeneutics, biblical studies, revealed theology, and so on. We believe that a vital measure of the value of a form of theological anthropology rests on whether it stems from or supports injustice or unfairness. Because of both the central commitment to justice and fairness that we believe must be part of any plausible form of Christian theism and because of the central role of Christian theism in this *Companion*, we need to take with great seriousness the charges of sexism and patriarchy raised by Frankenberry, Anderson, and others. In our view, we also need to appreciate the soundness of their reasoning: if a theological anthropology has the implications they articulate, it is essential either to reform it or, if reform is impossible, such a theological anthropology should be rejected.

Traditional Theological Anthropology: You've Got Male!

In this section we make use of many passages cited from the work of feminists in their critique of traditional theological anthropology. We believe it is important to consider those we address in their own words.

To introduce a portrait of recent philosophy from a feminist point of view, there is no better place to look than the prestigious *Stanford Encyclopedia of Philosophy*, which includes the entry "Feminist Philosophy of Religion." By way of background, many philosophers would agree with the assessment of the field of philosophy of religion along the lines of William Abraham, as outlined in the preface. During the 1950s and 60s, philosophical reflection on religion was largely hostile, based on a hyper-scientific empiricism (called logical positivism). When positivism collapsed by the 1970s, there was a massive revival of constructive philosophy of religion, along with a rise in criticism. This portrait of decline and re-birth is not, however, the storyline that Nancy Frankenberry paints in the *Stanford Encyclopedia*. Frankenberry describes mainstream philosophy of religion from the early 1970s onward in devastating terms, from the standpoint of gender. She singles out three philosophers who have contributed to Christian theological anthropology as leading examples of those who support patriarchy.

In the work of Swinburne, Plantinga, and Alston, "philosophy of religion was deployed in defense of the cogency of a standard form of western monotheism, in the service of a conception of 'God' that was patriarchal, and in the vested interests of staunchly traditional forms of Christianity."[1] Because none of the three philosophers Frankenberry cites *explicitly* claim that women are not equal to males in dignity and worthy of respect, nor do any of the three *explicitly* endorse a male-centered or patriarchal agenda, we must consider reasons for thinking of them as patriarchal beyond any of their own statements of allegiance and value. Two reasons may be advanced as to why we should think of them as patriarchal and male-centered.

One reason for thinking Swinburne et al. are guilty of the verdict "patriarchal" is that none of them have (or have not yet, Plantinga and Swinburne are both very much alive) devoted their work to critiquing the ways in which traditional religion has excluded women from positions of leadership and they did not argue vigorously against the vile ways in which males have oppressed females in the name of religion. Frankenberry writes about the difficulty of ignoring questions about gender.

---

[1]   N. Frankenberry, (2011), "Feminist Philosophy of Religion" in Edward Zalta (ed.), *The Stanford Encyclopedia of Philosophy* (Winter 2011 Edition), 4.

> *Feminists argue that philosophy of religion can hardly ignore questions of gender ideology when its very subject matter—religion—is riddled with misogyny and androcentrism. They point out that, historically, gender bias in religion has been neither accidental nor superficial. Elizabeth Johnson ... likens it to a buried continent whose subaqueous pull shaped all the visible landmass; androcentric bias has massively distorted every aspect of the terrain and rendered invisible, inconsequential, or nonexistent the experience and significance of half the human race. For philosophers studying the intellectual effects and belief systems of religions, the opportunity to critique and correct sexist and patriarchal constructions in this field is as ample as it is urgent, given the presence of gender ideology in all known religions. Not one of the religions of the world has been totally affirming of women's personhood. Every one of them conforms to Heidi Hartmann's definition of patriarchy as "relations between men, which have a material base, and which, though hierarchical, establish or create interdependence and solidarity among men that enable them to dominate women."*[2]

If Frankenberry is right, then a responsible theological anthropology must fully affirm women's personhood and must expose and condemn any anthropology that serves to directly or indirectly sustain the male domination of women. By not doing either, Swinburne, Plantinga, and Alston (henceforth SPA) may be judged patriarchal.

A second reason for seeing SPA as patriarchal is that traditional theism itself is patriarchal. Frankenberry depicts the God of theism as follows:

> *This supreme, ruling, judging, and loving male God is envisioned as a single, absolute subject, is named Father, and is conceived as standing in a relation of hierarchical dominion over the world. In ways both implicit and explicit, this construct tends in turn to justify various social and political structures of patriarchy which exalt solitary human patriarchs at the head of pyramids of power. Drawn almost exclusively from the world of ruling class men, traditional theistic concepts and images legitimate social and intellectual structures that grant a theomorphic character to men who rule and relegate women, children, and other men to marginalized and subordinated areas.*[3]

According to Frankenberry, the theology or philosophy of God in Christianity sets us up for a male-oriented anthropology. While it is obvious that in calling God "Father," one is thereby invoking a male title or metaphor, it may be just as male (though perhaps not as obviously) to think of the divine in terms of *ruling, judging,* and *exercising solitary power*. We note that this is not as obvious, because conceptually there seems no contradiction in supposing that a woman would rule, judge, exercise solitary power, and dominate others. Would a woman cease being a woman if she filled out such a domination-description? Bracketing that question for the moment, Frankenberry seems right that, historically, Christian tradition from the second century onward did think and speak of God in terms that were explicitly male (as in "Father" and "Son") and this accompanied the practice of not recognizing the equality of males and females and the practice of males oppressing women (not recognizing their equal right to own property, to have the same legal rights, and so on).

Frankenberry claims that the traditional distinction between God and the world enshrines an oppositional contrast in which one (God) is deemed superior to the other (the

---

[2] Ibid., 4.
[3] Ibid., 5.

world) and this is expressed negatively in a parallel hierarchical contrast what elevates males over females.

> *Insofar as Western monotheism has constructed the meaning of "God" in relation to "world" around binary oppositions of mind/body, reason/passion, and male/female, traditional theism remains complicitous with the very system of gender constructs and symbolic structures that underlie women's oppression. In the binary opposition between "God" and "world," the term "God" occupies the privileged space and acts as the central principle, the One who confers identity to creatures to whom "He" stands in hierarchical relation. Oppositional pairing of God/world has served in turn to organize other categories, such as heaven and earth, sacred and profane.[4]*

Anderson goes on to argue that the idea that God is maximally perfect, combined with thinking of God as Father (or as "He"), ensures a male bias:

> *Giving supreme perfection, and so authority, to the ideal of reason ensures the man has his ultimate gender ideal: the omni-perfect Father/God. Often there is still no awareness among philosophers of religion that their ideal is problematic; and this is re-enforced by divine, omni-perfect attributes; the latter serve as the core concepts and central topics in philosophy of religion. So, this patriarchal ideal ensures the dominant authority of men who remain blinded by their vision of perfection, unaware of the implications for the "rationality" of their beliefs concerning women, as well as non-patriarchal men.[5]*

Anderson and others embrace the importance of a perspectival approach to being male, female, desire, sexual passion, and more, rather than seeking a "God's eye point of view." The latter divine point of view is valorized by some philosophers (such as Taliaferro) in their theological anthropology as privileging a position of impartiality and non-bias. This is not right if Anderson is correct. Rather, such a point of view is like a disembodied vantage point, thinly disguised in its service of a male agenda. Anderson substitutes for an ideal or God's eye point of view, a yearning to search for truth and learning from others from one's own perspectival position. She distinguishes between a life-affirming yearning as distinct from a male pursuit of truth, love, and goodness in which the inquirer actually aspires to be God.

> *My contention is that yearning can continue to motivate the search for truth, love, goodness and justice without the one who craves or yearns necessarily aspiring to be fully rational, perfectly good and completely just; that is, without aspiring to be, in traditional theistic terms, God.[6] (Anderson 2001, 192)*

We cite Anderson further in extending her critique of traditional theological anthropology as we question whether this feminist critique is compelling. Before doing so, let us consider one alternative, positive conception of the divine that is explicitly advanced by a feminist in her anthropology and philosophy of God.

---

[4]   Ibid., 6.

[5]   "Why Feminist Philosophy of Religion?: An Interview with Pamela Sue Anderson" in Λogoi: *A Publication of the Center for the Philosophy of Religion of the University of Notre Dame*, 1 (2014), 12.

[6]   P.S. Anderson, "Gender and the infinite: On the aspiration to be all there is," *International Journal for Philosophy of Religion*, 50 (2001), 192.

FEMINISM AND THEOLOGICAL ANTHROPOLOGY

A Healthier, Holistic Feminist Theological Anthropology

In a series of publications, especially in *A New Climate for Theology: God, the World, and Global Warming*, Sallie McFague has done outstanding work in cajoling academic scholars to take seriously climate change and how the philosophy and theology of God can make a difference in our relationship with the world. Her alternative concept of the divine is framed by her rejection of traditional theological anthropology. Envisaging God as separable from the world promotes a conception of the world as bereft of God and of human beings having to approach God as some distant monarch.

> If I imagine God (deep down) to be a super-being, residing somewhere above and apart from the world, who created and judges the world but otherwise is absent from it, then I will conduct my affairs largely without day-to-day concern about God. If the God I believe in is supernatural, transcendent, and only occasionally interested in the world, then this God is not a factor in my daily actions.[7]

She proposes instead that if we think of the world as God's body and avoid a dualism of God and world, we have a more holistic understanding of love and a more immediate sense of the importance of caring for the world.

> What if the model was revised so that God as "person" would be not just mind, but also body? What if we did not insist on radical dualism between God and the world, with God being all spirit and the world being all matter or body, but imagined a model with God and the world being both? That is, what if the world were seen to be God's body, which is infused by, empowered by, loved by, given life by God?[8]

If McFague is correct, her re-conception of the divine offers a fuller foundation for environmental action. God cannot be adored or cared for instead of the creation. McFague's position is especially interesting because of its strong affirmation of a unity of God and world or creation, but she does not see the world and God as identical. "God is the source of all existence, the one in whom we are born and reborn. In this view, the world is not just matter while God is spirit; rather, there is a continuity (though not an identity) between God and the world."[9]

We return to McFague's theology of God and the world after considering the cogency of the feminist critique of traditional theological anthropology.

Are Patriarchy, the Oppression and Domination of Women, Children, the Marginalized, the Earth, and so on, Really Bad?

We propose that the problem with patriarchy, oppression, and the unjust treatment of the marginalized, the condition of the disabled and human mistreatment of the earth is that each of these practices reflects a profoundly false, twisted understanding of human

---

7   Sallie McFague, "Falling in Love with God and the World," *The Ecumenical Review*, 65, no. 1 (2013), 23.

8   Sallie McFague, *A New Climate for Theology: God, the World, and Global Warming* (Minneapolis, MN: Fortress Press, 2008), 71.

nature, gender, justice, and more. Or, if the practice is done out of virtually mindless habits and the oppressors have little to no understanding of why they are acting unjustly, their mindlessness is itself a grotesque failure, because this is a failure to recognize clear cases of injustice. So, we agree that any and all cases in which males dominate, oppress, exploit, manipulate others (female or male or some combination) is wrong. Given that we agree with Frankenberry, Anderson, and others, on this point, how might theism and traditional Christian anthropology impact or overshadow our shared conviction about injustice? Our response, to be developed below, is that believing that there is a just, all good God is to believe that any and all unjust action is profoundly against the will and nature of God. If it is obvious that male-domination etcetera is unjust (as it is obvious in our view), then anyone who believes in a just God is committed to believing that such male-domination is abhorrent to God.

When Anderson writes about divine perfection, there seem to be at least two issues to address. Recall that Anderson claims "Giving supreme perfection, and so authority, to the ideal of reason ensures the man has his ultimate gender ideal: the omni-perfect Father/God."[10] First, the way she puts her claim begs the question over what is sometimes called "projectivism"—the thesis that some thing (object, event, supposed reality) is not real but a projection of humans. No theist would claim to project perfection on the divine. Second, if you believe there is a perfect God and you believe that patriarchy is perfect, then there is a huge problem. But surely Anderson herself thinks patriarchy is anything but perfect. So, if she came to believe (for whatever reason) that there is a maximally perfect God, would this lead her to support patriarchy? Quite the opposite. We expect it would lead her to think that patriarchy is in conflict with the perfection of God. On this point, it should be appreciated that the whole Anselmian revival in philosophy of religion (which exalts in God as maximally perfect) places matters of justice and values at the very heart of philosophy of religion. The following claim by Anderson seems to ignore the Anselmian movement when she writes: "Generally justice as a regulative ideal is absent from masculinist philosophy of religion."[11]

The link Anderson supposes between theism and sexism needs to be questioned. Recall another passage, cited earlier, in which Anderson charges that believing in a perfect God will or can (or does?) make men "blinded by their illusion of perfection." This makes us think that Anderson is critiquing those who believe that patriarchy is perfect. Why not believe that those who think patriarchy is perfect are perfectly wrong, and belief in the perfection of God compels one to believe that any claims (backed by scripture or tradition) that God commands something (such as capital punishment for homosexuality) unjust are false?

Let's go back to Frankenberry's characterization of the philosophy of religion. It is true that some seminal figures such as Alston, Plantinga, and Swinburne did not single out the oppression of women as a core concern. That may have partly been because they were

---

[10]   Anderson, "Why Feminist Philosophy of Religion," 12.

[11]   Anderson, "Gender and the infinite: On the aspiration to be all there is," 204. Actually, the first philosophers to contribute to philosophy of religion consistently in English—rather than in Latin or French—were the Cambridge Platonists, a group of philosophers who were centrally concerned with the justice and goodness in their philosophy of God and theological anthropology. They strongly opposed the theological voluntarism of their day—if God wills X then X is good because God wills it. So, at the very foundation of philosophy of religion in the English-language—Cudworth is probably the first to use the term "philosophy of religion" and we get from him the first usage of terms like "theism"—the basic, foundational philosophical orientation of these early contributors was goodness and justice. While the central figures in this movement were male, Anne Conway is often classified with the Cambridge Platonists and she is credited with developing a non-Cartesian understanding of persons and a holistic understanding of God's relationship with the world.

principally working to defeat the wholesale dismissal of Christian theism and the charge that Christian faith was conceptually confused, nonsense. The stress on logic, dispassionate thinking, and such was partly a response to the charge that religious faith is a matter of blind faith and no reasoning whatever. Moreover, the critics of Christianity (Antony Flew, A.J. Ayer, Ronald Hepburn, Michael Martin, and more) nowhere argued that women were either fully persons or denied that women were fully persons. Antony Flew's appropriation of John Wisdom's famous thought experiment comparing belief in God to belief in an invisible gardener did not rest on seeing the gardener as either male or female. But PSA did defend a non-reductionist, non-materialist account of human nature, arguing for the reality and importance of freedom when freedom was under attack as at odds with a mechanistic materialism.

In assessing contemporary philosophy of religion, consider Anderson's description of the same era as Frankenberry.

> *Christian philosophy of religion assumed a narrow definition of what is "rational": rationality was defined by what it excluded; and these were things largely associated with women such as bodily life and desire. In contrast, the "man of reason" had the attributes of clarity, logical rigour and dispassionate thinking. The feminist critique of the "man of reason" reveals the attributes which restricted the role and use of reason to superior, white, Christian (Protestant) men: that is, to patriarchs![12]*

Actually, Swinburne, Plantinga, and Alston each affirm the reality of bodily life, desire, and a robust understanding of "reason" that includes far more than their empiricist counterparts. "Dispassionate" is not a term often used by PSA or others in philosophy of religion (a field that includes outstanding women philosophers such as Marilyn Adams, Sarah Coakly, Lynne Baker, Linda Zagzebski, Kathryn Tanner, Eleonore Stump, and others), but "dispassionate" might be used to refer to inquiry that is not driven by bias, prejudice, and particular passions that obscure impartiality (e.g. unjustified rage, vanity, envy). PSA and others defend the reality and importance of the body, desire, sensations, and personal identity. Again, if gender and race have not been major themes in their work that is partly because those attacking Christianity were focused on arguing that Christianity is conceptually incoherent; impossible due to the fact of there being any evil at all; or, if not impossible, vastly improbable given the magnitude of evil.

What about Anderson's characterization of seeking a God's eye point of view? Anderson suggests this is a view from nowhere, a disembodied abstraction. Her main criticism falls on Taliaferro for holding that moral inquiry consists in seeking impartiality, knowledge of all relevant facts, and an affective apprehension of the points of view of all relevant persons.[13] We suggest that this is not a view from nowhere, but from everywhere. If we inquire into whether to advance new, more restrictive laws protecting women and children (and all others who are marginalized) from abuse, we need to affectively appreciate the points of view of all relevant women, children, victims and victimizers. One might object that the victimizers are unworthy of our affective apprehension, but it is necessary to do this in order to understand why persons are victimizers and how to bring about reform and punishment. Appealing, literally, to God's point of view (in traditional Christianity), if God is all knowing, why wouldn't one claim that God knows what it is like to be an embodied woman or child and know why victimizers are perpetrators of violence? This is not disembodiment.

---

[12]   Anderson, "Why Feminist Philosophy of Religion," 12.

[13]   Charles Taliaferro, "The God's Eye Point of View: A Divine Ethic," in *Faith and Philosophical Analysis*, H.H. Harriet and C.J. Insole (eds) (Farnham: Ashgate Publishing, 2007).

Anderson makes a claim that strikes us as odd: "Why shouldn't rationality apply to women who do not try to get away from their bodies?" She writes:

> In excluding from "reason" questions of bodily matters and of non-straight categories, traditional philosophy of religion turned gay philosophers to feminist philosophy of religion. Today women, whether heterosexual or lesbian, gain a great deal of new insight for feminist philosophy of religion from gay men and other male feminists![14]

Imagine that Swinburne, Plantinga, and Alston are gay. Would discovering that these gentlemen were gay, in any way impact or alter our understanding or our estimation of the cogency of Swinburne's natural theology or Plantinga's epistemology, or Alston's contribution to the meaningfulness of religious language? We do not find anything particularly heterosexual or male about any of their positions such that, upon finding out that they are gay, transgendered or, more specifically, female lesbian identified, we would be compelled to revise our assessment of their work. As an aside, we have not identified our sexual orientation, and do not do so for a simple reason: we do not think that this should have an impact on our defense of traditional Christian theological anthropology.

To conclude: in this chapter we contest the feminist critique of the essential male-orientation of Christian theism as advanced by Frankenberry, Anderson, and others but, as feminists ourselves, we share with them a deep commitment to expose wrongful bias, discrimination, and prejudice in philosophy of religion and other domains of philosophy when it comes to gender as well as in all other areas in which persons are wrongfully marginalized. In a way, their critique makes the importance of theological anthropology abundantly clear. We believe that Frankenberry's and Anderson's work is of the utmost importance and value, for they make it evident that the criteria for a satisfying theological anthropology should include its providing the tools, and honoring the values, that enable us to be more just and fair with one another. Moreover, if Frankenberry and Anderson are right about the essential patriarchal nature of Christian theism, then they provide us good reason for seeking some theological or secular alternative. In this chapter, we have argued that Christian theism has the resources to critique and reform historical failures in justice and fairness, and that it invites all of us to advance ever more confidently in on-going inquiry into the ways in which theological anthropology may be emancipatory.

---

[14] Anderson, "Why Feminist Philosophy of Religion," 13.

PART III
Models for Theological Anthropology

Self-Organizing Personhood: Complex Emergent Developmental Linguistic Relational Neurophysiologicalism

Warren S. Brown and Brad D. Strawn

Introduction

For most of its history, the Christian church has been dominated by the view that persons have a dual (two-part) nature—body and soul. This position (*dualism*) asserts that humans are composites of two different parts, a material body and a non-material spiritual soul. These two parts are not equals in that the soul is considered to be superior to the body and to rule over it. In addition, the soul is immortal, while the body is mortal and transitory. The soul is often considered synonymous with the mind in that it is the source of human rationality, sociality, and spirituality. It is also posited to be the locus of personal identity.

This sort of dualism is difficult to maintain in the light of modern neuroscience in that there is scarcely any human capacity that has not already been shown to be products of identifiable patterns of brain activity, which also raises the problem of how a non-material soul would interact with a physical body. We have argued elsewhere that dualism is also problematic for reasons of practical theology and ecclesiology.[1] If the soul is superior to the body and rules over it, then Christian life must focus on caring for and nurturing the soul, first and foremost. One's body and outward behavior are secondary. Only if time and energy permit can attention can be paid to the physical, economic, and social well-being of other persons.

In psychology, philosophy, and theology there are a number of alternative models for capturing the fundamental nature of human beings and personhood, including Emergent Holistic Dualism, Emergent Monism, Dual Aspect Monism, and Nonreductive Physicalism, to name but a few. Very generally, these alternatives have the advantages of taking more seriously human neurobiology, and not needing to posit a distinct and separate entity—the soul—whose biblical, theological, and psychological status is uncertain, at best. In most of these alternative formulations, the concept of emergence plays a central role.

There are two important problems that are difficult to avoid in many of these models. First, while these views aspire to be holistic, there is often an implicit dualism that stems from attempts to preserve the inwardness of agency in a way that can be differentiated from the acting and interacting physical body. As we have argued elsewhere, dualism,

---

[1]   Warren Brown and Brad Strawn, *The Physical Nature of Christian Life: Neuroscience, Psychology and the Church* (Cambridge: Cambridge University Press, 2012).

whether explicit or implicit, is problematic in that it leads to an inward and individualist understanding of Christian spirituality.[2]

The second problem with these alternative models is their conceptual *simplicity* in referring to the nature of persons. For the sake of philosophical argument, positions and models are stated in conceptually simple abstractions that, in the case of human nature, hide much more than they reveal. Overly general and abstract models yield to forms of argument that are at considerable distance from anything that can adequately be about a functioning human being. For example, we have argued in the past for "nonreductive physicalism." While much can be elaborated from this position, it is itself a minimalist philosophical statement about the fundamental physical nature of humankind, but with the strong qualifier of having properties that are emergent and therefore not reducible to the properties of the elemental constituent parts. However, arguments for and against this position proceed on the basis of abstractions that, because of their simplicity, can systematically miss the point of the nature of persons.

Current philosophical arguments about human nature are paralleled by modern movements in theological anthropology, many of which have taken a more physicalist turn.[3] In addition, new understandings of biblical texts have called into question dualist views and suggested a more holist or physicalist reading of scripture, including unpacking categories and language impacted more by Greek philosophy than biblical exegesis.[4] However, progress in these areas is also stymied by shallow conceptual categories and incomplete knowledge of human psychology and neuroscience, such that the complexity of the person is not taken into account and potential contributions to a richer view of the physical aspects of human nature are ignored.

It is the conceptual simplicity of most holistic models that we wish to address in this chapter. We propose a more complex, and therefore more robust, view which we refer to using the cumbersome but richer title: Complex Emergent Developmental Linguistic Relational Neurophysiologicalism (CEDLRN, if you like acronyms). The point of labeling the position in this way is to make absolutely explicit the richness and complexity necessary for an adequate model of human nature. From this viewpoint, personhood is constituted by emergent properties which are the product of self-organizing processes within the hypercomplex neurophysiological systems of human beings, and which come about progressively over a long period of developmental, linguistic, and relational history. The discussions that follow are preliminary attempts to flesh out the elements of this complex model.

Neurophysiologicalism

We turn first to the idea of "neurophysiologicalism," since it is the noun that the other terms modify. The category "physical" (or even "biological") is too broad for a theory of human nature. "Neurophysiological," at minimum, refers to a biological system with a functioning nervous system—that is, complex networks of interactive neurons (neurons that are themselves complex functional systems). At the very least, neuropohysiology implies a high

---

2   Brown and Strawn, *The Physical Nature of Christian Life*, 2012.

3   Veli-Matti Karkkainen, *Creation and Humanity. A Constructive Christian Theology for the Pluralistic World*, vol. 3, to be published by Eerdmans, 2015.

4   J.B. Green, *Body, Soul, and Human Life: The Nature of Humanity in the Bible* (Grand Rapids, MI: Baker Academic, 2008).

level of biological complexity (hyper-complex in the case of a human being) and a dynamically interactive, ongoing functioning system. Without a view that explicitly encompasses this sort of system, one systematically misses critical points about human nature. For example, arguments about emergence in other sorts of physical system (e.g., solid state physics) miss major points about emerging properties within functioning neurophysiological systems.

The danger to be avoided is falling into the sort of category error that comes about by choosing categories that are too broad and abstract for the discourse at hand, and therefore discussions based on such categories hide the fundamental dynamic of what one intends to describe and characterize. Philosophical discourse, that proceeds on the basis of large abstract categories that have no inherent anchoring in human life and functioning, may be good philosophy, but such discourse is not very relevant to the topic of human nature as it is lived and experienced. Of course, philosophical and theological anthropology cannot recapitulate all of neurophysiology. However, these domains of discourse must meet half-way what is known in the field of human neurophysiology by at least expressing models in ways that allow the inherent complexity and basic functional properties of hypercomplex physical/neural systems like human bodies to be explicitly recognized.

Among other things, "neurophysiologicalism" implies ongoing dynamic feedback control of behavior, and a hierarchy of levels of processing and evaluation of moment-to-moment interactions with the world. Any attempt to conceptually halt this ongoing dynamic (as in philosophical arguments involving a "current brain state") have already missed the point of neurophysiological coupling with the environment via rapid feedback adjustments modulated by many layers of increasingly complex criteria of evaluation—such criteria becoming more spatially, temporally, whole-bodily extensive, and sophisticated at higher levels of a complex nervous system.[5]

To be clear, we mean "neurophysiologicalism" to refer to more than just the brain. Theories of *embodied cognition* make it clear that the brain interacts dynamically with all of the peripheral systems that control and sense the entire body. In essence, we think with records of experiences gained as our body interacts with the world. Human nature is emergent from more than just a complex brain, but from entire bodily systems of motor control and sensory feedback.

Finally, we would be equally happy with the term "neuro*psycho*logicalism" in that discussions of human nature are necessarily focused on the functional properties from which personhood emerges—that is, the neurophysiological processes that give rise to the psychological phenomena of thought, emotion, memory, planning, and religious experience. The question to be asked is whether there is merit in considering such critical properties of persons to be emergent from human brain-and-bodily neurophysiology, and for personhood to be further emergent from dynamic interactive patterns of such psychological phenomena.

Complex

The attribute of complexity in our model is meant to reflect not only the fact that the human nervous system is arguably the most complex structure known, but also the fact that that the theory of complex dynamical systems provides a robust functional model for explaining how the high-level properties of the human mind emerge and play a causal role in human life.

---

[5]   These ideas are developed more completely in Malcolm A. Jeeves and Warren S. Brown, *Neuroscience, Psychology and Religion: Illusions, Delusions, and Realities about Human Nature* (Radnor, Penn: Templeton Press, 2009).

First, the human brain is physically complex beyond what it is possible to imagine. The human nervous system is estimated to be composed of something like 100 billion neurons interacting over 100 trillion synapses. Despite the fact that potential patterns of interactivity are constrained by the physical architecture of the brain and nervous system (what is connected to what), due to the plasticity of each synapse and the possible degrees of functional connectivity over each synapse, the range of functional patterns that can be expressed is truly astronomical.

Degrees and forms of structural connectivity are as important as sheer size in contributing to the unique cognitive capacities of humans. Comparative neuroanatomy has made it clear that, while humans do not have the largest brains, they have a relatively larger cerebral cortex, and, most markedly, a very large prefrontal cortex. The area of the prefrontal cortex is roughly 4 percent of the total cerebral cortex in a cat, 10 percent in a dog, 12 percent in a macaque, and 17 percent in a chimpanzee; but in the human brain, it has enlarged to 29 percent of the total cerebral cortex.[6] Enlargement of the human prefrontal cortex has been found to result primarily from an increase in the amount of white matter—that is, interconnectivity.[7] Thus, the human prefrontal cortex is not simply larger, but more intensely and complexly interconnected within itself, and with other cortical and subcortical structures, than that found in our primate cousins.

Because of the complex, highly interactive, and functionally plastic nature of the human nervous system, the *theory of complex dynamical systems* is the most robust model for modeling its operative characteristics. When pushed far from equilibrium by environmental interactions, a complex dynamic system will emerge as elements self-organize into interactive *patterns* that are constituted by *relational constraints* between elements (e.g. neurons or neural sub-systems). Thus, the elements of the system come to work together in a coherent or coordinated manner to create a larger-scale functional system that can adapt to the demands of the physical, social, or cultural environment in complex and subtle ways. Thus, *aggregates* of disorganized elements become *systems* when the probability of each element doing one thing or another is altered, constrained, and entrained by interactions with other elements.

The physical requirements that are necessary for the self-organizational processes that give rise to a dynamical system and the emergence of higher-order properties, include: *complexity* (a very large number of elements, such as neurons); a high degree of *interconnectivity* (e.g., axons, dendrites, and synapses); two-way interactions (recurrent connections; feedback loops); and *nonlinear interactions* that amplify small perturbations and small differences in initial conditions. Thus, the complex and massively interconnected neuronal network that is the human brain, and most particularly the cerebral cortex, is well suited for the emergence of high-level causal properties-of-the-whole through dynamic self-organization, as described by this theory.

Emergent

Emergence denotes the fact that complex interactive *systems* can have properties that do not exist within the *elements* that make up the system. As noted above, dynamic systems theory

---

6   Joaquín M. Fuster, "Frontal Lobe and Cognitive Development," *Journal of Neurocytology* 31 (2002): 374–6.

7   P.T. Schoenemann, M.J. Sheehan, and L.D. Glotzer, "Prefrontal white matter volume is disproportionately larger in humans than in other primates," *Nature: Neuroscience* 8:2 (2005): 242–52.

gives the best account of how emergence takes place.[8] Due to instability in interactions with the environment, aggregates of interactive elements are forced to work together in a coherent or coordinated manner creating a larger-scale functional system. Once organized into a system, lower-level properties interact (bottom-up) with the relational constraints created by the higher-level patterns (top-down), without implying any exceptions to lawfulness at the micro-level. Continuing interactions with novel aspects of the environment cause repeated reorganizations that both allow adaptability and, at the same time, create increasingly more complex and higher-level forms of system organization. In the reorganization of a dynamical system, multiple smaller systems can become organized into larger systems. In this way, the processes of self-organization and repeated reorganization result, over time, in a nested hierarchy of more and more complex functional systems.

Organization of systems with respect to interactions with and feedback from the environment means that the system organization embodies *meaning* that is carried forward in the form of a memory of previous interactions and the relevant system reorganizations. By action and consequent feedback, a system learns to deal with a novel environmental challenge and also becomes prepared to deal with similar situations in the future. It is nature of the system organization that determines responses to future environmental events, not solely the characteristics of the constituent parts.

In this manner, the establishment of patterns of *constraint* between lower-level elements results in the emergence of higher-level properties that manifest *greater freedom*. The system has a substantially greater number of possibilities with respect to its interactions with the surrounding environment than it had prior to each new level of self-reorganization. "By enlarging and coordinating previously aggregated parts into a more complex, differentiated, systematic whole, contextual constraints enlarge the variety of states the system as a whole can access."[9] Thus, causal properties emerge from the processes of self-organization and the challenges that trigger reorganization.

Interestingly, complex, non-linear, near-chaotic dynamic systems manifest novelty. Even in rather small-scale computer models of dynamic systems, no two runs of the same system ever come out exactly the same. As neuroscientist Walter Freeman expresses it, "One profound advantage chaos confers on the brain is that chaotic systems continually produce novel activity patterns. … [T]he ability to create activity patterns may underlie the brain's ability to generate insight and the 'trials' of trial-and-error problem solving."[10]

Thus, dynamic systems theory specifies how truly emergent, non-reductive properties can be manifest by complex, interactive, near-chaotic, and contextually embedded physical systems—most particularly within hyper-complex physical human beings, as they interact with the social networks in which they are embedded. The emergent phenomena of mental processes (including thinking, deciding, consciousness, memory, language, representation, belief, etc.), operating as dynamic systems, create top-down influences on the lower-level neurophysiological phenomena whose activity constitute the mental processes themselves. Thus, one can also appreciate the fact that a different descriptive language will be necessary to do justice to the nature and activities of a system than is appropriate to use to describe the parts.

---

[8]   See Alicia Juarrero, *Dynamics in Action: Intentional Behavior as a Complex System* (Cambridge, MA: Bradford Books, 1999).

[9]   Ibid., 138.

[10]   Walter J. Freeman, "The Physiology of Perception," *Scientific American* 264 (1991): 78–85.

Developmental

How do we become the complex interactive persons that we are? During fetal and infant development, cells of the brain and spinal cord are forming into neurons, finding their place in the vast complexity of brain space, hooking up with neighboring neurons, and sending axons out to distant regions of the brain. During this process, the outcome is only very roughly pre-ordained by the genome. Contexts created by interactions with surrounding cells are critical to structural formation. Most importantly, the emerging *structure* is maximally open to *functional* organization as the physiology of the developing human responds to its internal milieu and to interactions with the external environment. The chaotic physical fumbling and amorous interactions of a newborn infant ultimately result in progressive adaptation to the physical, social, and cultural world in which the child inhabits.

Thus, the functional structure of the brain is formed ("wired") through a kaleidoscope of daily experiences. Genes contribute only a rough blue print of brain wiring, the rest is formed by a self-organizing process based on continued feedback from interactions with the environment. The development of intelligence, personality, and character, while influenced to some degree by genes, mostly takes place through complex interactions with the environment. Human beings are neither fixed at birth with certain immutable qualities via genetic endowment, nor are we a totally blank slate (*tabula rasa*) to be etched and inscribed by life experiences. Rather, the human mind is a combination of certain very general predispositions, and the experience-based emergence of mental capacities, personality, and character through a continuous history of situational and social interactions. Exploration, give-and-take, and trial-and-error with the physical and social environment fundamentally change us at the level of our neurons, even as adults. Within some genetic constraints, the brain is the sort of self-organizing system described above.

This experienced-based, self-organizing nature of human mind and personhood is significantly enhanced by the very slow physical development of the cerebral cortex that is a distinctive property of the human brain.[11] Whereas a chimpanzee has a nearly adult-like cortex (for a chimp) by the end of the second year of life, a similar degree of development is not reached in humans until four to five years later. In fact, the cortex is still maturing in the late teenage years. This slow development is particularly characteristic of the frontal lobes, areas critical for the most sophisticated processes of the mind. Prolonged physical development is important in allowing maximal opportunity for brain wiring to be sculpted by the physical, social, and cultural world of the individual. Thus, differences in mental power and sociality between humans and apes are not simply due to differences in the size of the brain, but also to the significantly extended opportunity for social and cultural learning to influence the organization of its fine structure.

The process of self-organization by which the open and dynamic brain and body of an infant becomes an increasingly complex mental system is referred to in modern developmental psychology as *meaning making*.[12] The idea is that the world has no innate meaning to an infant. Therefore, infants must actively engage the world to figure out what it is about. Meaning is inferred from feedback from action. The actions are, to begin with, quite random, with the possible exception of interactive eye-gaze and facial imitation of mom. These innate tendencies to orient to faces allow the infant to quickly begin to make social meaning. As children become more physically coordinated (that is, having begun to master

---

[11] Steven Quartz and Terrence Sejnowski, *Liars, Lovers, and Heroes: What the New Brain Science Reveals about How We Become Who We Are* (New York: Harper Collins, 2002).

[12] E. Tronick and M. Beeghly, "Infants' meaning-making and the development of mental health problems," *American Psychologist* 66, 2 (2011): 107–19.

motor meanings), they are increasingly able to explore their world, and to make more and more sensory meanings (visual, auditory, touch, kinesthetic). Their mental systems are becoming increasing complex and intelligent by constant sensorimotor interaction with their world. Meaning is made by action, not passively discovered by observation. For example, imagine how much children learn about space when they are suddenly able to crawl and move about.

The point we wish to emphasize is that intelligence, personality, and character are mostly "open programs" in the same way that some computer super-games have been created to learn game knowledge as they are played. The program itself gets progressively modified and improved by the experiences of trial-and-success and trial-and-error feedback as the game is played—so also with the developing brain of a child. Thus, our neural openness gives us a great advantage in mental flexibility, allowing our personhood to be shaped for unanticipated roles and challenges.

Linguistic

In terms of the emergence of human nature and qualities of personhood, the development of language is a game-changer. Sometime during the second year of life, language learning kicks into high gear and accelerates exponentially. With language, new, cognitive, social, and psychological capacities emerge that fundamentally alter personhood.

The capacity for language seems to have both a genetically related predisposition and a critical developmental (self-organizing) aspect. It rests upon a particular architecture within the brain that is present at birth. The existence of a genetic blue print for language has been suggested in studies using functional magnetic resonance imaging (fMRI) of brain activity. When pre-linguistic infants listen to speech, fMRI has shown evidence of localization of activity in left hemisphere language areas. However, it is also clear that language is impossible for children to learn outside of rich and constant language exposure from parents and other persons. Thus, mastery of language is a process of self-organization in response to a language dominant social environmental. That this genetically predisposed language system is highly malleable and plastic is illustrated by research that has shown that infants start life with the ability to tell the difference between all human language sounds (phonemes), but within a few years of hearing their native language, they progressively lose the ability to detect differences between sounds that do not occur in their native tongue.[13] If the mother tongue they are learning does not include a particular phoneme distinction (e.g., "ra" versus "la"), they soon are no longer able to "hear" the difference. In fact, if language is not heard and used at all during child development due to some form of social or sensory deprivation, the language capacity can suffer permanent loss. Linguist Susan Curtis has documented just such an outcome in the socially isolated case of Genie.[14]

The dependence of language on developmental self-organization from being embedded within a rich social and linguistic environment is illustrated in attempts to teach language to chimpanzees. Research in the 1960's and 70's suggested that minimal language-like abilities could be developed in adult apes when given intensive training. However, one chimpanzee,

---

[13] P.K. Kuhl et al., "Linguistic experience alters phonetic perception in infants by 6 months of age," *Science* 31 (1992): 606–8.

[14] Susan Curtis, *Genie: A Psycholinguistic Study of a Modern-Day "Wild Child"* (New York: Academic Press, 1977).

Kanzi, was remarkable with respect to the acquisition of language by a non-human primate.[15] Kanzi developed an English comprehension vocabulary that included more than 500 words, which is roughly equivalent to that of a two-and-a-half-year-old child. However, it is critical to note that, in contrast to prior attempts to teach language to adult apes, Kanzi was exposed from infancy to a rich language environment when he was present while his mother was attempting to learn a token language as part of a research project. He was consistently exposed to the token system being learned by his mother, as well as immersed in a human language environment via interactions with human caretakers and experimenters. Thus, despite his less adept chimpanzee cognitive capacities, self-organizing developmental processes allowed Kanzi to accomplish more nearly human language capacity.

As the capacity for language develops in children, it provides the basis for the emergence of important mental and social capacities, some of which have been outlined by anthropologist Terrence Deacon.[16] First, language distances behavior from the demands of immediate motivations and needs. Language can be used as a means of postponing gratification of immediate needs by considering alternative actions using language-dependent thoughts about the future. Second, the self-referential possibilities of language allow a person to have thoughts and express sentences that include the idea of "me." In this way, language facilitates the formation of a self-concept, allowing self-reflection, self-understanding, and projection of the self into the future. Third, language provides the basis for expanded empathy and an ability to understand the mental lives of others. We enter into, and become emotionally engaged by, the experiences of others through stories. Fourth, language facilitates a common mind among groups of people. Common semantics, metaphors, and stories form groups with similar understandings of life and the world around them. Children are brought into the worldview of their parents, family, and eventually wider social groups via language. Finally, ethical behavior is enhanced by language because it holds and communicates the values of communities in terms of statements and stories about what is "good" and "bad."

Story telling is particularly important in the emergence of personhood because it allows persons to know vicariously the experiences of others. Story-telling is particularly important in child development. Story narrative allows children to vicariously imagine new situations, "try out" various behaviors, and safely experience their positive or negative consequences, forming rich impressions in their minds about what is good and bad, right and wrong, and conducive or not to the well-being of others. Narrative memories also contribute to our understanding of our selves. This is illustrated in a rare neurological condition called "dysnarrativia" that is caused by damage to a particular part of the frontal lobe of the brain. Persons with this disorder are impaired in their ability to formulate a narrative history of their thoughts and experiences, even though they are quite aware at the moment of their circumstances and thoughts. Individuals with this disorder "lead 'denarrated' lives, aware but failing to organize experience in an action-generating temporal frame."[17] Most interestingly, these individuals are described as having lost their sense of self, suggesting a strong link between the capacity to narrate one's experiences and important qualities of personhood.

---

[15] Sue Savage-Rumbaugh and Roger Lewin, *Kanzi: The Ape at the Brink of the Human Mind* (New York: Wiley, 1994).

[16] Terrance Deacon, *The Symbolic Species: The Co-evolution of Language and the Brain* (New York: W.W. Norton & Co., 1997).

[17] Kay Young and Jeffrey L. Saver, "The Neurology of Narrative," *Substance: A Review of Theory & Literary Criticism* 30: 1/2 (2001): 78.

Relational

As we have described, it is impossible to formulate an adequate understanding of human nature and personhood without taking explicit account of the role of developmental processes in forming personhood, and the contribution of language to human cognitive and social capacities. It is equally impossible to formulate an understanding of human nature and personhood without an account of the fundamental relationality of humans. While some philosophical positions on anthropology give some recognition to human relationality, they don't seem to fully appreciate the power of human interpersonal interactions on the development of personhood, and the depth of its impact on what it means to be a person. The role of human relatedness on development cannot be overestimated.

The prolonged developmental openness of the human nervous system is obviously not sufficient to ensure the formation of personhood in a child. It needs to be coupled with innate behavioral tendencies to interact with other persons. As psychologist Andrew Melzoff has famously shown, even within hours of birth, infants will imitate the facial gestures of another person. Imitation of facial expressions begins a social give-and-take between parent and child.[18] Such tendencies to engage in reciprocal imitation builds into the cognitive system of a child the idea that others are "like me," an important step in the organization of an understanding of the mind of other persons (called Theory of Mind). Thus, based on innate primitive social inclinations, children form social relationships and social knowledge.

Psychologists have shown that human infants are born with a particular temperament, which by four months can be very broadly characterized as "inhibited" (20 percent of infants) or "bold/fearless" (40 percent), with the rest showing a mix of the two styles.[19] However, by four years of age, only 10 percent of children show such extremes in temperament. Thus, the experiences of life during these early years tend to modify these temperaments. In the self-organizing process of human development, being born *"some* way" does not equal being forever *"that* way." [20] Even more striking is research that bred monkeys to be primarily inhibited (fearful) or bold in temperament (presumably a genetically mediated selection process). Later, some of the fearful/inhibited infant monkeys were moved into a cage with uninhibited, nurturing foster mothers. They subsequently became less fearful and less "ramped up" physiologically, as indicated by a reduction in biochemical markers of stress and fear (such as blood levels of the stress hormones adrenaline and cortisol).[21] Relational experience significantly modified a genetically influenced temperament.

While the importance of early child environment and caregiver interactions have been demonstrated in extreme situations of deprivation,[22] more and more research is exploring the impact of early attachment experiences on the subsequent development of a person. Different qualities of the early caregiver–child relationship lead to core forms of self-organization that constitute the child's developing sense of self-in-the-world, self-and-other,

---

[18] Andrew Meltzoff and Jean Decety, "What imitation tells us about social cognition: A rapprochement between developmental psychology and cognitive neuroscience," *Phil Trans. Royal Society of London B*, 358 (2003): 491–500; Andrew Meltzoff, "The 'like me' framework for recognizing and becoming an intentional agent," *Acta Psychologica*, 124 (2007): 26–43.

[19] Research by Jerome Kagan described in Quartz and Sejnowski, op. cit., 125.

[20] Quartz and Sejnowski, *Liars, Lovers, and Heroes: What the New Brain Science Reveals about How We Become Who We Are*, 2002, 128.

[21] M. Champoux et al., "Serotonin transporter gene polymorphism, differential early rearing, and behavior in rhesus monkey neonates," *Molecular Psychiatry*, 7 (2002): 1058–63.

[22] Curtis, *Genie: A Psycholinguistic Study of a Modern-Day "Wild Child"*, 1977; Spitz, R., "Hospitalism: An Inquiry into the Genesis of Psychiatric Conditions in Early Childhood," *The Psychoanalytic Study of the Child*, 1 (1946): 53–74.

and emotional self-regulation. These core forms come together to create an identifiable style of adult relationships.[23]

As an outcome of developmental relational experiences, four basic attachment styles have been identified in children: securely attached, anxiously attached and avoidant, anxiously attached and resistant, and disorganized attachment.[24] An attachment style is a kind of internal working model for how relationships work. Through relating with caregivers, children learn how relationships operate, what to expect, and therefore how to predict and act accordingly based on their experiences with the environment. These internal models are not conscious but work in off-line ways as a kind of neurological hermeneutical activity of the brain for assessing, interpreting, and predicting different scenarios based on current and past experience.

Secure attachment doesn't just magically happen but is accomplished through a large number of child-caregiver interactions that bring about what has been called neural organization and integration.[25] Most researchers and theoreticians believe that it is the process of caregivers attuning to the child's internal states (these are primarily affect states) and bringing them into actions and words that facilitates development of affect regulation in the child and helps them eventually connect internal states with language.[26] This relational activity of affect attunement seems to provide a developmental environment characterized by a kind of safety for children as they experience new and often overly stimulating situations. This is very different from the experiences of anxiously attached children who, without a developmental environment rooted in comfort and safety, become easily overwhelmed by affect and interpersonal situations, and therefore learn to avoid or become overwhelmed by anxiety provoking interpersonal scenarios.

As we would expect from our understanding of the possibilities for reorganization in dynamical systems (such as the human brain), there is good news for children that did not experience a secure base from which to develop a secure attachment. Research has demonstrated that attachment styles can change if given new experiences over time.[27] While longitudinal research has indicated that attachment styles (i.e., characteristics of early relational organization) endure into adulthood and are predictive of later adult relationships, research has also shown that good friends, caring spouses, and good psychotherapy can ameliorate negative attachments styles and move individuals toward more secure styles (relationally provoked system reorganization).

With respect to relational styles and habits, it is also important how persons integrate conscious cognitive processes with affective tendencies. In one study, researchers found that mothers with personal insecure attachment styles were able to form secure attachment styles to their own babies if they were able to develop a coherent narrative of their own personal history.[28] Thus, narrative not only helps persons develop an understanding of the mind and experiences of others, but also has an integrative effect in bringing together

[23] Louis J. Cozolino, *The Neuroscience of Psychotherapy: Building and Rebuilding the Human Brain* (New York: Norton, 2002); Daniel J. Siegal, *The Developing Mind: How Relationships and the Brain Interact to Shape Who We Are* (New York: Guilford, 1999).

[24] M.D.S. Ainsworth, M.C. Blehar, E. Waters, and S. Wall, *Patterns of Attachment: A Psychological Study of the Strange Situation* (NJ: Erlbaum, 1978); M. Main and J. Solomon, "Discovery of an insecure/disorganized attachment pattern." In T. B. Brazelton and M. Yogman (eds), *Affective Development in Infancy* (pp. 95–124) (NJ: Ablex, 1986).

[25] Cozolino, *The Neuroscience of Psychotherapy*, 2004.

[26] Siegal, *The Developing Mind*, 1999.

[27] Research described in David J. Wallin, *Attachment in Psychotherapy* (New York: Guilford, 2007).

[28] Research described in Daniel Stern, *The Interpersonal World of the Infant: A View from Psychoanalysis and Developmental Psychology* (New York: Basic Books, 1985).

embodied internal processes of cognition and affect in ways that can create opportunities for reorganization of attachment styles and forms of emotional regulation.[29]

Conclusions

We began this chapter by arguing that most of the models currently framing the conversation about human nature suffer from two problems: (1) There is an implicit inner-outer dualism inherent in many models that otherwise presume to be monist; and (2) All of the current models express their basic understanding in a way that is stated too simply and therefore fails to bring into the conversation an array of dimensions of human nature that must be explicitly understood and taken into account before progress can be made. This chapter has focused on the second issue by putting forward a more explicit and complex model of human nature: Complex Emergent Developmental Linguistic Relational Neurophysiologicalism.

We have argued that we must not be content to merely philosophize about physicalism without being cognizant of the unique characteristics of neurophysiology. What is more, the human brain is the most complex structure and system known and that complexity must be explicitly acknowledged, as well as the value of understanding neurophysiology as a complex dynamical system. Adequate understanding of human nature must also take into account the progressive 10- to 20-year process of self-organizing neurocognitive development characteristics of human children, as well as the dramatic contribution to psychosocial capacities and human agency contributed by the acquisition of language. Finally, the deeply formative influences of inter-personal relatedness and socio-cultural systems must be taken into account.

It is our position that progress cannot be made in theories of human nature without this sort of explicit recognition of the depth and richness of what it means to be a human being and become a person. Given the state of understanding of complex systems, human cognition, neuroscience, child developmental, and relational psychology, it is time to move the discussion of human nature past the sparse models currently employed.

---

[29]   Siegel, *The Developing Mind*, 1999.

Physicalism, Bodily Resurrection, and the Constitution Account

Omar Fakhri

Introduction

This chapter is about bodily resurrection. More specifically, it is about whether bodily resurrection is feasible according to a physicalist account of human beings. I argue that bodily resurrection is less plausible given mainstream physicalism, but it is not less plausible given the constitution account.

In the first section, I criticize different options mainstream physicalism can take to make sense of bodily resurrection. All these options seem less than plausible. I spend more space on the first option, reassembly, because it seems to be *prima facie* the most natural option for mainstream physicalism. Then, in the second section, I show that the constitution account does not fall prey to the problems that infect mainstream physicalism.

Mainstream Physicalism and Bodily Resurrection

According to one branch of mainstream physicalism, a human being is identical to an organic animal. I am identical to a material object, which I call "my body."[1] This object contains my brain, heart, kidney, liver, and bones, among other things. Not every mainstream physicalist will agree with this. For instance, some would say I am identical to my brain as opposed to the entire material object I call "my body." Also some might hold I am not identical to my body but I am nothing "over and above" my body. For simplicity's sake, I ignore these distinctions. I assume I am identical to my body. Not much turns on this for the purposes of this chapter; the following arguments can be restated to accommodate this caveat.

Reassembly

In order for God to resurrect me at the day of resurrection, He must resurrect my body. At least this is the case if mainstream physicalism is true. Since I am identical to my body,

---

[1]   In Peter van Inwagen, "Philosophers and the Words 'Human Body,'" in *Time and Cause: Essays presented to Richard Taylor*, ed. Peter van Inwagen (Dordrecht: Reidel Pub. Co., 1980), pp. 283–300. In it, he rejects the use of the phrase "my body." To side step some of his worries, I use "my body" to mean "my body that is a living organism."

resurrecting me would be the same thing as resurrecting my body. At this point, problems immediately arise. How could God resurrect my body at the day of resurrection when my body is long gone by then? Suppose I die tomorrow from a car accident. My body would undergo a great deal of harm. My internal organs would be severely damaged. If the car accident is bad enough, parts of me might be missing. This is nothing in comparison to what my body would undergo after being buried for several decades. Time rots the flesh, leaving only the bones. Or worse, my family might decide to cremate me. In that case, my body would be destroyed, bones and all.

What would God need to do in order to resurrect me after the damage my body undergoes? One possible option is for God to create a body that is an exact replica of my body. This will not do. Creating a body that is a duplicate of my body and then resurrecting that body is not the same thing as resurrecting me. Although this other body would be qualitatively the same, it would be numerically distinct. There is one Omar and there can only be one Omar. Making duplicate Omars would produce Omar-clones, but they would not reproduce me. God knows better.

A better option is to reassemble the exact atoms that once composed me.[2] Once I am buried, my body would begin to decompose. While decomposing, atoms slowly leave my rotting flesh. God, being omniscient, knows which atoms these are and, being omnipotent, can exercise his power to gather all the atoms and use them to reassemble my body. If this reassembly brings back my body, then it would bring me back since I am just my body. At first glance, this second option seems more promising. Reassembling a material object by using the same parts is a step up from using new parts to make a duplicate. Consider this example. My watch begins to malfunction. After doing some research, I figure out I need to send different parts of the watch to different horologists across the country. This is the only way to get the watch fixed I am told. Once I get the parts back and reassemble them, I would have my watch back; the same watch I had before the reassembly. Like the watch example, God can do the same thing to my body; He can recollect all my parts and reassemble them. This option is the straightforward one for the mainstream physicalist to take.

Peter van Inwagen sees a problem with this option.[3] The problem, roughly, is this: the original object and the reassembled object have significantly different properties. He uses an example for the intuition pump. Suppose one of St Augustine's manuscripts was destroyed for whatever reason. By this time, the atoms that made up the manuscript are spread out all over the cosmos. God recollects all those atoms and reconstructs the manuscript. Would this be St Augustine's manuscript? Van Inwagen says "no" because this manuscript has different properties than St Augustine's manuscript. For instance, the reassembled manuscript did not exist during St Augustine's time because the original manuscript was destroyed shortly after his death. Moreover, the original manuscript had a different creator. Perhaps a fifth century monk created the blank manuscript and the ink that was used by St Augustine. In the reassembled manuscript, God is the cause of the blank manuscript, and He is also the cause of the ink being placed in such a way as to reproduce St Augustine's exact words.

Mark Johnston has an interesting response to van Inwagen.[4] According to Johnston, van Inwagen's objection does nothing more than point out an ontological distinction between immediate parts and remote parts. To see why Johnston thinks this, consider this

---

[2]   See Smith and Haddad, *The Islamic Understanding of Death and Resurrection* (New York: Oxford University Press, 2002), p. 146; and Caroline Bynum, *The Resurrection of the Body in Western Christianity* (New York: Columbia University Press, 1995), chapters 1, 3, and 6.

[3]   Perter van Inwagen, "The Possibility of Resurrection," *International Journal for Philosophy of Religion*, vol. 9, no. 2 (1978): pp. 114–21.

[4]   Mark Johnston, *Surviving Death* (Princeton: Princeton University Press, 2010), pp. 29–32.

reconstruction of the St Augustine example. Suppose St Augustine's manuscript was never destroyed. Rather, it was ripped in half, and each half was preserved throughout the years. Furthermore suppose archeologists from our time find the two pieces and reattach them. The two halves are immediate parts. Unlike the original example, the reassembly here seems to reproduce St Augustine's manuscript, not a mere duplicate. The difference between the two examples is this: the intuition behind the original example was based on remote parts whereas the intuition behind the second example is based on immediate parts. In order for God to reassemble the manuscript or me, He must work with the immediate parts.

Recall the original example. But now suppose St Augustine's manuscript was destroyed in the following way: a machine took the manuscript and slowly cuts each part of the manuscript in half. So it begins by cutting the whole manuscript into two halves. Then, it cuts each half into further halves, and so on. Eventually the machine will reach the mereological simples (assume we inhabit a world with mereological simples for the sake of this example), which do not have any parts. At this point, the machine would cease. Now suppose we reverse the process. We begin by collecting all the atoms that made up the manuscript, we start composing them by taking the atoms that were attached together from the last stage and join them together. Then take the atoms that were attached together from the stage before the last stage and join them together, so forth and so on. Each stage is a reassembly of two immediate parts into a whole, just like the reassembly of the two halves of St Augustine's manuscript in Johnston's example. If Johnston's example did its job, then the machine example should show that God could reassemble the completely destroyed manuscript, and it would not be a mere duplicate—or so the argument goes.

This fix will not do. At least my intuition about the example is not strong. I can grant that the machine example provides some favorable intuition. But those intuitions are not the sort of intuitions I would be confident in. I have strong and clear intuitions about whether two halves of St Augustine's manuscript can be joined together to make a whole. My intuitions there suggest that the result of joining those two halves is in fact St Augustine's manuscript. However, these intuitions leave me once we consider other cases. Cases like: all the atoms in St Augustine's manuscript instantly end up at the opposite corners of the cosmos, and stay floating there for thousands of years. Which parts would be immediate parts and which parts would be remote parts in that example? I am not sure. Moreover, at what stage of the division does the machine destroy the manuscript? Surely the manuscript is destroyed by the last stage. But if it is destroyed, then could the same manuscript survive destruction? Could any object survive destruction? If objects can survive destruction, then in what sense were these objects destroyed? These questions, at least to me, do not seem to have a clear answer. Likewise, I am not sure that the reassembled manuscript after complete destruction would be the same manuscript. I am not claiming that the machine example does not in fact show we can reconstruct the manuscript. Instead, I am claiming it is not clear whether it does show that.

There is yet a deeper problem. Suppose my intuitions are wrong. Suppose Johnston is right. Suppose even if all the atoms that compose St Augustine's manuscript were to immediately end up at separate corners of the cosmos, God can reassemble the manuscript, and it would be the same manuscript. The deeper problem is this: it seems possible—or maybe even an empirical fact—the atoms that compose me end up composing someone else after my body rots and crumbles. Or worse, someone digs up my body and eats my flesh. As a consequence, my body becomes part of someone else's body. How can God reassemble the two bodies at the day of resurrection if the two bodies share parts? He cannot.

Johnston has argued for a similar problem. He states the argument formally in the following way:[5]

1. Necessarily, two distinct things cannot become identical with one. (Necessity of Distinctness)
2. Necessarily, if at some time t after the death of a body x a body y comes together out of simple elements in such a way as to reproduce x's perimortem state then y is numerically the same body as x; that is, y is the very body x come back into existence. (The Auxiliary Principle)
3. Necessarily, the re-creation of a person's body is the re-creation of that person. (The Bodily Criterion)
4. It is possible that there be two people who have the same perimortem bodily state and then that a body y comes together out of simple elements at some later time t in such a way as to reproduce that common perimortem state. (Assumption)
5. It is possible that two distinct people become identical with one person. (From 2, 3, and 4, contradicting 1.)

The conjunction of (1)–(4) imply (5). But (1) and (5) produce a contradiction. So something has to give. Johnston thinks the obvious problem is the Auxiliary Principle.

The Auxiliary Principle says something like this: suppose I die today. Call the physical state that I am in at my death P. If God is able to recollect the very atoms that composed P and reassemble them to reproduce P, then he would have reproduced me and not a mere duplicate of me. Johnston thinks the Auxiliary Principle is the best bet for the mainstream physicalist (whose view is represented by premise 3), and it (coupled with some plausible premises) implies a contradiction. Hence, the Auxiliary Principle is necessarily false. Its truth is impossible.

As for premise 4, Johnston has the following story in mind. Suppose David dies in the 1800s; call the physical state that David was in at his death R. His atoms leave his body and begin to float around. Two hundred years later, John dies and somehow—perhaps because of how the world is constructed—ends up with the same physical state that David was in at his death. That is, as John ages and replaces his old atoms with new atoms, he slowly begins to replace the old ones with the atoms that composed David during state R. Once John reaches state R, he dies. As such, David and John both died in state R. Of course, the claim here is not that this story is in fact true. Rather, it is at least possible. If the John and David story is even possible, then God would not be able to bodily resurrect either John or David because it is impossible for two distinct people to become identical with one person. This is as good a reason as any to reject the Auxiliary Principle.

There is a hole in Johnston's argument. Suppose God encounters a situation like the one between David and John. Since it is impossible for two distinct people to become identical to one person, God cannot resurrect both David and John, even if this God is omnipotent (assuming omnipotence is restricted to logical possibilities). However, this should not be a problem for an all-rational God. Instead of resurrecting David and John at the stage they perished in, God can resurrect David at the stage he perished in and resurrect a younger stage of John, say when he was 20 years old. By doing this, God avoids the problem. And after all, the possibility of resurrection is what the mainstream physicalist is really after. As such, Johnston's argument does not impose any problems unless God must resurrect everyone at the stage they perished in. But there is no good reason to accept that claim.

---

[5]   Johnston, *Surviving Death*, p. 34.

Johnston cannot respond to this objection in the following way. We can think of a different example where 200 years after David's death, John ends up having the same atoms as David from age 20 until his death. For one, God can just resurrect an even younger John and let that John grow older in heaven. If Johnston takes it a step further and argues that at every stage in John's life, he has the same atoms as David, then that is just an odd case of reincarnation. We would not have two distinct persons in that case, but only one person who lives during two different time periods.

Despite this difficulty, there is a fix to this problem. Suppose David lived for 50 years and then died. His body completely recycled his atoms every ten years. So at age ten, he had completely different atoms than he did when he was born. The same goes for ages 20, 30, 40, and 50. If John, who lives 200 years later, has the same atoms as David from day one until his death, then John would just be a reincarnation of David and hence Johnston's argument will not work. But suppose that John dies having the same atoms that David had at age 50, Mike dies having the same atoms that David had at age 40, Steve dies having the same atoms that David had at age 30, and so forth and so on for Bob and Sam. Furthermore, we can suppose that John, Mike, Steve, Bob, and Sam have at least a subset of the atoms that belonged to David at every point in their life. This last claim screens off the possibility of God resurrecting a later or an earlier stage of John, Mike, Steve, Bob, or Sam. This fix seems to avoid the problems I raised earlier. If this is right, then so much the worse for the reassembly option.

Body Snatching

But perhaps God can salvage the cannibalism situation or Johnston's objection by body snatching. Van Inwagen takes this route.[6] God snatches your body and replaces it with a duplicate look alike to make sure no one ever eats you and to also make sure no one will share your atoms in the future. By doing this, God would be able to resurrect you at the day of resurrection because replacing your body with an indistinguishable body guarantees that your body would not become part of someone else's body.

Despite the speculative and implausible nature of body snatching, van Inwagen requires only the mere logical possibility of this scenario. Nonetheless, it does not work for the following reasons. When does God do the body snatching, before or after death? If it is right after death, then how can God snatch my body if, say, I was instantly disintegrated by a nuclear blast? This would require complete reassembly, and as we have seen, that is not the most plausible route. If God snatches my body right before death, then the account seems even more implausible. What (or who) would be the cause of my death if God snatches my body before I disintegrate from the nuclear blast? Would I never die? Would I die of natural causes in heaven? Or would God (or one of his angels) kill me? Surely there would be some serious moral issues with the latter option. Additionally, it is part of Christian orthodoxy that everyone (or almost everyone) dies before the final resurrection.[7] But maybe God snatches my body at the same time as my death—snatching and death are simultaneous. This option seems incoherent: suppose at t1 the nuclear blast takes place, and at t2 I die because all my atoms are instantly spread across the city. If God snatches my body at the moment of death, which is t2, then God would snatch a disintegrated body at that moment. This would of course defeat the purpose of body snatching.

---

[6] Peter van Inwagen, "The Possibility of Resurrection."

[7] "For as in Adam all die, so also in Christ all will be made alive" (1 Corinthians 15:22 NASB).

Although van Inwagen's account only requires the logical possibility of body snatching, his account is highly implausible. What I mean by this is that whether his account is logically possible is dubious. Van Inwagen's account seems to require God to do some morally questionable things that do not seem possible given God's all-loving and moral nature. As such, the account should be, at best, a last resort.

Spatiotemporal Gaps

Dean Zimmerman has a different proposal: spatiotemporal gaps.[8] Part of being a living organism is having the ability of self-maintenance. I am maintained in existence by my current intrinsic properties causing my succeeding intrinsic properties. I endure through time by self-maintenance. By immanent causation, my body directly causes my succeeding intrinsic properties. Zimmerman thinks it is at least possible that there could be a spatiotemporal gap with self-maintenance. In the normal case, my body at t1 directly causes my succeeding intrinsic properties at t2, and this process keeps recurring as long as I endure through time. With spatiotemporal gaps, the story is something like this: my body at t1 directly causes my succeeding intrinsic properties at t2. But then suppose I will die at t3. God makes it the case that my body, call it X, fissions right before death, which results in the creation of two bodies, call them Y1 and Y2. X directly causes Y1, and by doing so, Y1 will die at t3. On the other hand, X directly causes Y2, but there is a spatiotemporal gap, so Y2 appears at tn, where tn is whenever the day of resurrection is. The spatiotemporal gap then takes place between X and Y2 from t2 to the day of resurrection.

Zimmerman seems to commit himself to the closest continuer theory of personal identity.[9] In order for Y2 to be me at the day of resurrection, it must be the closest candidate in resembling X. If Y2 is the closest, then Y2 would be me. Zimmerman commits himself to this theory because otherwise it is difficult to say why Y1 isn't me and that Y2 is only some duplicate of me. If Y1 is me and Y2 is merely a duplicate of me, then I die at t3 and never make it to the day of resurrection. Some duplicate of me makes it, i.e., Y2 makes it. With the closest continuer theory, this problem does not arise.

Let us grant Zimmerman this theory of personal identity despite its many shortcomings.[10] It is not clear whether Zimmerman is logically committed to the closest continuer theory of personal identity.[11] But even while putting these worries aside, Zimmerman's account is not without flaws.

Here is a counterexample: suppose my body at t1 directly causes my succeeding intrinsic properties at t2. But then suppose I will die at t3. God makes it the case that my body, X, fissions right before death, which results in the creation of two bodies, Y1 and Y2. X directly causes Y1, and by doing so, Y1 will die at t3. On the other hand, X directly causes Y2, but there is a spatiotemporal gap, so Y2 appears at t10, where t10 is the day of resurrection. Now suppose I hire an organization that specializes in cryonics to freeze Y1 at t2 right before

---

[8]   Dean Zimmerman, "The Compatibility of Materialism and Survival: The 'Falling Elevator' Model," *Faith and Philosophy*, vol. 14, no. 2 (1999): pp. 194–212.

[9]   See Robert Nozick, *Philosophical Explanations* (Cambridge: Harvard University Press, 1981), pp. 27–70.

[10]   For a strong criticism see Katherin Hawley, "Fission, Fusion, and Intrinsic Facts," *Philosophy and Phenomenological Research*, vol. 17, no. 3 (2005): pp. 602–21.

[11]   See Jonathan Jacobs and Timothy O'Connor, "Emergent Individuals and the Resurrection," *European Journal for Philosophy of Religion*, vol. 2, no. 2 (2010): pp. 69–88. See Jacobs and O'Connor for a variant of the "falling elevator" account that does not require the closest continuer theory of personal identity.

death. Once they freeze my body, I die at t3. The company unfreezes my body and brings me back to life right at t10. At the day of resurrection there will be two equal candidates for being the successors of X, namely Y1 and Y2. But surely it is absurd that there would be two entities that are identical to me. Moreover, it would seem arbitrary to favor one of the bodies over the other since they are equally good candidates. The mere possibility of this case implies the absurdity of Zimmerman's account. I see no reason to deny the mere possibility. Hence, we should reject the account.

The Constitution Account

For the first section above, the strongest conclusion we should make is that bodily resurrection is infeasible given mainstream physicalism. Perhaps even this conclusion is too strong because I have not addressed every option in logical space.[12] But how could anyone accomplish such a task anyway? I am not sure. At any rate, in this section I argue that the problems present for mainstream physicalism—at least the accounts I have addressed—are not present for the constitution account. Hence, all things being equal, an advocate of bodily resurrection should prefer it over mainstream physicalism.

The Constitution Account and Bodily Resurrection

According to the constitution account—I have Lynne Rudder Baker's specific account in mind—a human being is not identical to his or her body. Rather, a human being is constituted by his or her body. For example, Plantinga (2006) takes a material object to either be an atom or something composed of atoms—where composition is a mereological concept. By contrast, constitution is not a mereological concept.[13] On the constitution account, x is a material object if and only if x, for all times when x exists, is ultimately constituted by some sum or other (different sums at different times) of physical particles. Constitution is a relation that is stronger than distinct existence but weaker than identity. Unlike identity, constitution is time bound and contingent. The constitution relation holds between primary kinds. Everything has a primary kind. Baker explains primary kinds in the following way: "A thing x's primary kind is the answer to the question, 'What, most fundamentally, is x?'"[14] For instance, a particular mallet is constituted at t by a sum of two cylindrical rods whose

---

[12] For instance, there is Locke's psychological continuity account in Locke, *An Essay Concerning Human Understanding* (New York: Dover Publications, 1959), book II, ch. XXVII, pp. 439–70. See Shoemaker, "Persons and their Parts," *Philosophical Quarterly*, vol. 7, no. 4 (1970): pp. 269–85. See Shoemaker for a more contemporary defense of the Locke account. For criticism, see D. Behan, "Locke on persons and personal identity," *Canadian Journal of Philosophy*, vol. 9, no. 1 (1979): pp. 53–75; John Perry, *Personal Identity* (Berkeley: University of California Press, 2008), and John McDowell, "Reductionism and the First Person," in *Reading Parfit*, ed. Jonathan Dancy (Oxford: Blackwell, 1997), pp. 230–50. Also see Lynne Rudder Baker, "Persons and the Metaphysics of Resurrection," *Religious Studies*, vol. 43, no. 3 (2007): see especially pp. 339–46, for criticisms of other options that a mainstream physicalist might take. Lastly, Trenton Merricks, "The Resurrection of the Body," in *The Oxford Handbook of Philosophical Theology*, eds Thomas Flint and Michael Rea (Oxford: Oxford University Press, 2009) deserves much attention, but I do not have the time or space to address his account here. I flag it for interested readers.

[13] Not all friends of constitution claim this. Like I said, I have Baker's account in mind. Some take it to be a primitive concept, and others even take it to be a mereological concept.

[14] Lynne Rudder Baker, "Christian Materialism in a Scientific Age," *International Journal of Philosophy of Religion*, vol. 70, no. 1 (2011): pp. 47–59, see especially p. 48.

primary kind is, say, wood, in certain circumstances. Baker is concerned with concrete particulars of primary kinds.

So the story is: a zygote develops in the womb and at a certain stage a person emerges from the organic body. Unlike mainstream physicalism, the organic body is not identical to the person. Rather, it constitutes the person. Things of the primary kind "personhood" and things of the primary kind "human organism" instantiate essentially the constitution relation. What makes a person is a first-person perspective. Unlike animals, human persons essentially have a first-person perspective. A first-person perspective is a nonreductive property. It cannot be reduced to simpler or more basic properties. Once a human person begins to learn a language and think of oneself as oneself, he or she develops a robust first-person perspective. Although babies do not develop a robust first-person perspective, they are still persons since they have a rudimentary first-person perspective and are of a kind (human organism) that typically comes to support a robust first-person perspective. The constitution account holds that a human organism constitutes a person. Since the relation here is constitution, I need not be constituted by this exact body. As long as I am embodied by a body that supports a first-person perspective I continue to be a person. The difference between a duplicate of me and me is that we have different exemplifications of the first-person perspective. This first-person perspective, according to Baker, is a dispositional property.[15]

With that in mind, let us return to the problems that faced mainstream physicalism. Reassembly is not a problem for the constitution account because the account can do fine without it. Since I am not identical to my body, at the day of resurrection God does not need to resurrect the exact body that undergoes death. As such, God does not need to worry about reassembling anything. There is also no need to worry about cannibalism or future people sharing my parts. Moreover, the constitution account does not need to postulate body snatching or spatiotemporal gaps because God does not need to preserve my body. Instead, at the moment of death, God can replace my body with another body and put me in whatever state until the day of resurrection.[16] By that time, God can either give me a new heavenly body and dispose of my old body, or let me keep the body I have during

---

[15] Not until recently, Baker has made it explicit that the first-person perspective is a dispositional property. See Lynne Rudder Baker, *Naturalism and the First-Person Perspective* (Oxford: Oxford University Press, 2013), pp. 169–82.

[16] Objection: some biblical passages seem to suggest that at the day of resurrection, we will be raised with our bodies instead of new bodies. See, for example, 1 Corinthians 15:42–55; also Jesus seems to appear to the apostles with the same body he was crucified in (Luke 24:39–40). In Thomas and Dominicans (1981), Supplement to the Third Part, question 79, St Aquinas endorses this view as well. Also, see Trenton Merricks, "The Resurrection of the Body and the Life Everlasting," in *Reason for the Hope Within*, ed. Michael J. Murray (Grand Rapids: W.B. Eerdmans, 1999), pp. 266–76, for another defense. What is there to say in response? First, I am taking the doctrine of bodily resurrection broadly construed, i.e. the doctrine given other major religions, not just Christianity. So a Muslim perhaps would be okay with this result. As such, I see these debates as more of an in-house debate between differing theological systems, so a full response is outside the scope of this chapter. Second, I will mention the following points as a response to the 1 Corinthians passage: first, there is good reason to think that St Paul thought Jesus' second coming would happen during his lifetime: see Barth D. Ehrman, *Peter, Paul, and Mary Magdalene: The Followers of Jesus in History and Legend* (Oxford: Oxford University Press, 2006), pp. 89–178. Second, it is not unlikely for St Paul to be talking about the believers who will be alive during the second coming; in other words, St Paul is describing, in 1 Cor. 15, what would happen to those who are alive during the second coming as opposed to those who have long perished. One commentary hints at this: "But if the end of our natural life is a prerequisite to the transformation that allows our participation in the eternal kingdom of God, then what will happen to those who are left alive at the time of Christ's coming and this world's demise? The answer is part of the mysterious wisdom of God's plan. 'We will not all sleep, but we will all be changed' (v. 51). In the same moment that the dead are raised, those who are alive will also be changed. Their perishable physical existence will be cloaked by the imperishable existence and immortality of a body transformed by God's power

my intermediate stage. With the constitution account, one need not worry about whether God is being deceptive for snatching my body and replacing it with a replica or whether spatiotemporal gaps are plausible.[17]

Objections and Replies

Lastly, I consider two objections against the constitution account. First, one might object that the constitution account is not, properly speaking, a physicalist account. Perhaps the idea here is that the stuff the first-person perspective is made out of is not physical. First, it is not clear what this even amounts to since the first-person perspective is not made out of "stuff"; and second there is no reason to think that physicalism is the thesis that everything is made out of physical stuff. The standard way of defining physicalism is this: "Physicalism is the thesis that everything is physical, or as contemporary philosophers sometimes put it, that everything supervenes on, or is necessitated by, the physical."[18] The constitution account holds that persons emerge from the physical—as long as we understand emergence to be nonreductive—and hence it is compatible with physicalism. Moreover, without a body, there is no person. So there is a strong sense in which the person is dependent on a physical body. How much more would one need? A person cannot be disembodied according to the constitution account; surely that earns the title physicalism. Maybe not mainstream physicalism, but physicalism nonetheless.[19]

The second objection is this: how can the constitution account provide us with an informative criterion for personal identity? In other words, what are the necessary and sufficient conditions that need to obtain for God to resurrect me and not someone else? This objection assumes that we need an informative criterion and that there are sufficient and necessary conditions to be obtained. Neither of those assumptions seems plausible. In fact, if what it means to be a person is to have the property of a first-person perspective and this property is irreducible to simpler properties, then we should expect a non-informative criterion of personal identity. Since the property of first-person perspective cannot be reduced to more fundamental properties, there cannot be an analysis to give.[20] What would the analysis be if there is nothing deeper to analyze? Anyone and everyone should agree that we need not give analyses of basic properties. Why should that change here? Giving an analysis assumes the first-person perspective is reductive. But why should we allow the interlocutor to beg the question against the constitution account in this way? Unless we get an independent reason as to why we need a criterion for personal identity, this objection

---

and surely as those who have died and been resurrected." W.A. Elwell, *Baker Commentary on the Bible* (Grand Rapids: Baker Books, 2000), 983.

[17]   See Baker, "Christian Materialism in a Scientific Age," for a fuller analysis.

[18]   D. Stoljar, "Physicalism," *The Stanford Enyclopedia of Philosophy*, ed. Edward N. Zalta URL = http://plato.stanford.edu/archives/fall2009/entries/physicalism/ (Fall 2009; accessed May 19, 2014), p. 1.

[19]   See the "Objections and Replies" section in Baker, "Personal Identity: a Not-so-Simple Simple View," *Personal Identity: Complex or Simple*, ed. Georg Gasser M. Stefan (Cambridge: Cambridge University Press, 2012), pp. 179–91.

[20]   P.F. Strawson, *Individuals: An Essay in Descriptive Metaphysics* (London: Routledge, 1990), pp. 87–116, argues that at least the concept of a person is not reducible to simpler concepts. If our concept of a person properly latches on to the world, then we have good reason—if Strawson's arguments are sound—to think that the first-person perspective is also irreducible.

does not get off the ground. Of course, I have not argued that we do not in fact need one. I just do not see a reason to think either way. The burden of proof is on both sides, so to speak.[21]

So on the constitution account, in order for God to resurrect me, He must bring it about that my first-person perspective is constituted by my resurrected body. This of course is a circular definition and hence uninformative. But so what? God being omniscient will know what first-person perspective is my first-person perspective, and He will act accordingly in the day of resurrection. As such, God can resurrect me or anyone else at the day of resurrection.[22]

Conclusion

I did two things in this chapter. First, I argued that reassembly, body snatching, and spatiotemporal gaps are not very plausible options for bodily resurrection. Second, I argued the constitution account avoids the problems that plague mainstream physicalism. Then, I responded to two objections. The constitution account has the right to be called a physicalist view. Lastly, I argued that even if the constitution account is committed to a non-informative criterion of personal identity, this is not a mark against the account.

It is worth noting that I did not argue for the truth of the constitution account, nor did I argue for the conclusion that mainstream physicalism is false. Rather, I argued for the following: if you want to accept the doctrine of bodily resurrection (broadly construed) and physicalism, then mainstream physicalism is a less plausible option; at least the options I considered are not obviously friendly to the doctrine of bodily resurrection. The constitution theorist, on the other hand, avoids the problems that plagued the three options we considered.

---

[21] In Trenton Merricks, "There are No Criteria of Identity over Time," *Nous*, vol. 31, no. 1 (1998): pp. 106–24, he argues that there are no criteria of personal identity.

[22] See Baker, "Personal Identity: a Not-so-Simple Simple View."

Anthropological Hylomorphism

Bruno Niederbacher, S.J.

In philosophical anthropology, hylomorphism is the view that human beings are compounds of matter (Greek *hylē*) and form (Greek *morphē*). In this chapter I first present a version of hylomorphism that is inspired by the Aristotelian tradition and explore some difficulties pertaining to it. Second I investigate how this version accounts for three central topics of Christian belief: the creation and beginning of an individual human being, the moral responsibility and moral status of human beings, and, finally, their bodily resurrection.

Aristotelian Hylomorphism in a Nutshell

The version of anthropological hylomorphism I am presenting here starts with the obvious fact that some entities we encounter are living entities. "To live, for living beings, is to exist."[1] For such beings, ceasing to be alive is ceasing to exist.[2] Thus, being alive is essential for living beings. Being alive is their first, basic, and constitutive activity. But what accounts for their being alive? The traditional answer is: the soul. The soul is often called the "cause and principle" of their being alive.[3] But what is the soul?

According to hylomorphism, the soul is a *form*. The corresponding term here is *matter*. A living earthly being, and thus also a human being, is defined as a form-matter-compound. I start by elaborating on the three key terms: form, matter, compound.

Form

Basically, one can distinguish two kinds of form: accidental and substantial forms. Accidental forms are forms which some actual existing entity of a certain kind can take on without ceasing to be the kind of entity it is. Thus, a lump of gold can become hot; a cat, for example, Sylvester, can become dirty; and a man such as Simon Peter can become bold. *Being hot* is an accidental form of the actual existing lump of gold, *being dirty* is an accidental form of Sylvester and *being bold* is an accidental form of Simon Peter. A substantial form, by contrast,

---

[1] Aristotle, *De Anima* II, 4, 415b13.

[2] See for example: Aquinas, *Summa Theologiae* III, 50, 4: "It belongs to the truth of a human being or an animal that through death the human being or animal ceases to be." Aquinas, *Quaestiones Quodlibetales* II, 2: "To be animated is a substantial difference; therefore to die is to be annihilated and not just altered."

[3] Aristotle, *De Anima* II, 4, 415b13.

is a form that makes something the kind of entity it is. Thus, *being gold, being a cat*, and *being human* are substantial forms. If an entity loses its substantial form it ceases to exist.

A soul is a substantial form of a living being. A living being is what it is and has the essential powers it has in virtue of its substantial form. Correspondingly, a human soul is the substantial form of a human being. Human beings are alive and have their human-specific powers in virtue of their souls. Their souls were traditionally considered to be rational souls.

Matter

In Aristotelian philosophy, "matter" in its most general sense means something that is determinable, something that has the potential to take on a form. Thus, what counts as "matter" varies from case to case. A lump of gold, for example, is already some existing entity with the substantial form of being gold. Now, imagine that the sculptor and goldsmith Benvenuto Cellini forms out of this the famous Salt Cellar called "Saliera." A hylomorphist would then say: the gold is the matter. It had the potential to take on the Saliera-form. The matter in question here is not prime matter, which is formless matter that exists only potentially. The matter in question here is called "proximate matter" which is already formed matter that has the potential to take on an accidental or a substantial form. Now, if a soul is a substantial form, what is the matter that is formed by that form? For Aristotle the matter in question is "a natural body which potentially has life, that is, a body which has organs."[4] Thus, he seems to consider the matter in question as proximate matter, matter which is proportioned to the form, matter that is able to receive, for example, a particular human form.

Compound

Some think of form and matter as the metaphysical parts that constitute a human being. On this view the form is a part which is added to the material part in order to constitute a compound; thus the question arises of how these two parts might form a unity. However, the version of Aristotelian hylomorphism I am presenting here does not speak in terms of parts at all. Aristotle thinks that even such concepts as *synthesis*, or *composite of matter and form* can be misleading.[5] The fact that a particular piece of gold is triangular consists neither in the conjunction of two parts, the gold and the triangularity, nor in the participation of the particular in the universal form of being triangular. "... the proximate matter and the form are one and the same thing, the one potentially, and the other actually."[6] Thus, matter and form are conceived of not as two separable parts that constitute a human being, but rather as potentiality and actuality. To say that matter is united with form is just to say that matter is actualized.[7] There is no human body as such that would be real independent of a human soul.[8] A dead body is no longer a human body. A dead body has taken on a different substantial form and can be called "a human body" only equivocally.

---

4 Aristotle, *De Anima* II, 1, 412a 21.

5 Aristotle, *Metaphysics* 1045b, 13.

6 Aristotle, *Metaphysics* 1045b 17–19.

7 Aquinas, *Sententia Libri De Anima*, 234: "... idem est materiam uniri formae, quod materiam esse in actu." See also: Aquinas, *Summa Theologiae* I 75, 1: "Anima ... non est corpus, sed corporis actus."

8 See: Runggaldier, Edmund, 2012: Unsterblichkeitshoffnung und die hylemorphistische Einheit von Leib und Seele. In: Karl-Ludwig Koenen/Josef Schuster (Hg.) 2012: *Seele oder Hirn. Vom Leben und Überleben der Personen nach dem Tod*. Münster, 95–123, here 100. Cf. Aquinas, *Summa contra Gentiles* IV, 99, 4.

Hylomorphism takes a human being to be one substance, one unit, with her human-specific powers. One can distinguish levels on which these powers are actualized: vegetative functioning, the ground level, is always actualized even when somebody is unconscious; conscious functioning is actualized when somebody perceives, desires, feels, thinks, acts intentionally, and so forth.

Anthropological hylomorphism is attractive because it corresponds with our experiences of ourselves as mind-body-units. It suffers neither the notorious difficulty faced by substance dualism, which is showing how mind and body are unified into a single whole, nor the problem faced by physicalistic monism, which is explaining our subjective experience.[9] Accepting Aristotelian substances as basic entities, "we do not have to reduce them to some complexes of ultimates of analysis or to construct them out of these ultimates. Substances as basic entities are not identical with their stuff and can be subjects of both bodily and intentional attributes."[10]

Disputed Issues

One or Many Substantial Forms?

The first disputed issue I consider concerns the question of whether the matter of a human being is formed by only one substantial form or by a plurality of substantial forms. Thomas Aquinas defends the view that every substance has but one substantial form. It would be a mistake, he says, to think that a human being has several substantial forms, for example, a form in virtue of which he falls under the supreme genus, *substance*, a second form in virtue of which he falls under the genus *animal*, a third form in virtue of which he falls under the species *human*. A human being has only one substantial form and that form is his rational soul. This one rational soul determines the whole human being in all his acts, even in his animality and corporeality. Aquinas's main reason for this claim is the following: if one allows a plurality of substantial forms, the first form would be the substantial form, and the other forms would merely be add-ons to some already actually existing particular form-matter-compound. There would already exist a subject with some nature, so the other forms would no longer be substantial, but rather accidental forms of that subject.[11] Note that this view does not imply that some already existing entity can receive a different substantial form than it already has. But it does imply that an entity ceases to exist as soon as it is formed by a new substantial form.

The doctrine of the unity of the substantial form was highly contentious. The Middle Ages witnessed a large debate about whether the four elements (earth, air, fire, water), out of which corporeal things were thought to be composed, keep their substantial form in a given body.

The context of the debate was mainly theological. It concerned the identity of the living body of Jesus with his corpse. If Jesus' body had just one substantial form, Jesus' rational

---

[9] Some of the problems of substance dualism and physicalistic monism are explored in James D. Madden, *Mind, Matter and Nature. A Thomistic Proposal for the Philosophy of Mind* (Washington, DC: CUA, 2013).

[10] Runggaldier, Edmund, 2006: The Aristotelian Alternative to Functionalism and Dualism. In: Bruno Niederbacher, Edmund Runggaldier (Hg.) 2006: *Die menschliche Seele: Brauchen wir den Dualismus?* Heusenstamm, 221–48, here 227.

[11] See for example: Aquinas, *Summa Theologiae* I, 76, 4.

soul, then this form was separated from his body when he died on the cross, and what was left had either no form at all or had taken on a new form.[12] Whichever route one chooses, the two bodies cannot be numerically identical, and thus neither can Jesus' resurrected body be identical with his mortal body. On the other hand, if there is a plurality of substantial forms, the corpse could still be formed by at least some of the same substantial forms as the living body.

The doctrine of the unity of form is also contentious from a biological or chemical perspective. Would it not be plausible to say that a human heart has its own form, that the liver has its own form, that a particular heart cell has its own form, that the molecules (e.g. glycose) have their own forms, that carbon atoms have their own form?

Aquinas struggled with these questions. In compounds, he says, the forms of the elements do not remain actually (*actu*) but only by power (*virtute*); that is, they are present by their powers, although not present as substances.[13] This thesis, however, is hardly conceivable and seems to lead to internal inconsistency. For in the case of the numerical identity of Christ's living body with his corpse, Aquinas speaks of a qualified numerical identity. The living body and the corpse, he says, are numerically identical in terms of their matter (*secundum materiam*), but not in terms of their substantial form (*secundum formam substantialem*).[14] But how could they be numerically identical "in terms of matter" if the matter of the living body did not have certain forms—at least the forms of the elements—that were present in the corpse?

Thus, there are good reasons to opt for the plurality-of-forms-view. This view does not imply that one and the same substance has a plurality of substantial forms. Rather, the same substance can have multiple components, each of which has its own form. As Gordon Barnes writes: "It is not the forms of the atoms that give being to this human being. The form of the atoms give being to atoms, and the form of a human being gives being to just that— a human being."[15]

What are Human Souls?

The second disputed issue I consider concerns the question of what a human soul is. According to hylomorphism a human soul is a substantial form of the body. But what exactly is a substantial form? An answer to this question that is in line with what has been said so far would be: a substantial form is the actualization of the potentiality to be something of a definite kind. Correspondingly, a human soul is the actualization of the potentiality to be a human being. Thus, substantial forms can only be understood properly within the conceptual framework of potentiality and actuality.[16]

Some philosophers are not satisfied with this answer. They ask: what is it "in a material object that, 'taken on its own, is merely potentially a K,' and what it is in a material object

---

[12]   See for example: Wilhelm de la Mare, *Correctorium fratris Thomae*, art. 31 (ed. Palémon Glorieux), p. 129: "… but if that body of Christ had no other form then the intellectual one, after its separation there remained only prime matter or another substantial form was introduced."

[13]   Aquinas, *Summa Theologiae* I, 76, 4 ad 4. See also: Aquinas, *De Mixtione Elementorum* II, 145–53. For a detailed exposition see: Decean, Christopher, 2000: Elemental Virtual Presence in St. Thomas, in: *The Thomist* 64 (2000), 271–300.

[14]   Thomas Aquinas, *Quaestiones quodlibetales* II, 1, 1.

[15]   Barnes, Gordon P., "The Paradoxes of Hylomorphism," in *The Review of Metaphysics* 56/3 (2003), 501–23, here 520.

[16]   See Runggaldier (2006), 234–6.

that 'actualizes the matter's potential to be a K'?"[17] Or "what sort of being is the actualization of a potentiality for humanity?"[18] I am unable to answer these questions properly here. I will just give some hints about how they might be dealt with.

First, one could counter by claiming that potentiality and actuality are primitive concepts. Non-primitive concepts can be defined by other concepts. But primitive concepts themselves cannot be defined. They can only be illustrated by examples.[19]

Second, one could counter that these questions are somehow misguided. They suggest that the form is an additional ingredient in a material object. But Aristotle did not think of substantial form this way. For him, the form is not "an additional part on par with matter—but constitutes the matter's being organized in such a way as to fulfill the functions and capacities that define a natural body of that kind. All living things have their form essentially, that is to say—by contrast with the case of artifacts—there is no object existing independently of a particular living thing which we can identify as potentially the matter of this living thing."[20]

Third, one could suggest that Aristotelian hylomorphism would not incorporate a real, ontological distinction between the form and the substance that is formed by it, and *a fortiori* between the human soul and the human being, but only a conceptual distinction: form and matter, soul and body, soul and human being would merely be ways of thinking of one and the same entity, one and the same substance. This suggestion, however, is contentious. For the hylomorphic explanation of substantial change seems to involve the separability of form and matter. If the generation of a thing belonging to a certain kind consists in the actualization of some matter that is potentially a thing of that kind, then matter must exist in some sense before the substantial form. Likewise, if the corruption of a thing of a certain kind consists in the separation of form and matter, the two must be real entities.[21]

Fourth, one could look to the Scholastic tradition for advice. Some Scholastic theologians understood the soul of an individual human being as the individual substantial form (*forma substantialis individualis*) of his body, which shows that for them the form is more than a mere aspect of one and the same entity. They would say: Simon Peter is an individual human being, and the form in virtue of which he is Simon Peter is the Simon-Peter-form. Aquinas thinks that this form is an immaterial, immortal entity created by God. But if a human soul is an individual substantial form, to which category does it belong? According to Aquinas, the human soul is a particular, a "*hoc aliquid*," but not a substance that falls under a natural kind.[22] Only the whole human being is a substance. Thus, according to this view the soul is not just an aspect of a living body, but an ontologically distinct entity. If one

---

[17] Michael Rea, "Hylomorphism Reconditioned," in *Philosophical Perspectives* 25 (2011), 341–58. "K" stands for a kind-term.

[18] Barnes 2003, 507.

[19] Compare: Barnes 2003, 506–7.

[20] McGinn, Marie, "Real Things and the Mind Body Problem," in *Proceedings of the Aristotelian Society* 100/1, 303–17, here 308.

[21] This argument is proposed by Barnes (2003), 510–11, who takes it from Peter Coffey, 1914: *Ontology, Or, The Theory of Being: An Introduction to General Metaphysics*, London, 152–3.

[22] Aquinas, *Summa Theologiae* I 75, 2 ad 1. See also: Aquinas, *De Spiritualibus Creaturis* 2: "... the soul cannot be called 'this something' if by this is meant a hypostasis or person, or an individual situated in a genus or a species. But if 'this something' is called everything that can *per se* subsist, then the soul is a this something." Francisco Suarez, in *Disputationes metaphysicae* XV, 5, speaks about the substantial form of a complex thing as an "incomplete substance." Note however that with this formulation Suarez did not intend to say more than Aristotle said. For Suarez wrote: "For the substantial form is an incomplete substance in such a way that it is the act of matter, the act (I say) or actually informing, or by its very nature instituted to form matter ..."

reads what Aquinas attributes to such human souls, for example to "subsist" after death without a body until resurrection, to operate intellectually, to have the beatific vision, to be punished, etc.,[23] then one cannot avoid the impression that he conceives of souls as very substance-like. Some rudiments of this can be found in the *Corpus Aristotelicum*.[24] However, this account seems hardly reconcilable with the original Aristotelian idea of the soul as an act of the body.

What and How Does the Soul Explain?

In Aristotelian philosophy form and matter are invoked to explain something. The matter of a hylomorphic compound explains certain of its general characteristics; the form explains some of its more specific characteristics.[25] The substantial form, then, is considered to be a formal cause. What the assumption of the soul explains is the life of a material body, its processes of nourishment and growth, perception and motion, desiring and thinking. And how does the assumption of the soul explain these processes? It does not do so in terms of efficient causality. The soul is not an agent which brings these processes about. Rather, the soul explains these processes in terms of formal causality. It is an explanation of the kind: the wood went up in flames because wood burns. The disposition of wood to catch fire explains why it burns. Applied to living things, this would amount, for example, to the following: Sylvester meows because he is a cat and cats meow. The disposition of the cat to meow explains why it meows. This, however, smacks of triviality and circularity. Thus, the question is justified: do formal explanations have any value?

One might describe the value of formal explanations by appeal to the contemporary debate about bottom-up and top-down causality. Naturalists usually believe only in bottom-up causality, according to which all causal effects are determined by the most basic particles of reality. Proponents of top-down-causality, on the other hand, believe that higher levels of reality can have causal effects on lower levels. They try to capture the relation between the whole and its parts by saying that the functions and potentialities of the parts are dependent on and determined by the kind of the whole of which they are parts. If there is such a thing as top-down causation, there might be a value in formal explanations: first, they provide an understanding of the parts of a certain kind of organism by showing how these parts are integrated in that kind of organism. Second, such explanations require knowledge of the essential properties of the kind of living being at issue. And this knowledge is supplied by the knowledge of the form of that kind of living being.[26]

---

[23] See for example: Aquinas, *Summa contra Gentiles* IV, 91.

[24] For example: Aristotle, *De Generatione Animalium* II, 3, 736b27–9, speaks of the "mind from outside." In *De Anima* III 5, 430a12–25, Aristotle speaks of the active mind (*nous poietikos*) as separated, unmixed, immortal, eternal.

[25] Cf. Jeffrey E. Brower, "Matter, Form, and Individuation," in Brian Davies and Eleonore Stump (eds), *The Oxford Handbook of Aquinas* (Oxford: OUP, 2012), 85–103, here 85.

[26] For a more extended treatment see: Josef Quitterer, "Lässt sich die Seele naturalisieren?" In: *Zeitschrift für Katholische Theologie* 133 (2011), 303–20, here 310–19.

Some Applications

The Creation and Beginning of an Individual Human Being

Christianity teaches that everything apart from God owes its existence to God's free creative act. This creative act not only brought the world into being but also efficiently causes it to remain in existence. Hylomorphism is compatible with this teaching. But one might ask: what does it mean for an individual human being, for example me, to be created by God? It means at least this: God, as the primary cause, brings about and keeps in existence a form-matter-compound that is me. Disputes arise about when in time somebody begins to exist. Hylomorphism as such has no clear answer and can be used to argue for very different positions. I would like to mention three:

(i) Late humanization: if the reception of a human form presupposes proximate matter, it is conceivable that several substantial forms might succeed and replace each other until a human being comes into existence. There would then be different kinds of beings involved in the development of a human being, each replacing its predecessor, until an organism has the disposition to receive a human form. And since the human form is the rational form, its reception would require (among other things) a developed brain.

Aquinas seems to have held a version of this successive ensoulment view. According to him, the individual human soul (the rational soul, an immaterial, immortal form), is created by God and infused into a body that was produced by the parents' generative act.[27] The *human* ensoulment happens at the time when the produced entity — already a form-matter-compound — is disposed to be newly formed by the human soul. Aquinas writes: "For, since the soul is united to the body as its form, it is united to the body as its proper act. Now the soul 'is the act of an organic body.' Therefore, the soul does not exist in the semen in act before the formation of the organs of the body."[28] Once Aquinas speaks about dead fetuses and distinguishes between those that have and those that have not yet received a rational soul. Of the latter, he says, nothing permanent will remain, whereas the souls of the former continue to exist after their death.[29] Following Aristotle, he says also in one place that the conception of males is not completed until the 40th day, whereas the conception of females is not completed until the 90th day.[30]

(ii) Humanization comes immediately after the possibility of twinning is excluded: this view starts with the hylomorphic premise that a human being is a single substance, an individual. Now we know that monozygotic twinning is possible. From a single fertilized egg two human beings might result. Whether twinning has occurred is clear after implantation. Thus, some might claim that before implantation there is no human being but rather a cluster of cells. This is taken to follow from the transitivity of the identity relation.

---

[27] Aquinas, *Summa Theologiae* I, 118, 3: "Therefore … we must simply confess that souls were not created before bodies but are created at the same time as they are infused into them."

[28] Aquinas, *Summa contra Gentiles* II, 89.

[29] See also: Aquinas, *Super Iob*, c. 3, l. 2: "But it is to consider that some die in the womb before the infusion of the rational soul which is alone immortal … Nothing permanent remains from such dead fetuses. Others die after the infusion of the rational soul; they subsist after death regarding the soul [*subsistunt secundum animam*] although they do not see the light of this world."

[30] Aquinas, *Commentary on the book of Sentences*, III, 3, 5, 2. This view, however, rests on erroneous ontogenetic assumptions, and some scholars say that Aquinas, had he understood modern developmental biology, would have held rather the position of early humanization. See, for example: John Haldane and Patrick Lee, "Aquinas on Human Ensoulment, Abortion and the Value of Life," in *Philosophy* 78 (2003), 255–78.

Let us call the predecessor "A," and one of the twins "B," the other one "C." Then, the argument can be posed in the way Lynne Rudder Baker does:

> *If A were identical to both B and C, then—by the transitivity of identity—B and C would be identical to each other. But B is clearly not identical to C. Therefore, A (the zygote) cannot be identical to B and C. A human organism cannot come into existence until there is no further possibility of "twinning"—about two weeks after fertilisation. ... Soon after implantation (the primitive streak stage), the embryo is an individual, as opposed to a mass of cells. At this point, there is an individual organism that persists through fetal development, birth, maturation, adulthood, until death.*[31]

This argument however has at least two weaknesses. First, before implantation what exists is not a "mass of cells" but rather an organism that organizes itself and interacts with its environment. Second, the pure possibility of monozygotic twinning does not speak against persistence. Thus, if no twinning occurs I see no reason why the embryo before implantation could not persist in the embryo after implantation. And this would mean that there exists a human being already before implantation. If twinning occurs, one could say that the predecessor either ceases to exist and twins come into existence or that the predecessor persists in one twin while the other is already a descendant of the first.

(iii) Very early humanization: some hylomorphists say that the ovum is "already a highly organized living cell, containing highly complex, specific information ... Hence the ovum is actually very close to readiness for rapid embryological development; it only requires fusion with the sperm and the activation that occurs with that fusion."[32] Thus, one could claim that the human form is already given at this very early stage.

Moral Responsibility and Moral Status

Christianity teaches that human beings are free moral agents, capable of performing morally good and bad actions, of being responsible for their actions, of sinning and being forgiven, and of receiving grace. Having moral responsibility requires being able to act on one's intentions and beliefs, to evaluate those intentions and beliefs, and, finally, to appreciate the fact that one acts and has acted in the past.[33] I cannot elaborate on this point here but only state that I see no reason why hylomorphism could not account for these abilities. It is in virtue of their human soul that human beings are able to exercise agency, have the intentional mental properties required for free action, and are able to have a first-person-perspective.

Christianity also teaches that all human beings have a special dignity, a moral status which prohibits their being treated in certain ways, such as being killed. How does hylomorphism account for moral status? Some philosophers in the tradition of John Locke distinguish between human beings and human persons. They say that something can be a living human organism without being a human person. For example, they might claim that a human fetus or even an infant is a human animal but not (yet) a human person, or

---

[31] Lynne Rudder Baker, "When does a person begin?" in *Social Philosophy and Policy*, 22 (2005), 25–48, here 27. Although Baker is famous for holding the Constitution view, her argument above is also available to a hylomorphist.

[32] See Haldane and Lee (2003), 273.

[33] See Lynne Rudder Baker, "First-Personal Aspects of Agency," in *Metaphilosophy*, 42(1–2) (2011), 1–16.

that somebody in a permanent vegetative state is a human being but not a human person. They thus think that personhood is a property that depends on other properties such as self-consciousness, rationality, and moral agency. There can be times in a human being's life when she does not have these properties, and times when she has them. Such philosophers consider being a person to be an accidental property of a human being, and some draw far-reaching moral conclusions from this view.

The hylomorphism advocated here precludes this dualism between human beings and human persons. Once something is configured by the human substantial form, that is, the rational form, it is a human person.[34] Accordingly, all human beings are human persons. The fact that somebody is prevented from performing certain activities does not prevent her from being a human person.

Hylomorphists are able to distinguish between *lacking* something and simply *not having* something. A hawk with a broken wing lacks the ability to fly. But an emu does not lack it because the ability to fly does not belong to the substantial form or nature of an emu. Similarly, somebody who suffers from dementia lacks the ability to use reason, but, say, a mouse does not lack it.[35] On the hylomorphic account, rationality is not considered to be an accidental form that a human being might have or not have, but rather as belonging to the substantial form of being human. This one substantial form is realized in a single human being, from the beginning to the end of her existence and in all her functions.

Resurrection

Christianity teaches that human beings die but that God will resurrect them to a life after death. This resurrection involves a body. The Bible says that the resurrected Jesus had a body, and that human beings will also receive an "incorruptible," "glorified," "spiritual," body.[36] The life of the world to come surely differs in many ways from the earthly life, but one thing is clear: it is the very same people who are here and there. This means that a human being, for example Simon Peter, who once lived on earth (SP_E), is numerically identical with the resurrected Simon Peter (SP_R). An important question is: what makes SP_E numerically identical with SP_R?

Let me first clarify the question. We are not asking the epistemic question of identity criteria; that is, we are not asking for indicators that justify us in believing that a particular human being at time t_1 is identical with another human being at time t_2. We are rather asking the ontological question of identity *conditions*: what makes a particular human being at time t_1 identical with another human being at time t_2?

Some might be tempted to think that the version of hylomorphism advocated here cannot explain the numerical identity between SP_E and SP_R and thus that hylomorphism is no viable anthropology for Christianity. The argument for this could start with the assumption of the continuous link (CL):

> (CL) The numerical identity between SP_E and SP_R is constituted by some sort of continuity between SP_E and SP_R.

---

[34] There could be a version of hylomorphism advocating such a dualism, for example, one that assumes a plurality of forms and takes the human being form as substantial form and human personhood as accidental form.

[35] Compare Anselm Müller, "Der neue Person-Begriff: Dualistischer Wolf im bioethischen Schafspelz," in *Niederbacher/Runggaldier* (2006), 75–98, here 89.

[36] See 1 Cor 15: 42–4.

It should be clear that not just any sort of continuity will do. The sort of continuity required for diachronic identity is often spelled out in terms of immanent causation: for SP_E to be numerically identical with SP_R there has to be an uninterrupted internal causal relation between SP_E and SP_R.[37]

The second premise in the argument is the claim that hylomorphists are unable to account for the continuous link between SP_E and SP_R. For hylomorphists must say that if SP_E dies he ceases to exist. If SP_E ceases to exist and is totally destroyed, he cannot stand in the required uninterrupted internal causal relation to SP_R. Think again of Bellini's Saliera. Imagine that a thief steals it, destroys it, and dissolves the gold it was made of in *aqua regia* acid. Could the original Saliera be restored? Bellini, if alive, could produce no more than a replica. And it seems that even the omnipotent God could not bring back the original Saliera. What applies to artefacts applies also to living beings. How could Sylvester or Simon Peter, once totally destroyed, exist again as numerically the same?

Aquinas accepts (CL), but rejects the second premise.[38] According to him, there is continuity both of form and of matter. First, there is continuity of form. This claim depends on an additional premise, namely that the human soul is an exceptional form that can "subsist" without matter.[39] This is a non-natural state of a human soul, but nevertheless a possible one, which is realized between the death of a person such as Simon Peter and the resurrection of his body. Second, there is continuity of matter. This claim is based on a reassembly view of resurrection. Some of the same material that composed Simon Peter's earthly body will compose his resurrected body. After all, we speak of "resurrection" rather than of "the assumption of a new body."[40] Thus, Aquinas thinks that the continuous-link requirement is fulfilled.

Aquinas's view, however, faces some problems. Let us begin with the continuity of matter. First, reassembly of some of the elemental stuff that once composed Simon Peter's body would not be sufficient for fulfilling the requirement that immanent causation be continuous. Second, Aquinas's view seems internally inconsistent. For it presupposes that some "stuff" of the human body can exist as numerically the same even when not formed by the substantial form. This seems to go against Aquinas's tenet that each human being has but one substantial form and that a human being's bodily parts are what they are only in virtue of being formed by that form. It also seems to go against Aquinas's view that a corpse belongs to a different kind than a living human organism. When the soul is separated from the body, what remains will be formed by a different substantial form that confers a different kind of being.[41] What is of a different kind cannot be numerically the same.

---

[37] Eric T. Olson expresses the idea of immanent causation in the following way: "*You* ought to cause *yourself* to continue existing. It isn't something that other beings or outside forces can do for you." See Olson, Eric T., 2010: "Immanent Causation and Life after Death." In: Georg Gasser (Hg.) 2010: *Personal Identity and Resurrection. How Do We Survive Our Death?* (Farnham: Ashgate, 2010), 51–66, here 56.

[38] See for example Aquinas, *Summa contra Gentiles* IV, 80: "What is not continuous seems not to be numerically identical." For a detailed account of Aquinas's position see: Bruno Niederbacher, 2010: *The Same Body Again? Thomas Aquinas on the Numerical Identity of the Resurrected Body*. In: Gasser, 2010, 145–59.

[39] See: Aquinas, *Summa Theologiae* I, 75, 2.

[40] Aquinas, *Scriptum super libros Sententiarum* IV, 44, 1, 1, 1 (Cf. Aquinas, *Summa Theologiae* III, Supp. 79, 1): "… if it were not the same body [*idem corpus*] that the soul reassumes, one would not speak of resurrection but rather of the assumption of a new body."

[41] Compare: Aquinas, *Sententia libri de anima* II, c. 1: "And hence it is that the body does not remain the same in kind when the soul is separated from it. For the eye and the flesh in the dead is called so only equivocally. … For when the soul is separated it is succeeded by a different substantial form which gives a different existence in kind because the corruption of one thing is not without the generation of another thing."

Now, one could respond that Aquinas does not need the reassembly view. All he needs is the continuous link on the part of the substantial form. According to Aquinas, the substantial form survives death and persists until the bodily resurrection, even though there is no matter which it forms during the interim period. When Simon Peter's substantial form, his rational soul, comes again to form matter, there will be numerically the same body, and there will be numerically the same human being. Aquinas writes: the existence (*esse*) of the rational soul, "which was that of the composite, remains when the body is dissolved; and when the body is restored in the resurrection, it is brought back in the very same existence [*esse*] which remained in the soul."[42] And thus the requirement of the continuity would be met, since the existence of the substantial form is never interrupted.[43] Although the existence of Simon Peter's soul is not sufficient for the existence of the human being Simon Peter, the existence of his soul is sufficient for making SP_E numerically identical with SP_R.[44]

The main problem with this solution is that it flies in the face of the simple idea of hylomorphism according to which the soul is the act of a body. Hence it seems to be true that this kind of hylomorphism is no viable anthropology for Christianity.

I would like to suggest a different strategy. This kind of hylomorphism might stand a chance if we could reasonably reject (CL). (CL) is based on a complex view (CV) of personal diachronic identity, which, for our purposes, can be stated as follows:

(CV) *The diachronic identity of a human being is constituted by further facts.*

The fact that a human being existing at one time is identical with a human being existing at another is due to the further fact that there is a continuous link of the proper kind. Depending on one's metaphysical views this continuous link is regarded as a sort of uninterrupted mental or physical continuity.

But (CV) is problematic. Space permits only a brief indication of the problems here.[45] First, there is the problem of graduality: continuity relations, whether mental or physical ones, admit of degree. But the relation of identity does not admit of degree. One could assume a precise threshold, but who has a justified idea about where it lies? Second, there is the problem of splitting: psychic- and/or physical-continuity relations could obtain between two successors and one common predecessor. As we noted above, sometimes twins develop from one fertilized egg. Both stand in the same kind of continuity relation to the organism from which they developed. But, due to the transitivity of identity, the successors cannot be identical to the predecessor. I do not claim that these problems of (CV) are insoluble. However, here I ask whether there is an alternative to (CV). It turns out there is: namely a simple view (SV) of diachronic identity which is the negation of (CV) and can be stated as follows:

(SV) *The diachronic identity of a human being is not constituted by further facts.*

---

[42]   Aquinas, *Summa contra Gentiles* IV, 81.

[43]   See Christina Van Dyke, "Human Identity, Immanent Causal Relations, and the Principle of Non-Repeatability: Thomas Aquinas on the Bodily Resurrection," in *Religious Studies*, 43 (2007), 373–94, here 389.

[44]   See Eleonore Stump, 2006: "Resurrection, Reassembly, and Reconstitution: Aquinas on the Soul." In: Niederbacher/Runggaldier, 2006, 153–74.

[45]   See for details: Harold W. Noonan, *Personal Identity* (London: Routledge, 1989), 128–68; Georg Gasser, Stefan Matthias (eds), 2012: *Personal Identity: Complex or Simple?* (Cambridge: Cambridge University Press, 2012).

Diachronic identity between human beings is a simple, "brute" fact: it is ontologically basic. Physical and psychic continuity relations might provide epistemic criteria for finding out whether a human being at one time is identical with a human being at another. However, such relations do not *make* the two identical. What makes them identical is just the fact that they are identical.

A hylomorphist account of resurrection that adopts a simple view of personal identity says: Simon Peter, a human being, a compound of form and matter, was created and sustained in existence by God until he died. When he died he ceased to exist. His resurrection is a re-creation, brought about by God. He is again a compound of form and matter, a human being, albeit with some new qualities and without some old qualities, and he is Simon Peter. He is identical with the Simon Peter who once lived on earth. What makes it true that SP_E is numerically identical to SP_R? It is just the fact that they are identical.

Some might think that this is logically impossible. They might hold that if somebody ceased to exist he or she cannot exist again as numerically the same at a later time. But I do not see that recreating Simon Peter implies a contradiction. Undoing past events would imply a contradiction, but recreating Simon Peter does not require this. Recreating him would be a new event, and thus almighty God could bring it about.[46] It would be something we human beings would have a hard time understanding, but it would not be contradictory.

A similar idea is expressed by William Jaworski: "God has managed to bring it about once already that some materials have a distinctively human structure and compose me and not someone else. Since it has been within God's power to do this at times before my death, there is good reason to think it remains within God's power to do this at times after my death."[47] And Aquinas himself wrote: "The divine power which brought the things into existence operates through nature in such a way that it can produce an effect of nature without it, as was shown above. Thus, since the divine power remains the same even when things are corrupted; it can restore the corrupted things to integrity."[48]

Conclusion

In this chapter I have presented one version of Aristotelian anthropological hylomorphism, which maintains the original idea of the human soul as the first act of a body. I sought to show that this anthropology not only accounts well for our experience of ourselves as mind-body units but also for central teachings of Christianity.[49]

---

[46]   Cf. Aquinas, *Summa Theologiae*, I, 25, 4 ad 1.

[47]   William Jaworski, "Hylomorphism and the Resurrection," in *European Journal for Philosophy of Religion* 5/1 (2013), 197–224, here 220.

[48]   Aquinas, *Summa contra Gentiles* IV, 81.

[49]   I am grateful to Katherine Dormandy, Joshua Farris, Georg Gasser, Josef Quitterer, and Edmund Runggaldier S.J. for reading previous drafts of the manuscript and giving me helpful comments.

Substance Dualism

Stewart Goetz

Mere Substance Dualism

In this chapter, I am not going to argue for substance dualism. I and others have done so elsewhere.[1] What I will do is explain why I believe substance dualism is the default position in theological anthropology. My explanation will draw heavily on the notion of common sense, which, as I understand it, consists of beliefs that arise directly out of the capacities of self-awareness (e.g., I am experiencing pleasure), sense perception (e.g., I see a tree), memory (e.g., I did not sleep well the past few nights), etc., which in part constitute human nature. Because I believe the authors of scripture were not philosophers writing for the purpose of questioning the metaphysics of ordinary people, I will assume that a hermeneutical method is sound only if it recognizes that the scriptural writers accepted the deliverances of common sense. In light of the concerns of this chapter, if a biblical writer addresses a topic (e.g., the afterlife) that raises ontological issues about the nature of a human being, one should assume that he espouses the anthropology of common sense, which is substance dualism.

So what is substance dualism? I take substance dualism (dualism, for short) to be the view that a human being is composed of two substances, a soul and its material (physical) body. While the academic establishment is for the most part firmly entrenched in its opposition to dualism, there is a general, if sometimes begrudging, acknowledgment that dualism is the view of the ordinary person. For example, the experimental cognitive scientist Jesse Bering has recently argued that human beings are believers in soul-body substance dualism.[2] As Bering sees things, Darwinian natural selection produced a cognitive system that gave rise to belief in commonsense soul-body dualism. According to the developmental

---

[1] See Stewart Goetz, "Dualism, Causation, and Supervenience," *Faith and Philosophy* 11 (1994): 92–108, "Modal Dualism: A Critique," in Kevin Corcoran (ed.), *Soul, Body, and Survival* (Ithaca: Cornell University Press, 2001), pp. 89–104, and "Substance Dualism," in Joel B. Green and Stuart L. Palmer (eds), *In Search of the Soul* (Downers Grove, IL: Intervarsity Press, 2005), pp. 33–64; Mark Baker and Stewart Goetz (eds), *The Soul Hypothesis* (London: Continuum, 2011); Stewart Goetz and Charles Taliaferro, *A Brief History of the Soul* (Malden, MA: Wiley-Blackwell, 2011); Charles Taliaferro, *Consciousness and the Mind of God* (Cambridge: Cambridge University Press, 1994); Richard Swinburne, *The Evolution of the Soul* (Oxford: Clarendon Press, 1986) and *Mind, Brain, and Free Will* (Oxford: Oxford University Press, 2013); John Foster, *The Immaterial Self: A Defense of the Cartesian Dualist Conception of the Mind* (London: Routledge, 1991); William Hasker, *The Emergent Self* (Ithaca: Cornell University Press, 1999); Dean Zimmerman, "Christians Should Affirm Mind-Body Dualism," in Michael Peterson and Raymond J. Vanarragon (eds), *Contemporary Debates in Philosophy of Religion* (Oxford: Basil Blackwell, 2003), pp. 314–27; and Robin Collins, "Modern Physics and the Energy Conservation Objection to Mind-Body Dualism," *American Philosophical Quarterly* 45 (2008): 31–42.

[2] Jesse Bering, "The Folk Psychology of Souls," *Behavioral and Brain Sciences* 29 (2006): 453–98.

psychologist Paul Bloom, all of us initially naturally develop a belief in dualism.[3] Similarly, the psychologist Nicholas Humphrey, in his recent book *Soul Dust*, recognizes the human inclination to believe in substance dualism.[4] Toward the end of his book, Humphrey points out that other scholars also acknowledge this ordinary belief in substance dualism.

Anthropologist Alfred Gell writes: "It seems that ordinary human beings are 'natural dualists,' inclined more or less from day one, to believe in some kind of 'ghost in the machine' ..." Neuropsychologist Paul Broks writes: "The separateness of body and mind is a primordial intuition. ... Human beings are natural born soul makers, adept at extracting unobservable minds from the behaviour of observable bodies, including their own."[5]

But what is a soul? For one thing, it is typically held to have the property of being simple, which means that it does not have any parts that are themselves substantive in nature. Additionally, as the philosopher David Barnett argues,[6] our naïve conception of ourselves includes the belief that we are simple entities. Thus, it is not surprising that we think of ourselves as souls. For example, C.S. Lewis wrote in *The Abolition of Man* "our souls, that is, ourselves,"[7] and in a letter of response to Mrs Frank L. Jones dated February 7, 1950 penned "*What is a soul?* I am. (This is the only possible answer: or expanded, 'A soul is that which can say I am')."[8]

A soul's substantive simplicity does not exclude its complexity with regard to its properties. In terms that I have used elsewhere, simplicity at the level of substancehood is compatible with complexity at the level of propertyhood.[9] Thus, a soul has properties like being able to think, being able to choose, being able to experience pleasure, and being able

---

[3]   Paul Bloom, *Descartes' Baby: How the Science of Child Development Explains What Makes Us Human* (New York: Basic Books, 2004).

[4]   Nicholas Humphrey, *Soul Dust: The Magic of Consciousness* (Princeton: Princeton University Press, 2011).

[5]   Ibid., p. 195. To be fair, while Bering, Humphrey, Bloom, Gell, and Broks maintain that human beings naturally believe in substance dualism, none of them believes in it. Sometimes one hears the following "flat-earth" objection to the common sense belief in dualism: "Sure, the authors of scripture were aware of themselves as souls. But they also were aware that the earth is flat. So much for the commonsense belief in dualism."
C.S. Lewis, the Oxbridge scholar in medieval and renaissance literature, was aware of this kind of objection in *The Discarded Image* (Cambridge: Canto, 1964, p. 20); we find him presenting the medieval model of the universe with its mobile spheres and in passing making the following comment: "There was no doubt a level below the influence of the Model. There were ditchers and alewives who had not heard of the Primum Mobile and did not know that the earth was spherical; not because they thought it was flat but because they did not think about it at all." Lewis's point was that common sense does not contain a belief that the earth is flat because it contains no belief at all about the topic of the earth's shape. It is true that as a matter of common sense ordinary people believe the earth is flat relative to the steps that they take and as far as their unaided eyes can see. But beyond these types of distances, ordinary people believe nothing about the earth's shape. However, Lewis reminds us that when the ancients did venture beyond common sense to consider the shape of the earth, they concluded that the "Earth is (of course) spherical" (ibid., p. 28). For a fine contemporary treatment of the invention of the idea of a belief in a flat earth, see Jeffrey Burton Russell's *Inventing the Flat Earth* (New York: Praeger, 1991).

[6]   David Barnett, "The Simplicity Intuition and Its Hidden Influence on Philosophy of Mind," *Noûs* 42 (2008): 308–35; "You Are Simple," in Robert C. Koons and George Bealer (eds), *The Waning of Materialism* (Oxford: Oxford University Press, 2010), pp. 161–74. I argued for the simplicity of the self in "Modal Dualism: A Critique." And see J.P. Moreland, "Substance Dualism and the Argument from Self-Awareness," *Philosophia Christi* 13 (2011): 21–35.

[7]   C.S. Lewis, *The Abolition of Man* (New York: HarperSanFrancisco, 2001), p. 72.

[8]   C.S. Lewis, The *Collected Letters of C.S. Lewis: Volume III; Narnia, Cambridge, and Joy, 1950–1963*, Walter Hooper (ed.) (New York: HarperSanFrancisco, 2007), p. 10.

[9]   Goetz, "Substance Dualism."

to experience pain. Given these multiple properties, a soul thinks, chooses, and experiences pleasure and pain.

The history of thought and contemporary philosophical literature contains a veritable host of views regarding the relationship between the soul and its body.[10] For example, up until the time of Descartes, it was commonly thought that the soul gives life to and causally interacts with its body, with death resulting from the soul's ceasing to impart this life. Descartes begged to differ about the soul being the source of life and maintained that the body is better thought of as a machine whose irreversible cessation of function results in the soul no longer being causally related to its body. And then there is the matter of how the soul is related to its body in terms of space (which is an issue about which I will have to say more toward the end of this chapter). Most philosophers prior to Descartes thought that the soul is located in its entirety at every point in space occupied by its physical body. The soul is wholly in its hand at the same time that it is wholly in its neck. Descartes seems to have maintained that the soul is not located in space at all. Some thought the belief that the soul is causally related to its body, which was accepted by both Descartes and those with whom he disagreed about the soul's spatial location, is itself false. Hence, we find those who defended the view known as occasionalism, according to which God causes events in the physical body on the occasion that the soul intends that it move, and others who defended the view known as pre-established harmony, according to which God created and "programmed" each body ahead of time to move like clockwork in ways that accord with the soul's intentions. But among those who disagreed about whether or not the soul causally interacted with its body, there was unanimity about the fact that God created and sustains the soul in existence *ex nihilo*. Quite recently, there has been much interest in the view known as emergent dualism, according to which the human brain, upon reaching a requisite level of developmental complexity, causes and continues to sustain the soul in existence.[11]

And the list of views goes on and on. For the purposes of this chapter, I am not going to argue for or against any of these views. Rather, I am going to regard them as species of a genus that I think of as mere substance dualism or mere dualism, after the idea of mere Christianity espoused by C.S. Lewis.[12] With Lewis as my guide, I regard mere dualism as a hallway or corridor, off of which there are many rooms. One room has "occasionalism" written above its door; another room has "causal interactionism" inscribed above its door; yet another has "life-giving soul" etched above it. Some rooms might be connected by interior doors so that if you enter one you can get into another without having to go back out into the main hallway. For example, the room for those dualists who believe the soul gives life to its body probably has an interior door that permits entrance into the room for those who think the soul occupies at least some of the space occupied by its physical body. However, the basic idea is that the main doors off the central hallway open into rooms that contain philosophical developments of the commonsense idea that we are souls that have bodies.

With this genus-species distinction in mind, in what follows I will for the most part not enter into any of the philosophical rooms but will remain in the hallway of common sense. By remaining there, I can avoid arguments among family members and focus my attention on mere dualism and its relationship to theological anthropology. For some time now, there has been a movement among those who are theologically literate to break ranks with the ordinary person and jettison mere dualism. The theologically literate, seemingly impressed by the materialistic spirit of the modern age, claim not to find substance dualism in the

---

[10] See Goetz and Taliaferro, *A Brief History of the Soul*.

[11] See Hasker, *The Emergent Self*.

[12] C.S. Lewis, *Mere Christianity* (New York: HarperSanFrancisco, 2001).

Jewish-Christian scriptures. It is to them that I principally want to speak in what follows. In doing so, I will interact at some length with the work of the New Testament scholar N.T. Wright.

What is Taught Versus What is Assumed

C.S. Lewis opened his book *A Preface to Paradise Lost* with the following admonition:

> The first qualification for judging any piece of workmanship from a corkscrew to a cathedral is to know what it is—what it was intended to do and how it is meant to be used. After that has been discovered the temperance reformer may decide that the corkscrew was made for a bad purpose, and the communist may think the same about the cathedral. But such questions come later. The first thing is to understand the object before you: as long as you think the corkscrew was meant for opening tins or the cathedral for entertaining tourists you can say nothing to the purpose about them. The first thing the reader needs to know about Paradise Lost is what Milton meant it to be.[13]

As I noted at the end of the previous section, those who are theologically literate are claiming not to find substance dualism in the Jewish-Christian scripture(s) with increasing frequency. Their conviction is often coupled with the assertion that the scriptures do not teach anything about philosophical anthropology, because they were, in Lewis's terms, neither intended to do nor meant to be used for this. For example, the New Testament scholar N.T. Wright says that "there are a great many things which have become central topics of discussion in later Christian thought, sometimes from as early as the late second century, about which the New Testament says very little; but it is assumed that, since the topic appears important, the Bible must have a view of it … ."[14] In Wright's view, while philosophical anthropology is an important topic, it is wrongly assumed that the New Testament writers must have purposefully taught something about it. Contrary to what many might think, scripture (at least the Christian New Testament) was not written for the purpose of teaching anything about the ontological makeup of a human being.

I believe a position like Wright's is eminently reasonable. However, I part ways with him where he proceeds to urge that it is wise, in light of scripture's pedagogical silence on philosophical anthropology, to jettison substance dualism.[15] My reasoning is that it does not follow from the fact that scripture does not teach anything about the ontological nature of a human being that scripture therefore assumes or presupposes no position on the topic. My position is that unless we have reason to think otherwise, we ought to assume that scripture itself simply presupposes what I summarized in the first section of this chapter as commonsensical, naïve, mere dualism.[16] My position is like that advocated by Lewis

---

[13] C.S. Lewis, *A Preface to Paradise Lost* (New York: Oxford University Press, 1942), p. 1.

[14] N.T. Wright, "Mind, Spirit, Soul and Body: All for One and One for All: Reflections on Paul's Anthropology in his Complex Contexts," http://www.ntwrightpage.com/Wright_SCP_Mind SpiritSoulBody.htm.

[15] Ibid.

[16] An excellent book that advocates this approach is John Cooper's *Body, Soul, and Life Everlasting: Biblical Anthropology and the Monism-Dualism Debate* (Grand Rapids, MI: Eerdmans, 1989, 2001).

with regard to Jesus and morality. Lewis maintained that the idea that Jesus brought a new ethical code into the world is simply absurd:

> *The idea ... that Christianity brought a new ethical code into the world is a grave error. If it had done so, then we should have to conclude that all who first preached it wholly misunderstood their own message: for all of them, its Founder, His precursor, His apostles, came demanding repentance and offering forgiveness, a demand and an offer both meaningless except on the assumption of a moral law already known and already broken. ... Essentially, Christianity is not the promulgation of a moral discovery. ... A Christian who understands his own religion laughs when unbelievers expect to trouble him by the assertion that Jesus uttered no command which had not been anticipated by the Rabbis—few, indeed, which cannot be paralleled in classical, ancient Egyptian, Ninevite, Babylonian, or Chinese texts. ... Our faith is not pinned on a crank.*[17]

According to Lewis, Christianity in its essence is not about the teaching of a new ethical code. Scripture simply assumes a moral law already known. If I am right, scripture is not about the teaching of a new (or any) philosophical anthropology. It just assumes an anthropology already known. And what it assumes is mere substance dualism.

The Irrelevance of Plato

If the scholars whom I cited in the first section are right about the commonsensical nature of dualism, we should not be surprised to find, and indeed we should expect to find, dualist "footprints" in scripture. And indeed we do find them. For example, there is the evidence of belief in ghosts. When the disciples saw Jesus walking on the sea, they thought he was a ghost (Matthew 14:26), and after the resurrection when Jesus was in the disciples' midst they thought they were seeing a spirit (Luke 24:37). Then there is the incident of Peter's appearance at Mary's house after Herod had jailed him. Those present insisted to a maid named Rhoda, who reported that Peter was at the door, that Peter himself could not be present but that it must be his angel (Acts 12:15). Each of these incidents confirms that substance dualism is the view espoused by ordinary people in scripture. Again, Lewis was spot on with the following comment: "[the early Christians] believed in [ghosts] so firmly that, on more than one occasion, Christ had had to assure them that He was *not* a ghost."[18] Moreover, Lewis would not let us forget the evidence of the Christian Old Testament (the Hebrew Bible):

> *From the earliest times the Jews, like many other nations, had believed that man possessed a "soul" or Nephesh separable from the body, which went at death into the shadowy world called Sheol: a land of forgetfulness and imbecility where none called upon Jehovah any more, a land half unreal and melancholy like the Hades of the Greeks or the Niflheim of the Norsemen. From it shades could return and appear to the living, as Samuel's shade had done at the command of the Witch of Endor.*[19]

---

[17] C.S. Lewis, *Christian Reflections* (Grand Rapids, MI: Eerdmans, 1967), pp. 46–7.
[18] C.S. Lewis, *God in the Dock* (Grand Rapids, MI: Eerdmans, 1970), p. 159.
[19] C.S. Lewis, *Miracles* (New York: HarperCollins, 2001), p. 237.

As Lewis said, other nations (peoples) believed in ghosts or shades. The Greek epic writer Homer comes immediately to mind. In *The Odyssey*, Book 11, there are numerous references to the ghosts of the dead which were in existence without their physical bodies. For present purposes, two quotations will suffice: "But first the ghost of Elpenor, my companion, came toward me [Odysseus]. He'd not been buried under the wide ways of earth, not yet, we'd left his body in Circe's house, unwept, unburied … . But I wept to see him now, pity touched my heart and I called out a winged word to him there: Elpenor, how did you travel down to the world of darkness?"[20] And "I [Odysseus], my mind in turmoil, how I longed to embrace my mother's spirit, dead as she was! Three times I rushed toward her, desperate to hold her, three times she fluttered through my fingers, sifting away like a shadow, dissolving like a dream … ."[21]

Now let us return to the Bible and consider the Apostle Paul's thoughts from 2 Corinthians 12:2–4: "I know a man in Christ who fourteen years ago was caught up to the third heaven—whether in the body or out of the body I do not know, God knows. And I know that this man was caught up into Paradise—whether in the body or out of the body I do not know, God knows—and he heard things that cannot be told, which man may not utter."[22] Wright, in commenting on this passage, says that he [Paul] never suggests that, if he wasn't embodied, it was his *psyche* which made the journey. The fact that he is uncertain about whether this experience was or wasn't "in the body" indicates that, for him, it wouldn't have been problematic if the body *had* been involved. For him, the body could just as well have been carried up to heaven … Equally, of course, the fact that he can consider the possibility that the experience might *not* have been "in the body" does indeed indicate that he can contemplate non-bodily experiences, but as will become clear I don't think one can straightforwardly argue from this to what is now meant, in philosophical circles, by "dualism" …[23]

For the sake of argument, I will concede that Wright is correct about the following: one cannot straightforwardly *argue* from Paul's comments in these verses for the existence of a substantive soul and the truth of dualism. But why not think that in this context Paul is simply working with a commonsense, dualist anthropology? The most plausible reading of the text implies that Paul, like other ordinary human beings, simply presupposes a dualist soul-body distinction and it is his assumption of this distinction that informs and makes intelligible his comment about his journey to the third heaven and the possibility that it might have been made "out of his body." Paul conceptually captures this soul-body distinction here and elsewhere (cf. 2 Corinthians 5:1–9) in terms of a self-body distinction,[24] because it is part of common sense to equate the soul and the self (e.g., my soul (I) doth magnify the Lord). The fact that the word *psyche* is not used is thoroughly irrelevant.

One other example from scripture should suffice. Consider the passage where Jesus asks his disciples "Who do people say that I am?" He is told that some think he is John the

---

[20] Homer, *The Odyssey*, trans. by Robert Fagles (New York: Viking, 1996), p. 251; Book 11, lines 56–63.

[21] Ibid., p. 256; Book 11, lines 233–7.

[22] The quotation is from *The Holy Bible: Revised Standard Version* (New York: Thomas Nelson and Sons, 1952).

[23] Wright, "Mind, Spirit, Soul and Body," pp. 6–7.

[24] It is significant to note here that Wright in his magisterial *The Resurrection of the Son of God* (Minneapolis: Fortress Press, 2003, p. 369) reads 2 Corinthians 5:6–10 dualistically. He points out that death is the dissolution of the present body, whereupon the believer lives away from the body (disembodied) and at home with the Lord before the resurrection. John Cooper has reminded me that if dualism is not true, then the human Jesus did not exist between Good Friday and Easter morning, and this leads to a "weird" reading of Luke 23:43: "today you [one of the two crucified criminals] will be with me in Paradise."

Baptist, others that he is Elijah, and others that he is Jeremiah or one of the prophets (Matthew 16:13–14). Even Herod, who had John the Baptist executed, wonders if Jesus is John (Matthew 14:2). Given that it is reasonable to assume that the Baptist's body could be easily located, ordinary people, including Herod, could naturally have been thinking that Jesus was John's soul re-embodied.[25] Moreover, dualism fits best with the idea that Jesus cast out unclean spirits from people. If materialism had been the commonly accepted view and selves or persons were believed to be material objects with at most immaterial psychological properties (what is commonly referred to as the dual-aspect theory), it is doubtful that those who followed Jesus would have as readily appealed to the notion that he expelled unclean spirits (e.g., Mark 1:27). Given that they were apparently intellectually comfortable with the dualistic/animistic metaphysics of demon expulsion, it is hard to dismiss as thoroughly implausible the idea that people might have believed John's soul (spirit) was re-embodied in Jesus.

What we have in these passages from the Bible and Homer is mere dualism, which is a pre-philosophical conception of the soul-body distinction. What Wright (and others like him) seemingly finds impossible to do is understand that there is a distinction between mere dualism and philosophical dualism. Wright appears to find it difficult to keep clear the distinction between someone like a disciple of Jesus who believes in the soul and thinks that he might be seeing a ghost, and a philosopher like Plato who philosophizes about the soul.[26] Here are some representative comments from Wright: "when Paul and the gospels use the

---

[25]   Wright wrestles with what might be going on in the minds of people like Herod concerning John the Baptist. He points out that the general theological view at the time was that the resurrection of the dead would happen to all the righteous dead simultaneously (who would be existing disembodied in the intermediate state), not to an isolated individual, but reminds us that in the case of Herod and his court we do not have "the most accurate indicators of mainstream second-Temple Jewish belief" (*The Resurrection of the Son of God* [Minneapolis: Fortress Press. 2003], 413). Might it not be the case, then, that with Herod we have an expression of the ordinary human belief in the possibility of re-embodiment of a soul, in this case John's soul? Wright cautions against this reading because that "would normally require the soul to pass into a newborn, or newly conceived, child, whereas Jesus was a fully grown man, of about the same age as John" (*The Resurrection of the Son of God*, 413–14). But with Jesus and John, things were hardly normal, as anyone who knew of their ministries understood. And the abnormal could provide reason to consider the possibility of re-embodiment at a time other than when it was normally thought to occur. Wright concludes that "[p]erhaps the simplest explanation for why Herod said what he did … is the general idea, current at least since the Maccabees and Daniel, that Israel's God would vindicate a righteous sufferer, and that Herod might well think of John in that way" (*The Resurrection of the Son of God*, 414). However, if this is all Herod was thinking, it remains a mystery why he would think Jesus was John. To vindicate John, Jesus need not be John.

[26]   I say that Wright seemingly finds it difficult to keep clear the above distinction because in some of his scholarly work he has clearly argued that the mainstream Jewish view in the immediate centuries leading up to and including the life of Jesus was that bodily resurrection presupposed continued existence in an intermediate state between bodily death and re-embodiment: "[A]ny Jew who believed in resurrection, from Daniel to the Pharisees and beyond, naturally believed also in an intermediate state in which some kind of personal identity was guaranteed between physical death and the physical re-embodiment of resurrection" (N.T. Wright, *The Resurrection of the Son of God* [Minneapolis: Fortress Press, 2003], 164). In this context, the expression "the resurrection of the dead" itself warrants comment. As Wright points out (The New Testament and the People of God [Minneapolis: Fortress Press. 1992], 320–34; cf. Cooper, *Body, Soul & Life Everlasting: Biblical Anthropology and the Monism-Dualism Debate*, pp. 101–3), one must be careful about using linguistic expressions as the basis for determining what people believe about the nature of the afterlife. Wright notes that just as it is possible to use language about the soul and life after death to refer to the idea of physical resurrection, so also it is possible to use language about physical resurrection to refer to the idea of the soul and life after death. Thus, he makes clear that it is erroneous to conclude from the fact that the Pharisees are consistently described in the Gospels and extra-biblical sources as believing in the resurrection of the dead that they did not believe in the existence of a soul that would receive a new body in the future. They did believe in the soul's existence and its future re-embodiment, as Wright notes with the support of various texts. And it should not be forgotten at this point that the apostle Paul was a Pharisee.

word *psyche*, it is clear that they are not using it in the sense we'd find in Plato"; "Jesus in the Sermon on the Mount challenges his hearers not to worry about their *psyche*, what they shall eat or drink, or about their *soma*, what they shall wear. The distinction is clear, and has nothing whatsoever to do with Platonic or quasi-Platonic dualism"; "In the famous passage [from 2 Corinthians] 4.16–5.10 we find the contrast between the outer person and the inner person, the *exo anthropos* and the *eso anthropos*, but this does not denote a Hellenistic dualism of body and soul."[27]

But it simply does not follow from the fact that what Jesus and Paul say has nothing to do with Hellenistic or Platonic dualism that it also has nothing to do with mere dualism. One might think that the problem for Wright is that he believes one cannot remain in the main hallway of mere dualism but must enter the room with "Hellenistic-Platonic Dualism" written above the door. However, at times it is hard to avoid the conclusion that his problem is more serious: he cannot even recognize the distinction between the hallway and the rooms off of it.

From Mere Dualism to Philosophical Dualism

The Bible and Homer contain accounts of ordinary people who believed in a difference between ghosts and bodies. These ordinary people believed mere dualism. The philosopher David Barnett (see the opening section) talks about a naïve conception of ourselves as substantively simple entities. One might wonder about the relationship between two ideas about ourselves. If ordinary people believe in ghosts and these ghosts take bodily forms, how can these ordinary people also believe that they are simple entities? After all, a body is ordinarily thought of as a thing that can be divided into substantive parts and a ghost is something that has a bodily shape. How, then, can a ghost be substantively simple? Do ordinary people believe that it is substantively simple?

The answer is that these questions do not occur to ordinary people. When at some point they do occur (when ordinary people became philosophers), we know that they do not relinquish the belief that souls exist and are substantively simple. But retaining this belief requires that they check into one of the rooms off the main hallway. For example, by the time that we get to Augustine, a fairly well developed concept of the soul has been developed that harmonizes nicely with the ordinary person's belief in the soul's existence as a ghost. According to Augustine, the soul is located in space but not in the same way that a material body is located in space. A material body occupies space by having each of its substantive parts occupy space. Smaller parts occupy smaller spaces while larger parts occupy larger spaces. The main point is that the material body *as a whole* is not present in each of the regions of space that are occupied by its parts: "Each mass that occupies space is not in its entirety in each of its single parts, but only taken together. Hence, one part is in one place; another in another."[28] This way of occupying space is by diffusion. But the soul, though located in space, is not diffused. In other words, the soul, because it does not have substantive parts, does not occupy space by means of its substantive parts occupying sub-regions of space. Instead, it is present in its entirety at one time not only in the entire space that is occupied by its material body but also in each of the sub-regions of space occupied by its body's parts. The following are Augustine's own words:

---

27   Wright, "Mind, Spirit, Soul and Body," pp. 6, 8, 10.
28   St Augustine, *The Immortality of the Soul*, trans. by Ludwig Schopp (New York: CIMA Publishing Company, 1947), 10.17.

[Because] it is the entire soul that feels the pain of a part of the body, yet it does not feel it in the entire body. When, for instance, there is an ache in the foot, the eye looks at it, the mouth speaks of it, and the hand reaches for it. This, of course, would be impossible, if what of the soul [that] is in these parts did not also experience a sensation in the foot; if the soul were not present, it would be unable to feel what has happened there. ... Hence, the entire soul is present, at one and the same time, in the single parts, and it experiences sensation as a whole, at one and the same time, in the single parts.[29]

And again:

But if a body is only that which stands still or is moved through an area of space with some length, breadth and depth so that it occupies a larger place with a larger part of itself and a smaller place with a smaller part and is smaller in a part than in the whole, then the soul is not a body. It is, of course, stretched out through the whole body that it animates, [but] not by a local diffusion . ... For it is at the same time present as a whole through all the body's parts, not smaller in smaller parts and larger in larger parts, but more intensely in one place and less intensely in another, both whole in all parts and whole in the individual parts.[30]

This account of how the soul occupies space was for the most part retained by medieval philosophers like Thomas Aquinas.[31] It is only when we reach Descartes that we encounter a radical shift in thought about the soul's relationship to space and must move to a different room off the central hallway. According to Descartes, it certainly seems as if the soul occupies space (for a reason like that given by Augustine) and is ghostlike. He said in his Meditation II that before engaging in his meditations, "I imagined that [the soul] was something extremely rare and subtle like a wind, a flame, or an ether, which was spread throughout my grosser parts."[32] However, reflection led him to believe that the nature of the soul is such that it cannot be located in space. To explain why, he contrasted the soul's nature with that of a body. Here is what Descartes says about the nature of a body in the second of his *Meditations*:

By the body I understand all that which can be defined by a certain figure; something which can be confined in a certain place, and which can fill a given space in such a way that every other body will be excluded from it; which can be perceived either by touch, or by sight, or by hearing, or by taste, or by smell: which can be moved in many ways not, in truth, by itself, but by something which is foreign to it, by which it is touched ... : for to have the power of self-movement, as also of feeling or thinking, I did not consider to appertain to the nature of body ... .[33]

Later in Meditation VI, Descartes further defines the nature of a body: "I possess a distinct idea of body, inasmuch as it is only an extended and unthinking thing ..." Moreover, "body is by nature always divisible ..."[34] According to Descartes, then, a body is that which is

---

[29]   Ibid., 16.25.

[30]   St Augustine, *Letters* 156–210, trans. by R. Teske (New York: New City Press, 2004), 166.2.4.

[31]   See Goetz and Taliaferro, *A Brief History of the Soul*, Chapter 2.

[32]   René Descartes, *The Philosophical Works of Descartes: Volume I*, trans. by E.S. Haldane and G.R.T. Ross (Cambridge: Cambridge University Press, 1967), p. 151.

[33]   Ibid., p. 151.

[34]   Ibid., pp. 190, 196.

extended with a certain shape or figure in a given space, is divisible into parts that are themselves extended, shaped, etc., is moveable but not capable of self-movement, and is perceivable by one or more of the five senses.

What does Descartes say about the nature of the soul? Basically, its nature is the exact opposite of that had by a body. A soul (mind) is a thinking thing and a thinking thing is a thing that is not extended: "I rightly conclude that my essence consists solely in the fact that I am a thinking thing [or a substance whose whole essence or nature is to think]. And ... inasmuch as I am only a thinking and unextended thing ... it is certain that this I (that is to say my soul by which I am what I am), is entirely and absolutely distinct from my body."[35] Moreover, "in the first place ... there is a great difference between mind and body, inasmuch as body is by nature always divisible, and the mind is entirely indivisible."[36] And again:

> [M]ind and body ... are really substances essentially distinct one from the other ... . This is further confirmed ... by the fact that we cannot conceive of body excepting in so far as it is divisible, while the mind cannot be conceived of excepting as indivisible. For we are not able to conceive of the half of a mind as we can do of the smallest of all bodies; so that we see that not only are their natures different but even in some respects contrary to one another.[37]

Finally, Descartes says the following about the lack of movement of the soul:

> I observe also in me some other faculties such as that of change of position ... which cannot be conceived ... apart from some substance to which they are attached, and consequently cannot exist without it; but it is very clear that these faculties ... must be attached to some corporeal or extended substance, and not to an intelligent substance, since in the clear and distinct conception of these there is some sort of extension found to be present, but no intellection at all.[38]

The following, then, encapsulates Descartes' conception of the nature of the soul: a soul is non-extended and, thereby, without any shape in a given space, is not divisible into parts and is not moveable in the sense that it cannot change spatial position. Therefore, Descartes believes that a soul is not located in space, period.

It is not my purpose in the least to arbitrate between the conflicting accounts of the soul's relationship to space and, thereby, the idea of its being a ghost. My purpose is far more limited in scope. It is merely to make clear that there is a clear divide between mere dualism and philosophical accounts of dualism. Ordinary people believe in the former and rarely acquire a belief of the latter kind. Yet, when theologically literate people like Wright attack substance dualism as an anthropological account that is not found in scripture, they inevitably attack philosophical accounts of dualism (again, Plato and/or the Greeks are their standard targets). The correct response to them is that of course philosophical accounts of dualism are not found in scripture, not only because it is not a purpose of scripture to teach philosophical anthropology but also and more basically because scripture is written to and about ordinary people. However, it in no way follows from this that scripture does not presuppose an anthropological view of human beings. It most certainly does. And what it

---

[35] Ibid., p. 190.
[36] Ibid., p. 196.
[37] Ibid., p. 141.
[38] Ibid., p. 190.

presupposes is mere dualism. Stated one other way, scripture presupposes generic dualism without embracing any species of dualism. It stays in the main hallway without ever entering any of the rooms off it.

Theological Implications of Soul-Body Dualism

Four implications of soul-body dualism for philosophical and theological anthropology immediately come to mind.

First, soul-body dualism resonates with ordinary people, which makes a religion like Christianity readily intelligible to them. This is not something to be taken lightly. If one jettisons dualism, it becomes increasingly difficult to defend the idea that Christianity is a religion for the masses.

Second, as the editors of this volume pointed out in the invitation letter to contributors, soul-body dualism has been the dominant anthropological view throughout the Christian ecclesiastical tradition. To reject it would be to break radically with that tradition. This is a fact that needs to be recognized and remembered.

Third, at the center of the Christian religion is the incarnation of God in Jesus of Nazareth: God, an immaterial being, resides in and causally acts upon a human with a material body. C.S. Lewis put the point this way: "our own composite existence is not the sheer anomaly it might seem to be, but a faint image of the Divine Incarnation itself—the same theme in a very minor key."[39] Hence, if one were, say, to reject interactionist substance dualism because the concept of causal interaction of an immaterial soul on its material body faces insurmountable philosophical and scientific objections, then one would be even more hard pressed not to reject the idea of the incarnation itself for the same reason or reasons. If there are good reasons that undermine the former, those reasons are equally good at undercutting the latter.

Fourth, there is good reason to think that if life is to be meaningful in the sense that things ultimately go or fit together in a coherent way (e.g., justice is achieved; people experience the kind of happiness that they so deeply desire), then there must be an afterlife in which these things are accomplished.[40] Of course, this entails that the same persons who existed in this life must persist or endure as numerically the same individuals into the next life. This persistence seems most naturally to require the existence of the soul, for two reasons.

First, the soul alone seems to persist in the requisite way (that is, as the numerically same individual) in this life. After all, the bodies that we possess in this life do not endure numerically the same through time. Indeed, they are constantly taking on and losing parts. Most, if not all, of the parts of our bodies are replaced every seven or so years.

Second, even if, as on the Christian view, the afterlife is bodily in nature through the resurrection of the dead, not only is it counterintuitive to think that the numerically same parts that at one time or another composed our bodies in this life need to be reassembled in order for us to exist bodily in the next life, but also there are potential problems that arise for such reassembly. After all, it is not the least implausible to think that the elements composing the body of one person in this life could be constituents of another person's body during his or her life. Were this to occur, whose body would get those parts? Augustine and

---

[39] Lewis, *Miracles*, p. 178.
[40] See Stewart Goetz, *The Purpose of Life: A Theistic Perspective* (London: Continuum, 2012).

Aquinas wrestled mightily with this problem and the reader can see for him- or herself what they had to say about the issue.[41]

I am not aware of a place in the Christian creeds where it is stated that the resurrection body must and/or will be composed of the numerically same parts that composed the human body in this life. And I think this is for good reason, because, as just suggested in the previous paragraph, the requirement of numerical sameness of parts for resurrection seems unnecessary and extremely difficult, if not impossible, to meet. C.S. Lewis on occasion took the opportunity to weigh in on the issue of the identity of the resurrection body and when he did he came down decisively against the idea that to be raised from the dead is to have the numerically same parts of one's earthly body, which during life have been organically integrated into a whole and "[a]t death … [fall] back gradually into the inorganic,"[42] reassembled:

> I agree … that the old picture of the soul re-assuming the corpse — perhaps blown to
> bits or long since usefully dissipated through nature — is absurd. Nor is it what St.
> Paul's words imply.[43]

We must, indeed, believe the risen body to be extremely different from the mortal body … It is presumably a foolish fancy (not justified by the words of scripture) that each spirit should recover those particular units of matter which he ruled before. For one thing, they would not be enough to go around: we all live in second-hand suits and there are doubtless atoms in my chin which have served many another man, many a dog, many an eel, many a dinosaur. Nor does the unity of our bodies, even in this present life, consist in retaining the same particles. My form remains one, though the matter in it changes continually. I am, in that respect, like a curve in a waterfall.[44]

But enough about the nature of the resurrection body. Why have a body at all in the afterlife? Once again, I will turn to Lewis for some thought-provoking ideas. He wondered if the kind of "matter" that will compose the resurrection body will be material in the sense of being different from what is psychological, mental, or ideational in nature. Thus, he speculated in the spirit of idealism (the view that what is "material" is nothing more than ideas or sensations in the soul) that the resurrection body will be "inside the soul": "[a]t present we tend to think of the soul as somehow 'inside' the body. But the glorified body of the resurrection as I conceive it — this sensuous life raised from its death — will be inside the soul."[45] Lewis said that "in this life matter would be nothing to us if it were not the source of sensations."[46] It is sensations that Lewis believed are ultimately important to us and, hence, "[w]e are not, in this doctrine [of the resurrection of the body], concerned with matter as such at all; with waves and atoms and all that. What the soul cries out for is the resurrection

---

[41] Cf. St Augustine, *The City of God*, trans. by Marcus Dods (New York: The Modern Library, 1993), Book XXII; and St Thomas Aquinas, Compendium Theologiae, trans. by Cyril Vollert, S.J. (St. Louis: B. Herder Book Co., 1947), Chapters 153–61. http://dhspriory.org/thomas/Compendium.htr; *Summa Contra Gentiles: Book Four; Salvation*, trans. by Charles J. O'Neil (Garden City, NY: Image Books, 1957), Chapters 79–80.

[42] Lewis, *God in the Dock*, p. 33.

[43] C.S. Lewis, *Letters to Malcolm: Chiefly on Prayer* (New York: Harcourt, 1992), p. 121.

[44] Lewis, *Miracles*, pp. 244, 246–7.

[45] Lewis, *Letters to Malcolm*, p. 122.

[46] Ibid., p. 121.

of the senses."[47] This is because in our present life matter, as depicted by physics (that is, in largely mathematical terms), lacks those properties that are of ultimate concern to us:

> *You know ... that the "real world" of our present experience (coloured, resonant, soft or hard, cool or warm, all corseted by perspective) has no place in the world described by physics or even by physiology. Matter enters our experience only by becoming sensation (when we perceive it) or conception (when we understand it). That is, by becoming soul. That element in the soul which it becomes will, in my view, be raised and glorified; the hills and valleys of Heaven will be to those you now experience not as a copy is to an original, nor as a substitute is to the genuine article, but as the flower to the root, or the diamond to the coal. It will be eternally true that they originated with matter; let us therefore bless matter. But in entering our soul as alone it can enter—that is, by being perceived and known—matter has turned into soul ... .[48]*

But Lewis was not done. In thinking of the resurrection of the body and the world it inhabits, he creatively suggested that perhaps we should be thinking of a power of the soul to imaginatively create a public sensuous life at will. Such a life "need no longer be private to the soul in which it occurs. I can now communicate to you the fields of my boyhood ... only imperfectly, by words. Perhaps the day is coming when I can take you for a walk through them."[49]

From the foregoing comments of Lewis about the resurrection body, it is clear he believed not only that a person's body in the resurrection will not include the parts had by his or her body in this life, but also that the nature of the resurrection body will be different from that of the human body (the resurrection body will be a different kind of body). Moreover Lewis rightly thought that there is a deep functional unity involved in embodiment in which the value of having a body is a great good of an instrumental kind: the body is good insofar as it is a source of good sensations. And sensations are important because they are part and parcel of our happiness. But our happiness is a subject for another day. For now, it is enough to say that on Lewis's view the soul is that which experiences happiness that in part is provided by its body. And here we have returned full circle to substance dualism.[50]

---

[47] Ibid.

[48] Ibid., p. 123. In saying matter enters experience only by becoming sensation, Lewis probably meant that all we know about the nature of material objects is how they appear to us in sensation, which is to say that we really do not know anything about the intrinsic nature of matter.

[49] Ibid., p. 122.

[50] I want to thank John Cooper and Joshua Farris for helpful comments on an earlier draft of this chapter.

ASHGATE
RESEARCH
COMPANION

The Human Person as Communicative Event: Jonathan Edwards on the Mind/Body Relationship

Marc Cortez

Jonathan Edwards' metaphysics has received considerable attention from people writing on issues like idealism, empiricism, dispositionalism, Neoplatonism, occasionalism, panentheism, and theocentrism, to name just a few.[1] And others have delved into anthropological issues like his view of the affections, volition, free will, and original sin.[2] However, relatively little attention has been given to the ways in which Edwards' general ontology impacts his approach to human ontology—in particular, his view of the mind/body relationship. That is unfortunate given that Edwards' ontology offers unique resources for today. First, Edwards' ontology offers a perspective on the human person that differs radically from the materialism most commonly encountered in the modern world. As we will see, Edwards maintains an idealist ontology that is hostile to materialism in any form.[3] Although some might be inclined to reject his conclusions on that basis alone, he offers a unique perspective from which to challenge modern assumptions about what it means to be human. Secondly, although Edwards' metaphysics can be understood in several ways, it seems likely, as we will see, that he should be viewed as affirming some form of panentheism.[4] Given the growing popularity of panentheistic ontologies for understanding

---

[1]   For examples of each, see Leon Chai, *Jonathan Edwards and the Limits of Enlightenment Philosophy* (Oxford: OUP, 1998); Perry Miller, *Jonathan Edwards* (Meridian, 1959); Sang Hyun Lee, *The Philosophical Theology of Jonathan Edwards* (Princeton: Princeton University Press, 2000); Stephen H. Daniel, "Edwards' Occasionalism," in *Jonathan Edwards as Contemporary* (ed. Don Schweitzer; New York: Peter Lang, 2010), pp. 2:1–14; Oliver Crisp, "Jonathan Edwards' Panentheism," in *Jonathan Edwards as Contemporary*, pp. 107–25; and Michael J. McClymond, "God the Measure: Towards an Understanding of Jonathan Edwards' Theocentric Metaphysics," *Scottish Journal of Theology* 47.1 (1994), pp. 43–59.

[2]   E.g., John E. Smith, "Editor's Introduction," *The Works of Jonathan Edwards* (New Haven: Yale University Press, 2009), pp. 1–83; Perry Miller, "Jonathan Edwards and the Sense of the Heart," *Harvard Theological Review* 41 (1948), pp. 123–45; Norman Fiering, "Will and Intellect in the New England Mind," *William and Mary Quarterly* 29 (1972), pp. 516–58; Allen C. Guelzo, *Edwards on the Will: A Century of American Theological Debate* (Eugene: Wipf & Stock, 2008); and Oliver Crisp, *Jonathan Edwards And The Metaphysics Of Sin* (Aldershot: Ashgate, 2005).

[3]   Although, as Wallace Anderson states, "there is no evidence that he studied the work of any recognized materialist" during the period in which he developed the basics of his ontology ("Editor's Introduction," *WJE* 6:54), Edwards viewed materialism as a direct threat to historic Christian doctrines like the existence of the soul, heaven and hell, angels and demons, and the very being of God himself.

[4]   See esp. Crisp, "Jonathan Edwards' Panentheism."

both the God/world and mind/body problems,[5] studying Edwards may offer insight into the unique strengths and weaknesses of this approach to the mind/body relationship.[6]

We will approach the task of understanding Edwards' anthropological ontology in three steps. First, I summarize Edwards' general metaphysics as the necessary background for understanding his ontology of the human person. Then I explain Edwards' particular approach to the mind/body relationship. And finally I draw a few conclusions about the significance of Edwards' ontology for today. Although I argue that Edwards' approach comes with some important strengths, I also point out several areas that need to be addressed before an Edwardsian ontology can be a viable candidate for understanding the mind/body relationship today.

Life, the Universe, and Everything

To understand Edwards' ontology of the human person, we need first to discuss his approach to ontology in general. Given the range and diversity of Edwards' metaphysical writings, however, that is a daunting task. So my comments in this section will be necessarily brief and will run the risk of raising more questions than they answer. Nonetheless, before we can turn to the mind/body question, we will need some idea of how Edwards understands the God/world relationship in general.

God as Absolute Being

Edwards has a radically theocentric ontology.[7] In his early essay "On Being," Edwards offered an argument for the existence of God based on the premise that it is absolutely necessary that some being exist. And this necessary being must also be eternal, omnipresent, and immaterial. Which, of course, means that this being is God himself.

But Edwards takes this a step further by claiming that we could also identify this necessary, eternal being with "space," even going so far as to say that "space is God."[8] This suggests that Edwards views God as the field of being in which all other things find existence. Everything exists "in" God. Although this is an early essay and Edwards does not make much use of this spatial analogy elsewhere, the idea that creation finds its being "in" God will remain prominent throughout his writings.

From this, we can appreciate why Edwards argues that God is the only true substance. For Edwards, *substance* in its most proper sense refers to "something that really and properly subsists by itself and supports all properties" (*WJE* 6:125). So, for Edwards, two criteria must hold for something to qualify as a true substance. First, it "subsists by itself." In other words,

---

[5]   E.g., Ian Barbour, *Religion in an Age of Science* (San Francisco: Harper and Row, 1990); Idem., *Nature, Human Nature, and God* (Minneapolis: Augsburg Fortress, 2002); Philip Clayton and Arthur Peacocke, *In Whom We Live and Move and Have Our Being: Panentheistic Reflections on God's Presence in a Scientific World* (Grand Rapids: Eerdmans, 2004); and Arthur Peacocke, *Theology for a Scientific Age: Being and Becoming—Natural and Divine* (Oxford: Basil Blackwell, 1990).

[6]   We need to keep in mind, of course, that panentheism comes in a variety of forms. So Edwards' ontology merely illustrates one panentheistic approach to mind/body issues.

[7]   See McClymond, "God the Measure."

[8]   Jonathan Edwards, *The Works of Jonathan Edwards: Volume 6—Scientific and Philosophical Writings* (New Haven: Yale University Press, 1980), p. 203. Henceforth, references to *The Works of Jonathan Edwards* will be abbreviated as *WJE* and cited by volume and page number (e.g. 6:203).

it cannot receive its being from some other entity. And second, it is that which supports all properties, and, therefore, is not itself a property of some other substance.

From what we saw above, though, only God meets the first criterion. Clearly all created beings fail to subsist in themselves since they depend on God's necessary being for their existence. And, as I argue later, God alone meets the second criterion as well. So, for Edwards, "Speaking strictly there is no proper substance but God himself" (WJE 6:215).

Thus, Edwards has a radically God-shaped ontology. God is the only true substance in the world, the necessary ground of all being. As Michael McClymond and Gerald McDermott state, "If there is a single theme that draws together the many disparate lines of thought in Edwards's metaphysical and scientific writings, it might well be theocentrism. For Edwards, God was the measure of all things."[9] Or, as Edwards states, "God is the prime and original being, the first and last, and the pattern of all, and has the sum of all perfection."[10]

But what does that mean for the reality of non-divine things? Is there any sense in which we can talk about bodies and souls have any real, substantial existence? Or does Edwards collapse created reality so completely into the being of God that there remains no real distinction?

The Material World as Divine Event

In his essay "On Atoms," Edwards argued that what we call "physical" things are nothing more than the ways in which conscious beings perceive a particular kind of God's actions. When we perceive something to be "physical," we are simply noting that it is solid—i.e. it resists being penetrated by other physical things. So I perceive my desk and my coffee cup both to be "physical" because, when I place the cup on the desk, they resist each other—i.e. the cup does not penetrate the desk. But Edwards argues that this resistance is not actually a property of some underlying physical substance. Instead, it is the direct expression of God's power. The "solidity" is nothing other than God creating "resistances" in this particular place and time. So what I perceive to be two "material" objects is actually the very activity of God. Thus, as Edwards says "the substance of bodies at last becomes either nothing, or nothing but the Deity acting in that particular manner in those parts of space where he thinks fit."[11]

But Edwards presses the idea that we exist "in" God even further. For Edwards, "nothing has any existence anywhere else but in consciousness."[12] This is because all the properties of material bodies require some conscious being for their expression. What does it mean to say that a body has the property of being red except to say that the body has appeared to some conscious being in such a way as to elicit the perceptual experience of redness? Similarly, what does it mean to say that a body is "in motion," except to say that some conscious being perceives that the relation of the body relative to other bodies has changed? And Edwards argues that this is true of all the properties of material bodies. But, as we've seen, Edwards did not assume that there must be some "substance" lying behind or beneath these perceived properties. Instead, he contended that the essential reality of material bodies

---

[9]   Michael J. McClymond and Gerald R. McDermott, *The Theology of Jonathan Edwards* (New York: OUP, 2011), p. 106.

[10]   WJE 6:363.

[11]   WJE 6:215.

[12]   WJE 6:204.

lies in their being perceived by conscious beings.[13] Thus, "the material universe exists only in the mind" (WJE 6:368).

So, for Edwards, a material body is simply the result of God acting in such a way as to produce the experience of certain properties in the mind of some conscious perceiver. But this means that a material body is much more of an "act" or "event" than it is a "thing" or "substance." Although Edwards will still refer to material things as substances on occasion, he has radically redefined what he means by the term.

But an event-oriented ontology like this would seem to rob the material world of having any meaningful existence of its own. Although Edwards would agree that the material world does not (and should not) have any existence "of its own," he does allow for the material world to have a particular mode of existence. As he describes it,

> And indeed, the secret lies here: that which truly is the substance of all bodies is the infinitely exact and precise and perfectly stable idea in God's mind, together with his stable will that the same shall gradually be communicated to us, and to other minds, according to certain fixed and exact established methods and laws: or in somewhat different language, the infinitely exact and precise divine idea, together with an answerable, perfectly exact, precise and stable will with respect to correspondent communications to created minds, and effects on their minds. (WJE 6:344)

So, despite the dynamism of Edwards' event-ontology, there are two stable elements grounding the existence of my desk: the "perfectly stable idea in God's mind" and the "fixed and exact established methods and laws." In other words, God has a stable idea of my desk, and he has established certain laws by which he consistently chooses to convey that stable idea to my consciousness so that I can have the perceptual experience of my desk that I am now having. These two things mean that my desk has a stable existence. And indeed, Edwards does not deny that material things have "substance," as long as we understand that substance to be God's own action: the "very substance of the body ... is nothing but the divine power, or rather the constant exertion of it" (WJE 6:351). So Edwards can use substance-language when speaking of material objects, though in a highly nuanced manner.

This framework also helps explain how Edwards deals with the question of whether my desk continues to exist even when no conscious being is in the room to perceive it. Edwards does not want to say that the desk continues to "exist" simply because it remains a stable idea in God's mind. Instead, Edwards draws on the notion that everything in the material world is connected. So my desk stands in a particular relationship with everything else in my office. And all of that, in turn, stands in a particular relationship with the rest of my house. So, even when I'm in the kitchen and perceive only the contents of that room, God has chosen to constitute my perceptual experience of the kitchen in a way that "supposes" the existence of my office and the desk it contains. For Edwards, even the minutest particle in the universe stands in some relation and has some impact on everything else. So my conscious experience of my kitchen presupposes the existence of everything that exists in the universe.[14]

---

[13] Edwards argues that we tend to think of material beings as substances because we recognize that something must cause and uphold the properties that we perceive, but we fail to realize that God himself is the "something" that lies behind the properties (WJE 6:380).

[14] It may be fair to say that Edwards views the entire universe as a interconnected set of properties that is, to some degree, perceived all at once by any conscious being. Thus, the entire universe finds its being in the mind of any conscious knower.

And this "supposition" is done in accordance with the patterns of God's consistent action. So, although the desk doesn't have the same kind of existence that it would if I were directly experiencing it, it maintains a kind of virtual existence that comes through the stable idea in God's mind expressing itself through consistently determined laws or patterns in God's creative activity.[15]

Thus, material beings are nothing more than God acting in such a way that conscious beings experience the properties that we associate with material things. But, for Edwards, this means that "the universe is created out of nothing every moment" (*WJE* 6:241). Since the material world is not comprised of enduring substances, there is nothing to "continue" from one moment to the next. Every moment, the entire universe receives being a new act of God. But this re-creation is not an arbitrary act whereby the universe in the next moment might be radically discontinuous with the universe in the present moment. God still has his "stable idea" of the universe, and he still acts according to the fixed and law-like patterns that he has established. Thus, the universe that he creates in the next moment flows from and is consistent with the state of the universe in the present moment, even though there is no direct causal link between the two states of the universe other than the divine act itself.[16]

The Immaterial World as Conscious Event

But most of what we've said thus far refers specifically to non-conscious, material bodies. Such a body is clearly not a proper substance because "it is absolutely dependent on the conception of the mind for its existence" (*WJE* 6:368). But these are not the only kinds of entities in the world. What about conscious entities? They play an important role in Edwards' ontology. What can we say about their ontological status? Could they qualify as proper substances in Edwards' sense?

As Oliver Crisp points out, it is entirely possible to maintain Edwards' idealist view of the material world and still believe in the existence of immaterial substances.[17] So he argues

---

[15] Sang Hyun Lee explains Edwards' ontology as "as a dynamic network of dispositional forces and habits" (*The Philosophical Theology of Jonathan Edwards*, p. 4). "When God creates an entity, what he does is essentially to establish a nexus of laws" (p. 79) that are "ontologically abiding powers" possessing "a mode of reality even when not in exercise" (p. 7). Thus, these powers continue to exist irrespective of whether they are in any conscious mind. Although Lee's account is helpful in a number of respects, I remain unconvinced that Edwards thinks of material beings as having any kind of existence apart from consciousness. As Edwards states, things exist "nowhere else but either in created or uncreated consciousness" (*WJE* 6:204) and "all existence is mental" (*WJE* 6:341). It seems more likely, as Oliver Crisp argues, that Edwards views material beings as "simply bundles of attributes that continue to exist through the constant activity of God" ("Jonathan Edwards' Ontology: A Critique of Sang Hyun Lee's Dispositional Account of Edwardsian Metaphysics," *Religious Studies* 45 (2009), p. 6). Their continuous being when not directly perceived by human consciousness is grounded in the "stable idea" of the divine *and* in creaturely consciousness as the necessary supposition of what we do perceive.

[16] Here again Lee appeals to dispositional states as "abiding" principles to avoid the conclusion that Edwards was a true occasionalist. Although God does move the universe "from virtuality to full actuality" every moment, the established laws endure (*The Philosophical Theology of Jonathan Edwards*, p. 63). But, as I have argued, the "abiding" aspect of the universe comes from God's consistent action, not from anything inherent in the created world. So Edwards does see the universe as created anew every moment, but this does not mean that its successive states are entirely unrelated. (See also Norman Fiering, *Jonathan Edwards's Moral Thought and Its British Context* (University of North Carolina Press, 1981), pp. 270–80, 307–8; Oliver Crisp, "How 'Occasional' Was Edwards," in *Jonathan Edwards: Philosophical Theologian* (eds Paul Helm and Oliver Crisp; Aldershot: Ashgate, 2004), pp. 61–77; and Stephen H. Daniel, "Edwards' Occasionalism").

[17] Crisp, "Jonathan Edwards' Ontology," p. 6.

that Edwards is best understood as affirming "an ontology where there are uncreated and, in a qualified sense, created substances (i.e. divine and human minds)."[18] But what exactly does it mean to refer to a created mind as a substance, even in a qualified sense? Since created minds are not self-subsistent—they too must be re-created every moment—they clearly fail to meet Edwards' first criterion for being a substance. But maybe human minds can still be that which supports particular properties (Edwards' second criterion). It could be that created minds are substances that God creates every moment as the ground for their particular properties. Thus, although created minds would not be true substances, they could be substances in a qualified sense.

And Edwards does refer to created minds and spirits in ways that would suggest that Crisp's reading is correct. In "On Being," he contrasts spirits and material beings by saying, "spirits only are properly substance" (WJE 6:206). And in another place, "spirits are much more properly beings, and more substantial, than bodies" (WJE 6:238). And, in both cases, the difference is that bodies depend on created minds for their being, but created minds do not depend on any other created thing for their being.

Nonetheless, in Edwards' ontology, we should not view created minds as immaterial substances that bear properties. Indeed, I think this is to make the same mistake with minds that Edwards thinks we so commonly make with respect to material bodies—namely, recognizing that something must lie behind the properties, but failing to realize that the "something" is God himself. For Edwards, the essential property of created minds is consciousness: "A mind or spirit is nothing else but consciousness" (WJE 6:342). It would be most consistent with the rest of Edwards' ontology to conclude that human minds are simply the direct action of God to produce the property of consciousness in the world moment-by-moment. Thus, God creates material beings by producing the properties of material bodies (e.g. solidity) and at the same time produces the properties of immaterial minds (consciousness) to perceive those material properties. Thus, created minds are still "more substantial" than material bodies in that they are conscious knowers, and thus closer to God's own being, but they are not true substances either as self-subsistent entities or as that which lies behind particular properties.

Created minds, then, are no less "events" than material bodies. Indeed, the two are part of the same event in which God creates a world to be known and minds to do the knowing. And, in this sense, we can understand Edwards' ontology as a communicative event.[19] In the creative act, God communicates his own glory through the properties of the material world to created minds. As we noted earlier, Edwards' ontology is radically theocentric.

The Law of the Union Between Soul and Body

Now that we've developed some understanding of Edwards' general ontology, it remains for us to consider what this has to do with his understanding of the mind/body relationship in particular. Probably the best summary of Edwards' understanding of the mind/body relationship comes from his discussion of original sin:

---

[18] Crisp, "Jonathan Edwards' Ontology," p. 8.

[19] On the importance of "communication" for understanding Edwards' ontology, see Stephen H. Daniel, *The Philosophy of Jonathan Edwards: A Study in Divine Semiotics* (Bloomington: Indiana University Press, 1994).

Again, the body and soul of a man are one, in a very different manner, and for different purposes. Considered in themselves, they are exceeding different beings, of a nature as diverse as can be conceived; and yet, by a very peculiar divine constitution or law of nature, which God has been pleased to establish, they are strongly united, and become one, in most important respects; a wonderful mutual communication is established; so that both become different parts of the same man. But the union and mutual communication they have, has existence, and is entirely regulated and limited, according to the sovereign pleasure of God, and the constitution he has been pleased to establish. (WJE 3:398)

From this summary, we can see that Edwards viewed the human person as comprising two things with radically different natures—body and soul—which are united by God in a particular order to constitute one human person. And the language that he uses here is surprisingly traditional, almost Cartesian. It is only when you understand this description in the context of his overall ontology that you begin to see how radically different his conception of the human person is from both materialism and substance dualism.

The Radically Different Natures of Soul and Body

We have already addressed most of what needs to be said regarding the fundamentally different natures of soul and body. The basic difference is that the soul is conscious and the body is not. In other words, like all other "material" things, the human body is the moment-by-moment product of God's activity in a particular time and place to create a phenomenal experience for conscious beings. And the soul is the moment-by-moment product of God's activity in a particular time and place to receive that phenomenal experience.

Thus, at the most basic level, there is no ontological difference between the mind and the body. Neither are proper substances, and both are equally and continuously the result of God's creative activity. Indeed, Edwards spends far more time discussing the relationship between God and creation because he seems to view this as the only fundamental ontological distinction.

The real difference between soul and body, then, is one of function. Edwards' event-ontology means that every moment God directly produces the world as an expression of his own glory. Bodies and souls together constitute the two inseparable moments in that one event. In the first moment, God acts so as to make his glory available, and in the second he makes his glory consciously perceived.

But Edwards can also talk about body and soul as being different with respect to their relative properties. Bodies have properties like colour, solidity, and location. Souls, on the other hand, have none of these properties and are purely conscious beings.

The sharp differentiation between soul and body becomes even more clear when we consider the possibility of body/soul separation, which Edwards maintains is the state of the human person in heaven (*WJE* 2:113). We don't know much about the nature of such a state, but the fact that it is possible confirms that body and soul are very different entities.

Thus, although body and soul are ontologically similar in being to God's own actions, they comprise different sets of properties that serve different functions in Edwards' ontology.

The Union of Soul and Body

Despite these differences, body and soul are still united in a single human person. As Edwards says, "the appellative, 'man,' or the proper name of any particular man, is the name of a whole, including the different parts of soul and body" (*WJE* 3:308).

But what makes it the case that my soul is united to this particular body? Or stated differently, how is the relationship between my soul and my body any different from its relationship to any other material thing?

This is particularly challenging for Edwards in that he does not think that souls occupy space in the same way as bodies.

> *And why should we then form such a ridiculous idea of spirits, as to think them so long, so thick, or so wide; or to think there is a necessity of their being square or round or some other certain figure? Therefore spirits cannot be in place in such a sense, that all within the given limits shall be where the spirit is, and all without such a circumscription where he is not.* (WJE 6:338)

But that means bodies and souls cannot be related through proximity. My soul is not "in" my body any more than it is "in" my desk. And that means that the body/soul union cannot be established through any kind of identity between the soul and the brain. As Edwards says, "the seat of the soul is not in the brain" (*WJE* 6.352).

But if my soul is not in my body, or my brain, any more than it is in my desk, what makes it the case that my body is united to my soul and not the desk? Edwards addresses this issue through another appeal to phenomenal experience:

> *... all created spirits have clearer and more strongly impressed ideas of things in one place than in another, or can produce effects here and not there; and as this place alters, so spirits move. In spirits united to bodies, the spirit more strongly perceives things where the body is, and can there immediately produce effects, and in this sense the soul can be said to be in the same place where the body is.* (WJE 6:338–9)

In other words, I am united to my body in the sense that the phenomenal experiences produced in me by my body are stronger and more distinct than the phenomenal experiences produced by other bodies. And, since all phenomenal experience is the direct result of God acting moment-by-moment to create bodies that produce phenomenal experiences in conscious beings, the fact that I have clearer and more distinct phenomenal experiences of my body is simply the product of God's creative activity.

So his first argument for the uniqueness of the body/soul relationship is through phenomenal experience. But Edwards also argues that body and soul are united through a unique "causal" relationship, which takes us to our next point.

The Mutual Communication between Body and Soul

Edwards also talks about the "mutual communication" between soul and body. And by this he means that body and soul mutually affect one another, but always in such a way that the soul leads and the body follows.

Edwards clearly affirms that changes in the soul effect changes in the body.

> *And God has so made and established the human nature, the soul being united to a*
> *body in proper state, that the soul preferring or choosing such an immediate exertion*
> *or alteration of the body, such an alteration instantaneously follows.*

Indeed, "so subject is the body to the mind … that there can't be so much as an intense thought, without an effect" on the body (*WJE* 2:132). Clearly there is a strong communication of influence from the soul to the body.[20]

And this is how it should be since God has constituted the body/soul relationship in such a way that the soul is in charge. Only the soul "is properly and directly the subject of precepts or commands" (*WJE* 302). And only the soul is "the proper seat of affections," from which flows all human action (*WJE* 2:98).

But, despite this strong emphasis on how the soul affects the body, Edwards also affirms that this truly is a *mutual* communication. So he argues that bodily states can be "an occasion of affections in the mind" (*WJE* 2:269). And in his discussions of revivals, Edwards showed remarkable sensitivity to the many ways that bodily states impact the soul.

The restrained language here of the body merely providing an "occasion" for something to happen in the soul raises an important question. What exactly does it mean for soul and body to affect each other? As we discussed earlier, Edwards' occasionalism means that every moment God creates the universe anew. So it would seem difficult for Edwards to have any concept of creaturely causation.[21] But, if this is the case, how can souls or bodies have any impact on the other?

Consider the problem in this way. If the state of my soul (S1) at one moment (T1) is followed in the next moment (T2) by some state of my body (B2), what is the relationship between S1 and B2? Given Edwards' occasionalism, it seems impossible to say that S1 directly produced B2 since there is nothing of either B or S that endures from T1 to T2. So anything that S1 may or may not have done with respect to B1 can have no direct influence on the state of B2. And, of course, the same logic would hold if we inverted the scenario and tried to understand how the body can have any causal effect on the soul.

But, as I argued above, the solution comes from the idea that creaturely entities "exist" by virtue of a stable idea in the mind of God and his sovereign determination to act according to fixed laws or patterns. At T1, God created S1 with its particular properties. Because God has determined that he will act in consistent (patterned) ways with respect to creation, what he creates at T2, though not directly produced by the state of anything at T1, will be consistent with that state. So, when God creates B2, he does so because it is consistent with the state of S1. In this way, it is even possible to speak of S1 as "causing" B2 if we mean by this that the state of S1 is causally relevant to the production of B2.[22]

---

[20] Edwards even explains how he thinks the soul effects these changes on the body. Although the soul does not reside in the brain, it makes sense to identify the brain as the nexus of the soul's interactions with the body "because ideas that come by the body immediately ensue only on alterations that are made there, and the soul most immediately produces effects nowhere else" (*WJE* 6:339). More specifically, the soul influences the body by causing the brain to emit "animal spirits," which go out to the rest of the body and cause the necessary effects (*WJE* 6:246).

[21] Oliver Crisp argues convincingly that Edwards' occasionalism is inconsistent with viewing creaturely beings as secondary causes in the traditional sense ("How Occasional Was Edwards' Occasionalism?").

[22] Thus, Edwards prefers to use the language of one creaturely event being the "occasion" for another, rather than serving as "a cause, most properly speaking" (*WJE* 1:181).

The Human Person as Communicative Event

Putting all of the pieces together, we can say that, consistent with his general ontology, Edwards views the human person as a communicative event. In other words, the human person is an event in which God creates the properties of the material world and communicates them to some conscious mind, which he creates in the same moment, so that the material properties are received and known by the conscious mind. Of course, this is true of his ontology as a whole. But, in the body/soul union that constitutes a human person, you have a far more immediate and intimate instantiation of this communicative process. It is most particularly in the human person, then, that God's glory is communicated in creation.

Prospects for an Edwardsian Ontology Today

Although Edwards' anthropological ontology will certainly strike many readers as insurmountably "odd," its stridently anti-materialist voice sounds ever so off-key in our largely materialist world. Nonetheless, I find much to appreciate in his unique approach. First, although I have some reservations about Sang Hyun Lee's dispositional understanding of Edwards' ontology, I agree with the conclusion that Edwards' anthropological ontology is dynamic and relational in ways that create the possibility for interesting dialogue with contemporary science.[23] A world made of quantum fields, subatomic particles, and even vibrating strings is far more fluid, dynamic, and relational than tends to be the case with ontologies based on discrete substances. This more modern understanding of the "physical" universe, though, seems quite consistent with Edwards' view of a world that comes to be moment-by-moment through the law-like activity of God.

I also appreciate that Edwards' ontology offers a surprisingly high view of the material world and, in particular, human bodies. One might expect that an idealistic system like Edwards' would ultimately denigrate physicality. But, as we've seen, the material world is God's own action. Thus, like all of God's actions, it must be good and valuable. And, since it plays an essential role as one moment in the "communicative event," the material world clearly plays a vital role in Edwards' ontology.[24]

Finally, Edwards' ontology helps illustrate how a panentheistic ontology can ground everything in God's own being while still retaining some distinction between God and creation. Although some have argued that Edwards fails at this very point,[25] Edwards clearly distinguishes between God himself and the properties that he creates in his communicative action. Of course, that does not mean Edwards' panentheistic approach to the human person is entirely adequate, only that it illustrates one way in which panentheism may provide resources for maintaining a God/creature distinction.

---

[23] See esp. Lee, *The Philosophy of Jonathan Edwards*, pp. 76–114. Some scholars have appropriated Lee's insight into their own anthropological projects (e.g. Mark Graves, *Mind, Brain, and the Elusive Soul: Human Systems of Cognitive Science and Religion* (Aldershot: Ashgate, 2008), pp. 189–90, and F. LeRon Shults, *Reforming Theological Anthropology: After the Philosophical Turn to Relationality* (Grand Rapids: Eerdmans, 2003), p. 34).

[24] For more on this, see esp. Sang Hyun Lee, "Jonathan Edwards on Nature," in *Faithful Imagining: Essays in Honor of Richard R Niebuhr* (eds Wayne L. Proudfoot, Albert L. Blackwell, and Sang Huyn Lee; Atlanta: Scholars Press, 1995).

[25] E.g. Clyde A. Holbrooke, *Jonathan Edwards, The Valley and Nature: An Interpretive Essay* (Lesiburg: Bucknell University Press, 1987).

And I find much to value in Edwards' vision of the entire universe as God's own self-expression, the moment-by-moment communication of God's own beauty to the beings that he creates and sustains to be participants in the divine self-expression.

Despite these points of appreciation though, I would like to register at least a few concerns at the same time. Unfortunately, at this stage of the argument, we do not have adequate space to develop these arguments in full. So that will need to remain the task for a future project. Nonetheless, let us briefly explore a few potential weaknesses in Edwards' anthropological ontology.

First, Edwards' approach manifests a complete lack of attention to the significance of the person and work of Christ for understanding the nature of humanity.[26] Although Edwards himself expresses a high view of the incarnation, it is startling how little this factors into his theological anthropology. Indeed, I have yet to find any place in Edwards' writings where he uses the incarnation as an explicit starting point for reflecting on human ontology. As I have argued elsewhere, Christology should serve as the fundamental ground for any adequately Christian anthropology.[27] And this has decisive implications for our understanding of human ontology.

Even more surprising, Edwards does not even seem to explore the reverse logic: how his vision of human ontology impacts his understanding of the incarnation. If we view the body and human soul of Christ through the lens of Edwards' event-ontology, do we end up with an adequate view of the incarnation? That is a difficult question to answer at this point since Edwards does not seem to have addressed it himself.[28]

Additionally, although I earlier expressed appreciation for Edwards' high view of creaturely reality and the human body, there are still some concerns regarding his view of the created order. Most importantly, when Edwards discusses human persons living a disembodied existence in heaven, he describes them as living a complete human life with the full range of affections and as continuing in their purpose as conscious knowers of God's glory.[29] But that suggests that human bodies really are not essential for full human life and for carrying out God's purposes. If so, then it would seem that Edwards' ontology, at that point at least, is inadequate given the narrative of redemption and its emphasis on creation, incarnation, and resurrection, all of which are inherently embodied realities.[30]

Finally, I still have some questions about whether Edwards' approach provides adequate ground for personal identity through time. His occasionalism renders it impossible to ground personal identity in any kind of creaturely continuity. So his solution is to argue that God can treat discrete entities as comprising a single whole and that this is adequate for grounding the identity of creaturely beings.[31] Thus, personal identity seems to be grounded in the divine will alone, which raises questions for, among other things, moral responsibility.

---

[26] This is particularly surprising since his emphasis on the Son as the only perfect expression of the Father's self-knowledge would seem the perfect starting point for connecting Christology and anthropology more explicitly.

[27] Marc Cortez, *Embodied Souls, Ensouled Bodies: An Exercise in Christological Anthropology and Its Significance for the Mind/Body Debate* (London: T. &. T Clark, 2008).

[28] I acknowledge, though, given the breadth and diversity of Edwards' writings, it is possible that Edwards has addressed these issues elsewhere.

[29] See *WJE* 2:113.

[30] I also wonder if Edwards' language of bodies being "lower" and "less substantial" than souls suggests an implicit denigration of creaturely realities even though that is not his intent in these passages.

[31] See *WJE* 3:397–402; see also Paul Helm, "A Forensic Dilemma: John Locke and Jonathan Edwards on Personal Identity," in *Jonathan Edwards: Philosophical Theologian*, 45–59 and Oliver Crisp, *Jonathan Edwards and the Metaphysics Of Sin*, chapter 5.

We could strengthen this account of personal responsibility somewhat in two ways. First, we could point out that God has determined to act in law-like ways with respect to creation. So my identity is continuous with the "me" who existed a moment ago because God has decreed that he will create each successive version of "me" in ways that are consistent with each prior version. Thus there is continuity in that each state of "me" bears a particular relation to each prior state that is true of no other entity. So personal identity is not entirely arbitrary, but it is still not grounded in anything that persists from one moment to the next. Second, we could appeal to Edwards' explanation of our identity with Adam in his volume on *Original Sin*.[32] There he seems to suggest that God can, in his divine sovereignty, group creaturely entities in such a way that even in their discrete particularity they comprise metaphysically real unities. Thus, in the case of Adam and other humans, God can treat them as a singular entity (i.e. humanity) because he has sovereignly determined to group them that way.[33] In the same way, my identity through time could be grounded in God's sovereign determination to count these seemingly diverse expressions as different parts of the metaphysical whole that is "me."[34] Whether such explanations suffice to ground a robust view of personal identity through time requires closer study than we can engage at this point.[35]

To conclude, Edwards offers a fascinating and all-encompassing view of the universe in general and the mind/body relationship in particular. If nothing else, his ontology offers a refreshingly different perspective that is deeply theological while still being sensitive to the insights and contributions of philosophy and the sciences. Regardless of whether modern thinkers are willing to embrace such a radically idealistic understanding of the universe, his approach is worth studying further.

---

[32] See esp. Oliver Crisp, *Jonathan Edwards and the Metaphysics of Sin* (Farnham: Ashgate, 2005), chapter 5.

[33] Although this could be construed in an entirely arbitrary manner—i.e. God could sovereignly create a metaphysical unity out of butterflies, humans, and popcorn-flavored jelly beans—Crisp rightly points out that there may be certain ways of carving up matter that are more fitting for divine purposes, and therefore privileged in a way that other, equally arbitrary objects … are not" (ibid., 100).

[34] This approach would make Edwards' view of personal identity quite similar to those modern philosophers arguing for some kind of four-dimensionalism (see esp. Theodore Sider, *Four-Dimensionalism* (Oxford: Clarendon, 2001)).

[35] Interestingly, though, this approach to personal identity would have a much easier time accounting for continuous identity through death and resurrection. As long as any post-resurrection form of "me" was created as a consistent expression of the pre-resurrection state of "me," we could affirm that it is the same "me."

Why Emergence?

William Hasker

Reductionism, Creationism, Emergentism

"And the LORD God formed man of the dust of the ground, and breathed into his nostrils the breath of life, and man became a living soul" (Genesis 2:7, KJV). But what is a soul? It is not too difficult to give a functional definition of a soul—to say what a soul *does*. The soul is that in us which feels and thinks, which makes decisions and sometimes incurs guilt. Above all, the soul is that by which we reach out to God. In a word, the soul is the inward center of all our thoughts, feelings and actions, indeed of all of our experiences. But saying these things leaves some important questions unanswered. What is the *nature* of the soul—that is, what *kind of thing* is it? And what is the *origin* of the soul—where does it come from? It is the purpose of this chapter to consider these questions.

There are three basic sorts of answers to our two questions; they go under the labels of *reductionism, creationism,* and *emergentism*. The core idea of reductionism is that more complex entities are built up, according to understandable laws and principles, from simpler entities combined and arranged in the right way. A key phrase for understanding reductionism is "nothing but"; the complex entities are "nothing but" the simple entities, properly arranged and interacting. Many examples of reduction come from the sciences. The many thousands of kinds of materials in the world are nothing but substances built up out of just 90-odd chemical elements, combined in various complex ways. These elements, in turn, are built up out of a still smaller number of elementary particles: primarily protons, neutrons, and electrons, but quite a few others have recently been added. And so on. Applied to the human mind or soul, the idea is that the mind is "nothing but" the complicated functioning of the neurons of which the brain is composed, operating according to the standard laws of physics and chemistry. Proponents of scientific reductionism harbor the dream of a "final theory"—a fundamental theory of physics, utilizing a relatively small number of laws, which in principle would enable us to explain and predict absolutely everything that takes place in the physical universe.

Not a great deal will be said here about reductionism, because this approach holds few attractions for those who desire to gain an understanding of the human person that is helpful for theology. Reductionists are strongly inclined to deny or minimize the "higher" functions of the soul, so as to make them less of an obstacle to the reductionist program. Reasoning is simply the mechanical operation of the brain, churning out the answers to questions computerwise, according to "programs" encoded in the brain. Morality is "nothing but" the codification of behaviors which have proved, over the course of evolution, to be conducive to individual or group survival. Reductionists generally do not believe in free will, in the sense according to which we sometimes really have a choice between two or more different ways in which our lives shall unfold. Since the mind is nothing but the operation of the brain, it stands to reason that when the brain ceases to function and decomposes, that is the end of the human being. As has been noted, there is little here that should appeal to anyone wishing to construct an adequate theological anthropology. One caution is needed, however: opposition to reductionist views of the human person should not lead us to denigrate the whole idea of reduction and reductive explanation. Successful reductive explanations are the meat and drink of the physical sciences; a few examples were already suggested above. Our objections to the misuse of such explanations should not lead us to reject this type of explanation where it is feasible and useful.

Creationism, in contrast to reductionism, has proved to be quite appealing to religious believers seeking to understand the human soul. Indeed, it has been by far the majority view, though not accepted by everyone. Creationists concerning the soul do not hold merely that the soul is created by God in the general sense in which oceans, mountain ranges, trees, and stars are created entities. These sorts of things are indeed part of God's creation, but individual trees, stars, and mountains come into being through natural processes, which we at least roughly understand. God, we say, is the "primary cause" of the existence of these things, but they have "secondary causes" in the form of other created things. Creationists concerning the soul, however, hold that each individual human soul is *directly and individually* created by God; created *ex nihilo*, "out of nothing," and not through any natural process. It seems natural to see this view as reflecting the individual, personal care which God manifests towards each and every human being; it also emphasizes the fundamental difference between humans and animals—or, we should more properly say, between humans and *other* animals. Nevertheless, the view faces some formidable difficulties. We return to this topic shortly.

Before that, however, we need to consider the third class of views, emergentism. The basic idea of emergence is that, when certain elements are assembled and related to each other in a certain way, something new and surprising can appear—something we would not have anticipated, merely on the basis of what we knew beforehand about the elements. Yet the new thing is not "added from the outside," as is the case with creationism; rather, it appears as a natural consequence of the elements in their combination and relationship. Map out on a graph the geometric points that satisfy a certain equation, and something new appears: a fractal pattern, sometimes elegant and surprisingly beautiful. There are many candidates for emergence in the natural sciences: examples include the emergence of complex crystalline structures out of material that formerly had no such structure, and the emergence of elaborate group behavior from swarms of insects that individually give no evidence of such behaviors. Applied to the human mind, emergentism implies that consciousness, thought, rational volition, and so on make their appearance naturally as a result of the structure and functioning of the human brain and nervous system. It can be seen that in a sense emergentism is a mediating view between reductionism and creationism. Unlike reductionists, emergentists do not seek to "reduce" mental phenomena to their material base, in the process depriving them of much of the significance we ordinarily take them to possess. But unlike creationists, emergentists do not view the mind and its powers as being, as it were, injected from outside into the human biological system. Instead, the soul appears naturally, given the appropriate physical organization and function of the body and brain. It is worth pointing out that while the idea of emergence as such is fairly recent, it does have a certain affinity with *traducianism*, the view that a person's soul is somehow derived from her parents, as a result of the natural process of reproduction. In the history of Christian thought traducianism has vied for acceptance with creationism. Augustine, for example, hesitated between traducianism and creationism; it seemed to him that traducianism made it easier to understand the transmission of original sin from Adam and Eve to their posterity. Emergentism can well be viewed as a contemporary version of traducianism.

Given this initial characterization of the three types of views, we proceed to evaluation. As already noted, reductionism has little appeal and need not be further considered. Creationism, however, calls for our close attention. The common versions of creationism are generally modeled on the dualism of René Descartes,[1] according to which body and mind are two radically different kinds of substances. The body is physical through and through; it has all the natural, physical properties we are familiar with through the physical sciences, but in itself it has no trace of mental properties such as thought or even sensation. The mind is the "thinking thing"; its essential characteristic is consciousness and conscious thought, with everything that goes along with that. The mind, however, has no physical properties whatsoever: no electric charge, no mass, not even (in most versions) a location in space. But in spite of the radical difference between mind and body, the two do interact: the mind receives information from the body and brain, and the body in turn carries out the decisions made by the mind. The mind, according to creationism, is infused by God early in the development of the organism; it is united with the body throughout the course of a person's life, but in no way does it owe its origin or its continuance to the body.

For some readers, creationism may seem so natural and plausible that there is little need to consider alternatives. Nevertheless, it does face difficulties, as we shall see. But there is one highly publicized objection that is not nearly as formidable as is often thought: the notorious "problem of mind-body interaction." The objector asks, "How can the mind, which has no physical attributes whatsoever, make a difference to the functioning of the physical brain and body?" When no convincing reply to this "how" question is forthcoming, it is assumed that the credibility of dualism has been dealt a decisive blow. This, however, covertly assumes that we *do* understand causation in the body-to-body cases, as in the classic example of two billiard balls colliding and rebounding in different directions. But as David Hume showed long ago, this simply is not the case. We know that the balls *do in fact* act like this, rather than exploding, coming immediately to a dead stop, or passing through one another without resistance. And because we have witnessed this many times, it has come to seem "natural" to us, and we have the illusion that we understand what is going on. At bottom, however, we cannot claim to have rational insight into the *why*; we simply have to say, "that is just what happens."[2] But surely, there are few other things that "just happen" as often (and without striking us as unusual or surprising) as the fact that our conscious experiences influence, and are influenced by, the state of our physical bodies. This objection, then, can be simply dismissed, in spite of the fact that many still take it seriously, even sophisticated philosophers who ought to know better.

But while the bare fact of mind-body interaction does not pose a serious problem for creationism, the *intimate and pervasive dependence* of mental processes on one's bodily condition is harder to reconcile with that view. It is easy to see that, if the body or nervous

---

[1]   It should be said that there is another type of creationism, derived from the thought of Thomas Aquinas, that also has a number of contemporary defenders. Thomistic dualism has some advantages as compared with Cartesian dualism; it also has difficulties of its own, as well as sharing some of those enumerated here. For discussion, see my "The Dialectic of Soul and Body," *American Catholic Philosophical Quarterly* 87:3 (Summer 2013), pp. 495–509; an expanded version, under the same title, will be found in *Contemporary Dualism: A Defense*, edited by Andrea Lavazza and Howard Robinson (London: Routledge, 2013), pp. 204–19.

[2]   At present our most fundamental theory about the nature and behavior of matter is quantum mechanics. The theory is accepted because of the wide-ranging and astonishingly accurate predictions that are made from it, but it is a commonplace among the experts on this theory that *no one really understands* why matter behaves in the (sometimes very strange) ways the theory describes. Yet all of the "ordinary" causal interactions, which we imagine that we do understand, are the result precisely of these mysterious quantum interactions!

153

system are impaired, the mind might be lacking in sensory input, or might not be able effectively to control the muscles that produce movement. But why should *consciousness itself* be interrupted by a blow on the head, or by the action of an anaesthetic? And why should damage to the brain produce major alterations (as sometimes happens) to a person's character and personality? A particularly telling example is the phenomenon of *visual agnosia*. Persons suffering from this condition are unable to identify familiar faces, or to read the expressions on other people's faces. This is not due to a lack of visual acuity or to a deficit in general intelligence. Rather, this rather subtle ability to interpret one's visual input is lost due to damage in a specific small region of the brain—and this is only one example among many of the same sort.[3] Creationists have yet to produce a convincing explanation for this pervasive dependence of mind upon body, a dependence which from their point of view was hardly to be expected.

Further difficulties arise when we consider the relationship of humans to non-human animals. If human bodies, as such, are unable to have thoughts, sensations, or any other kinds of conscious experiences, the same must be true of animals. Descartes himself had a simple solution to this problem: animals in fact *do not have* sensations or any other kind of conscious experiences; they are mere automata, and it is simply an illusion that, when you come home and your dog jumps up and wags his tail, he is happy about your return. (This was not merely an eccentric philosophical idea; it had practical implications. Some followers of Descartes's view practiced vivisection with no concern for the pain they were causing their victims: the subjects of the experiments were not, in fact, experiencing anything at all, in spite of the illusion on the part of naïve persons that the animals were suffering excruciating pain!) Clearly we cannot follow Descartes in this, so the creationist is forced to attribute divinely created souls to animals—not necessarily souls in every respect equivalent to human souls, but souls that are adequate to the sort of thoughts and experiences the animals do seem to have. But now a problem arises: how far do we carry this? How far down the "scale of life" do we find these divinely-created souls? Of course, it is difficult for anyone to say with confidence just which simpler life-forms have conscious experience, and which do not. The problem, however, is that any answer the creationist can give tends to be embarrassing to his view. If the bar for consciousness is set high (one well-known philosopher thought it absurd to suppose that fish have experiences), this looks like a questionable prejudice against "lower" life-forms. Not as bad as Descartes's prejudice, perhaps, but still bad enough! But if we are generous in assigning souls to lower life-forms (another philosopher referred, only partly in jest, to "brother worm"!), we have the unappealing notion of God's creating souls by the billions for spiders, mosquitoes, and intestinal parasites. And then there is the problem of what becomes of all those souls when the creatures perish: since the souls don't depend for their existence on anything physical, it is hard to see how the death of a mosquito can extinguish its immaterial soul.

Yet another (and to my mind, powerful) objection appears when we try to connect creationism to the process of biological evolution. To be sure, raising this objection presupposes that there was in fact an evolutionary process, relating all of the creatures on our planet to one another by their descent from one or a small number of primitive life-forms. I believe the evidence overwhelmingly supports the claim that such a process occurred, but we obviously can't enter into that debate here.[4] It is clear in any case that anyone who accepts a view of the mind/soul that requires one to reject an evolutionary view of life's

---

[3]   See Neil R. Carlson, *Physiology of Behavior*, 5th ed. (Boston: Allyn and Bacon, 1994), pp. 171–80.

[4]   I find the evidence that *an evolutionary process occurred* completely convincing. This does not, however, entail that the prevailing "neo-Darwinian synthesis" provides a complete and adequate explanation of that process.

history incurs a heavy burden in the debate about the nature of persons. The problem is not merely that one is coming into conflict with a view that is widely accepted in our society; we should not, after all, be overly intimidated by prevailing intellectual fashions. The real burden lies in the need to provide a convincing alternative explanation for the immense, and ever-growing, body of data that supports belief in the evolution of life on the earth.

Unfortunately, creationism concerning the soul is difficult to reconcile with any plausible version of evolutionary biology. Evolution presents us with a very long and complex story in which, over hundreds of millions of years, the most primitive life-forms gave rise *through a natural process* to the complex kinds of life we observe today, including human life. The question is, how do the divinely created souls fit into this story? More complex animals, with greater cognitive powers, require "higher," more powerful souls; a highly developed brain is useless to an animal if the animal's soul is unable to utilize it effectively. And on the other hand, even a high-level soul is of little use if the required cerebral machinery is not in place. (Tragically, this situation is illustrated in the case of some human beings with damaged or defective brains.) We cannot suppose that God waits until the brains have evolved through natural selection, and then supplies the requisite soul with its advanced capabilities: lacking the right sort of soul, the advanced brain would be non-functional and would not be conserved through evolutionary selection. Perhaps we might suppose that God simultaneously brings about a change in the genetic mechanism (DNA and so on), and also supplies a new, more powerful soul to take advantage of the improved cognitive hardware. But this would not by any means be evolution *as a natural process*, and we can confidently predict that it would be rejected by evolutionary biologists, theists, and atheists alike. The truth is that creationism concerning the soul just does not fit at all comfortably with an evolutionary account of life. This fact creates a significant burden for creationism, though one of which its proponents have often seemed to be unaware.[5]

Emergentism, in contrast, is completely free from these objections against creationism; indeed in some cases it is able to turn the problematic features to its advantage. It is true that we lack deep insight into the way in which the mind is produced by the body and brain. But given that it is so produced, causal interaction is built in right from the beginning; it does not need to be added later as a separate assumption. Furthermore, the generation of the mind by the brain makes it much easier to understand the intimate, fine-grained dependence of mind on brain that we find to be the case, as compared with the situation for creationism. Emergentism has no problem with the souls of animals: non-human animals (those that enjoy any sort of conscious experience at all) have souls appropriate to the kinds of being they are, souls that are generated by their own nervous systems. Furthermore, emergentism provides a remarkably appropriate fit with an evolutionary account of the history of life on earth. It is possible, to be sure, to maintain an emergentist view of the mind even if one rejects the evolutionary narrative.[6] Doing so, however, sacrifices one of

---

[5]   I mention here two especially eminent examples. Richard Swinburne's *The Evolution of the Soul*, revised edition (Oxford: Clarendon Press, 1998), is one of the best recent defenses of Cartesian dualism. Swinburne is deeply engaged with science, and has no interest in rejecting evolution. Yet he never discusses the tension between evolution and his creationist view of the soul. In Alvin Plantinga's *Where the Conflict Really Lies: Science, Religion, and Naturalism* (Oxford: Oxford University Press, 2011), he devotes two entire chapters (63 pages) to alleged conflicts between Christian faith and evolution, and evolution is referred to frequently throughout the rest of the book. Yet he also never mentions the tension between evolution and his own, presumably creationist, view of the soul.

[6]   An example of this combination is J.P. Moreland. Moreland presents his view of the soul in both a creationist and an emergentist version (see Chapter 6, "Substance Dualism and the Body: Heredity, DNA, and the Soul," in J.P. Moreland and Scott B. Rea, *Body and Soul: Human Nature and the Crisis in Ethics* (Downers Grove: InterVarsity Press, 2000)). Moreland has stated that the emergentist version

the main attractions of the emergentist view with little or no compensating advantage. Emergentism presents us with a compelling picture of the co-evolution of mind and brain. Genetic changes which lead to a more highly-developed brain lead in turn to the emergence of a more sophisticated mind, a mind which has a more accurate grasp of its environment and responds in ways that enhance survival and reproduction. These improved responses in turn lead to the conservation of the genetic changes and to their becoming established in the population. Indeed, this feature of emergentism amounts to powerful argument in favor of emergentism over reductionism—an ironic result, in view of the materialist and reductionist bias of many evolutionary thinkers. Reductionism, however, faces a fundamental difficulty precisely in accounting for the evolution of the conscious mind. Reductionist views insist that the physical world cannot be affected by anything non-physical, such as a thought or an emotion. All the causal work is done, according to these views, by the basic physical entities; this is known as the "causal closure of the physical domain." Evolutionary selection, however, can operate only on physical structures and physical behavior, so if conscious thought has no effects in the physical realm it becomes invisible to evolutionary selection, and cannot (except by accident) be improved by selection. To give a graphic example, materialist evolutionary theory may be able to give a plausible explanation of why, when a group of primitive hominids are threatened by a predator, they will remove to a safer location—say, by climbing a tree. But materialist evolution has no explanation whatever for the fact that their conscious mental state corresponds to "Let's get out of here before that saber-tooth cat arrives," rather than "Isn't this a delicious meal of baboon meat!" But an evolutionary theory that can give no account of the evolution of consciousness is defective at a fundamental level.[7] (I do not mean to imply, by the way, that once consciousness is recognized as having causal powers, Darwinism provides us with a complete and adequate account of the development of the mind. I suspect, on the contrary, that quite a lot more is needed. But without a recognition of consciousness as causally effective, the account of mental evolution can't even get started.)

This, then, is my answer to the question, "Why emergentism?" I believe that, even apart from evolutionary considerations, emergentism enjoys significant advantages as compared with both reductionism and creationism. Add in an evolutionary perspective, and the advantage becomes decisive. Or so I say! There is more that needs to be done, however, before the case can be considered complete.

Varieties of Emergentism

At this point it is appropriate to remind ourselves that reductionism, creationism, and emergentism are *kinds* of views, not single, well-articulated theories. There are a variety of reductionist views on offer, as well as several different creationist views, and certainly there are various forms of emergentism that have been proposed. In order to begin sorting these out, I focus on the question, "What precisely is it that emerges?" Different answers to this question yield a series of progressively stronger emergentist positions.

---

is the one he prefers, but Moreland rejects evolution in favor of "progressive creation," in which God creates new types of life *ex nihilo* from time to time as the earth becomes ready to receive them. For comment see "The Dialectic of Soul and Body," pp. 209–15 in Lavazza and Robinson, eds, *Contemporary Dualism.*

7   For this objection see my "What Is Naturalism? And Should We Be Naturalists?" *Philosophia Christi* 15:1 (2013), pp. 21–34; also, *The Emergent Self* (Ithaca: Cornell University Press, 1999), pp. 75–9.

The first answer to that question is that what emerges are *mental properties* and *mental events*—in particular, *conscious experiences*. It seems evident that these sorts of items are essential to any possible account of the mind/soul; without them, there is no mind to discuss. These things are not always viewed as emergent, but that is what they must be, given that they cannot be reduced to anything that is purely physical. Reductionists, to be sure, have invested an enormous amount of effort in the attempt to show that mental properties are reducible, either to behavioral properties, or to neurophysiological properties, or (the current favorite) to functional properties. These efforts at reduction have not been particularly successful, as we might expect: it just seems evident on the face of it that, for instance, the mental property of hoping that the Cubs will at last win the World Series is not the same as any physical property, however complex, of the neural assemblages in a person's brain. The frustration that has attended these efforts at reductionism has led some philosophers to embrace *eliminative materialism*, the view that desires, purposes, intentions, and conscious experiences in general as they are ordinarily conceived, simply *do not exist*—that our belief in these things is merely evidence of our adherence to a primitive theory, called "folk psychology," which like other primitive theories is destined to be replaced, in this case by a more adequate, and thoroughly physical, theory of the mind (a theory which, unfortunately, does not yet exist). Most of us, however (including most philosophers) find this incredible, which means that mental properties and mental events *do exist*—and if they cannot be reduced to physical properties, they must be considered as being emergent. The view that the *only* thing that emerges in the case of the mind are mental properties is often termed *non-reductive physicalism*; the view is "physicalist" with the sole exception of those properties. This label, and the view itself, have been criticized by Jaegwon Kim, who has argued forcefully that any physicalist view worth its salt needs to be reductionist.[8] In spite of this criticism, however, the name is still in common use, and we can accept it as a label, while recognizing that views so called may still be reductionist in other ways.

A second answer to our question is that what emerges, in addition to the mental properties, are *novel causal powers* that are associated with those properties. An example: when a person becomes angry, this often has results, not only for subsequent mental states, but for what happens in the physical world, results ranging all the way from loud and emphatic protests to acts of violence. And these results are different than what would have happened apart from that emotion. One might think that the emergence of such powers goes without saying, given the emergence of mental events and properties, but in fact it does not. Philosophers inclined towards physicalism often insist that the mental event (in this case, the feeling of anger) is itself the result of the person's physical brain-state, and that *any subsequent physical events (the physical reaction to the anger) are also the result of the physical brain-state*, operating throughout according to the standard laws of physics and chemistry. This strongly suggests that the view in question is one of *epiphenomenalism*, according to which mental properties and mental events are merely the accompaniments of the physical properties of body and brain; in themselves, the mental properties do no work and have no causal effects. This however is massively implausible, and most physicalists are determined to resist it, suggesting instead ingenious ways in which we may after all consider the mental properties as being causally effective. The success of these attempts is dubious, but in any case physicalists uniformly insist on the *causal closure of the physical domain*, which means in effect that any event that has a cause at all has a sufficient physical cause. (The qualification is needed because quantum mechanics seems to tell us that some micro-events are purely random and uncaused.) This view, however, has consequences that are truly

---

8   See Jaegwon Kim, "The Myth of Nonreductive Materialism," in *Supervenience and Mind: Selected Essays* (Cambridge: Cambridge University Press, 1993), pp. 265–84.

mind-boggling. For instance, it means that one never in fact performs an action *because* one consciously decided to perform it; rather, *both* the physical action and the decision to perform the action are entirely the result of physical brain-states, states over which one has no conscious control whatsoever. The view also implies that one never accepts the conclusion of a process of reasoning because one has followed the argument and has seen, rationally, that the conclusion follows from the premises; rather, one's acceptance of the conclusion is, once again, entirely the result of one's physical brain-state, a state which is in no way guided by the laws of logic or the principle of sound reasoning, but simply by the laws of physical cause and effect. The argument given in the previous section, to the effect that a reductionist view of evolution can have no explanation for the development of conscious thought, presents one more example of the unfortunate consequences of the doctrine of causal closure. Emergentists of this second sort reject that doctrine, and insist that *because of the occurrence of conscious mental events things go differently on the micro-level than they would go in the absence of such events.* This is an important conclusion, one that upsets much of the thinking that underlies contemporary naturalism concerning the human person. This kind of view is often said to involve "downward causation," because the "higher" mental level is held to exert causal influence on what happens at the "lower" level of neurons in the brain. However, there is quite a bit of confusion surrounding the notion of downward causation, so it may be best to avoid that term unless it is accompanied by careful explanations. There is not at present any generally accepted label for the kind of view under discussion here; we might be tempted to call it "non-reductive physicalism," but as we have seen that name is already preempted for another use. I have suggested elsewhere that the view might be termed the *theory of emergent material persons* (the EMP theory),[9] and perhaps this label can serve our present purposes.

The theory of emergent material persons will seem to many a plausible candidate for the metaphysical component of a theological anthropology. In fact, several contributors to this volume embrace views of this general sort. However, there are reasons to think such a view may in the end not be adequate. Some of these reasons are more strictly theological; we will attend to them briefly later on. But there are also purely philosophical difficulties. Consider once again the emergent mental properties which play a role in this view. Timothy O'Connor (himself a leading proponent of the EMP theory) has pointed out that these properties are *non-structural*, meaning that the property's instantiation "does not even partly consist of the instantiation of a plurality of more basic properties by the entity or its parts."[10] Some examples may help to clarify this point. A person's standing upright consists in the fact that her limbs are aligned with one another, and with the surface of the earth, in a certain way. (These relationships would be quite different if she were sitting, or lying down, or running.) A person's weighing 150 pounds consists in the fact that each of his various parts (arms, legs, torso, head, and neck) has a certain weight, and these weights add up to 150 pounds. My shoveling the snow in my driveway consists in my hands gripping the handle of the shovel, my feet, legs, and torso being positioned so as to support my holding the shovel, and my arms pushing the blade of the shovel under a heap of snow, lifting it, and tossing it off to one side. All these are *structural* properties; the properties of the person as a whole (standing upright, weighing 150 pounds, shoveling snow) consist of properties of, and relations between, various parts of the person, in relation to the surrounding environment. But now consider my thinking to myself the thought that "Non-reductive physicalism is not adequate as a theory of the mind." How are we to analyze the structure of this event, in

---

9   See my "Do My Quarks Enjoy Beethoven?," forthcoming.
10   See Timothy O'Connor and Jonathan D. Jacobs, "Emergent Individuals," *The Philosophical Quarterly*, vol. 53, no. 213 (October 2003), p. 541.

a way paralleling the other examples? Which parts of me are relevant, and what are those parts doing? Without doubt it is true that, when I am thinking this thought, certain neurons in my brain are firing in a particular pattern. But in which of these events does my thinking that thought *consist*? Certainly no one of my neurons is thinking that entire thought. Perhaps we could divide the thought into bits of some sort, and assign each of the bits to one neuron. But doing this would not, it seems, bring us any closer to our goal. We would then have many different neurons, each entertaining some tiny fragment of the thought, but we would still have no insight at all into whatever it is that *thinks the entire thought*, "Non-reductive materialism is an inadequate theory." What we need is a *single thing* that grasps and affirms that thought—and as yet, nothing of the sort has come into our view. Three centuries ago, the philosopher Leibniz wrote,

> *In imagining that there is a machine whose construction would enable it to think, to sense, and to have perception, one could conceive it enlarged while retaining the same proportions, so that one could enter into it, just like into a windmill. Supposing this, one should, when visiting within it, find only parts pushing one another, and never anything by which to explain a perception. Thus it is in the simple substance, and not in the composite or in the machine, that one must look for perception.*[11]

It is a mistake to suppose that the problem arises because of the limitations of Leibniz's science. If we find his "parts pushing one another" implausible as the vehicle of thoughts, how would replacing those parts with silicon chips, or with neurons, make things any better? The problem does not lie in the pushes and pulls but rather in the *complexity* of the machine, the fact that it is made up of many distinct parts, coupled with the fact that *a complex state of consciousness cannot exist distributed among the parts of a complex object.* The payoff of the argument comes in its final sentence: "it is in the simple substance, and not in the composite or in the machine, that one must look for perception." This is the unity-of-consciousness argument, and it poses a serious problem for views which, like the EMP theory, affirm that human beings are composed of physical stuff and nothing else. What is sometimes said in response is that the subject of experience is the "person as a whole"—that is, the body as a whole. But if this is intended as an answer to the unity-of-consciousness argument it is simply an evasion. The body as a whole, on this view, consists ultimately of those microphysical particles and nothing more. To say that there is something going on here—something done *by that body*—which can't be accounted for by anything done by those particles, either individually or in their interrelationships, verges on incoherence. To repeat: there is (by hypothesis) nothing there to do anything, *except* for those very same particles.[12]

These considerations have prompted yet another answer to the question, "What emerges?" What emerges, on this third view, is not merely mental properties and experiences, and not merely new causal powers, but a *new individual*, a *subject* that *has* those experiences and *exercises* the causal powers in question. In view of the considerations explored in the last paragraph, this new individual *is not composed* of the elementary particles of physics—otherwise, the argument would get started all over again, with the same result as before. So the new individual is an *emergent immaterial entity*, an "emergent self" which *as an undivided whole* undergoes conscious experiences of various kinds, acquires knowledge of itself and the world in which it lives, and carries out actions which serve (or are intended

---

[11] Gottfried Wilhelm Leibniz, *Monadology*, in Nicholas Rescher, *G.W. Leibniz's* Monadology: *An Edition for Students* (Pittsburgh: University of Pittsburgh Press, 1991), par. 19.

[12] For more on the unity-of-consciousness argument, see *The Emergent Self*, pp. 122–46; also, "Do My Quarks Enjoy Beethoven?"

to serves) its ends and desires. By now this new individual is beginning to sound quite a bit like the soul posited by creationist versions of dualism; there are, however, some important differences. The emergent self is generated by the organic body through a natural process, rather than being inserted into the body from outside. It is also sustained in its continuing existence by the body and brain, and both its powers and its activities are intimately related to and dependent on the condition and functioning of the brain. And unlike most versions of creationist dualism, the emergent self is located in space: it exists in the region occupied by the brain and nervous system by which it is generated. Nevertheless, in spite of these differences the postulation of such a soul makes this view a version of dualism; indeed of substance dualism and not of mere property dualism. Hence the name given to the view: *emergent dualism*.[13]

It was mentioned above that the EMP theory may run into theological difficulties. Now, great care is needed when one undertakes to criticize philosophical theories of the person on the basis of the biblical text. It can't be emphasized too strongly that the Bible *does not have* a developed philosophical theory of the human person; this is an area in which proof-texting is very much out of place. But if scriptural passages consistently, and over a broad range of texts, seem to imply something about the human person that is contradicted by a philosophical theory of the person, this raises legitimate questions. There is reason to think that the New Testament consistently assumes that human beings are able to persist, without an ordinary physical body, between a person's death and the final bodily resurrection, something that would be impossible if humans consist entirely of ordinary matter.[14] A more crucial question, however, is raised by the very concept of resurrection. Clearly, there is no difficulty in the thought that God is able to craft a "resurrection body" that is as similar as one might wish to the body of a person that has perished, and to do so either out of the very same matter (to the extent that it is still available) or out of new matter. But if this is done, what makes it the case that the person thus constituted is *the very same individual* that previously perished? On the face of it, when a person, consisting solely of ordinary matter, dies, and her body decomposes (part of the matter perhaps being incorporated into other bodies or even annihilated in a nuclear explosion)—when that happens, that person ceases to exist, and any similar person subsequently created would be a new individual. Appeals to divine omnipotence at this point are of no use; before we can appeal to God's power to accomplish a task, it must be established that the task in question can be described in a way that is logically coherent; otherwise, we are saying God can do something nonsensical. Now, this remains an area of major controversy, and we can't go into the details here. However, there is reason to think that all of the solutions to this problem proposed by Christian materialists are unsuccessful; that at least is my own view of the matter. If so, then views in which human persons are wholly material beings are simply unacceptable for the purposes of Christian theology.[15]

Emergent dualism, on the other hand, suffers from no such objection. As is the case for creationist versions of dualism, the identity of the person is guaranteed by the soul, which persists after bodily death and is invested in a transformed, glorious body in the resurrection.

---

[13] For more on emergent dualism, see *The Emergent Self*, pp. 171–203.

[14] See John W. Cooper, *Body, Soul, and Life Everlasting: Biblical Anthropology and the Monism-Dualism Debate*, 2nd ed. (Grand Rapids: Eerdmans, 2000); also John W. Cooper, "Exaggerated Rumors of Dualism's Demise: A Review Essay on Body, Soul, and Human Life," *Philosophia Christi* 11:2 (2009), pp. 452–64.

[15] *The Emergent Self*, pp. 204–35; for a more recent discussion, see my "Materialism and the Resurrection: Are the Prospects Improving?," *European Journal for the Philosophy of Religion* 3:1 (Spring 2011), pp. 83–103.

To be sure, special divine assistance may be needed to sustain the soul during the interval when it lacks its ordinary support from the body. (Something similar to this is needed also by creationists: creationist views generally imply that the soul is dependent on the body in some respects (e.g., sensory capacity and memory) that are essential to its normal function.) But the problem of the identity of the resurrected person with the individual who previously lived, a problem which is extremely difficult for physicalist views, simply does not exist for emergent dualism.

It has been argued that emergentist views are preferable to both reductionist and creationist views of the human person, and further that of the available emergentist views emergent dualism is the most satisfactory, from both a philosophical and a theological point of view. The reader is invited to consider this option carefully, investigating both its merits and its challenges, and comparing it with its leading competitors, which I take to be creationist dualism and the theory of emergent material persons. It may be that you, too, will come to love it.

To be sure, special divine assistance may be needed to sustain the soul during the interval when it lacks its ordinary support from the body. (Something similar to this is needed also by creationists.) Creationists generally view simply that the soul is dependent on the body in some respects (e.g. sensory capacity and memory) that are essential to its normal function.) But the problem of the identity of the resurrected person with the individual who previously lived, a problem which is extremely difficult for physicalist views, simply does not exist for emergent dualism.

It has been argued that emergentist views are preferable to both reductionist and creationist views of the human person, and further that of the available emergentist views emergent dualism is the most satisfactory, from both a philosophical and a theological point of view. The reader is invited to consider this opinion critically, investigating both its merits and its challenges, and comparing it with its leading competitors, which I take to be creationist dualism and the theory of emergent material persons. It may be that you, too, will come to love it.

PART IV
Theological Models of the *Imago Dei*

A Substantive (Soul) Model of the
Imago Dei: A Rich Property View

Joshua R. Farris

Kathryn Tanner contributes a thoughtful Christological view of the "image of God" where humans become an image through participation in Christ (as the archetype where we are the ectype), which I call a Christ-participatory view.[1] As such, she offers a defensible, yet open to question Christological reading of the Creation narrative of the "image" (instead of humans imaging God or Trinity; Christ is the image). In this way, she posits a view that is strikingly in contrast with a view characteristically described as a substantive view, a natural "image," and an intrinsic image.[2] My goal is to constructively compare and contrast Tanner's *imago* view with a view that is more in line with "western" and Augustinian (used as a term of art) intuitions and is more in keeping with a plausible account of scripture.[3] Justification for this aligning with an Augustinian tradition finds support in Augustine's referring to the soul (and all its features) as an "image" of God.[4] By interacting with Tanner, I hope to show that one can affirm a view in line with a substance view that is able to accommodate Tanner's concerns and incorporate some of the insights from Tanner's external Christ-participatory view. In order to do this, I suggest a more finely grained account of a substantive view is required with the use of intrinsic teleology.[5] In this chapter, I argue that both views satisfy contemporary theological desiderata for the "image" from creation, Christology, and teleology. However, I suggest that the substance view I advance is superior in its accounting

---

[1]   See Kathryn Tanner, *Christ the Key* (Cambridge, UK: Cambridge University Press, 2010). Image often refers to the King and his subjects in the Ancient Near East, which serves as part of the historical context for the Genesis narrative.

[2]   There are two good philosophical reasons for affirming a natural/substance view of the image of God from the stability of dignity and natural knowledge of God.

[3]   By western, or Latin, I mean to affirm a view that gives priority to human psychology, interprets the "our" in the Creation narrative (i.e. Genesis 1) as a reference to the trinity, and gives some priority to nature as the ground of grace.

[4]   See Augustine (*On the Holy Trinity*, 14.4 in Nicene and Post-Nicene Fathers, vol. 3). While he does refer to the capacity of reason he also refers to the "immortal substance." Augustine is commonly known as one who uses the "mind" as substance as an image of the Divine, not simply conscious phenomenological states (as with John Locke). For a useful historical defense see Stephen Menn, *Descartes and Augustine* (Cambridge, UK: Cambridge University Press, 1998), chapter 4. Also see David Meconi S.J., *Augustine: Augustinian Theology of Deification* (Pennsylvania: CUA Press, 2013), chapter 1.

[5]   Something like this understanding of individual souls has been called a "soupy metaphysics" by Russell. See Howard Robinson, "Substance Dualism and its Rationale," in *Free Will and Modern Science*, ed. Richard Swinburne (Oxford: OUP, 2011), 172. By teleology I mean to suggest that substances are goal-oriented by nature such that the nature of the thing functions according to purposive laws and has passive and active liabilities.

for the Creational data from scripture, providing a stable ground for personal identity and the "image," and providing a ground for making sense of teleological union with Christ.

On the substance view I advance, individual human souls are the "image" necessarily and essentially,[6] yet have other accidental and telic properties that are actualized in an appropriate dynamic structural context.[7] I suggest that the "image" is a rich property of the human soul (this kind of property is synonymous with the human soul as substance where the primary referent is the soul and the property it carries along). This particular property is a unique property or set of properties that each human soul bears essentially and necessarily.[8] In order to contrast the views and show how my view has some advantages, I proceed in the following way.[9] First, I define and situate the views. Second, I illustrate both views and show that analogies are intended to illuminate a metaphysical story, but on Tanner's Christ-participatory view it is difficult to see how this is the case. Third, I argue that my substance view provides a more promising ground for scripture. Fourth, I suggest that the substance view here provides a stable and enduring ground for persons and the image. Finally, I conclude with some summary thoughts on how the substance view incorporates Tanner's insights.

In the course of the chapter, I contrast Tanner with the Augustinian (as a term of art) view I put forward as more satisfying (potentially superior), yet before I do I must situate the discussion in its historical and contemporary setting—albeit briefly.

Situating the *"Imago"* in the Contemporary Discussion

Marc Cortez has recently offered a set of desiderata for the image of God that is largely accepted by most in the contemporary literature. For my purposes here, I mention these characteristics of the "image" for the purpose of facilitating the discussion between Tanner's Christ-participatory view and the Augustinian substance view I put forward. In summary, the image of God (1) reflects God in creation, (2) image and "likeness" are mostly

---

[6]   Tanner does not affirm that souls are images in themselves, but she gives a much greater place to the body. She seems to be working with a variation of hylomorphism as a model of anthropology as she states on p. 50, but it is not entirely clear. See Kathryn Tanner, *Christ the Key* (Cambridge: Cambridge University Press, 2010), 50–53. She is critical of any sort of dualism, which I am working with here in my understanding of the *imago Dei*.

[7]   On a Cartesian model of anthropology (which I am working with as a kind of term of art; where this variation of Cartesianism (not strictly identical to what Descartes states) is more robust and has the resources to accommodate biological evolutionary concerns), human nature can be a reference specifically to the soul or the soul in relation to a body. In this case, I am working with the latter, however one might be able to work something similar out on the former. With reference to dynamic structural contexts it is important to note on this theory of the *"imago Dei"* that relational contexts (in which case relations are not rock bottom) become not only important but causally necessary for human flourishing. One might object that this creates problems in light of the "intermediate state," but I am not certain that it does.

[8]   Without making a sharp ontological distinction between "image" and "likeness" and stressing the scriptural terms too far, this allows for the conceptual and/or modal distinction between man as a stative reflection or similar being to God and his coming to be more like God. According to Meconi, Augustine makes a distinction between "image," "likeness," and "equality." Furthermore, Augustine says that human souls bear the "image" and that "likeness" is predicable of "image," but other creatures could bear likeness yet not the image. Additionally, while humans bear the image they are not equals with God. See Meconi, *The One Christ*, 37.

[9]   This will require an article in itself where I explore the relationship of the "imago Dei" to transformational views.

synonymous, (3) the "image" includes all humans, (4) sin affects the "image," (5) the "image" is Christological in nature, (6) the "image" is teleological in nature.[10] In his discussion of the main contenders, Cortez lists the structural "image," the functional "image," the relational "image," and the multifaceted "image." In brief, the structural image is that view where the image is identified with a particular facet or capacity(s) in man (e.g. free-will, rationality, conscience). The functional image, which is commonly affirmed among biblical scholars today, is that view which identifies the "image" with human "doings" or "activity," not with structural capacities. The relational image, commonly accepted among systematic theologians since Barth, is the view that human images are identified with "relations" where humans are essentially and fundamentally related to God and other beings. Finally, the multi-faceted view is that view which identifies the structural, functional, and relational views or some combination with the "image." All four views have their strengths and weaknesses, and my purpose is not to criticize them but to put forward two views that have some similarities to the views mentioned by Cortez, yet are distinct in that they are holistic referring to all aspects of man as an image bearer—albeit in a different way.[11] Both Tanner's view and the substantive view adequately account for the above-mentioned desiderata (e.g. being reflections of God in creation, Christological, teleological etc.). Specifically, I am interested in contrasting the views in light of the "image" as a reflection of God at creation, as Christological, and as teleological.

Describing the Two Views

Tanner describes the "Image" as that which is Christ (cf. Romans 8:29–30 and 2 Cor. 4:4 where believers image Christ, which seems to be support for Tanner's view, but I situate this as a building upon the creational image).[12] It is only by having a relationship in Christ's life that humans become images.[13] This is a view often associated with the Patristic fathers and, supposedly, strongly characteristic of Eastern Orthodox developments of the "Image" (namely, Christ = Image while humans are in process as images). In this way, humans are in the Image or take on properties according to the Image only in virtue of this relational participation in the Logos. In one sense, humans never truly become an image and do not begin as an "image"—except externally in the sense that there is nothing in the respective individual nature that bears this image or is this image—but they may come to resemble the Image. However, even the resembling of the Image is a manner not proper to one's nature, and neither is it internal.[14] Humans externally reflect the Image thereby becoming images as a property on a sliding scale. Thus, humans are images through exterior illumination where humans glow with the light of another.[15] Tanner explains the notion that humans are images in terms of Divine presence, which shapes human nature,

---

[10]   See Marc Cortez, *Theological Anthropology: A Guide for the Perplexed* (London: T. & T. Clark, 2010), 16–17.

[11]   It is arguable that both relational and functional views require relata, and presume ontological commitments.

[12]   Kathryn Tanner, *Christ the Key* (Cambridge: Cambridge University Press, 2010), 4, 5, and explicitly 13.

[13]   Ibid., 2 and 8.

[14]   Ibid., 15.

[15]   Ibid., 15.

Karadou

> By attaching ourselves to the incomprehensible that has attached itself to us in becoming incarnate for this very purpose, we become in the strongest sense incomprehensible ourselves. One with Christ, incomprehensible in his divinity, we take on the very incomprehensibility of the divine rather than simply running after it, working to reproduce it in human terms.[16]

Only through attachment to the Divine and continuous illumination will humans bear the Divine light as images. Thus, on Tanner's view there is not a substance or property that is the primary reference for the image. Neither is there a unique "natural" image relevant to human beings. Thus, *prima facie*, Tanner's view seems to satisfy the desiderata listed above in that it satisfies both criteria of being teleological and Christological. In fact, she is explicit about the fact that "image" is directed toward man's eschatological completion via union with Christ such that Christ is *the* Image of God in the truest sense of the term. Her view also has a place for the "image" at creation, yet, as I state above, Tanner holds that humans are not truly "images" apart from participation. The difficulty is that the Tanner view has no explicit metaphysical entity in terms of the creational "image," as found in substance and structural views. Neither does it give a sufficient role to the capacities making the process of "imaging" possible, thus making the position seemingly vacuous. On these grounds, it seems there is room for arguing that Tanner's view could give more attention to the capacities, means, and the ground for humanity's imaging the Divine.

Tanner's view

Augustinian view

In contrast, a western or Augustinian view has a place for a natural (e.g. internal and real) substance view of the image that truly refers to individual human substances.[17] By saying this, I mean to affirm the notion of a stable thing that truly images God in both administrations (by which I mean to convey God's dealings with people in the covenants) found in the Old and New Testaments. On this view, one can accurately describe the image as truly referring to individual human beings in contrast to something we know not what. In this way, it is accurate to say that an individual human is an "image." Similar to Tanner's view, this view has a robust place for Christ as the Image. Yet, one can hold to Christ as the Image in two distinct senses. First, Christ in his humanity is properly an image in the perfected and full sense of the term. Christ in his humanity is the exemplar for humanity and becomes the paradigm for humanity.[18] Additionally, he is the first "image" to fully and completely exemplify what it means to be human (Rom. 8:29–30; 2 Cor. 4:4). This is important to note because all humans bear the "image," but they do not bear this fully and completely (again human souls bear a rich property). Second, one can hold to a distinct view of the Image in virtue of Christ's divinity as the "perfect" representation of God to humans (Colossians 1:15). In this way, humans only come to exemplify this "image" through their redemptive union to the Logos via his humanity. This I explain further when contrasting Tanner's use of scripture with the view I advance. Similar to *imago* views highlighting specified capacities, I suggest that this view or some similar view can highlight the "image"

---

[16]   Ibid., 57. Leading up to this, Tanner develops her anthropology as open-ended, indeterminate, unlimited, and unbounded needing the filling of Divine energy (see 38–57). In the quote above, we see Tanner's apophatic theology and anthropology, which is distinct from Augustine's view that humans bear a determinate structure.

[17]   Tanner explicitly distinguishes her view from a more western/Augustinian view, see Tanner, 3 and 5. Whether this is historically accurate is not the issue I am concerned with nor do I wish to enter into the various interpretive difficulties on Augustine, other Western Fathers or Roman Catholic views in general. What I have stated regarding Augustine is purely for motivating a description.

[18]   *Christ The Key*, 14, 17, and 35.

as these capacities/properties are united to a substance.[19] Thus, one can stave off objections from isolated capacities.[20] One can have a holistic view that incorporates all aspects of humans via a rich property. Through the course of this chapter, I work with a particular model of anthropology known as compound substance dualism. By this, I mean to convey the idea that persons are soul-substances that are pluri-potent, referring to a single simple entity that gives rise to a plurality of properties and powers. Yet, souls as substances are able to exist and function in compound dynamic structures wherein the soul's properties and powers actualize teleologically in particular contexts and dynamic structures. I suppose that some similar model of anthropology could be developed along similar lines with some minor adjustments, *mutatis mutandis*.[21]

Historically Situating the Two Views

Tanner convincingly shows that her view is comfortably situated in patristic thinking on the "image." Furthermore, Tanner's view is recognized as a view that is largely patristic in its characterization. For the purposes of gaining a better understanding of Tanner's view to the patristic literature, I refer the reader to her writings on the matter.

As to an Augustinian view I posit there is some contemporary support and it is comfortably situated in the Medieval and Reformation literature. One contemporary defender of a similar view highlights the fact that the "image" is not primarily a reference to a function or a relation but to a substance of a natural kind. J.P. Moreland in his recent book *The Recalcitrant Imago Dei* posits not a structural view of the image but a kind of substantive view. Distinct from offering a view identifying the "image" with one faculty or an isolated property (or properties) (i.e. the structural approach), Moreland identifies the "image" with a kind of being (namely a "soul" or "human soul") that bears a set of properties/features including consciousness, free will, self, and intrinsic value, which underlies human relations and functions.[22] I suggest that this view is a variation of a substance/substantive view similar to an Augustinian view advanced here and both views find traction in the tradition of the Church. It ought to be unsurprising that Protestant Reformed literature shares much

---

[19] The underlying ontology I am assuming is a substance-property ontology that undergirds powers, events and relations. This has often been referred to as the traditional account in contrast to relational ontologies, event ontologies, or powers ontology. See R. Harre and E.H. Madden, *Causal Powers* (Basil: Blackwell Publishing, 1975); Brian Ellis, *Scientific Essentialism* (Cambridge: Cambridge University Press, 2001); Richard Swinburne, *Mind, Brain, and Free Will* (Oxford, UK: OUP, 2013), chapter 1. Also see E.J. Lowe, *Personal Agency* (Oxford, UK: OUP, 2008), see especially the introduction and chapter 1.

[20] *Christ the Key*, 1.

[21] Other models that one could draw from would include composite variations of substance dualism or hylomorphism.

[22] See J.P. Moreland, *The Recalcitrant Imago Dei: Human Persons and the Failure of Naturalism* (London, UK: SCM Press, 2009), 4–5. A common objection to substantive or structural views is that one must isolate and pick a faculty or quality as the distinguishing mark, but on a substance view (as I am construing it) that falls under kinds this is not necessarily the case. While the most immediate properties of various capacities are the most likely candidates for the "image" because they provide the means and are presupposed in relations, the "image" is not limited to them. Furthermore, one advantage a substance view might have over a "structural" view is that on a "structural" view where one quality is chosen you might argue that that quality is possessed to varying degrees, but with substance views there is a fact to the matter. In his useful article on the image of God, Aku Visala develops a structural view in contrast to a substance view. See his "*Imago Dei*, Dualism, and Evolution—A Philosophical Defense of the Structural Image of God," Zygon, *Journal of Religion and Science*, 49(1), March 2014.

with Augustinian thinking. The *imago Dei* view advanced here is commensurate with the Medievals, Roman Catholicism, and much Reformed Scholasticism. Thomas Aquinas, for example, in line with Augustine, argues that man is an "image of God" at creation, post-fall, and post-redemption in terms of the soul. His distinction between Christ as an image and man as an image has to do with the former being a perfect "image" and the latter an imperfect "image" in contrast to Tanner's distinction of a "weak" and "strong" image, which I discuss below.[23] The Reformers commonly referred to the creational and/or natural "image" as a reference to human beings as a whole. Some highlighted "rationality" and others highlighted the soul as substance in keeping with Calvin's view that the "proper seat" of the image is to be found in the soul and its powers.[24]

Illustrating Both Views

Tanner illustrates her view with the use of a mirror whereby humans become the "image" through reflecting Christ's image.[25] Tanner explains,

> Although showing off the light of the divine image itself—and in that sense good images of God themselves—they would always be doing so only by exterior illumination, by glowing with a light that remains another's, and not by some phosphorescent assimilation of that light into their own nature as an acquired created property. The human "becomes pure and luminous in contact with the true supernal purity; in such an atmosphere it even itself emits light, and is so filled with the radiance, that it becomes itself a light ... We see this even here, in the case of a mirror, or a sheet of water, or any smooth surface that can reflect the light; when they receive the sunbeam they beam themselves.[26]

In keeping with the worry above, the mirror analogy must have a particular set of properties and faculties to perform the reflective function. It may also be accurate to identify Tanner's understanding of the human "image" as a piece of glass where the light of the son shines through the glass to all the various parts of human nature, yet also shining outward beyond the individual. However, it is my intuition, along with others broadly aligning with

---

[23] See Thomas Aquinas, *The Basic Writings of St. Thomas Aquinas*, trans by A. Pegis, 2 vols, Pontifical Institute of Mediaeval Studies (New York: Random House, 1945). See ST I.93.1 ad2 and 93.2 ad1. Aquinas affirms that the natural creation is preserved and perfected by grace. "Grace does not do away with nature, but brings it to perfection" (ST I.1.8 ad2).

[24] John Calvin, *Institutes of the Christian Religion*, ed. John T. McNeill, trans. Ford L. Battles (Louisville: Westminster John Knox Press, 1960), 1.15.2, 3. "Editor's Introduction," in William Ames, *The Marrow of Theology* (Grand Rapids, Baker Books, 1968), 11. *Westminster Confession of Faith*, in *Reformed Confessions Harmonized*, ed. Joel R. Beeke and Sinclair B. Ferguson (Grand Rapids: Baker Books 1999), 39. Others that follow a Calvinian view including William Ames, Westminster divines, Francis Turretin, and Peter van Mastricht. It is not accurate to portray Calvin's view as isolating one property or faculty at the exclusion of others. In fact, Calvin was holistic wherein he included the body in the image (albeit contingently). A proponent of compound substance dualism can include the body because the soul bears first-order properties that are actualized in the context of embodiment. Additionally in the above section of the Institutes, Calvin had a place for man as an image in relation to Christ.

[25] Tanner, 15. She explicitly uses the examples of a mirror and a clear body of water that reflects light to illustrate her view on the image.

[26] See Tanner, 15. She also cites Gregory of Nyssa, "On Virginity," 336.

Augustinian intuitions, that humans have being and "image" God intrinsically. I liken the human soul as an "image" to a light bulb.

I like to think of the human soul's relationship to other particulars in terms of a light bulb. Light bulbs serve to highlight the teleological and Christological aspects of a substantive view. Light bulbs have several features and give rise to specified properties analogous to souls. A light bulb exists as a substantial entity. Light bulbs are the kinds of entities that function in a dynamic structure of energy transfer to the light bulb. If we use the example of an incandescent light bulb that is electric, then light is produced by an electric current passing through a filament wire that is raised to a high temperature. Certainly there are various specifications and limitations to light bulbs. Yet, the light bulb holds some promise as an analogy for the soul as an "image." First, both are substances existing with specified properties and powers. Second, both substances you might say are goal-oriented. The purpose of the light bulb is to shine light and the purpose of the human soul is to shine forth God's light (i.e. a metaphor for glory). Third, both exist in a dynamic structure of inputs and outputs. Light bulbs require an energy source, namely a socket. The energy source gives power to the light bulb as it is connected via the socket and transferred through a wire. Analogously, human souls (construed as souls with aptness for bodies) depend in some functional and phenomenological sense on bodies and other persons through which they have appropriate mental and volitional functioning.[27] Fourth, both light bulbs and souls have greater potential in a larger compound structure. For example, light bulbs that are united in an overall compound structure with other light bulbs will give off greater light and heat. One might argue that bulbs have no light or heat without being placed in sockets, and this may be the weakness with the analogy. Human souls have greater teleological capacities in a relational dynamic with other human souls. While glory is closely related to the "image," glory is greater in conjunction with other human souls. The situation with several light bulbs giving off greater light is analogous to a communion of the saints where perfect unity occurs in Christ's body in eschatological glory. Fifth, and finally, both the light bulb and human souls have the potential for something greater than their standard properties. It is conceivable that light bulbs could be re-structured for greater wattage. Analogously, human souls that are changed by the interior work of the Holy Spirit have potential for that which is beyond their original capacities. As such, both the light bulb and the human soul require and depend upon an external cause for the "greater wattage."

While both the analogies for the Christ-participatory view and the "substance" view have strengths and weaknesses,[28] they do serve to highlight important aspects of the desiderata mentioned above. The Christ-participatory view analogy highlights the nature of humans as teleological and requiring the light of Christ. The weakness of the analogy, which is also a potential weakness of the view in general, is that the mirror analogy requires certain specified properties and capacities to accomplish the reflective function. On the analogy of the "substance" view, the weakness is in showing a relationship between the soul's fundamental capacity (as a metaphysical simple that gives rise to powers and relations) and the light bulb's initial capacity. The strength of the analogy is in highlighting how it is that a substance could have teleological properties. The light bulb gives us some conceptual grasp on how an entity can come to be both goal-oriented and related to another concrete particular as a source of power and as an entity that the bulb's light participates in. While all analogies break down at some level, there is an advantage with the light bulb analogy for the substance view. As it goes, analogies are used for highlighting and illuminating the

---

[27] See Richard Swinburne, *The Evolution of the Soul* (Oxford: OUP, 1997), see the latter of chapter 15.

[28] Thanks to Marc Cortez for helping clarify the weaknesses of the analogies.

truth of a theological position. The light bulb in this instance illuminates the substance view of the "image" because there is a metaphysical story standing behind the analogy. However, it is difficult to see how the mirror analogy illuminates Tanner's view because it lacks a clear metaphysical story of what human persons and the image are by nature. In order to do this, Tanner's view requires further elaboration in terms of a substance (e.g. hylomorphic), a property, or a power (e.g. the will). Next, there is a second way in which the "substance" view with intrinsic teleology surpasses the Christo-participatory view in how it accounts for the scripture's narration of the creational and teleological "image."

Tanner's View and Use of Scripture

Tanner's Interpretation of the Creational *Imago*

Tanner's treatment of the Creation narrative (e.g. Genesis 1:26–7), in keeping with what she sees as the dominant patristic reading, is to make much of the fact that we were not made as images of God, but "in" or "according to" the image/Image.[29] The Image that is primarily referenced here is Christ. She offers support for this interpretation by suggesting that Christ is referred to as the "image" cosmically referenced in the NT (cf. Col. 1:15–21). By contrast, Augustinian views have seen Genesis as primarily referencing humanity. Support in favor of the latter is two-fold. First, there may be exegetical evidence supporting the primary reference to humanity. Arguably, the creation narrative reaches its penultimate climax in the creation of humanity. When reading the creation narrative it seems that God reaches the pinnacle of his creation when he creates humans as images of the Divine, highlighting the product not process. In addition, this historically makes sense in light of "images" in the Ancient Near East as referencing Kings or Divine entities. Theologically, then, human beings are the "images" of God and come to bear properties representing God (i.e. functionally). As representatives, humans have an important typological function according to scripture that finds fulfillment in Christ the archetype. Second, when we consider other passages in the OT and NT it is important that we see finer distinctions than simply Christ as the image identical to all images found in scripture. Tanner's use of scripture in this instance of the creation narrative is an instance of theological interpretation, as is what I have offered here, but the problem with Tanner's interpretation is that she seems to short-circuit (no pun intended) the process of theological interpretation by not sufficiently taking into account the literal and historical lens by which to constructively read this passage. Finally, I propose that Tanner's reading of scripture might not pay sufficient attention to the details of the scripture's differing "images," wherein it seems to affirm a distinctive *"imago Dei"* category to humans in creation in contrast with a salvific or redemptive category concerning Christ.

Tanner's Omission of Relevant Scripture's Pointing to a Creational/Natural Substantive View

Consider Genesis 9:6, "Whoever sheds man's blood, By man his blood shall be shed, For in the image of God He made man" (NAS). 1 Corinthians 11:7, "For a man indeed ought not to have his head veiled, forasmuch as he is the image and glory of God: but the woman is the

---

[29] Ibid., 4.

glory of the man" (NAS). James 3:9, "Therewith bless we God, even the Father; and therewith curse we men, which are made after the similitude of God" (KJV). Again, I take the terms "image" and "likeness" as almost synonymous. While it may be generally true to say that all of creation has a likeness to God it seems that James is saying something specific and unique about human creatures. In this passage we have an example where humans are created in the image of God. Significant for my purposes here, the author uses the word *ginomai* as a perfect participle, which signifies the notion of an action that is past tense with abiding result.[30] Herein we see a link between humans in the OT and the NT. New Testament and patristics scholar Ben Blackwell has rightly referred to NT passages as creational "images" and others as telic "images" where humans are rightly ordered toward Christ. He says, "In Paul, image language can refer to a creational cosmology (1 Cor. 11:1–7), but more often it refers to the telos of humanity as believers are conformed to or transformed into the image of Christ."[31] Unfortunately, Tanner does not constructively appropriate these passages into a systematic whole. If we are to take 1 Corinthians 11:7 and James 3:9 seriously, then we would with Aquinas and Calvin see the "image" as a *leitmotiv* between the OT and the NT where humans are central to God's redemptive plans and purposes. It is not uncommon for contemporary theologians to either omit a discussion of these passages or dismiss them, as it were, with the wave of a hand. For example one recent theologian interprets the 1 Corinthians and James passages as Paul's making a statement "in passing," and thus by implication they deserve no serious constructive attention.[32] However, by taking these passages seriously and constructively reading them with the OT and other theological tools it seems sensible to say that the image finds its reference to humans; this image is a feature or property of all humans, and immutably persists during all periods of Divine administration. Certainly Tanner, or a proponent of a similar view, might respond and argue that because humans are created to reflect Christ's image they receive the universal benefits across Divine administrations. Thus she and others might interpret these two passages along Christ-participatory lines. One difficulty for this view is common to most relational ontologies from degrees. On these relational and participatory ontologies, it still seems that the image is predicable upon the degree to which humans relate to the Divine, and they relate to the Divine via the incarnate Logos. Hence benefits still appear to be as a property on a sliding scale. As such, interpreting the 1 Cor. and James passages along Christ-participatory lines seems to mitigate against the absolute nature in which the authors identify humans as images. Tanner, along with others (e.g. many in the East), may be willing to affirm the consequence that humans do not immutably persist as images of the Divine.

---

[30] See Anthony A. Hoekema, *Created in God's Image* (Grand Rapids, Michigan: Eerdmans, 1986), 18.

[31] See Ben C. Blackwell, *Christosis: Pauline Soteriology in Light of Deification in Irenaeus and Cyril of Alexandria* (Tubingen, Germany: Mohr Siebeck, 2011), 256. Blackwell does not mention James 3:9 specifically in this context, however it seems clear that this passage would be an explicit reference to the "image" found in the creation narrative. The appropriate translation of James is often "likeness" or similarity, but I see these terms as nearly synonymous with "image." In footnote 8 on p. 256. However, I realize one could read this from the perspective of Christological-participatory view. Blackwell, for example, would read the creational image from the perspective of the end of humanity, and I would read this creational image from the perspective of creation looking forward.

[32] See Ian A. McFarland, *The Divine Image: Envisioning the Invisible God* (Minneapolis: Fortress Press, 2005), 1. McFarland, in a footnote, offers a brief explanation as to why he does not give the 1 Corinthians passage much weight by stating that it contradicts the creation narrative that includes women in the image, but I am not sure that the passage requires an interpretation of the sort suggested by McFarland.

Tanner's Use of the Image in the New Testament

There are a variety of NT passages referring to an image which Tanner takes as clear references to the *imago Dei* of the OT. If Tanner is correct, then all OT references are primarily and ultimately references to Jesus Christ the Logos. However, I am not sure this is the case. In fact, a finer distinction that is deserving of attention is that some references to the "image" in the NT are distinctly referring to Christ's divinity. One specific example is Colossians 1:15, "The Son is the image of the invisible God, the firstborn over all creation." While this passage is often identified with the "image of God," I suggest with Gerald Brey that this is a unique title for Christ highlighting his deity, rather than his humanity, as an image.[33] By contrast, in the OT I would suggest that the "image" referenced is normally a reference to the human image for God as a unique title for human beings. There are several indications that this "image" is not identical to the human image of God, because Christ here is imaging the invisible God (v. 15, 16).

Furthermore, Paul delineates other characteristic ascriptions to the image as the fullness of deity (v.19), and he is pre-existent (v. 16). Certainly, I am not suggesting that there isn't any notion of Christ's humanity implicit in this text, but Paul is primarily expounding upon Christ as the "image of the invisible God." What is important to note is that Paul highlights properties of Christ that are not predicable of humans. Furthermore, we see that "believers" are to "put-on" the new self. Thus, believers are to image Christ, but this is a specifically "redemptive" category, which is not to exclude the creational image.[34] Certainly there are overlaps between the creational image and the redeemed image in that human beings persist, but the two are distinct in the language of scripture in that we have creational images and redeemed images. Tanner might read these NT passages as supporting her Christological-participation image, given the NT provides further clarity on the OT or that a canonical reading of the Bible guided by the tradition might lend itself to such an interpretation. I suppose this line is a possibility, but if there are passages that clearly refer to the creational image and others that distinctively refer to Christ and our relationship to Christ, then we seem to have more varied and complex definitions of "image" as doctrinal categories that deserve explanation. Tanner offers an explanation, but it seems to me less than sufficient to adequately account for all the passages of scripture. She offers a two-tiered understanding of the "image."

In the end, both views have a way of organizing the data of scripture concerning humans as images. The Christ-participatory view arranges the data on the "image" solely to Christ as the concrete particular deserving the primary reference of the "image." Contrastively, the "substantive" view organizes the data on the "image" as referring primarily to human beings holistically as they point to Christ. The challenge for the Christ-participatory view is that it either does not affirm or sufficiently highlight the substance or the structural aspects in order to account for scripture's narration on human beings. As shown here, there is some textual evidence to suggest that the creational "image" primarily refers to human beings and that, taken as a whole, the data of scripture can be accounted for in terms of a

---

[33] Gerald Bray, "The Significance of God's Image in Man," *Tyndale Bulletin* 42.2 (Nov. 1991), 195–225.

[34] One could take this in the direction of the Medievals and some Reformers by considering a natural and supernatural distinction, but this would take me too far afield. While I see a transformational account of human beings in scripture narrated for us, I do not see this as necessary given what I have argued here with respect to a rich-property soul view that has telic-properties.

substance view.[35] I suggest that the scriptures narrate a more complex picture of the "image" in terms of a *creational* "image" and *redemptive* "image." While intimately related, the two are distinct in the language of scripture. One refers primarily to human beings and the other refers to humans in relational union with Christ.[36] Finally, there is a third way in which the "substance" view is superior in terms of categorizing the "image" by incorporating the insights of the Christ-participatory view.

Tanner's Two-tiered Understanding of the Image

Tanner's Christ-participatory view has a place for ways of speaking about the "image." She posits that humans image God as weaker and stronger images. By contrast, I suggest that there is something more like three ways to speak about the image, and specifically two ways that seem explicit in scripture.

Tanner offers what she refers to as a weaker image. On the weaker sort of image, Tanner argues that all created things image God in some very attenuated sense by being effects of the Divine cause, which is in some ways similar to an Augustinian view. In the manner that each entity participates in the Divine, so it comes to image God in this weaker sense.[37] Tanner says that humans are unique as a property on a sliding scale by way of having certain capacities that set them apart from other created beings. What is unclear is how to make sense of this as an image when Tanner argues that there is no sense in which created things are Divine or share Divinity nor does she offer a description of what is doing the imaging or representation.[38] Tanner develops a notion of human beings and the "image" in relation to humans that is apophatically driven and characteristically described as unbounded, open, and unformed like "fluid wax needing a seal."[39] Nonetheless, this sort of weak imaging can be easily accommodated on the view I posit here, according to which one takes humans as souls that give rise to a set of specified properties.[40] While this aspect of the Christ-participatory theory can be accommodated, it does not have an explicit place in the narrative flow. Again, while this might be identified with creational images it does not fit the narrative very well because all creatures can come to bear this in virtue of participation, but this does not hold the unique status that humans as image bearers do. Furthermore, the scripture's use of "image" never refers to animals as images (although they may share some resemblance). Instead I suggest with a "substance" view that there are two predominant ways in which scripture narrates the "image." Instead, the creational "image" refers to humans as set apart

---

[35]   One might object by stating that there is no scripture that explicitly supports a substance (or, a structural) view, but this is true of other views. However, if the "image" referring to humans persists through the fall, redemption, and glory, then, some substance, property, or capacity that is internally fixed would sufficiently account for this implicit teaching.

[36]   See Oliver Crisp in this volume, "A Christological Model of the *Imago Dei*." In it, Crisp helpfully highlights the fact that relational views may not be distinct from substance views, instead, they "extend" and "supplement" the entity.

[37]   Kathryn Tanner, *Christ the Key*, 10–12.

[38]   Ibid. 54. How this actually resembles God is unclear, on her view, given her apophatic (i.e. Divine knowledge gained negatively as the contrary of what humans know positively) foundations.

[39]   Ibid. 53–60.

[40]   Tanner could make a Barthian move and say that there is something distinctive about humanity in terms of creation apart from our union with Christ via Divine choice, with no predication of intrinsic value placed on humans as image bearers.

from the rest of creation. While there may be some weak sense in which all of creation reflects God it never receives a unique title.

Tanner also has a place for a stronger image. The stronger images are those images that participate in Christ as the one and only true Image. Humans are unique in that they are created with the Divine intent to participate relationally in the Logos and by this they only come to image the Divine externally. In contrast, I suggest that the Augustinian view here has a strong image whereby human beings as soul-substances bear the image naturally, essentially, and immutably, which forms the base for a substantive view of the image of God. Furthermore, this is a distinctive feature/property of humans, not of all creation.[41] In this way, image-bearers are the building blocks that God works with in his redemptive plan to raise them above what is natural.[42] Having said this, I would like to add one further systematic category to the discussion that resembles Tanner's version of the stronger image in important ways.

I put forward a distinct category that does not exclude the created/natural image, but builds upon it. I refer to this as the *imago Christi.* I suggest that, in keeping with scriptural categories, we add one further doctrinal category that is distinct from the image of God albeit intimately related. The image of Christ is a purely redemptive category that humans only come to instantiate as a gift given by the Holy Spirit working internally in "saints" to bring about a union with the Logos. In this way, this property or set of inter-related properties/powers occurs through union with the Logos as the entrance to theosis, whereas according to Tanner we become images primarily through our participatory union with Christ as the second person of the Trinity. For Tanner then, the process of theosis/deification is the process whereby we come to reflect the "image" or the light given to us. While not mitigating the natural substantive image, this allows for a distinction between a creational image and a redeemed image, according to the categories derived from scripture.[43] Through union we are able to participate in what is not ours by nature, yet this becomes internal to the workings of the *imago* substance. It is only in the context of becoming a part of Christ's body like a compound structure that we can come to bear specified properties/powers. One might argue that this would be implied by nature. As a result, grace would become unnecessary. However, one must keep in mind that this is only passively received and contingent or accidental to nature. Herewith, we have a view beginning to resemble something that both Augustine and Aquinas would affirm. Yet, this is not limited to the Medievals or Roman Catholics. Instead we have something like this in the works of Calvin and many Reformed Scholastics. What is different about this rich-property of substance view is that it highlights aspects of the Medieval and Reformation views that are otherwise subtle, namely the eschatological end of man and the Christological aspect of man's image. In virtue of our

---

[41] This is a common Reformed view where the image refers to the soul primarily, yet also to the body as a functional integrative unity such that the whole of man bears the image. Augustine affirms that human souls are images not simply in the image. See *De Trinitate* 15.7.11 and 15.23.43. For support of this in the secondary literature see Peter Burnell, *The Augustinian Person* (Washington, DC: The Catholic University of America Press, 2005), 187. Also see David Meconi, *The One Christ*, 54. Unlike other Patristics, Augustine affirms that only human souls are images that always carry along a likeness or resemblance, but that which is not an image can bear a likeness.

[42] Not all Reformers hold that the image will be raised higher than man's natural state, but they do all hold that Christ "restores" the image and the soul/body.

[43] Again, how one philosophically parses out the nature of the scriptural categories might be different here, but what seems difficult for a view like Tanner's is that all distinction in "image" seem relegated to Christ. Herein, there is a lack of an account for a clear distinction between human images and the Divine image as Christ. If one were to assume the doctrine of Theosis on the substance view I am positing, one would affirm a transformational account of human beings via redemption.

souls' uniting to Christ's body in conjunction with other souls, we have something greater than created natures. I like to think of this as a compound structure whereby we have a set of light bulbs connected together and united to one source. As a result of this cooperative interaction between the light bulbs a profound brightness emerges. In a similar way, as the saints are united to Christ as the source of light, the saints come to bear other properties, which elevate normal created capacities.

In the end, both views are able to account for the language of scripture regarding the image, but the language is explicit enough so as to make a finer distinction between creational images and redeemed images. I suggest that a "substance" view is able to accommodate both the creational aspects whereby humans are truly referred to as images, and is also able to accommodate the notion of a redeemed image presumably better than the alternative in virtue of the fact that the creational image persists across the narrative and the Christ-image is only had relationally (i.e. contingently). Thus, humans bear the "image" under ordinary conditions, but its manifold expression is only seen under extra-ordinary conditions (i.e. eschatologically).

Substance, Image, and Teleology

While many relational and participatory ontologies exclude substance ontology or place them in the periphery, the view posited here does no such thing.[44] In keeping with much of the Christian tradition (elevating the notion of substance and its properties), the intuition of substance still has a crucial role to play, for example, in distinguishing God from his creation and man from other created entities. First, via a teleological view of substance, it secures the intuitive ground for relations and functions, namely the *relata* that accounts for Divinely designed relations and functionality. Second, it secures the plausibility of accounting for the scriptural data that arguably teach that we have an enduring and immutable entity. Third, like many eschatological or Ecclesiological views, this view has a relationship to the completion of the Divine plan. Like the light bulb that is united with other bulbs connected to one source, souls could contribute to man's (taken as a whole or as one kind) overarching purpose as "one" collective whole. This would be something like a broader view of substance, namely a dynamic compound structure (i.e. the redeemed community).[45]

A helpful analogy for the souls existing in a larger compound structure can be assisted by thinking about the soul–body relationship. Swinburne discusses the goodness of the body as a public region of space for the soul. He lists four things involved in having a body: it provides a public region of basic control, it provides a region for acting and perceiving, it provides a "machine room" for actions and perceptions, and it is a source of desires.[46] In a similar fashion we might say that the body of Christ extends the spatial region by which

---

[44]   It may be that participatory views assume some sort of substance ontology, and see these as distinct issues. This may be, but it is unclear on Tanner's view and on other views whether substance has a place. If a proponent of a Christ-participatory view affirms substance ontology, then the difference between what I have suggested is that the "image" is most fundamentally and necessarily a substantive matter, not an activity.

[45]   See Robert Koons, *Realism Regained* (Oxford: OUP, 2000), 145, 153.

[46]   See Swinburne, "What is So Good about Having a Body?" in *Comparative Theology: Essays for Keith Ward* ed. T.W. Bartel (London, UK: SPCK, 2003), 134. By entering into these new relational contexts, we gain something new that is rooted in the "perichoretic" relation of the Logos in union with human nature such that our natures are re-structured and experience a finite and contingent unity beginning to resemble the Trinity.

we as God's image-bearers can affect and influence the world.[47] In this way, becoming a part of Christ's body involves two distinct additions to creational images. First, by way of linking up with other image-bearers tied to the one who fully bears the image of God, our powers and properties become actualized and strengthened. Human powers are enhanced in these Divinely ordained contexts. Second, in virtue of our unity with Christ as the infinite and perfect image of Divinity, this opens the door to transformational views of persons,[48] similar to the adjusted incandescent light bulb that is situated in a structural context with other light bulbs where its capacity is higher than normal. Through cooperation among the various light bulbs we have not only greater capacity for light, but we have something above and beyond the natural capacity of the light bulb that exceeds the powers of the individual parts—something like novel emergent properties. Thus, a "substance" view of this sort incorporates some of the virtues of the Christ-participatory view, namely, that the image is teleological and Christological.

Conclusion

As the reader can see, there are similarities between Tanner's Christ-participatory view and the substantive view posited here. Proponents of both views have a place for the creational image. Both affirm the teleological nature of man and the fact that man is goal-oriented and both affirm a radically Christological aspect of the image. Having said this there are some dissimilarities. I will first address the benefits of the substance view. Substantive views are holistic in that the image refers to the soul (man's core) essentially and his body contingently. Additionally, it provides a stable ground for personal identity and the image. As a more nuanced accounting of the image, the substantive view seems to offer a more consistent accounting of scripture's varied and complex portrayal of the image. By contrast, there are some challenges with the Christ-participatory view. Tanner's view may be holistic, but it is difficult to tell what humans are by nature or in creation apart from grace. It appears that Tanner must affirm a property, concerning persons and the image, on a sliding scale, which is similar to a common view in the East of Divine Energia as constitutive of man. Furthermore, using sliding scale language seems to be in tension with the language of scripture because the authors of scripture seem to predicate properties to stable substances. A final worry, Tanner stops short of integrating important passages of scripture, which the substance view I advance takes into account quite naturally. Another distinction is that a proponent of a substantive view affirms that humans have an internal structure in contrast to Tanner's notion that persons exist in a state of absolute openness. In the final analysis, both views are able to account for the above-mentioned desiderata (i.e. the creational image, teleological image, and Christological image), yet in positing a variation of the substantive image I have suggested that it is superior with respect to accounting for the notion of creational and telic aspects of the image as narrated by the Christian scriptures.[49]

---

[47] Ibid. Richard Swinburne has something useful in terms of analogy for this view when he discusses the relationship of the soul to the body and the benefits the soul gains via the body.

[48] However, the view here does not entail transformational views, but it is compatible with it. This is the subject of another paper.

[49] Thanks to the participants of the Southwest Region and Annual Evangelical Philosophical Society 2014 where I presented distinct yet overlapping drafts. Thanks to Jonathan Chan for reading an initial draft. Thanks also to Ben Blackwell, Marc Cortez, R.T. Mullins, Charles Taliaferro, and Thomas Carroll Lambert for their helpful comments.

Why the *Imago Dei* Should Not Be Identified with the Soul

Joel B. Green

Traditionally, when the question of human uniqueness is raised in theological discussion, the answer has centered on two theological loci, human creation in the divine image and human possession of a soul.[1] The importance of the soul in this respect is more widely shared, as evidenced, for example, in the mid-twentieth century work of self-proclaimed agnostic-cum-atheist Isaac Asimov, whose book, *I, Robot*, portrayed robots with qualities that others might have reserved for humans. Robbie the robot practices love and kindness, we are told, and his young companion, Gloria, regards Robbie as her friend. Gloria's mother is unimpressed, noting that Robbie is "nothing more than a mess of steel and copper in the form of sheets and wires with electricity"; it lacks humanity for "it has no soul."[2] Readers of scripture want to say more, of course, taking their point of departure from the celebrated if contested phrase, "Let us make humanity in our image" (Genesis 1:27).[3] According to long-held views among Christian theologians, human creation in the divine image is realized in the human possession of a soul, that is, these two theological loci are often reduced to one, with the soul understood as the particular consequence of creation in God's image. Here is proof that humans are unique among God's creatures, and, for many, the basis of theological-ethical views concerning human dignity and the sacredness of human life as well as the necessary ground for the human's capacity to enter into and enjoy a relationship with God.

My argument in this chapter is straightforward. I intend to show that the identification of the human soul with creation in God's image is alien to scripture and, in fact, should be abandoned. My encouragement that theologians abandon this identification is not simply a biblicist move, however. That is, I am under no illusion that Christian theology simply derives from the Bible. Nor do I imagine that those who accept my argument will necessarily take the further step of rejecting outright the need for a metaphysically separate entity other than the body, such as a "soul" or "spirit," to account for human capacities and distinctives. Instead, recognizing that creation in God's image is itself a biblical datum, one that is introduced into theological discussion only because this language appears in Genesis 1 (and only a handful of related texts in the Old and New Testaments), I urge that our thinking about the divine image ought to take its point of departure from scripture.

---

[1]   For two voices that span much of the twentieth century, e.g., cf. H. Wheeler Robinson, *The Christian Doctrine of Man* (3rd edn; Edinburgh: T. & T. Clark, 1926); Paul K. Jewett, *Who We Are: Our Dignity as Human: A Neo-Evangelical Theology* (ed. Marguerite Shuster; Grand Rapids: Eerdmans, 1996).

[2]   Isaac Asimov, *I, Robot* (New York: Doubleday, 1950), 9, 23.

[3]   Unless otherwise indicated, biblical citations follow the Common English Bible.

Since scripture does not associate the *imago Dei* with the human possession of a soul, or otherwise identify the human "self" with the *imago Dei*, theologians should sever the link between the two. What is more, they should accept that attempts to identify God's image with the human soul — and, indeed, to introduce the idea of a human soul into the creation accounts in Genesis — owes far less to scripture itself and far more to the forms of Platonism alive in the early centuries of the Common Era.

God Creates Humanity

For our discussion, the crucial text is Genesis 2:7, which reads in the Authorized Version (1611), "And the LORD God formed man of the dust of the ground, and breathed into his nostrils the breath of life; and man became a living soul." I discuss this assertion in more detail below, but we can begin to get a sense of where study since the 1600s has taken us by referring to more recent translations. For example, the New International Version (1984) reads: "the LORD God formed the man from the dust of the ground and breathed into his nostrils the breath of life, and the man became a living being"; the New Revised Standard Version (1989) reads: "the LORD God formed man from the dust of the ground, and breathed into his nostrils the breath of life; and the man became a living being"; the New American Bible (1991) reads: "the LORD God formed man out of the clay of the ground and blew into his nostrils the breath of life, and so man became a living being"; and the Common English Bible reads: "the LORD God formed the human from the topsoil of the fertile land and blew life's breath into his nostrils. The human came to life." Notice that none of these more recent English translations use the term "soul," thus exemplifying an easily documented trend away from using the term in English translations since the rise of modern biblical studies. Interestingly, according to the eighteenth-century lexicographer Samuel Johnson, during the time of the Authorized Version's production "soul" might refer to "vital principle" or "interior power," or simply "human being." However, the first definition he provides, "the immaterial and immortal spirit of man,"[4] coheres well with the definition found in twenty-first century Oxford Dictionaries, where "soul" is used first in the sense of "the spiritual or immaterial part of a human being or animal, regarded as immortal."[5] Apparently, biblical translators have ceded the term "soul" to popular usage, where it customarily refers to an immaterial, immortal part of a human, while noting that the Hebrew and Greek terms used in the Bible (*nefesh* and ψυχή, respectively) are not very well lexicalized in this way. According to a widespread theological tradition, however, Genesis 1–2 bears witness to the special creation of the human soul as the particular manifestation of human creation in God's image and likeness, with human possession of the soul both distinguishing humanity from the rest of God's creatures and elevating the human to a position of supremacy over

---

[4]   Samuel Jackson, *A Dictionary of the English Language* (Dublin: W.G. Jones, 1768), n.p.

[5]   "Soul," http://oxforddictionaries.com/definition/english/soul?q=soul (accessed 3 December 2013). Interestingly, however, the Oxford English Dictionary lists this sense second, after "an essential principle or attribute of life, and related senses" ("Soul," http://www.oed.com [accessed December 3, 2013]).

creation. A number of early Christian readings of the text follow just such an interpretive path.[6] A closer examination of this text is therefore necessary.[7]

"God formed the human from the topsoil of the fertile land"

Given our present concerns, this phrase is important for two reasons. First, and negatively, the text says nothing about God's forming from the topsoil a human "body" subsequently in need of a human "soul" or "spirit." Rather, God uses the topsoil to form a "human" — in the Hebrew text, 'dm ("a person," "a human"); in the Greek text, ἄνθρωπος ("a human being"). We find here no hint that (only) the physical or material or corporeal "part" of the human being was created from the loose, earthy topsoil, with some additional "part" of as-yet-unknown origins to be added later.

Second, the language our writer uses identifies the human being with the rest of creation; in particular, the text draws attention to the transitory, humble character of human life, which is shared with the rest of God's creatures. Like the human being, "all the wild animals and all the birds in the sky" are "formed from the fertile land" (Genesis 2:19; the same verb ytsr, "to form," appears in vv. 7, 19). The human being is composed of "topsoil" ('pr, traditionally translated as "dust"), a claim repeated in the curse of Genesis 3:19: "By the sweat of your face you will eat bread — until you return to the fertile land, since from it you were taken; you are soil, to the soil you will return." According to the psalmist, all of humanity is composed of the stuff of the earth, and this is cause to reflect on human mortality and fragility: "Because God knows how we're made, God remembers we're just dust" (Psalm 103:14). The phrase "return to dust" appears elsewhere in the Old Testament (e.g., Psalms 90:3; 104:29; 146:4), associating humanity's dusty origins and make-up with human transience. For Ecclesiastes, humans and nonhuman animals are the same in this respect: "Where human beings are concerned, God tests them to show them that they are but animals because human beings and animals share the same fate. One dies just like the other — both have the same life-breath. Humans are no better off than animals because everything is pointless. All go to the same place: all are from the dust; all return to the dust" (Ecclesiastes 3:18–21).[8]

"God ... blew life's breath into his nostrils"

Having formed the human being from the earth's topsoil, God next breathes life's breath into the human. This is a potent affirmation that human life is dependent on the God who gives life (cf. Job 32:8; 33:4). What we might say of humans, though, Genesis also says of nonhuman animals. In preparation for the story of the flood, for example, God undertakes "to destroy from under heaven all flesh in which is the breath of life" (Genesis 6:17, NRSV), and Noah brought onto the ark "two and two of all flesh in which there was the breath of

---

[6]   This was not universal, however. See, e.g., Kallistos Ware, "The Soul in Greek Christianity," in *From Soul to Self* (ed. M. James C. Crabbe; London: Routledge, 1999), 49–69; Andrew Louth, ed., Genesis 1–11 (*Ancient Christian Commentary on Scripture* 1; Downers Grove, IL: InterVarsity, 2001), 47–53; M.C. Steenberg, *Of God and Man: Theology as Anthropology from Irenaeus to Athanasius* (London: T. & T. Clark, 2009).

[7]   For a similar brief, and for more details, see Lawson G. Stone, "The Soul: Possession, Part, or Person? The Genesis of Human Nature in Genesis 2:7," in *What about the Soul? Neuroscience and Christian Anthropology* (ed. Joel B. Green; Nashville: Abingdon, 2004), 47–61.

[8]   The subsequent question concerning the destination of "life-breath" (Ecclesiastes 3:21) is answered in Ecclesiastes 12:7: "the life-breath returns to God who gave it." See L. Wächter, "'pr," in *Theological Dictionary of the Old Testament* (vol. 11; ed. G. Johannes Botterweck, Helmer Ringgren, and Heinz-Josef Fabry; Grand Rapids: Eerdmans, 2001), 257–65.

life" (Genesis 7:15, NRSV). The writer later reports, "Every creature took its last breath: the things crawling on the ground, birds, livestock, wild animals, everything swarming on the ground, and every human being. Everything on dry land with life's breath in its nostrils died" (Genesis 7:21–2). Accordingly, although it is true that God animates the dusty form, the invigoration of the human being does not distinguish the human from the rest of God's creatures but, like humanity's dusty origins and composition, the gift of life's breath is a sign of humanity's essential solidarity with nonhuman creatures.

"The human came to life"

We come finally to the primary point, namely, the outcome of God's formation of the human being from the earth's topsoil and God's giving the human being life's breath. In the words of the Authorized Version, "man became a living soul." The Hebrew term in question, rendered by the Authorized Version as "soul," is *nefesh*, used almost 800 times in the Hebrew scriptures. The basic meaning of the word is "throat," which makes sense of the range of uses in the Old Testament where the term refers to "breath" or "neck," for example. In Israel's scriptures, *nefesh* is often used with reference to the whole person as the seat of desires and emotions (though not to the "inner soul" as though this were something separate from one's being). In fact, *nefesh* is well-translated in many places as "person," or even by the personal pronoun "I" (e.g., Leviticus 2:1; 4:2; 7:20). It denotes the entire human being, but can also be used with reference to nonhuman animals (e.g., Genesis 1:12, 24; 2:7; 9:10). As H. Seebass summarizes his extensive study of the term, people in the Old Testament "… do not think of themselves in a subject-object relationship (spirit and soul); the subject in particular is not thematic. On the basis of being alive, of individuation within life, of perceiving life as an in-and-out rhythm (breathing?), they find themselves to be living quanta with respect to *hayyim*, life."[9]

Stated negatively, Genesis 2:7 does not picture the creation of the human being as a process leading, finally, to his receiving a soul; the soul is not a "thing" to be given and received or possessed. Nor is the human simply being equated with a metaphysically separate entity separate from the body, a "soul," as if the text could be taken to imply that the human is a soul that comes to inhabit a body.

Stated positively, Genesis 2:7 pictures the consequence of God's formation and animation of the human as the human's becoming a "living *nefesh*." I have left this phrase untranslated for the moment in order to draw attention to its parallel use in its local context:

> So God created the great sea monsters and every living creature that moves, of every kind, with which the waters swarm, and every winged bird of every kind (Genesis 1:21, NRSV).
>
> And God said, "Let the earth bring forth living creatures of every kind: cattle and creeping things and wild animals of the earth of every kind" (Genesis 1:24, NRSV).
>
> God said, "See, I have given you every plant yielding seed that is upon the face of all the earth, and every tree with seed in its fruit; you shall have them for food. And to every beast of the earth, and to every bird of the air, and to everything that creeps on the earth, everything that has the breath of life, I have given every green plant for food" (Genesis 1:30, NRSV).

---

9   See H. Seebass, "nfsh," in *Theological Dictionary of the Old Testament* (vol. 9; ed. G. Johannes Botterweck, Helmer Ringgren, and Heinz-Josef Fabry; Grand Rapids: Eerdmans, 1998), 497–519 (503–4); note especially Seebass' excursus, "The Translation 'Soul'" (508–10).

In each of these three texts, the italicized phrase represents the English translation of the phrase marking the result of God's formation of the human being in Genesis 2:7: *nefesh hayyah*. To these texts we can add another. After the human being's creation in Genesis 2:7, God moves in his search for a partner for the human to create nonhuman animals. This process recapitulates what we saw with the creation of the human being: earthy origins leading to *life*. "So out of the ground the LORD God formed every animal of the field and every bird of the air, and brought them to the man to see what he would call them; and whatever the man called every living creature, that was its name" (Genesis 2:19). In this text, "living creature" translates the same phrase used of the human being, *nefesh hayyah*. Like him, the nonhuman animals are earthy creatures made to be a "living *nefesh*." Clearly, then, "soul" is not for the Genesis story a unique characteristic of the human person; humans are not distinctively human on account of their purported possession of a "soul." Indeed, one might better translate Genesis 2:7 with reference to the divine gift of life: "the human being became fully alive" (my translation) or "the man became a living being" (NIV, NRSV, NAB) or "the human came to life" (CEB).

Because many in the early church read Israel's scriptures not in Hebrew but in Greek, I should draw attention to the fact that these exegetical observations are not specific to the Hebrew text. Genesis 2:7 identifies the result of God's creation of a human being (ἄνθρωπος) with these words: καὶ ἐγένετο ὁ ἄνθρωπος εἰς ψυχὴν ζῶσαν, "and the human became a living being" (New English Translation of the Septuagint). The phrase "living being" also appears in Genesis 1:21 (ψυχὴν ζῴων), 24 (ψυχὴν ζῶσαν), 30 (ψυχὴν ζωῆς); 2:19 (ψυχὴν ζῶσαν), again demonstrating incontrovertibly that the creation stories in Genesis know nothing of the human possession of a soul (or the identification of the human with a soul) as a way of distinguishing humans from nonhuman animals. In fact, as with the Hebrew term *nefesh*, so the Greek term ψυχή refers broadly to "life." The term does not mean "soul," as this term is used among those who hold to anthropological dualism (or a tripartite account of the human being: body, soul, and spirit), though it can have this sense when framed in ways more at home in some strands of Greek philosophy than in Israel's scriptures—that is, when anthropological dualism has already been established.

As Old Testament scholar Lawson Stone observes, it nonetheless remains the case that assumptions grounded in anthropological dualism have often prevented even learned readers from taking seriously these observations. "For example," he writes, "the medieval Jewish exegete Rashi noted this equation, but argued that the human *nefesh* "is the most highly developed of all of them, because to him was granted understanding and speech." He was forced to this view because earlier he programmatically claimed that "there were two formations—a formation of man for this world, and a formation of man for the resurrection ... [God] made him of both, of earthly and of heavenly matter: the body of the earthly, and the soul of the heavenly."[10] Stone observes that Calvin, too, noted the linking of "living *nefesh*" to both humanity and animals, but explained this in terms of the "lower faculty of the soul."[11] Calvin's reference to the soul's "lower faculty" is telling, since, as we will see shortly, it reveals his dependence on a tradition of interpretation drawn from readings of scripture heavily determined by Middle Platonism.

---

[10] Stone, "Soul," 55 (citing Pentateuch with Targum Onkelos, Haphtaroth, and Rashi's Commentary [New York: Hebrew Publishing, 1965], 1:10).

[11] Stone, "Soul," 55 (citing John Calvin, Genesis [Edinburgh: Banner of Truth, 1965 (1554)], 1:112).

An Important Corollary

We have seen thus far that the term *nefesh* (or ψυχή) in Genesis 2:7 does not refer to a part of the human being, nor to the human's possession of a metaphysically separate entity distinguishable from the human body such as a "soul" or "spirit." Indeed, this text provides no basis at all for imagining that the human being is comprised of parts, or that some part of the human being is "spiritual" as opposed to "earthy" (or material). Moreover, the phrase our writer chooses—*nefesh hayyah*—binds the human to nonhuman creatures; it manifestly does not distinguish between them.

Momentarily stepping back from exegetical detail, we can summarize the perspective on humanity disclosed in Genesis 1–2 in terms of continuity and difference. Humans are like other living things in their being created by God and thus in their relation to him. Like them, humanity is formed from the stuff of the earth. "Humans are wholly embedded in creation," LeRon Shults rightly observes, "and no special part of humanity, not even the mind, escapes this creaturely continuity."[12] Vegetation is for both humans and nonhuman animals (Genesis 1:30). Nonhuman animals share with humans the command to reproduce, increase, and fill the seas and the earth (Genesis 1:22). And, as we have seen, humans and nonhuman animals are both composed of the stuff of the ground and both are living creatures divinely animated. However, humans are unlike other creatures in that humanity alone is created after God's own likeness, in God's own image. God's image, not the soul, is the distinguishing characteristic of the human family in relation to the rest of creation.

As is widely acknowledged, the text of Genesis gives us little with which to work in terms of spelling out the nature of humanity's creation in God's image.[13] What we have seen thus far, though, is that it gives us no basis for supporting what is variously called a structuralist, substantialist, or essentialist understanding of the divine image in which humanity is created. That is, the divine image cannot be understood in terms of the claim that humans have a soul. A string of other, closely related interpretations of the divine image (particularly relational, vocational, and covenantal views)—views that explicate God's image in terms of a way to be and a call on our life together as humans—more readily find a home, both in the Old Testament[14] and in a short series of biblical texts that reflect openly on the question, What is a human being? (Psalms 8:144; Job 7; Hebrews 2:6–9).[15] Even here, though, it is important to accentuate what Genesis 1–2 emphasizes regarding the essential

---

[12] F. LeRon Shults, *Reforming Theological Anthropology: After the Philosophical Turn to Relationality* (Grand Rapids: Eerdmans, 2003), 164.

[13] Among Old Testament scholars, cf., e.g., Brevard S. Childs, *Biblical Theology of the Old and New Testaments* (London: SCM, 1992), 567; John Goldingay, *Old Testament Theology*, vol. 2: *Israel's Faith* (Downers Grove, IL: InterVarsity, 2006), 518; more generally, Richard S. Briggs, "Humans in the Image of God and Other Things Genesis Does Not Make Clear," *Journal of Theological Interpretation*, 4, no. 1 (2010): 111–26.

[14] On the interpretation of the *imago Dei* in Genesis 1, see especially J. Richard Middleton, *The Liberating Image: The Imago Dei in Genesis*, 1 (Grand Rapids: Brazos, 2005); Middleton critiques the substantialist and relational views in favor of his own proposal that "the imago Dei refers to humanity's office and role as God's earthly delegates, whose terrestrial task is analogous to that of the heavenly court" (p. 60), though in fact this emphasis on status and role can be seen as adding important nuance to a relational orientation. For a complementary perspective, see W. Sibley Towner, "Clones of God: Genesis 1:26–8 and the Image of God in the Hebrew Bible," *Interpretation* 59 (2005): 341–56. For further theological assessment, see Stanley J. Grenz, *The Social God and the Relational Self: A Trinitarian Theology of the Imago Dei* (*The Matrix of Christian Theology*; Louisville, KY: Westminster John Knox, 2001).

[15] See the useful discussion of these texts in Patrick D. Miller, "What Is a Human Being? The Anthropology of Scripture," in *What about the Soul? Neuroscience and Christian Anthropology* (ed. Joel B. Green; Nashville: Abingdon, 2004), 63–73.

solidarity of human and nonhuman creatures and to articulate the distinction between human and nonhuman creatures less in terms of different capacities and more in terms of the relative degree to which they manifest those capacities.[16]

The Soul of Humans and the Soul of Animals

It remains, then, for us to discuss the rise and spread of an alternative interpretive tradition, one that finds in these accounts of humanity's creation grounds for linking the divine image with God's gift of a human soul (distinguishable and separable from the human body). Stone theorizes that the raw materials for this alternative were near at hand in the vital belief in the afterlife among Babylonians, Assyrians, Egyptians, and Canaanites, and in the widespread use of Israel's scriptures in Greek translation in the Second Temple period. He asks, "If nothing in Gen 2:7 supports the notion that humanity was endowed, by a special act of divine creation, with an intangible, immortal, and personal 'soul,' the question must be asked, From where did such an interpretation of the Old Testament arise?" His response:

> The existence of beliefs in the afterlife and the immortality of disembodied human personality in the ancient Near East explain why these notions eventually became part of Jewish and Christian thought. Eventually, the religious veneration of the dead that pervaded the cultures of antiquity found its way into the biblical communities. The transformation of nefesh into immortal, disembodied human consciousness probably began no later than the moment a Greek translator of the Old Testament decided to use psyche (often translated as "soul") as the equivalent for nefesh. That choice created the danger that a Hellenistic reader, ignorant of the biblical rejection of the cult of the divinized dead, would assume that psychē meant in the Old Testament the same thing that it meant in the surrounding culture. As far back as Homer, the body denoted simply the carcass, a corpse, stripped of the dynamism of human personality. Plato even understood the body as a tomb, and saw death as the final release of the soul. Of course these were not the only alternatives. Aristotle's views on the soul were not as distant from the Old Testament as Plato's, for example, yet the dominant view was more generally derived from Plato. Thus, the cultural setting provided the tools for transforming the Old Testament's "this worldly" sense of nefesh into an "other worldly" concept.[17]

Even if Stone somewhat exaggerates the pervasiveness of Platonic influence in Roman Hellenism,[18] his basic hypothesis is a sound one.

---

[16]   Cf. Warren S. Brown, "Cognitive Contributions to Soul," in *Whatever Happened to the Soul? Scientific and Theological Portraits of Human Nature* (ed. Warren S. Brown, Nancey Murphy, and H. Newton Maloney; *Theology and Science*; Minneapolis: Fortress, 1998), 99–125; Joshua M. Moritz, "Evolution, the End of Human Uniqueness, and the Election of the Imago Dei," *Theology and Science* 9, no. 3 (2011): 307–39.

[17]   Stone, "Soul," 57.

[18]   In fact, Greek thought and Greek influence during this period was more variegated than is often assumed; cf., e.g., the opening chapters of John P. Wright and Paul Potter, eds, *Psyche and Soma: Physicians and Metaphysicians on the Mind-Body Problem from Antiquity to Enlightenment* (Oxford: Clarendon Press, 2000): Hippocratic medicine (Beate Gundert); Plato (T.M. Robinson); Aristotle (Philip J. van der Eijk); a cluster of Hellenistic philosophers and physicians, from Epicurus to Galen (Heinrich von Staden), and Paul (Theo K. Heckel); Dale B. Martin, *The Corinthian Body* (New Haven: Yale University Press, 1995),

To borrow a metaphor, in the working of crossword puzzles, themes—like "Scottish History" or "State Capitals"—orient people by providing broad clues concerning the specific words needed to complete the puzzle.[19] By way of analogy, if one is working within the matrix of ancient cults of the dead and/or within the horizons of Platonic philosophy and its developments, then it would seem only natural to find in the term ψυχή a reference to the soul of anthropological dualism, irrespective of the narrative context provided by Genesis 1–2 (or, indeed, by the Old Testament as a whole). Still more can be said regarding the development of this interpretive tradition, however.

We observed in passing Calvin's reference to the soul's "lower faculty," itself representative of a broader understanding of "soul." Pierre Gassendi (1592–1655), for example, had claimed in his Syntagma that animals must have souls since they apparently possess a memory, a capacity for reason, and other traits typically associated with the soul. What, then, distinguishes humanity from "brutes?" Scientist-philosophers of the period thought in terms of two souls—the first a material soul, characteristic of both humans and nonhuman animals, and the second an immaterial and immortal soul, found in humans alone. The founder of neurology, Thomas Willis (1621–75) distinguished between the Corporeal Soul (common to humans and animals) and the Rational Soul (superior to the Corporeal Soul, found in humans only)—a hoary distinction indeed, according to Willis, who observed it among "divers Authors both Ancient and Modern and both Philosophers and Theologists."[20] His own work focused on the "animal soul" (in both humans and nonhuman animals), even if he consistently attributes what might otherwise be regarded as soulish capacities (cognition, volition, affect, imagination, memory, et al.) to the brain and central nervous system. As Paul Cranefield summarizes, "The soul of brutes, in the hands of Willis, really seems to be simply a handy name for the assemblage of anatomical and physiological mechanisms which underlie psychological processes."[21]

I mention Willis because it is no exaggeration that his work marks the beginning of the end of the viability of belief in a "soul" from the perspective of the natural sciences, neurobiology in particular.[22] Taking the discussion in the other direction, we find an emphasis on the soul, particularly lexicalized as the "rational soul," as the distinguishing characteristic of human beings among a number of church fathers of the second and third centuries.[23] Thus, in Clement of Alexandria (ca. 150–ca. 215) we find an example of what will become a standard Christian usage.

3–37; Paul S. MacDonald, History of the Concept of Mind: Speculations about Soul, Mind and Spirit from Homer to Hume (Aldershot: Ashgate, 2003); Richard Sorabji, "Soul and Self in Ancient Philosophy," in From Soul to Self (ed. M. James C. Crabbe; London: Routledge, 1999), 8–32.

[19] This metaphor was suggested to me by John J. O'Keefe and R.R. Reno, Sanctified Vision: An Introduction to Early Christian Interpretation of the Bible (Baltimore, MD: The Johns Hopkins University Press, 2005), 45.

[20] Thomas Willis, Two Discourses concerning the Soul of Brutes, Which Is That of the Vital and Sensitive of Man (trans. Samuel Pordage; Gainesville, FL: Scholars' Facsimiles and Reprints (1971 [1683]), 38.

[21] Paul F. Cranefield, "A Seventeenth Century View of Mental Deficiency and Schizophrenia: Thomas Willis on 'Stupidity or Foolishness,'" Bulletin of the History of Medicine 35 (1961): 291–316 (306).

[22] Cf. Joel B. Green, "Science, Religion, and the Mind-Brain Problem: The Case of Thomas Willis (1621–1675)," Science and Christian Belief 15 (2003): 165–85; Carl Zimmer, Soul Made Flesh: The Discovery of the Brain—and How It Changed the World (New York: Free, 2004).

[23] The following material is adapted from Joel B. Green, Practicing Theological Interpretation: Engaging Biblical Texts for Faith and Formation (Theological Explorations for the Church Catholic; Grand Rapids: Baker Academic, 2011), 86–92.

Rightly then Moses says, that the body which Plato calls "the earthly tabernacle" was formed of the ground, but that the rational soul was breathed by God into man's face.[24] For there, they say, the ruling faculty is situated; interpreting the access by the senses into the first man as the addition of the soul.

Note how this theologian acknowledges the role of Platonic categories as the interpretive frame within which to read Genesis 1–2. Thus: "Wherefore also humanity is said 'to have been made in [God's] image and likeness.' For the image of God is the divine and royal Word, the impassible human; and the image of the image is the human mind" (Stromata 5.14).[25] Throughout Clement's work the "rational soul" is the governing seat of the human being, the location of the intellect, the human being as he or she is addressed by God.

So thoroughly has Platonic thought made its mark that Tertullian (ca. 160–ca. 225) entitles chapter 16 of his treatise *On the Soul*, "The Soul's Parts: Elements of the Rational Soul." He begins: "That position of Plato's is also quite in keeping with the faith, in which he divides the soul into two parts—the rational and the irrational."[26] Tertullian goes on to emphasize the importance of the rational soul as the seat of communion with God and Christian living, in contrast with the irrational element, which is controlled by sin and the devil.[27]

It is in Origen (184/5–253/–4), whose career began in Alexandria, that we find among early church theologians the most extensive use of the phrase "rational soul." For example:

But if one were to take the change as referring to the soul of Jesus after it had entered the body, we would inquire in what sense the term "change" is used. For if it be meant to apply to its essence, such a supposition is inadmissible, not only in relation to the soul of Jesus, but also to the rational soul of any other being. (Against Celsus 5.14)[28]

Notice Origen's assumptions that a soul could "enter the body" and that "rational souls" are incapable of essential change. In *Against Celsus*, he seems to agree with Celsus' Platonic anthropology:

In the next place, [Celsus] expresses his approval of those who "hope that eternal life shall be enjoyed with God by the soul or mind, or, as it is variously called, the spiritual nature, the reasonable soul, intelligent, holy, and blessed"; and he allows the soundness of the doctrine, "that those who had a good life shall be happy, and the unrighteous shall suffer eternal punishments." (8.51)[29]

This is especially telling since Origen thus finds a point on which he and Celsus agree, namely, the nature of the "reasonable soul," now identified with "soul," "mind," and "spiritual nature." In classical Platonism, the "rational soul" is really a shorthand way of

---

[24]   This reference to breathing into the human being's "face" indicates that Clement, like Philo before him (see below), is reading the text in its Greek form: ὁ θεὸς … ἐνεφύσησεν εἰς τὸ πρόσωπον αὐτοῦ (Genesis 2:7).

[25]   Clement of Alexandria, "The Stromata, or Miscellanies," in *Ante-Nicene Fathers* (vol. 2; ed. Alexander Roberts and James Donaldson; reprint ed., Peabody, MA: Hendrickson, 1994 [1995]), 299–567 (466).

[26]   Tertullian, "A Treatise on the Soul," in *Ante-Nicene Fathers* (vol. 3; ed. Alexander Roberts and James Donaldson; reprint ed., Peabody, MA: Hendrickson, 1994 [1995]), 181–235 (194).

[27]   See the helpful analysis in Steenberg, *Of God and Man*, 55–103.

[28]   Origen, "Origen against Celsus," in *Ante-Nicene Fathers* (vol. 4; ed. Alexander Roberts and James Donaldson; reprint ed., Peabody, MA: Hendrickson, 1994 [1995]), 395–669 (504).

[29]   Origen, "Origen against Celsus," 658.

referring to a particular species or power of the trifunctional soul. In Origen, it simply is the soul. Especially interesting for our purposes is the hallmark of the rational soul, namely, its identification with the "image of God," as when Origen claims that human beings "have been created in the image of God, for the image of the Supreme God is his reason" (*Against Celsus* 4.85).[30]

These early church theologians were not innovating when they interpreted humanity in this way, though neither were they simply following Plato. The phrase in question, "rational soul" (λογικὴ ψυχή), is used at the turn of the Common Era as a shorthand for referring to an aspect of the soul, as this was expounded in Plato. By the end of the fourth century AD, however, the phrase had become thoroughly standardized and Neoplatonized, such that it referred to the human soul, pure and simple.

We look in vain for the phrase "rational soul" (λογικὴ ψυχή) in the Old and New Testaments. Nor is it found in the surviving works of Plato and Aristotle. Plato had spoken of a complex inner person, a soul comprised of either two or three species or powers,[31] the most important being reason or rationality (λόγος ["reason"] or λογιστικός ["invested with reason, rational"]). In many cases in ancient sources, "soul" simply denotes a human person—a usage found, for example, in Acts 27:37, where Luke writes, "In all, there were two hundred and seventy-six of us [αἱ πᾶσαι ψυχαί] on the ship," but "soul" could also be used of nonhuman creatures. Accordingly, modifying a "soul" as "rational" would immediately signal that the author was talking about humans rather than plants or nonhuman animals. Here is the basis for later talk about lower and higher faculties of the soul, or of different souls for humans and nonhuman animals.

The earliest, clear instances of the phrase "rational soul" come from the first-century Alexandrian Jew Philo (30 BC–45 AD), who worked with Platonic categories to distinguish between irrational souls (created with the bodies of humans and nonhuman animals) and rational souls (created earlier, prior to their taking up lodging in human bodies). Sketching God's creation of the world, Philo observes, "He made man, and bestowed on him mind par excellence"[32]—which he then labels "the soul of the soul" (ψυχῆς τινα ψυχήν; my translation; *On the Creation of the World* 21 §66).[33]

Philo's exegesis of Genesis 1–2 equates the "rational soul" with God's image in Genesis 1:

> *Accordingly, the great Moses has not compared the nature of the rational soul to anything created, but spoke of it as the image of that divine and invisible Spirit—as though it were a coin stamped and impressed by God's seal, the engraving of which is the everlasting Word. For he says, "God breathed into his face the breath of life."* (*Concerning Noah's Work as a Planter* 2.5 §§18–19; my translation)

Philo identifies the soul with God's image similarly in his treatise On the Creation of the World:

---

[30] Origen, "Origen against Celsus," 535.

[31] His favored terms were γενεά ("class, kind") and εἶδος ("class" or "kind"), rather than, say, μέρος, which would signify "part." Indeed, it is difficult to imagine "parts" of a thing regarded as immaterial. See MacDonald, *Concept of Mind*, 37–54; T.M. Robinson, "The Defining Features of Mind-Body Dualism in the Writings of Plato," in *Psyche and Soma: Physicians and Metaphysicians on the Mind-Body Problem from Antiquity to Enlightenment* (ed. Jon P. Wright and Paul Potter; Oxford: Clarendon Press, 2000), 37–55.

[32] Unless otherwise noted, translations of Philo follow Philo (10 vols.; trans. F.H. Colson and G.H. Whitaker; Loeb Classical Library; Cambridge, MA: Harvard University Press, 1929–62).

[33] See Eduard Schweizer et al., "ψυχή κτλ," *Theological Dictionary of the New Testament* (vol. 9; ed. Gerhard Friedrich; Grand Rapids: Eerdmans, 1974), 608–66 (635).

After all the rest, as I have said, Moses tells us that humanity was created after the image of God and after his likeness [Gen. 1.26]. Right well does he say this, for nothing earthborn is more like God than humanity. Let no one represent the likeness [of God] as one to a bodily form; for neither is God in human form, nor is the human body God-like. No, it is in respect of the mind, the sovereign element of the soul, that the word "image" is used. (23 §69)

For Philo, then, Genesis provides two accounts of the creation of humanity. Attributing the authorship of Genesis to Moses, he writes:

After this he says "God formed man by taking clay from the earth, and breathed into his face the breath of life" (Gen. ii.7). By this also he shows very clearly that there is a vast difference between the man thus formed and the man that came into existence earlier after the image of God [that is, according to Gen 1:26–8]: for the man so formed is an object of sense-perception, partaking already of such or such quality, consisting of body and soul, man or woman, by nature moral; while he that was after the (Divine) image was an idea or type or seal, an object of thought (only), incorporeal, neither make nor female, by nature incorruptible.

It says, however, that the formation of the individual man, the object of sense, is a composite one made up of earthly substance and of Divine breath: for it says that the body was made through the Artificer taking clay and moulding out of it a human form, but that the soul was made originated from nothing created whatever, but from the Father and Ruler of all: for that which He breathed in was nothing else than a Divine breath ... (On the Creation of the World 46 §135)

Going on at length to prove the splendor of the human body God created, Philo remarks how God chose the very best clay, the most pure material to form the body; after all, "a sacred dwelling-place or shrine was being fashioned for the reasonable soul, which man was to carry as a holy image, of all images the most Godlike" (*On the Creation of the World* 47 §137). Here and elsewhere in his writings, then, we find a Platonizing interpretation of the relevant passages in Genesis 1–2, whereby Genesis 1:26–7 concerns the creation of the invisible, immortal human being (the soul, God's image), and Genesis 2:7 recounts the creation of the visible, mortal human (the body, into which is placed the soul, God's image).

Note, then, the interpretive path of the phrase "rational soul." It has precursors in Platonic thought. It is never found in scripture; irrespective of how they might have been influenced by Hellenistic thought, the New Testament authors never use the phrase and, indeed, never reflect on Plato's complex notion of the soul. It is picked up by the Middle Platonist Jewish thinker Philo, for whom it functions centrally to interpret Genesis 1–2 to the world of Roman Hellenism. Echoing Philo's language and thought, Clement, Tertullian, and Origen each came to view the rational soul as the most characteristic human self. To be clear, none of the writers of New Testament texts exhibit influence from this stream of the Platonic tradition,[34] and we look to them in vain for some of the prominent thought-patterns found

---

[34] This claim is disputed in George H. Van Kooten, *Paul's Anthropology in Context: The Image of God, Assimilation to God, and Tripartite Man in Ancient Judaism, Ancient Philosophy and Early Christianity* (WUNT 232; Tübingen: Mohr Siebeck, 2008), whose presentation of Philo's anthropology is far more convincing than his presentation of Paul's; indeed, for Van Kooten we learn how to read Paul above all by reading the apostle through Philo—this in spite of the fact that the apostle provides nothing comparable to the exegesis we find in Philo's works (and, as I have observed, the telling phrase "rational soul" [λογικὴ ψυχή] is altogether missing in Paul's correspondence). That is, Philo's work with Greek philosophy is clear because Philo himself makes it clear, whereas Paul's engagement with and dependence on

in the early church writers mentioned above—who attributed the will to sin to the soul, for example; who attributed immorality to the soul; or who imagined that the body, a thing corporeal, must be governed by a thing incorporeal, that is, by a soul. The New Testament writers simply do not portray humans in this way, nor do they evidence this way of reading the creation of humans in Genesis 1–2.

Conclusion

Careful consideration of what Genesis 2:7 does affirm about the creation of the human being demonstrates, negatively, that this text knows nothing of a human soul and, then, that the attempt to identify the divine image with the human soul is alien to the creation accounts of Genesis 1–2. Study of this text demonstrates, positively, the formation of the human person from the stuff of the earth and the essential solidarity with nonhuman animals. Although much more needs to be said about the divine image, what can be said thus far is that the divine image cannot on the basis of Genesis 1–2 be identified with the soul. In fact, attempts to do so owe their logic not to the text of Genesis, nor to reflection on the creation of humanity found elsewhere in the Old and New Testaments. Instead, the exegetical-theological tradition that finds the soul of anthropological dualism in Genesis 1–2 and that posits the identification of the divine image with this soul in Genesis 1–2 is deeply indebted either to Philo's Middle Platonism or to the same philosophically guided interpretive moves he made. Someone might want to continue arguing for a structuralist or substantialist or essential identification of the divine image with the soul, but the one who does so should recognize and acknowledge that this requires a decisive departure from scripture's own witness.

Greek thought becomes transparent only by reading Paul through Philonic lenses. See my review: Joel B. Green, review of George H. van Kooten, *Paul's Anthropology in Context: The Image of God, Assimilation to God, and Tripartite Man in Ancient Judaism, Ancient Philosophy and Early Christianity, Review of Biblical Literature* [http://www.bookreviews.org] (2011). Contra Van Kooten's reading of the evidence, see, too, Graham J. Warne, *Hebrew Perspectives on the Human Person in the Hellenistic Era: Philo and Paul* (MBPS 35; Lewiston, New York: Mellen, 1995).

The Dual-Functionality of the *Imago Dei* as Human Flourishing in the Church Fathers

Fr. David Vincent Meconi, S.J.

In his attempt to locate a convergence between the divine Demiurge and the human soul, Plato exuberantly taught that when this father (πατήρ) of all saw how that which he brought into being was moving and alive, he rejoiced and was resolved to make the copy even more like its paradigmatic original (ὅμοιον πρός τὸ παράδειγμα).[1] Yet, the joy of the gods would need to overcome the vicissitudes of this world and the weakness of human dissimilitude. Since this visible and thus fluctuating order is contrary to the divine world—Socrates bemoans in the *Theatetus*—evils here necessarily haunt us. That is why Socrates next exhorts his interlocutor Theodorus that he must, "flee out of this world to the other, which means becoming like God (ὁμοίωσις θεῷ) in so far as one is able."[2] In this Platonic view, the visible world is a faded copy of the model in which it necessarily participates; and while nowhere is the human person singled out explicitly as a divine image, Plato does see how the human capacity for divinity resides in the soul. The truest nature of the human psyche is accordingly actualized through godly mimesis, and it is Plato who establishes such concepts as divine similitude, *homoiosis*, and participation in God, as the means by which the human soul is finally fulfilled.

Early Christian thinkers drew from these same Platonic themes of participation and theosis to exegete the creation narratives found in Genesis. To understand how the *imago Dei* is seen to function in the foundational thinkers of Christianity, we shall focus our thoughts on Gen. 1:26–8 where a doctrine of humanity's imaging God is given a dual purpose. It is both a matter of heavenly deliberation ("Let us …"), as well as a matter of relating to God's good creation ("Be fertile … subdue the earth and have dominion …"):

> Then God said: Let us make human beings in our image, after our likeness. Let them have dominion over the fish of the sea, the birds of the air, the tame animals, all the wild animals, and all the creatures that crawl on the earth. God created mankind in his image; in the image of God he created them; male and female he created them. God blessed them and God said to them: Be fertile and multiply; fill the earth and subdue it. Have dominion over the fish of the sea, the birds of the air, and all the living things that crawl on the earth (Gen. 1:26–8).

---

[1] *Timaeus* 37C; unless otherwise noted, all translations are mine.

[2] *Theatetus* 176B.

This celebrated passage is admittedly a rather isolated text within the whole of revelation, but it has occasioned rich and unmatched insights. Here the human person is undoubtedly a faint icon of God's fullness, while also being somehow inextricably related to the material order.

Focusing mainly on how the first Christian theologians elucidated Gen. 1:26–8, this chapter constructs a patristic anthropology by arguing the following four points. The first is to show how the very function of an "image" is both to unite and distinguish. The created human image is like God, because like God it enjoys the capacity for reason as well as interpersonal relationality. Yet, at the same time, the image in humanity is always other than and essentially different from God, forever separating copy from Model. This is how the church fathers saw in Adam the primal *mikros kosmos*, a being whose essence was once both united to the spiritual realm as well as inextricably linked with the material order. The primal call of all humans, therefore, is to function on two levels—on both the intellectual and spiritual, as well as on the earthly and corporeal.

The second section will take up the various ways the *imago Dei* functions by way of alterity. The human creature is brought about in and through relationship. Not only is the very soul itself created relationally, the hortatory "Let us make" (Gen. 1:26) roots the very beginnings of humanity in a divine conversation between persons who wish to share their own interpersonal communion. Genesis next depicts Adam as one made "to" the image and likeness, suggesting that the human person is not an unqualified image. This is the role of the Son, the perfect image of the Father (see Col. 1:15). The Son of God is therefore revealed to be the model and goal of every created human image, the one on whom all created personhood is patterned. That is why Paul can name Adam the foreshadowing or type of the one yet to come (τύπος τοῦ μέλλοντος / *forma futuri*; Rom. 5:14). Adam's hylomorphism bespeaks of the perfect Image's becoming human in the incarnation of Christ. Moreover, human images are created "male and female" (Gen. 1:27), and are thus made for intimate interpersonal union. This first couple is also given the commands to "subdue the earth" and to "have dominion over" all other living things (Gen. 1:28). Because of this, early theologians saw that the image of God inherent in each human person commits us to love, service of neighbor, and to faithful stewardship over the rest of creation.

The third set of reflections examines the human person as made "in the image and the likeness" of God, and not in the image of any other creature. God alone can provide the ultimate fulfillment of human life. The ultimate purpose of all human functionality is divine union. Those made in God's image are to live lives so as to allow God to fulfill that image and thus become like God. Early Christian thinkers followed earlier religious and philosophical traditions in arguing that the human person is made for deifying union. However, understood in the context of humanity's embodiment and interpersonal relationality, the Christian perspective emerges as the most amplified and "world friendly" understanding of the divine image possible.

To conclude, the final section weaves these earlier images of functionality together in order to show how this understanding of the *imago Dei* is the antidote to those who relegate the divine image in humanity to a heavenly purpose only. In this final part, I conclude by arguing that the human person is called to be God's corollary on earth: to be rooted firmly in the affairs of creation while always living as an eternal citizen of heaven.

Created to Function in Heaven and on Earth

The American philosopher and psychologist, William James (d. 1910), described the ever-elusive present, not as a "knife's edge" but as a "saddle back" type of creature. The fleeting "now" is that upon which those caught up in time "sit perched" so as to be to look concurrently into two differing directions: "The unit of composition of our perception of time is a *duration*, with a bow and a stern, as it were—a rearward and a forward-looking end."[3] This simultaneity of the present reflects the concurrence of the *imago Dei*, made to be at once both reflective of the divine as well as united with the created order. As a "saddle back" reality, humanity's imaging of God is poised to look both "forward" to the heavens and "rearward" toward the earth.

The human person is both related to God as well as distinct from God—similar to the divine but always and everywhere other than the divine. The *imago* is a mirrored reflection which is both the copy of the model reflected, as well as the absolute other, different from the mirrored archetype. The divine image in the human person accordingly links men and women both to God *and* to the created order from which they come. Both loci are integral and indispensable to human excellence: neither are temporary burdens to be overcome or dismissed, but, rather both are inherent of what it means to be fully human. So in order to understand in what the human person's imaging God consists, we shall concentrate on the two origins of the human person as suggested in Genesis: the creator in whose image and likeness the human is made, and the created order from which both man and woman, albeit each in his and her own way, appear.

For the most part, early Christian thinkers followed Philo of Alexandria's lead and located the divine image in the human soul.[4] For Philo, the divine nature may be concealed to the senses of creatures but the divine Logos can in fact be known through the *logoi* borne by human images of God. The mind is where the *capax Dei* and thus the *similitudo Dei* can be actualized: the capacity for reason and freedom of the will are the differentiating characteristics of the human person. While striving not to deprecate or neglect the bodily dimension of human life, Christian thinkers have tended to locate the divine image within the spiritual—in the *psyche, mens,* or *anima.*[5] Such localization internalizes the drama of human salvation. God is now understood to reveal himself mainly within the mind. The divinely-imaging soul is thus the place where God personally meets his creatures, the stage where the divine and human encounter is realized.

Athanasius (d. 373) placed the divine image in that which is "immortal and invisible" (ἀθάνατον ... καὶ μὴ βλεπομένην) in men and women.[6] But he went on to argue that through the exercise of this spiritual capacity, humans can affect a likeness in things visible and material. That is, as media between heaven and earth, those made in God's image can help render the cosmos more Godlike. This mandate to instantiate the divine everywhere arose early in the Alexandrian Catechetical School. Clement of Alexandria (d. 215) originally taught that the true Christian wise man (ὁ γνωστικὸς), pursues "God's own image and likeness by imitating God as far as he is able. This one is lacking in nothing that pertains to that likeness: self-mastery, perseverance, the practice of virtue, and restraining the

---

3   William James, *The Principles of Psychology*, vol. 1 (Harvard University Press [1890] 1981) 574.

4   See Philo, *On the Confusion of Dreams* §147–8; *On Creation* 6.23.

5   For human reason as the primary way the soul images God, see: Tatian, *Address to the Greeks* §12; Origen, *On First Principles* 4.37; Ambrose, *Hexameron* VI.7–8; St Augustine, *On the Trinity* [*Trin.*] 12.12, 14.4.

6   Athanasius, *Contra Gentes* §34; *Contra les païens, Source Chrétiennes* 18 bis, ed., Pierre-Thomas Camelot (Paris: Éditions du Cerf, 1977) 164.

passions ..."[7] These selections help illumine the pioneering Christian position: while the human creature resembles the invisible God principally through the mind's inner-workings, the effects of the divine image are also necessarily realized bodily.

Liturgically this dual-functioning comes through beautifully when ecclesiastics explain the nature and purpose of the visible sacraments. Take, for example, a homily preached to the baptized on the holy night of the Easter Vigil. These *infantes* are enlightened through water and oil to know not only who God is but who they themselves, precisely as his images, are:

> Now that you have been schooled in this honored, glorious and all-holy creed, it is time
> to learn what you yourself are. As a human person, you enjoy a two-fold (διπλοῦς)
> nature. You have been fashioned out of both soul and body (ἐκ ψυχῆς καὶ σώματος),
> and as we just heard, the same God we worship is the also the creator of both soul as
> well as body. Understand that you are a self-governing soul—the most noble work
> of God—created in your creator's own image and because of that, God gives the soul
> immortality. To you, a vivified, rational and immortal being, God has bestowed these
> gifts and has given your soul the power to act as it desires.[8]

Here Cyril of Jerusalem (d. 386) teaches his flock that in their study of the creed and subsequent coming to learn who the Model of all reality is, God's "copies" should have come to greater insight into their own nature and *telos* as well.[9] Yet notice that just as the spiritual effects of the *imago Dei* can be realized bodily, the body also affects the *imago Dei*, a point made most often in liturgical texts and sermons where the material conveys God's otherwise invisible presence. In the waters of baptism, the human body is drawn into the divine encounter.

This text is indicative of an early ecclesial anthropology, made often by bishops especially at the Easter vigil where the catechumens approach the sacraments for the first time. While giving precedence to the soul, Cyril is careful to teach each of his congregants that they are neither wholly spiritual nor entirely bodily. They are each a two-fold nature of spirit and matter and that is why the creedal adherence they intellectually expressed in their conversion must now be realized through such visible vehicles as water and oil, bread and wine.

Fittingly, the first great Christian thinkers depicted Adam as the summation of creation, a *mikros kosmos* and sort of "second world" combining both the visible and the invisible realms. For the human person alone testifies to how God:

> took from already existing matter a body and placed his own breath within, which
> the Logos knew to be an intelligent soul and an image of God. This was a new sort
> of second world (κόσμον δεύτερον). God placed the man, great in littleness on the
> earth. God made him a new sort of angel, a mingled worshipper, fully initiated into
> the visible creation, but only partially into the intellectual. He was made a king over
> all the earth, subject only to the King above. He is both of the earth and of heaven,
> temporal and immortal, visible and yet rational. He is made half-way between

---

7   Clement of Alexandria, *Stromata* 2.19; PG 8.1040B.

8   Cyril of Jerusalem, *Catechetical Lectures* 4.18; PG 33.477A–480A. Augustine too will call the imaged soul the *praecipuum Dei opus* ("chief work of God"), *Literal Meaning of Genesis* (*Gn. litt.*) 6.12; CSEL 28.185.

9   This is reminiscent of *sermo* 272 wherein Augustine also teaches his *infantes* (Pentecost, 408) that by gazing upon and receiving the Body of Christ, they come to see who they too are—namely, the body of Christ! "So if it's you that are the body of Christ and its members, it's the mystery meaning you that has been placed on the Lord's table; what you receive is the mystery that means you"; trans., Edmund Hill, *Sermons* 230–272B (Hyde Park, New City Press, 1993) 300.

*greatness and lowliness. In one person is combined spirit and flesh: spirit, due to the
kindness bestowed upon him, flesh, because of the height to which he had been raised.*[10]

In this unique hylomorphic nature, God's creative glory shines not only in the angelic
loftiness of reason, but also in the brutal realities of flesh and mortality. Adam thus unites
in himself all reality (foreshadowing the perfect union of even divinity and humanity in the
New Adam). Origen asks why we are so surprised when Christ calls his followers the light
of the world when our divine image already contains the sun and the moon, as each one
is a "universe in miniature" (*mundum parvulum*).[11] According to Augustine, even the very
name ADAM represents all the being represented metaphorically by the four winds of the
earth: the Anatolê (the East wind), Dysis (West), Arctos (North), and the Mesêmbria (from
the South).[12]

In the words of Norris Clarke, a truly unique Christian anthropology arose with the
church fathers reflecting on how the human person is called to function as a "frontier being."
The human person is the only creature who can legitimately "integrate within itself all the
levels of the universe, but in particular it binds together into one the two great disparate
dimensions of reality, the material and spiritual worlds, which were so much at odds with
each other in the Platonic universe."[13] Having been made a frontier being, bearing traces of
both heaven and earth, the human person lives on earth but longs for heaven, born in time
but made for eternity.

The man or woman of antiquity teetered between two very evident worlds. The divine
moved all around and "above" them; the terrors of nature and the obviousness of materiality
surrounded them from "below." Between immutability, true beauty and unity, on the one
hand, and non-being and destructive divisiveness, on the other, Plato placed his *meristes*—
a dividing being (*Timaeus* 35A), and Plotinus put his *metherion*—a boundary being (*Enneads*
iv.4.3). What the purely Greek view could not conceive of, however, was the Christian
teaching that it was the whole person, the *anthropos*, who was this glorious microcosm and
not simply the *psyche* or the soul alone.[14] The "middle being" of Greek thought remains
divided until he sloughs off the material and ascends fully and unregrettably to the world
of eternity above. This view becomes most evident in the various systems of Christian
Gnosticism, wherein one divine being brings the excellence of spirit about, while another
deity proves responsible for generating the baseness of body. This must be a clear affront
to a truly Christian anthropology where the one and same God freely creates both soul and
body, longs to be made personally present through both male and female images of himself.

---

10   Gregory of Nazianzus, *Oration* 38.11; PG 36.321C–324A.

11   Origen, *Fifth Homily on Leviticus* 2; PG 12.449C.

12   Augustine, *Tractates on the Gospel of John* 10.12. In the world of Latin numerology, ADAM also
adds up to 46, also the same number of years it took Herod to build the temple in Jerusalem; Augustine
of course here sees another way Adam then prefigures the true temple of Christ's body (see also
Augustine, *Expositions on the Psalms* 95.15).

13   Norris, Clarke, "Living on the Edge: The Human Person as 'Frontier Being' and Microcosm,"
International Philosophical Quarterly 36.2 (Issue 142; 1996) 183–99; 188.

14   To account how the body, even *qua* body, had a role in imaging God, most argued simply
that the human person's erect posture was a sign that this enfleshed being alone was made for God
(see Leviticus 26:13: "I, the Lord, am your God, who brought you out of the land of Egypt to be their
slaves no more, breaking the bars of your yoke and making you walk erect"). Able to gaze upon the
heavens unlike any other animal, the human person was clearly unique throughout the visible world;
e.g., Gregory of Nyssa, *On the Making of Man* §8; Augustine, *De Diversis Quaestionibus* no. 51. While most
church fathers stressed, the soul as the primary locus for the *imago Dei*, we know of one group out of
Mesopotamia named by Epiphanius as the Audians (viz., *Panarion* §70), who taught that the image of
God was encapsulated by the human body.

Various Gnostic sects justified their deprecation of the body not from some secret text but from a "secret" reading of scripture. In the second and third centuries the Genesis narrative began to be read in a way that deprecated the terrestrial. Thinkers such as the Roman philosopher Valentinus (d. c. 160) noticed that whereas Genesis originally describes God as creating man "in our image, after our likeness" (Gen. 1:26), the very next verse depicts humanity now as embodied and sexualized as being made in the image only: "God created mankind in his image; in the image of God he created them; male and female he created them" (Gen. 1:27).[15] The promise of divine likeness has jarringly fallen away. Gnostics seized on this dissonance between verses in order to teach that becoming like God was inimical to humanity's corporeality and subsequent sexual engendering and differentiation. Ironically, perhaps, it would thus prove to be the Christian Gnostics who took the Platonic principles of a higher world to a disastrous conclusion. This world, no longer a faint refraction of the eternal, has lost its divine likeness and must now be shed; fulfilling the divine image in each human now means disembodiment and denial of desires. Descent is decay, and if the soul wishes to recover its divine similitude, it must flee the historical and the relational. Or in the words of John McGuckin, "Platonism, however, never placed more emphasis on the idea of image than [its divine resemblance—*syngeneia*], for the simple reason that it was a notion indissolubly bound up with the world of the sensible and, as such, part of the fabric of the illusory."[16] Seeing how the *imago Dei* is called to operate on both the heavenly and terrestrial levels, however, Christian anthropology embraces the body as not only divinely intended, but also as an indispensable constituent of human nature allowing the *imago Dei* to function fully.

Accordingly, not all interpretations juxtaposing Gen. 1:26 and 1:27 were intentionally inimical to the Christian hylomorphic view. Many fathers used the omission of *imago* in Gen. 1:27 in order to emphasize humanity's need to collaborate with God's intent to make all more and more like himself. The first to reflect deeply on the implications of these passages, Irenaeus of Lyons (d. c. 202), argued that the first man was created directly through "the two hands of God," the Logos and the Spirit, giving Adam his divine image. The eternal likeness to God, however, would be a state Adam would have to realize through virtuous living: "For he made man the image of God; and the image of God is the Son, after whose image man was made; and for this cause he appeared at the end of times that he might show the image (to be) like unto himself."[17] Here a division between image (*imago*) and likeness (*similitudo*) is made: while image is something innately given the rational soul, the likeness to God is something that must be achieved by union with the Son of God who has become visibly incarnate. Only through cooperation and obedience are men and women able to be elevated and divinely transformed: "For Irenaeus, image is both form and substance, and likeness is the saving action by which the spirit raises man to God."[18] So, while all persons are *imagines*, only the saints will prove to be *similitudines*.

To achieve such sanctity, Origen insisted that the "likeness" omitted in Gen. 1:27 was purposeful. The omission was in fact God's own invitation for the human soul to cooperate

[15] For more on the history of this reading, see Mark Edwards, *Catholicity and Heresy in the Early Church* (Farnham, Surrey: Ashgate, 2009), 14–20.

[16] McGuckin, "Image of God" in *The Westminster Handbook to Origen*, ed. John McGuckin (Louisville: Westminster John Knox Press, 2004), 132.

[17] *Demonstratio* §22; trans., Iain MacKenzie, *Demonstration of the Apostolic Preaching* (London: Ashgate Publishing, 2002) 107. This Irenaean understanding of image is captured by Philaster (d. c. 397), Bishop of Brescia, reserving *similitudo* only for souls graced with faith: "Imago enim dei id est anima omnis hominis, facta ex nihilo: similitudo autem in fide uita nisi cognita fuerit a deo, appellari non potest dei imago similis"; *Liber de Haeresibus* §109; CCL 9.301.

[18] *Irenaeus of Lyons*, Eric Osborn (Cambridge University Press, 2001), 217.

with his undying grace. That is, God created the human person in his image, and is intentionally silent about the likeness because scripture,

> means to say nothing else than that, whereas the human person has obtained the image in the dignity of our first condition, the perfection of the likeness is laid up for him only at the consummation. The purpose for this was that humanity should acquire such likeness for itself through earnest efforts to imitate God. In this way, while the possibility of attaining perfection was given to the man in the beginning, through the honor of "the image," even so he should, in the end, obtain for himself the "perfect likeness" by the accomplishment of these works.[19]

Origen maintains that whereas the likeness is promised humanity, it will not be achieved until all creation is brought back into union with the God from whom all has turned away. This return, he emphasizes, is affected by the individual's mimesis—explained here in terms of effort and work. In imitating the divine, Christians come to realize the likeness of God which awaits them.[20] This function of the created image to attain the "perfect likeness" is actualized by the descent of the divine Word into human flesh. Adam's hylomorphic imaging of God foreshadowed the incarnation of God, the Second Adam (see Rom. 5:14), and it is to this exact image of the Father we now turn.

Made to Function Relationally

As Christians came to understand the man Jesus as the perfect image of the Father (see Col. 1:15), the need for a more precise theology of image arose. The Logos is the divine image *simpliciter* (2 Cor. 4:4; Col. 1:12–16; Heb. 1:3), being by nature the perfect reflection of the Father. Human persons, on the other hand, are created so as to be made sons and daughters through grace. We read that "Adam was one hundred and thirty years old when he begot a son in his likeness, after his image" (Gen. 5:3). A child enjoys both image and likeness of the one who begets him or her. In their disobedience, created images however turned away from God; consequently, the image, albeit diminished, still served as a testimony to human dignity (Gen. 9:6) and cried out for healing. The Father reestablishes union with those made in his image by sending his perfect and eternal image into human flesh. Through this incarnation, the Father works to conform his children "to the image of his Son" (Rom. 8:29) and thereby not only restore humanity's discolored image but to renew it unto himself.

Early theologians were right to see that as created, Adam was incomplete and was brought about in order to yearn for more. Made "to the image" (κατ' εἰκόνα/ad imaginem) and "to the likeness" (καθ' ὁμοίωσιν/ad similitudinem) implied that Adam had an innate dynamism toward the divine but in himself was no way divine. The prepositional phrase suggests the created image is not yet a full image but is instead progressing to(ward) the

---

[19] *Peri Archon* 3.6.1; PG 11.333B-C. For more here, see Mark Edwards, *Origen Against Plato* (Farnham, Surrey: Ashgate, 2002) 102–4; Origen seems to understand that the divine likeness is realized only when the human soul is resurrected and made righteous, cf. *Contra Celsum* 4.30.

[20] Other thinkers granted all creation the divine image but conversely argued that it was the image which would be granted to those who cooperate with God. Given the importance of procreation in the Genesis narrative, fruitfulness being the first commandment to our protoparents, Clement of Alexandria maintained that one fulfills one's *imago* through cooperating with God in bringing about other persons: "The human person becomes an image of God (Εἰκὼν ὁ ἄνθρωπος τοῦ θεοῦ γίνεται) in that he cooperates with him in the procreation of other human persons"; *Paidagogos* 2.10; PG 8.497B.

perfection in and for whom it was created. In both Greek and Latin, the prepositions κατὰ and *ad* denote an active and dynamic propulsion of one existent toward another. It implies an adventitious and participatable attribute desired for by a reality somehow incomplete without it. In other words, the construction of Gen. 1:26 both an intrinsic resemblance between paradigm and copy, as well as the copy's inherent propulsion to become like the model from which it is derived.[21]

Saint Augustine was the first to descry the *imago*'s relationality as constituted by inter-personality, but even within the *imago* lies a relationship comprising the nature of rational mind. This intra-personal relationship is naturally triadic; if the human person is created in the image of a Triune God, it follows that there must be a trinity locatable within each person. Augustine came to explain this triad in terms of memory, intellect, and will, spending the second half of his *De Trinitate* trying to discover this *imago triplex*. After first entertaining the triad of *mens, notitia sui,* and *amor sui,*[22] he then proffers *mens sui, intellegit se,* and *diligit se.*[23] But these (and other possible) models fail because they are solipsistic and cannot reach their true purpose. As long as the mind remembers, knows and loves itself—or any other creature, for that matter—it utterly fails as an *imago Dei*.

This is why Augustine's only correct answer to how the human person images and is like God is when the mind remembers (*memoria Dei*), understands (*intelligentia Dei*) and loves (*amor Dei*) the one in whose image it is created:

> And when [the human mind] does this (i.e., remembers, understands, and loves God)
> it becomes wise. If it does not do it, then even though it remembers and understands
> and loves itself, it is foolish. Let it then remember its God to whose image it was made,
> and understand and love him. To put it in a word, let it worship the uncreated God,
> by whom it was created with a capacity for him and able to share in him.[24]

This is the highest "human honor," to be found in the mind's functioning so as to be united with the one in whose image it has been impressed.[25] For Augustine, the mind is the divine image not simply because of its triadic functions of memory, intellect, and will, but the mind images God because it is made to be in union and thus activated by the Trinity. As such, it is not memory, intellect, and will that image God, but these three operations in a dynamic adherence to divine persons, each in its proper manner. The image of the Triune God, therefore, is not comprised of three static powers but of three relationships in union with the source of their being and particular operations.

For the Christian mind, to be in relationship with other persons is the only way the *imago Dei* is fully actualized. This was the basis of early ethics. Humanity's innate imaging of God was not something reserved only for believers and the baptized. It is what united all humans

---

21   For the use of "ad" in the Latin Fathers' exegesis of Gen. 1:26, see Olivier Du Roy, who argues that the "ad" signifies a particular relation of resemblance ("relation particulière de resemblance") as well as an orientation and movement toward an existent's unifying principle; cf. *L'intelligence de la foi in la Trinité selon saint Augustin: Genèse de sa théologie jusqu'en 391* (Paris: Études augustiniennes, 1966) 361. Vladimir Lossky sees the Septuagint's κατά as "loaded with a promise of future theology, denoting a progress of tradition, a 'preparation for the Gospel' in light of revelation," *In the Image and Likeness of God* (Crestwood, NY: St. Vladimir's Seminary Press, 1974), 137.

22   *Trin.*, 9.4.4; CCL 50A.297.

23   *Trin.*, 14.8.11; CCL 50A.436.

24   *Trin.* 14.12.15; trans., Edmund Hill, *Trinity* (Hyde Park, NY: New City Press, 1991), 383; cf. *Trin.* 15.42.

25   *Trin.* 12.11.16: "Honor enim hominis uerus est *imago et similitudo dei* quae non custoditur nisi ad ipsum a quo imprimitur"; CCL 50.370.

together into one potential family. As the Cappadocians especially knew, identifying the *imago* in all one meets is the beginning of charity. Sin may diminish God's image and likeness but it never removes it completely. "If you were my child, your life would be marked by my own good qualities. I do not recognize in you the image of my nature."[26] Recognizing the inherent image moves one to charity for and service to the other; even when sullied and perhaps unrecognizable, the image in each person remains the basis of their inalienable dignity and human worth. As Jaroslov Pelikan notes, "The doctrine of the image of God served, therefore, as a key to Cappadocian social ethics."[27] Insistent as the early Christians were in their eleemosynary activities, they knew that they could only recognize the *imago Dei* in others but they could never find ultimate fulfillment in others. Of course, Augustine's famous *cor inquietum* is most noted for this—our hearts are restless until they rest, not in any creature, but in God.[28] "Not in likeness to the created world, but in being in the image of the nature of the One who begot him" (κατ᾽ εἰκόνα γεγενημένου)[29] As such, we now turn to the one union that alone can bring lasting joy and fulfillment, deifying unity with God himself.

Image Fulfilled: You Too Are Gods

At the funeral of his dear friend, Basil the Great, Gregory of Nazianzus related how Basil agreed with the church's enemies that all humans *qua* creatures are subject to earthly limitations; but Basil also outmaneuvered and defied those who expected Christians to worship the emperor, by co-defining the human person as the only creature called to rise above all temporal restrictions in order to become God (καὶ θεὸς εἶναι κεκελευσμένος).[30] Here the image of God reaches its highest and ultimate function—namely, to become deified and thus one with God himself. In the Platonic tradition out of which the church fathers theologized, it belonged to the nature of an image to imitate the model from whence it is derived. To Christian thinkers, while all things may be like God, the human person alone is in his image, and thus the only creature made to receive and appropriate the divine nature (see 2 Pet. 1:4).

Clement of Alexandria was the first Christian to use the term θεοποιεῖν in any meaningful soteriological sense.[31] Dionysius the Areopagite was the first to define the term, as "the attaining of likeness to God and union with him so far as is possible."[32] But it was Athanasius who gave the Christian tradition its most lasting expression of deification in Christ: "God became human so humans could become gods."[33] Here the *imago Dei* receives its most robust

---

[26] Gregory of Nyssa, *Homily on the Lord's Prayer* §2; PG 44:1144.

[27] Jaroslov Pelikan, *Christianity and Classical Culture: The Metamorphosis of Natural Theology in the Christian Encounter with Hellenism* (Yale University Press, 1993) 124. For an excellent synopsis into how the Christian view of the *imago Dei* aided the dignity of women and others on the peripheries of Graeco-Roman society, see Nonna Verna Harrison, *God's Many-Splendored Image* (Grand Rapids, MI: Baker Books, 2010), 92–106.

[28] *Confessions* 1.1.1: "You stir us so that praising you may bring us joy, because you have made us and drawn us to yourself (*ad te*) and our heart is unquiet until it rests in you"; trans., Maria Boulding, as in *The Confessions*, ed. and annotated by David Meconi (San Francisco: Ignatius Press, 2012) 3; the Latin *quia fecisti nos ad te* hearkens the *ad* of Gen 1:26; CCL 47.1.

[29] Gregory of Nyssa, *On the Making of Man* §16; PG 44.179B.

[30] Basil of Caesarea, used at his own funeral by Gregory of Nazianzus, *Oration* §43.48; PG 36.560A.

[31] See Protrepticus 1.8; Paedagogus 1.6.26.

[32] *Ecclesiastical Hierarchy* 1.3; PG 3.376A.

[33] Athanasius, *De Incarnatione* §54; PG 25.192B.

purpose: not only to be fulfilled in God but to become like him. Theologians who stress the deifying consequence of the incarnation hold that the fallen image in humanity is not only restored to what was lost in Eden but made even infinitely more glorious—to become heaven itself.[34]

St Augustine was the first to notice that the original images, Adam and Eve, created on the sixth day were created incompletely. Augustine's very careful reading of Genesis alerted him to how the sixth day did not receive its own conclusion. Whereas other days of creation cease with the divine declaration, "and God saw that it was good," we read at the eve of the sixth day that, "God looked at *everything* he had made and he found it very good. Evening came and morning followed, the sixth day" (Gen. 1:31). Here Augustine comments that God "did not say individually about the human creature, as in the other cases, *And God saw that it was good,* but after the man was made and given rights, whether to rule or to eat, he concluded about them all: *And God saw all the things that he had made, and behold they were very good.*"[35] Adam and Eve were created incompletely because as images of God, that image had still to be fulfilled. Augustine goes on to note that this promise was also the cause of humanity's downfall.

Made to be like God, the one thing which Adam and Eve lacked was the very one thing the Enemy could have used to entice Adam and Eve's disobedience. According to Augustine, every image longs to be like the Model from whence it comes.[36] Therefore, when Satan promised Adam and Eve divinity—you will be like gods (Gen. 3:5)—he was not so much lying as he was usurping his power in promising something which was of course never his to grant. A clever exegesis emerges. Augustine argues that on the natural level, the first couple had everything perfectly (for this is precisely what Eden represents), but they still lacked one unfulfilled promise. The only reality due to them that was still lacking was their divine transformation. This therefore is the only good with which the Enemy could have tempted them. The image of God in every human soul orients each image toward God and humans accordingly spend their lives searching to have that divine image fulfilled and the divine likeness realized.

As mentioned, Irenaeus of Lyon was the first to notice that image and likeness were separated in the original creation of the human person. For Irenaeus, however, this was not a diminishment or a lessening but an invitation to see this world as the place where one could become like God and thus fulfill the ultimate human vocation. Irenaeus is unique among the Fathers in his depiction of Adam and Eve as innocent children who must learn to navigate their way in this world:

---

[34] This is perhaps best seen in Augustine's emphasis that while in Eden humans were able not to sin and able not to die (*posse non peccare/posse non mori*) but in Christ now, the elect are actually unable to sin, unable to die (*non posse peccare/ posse non mori*); *Literal Meaning of Genesis,* 6.25; CSEL 28.197. Origen's *8th Homily on Jeremiah* appears to be the first instance that the Christian is to become heaven, becoming a very influential trope in later oriental fathers. See, for example, Isaac of Ninevah (d. 700): "Purify yourself and you will see heaven in yourself. In yourself you will see angels and their brightness, and you will see their Master with them and in them"; *Ascetic Treatises* §43.

[35] Augustine, *Literal Meaning of Genesis* 3.24.36; trans., Edmund Hill, *On Genesis* (Hyde Park: New City Press, 2002), 239. For Augustine's view on our becoming gods in Christ, see my *The One Christ: St. Augustine's Theology of Deification* (Catholic University of America Press, 2013).

[36] Very early on he provided a philosophical answer to this imaging, depicting himself [A] talking with Reason [R] personified. [R]: Does it not seem to you that your image in a mirror [*imago tua in speculo*] wants, in a way, to be you and is false because it is not? [A]: That certainly seems so. [R]: Do not all pictures and replicas of that kind and all artists' works of that type strive to be that in whose likeness they are made? [A]: I am completely convinced that they do; *Soliloquies* 2.9.17; trans., Kim Paffenroth, *Soliloquies* (Hyde Park, New City Press, 2000), 72–3; see also, *Contra Academicos* 3.17.39 as well as *De Vera Religione* §44.82.

> *Human persons had first to be created and only then were they able to grow and mature. Having grown, they were meant to become adults and after growing in this way, to reproduce and beget other. Having multiplied, they were then to become strong, and having become strong, finally to be glorified and once glorified, to behold their Lord … the fitting expression of their union with God.*[37]

Made to function on two levels, Irenaeus stresses a point often overlooked in theological discourse: God has made his imaged creatures to mature, to develop their faculties, to ripen and thus to grow in ever closer union with him. God has set the terrestrial stage for his creatures, *not only* as a heavenly propaedeutic but as the arena where they discover who they are. Process and the slow contours of conversion are now holy, given uniquely to embodied images of God.

The *Imago Dei* Functions Against the Stern-minded

The Father of Western monasticism (and a saint in the East), John Cassian (d. 435), conveys the following hagiography with brio and satisfaction. It involves a man eponymously named Patermutus, the silent father who seeks entrance into a desert monastery. In his *Institutes*, Cassian relates this story, indicating that it is "worthy of remembrance" for the true and holy obedience it illustrates.

Patermutus arrives at the monastery of Abba John deep in the Egyptian Thebaid. Desirous to attach himself to the monastery widely known for its rigor and asceticism, Patermutus is finally allowed entrance and appears on the threshold with his eight-year-old son. In order to test Patermutus' obedience, the Abbot in full view of all present begins to slap the child and berate him; Patermutus does not flinch and seems even glad to offer up this suffering of his son, we read, "unmoved" by the boy's cheeks "streaking with the dry traces of tears." Such apathy was obvious "out of Patermutus' love for Christ." After such beatings and blows, the final test came when the Abbot tells Patermutus to throw his only son off the walls of the monastery into the Nile many stories below. Cassian recalls how Patermutus gladly embraced this challenge "as if he had been ordered to do so by the Lord" himself, and hurled the boy headlong. Fortunately, we later learn, the Abbot had brothers stationed at the river's edge to snatch the boy safely. The story ends by telling us that the father's "faith and devotion were so acceptable to God that they were immediately confirmed by divine testimony."[38] Such feats of supposed Christian heroism run throughout the genre of monastic desert theology.

Two recent works acknowledge what the story of Patermutus suggests: there is a strand of Christianity that relegates all to the heavenly and thereby belittles all that has to do with embodiment, human relationship, and what makes living as a creature meaningful. In her magisterial work on theodicy, Eleonore Stump uses Patermutus (as well as other notable Christians) to show how a certain "stern mindedness" has crept into

---

[37] Irenaeus, *Aduersus Haereses* 3.38.3; *Contre les hérésies*, Livre IV, ed. A. Rousseau, B. Hemmerdinger, C. Mercier, L. Doutreleau, *Sources Chrétiennes* 100 bis (Paris: Éditions du Cerf [1965] 2006), 954–6. The classical line of Irenaean deification runs: "For this is why the Word became human and the Son of God became the Son of Man, so that the human person through communion with the Word, would become a child of God" (*Adu. Haeres* 3.19.1).

[38] Cassian, *Institutes* 4.27; trans., Boniface Ramsey (Mahwah, NJ: Paulist Press, 2000), 92–3.

the tradition.[39] By "stern minded," Stump means a misplaced piety which manifests itself as a Christian rigor which relegates the desires of one's heart to needless distractions. The stern minded eschatologically consign all they purport to value to the heavenly kingdom. Consequently, they pride themselves for not being moved by loss of friend or family, and they strive not to be mindful of their own bodily selves, their mind's cares, or their heart's desire.[40]

Stump's lectures reveal a pessimism which many attribute to Augustine. Take, for example, Frances Young's recent compilation of her 2011 Bampton Lectures. In her conference on the *imago Dei*, "From Image to Likeness," she blames the Augustinian emphasis on original sin for Christianity's unfortunate "reinforcement of personal guilty, with resultant self-deprecation masquerading as humility."[41] Augustine's highlighting of original sin (especially as ratcheted up against the self-sufficient Pelagians) is surely responsible for some of the western church's missteps. But for my purposes, I want to argue that what Stump has labeled "stern mindedness" and Young sees simply as "pessimism," is actually traceable to the loss of the dual-functionality of the *imago Dei* in the writings of certain desert fathers.

This loss of the earthly aspect of the *imago Dei* arose through the exaggerated rigor and extreme asceticism stressed by the post-Constantinian desert movements. Such rigorism entered theology after the legalization of Christianity in 313 when the more zealous headed off into desolation; when warfare with the Roman Empire ended, some left for the desert to engage in greater battle with Satan and the wastelands of one's own soul. From here the Church received a tradition of treating one's most precious loves as nothing more than distractions, and a new strand of living as angels on earth arose.

Take the young Acacius who submitted himself to an elder knowing that this Abba would torment him daily. In his chapter on holy obedience, John Climacus (d. 606) tells us that each morning Acacius would come out of his cell with a "black eye, or a bruised neck or head" only to hear his brothers in community cry daily, "Well done, well done, put up with it, and it will be for your own good."[42] For nine years this young monk submitted himself to the beatings of a maniacal older Abba, earning the esteem of those in the community who supposedly, in all Christian charity, cared about both men. In any desert anthology, we read of great tales of life-long fasts, sleepless nights, and feats that defy human sensibilities—the Syrian, Simeon Stylites (d. 459), who lived 37 years atop a large pillar; or his Irish version, Kevin of Glendalough (d. 618) who kept his arms outstretched

[39]   Eleonore Stump, *Wandering in Darkness* (Oxford University Press, 2010).

[40]   Stump uses the power of narrative throughout to reinforce her argument, here citing such saints as Anselm and Teresa of Avila (see pp. 426–30), exhorting their interlocutors not to be moved by this world or even by the deaths of friends and family. As a Jesuit, I see in Teresa's contemporary, St Ignatius of Loyola (d. 1556), a very different Christian anthropology and approach to the world. At the beginning of his *Spiritual Exercises*, for example, the *Principle and Foundation* states that human persons are created to praise, reverence, and serve God and thereby to save their souls. But then the next line is indicative of Ignatian spirituality: all things (*omnia*) on the face of this earth are given to help each attain the end for which he or she has been created. God unites himself to those made in his image through created media, the humanity of his incarnate Son above all. The stern-minded Christian forgets this and relegates all divine image and likeness to the heavenly, to the spirit. The result is a spirituality in which "God alone matters" (a popular—and telling—phrase which appears over 150 times in the writings of St Louis De Montfort (d. 1716), but never once in Ignatius).

[41]   Frances Young, *God's Presence: A Contemporary Recapitulation of Early Christianity* (Cambridge University Press, 2013), 182.

[42]   Climacus, *The Ladder of Divine Ascent* §4; trans., Colm Lubheid and Norman Russell (Mahwah, NJ: Paulist Press, 1982), 115.

in a cruciform imitation of Christ so transfixed, that birds nested in the holes they pecked into his hands and arms.[43]

While never denigrating Christian saints nor the practices that helped school them in sanctity, I do want to argue that such extreme forms of external piety arose with the loss of the *imago Dei* in the desert fathers. In its exuberance to portray life in Christ as a new heaven, early eremitic theology insisted that the extreme Christian combatant must remove from him or herself all traces of this world. In the writings of these desert theologians, the *imago Dei* as portrayed in Eden is scarcely present. We instead encounter a theological anthropology more insistent on the extinguishing of human desires and the recalibration for the human soul away from any earthly attachments or cares to exclusively heavenly realities. To achieve this, hermetic nomenclature often employs imageries of savagery, to sever one's will, or to become a corpse for the sake of obedience, for example.

The various versions of Platonism which most of the desert thinkers would have either been directly trained in or simply picked up as being the relative *literati* of their day, reduced the tapestry of reality into a binary distinction between two worlds, one beautiful and the only true goal, the other moribund and to be fled. Here the basic principles of Platonism are spiritualized into a certain form of Christian mysticism. In Plato's central distinction between the spiritual, intelligible order and the corporeal and thus dissipating order, only the former world is to be understood as fully real and therefore fully worthy of human allegiance and energy. The visible world of flesh and of flea is to be dismissed and transcended.

While always striving to maintain the goodness of all things, the human body and need for sensation included, Plotinus often explained the salvific return to the One as fleeing the multiple distractions of this world. Only then can the soul begin to shake off the stupor embodiment induces: "I am puzzled how I ever came down, and how my soul has come to be in the body when it is what it has shown itself to be by itself, even when it is in the body."[44] For a very strong segment of the Greek tradition, to become whole is ultimately to cease to "look rearward" to the corporeal, historical, and earthly. Again, it is Plotinus who describes the perfect life as that which transcends the grief and sorrow of this world. Knowing that one's well-trained soul is now united with the One, "Even if the death of friends and relations causes grief, it does not grieve him but only that in him which has no intelligence, and he will not allow the distresses of this to move him."[45]

Such lines in Neoplatonism (as well as the central tenets of Stoicism and Middle Platonism), converge with stern minded Christianity by erring in thinking that if God alone must matter, all other objects of desire must be frightfully eliminated. An influential ascetic writer, Dorotheus of Gaza (d. c. 565), for example, held that, "if we wish to be wholly liberated from our passions we have to learn to cut off our will (κόπτειν τὰ θελήματα

---

[43] For these extreme feats of Christian other-worldliness, see G.S. Sloyan, "Piety Centered on Jesus' Sufferings and Some Eccentric Christian Understandings of the Mystery of Calvary," *Worship* 67:2 (1993), 98–123. For an illuminating overview of the influence of Simeon, see *The Lives of Simeon Stylites*, trans., Robert Doran (Kalamazoo: Cistercian Publications, 1992). Such stern mindedness is not a relic of the past. In his otherwise excellent spiritual classic, *God Within Us*, Raoul Plus, S.J. (New York: P.J. Kennedy, 1924), approvingly tells a story of "a pious woman" who "after many years of childlessness, gives birth to a daughter. The child is put in her arms, that she may embrace it. 'No,' she says, 'I will wait until she has been baptized.' How many mothers have such ardent faith as this?" p. 30. Far from edifying (dare we name her?) *Matermutus* should be corrected by the wider Christian tradition for her failing to embrace all of creation as inherently good and all persons, regardless of creed or even behavior, as innately worthy of honor and charity.

[44] *Enneads* IV.8 [6].1; trans. A.H. Armstrong, *Enneads*, vol. IV, Loeb Classical Library (Harvard University Press, 1984), 397.

[45] *Enneads* I.4 [46].4; Armstrong, *Enneads*, vol. I, op. cit., 185; this is the *prima facie* tenor of the selection (viz., *The Interior Castle*) from Teresa of Avila as cited by Stump, op. cit., 424.

ἡμῶν) and so, with God's grace, we can eventually progress until we reach freedom from desire (τὴν ἀπροσπάθειαν)."[46] In the stern-minded way of understanding both God and those persons made in his image, creatures must so die to themselves that they no longer have a self to offer; they must so die to their peculiarities and individual uniqueness that they refuse to have a personal identity or their own center of consciousness.

But in creating God has chosen not to be alone. Whereas the Neoplatonic tradition saw salvation as the *flight of the alone to the Alone*, Christianity stresses both the inherent goodness and beauty of the divine as well as the participatory goodness and beauty of the created order.[47] In creating God has relinquished his claim to be "all," but has chosen now to share his being and life and attributes, becoming "all in all" (πάντα ἐν πᾶσιν; 1 Cor. 15:28). This is a key passage in Christian anthropology: in creating, the God of Genesis longs to share his life with those of an ontologically distinct order, and in making those in his own image, God wants other persons to reflect him precisely while remaining "other" and distinct in their creaturliness.

Conclusion

Like the two-headed deity Janus who looks both forward and backward, the Christian understanding of the human person as an image and likeness of God is also two-pronged. The *imago Dei* simultaneously claims that the human person is inseparable from God yet remains always essentially distinct from the divine. That is, the life of the human animal is simultaneously a radically incessant relationship with the underived Trinity, but also the recognition that this creature will always remain dependent and contingent. In creating each person toward his own self, God has put in the soul a prolepsis to find and to become one with him. We are made for this relationship and anything else we consider "ultimate" will only disappoint.

This chapter has attempted to argue that the most foundational of Christian theology sees the essence of the human person as a divine image—that is, made both for divinity but always as a created image whose full flourishing will be found not by destroying one's created otherness but by finding the divine in that otherness. This is opposed to the "stern-minded" Christian view wherein one's holiness is marked by the tranquility one has in God alone, in an *apatheia* that even the death of a parent or sibling cannot touch. This chapter returned to many sources of the Christian tradition to show that the term image enjoyed an important pedigree in Hellenic, Hebrew, and Christian thought. In each, "image" was used to represent both the closeness to as well as the difference from God; it both united a creature to its Model, while at the same time introduced insurmountable non-identity. When read in the Genesis account in light of the perfect image of God made flesh, Christian theologians were able to stress how the excellence of human life had to incorporate matters of creation. This means that to recognize the goal of one's life in Christ is ultimately to be opened to a transformative and divinizing relationship with the one in whose image each person has been made.

---

[46] Dorotheus of Gaza, Discourse §1; *Œuvres spirituelles*, trans., Lucien Regnault and J. de Préville, vol. 92, *Sources Chrétiennes* (Paris: Éditions du Cerf, 1963), 176; see also, *Dorotheos: Practical Teaching on the Christian Life*; trans. Constantine Skouteres (Athens: Constantine Scouteris, 2000), 81.

[47] *Enneads* VI.9 [9].11; Armstrong translates this famous line as: "This is the life of the gods and of godlike and blessed men, deliverance from the things of this world, a life which takes no delight in the things of this world, escape in solitude to the solitary," *Enneads*, vol. VII, op. cit., 345.

As a creature, the *imago Dei* is always other, as image always connected; it is therefore never absorbed (abolished) or separated (autonomous). Yet the stern-minded tend to absorb, to deny the inherent goodness of creation and thus of alterity, positing all not only in God but as God, reducing the created order to a temporary interruption or to a hurdle or test. But the Creator himself tells us to be faithful stewards, to find and love him in our neighbors, to pray for bread. Because God's image is found in creation, creation not only matters, it becomes our only way back to God. That is what the incarnation is essentially about: once the perfect imprint and image became human, no image could ever come back to God now except through the human.

Ecclesial-Narratival Model of the *Imago Dei*

Dominic Robinson, S.J.

This chapter aims to outline in brief the development in Christian anthropology of what has been termed an 'ecclesial' and 'narratival' view of the doctrine of the *imago Dei*. Through this my contribution to the volume will above all be of an ecumenical nature. My study aims to demonstrate how Catholics and reformed Christians in particular may move forward in a constructive dialogue about how we understand the human person in the context of Christian faith.

An 'ecclesial' and 'narratival' view sees our human identity as the *imago Dei* as teleological and Christological. Human identity is expressed in its orientation towards a goal. According to the tradition, the goal of humans is God. This finds its root in Christ who is seen as the perfect image of God and the perfect image of humanity. To be rooted in Christ is to flourish humanly in the world as the Body of Christ in whose redemption we are incorporated. In both Catholic and Protestant traditions this teleological and Christological understanding of the *imago Dei* has been placed in the context of the narrative of redemption and comprises a relational union with others participating in the Body of Christ, thus suggesting also a strong ecclesial dimension.

For the purposes of this chapter the history of the doctrine will be divided into three parts: the Patristic period, the Reformation and the post-Vatican II period. In doing so, for reasons due to shortage of space, I focus on particular theologians who represent the key moves in the development of the doctrine. As such I do not attempt to cover every theologian or Church document, which has considered the doctrine. Rather, I attempt to show simply how there is a development of a tradition across Reformed and Catholic interpretations which sees human identity as the *imago Dei* as Christological and teleological, that is what has been described as an 'ecclesial' and 'narratival' model. So I am simply offering a set of important historical themes concerning the *imago Dei* for the purpose of drawing out some modest constructive contribution toward the end, not attempting to cover the whole history of the doctrine.

Let us first of all turn to the Patristic period. I turn first here to Augustine then to Irenaeus. This might seem at first sight unusual as Irenaeus preceded Augustine. However, Augustine is the principal source of the interpretations of the doctrine in the tradition while Irenaeus represents a nuanced perspective, which is integrated into the tradition in some more modern theology.

Augustine

A key figure in the development of the doctrine during the Patristic period is Augustine. He becomes the source of much later tradition. Augustine identifies humanity's being created in the *imago Dei* in teleological and narratival terms. We are created 'ad Imaginem' with the interior ability to participate in Wisdom, that is oriented towards a goal that is God, to participate in the life of the true image of God. For Augustine the image of God himself is also Christological. The true image is the second person of the Trinity, the Word. It is according to this relationship to the true image of God himself that humanity is created 'ad Imaginem'. Humanity itself is not in fact the *imago*, the image of God as though we reflect God in a mirror. Rather humanity is placed in a special teleological relationship with God. This basic relationship marks off humanity from all other creatures.[1]

There is, then, a basic intrinsic difference between God and humans made 'ad Imaginem Dei' which marks a chasm between us and God and so suggests the need for a central narrative of redemption. From this position Augustine develops the framework of his theological anthropology as part of a wider theology of humanity's redemption in Christ. Our human nature, despite the Fall, still yearns for this state of 'beatitudo', 'blessedness' and 'happiness'. We all have as part of our nature, because we are oriented 'ad imaginem Dei', an 'appetite' for 'blessedness', made as we are according to the image of God.[2] So how can we be saved? The basic answer for Augustine was to follow St Paul's teaching in Romans. Our salvation came through Jesus Christ. God incarnate in Jesus Christ gave his life as a ransom for the human race. Salvation comes through the sacrifice of Christ.

> Since men are in this state of wrath through original sin – a condition made still graver and more pernicious as they compounded more and worse sins with it – a Mediator was required, that is to say, a Reconciler who by offering a unique sacrifice, of which all the sacrifices of the Law and the Prophets were shadows, should allay that wrath. Thus the apostle says, 'For if, when we were enemies, we were reconciled to God by the death of his Son, even more now being reconciled by his blood we shall be saved from wrath through him.'[3]

Human beings, although created in God's image, cannot attempt to be saved themselves. They can only be saved by Christ who has paid the ransom for them. 'But now, can that part of the human race to which God hath promised deliverance and a place in the eternal Kingdom be restored through the merits of their own works? Of course not! For what good works could a lost soul do …?'[4] Our own human nature, despite our being made 'ad imaginem Dei', cannot save us. We need a Saviour who is Jesus Christ.

Human beings after the Fall can do nothing except through Christ but this does not mean that we are merely passive spectators in the special relationship with God according to whose image we are made. Augustine also opens up a teleological picture of the relationship oriented towards 'beatitudo' in the 'heavenly Jerusalem'. As such he prepares the ground for a Christian anthropology that makes us participants within Christ's body, the Church. In becoming participants in His Body we grow toward his likeness. These will be important themes to which we will return later.

---

[1] St Augustine, *De Diversis Quaestionibus* LI.2. English translation in Eugene TeSelle, *Augustine the Theologian* (New York: Herder and Herder, 1970).

[2] St Augustine, *Enchiridion on Faith, Hope and Love* (Philadelphia: Westminster Press, 1955), VIII.25.

[3] Ibid., VIII.33.

[4] Ibid., VIII.30.

Irenaeus

Although tradition had taught that Irenaeus provided a direct link with the teaching of the apostles, the less voluminous writings of this Greek Father did not take root to the same extent as the prolific Augustine. However, he is an important link for us in the development of an 'ecclesial' and 'narratival' model of the *imago Dei* which combines the call to be part of the Body of Christ with a call to grow in his likeness. While it is not always clear through the scant original material we have exactly what Irenaeus believed, he presents a clearer vision of the *imago Dei* as Christological yet teleological than that which was to become a rich Augustinian tradition in the Church.

Irenaeus made a sharper distinction between the Greek terms 'εικών', translated into Latin as *imago* and English as 'image', and 'ομοίωσις', translated into Latin as 'similitudo' and English as 'likeness'.[5] For Irenaeus our being made in God's 'image' was of great significance to understanding why Adam fell and so humanity's retention of this 'image' after the Fall through Christ becomes the key to his view of our relationship with God now. Adam's being created with the ability to choose freely and to reason meant that he was not created in God's actual 'likeness'. Thus he was in fact divided from God at the very outset in a different and far greater way than taught by Augustine. He was not just mutable and so distanced from the God who is immutable, as Augustine had taught. In fact he was also, from the very outset, created in a child-like state of imperfection that necessarily tended towards acting in a way that distanced him from God.[6] When God infused into the first human being 'the breath of life' this did not constitute him at this stage as an adopted son of God. Rather '[I]t was by a long process of response to grace and submission to God's will that Adam, equipped as he was with free choice, was intended to advance towards ever closer resemblance to His maker.'[7] The opportunity of this fresh start, this life's pilgrimage back towards God, is offered to us, through and only through the grace of Christ. As with Augustine we cannot work our way back to God on our own. However, whereas Augustine has focused more on the retention of our original sin and the possibility, or in the case of some inevitability, of our damnation, Irenaeus has focused more on how the grace of Christ offers humanity in general a fresh start.

Irenaeus develops the teaching of St Paul to present a very particular understanding of our redemption. 'Because of His measureless love He became what we are in order to enable us to become what He is.'[8] In other words the point of the incarnation was to draw us human beings into Christ, the one who is fully God and fully human. What we lost in Adam we are now enabled to regain in Christ as God's purpose is, as Paul had written, 'to sum up all things in Christ'.[9] Christ is the 'second Adam', heralding a fresh start, as he has 'recapitulated in Himself all the dispersed peoples dating back to Adam, all tongues and the whole race of mankind, along with Adam himself'.[10]

What are the implications of these divergent Patristic models? Whereas Augustine emphasises how the Fall led to God's punishment and damnation of the human race, for Irenaeus the Fall leads to negative consequences as we lose our 'likeness' to God; and this is

---

[5]   I am indebted here to the translation and paraphrasing of Irenaeus' views in J.N.D. Kelly, *Early Christian Doctrines*, 4th edn (London: Adam and Charles Black, 1958, 1968), 171, of the Greek text in Migne, *Patrologiae Graecae, Tomus VII* (Paris: Garnier Fratres and J.-P. Migne Successoris, 1882).

[6]   Ibid., 171, referring to *Adversus Haereses* 4, 38, 1–3.

[7]   Ibid., 171, referring to *Adversus Haereses* 4, 37, 1; 4, 38, 3.

[8]   Ibid., 172, referring to *Adversus Haereses* 5, Preface.

[9]   Ephesians 1:10.

[10]   Ibid., 173, translating *Adversus Haereses* 3, 22, 3.

all part of the necessary environment for human growth. But for both it is Christ who offers us the possibility of being restored in his mystical body. So Irenaeus gives a clearer account of a model of *imago Dei* which is 'ecclesial' and 'narratival'. For Augustine the emphasis here is on our redemption to our lost former state. For Irenaeus it is a constant renewal and regeneration through the ongoing redemptive power of Christ. In both the hallmark of the doctrine is both teleological and Christological and paves the way for a narrative rooted in redemption and incorporation into Christ's Body.

Luther

The issue of what caused the Reformation is very complex, involving political and cultural considerations as well as theological. However, in theological terms, differing perspectives on the relationship between God and human beings were at the heart of the dispute. Reformation theology still accepted in general terms the narratival account of Christian anthropology inherited from the Fathers. Human beings have a special dignity and special relationship with God as they are made in his image. They fall from the perfect image in which they were created. Jesus Christ, through his death and resurrection, redeems us. So much is agreed and thus is common ground. But it is in the particular understanding of the Christological force in this narrative that we find crucial points of departure.

Luther believed that medieval theology's concentration on the role of human nature in the God–human relationship after the Fall implied our ability to work our way back to God to the extent that an affirmation of belief in the total gratuity of salvation in Christ was jeopardised.[11] His intention was to correct this error and reclaim the true teaching of scripture and rightful Christocentric account of what it means to say that we are creatures made in God's image. For Luther humanity's creation in God's image does not entail the natural ability to prepare for God's justice that had characterised some medieval theology. Human beings are called simply to accept that as creatures made in his image we have been put right with God through the redemptive sacrifice of his Son Jesus Christ.

Luther's role in the development of theological thinking on humanity's creation in God's image is important. He rejects the up to this point accepted notion of the earthly pilgrimage culminating in the beatific vision such as we found in Augustine, or at least in the Platonic part of his thought, in Irenaeus and the Greek Fathers, and through to Aquinas and medieval theology. Instead he introduces a wholly different emphasis in Christian anthropology, stressing how humanity's identity can only be defined in terms of Christ's justification. In so doing Luther was not merely returning to the strand of Augustine's thought that stressed the human being's need of redemption. He is not merely saying that in the Fall God's image in humanity has been distorted and we rely on God's grace to restore us or, as Irenaeus would have it, Christ restores us as part of his plan to bring us to our fuller maturity. When we examine Luther more carefully we find a very radical Christocentric account of human identity before God that claims to represent faithfully the teaching not of any early Church Father or medieval writer but of St Paul, especially in his letter to the Romans.

To accept 'justification by faith alone' in fact answers all questions about our human identity as creatures made in God's image and entails the freedom of the Christian. Not

---

[11] Here I am giving a general introduction to Luther's thought, based in particular on his *Preface to the Latin Works*, in *D. Martin Luthers Werke: Kritische Gesamtausgabe*, vol. 54 (Weimar: Böhlau, 1938), 185.12–186.21. For a fuller account please see my monograph *Understanding the 'Imago Dei'* (Burlington, VT: Ashgate, 2011), 17–19.

to accept God's justification of us in Christ is for Luther a rejection of our true identity as creatures made in the perfect image of God who is Christ. However, if our true identity as creatures made in God's image lies in simply accepting that we are here and now right with God there is another question we must address. Has the narrative of Christian anthropology become purely passive, or in fact has narrative been written out of the doctrine altogether as we arrive at a rather static, mechanical view of the *imago Dei*? Is Luther saying that in fact all human beings are saved and that is the bald fact we are called to accept? In a complex and multi-faceted theological picture the Church Father Origen had taught universal salvation in Christ after the Fall and this had been condemned as heresy. It is unclear from Luther's writings how he saw this issue. Some scholars believe that his call to be assured of salvation amounted to a belief that we can hope that we are all saved. However others note his emphasis on the elect and see in his picture the teaching that, while we can all hope, some are saved and others condemned.

Nevertheless, regardless of this uncertainty over universal salvation, Luther leaves theology with a model of *imago Dei* which, while claiming that humanity is free in accepting the righteousness of God in Christ, at the same time portrays the believer's relationship with God as necessarily passive. There appears to be little room for a teleological and so narrative perspective in the special relationship between God and humans. On the one hand Luther's new model, in placing renewed emphasis on Christ, may be said to cut through the medieval preoccupation with our ability with God's grace to become once again like God. However, in doing this and giving the glory back to God in Christ, the human person's creation in God's image ceases to involve a reciprocal relationship with God played out actively on our earthly pilgrimage.

The Second Vatican Council[12]

In the teaching of the Second Vatican Council we have a presentation of the doctrine that integrates the Christocentric and teleological narrative and places it in a more focused ecclesial context than was present in the Fathers. Here we find a renewed understanding of the doctrine that finds its meaning and destiny in the gift of Christ. Yet this is placed in the context of a theology of deification that looks not so much vertically towards God but looks horizontally towards our fellow humans. Vatican II was to teach that, through common baptism, Christ has joined himself to fallen humanity and restored it to a special dignity as we are called into his company here on earth. It is in the documents *Lumen Gentium* and *Gaudium et Spes*[13] that we are to find this emphasis. *Lumen Gentium* was to set forth a vision of the vocation of each human being as, through baptism, called to participate here on the earth in the life and mission of Christ in which we have already been constituted as a pilgrim people.

This does not amount to a break with Catholic teaching and the tradition of the Council of Trent. Trent had stated this teaching implicitly but expressed it in a different way for

---

[12] I move to the teaching of the Second Vatican Council in order to highlight the integration of themes in Augustine and Irenaeus and in Luther. The contribution of other reformers, notably Calvin, and of the response within Catholic theology in the Council of Trent, is significant, but not discussed here in this short chapter. For a fuller treatment of this see my monograph, *Understanding the 'Imago Dei'*, 20–24.

[13] Second Vatican Council, *Lumen Gentium* [hereafter referred to as LG], and *Gaudium et Spes* [hereafter referred to as GS].

a different time. Rather it represents a continuity and development of Trent's teaching. For Trent, perceiving the need to correct Reformation theology's stress on the passivity of the God–human relationship, our call to a life of holiness emphasised the struggle of the individual's ascent back to God as fallen creatures. So it laid great emphasis on our ultimate sanctification, on our becoming less earthly and more like God, that is, through what became known as 'mortification'. 'Mortification' for the Tridentine Decree on Justification is the 'mortificando membra carnis suae', translated by Tanner as 'putting to death what is earthly in themselves'.[14] This now was to be expressed in a renewed focus on our common baptismal dignity expressing a common identity in Christ who calls us into his company as his Body, the Church.

For *Lumen Gentium* the baptised are called into a relationship with Christ, the new Adam in whom they have been reborn. So in our baptism we are already marked as holy in Christ. All are called 'by God not in virtue of their works but by his design and grace, and justified in the Lord Jesus' (LG 40). Those 'justified in the Lord Jesus' 'have been made sons of God in the baptism of faith and partakers of the divine nature, and so are truly sanctified' (LG 40). While some may argue that, in rooting the doctrine firmly in Christ, the Council was on a basic level heeding the insights of the Reformation, the shift in emphasis is a more subtle and dynamic vision of the insights of Catholic doctrine that are present in the Patristic period. It takes us further into discussion of the mystery of the human person and our role in the world as members of his Body the Church. It is above all *Gaudium et Spes* which develops these themes.

Christ, states # 22, is the "image of the invisible God' (Col. 1:15),[15] is himself the perfect man who has restored in the children of Adam that likeness to God which had been disfigured ever since the first sin. Human nature, by the very fact that it was assumed, not absorbed, in him, has been raised in us also to a dignity beyond compare' (GS 22). Christ not only puts us right with God but explains our vocation and special dignity as creatures made in God's image. For Christ is construed here not as counter to fallen human nature. On the contrary it is Christ's own humanity, assumed and not absorbed, which joins him to our humanity and represents to us the perfect image of God. Our humanity is not lost. Rather our human nature is, through him, as Ladaria puts it 'exalted to its supreme dignity'.[16]

Thus each human being made in God's image and reborn in Christ is above all worthy of great respect and his or her vocation is not simply to return to the Creator but to make Christ present here on the earth. Our ongoing relationship with Christ involves a communal and social dimension. So *Gaudium et Spes* was able to outline a belief in the essential dignity of the human being who, while made for God we must affirm 'by his innermost nature [man is] a social being' (GS 12). Our vocation is to grow in our likeness to Christ but this cannot be construed in any way as purely individualistic or divorced from the reality of life here on earth. Rather, because in baptism we are conformed to Christ, image of the invisible God on earth, we are called to active participation in his mission in the life of the Church in the world. So *Lumen Gentium* can proclaim:

> It is therefore quite clear that all Christians in any state or walk of life are called to
> the fullness of the Christian life and to the perfection of love, and by this holiness a
> more human manner of life is fostered also in earthly society. In order to reach this
> perfection the faithful should use the strength dealt out to them by Christ's gift, so

---

[14] Council of Trent, Decree on Justification, # 10.

[15] Cf. 2 Cor. 4:4.

[16] Luis Ladaria, 'Humanity in the Light of Christ in the Second Vatican Council', in *Vatican II: Assessment and Perspectives*, R. Latourelle, ed. (New York and Mahwah: Paulist Press, 1989), 391.

that, following in his footsteps and conformed to his image, doing the will of God in everything, they may wholeheartedly devote themselves to the glory of God and to the service of their neighbour.[17]

Our conformity to God's image directs us outwards to our fellow humans. This ecclesial dimension flows into the Second Vatican Council's renewed emphasis on the Christian disciple's active role in society. *Gaudium et Spes* goes on to proclaim the need to transcend an individualistic morality. The keynote is the fundamental respect for each human person as a child of God in Christ and the heightened role of the Church in building up a society that promotes this. This has become more and more the orientation of the postconciliar Church in its social and ethical teaching.

In short, Vatican II has brought two motifs to the fore. On the one hand the Council wished to emphasise how Christ is the answer to all questions about our human identity. However, it also wanted to reassert that we cannot simply passively accept our justification. Christ calls us into a relationship with him that at one and the same time affirms our special dignity as creatures made in God's image and draws us into his company. This directs us outwards towards others as partners on his mission as the Church. Our ongoing relationship with him is not just about our future destiny but represents a communal call to build up the Body of Christ here on the earth. It is about our destiny yet is rooted in our membership of the Church through participation in the Body of Christ. Thus a more fully 'ecclesial' and 'narratival' understanding of the *imago Dei* has, through ecumenical integration, taken root in postconciliar Catholic theology.

Hans Urs von Balthasar

One key interpreter of the tradition coming down through Vatican II has been Hans Urs von Balthasar. I single him out in this chapter because it seems that he incorporates much of the tradition from the Fathers and the Reformation in presenting a dynamic 'ecclesial' 'narratival' view of the *imago Dei* expressive of the Vatican II hermeneutic.

Balthasar owes much to his Protestant dialogue partner Karl Barth. It is principally from Barth that he discovers the insights of Reformation Christian anthropology. In particular Balthasar is interested in Barth's objection to any theological system that gave glory to human beings rather than gave the glory to God. For Balthasar human identity is clearly rooted in the person of Christ and his involvement in human lives. So Balthasar's Christian anthropology is not above all working in the traditional Catholic framework of Trent, Aquinas and a more teleological interpretation of Augustine. Rather he is placing his emphasis on how our lives are transformed through the appearance of Christ on the human horizon as the revelation of God.

So our Christian response to God is not first and foremost about a quest for God in the next life. Rather the 'Gestalt' is a human person Jesus, with real flesh and blood, who in the world here and now is immersed in our human condition, and through this meets us. The emphasis is not so much that we sinners need to turn to God. God comes to us in Christ as the beautiful immersed in the ugliness of our world. Precisely in this appearance of Christ on the horizon of our lives is our personal loving call to participate with him on his mission here and now. To this we cannot but respond as actors in this drama of the beautiful amidst

---

[17] LG, # 40.

the ugly. The Christocentric narrative draws us into a call to be incorporated in the Body of Christ, the Church.

Balthasar expresses these insights above all through dramatic narrative. In particular the narrative is rooted in the drama of Christ's descent into the underworld.[18] In doing so he places Christian anthropology in the context of the redemptive action of Christ. In the underworld Christ is at one with humanity in humanity's ugliness. 'By it [the descent into the underworld]', says Balthasar, 'Christ takes the existential measure of everything that is sheerly contrary to God.'[19]

Balthasar emphasises how this final act of Christ's obedient engagement in the plight of humanity, disfigured through disobedience, is necessary in an account of redemption. 'The Son', he states, 'must "take in with his own eyes what in the realm of creation is imperfect, informed, chaotic", so as to make it pass over into his own domain as the Redeemer'.[20] It is this action of Christ on Holy Saturday, when he is at one with the fallen, which then draws us back to him on our pilgrimage through life. This pilgrimage now ties us to Christ as we follow him as disciples on mission here on earth and it culminates in our oneness with him in Heaven. Thus, through Christ's call into his company, the more teleological vision of human pilgrimage and deification comes into play as Balthasar now returns to the Early Church Fathers to develop a fundamentally Christocentric but also dramatic and aesthetic theological anthropology which emphasises our earthly encounter with and participation in Christ's mission. Irenaeus' perspective, as well as Augustine's, is significant for him. 'The vision of chaos by the God-man has become for us the condition of our vision of the Divinity.'[21]

Absolutely central to his scheme is the fact that human beings are fundamentally indefinable except through reference to Jesus Christ. So Balthasar cannot appropriately define how we are created *imago Dei* except through proclaiming how it is Christ who has restored us to our divinely willed dignity:

> In a Christian theodramatic theory we have the right to assert that no other, mythical or religio-philosophical anthropology can attain a satisfactory idea of man, an idea that integrates all the elements, but the Christian one. It alone can release man from the impossible task of trying, on the basis of his brokenness, to envisage himself as not broken, without forfeiting some essential aspect of himself in the process. It releases him from this burden by inserting him, right from the start, into the dramatic dialogue with God, so that God himself may cause him to experience his ultimate definition of man.[22]

Thus, starting from a firm belief in Christ's immersion in the world, a Weltanschauung based on the incarnation and Trinitarian love *ad extra*, Balthasar can weave a picture of a relationship between a broken God and a broken humanity, of humanity's brokenness in relation to God's love. Indeed God draws us to himself as lover through his very victorious brokenness that extended to the point of meeting us in the ugliness of the underworld. The drama of the relationship between God and his creation will be one of an interplay between

---

[18] Hans Urs von Balthasar, *Mysterium Paschale* (Edinburgh: T. and T. Clark, 1990), 164–81 [hereafter referred to as MP].

[19] MP, 174.

[20] Ibid., 175. Balthasar states that he is quoting from the Gospel of St John.

[21] Ibid., 175, quoting St Irenaeus, *Summa Alexandri* 3.7.1.1. *Quaracchi* 4, 205 (Balthasar's own notes).

[22] Hans Urs von Balthasar, *Theo-Drama: Theological Dramatic Theory II: Dramatis Personae: Man in God* (hereafter referred to as TD) (San Francisco: Ignatius Press, 1990), 343.

God's 'infinite freedom' in love and humanity's 'finite freedom' to respond or not to that love as God in Christ opens us to its possibility. This is what our lives will be about. This is the essence of our humanity. '... if we want to ask about man's "essence", we can do so only in the midst of his dramatic performance of existence. There is no other anthropology but that which is rooted in the drama of the narrative of Christ's redemption and call into his company'.[23]

So Balthasar, on the one hand, can hold firm to the necessity of understanding the human being's special dignity only in terms of God himself in Christ. Thus we might say that he is following Barth in his perceived return to the Fathers of the Early Church. All the glory is given to God. Any philosophy or anthropology which tries to find a way to God is to be rejected. Yet, at the same time, Balthasar's multi-faceted view wants to allow for some kind of innate human quest for relationship with the infinite. Human beings are opened up to the beauty of the love of God in the Christ who meets them in their sinful state. They can move and ought to respond to the beckoning of Christ to fulfill their desire for the infinite. The human being is on a journey from finitude back to infinity, to God himself. These latter themes are much more in keeping with the traditional Catholic understanding of grace co-operating with nature. However, Balthasar's aesthetic and dramatic understanding of this is closely tied to a post-Vatican II understanding of the human beings' response to grace as an actual incorporation into the life of Christ who has claimed him. Drawn into Christ's company we live out our call not in isolation but in relation to others, as we are constituted as Christ's disciples on a mission.

It is in the meeting of these strands to his thought that we find in Balthasar a distinctive new ecumenical contribution to the postconciliar understanding of *imago Dei*. In particular we find in his writings a new evaluation of the Reformed Tradition. This aspect of his thought enables him to appreciate the work of Barth and the Reformation while developing a fundamentally Catholic postconciliar understanding of the graced dignity and freedom of the human person called into Christ's company and so placed with him on his mission in the Church.

Conclusion

This chapter has attempted to trace some of the themes which outline the development of an 'ecclesial narratival' doctrine of the *imago Dei* for today. In the Patristic period Augustine is an important primary theological source. He stressed how in the Fall the divine image is distorted through our sin. Thus our reliance on the grace of Christ to restore the image becomes also a very powerful motif. Future theology will tend to place a similar emphasis on our need for a saviour. However the tradition will interpret Augustine in different ways. In very general terms we might conclude that, at first blush, Reformation theology will want to stress human passivity through a firm belief in the absolute inability of humanity to participate in the divine life after the Fall. God's image in us is restored and we simply are to accept that in faith. On the other hand a more Catholic apologetic theology, while clearly accepting Augustine's belief in the necessity of grace and condemnation of Pelagianism, will look to Augustine's Platonism, his picture of humanity's pilgrimage back towards a vision of God, actively worked out through a life of virtue.

---

[23] TD II, 335.

Both Catholic and Reformed theology, however, will also be influenced by other significant perspectives in the history of the tradition. They will turn not just to Augustine, but also to the earlier Irenaeus. In rediscovering Irenaeus they will find a complementary vision that distinguishes more sharply between our creation in God's image, which at the Fall is distorted but in some way retained, and our creation in his likeness, which we lose but strive to regain through life. Rather than stress damnation and salvation, Irenaeus sees our imperfection as a necessary aid to our growth as we are restored to Christ's image.

The Reformation itself was to react strongly to the more philosophical and scientific medieval approach to the doctrine of *imago Dei*. The Reformers were to reject the move to express human identity in terms of divine possibility and ascent to God. Thus, in general terms, we might say that the sixteenth-century theological world became something of a battleground between this Reformation emphasis on human passivity in the face of Christ's once-and-for-all restoration of the divine image after the Fall and the Catholic emphasis on our active participation in a relationship with Christ as we worked to achieve our divine destiny in Heaven. The Reformation position was laid out especially in Luther's doctrine that we are 'justified by faith alone'. The Council of Trent, on the other hand, responded to the Reformation by reaffirming a strong belief in the compatibility of a belief in God's grace in Christ with the more teleological portrayal of the human path back to God. In particular Trent stressed that we co-operate with grace through mortification, putting to death what is earthly in ourselves in order to find our way to Heaven.

It was the Second Vatican Council, in the documents *Lumen Gentium* and *Gaudium et Spes*, that was to develop a more dynamic and integrated Catholic vision of the human being's creation in *imago Dei*. While clearly holding to the Tridentine vision of the compatibility of grace and human nature after the Fall, and rejecting the doctrines taught by the Reformers, Vatican II was able to set forth a picture of the vocation of each human being which placed greater emphasis on how through our common baptism we are called to participate here on the earth in the life and mission of Christ in which we have already been constituted as a pilgrim people. Thus a new ecclesial Christocentric emphasis was placed on our special dignity here on earth as creatures made in his image. This makes way for a theological narrative in which God calls us here and now to build up the Kingdom as a community rather than to work out our own divine destiny in the heavenly Jerusalem.

In focusing on Hans Urs von Balthasar we see this ecclesial narratival model in closer focus. Balthasar learns much from Barth and the Reformation tradition. Christ is primary and paramount in his thought. Yet he will integrate this into a fundamentally Catholic tapestry of human life drawn into the company of Christ with whom we are placed on mission. Dramatic narrative will help him to present this perspective and shed light on the tradition he studies in detail. Through these categories, also, and notably his interpretation of Barth, Balthasar will attempt to form a model of *imago Dei* which suggests infinite possibility in a dialogical encounter between God and humans. This is more of a vocational model. Christ is still at the apex but calls us to live out our destiny actively as his companions on his mission in his Body, the Church.

A Christological Model of the *Imago Dei*

Oliver Crisp

> *The concept of the image of God is at the heart of Christian anthropology.*
> —Anthony Hoekema[1]

What is the "image of God"? What is it for human beings to be created "in God's image"? There are a number of different answers to these questions in the Christian tradition. This chapter sets out and recommends one particular account. Call it, *the Christological doctrine*. On this view the image of God is borne by one individual, Christ. Other human beings are made in the image of God to the extent that they are conformed to the likeness of Christ. We might say that they are ectypes of the archetype of the divine image in Christ. Rather like the prototype of an automobile and the production model that is based upon the blueprints of the prototype, Christ is the "prototypical" human. We are made in *his* image, as it were, so that we reflect God in some measure as we image Christ, the God man.

In the biblical tradition human beings are said to have been created in the image (*zelem*) and likeness (*Demut*) of God (Gen. 1:26–7). There has been much theological debate about whether the terms "image" and "likeness" in the Primeval Prologue to Genesis are synonyms, or should be distinguished as two different states or stages of human moral development. However, it appears that these two terms refer to the same thing, namely, the human person taken as a whole, acting as the divine representative on earth (*tselem*).[2] By contrast, in the New Testament Christ is said to be the image (*ikon*) of the invisible God, the firstborn over all creation, by whom all things are made (Col. 1: 15), the exact representation of the being of the Father (Heb. 1:3), and the image of God (2 Cor. 4:4). St Paul tells us in Rom. 8:29 that, "those whom he foreknew he also predestined to *be conformed to the image of his Son*, in order that he might be the firstborn among many brothers." On the basis of such biblical claims St Irenaeus writes,

> For in times long past, it was said that man was created after the image of God, but it was not [actually] shown; for the Word was as yet invisible, after whose image man was created, Wherefore also he did easily lose the similitude. When, however,

---

[1] Hoekema, *Created in God's Image* (Grand Rapids: Eerdmans, 1986), 66.

[2] This is an instance of Hebrew parallelism. For discussion, see Richard J. Plantinga, Thomas R. Thompson, and Matthew D. Lundberg, *An Introduction to Christian Theology* (Cambridge: Cambridge University Press, 2010), 182–5. Also relevant are R.W.L. Moberly, *The Theology of The Book of Genesis*, Old Testament Theology Series (Cambridge: Cambridge University Press, 2009), ch. 2; Gehard von Rad, *Genesis* (Philadelphia: Westminster Press, 1961), 56; William Dyrness, "The *Imago Dei* and Christian Aesthetics," *Journal of the Evangelical Theological Society* 15.3 (1972): 161–72, esp. 162.

the Word of God became flesh, He confirmed both these: for He both showed forth the image truly, since He became Himself what was His image; and He re-established the similitude after a sure manner, by assimilating man to the invisible Father through means of the visible Word.[3]

Similarly, St Athanasius writes that after the Fall, God was faced with the prospect of a defaced image in human beings:

What, then, was God to do? What else could He possibly do, being God, but renew His Image in mankind, so that through it men might come once more to know Him? And how could this be done save by the coming of the very Image Himself, our Saviour Jesus Christ? Men could not have done it, for they are only made after the Image; nor could angels have done it, for they are not the Images of God. The Word of God came in His own Person, because it was He alone, the Image of the Father, who could recreate man after the Image.[4]

The argument that follows takes its point of departure from these patristic accounts of the image of God as they reflect the biblical traditions. It has three parts. In the first, two traditional approaches to the doctrine of the image of God are set out and assessed. Then, in a second section the Christological doctrine is offered as an alternative to the two traditional approaches to the divine image. In a third section some objections to this model are considered.

Two Approaches to the Divine Image

Often in historic discussion of the image of God it has been identified with some capacity or power, or something about the nature of human beings that sets them apart from other creatures. Thus John Calvin writes that,

although the soul is not the man, there is no absurdity in holding that he is called the image of God in respect of the soul; though I retain the principle which I lately laid down, that the image of God extends to everything in which the nature of man surpasses that of all other species of animals. Accordingly, by this term is denoted the integrity with which Adam was endued when his intellect was clear, his affections subordinated to reason, all his senses duly regulated, and when he truly ascribed all his excellence to the admirable gifts of his Maker. And though the primary seat of the divine image was in the mind and the heart, or in the soul and its powers, there was no part even of the body in which some rays of glory did not shine.[5]

---

[3]   Irenaeus, *Against Heresies* in *Ante-Nicene Fathers, Vol. 1: The Apostolic Fathers, Justin Martyr, Irenaeus*, eds. and trans. Alexander Roberts and James Donaldson (Peabody, MA: Hendrickson Publishers, 1994 [1885]), V. XVI. 2, p. 544.

[4]   St Athanasius, *On the Incarnation*, §13, trans. A Religious of C.S.M.V. (Crestwood, NY: St. Vladimir's Seminary Press, 2003).

[5]   John Calvin, *Institutes of The Christian Religion*, ed. John T. McNeil, trans. Ford Lewis Battles (Philadelphia: Westminster Press, 1960 [1559]), 1. 15. 3.

This is not just a Protestant approach to the divine image. Similar ideas can be found in the *Catechism of the Catholic Church*, which states "By virtue of his soul and his spiritual powers of intellect and will, man is endowed with freedom, an 'outstanding manifestation of the divine image.'"[6]

This sort of view is often referred to as *the substantive account of the image of God*, since it equates the image with something substantive about human beings, such as possession of an immaterial substance, or soul, or certain powers associated with the soul or the human person, such as rationality.[7] (These are not mutually exclusive, of course. For instance, one might identify the divine image with rationality *as exemplified by* the human soul.) Calvin represents a substantive account of the divine image in human beings, in keeping with the Augustinian tradition in which he stands. For Calvin, the divine image shines in all parts of unfallen humanity, but is especially present in the soul with its various powers, especially the powers of the intellect and affections, rightly governed by reason. It is this pristine state from which human beings fell in Adam, so that fallen human beings bear at most a defaced remnant of this divine image that requires the secret work of the Holy Spirit to be renovated and restored.[8]

The problems with this doctrine are well known. Here are some of the most obvious. First, if the image of God is a capacity or power (construed broadly to include things like the capacity to think, and therefore, rationality, as in the *Catechism of the Catholic Church*) it is difficult to demarcate human beings from other sorts of created entity. Do certain sorts of simians have such rationality? Do dolphins? Surely angels do. Yet the image of God is usually thought to be a property of human beings alone among God's creatures. If that is right, then the divine image cannot be identified with rationality, for it is not at all clear that that is a characteristic unique to human beings.

This approach also raises worries about the measure of the given power or capacity necessary to exemplify the image. Take rationality once more, since it has been a popular candidate in historic discussion of the topic.[9] What are we to make of human beings that fail to exemplify this capacity, like those in utero, or infants, or those who are severely mentally impaired, or in permanent vegetative states, or that are born encephalic?

---

6   See *The Catechism of the Catholic Church* III. I. 1 Art. 1, 1705 located online at: http://www.vatican.va/archive/ccc_css/archive/catechism/p3s1c1a1.htm. Some of the Protestant Confessions are more ambiguous, e.g. *The Westminster Confession*, which says this: "After God had made all other creatures, He created man, male and female, with reasonable and immortal souls, endued with knowledge, righteousness, and true holiness, after His own image" (WCF IV. II). Wolfhart Pannenberg makes it clear that "The classical understanding of the divine likeness in Christian theology relates it to the soul." Wolfhart Pannenberg, *Systematic Theology Vol. 2*, trans. Geoffrey Bromiley (Grand Rapids: Eerdmans, and Edinburgh: T. & T. Clark, 1995 [1991]), 206. This is broadly correct. For a recent and accessible account of the image of God that equates it with possession of a soul, see J.P. Moreland, *The Recalcitrant Imago Dei: Human Persons and the Failure of Naturalism* (London: SCM Press, 2009).

7   Sometimes this substantive view is called the structural view (thus, Hoekema). However, the benefit of the former appellation is that it makes clear the fact that according to this way of thinking, the image of God is something about human beings that is essential or substantive, e.g. a property, power, or nature that belongs to a certain sort of entity.

8   Calvin is a somewhat frustrating interlocutor on this matter because he appears to say different things in different places in his corpus about whether the divine image has been effaced post-Fall, or merely severely damaged. In keeping with most Calvin interpreters, I am reading him as a proponent of the latter, less extreme view, which does seem to represent the preponderance of his writings on this matter.

9   See Thomas Aquinas, *Summa Theologiae* I. 93. 6. The patristic discussion of the divine image has informed all subsequent debate in Christian theology. For an interesting recent treatment of this material, see Frances Young, *God's Presence: A Contemporary Recapitulation of Early Christianity* (Cambridge: Cambridge University Press, 2013), ch. 4.

For most Christians, moral intuitions will press in the direction of including most if not all such entities within the bounds of human personhood. Yet none of these sorts of individuals actually possess rationality (though some may have the dispositional property of rationality, such as infants). But then it looks like there are some humans (perhaps, human persons) that lack a necessary condition for being made in the divine image, which is an outcome few Christian theologians will want to embrace given that the divine image is not usually thought to be something accidental, but essential to human persons. (Humans are, after all, said to be *made in* the divine image in Gen. 1:26–7.)

As we have seen, Calvin is more expansive in what he thinks falls under the image of God. He includes the body as a part of human beings in which the rays of the image shine. Following his lead, other Reformed theologians have also argued that the whole human person must be included within the notion of the divine image, not merely human rationality, or even a human soul. But it is difficult to see how the defender of a substantive doctrine can make good on this claim, since God is essentially disembodied. How can a corporeal body be said to be made in the image of an essentially immaterial agent, like God? This seems to be a straightforward category mistake.[10]

Suppose the claim is that God's image in human beings is essential, and has to do inextricably with rationality. Presumably, human beings image God in this respect in virtue of having the capacity for a certain sort of complex mental life. Even if one thinks that human beings are material objects, as with physicalism, this does not necessarily mean that human bodies are in the image of God. All it requires is that humans exemplify certain properties requisite for certain mental states, like rationality. Since properties are not physical objects, it makes no sense to say that the instantiation of those properties in human beings has to do with the corporeality of human beings, as if being embodied were somehow a constituent of the divine image in human beings.

Having said that, although this approach appears to be mired in difficulties, which is why many contemporary theologians have begun to look elsewhere for ways of conceiving the image of God, I do not claim that the defender of such a position is without resources or potential responses. Nevertheless, there are significant obstacles in the way of an attempt to rehabilitate this approach to the image of God without recourse to supplemental theses and additional arguments—as we shall see in due course, when considering the Christological doctrine.

More recently, theologians have thought that a better way of characterizing the image as it is set forth in Gen. 3 is what is often called *the relational account of the image of God*. On this view, human beings bear the divine "image" as they relate to one another and to God, and act as divine regents over the created order. Thus, David Fergusson writes:

> In its Hebraic context, the divine image refers not to the possession of an immortal
> soul (as in the Greek tradition) but more to the role exercised by human beings in
> the cosmic order. As those who can hear and obey the divine word, human beings
> are charged with acting on God's behalf in relation to one another and to the rest of
> creation. This more functional or relational account of the divine image makes better

---

[10] Herman Bavinck is one Reformed theologian that thinks human bodies must be included within the ambit of the divine image in humans. Greshen Machen resists this for the reasons given here. A useful discussion of these matters can be found in Hoekema, *Created in God's Image*, 67–8. Hoekema sides with Bavinck. He says, "If it is true that the whole person is the image of God, we must also include the body as part of the image" (ibid., 68). We shall see that Hoekema's intuition, which reflects the Primeval Prologue in Genesis, can be included within the Christological doctrine. This is one reason for preferring it to what we might call the *merely* substantive doctrine.

sense of the succeeding verses that speak of the roles of human beings in the world already made.[11]

Although variations on the relational doctrine are in the ascendency in biblical studies and modern theology, there is reason to doubt that this really captures all that is meant by the divine image in human beings. For one thing, it does not really do justice to the claim in Gen. 1:26–7 that human beings are made *in* or *after* God's image, unless one connects this image to those versions of social trinitarianism, according to which there are three centers of consciousness in the divine life relating to one another in eternal perichoresis. Then human beings image God as they (somehow) reflect this irreducible relationality within the Godhead. However, for those that find such social views of the Trinity unappealing (such as the present author), or who find the supposed connection between the divine life, human relationality, and the image of God, tenuous or even implausible, this provides no motivation for a relational doctrine of the image of God.

One might hold to a relational view of the divine image without appeal to social trinitarianism, however. For instance, it might be that the divine image has to do with oversight and care for the creation, with human beings acting as divine vice-regents, relating to one another, to the other creatures over whom they have a certain derived authority and responsibility, and to God their creator. This seems to be what Fergusson has in mind in the passage just cited.

However, as with the substantive doctrine, it is not clear how this adequately distinguishes human beings from other entities. That is, it is not apparent from such a characterization of the divine image why *only* human beings bear it. Other creatures relate to one another, to the rest of the creation, and (possibly) to their creator. Certainly angels do this. Yet they are not traditionally thought to be image-bearers in the way that human beings are. It might be thought that there is something about the divinely-bestowed role of overseeing the creation that makes human beings unique. In virtue of this role they relate to the creation (and to God) in a way that no other creature does, not even angels. There is textual and exegetical support for this view. However, this also presents challenges for contemporary constructive theologians. For instance, some are uncomfortable with notions of human "dominion" over other creatures, which seem to them to be quaint or imperialistic, even speciesist. However, suppose some mileage can be gotten from the notion that human beings have a unique role in overseeing the created order, how does this in-and-of-itself provide a reason for thinking that this exhausts what is meant by the divine image? How does it account for the way in which the New Testament identifies the image with Christ and the redeemed? At the very least this reading of the biblical material leaves a number of important theological questions unanswered.

In recent theology there have been other attempts to find a relational basis for the image of God that does not fall foul of this worry about human uniqueness. One example can be found in the systematic theology of the Lutheran, Robert Jenson. He has argued that "our specificity in comparison with the other animals is that we are the ones addressed by God's moral word and so enabled to respond—that we are called to *pray*." Jenson goes

---

[11]   David Fergusson, "Creation" in John Webster, Kathryn Tanner, and Iain Torrance, eds, *The Oxford Handbook of Systematic Theology* (Oxford: Oxford University Press, 2009), 74. Other influential modern theologians that espouse a relational view of the image of God include Karl Barth, Jürgen Moltmann, and Wolfhart Pannenberg. It is a view one can find among Christian philosophers too. One example is Kevin Corcoran. See *Rethinking Human Nature: A Christian Materialist Alternative to the Soul* (Grand Rapids, Michigan: Baker Academic, 2006), 81. I owe this reference to Joshua Farris.

on to say that "the final specification of 'the image of God' is love."[12] Is he right about this—can the divine image be identified with certain relations humans normally possess, and specifically with loving and praying? Although these might be thought improvements upon the medieval notion that the image was to be identified with, or (at least) intimately bound up with, rationality, these alternatives do not appear able to overcome the worry about human uniqueness. Are we to say of those incapable of prayer (e.g. patients in a permanent vegetative state, and so forth), or those that do not pray that they have nothing of the divine image, or, alternatively, only some reduced amount of it? As for those who are impaired in their capacity to love (e.g. sociopaths, the severely mentally handicapped), do they possess less of the divine image because they are incapable of appropriately giving and receiving love?

This does not seem at all theologically satisfactory. For one thing, it suggests that certain human individuals suffering from particular personality disorders like sociopaths, or from particular mental incapacities, do not instantiate the divine image in the same manner as do other human beings. But, as with the objection from human uniqueness applied to substantive views, so too here: an argument for the image of God that excludes *ex hypothesi* a certain group of human persons from consideration, or calls their inclusion in the divine image into serious question, is hardly theologically satisfying if the image is thought to be an essential human characteristic.

In addition to these worries, it could be objected that relational views of the divine image rely upon implied ontological claims that render them, at bottom, substantive after all. J.P. Moreland writes, "Even if we functionalize the image or treat it in largely relational terms ... it is still true that a thing's functional abilities or relational aptitudes are determined by its kindedness," i.e. by the natural kind to which it belongs. "Thus, even the functional, relational aspects of the image of God have ontological implications."[13] Thus, if humans do represent God in their dominion over creation they do so because they have the requisite properties and powers by means of which they exercise such dominion. Alternatively, if humans image God in their interpersonal relations (which, some suppose, are analogs to divine relationality) then this obtains just in case the humans in question have certain powers and properties, and are the sort of thing that can exemplify relationality (like God). So it looks like the relational account of the divine image depends upon ontological claims of the sort we find in the substantive account. If that is right then relational accounts of the divine image are not really distinct from substantive views, but supplement or extend them.

Yet these are not the only alternatives on the doctrine of the image of God.[14] Suppose human beings image God as they are conformed to the image of Christ, who, being the Son of God incarnate, is the image of the invisible God (i.e. the image of the Father) in human flesh. Such a notion provides the basis for a Christological gloss on Gen. 1 that makes sense of the New Testament claims about the relation between Christ as the principle image-bearer, and fallen human beings as those that are being conformed to the divine image by being united to Christ. It is this doctrine, which is very ancient indeed, and can be traced back to

---

[12]   Robert W. Jenson, *Systematic Theology Vol. 2: The Works of God* (New York: Oxford University Press, 1999), 58–9 and 72, respectively.

[13]   Moreland, *The Recalcitrant Imago Dei*, 4. Hoekema makes similar claims in *Created in God's Image*.

[14]   Joshua Farris distinguishes between a functional and relational view of the image of God. However, it is not clear to me from the examples he provides that there is a real difference between these two views, so I have conflated them. See Farris, "A Fresh Immaterial Substance View of the *Imago Dei*: Refashioning a Substance View in the spirit of the Tradition for Contemporary Times," forthcoming in the *Heythrop Journal* (2015).

patristic theologians like Irenaeus and Athanasius, that we will explore in the remainder of the chapter.

I argue that it is an improvement on various iterations of the substantive and relational doctrines of the image of God because it is able to include within the scope of the divine image the whole human being, not just certain powers or capacities that supposedly distinguish humans from all other creatures. What is more, it provides a reason for thinking that there is an important relational dimension to the image of God because those made in his image are conformed to the likeness of Christ. Finally, by making Christology the theological frame for discussion of the divine image, it provides a reason for thinking that human beings possess the divine image in a way that it is not present in other creatures. This is an important consideration given the amount of ink that has been spilt trying to discover some reason for thinking that the image of God is unique to human beings.

The Christological Argument

Traditional substantive accounts of the image of God often make reference to the importance of Christ as an archetype of the divine image. Thus, the *Catechism of the Catholic Church* states that, "It is in Christ, 'the image of the invisible God,' that man has been created 'in the image and likeness' of the Creator. It is in Christ, Redeemer and Savior, that the divine image, disfigured in man by the first sin, has been restored to its original beauty and ennobled by the grace of God."[15] The idea seems to be this: Adam and Eve were endowed with the image of God, understood as possession of a human soul, and the intellectual powers of rationality and will. As a consequence of the Fall, these gifts were impaired. Christ is the Second Adam (as per Rom. 5: 12–19). He possesses in an untarnished state the divine image because he is without sin (Heb. 4: 15). Fallen human beings can have the divine image repaired in them by the secret working of the Holy Spirit in regeneration and sanctification, conforming fallen human beings to the image of God in Christ.

Yet this is not the only way to understand the excerpt from the *Catechism of the Catholic Church*. In keeping with Fathers like Irenaeus and Athanasius, it could be read in a rather different manner, one that makes the divine image not merely something that Christ repairs, but rather something that he instantiates as the archetype and divine *eikon*. On this way of thinking, human beings are made in the image of God *by being made in the image of Christ*. An illustration will help make this clearer. Imagine Michelangelo's statue of David. There is an original statue, carved from a single slab of marble and housed in the *Accademia di Belle Arti* in Florence, Italy. There are also multiple copies of this artistic marvel, including several in the environs of Florence itself. What relationship do the copies bear to the original? We might say that they reproduce the physical properties of the original—often in a different medium, such as bronze. Suppose we take a cast the original marble statue, and from this generate ten impressions in bronze. Then, we have ten copies of the original. Although the copies are in bronze not marble, they look almost identical to the original from which they have been cast (allowing for minor differences and defects that are incorporated in the replication process). Yet the ten bronzes are clearly copies or facsimiles of the original. This would be true even if they were composed of the same material.

Now, suppose Christ is like the original statue. Just as the marble slab that felt the impress of the hands of Michelangelo is the original from which the facsimiles in bronze

---

[15] *Catechism of the Catholic Church*, 1701.

were derived, so Christ is the "original," the archetypal human being who bears the image of God. Although (according to classical Christian theology) human beings are descended from an original human pair, they are not made in the image of Adam and Eve, strictly speaking. Rather, on this way of thinking, Eve, Adam, and every other human being is made in the image of Christ, who is the image of the invisible God. Hence, the divine image you and I bear is, as it were, a facsimile of that image borne by Christ; it is ectypal. Although he lived long after any first putative human community, he is the one who bears the archetypal divine image, after whose divine image the rest of humanity is fashioned.

In a recent essay on this topic, Mark McLeod Harrison says "When a 'regular' human is made, she is made from scratch as a copy of God. But Jesus pre-exists his human incarnation and thus, in a sense, *he copies humans* when he is made the incarnate God. Whereas we all resemble one another because we copy God, Jesus resembles us because he copies us."[16] It seems to me that McLeod Harrison is right about this, from a certain point of view. In a sense the human nature of God the Son is a copy of the sort of nature all other human beings possess, yet without sin. In his respect he "copies humans" when he becomes incarnate. However, without further explanation this could be misleading from the standpoint of the Christological doctrine of the divine image with which we are concerned here. For on this view it is not merely that Christ possesses a copy of human nature in virtue of his assumption of human nature. That is true, of course. But it is not terribly theologically interesting. Much more important, for the present argument, is the claim that God has ordained from before the foundation of the world that Christ would be the archetype of true humanity, and that his human nature (in hypostatic union with God the Son) would be the blueprint for all other human natures. He is the image of God as the New Testament declares. And his being the image of God has to do with the fact that God makes human nature capable of bearing union with the divine, and capable of bearing the divine imprint or image in order to do so.

Another illustration: Suppose I wanted to go to a masquerade. In order to do so, I need to purchase a disguise. It needs to "fit" my face. So I have a mask made that conforms to the contours of my visage. It would not fit your face in the same way because it is bespoke; it is made to fit me, not you. In a similar manner, the human nature of Christ is fashioned in order that it might conform to, and be in personal union with, God the Son. What I am suggesting is that in order to do this, God ordained that human nature have certain properties and powers that would mean that the particular human nature God the Son assumes at the first moment of his incarnation conforms to, and is capable of being in personal union with, a divine person. Human nature is created in order that it might reflect the divine image, and in order that it might be united to God. In the case of Christ that union is unique and personal; he has metaphysical ownership, as it were, of the human nature he assumes (just as I have ownership of my human nature). But all human beings have a nature that is capable of such hypostatic union in principle. And all human beings are given a nature that has the requisite image of God so that God the Son may unite himself with human nature. Indeed, Christ is the archetype, whose human nature is the blueprint for all other human natures.

This goes a considerable way towards explaining why the image of God we bear includes the whole of human nature (whatever that turns out to be). It is not just that I bear the divine image in my soul (if I have a soul), or in virtue of having rationality, or the capacity to love, or pray, or whatever. Rather, I bear the divine image in virtue of the fact that human nature is in principle created with the capacities and powers necessary and sufficient to be

---

[16] Mark McLeod Harrison, "On Being the Literal Image of God," *Journal of Analytic Theology* 2 (2014): 158.

in hypostatic union with a divine person.[17] This includes both my mind (and soul, if I have a soul), and body rightly configured. To abstract from human nature one aspect that is in the likeness of God is to divide what is united in Christ. He assumes a complete human nature, not merely human rationality, or a human soul (if humans have souls). It is his whole human nature that images God by being made with the capacity for hypostatic union with a divine person.

What is more, this picture of the divine image makes sense of Calvin's worries about the vitiation of that image because of human sin. Suppose with much traditional, classical Christian theology that there is a primeval Fall from grace that entails the moral defacing of the divine image in human beings thereafter. We bear a defaced image, whereas Christ who is without sin, bears the perfect image. Our image must be restored through the secret working of the Holy Spirit in regeneration. Christ's human nature does not require such repair because it is miraculously generated without sin (Heb. 4:15). For this reason he is able to act in such a way as to provide the restoration of that image in fallen human beings through an act of atonement (whatever the mechanism is by means of which he brings about that state of affairs). That is, because he does not bear a defaced divine image, he is able to act on behalf of those that do bear a defaced divine image, providing the means by which that image may be restored in redemption.

Thirdly, this view dovetails the New Testament emphasis upon Christ as the *eikon* of God with the Old Testament view of the Primeval Prologue to Genesis, according to which the image of God has to do with representing the divine on earth. Peter Enns expresses this consensus view amongst biblical scholars when he writes that the image of God in Genesis "refers to humanity's role of ruling God's creation as God's representatives." He goes on,

> We see this played out in the Ancient Near Eastern world, where kings were divine image bearers, appointed representatives of God on earth. This concept is further reflected in kings' placing statues of themselves (images) in distant parts of their kingdom so they could remind their subjects of their "presence." Further, idols were images of gods placed in ancient temples as a way of having a distant god present with the worshipers.[18]

According to Enns, the image of God in Genesis is not "that spark in us that makes us human rather than animal" such as reason, the soul, and other candidates put forward by defenders of the substantive view of the divine image. Instead, it has to do with representing God in the world.[19]

But this makes complete sense if we understand the divine image according to the Christological view. If Christ is the archetype of humanity, then the representational role the image of God plays in Genesis is consistent with the Christological focus of the New Testament. For then Christ is the archetypal human being, who represents God to humanity and humanity to God in his incarnation. He is also the prototypical human being, after

---

[17] Compare a suit of armor, which in principle provides necessary and sufficient protection from sword thrusts. However, it only actually provides me this protection if I am wearing the suit when attacked by another knight. Just so, human nature in principle has the necessary and sufficient conditions for hypostatic union with God, but will only actually be in such union if assumed by a divine person.

[18] Peter Enns, *The Evolution of Adam: What The Bible Does and Doesn't Say About Human Origins* (Grand Rapids: Brazos Press, 2012), xv. Cf. J. Richard Middleton, *The Liberating Image: The* Imago Dei *in Genesis 1* (Grand Rapids: Brazos Press, 2005), 121, where Middleton also opts for this sort of reading of the divine image in Genesis.

[19] Enns, *Evolution of Adam*, xv.

whose image all other human beings are fashioned. Humans are able to represent God in the world in virtue of being made in the image of the God-man, the archetypal image-bearer.

This means that there is a very good biblical and theological case to be made for the Christological view. It is able to incorporate the central issues of both the substantive and relational views of the divine image, and to reconcile the apparent tensions between Old and New Testament material concerning the nature of that image. It also provides a way of thinking about humanity that is shaped by specifically Christological concerns, rather than more general theological or philosophical ones. For these reasons it seems to me that the Christological view has much to commend it.

Objections

However, there are objections to this Christological alternative to the merely substantive and merely relational views (understood as discrete, independent positions). The first and most important is this: Can Christ be the archetypal image and we the ectypes when the New Testament connects bearing the image that Christ renews with redemption? That is, it looks like those who bear Christ's image are the redeemed, not all of humanity (cf. Col. 3:10; Eph. 2: 10; 4.24). As Wolfhart Pannenberg puts it, "Christian theology must read the OT saying about our divine likeness in the light of the Pauline statements that call Jesus Christ the image of God ... and that speak of the transforming of believers into this image." When the Pauline doctrine is examined, it is clear that "Participation in the likeness attributed to Christ is promised only to believers."[20]

However, this reading of the biblical material is not the only one possible. Here is an alternative that is consistent with the Christological doctrine. God eternally ordains that Christ be the archetype of human beings. The creation of human beings is in the "image" of Christ, as embodied rational animals capable in principle of being hypostatically united to a divine person. The first humans possess the nature of embodied rational animals modeled on Christ. The first human community falls from grace, thereby vitiating the embodied rational nature they each possess, and disrupting the relations in which they stand to one another and to God whose vice-regents they are. The restoration of this image obtains through the redemptive work of Christ, applied to believers through the secret work of the Holy Spirit in regeneration. Those united to Christ by this work of salvation are in a process of sanctification that includes the renewal of the divine image, which will be completed in the afterlife, whereupon they will be elevated to a moral state that enables them to enjoy the eschatological vision of God (*visio dei*).

This way of understanding the Pauline material does justice to both the OT texts about the embodied divine image and the role human beings play as divine representatives on earth. It also makes sense of the way in which the NT material identifies the divine image with Christ, as well as the way in which its renewal is correlated to redemption in Christ.

A second, related objection is this. How can an entity that begins to exist later than the first in a series be the archetype or prototype for the series? Normally one would expect a prototype to begin to exist chronologically prior to the production model, for obvious reasons: the prototype is tested and examined in order to make sure that the production line models are up to specification, and work properly. However, according to the Christological

---

[20] Pannenberg, *Systematic Theology Vol. 2*, 208. Compare Friedrich Schleiermacher, *The Christian Faith*, trans. H.R. MacIntosh and J.S. Stewart (Edinburgh: T. & T. Clark, 1999 [1830]), §89, which makes a similar point in a rather more indirect manner.

doctrine Christ begins to exist a long time after human beings appear on the scene. This seems deeply counterintuitive; some explanation is surely required.

However, this objection only goes through if Christ is *merely* human. That is, it would obtain if Christ is merely a human person. For then his being the prototypical human being, the archetype of all subsequent humans would make no sense because he begins to exist at a moment chronologically subsequent to the first moment at which human beings began to exist. However, there is very good theological reason for resisting this position. The Christological doctrine depends on two classical Christological claims. The first is that Christ is the God-man, a divine person to which is joined a human nature. The second is that he is eternally generated according to his divine nature so that his divine nature pre-exists his human nature, although his human nature begins to exist at a particular moment in time. God has ordained that the human nature God the Son assumes the prototype of all other human natures. Although in one sense the concrete particular that is his human nature begins to exist subsequent to the moment at which the human race begins to exist, it is possible for his human nature to be the archetype of all other human natures because its generation is eternally in view, as it were, in the mind of God logically prior to his ordination of all subsequent human beings. What is more, it is eternally ordained that this be the human nature God the Son assumes. For this reason Christ is able to say in the Fourth Gospel, "before Abraham was, I am" (Jn. 8:58).

This state of affairs is rather like one in which an author plans a work of science fiction. Suppose she begins the process with the protagonist, the heroic leader of a race of aliens. This leader is introduced some way into the narrative, situated in a make-believe history that includes a complex backstory about the race of which he is a member. Nevertheless, the characteristics of the race were conceived prior to the writing of the narrative in which the leader is situated. They were based upon the characteristics of the leader, who was the first element in the fiction thought of by the author. She inserts the protagonist some way into the narrative though in point of fact he was envisaged by the author prior to any other character in the book. *Mutatis mutandis*, Christ is ordained (not conceived!) as the prototypical human being, the archetype of the whole race, logically, though not chronologically, prior to the existence of any of human being in the mind of God.[21]

A third objection is this. Does the Christological doctrine require a first human pair? More generally, is such a doctrine consistent with an evolutionary account of the generation of human beings? Let me address these two related concerns in order. First, I do not think that the doctrine *requires* a first human pair, understood to mean a first specially created human pair from whom all other humans are descended by normal generation. One could assume a story according to which human beings gradually emerge from earlier ancestors over time, including the complex history of evolutionary development that such stories entail in the current scientific literature on human origins. This does no violence to the Christological doctrine; it is consistent with it. For on this view, God ordains Christ as the human archetype, and then sets in motion (and superintends) the created order, in which the emergence of human life over vast aeons of time is an intended outcome. This might be true even if the particular biological steps towards this goal are not "fixed" by divine decree, just as the outcome of a battle with an invincible pugilist is known in advance even if the particular stages of the fight are not. Suppose for the sake of argument that this is right. Then, God ordains that human beings will emerge at a certain stage in evolutionary development even if he does not ordain the stages of development that precede it. Moreover, he ordains that the humans that emerge conform to the image of Christ.

---

[21] I have dealt with the election of Christ in more detail in Crisp, *God Incarnate: Explorations in Christology* (London: T. & T. Clark, 2009), ch. 1.

Exactly how the emergent human community falls from a state of moral innocence, vitiating human nature, is more difficult to discern given this framework. Perhaps hominids reach a particular stage of social, moral, and physical development at a particular moment in pre-history, the time at which *homo sapiens* begin to exist as a stable hominid community. Very soon after this, there is some moral disruption that corrupts these early humans. After that, the rest of the creation-fall-redemption arc of the biblical metanarrative follows without much perturbation. The Christological doctrine is consistent with this story. It, or something very like it, is not beyond the bounds of the broad contours of contemporary evolutionary theory as far as I can discern. In which case, the Christological doctrine is consistent with at least one such story, though it is also consistent with the traditional theological account of the Fall of an aboriginal human pair.

A fourth and final objection has to do with the limit cases that entangled the merely substantive and merely relational accounts of the divine image. Recall that in each case worries were raised about certain sorts of human beings that did not appear to be a good "fit" with the notion of the divine image in view. Does the Christological view fare any better on this score? Can it account for those, like the severely mentally impaired, or infants, or those born encephalic, who are what we might call (in a non-pejorative sense of the word) *liminal* cases of human beings? I think it can, although I can only indicate here how to respond to some of these cases. Earlier I indicated that Christians normally have views about physical or mental impairment (including the lack of certain important physical constituents like a brain in the case of the encephalic) that do not necessarily exclude such entities from counting as human beings, even human persons. On that assumption, let us apply benefit of the doubt reasoning to our three cases. Of these, human infants are rather different because they are not physically or mentally impaired, only immature in some respects (e.g. with respect to the exercise of rationality). Nevertheless, is it the case that humans that are physically and/or psychologically immature or impaired in some significant respect fail to bear the divine image? I don't see why. Human beings gain and lose parts all the time. So, it cannot be that just in virtue of losing a physical part the humanity of our liminal cases is in question. Nor can it be the case that the humanity of infants is in question in virtue of their being physically and psychologically immature. Although the divine image may be underdeveloped or impaired in some respects in each of the three liminal cases (vis. the substantive and relational aspects of the image) all three are the sorts of entity that are capable of bearing hypostatic union with God. And all three sorts of entity belong to the natural kind of which Christ's human nature is also a member. Hence, I conclude that in each of the three cases the entity in question is arguably both human and an image bearer, although the instantiation of that image may be immature (in the case of infants) or impaired (in the case of the severely mentally handicapped and the encephalic).

Conclusion

I have argued that a version of the Christological doctrine for the image of God is able to give a more satisfying and comprehensive account of the divine image than those versions of the doctrine that privilege either the substantive or the relational aspects of the image. It also makes good sense of the biblical traditions—indeed, better sense then merely substantive or merely relational accounts. It is also able to meet several important objections. Given its ecumenical importance and its deep roots in patristic theology, a version of this doctrine has much to commend it. It may also provide resources for other theological loci, such as the doctrines of original sin and of atonement. For these reasons it seems to me that the

Christological doctrine has much to commend it. There are other concerns the doctrine raises that have not been dealt with here. For instance, the nature of the divine image has not been elucidated in detail,[22] nor has the question of how the Christological doctrine helps make sense of the vitiation of the image in Adam and its repair in regeneration been addressed in sufficient detail (and I am sure there are other concerns besides these). However, I trust that enough has been provided to give the reader an indication of how these two issues might be addressed in a more expansive account of the doctrine.

---

[22] This is where Mark McLeod Harrison's essay is useful. He is sympathetic to the patristic doctrine of Christ as the *ikon* of God, even if he may not agree with the particular way in which I have construed that doctrine here.

PART V
Human Nature, Freedom, and Salvation

Free Will and the Stages of Theological Anthropology

Kevin Timpe and Audra Jenson

The Stages of Theological Anthropology

Our primary goal in this chapter is to explore the role of human free will in theological anthropology.[1] More specifically, we aim to address how human freedom relates to the progression from the *status integritatis* through the *status corruptionis* to the *status gloriae*.[2] In exploring these three stages of theological anthropology, we will contrast libertarian and compatibilist views of what humans are and are not able to freely do at each stage.[3] We will argue that either account can give an acceptable account of these stages. There may well be either philosophical or theological reasons for preferring libertarian or compatibilist

---

[1] In this chapter our focus will be on human free will. For an account of divine free will, see chapter 7 of Kevin Timpe, *Free Will in Philosophical Theology* (London: Bloomsbury, 2013). We also won't be addressing the issue of the free will of angels, although it would probably parallel the stages that we outline here.

There are also issues about the relationship between free will and human nature that we cannot explore here. Most important here, perhaps, is the relationship between how we understand free will and debates between substance dualists, hylomorphists, and materialists regarding human nature. For relevant scholarship on these issues, see, among others, Richard Swinburne, *Mind, Brain, and Free Will* (New York: Oxford University Press, 2013); E.J. Lowe, *Personal Agency: The Metaphysics of Mind and Action* (New York: Oxford University Press, 2010); Helen Steward, *A Metaphysics for Freedom* (New York: Oxford University Press, 2012); Peter van Inwagen and Dean Zimmerman, eds, *Persons: Human and Divine* (New York: Oxford University Press, 2006); S.C. Gibb, E.J. Lowe, and R.D. Ingthrosson, *Mental Causation and Ontology* (Oxford: Oxford University Press, 2013); Steward Goetz, *Freedom, Teleology, and Evil* (London: Continuum, 2011); Kevin Corcoran, *Rethinking Human Nature: A Christian Materialist Alternative to the Soul* (2006); James Madden, *Mind, Matter, and Nature: A Thomistic Proposal for the Philosophy of Mind* (Washington, DC: The Catholic University of America Press, 2013); Nancy Murphy and Warren Brown, *Did My Neurons Make Me Do It? Philosophical and Neurobiological Perspectives on Moral Responsibility and Free Will* (New York: Oxford University Press, 2007).

[2] The *status integritatis* is sometimes referred to as the *status naturae elevatae* or the *status iustitiae originalis*. The reasons for this last name will be made clear in the third section below. See, for example, Ludwig Ott who describes the *status naturae elevatae* as "the primitive state of the first human beings before the fall through sin in which they possessed both the absolute supernatural gift of sanctifying grace as well as the preternatural gifts of integrity" (Ludwig Ott, *Fundamentals of Catholic Dogma*, trans. Patrick Lynch (St. Louis: B. Herder Books Co: 1955), 105). An alternate phrasing for these states that is especially widespread among Reformed theologians is: (a) *posse peccare/posse non peccare* (able to sin/able not to sin; (b) *non posse non peccare* (not able not to sin); (c) *posse non peccare* (able not to sin); and (d) *non posse peccare* (unable to sin).

[3] Though in what follows we treat these stages as historical, some theologians approach them instead as merely possible states. See, for example, the discussion in Ott, 105f.

accounts;[4] we do not think, however, that the desire to affirm the traditional claims of theological anthropology regarding the stages pushes one toward either of these views.

As Marc Cortez notes in a recent introduction to the topic, "theological anthropology takes the human person as an important object of theological reflection because the triune God has drawn the human person into the theological narrative and, consequently, has made a theological understanding of the human a necessary and vital aspect of the theological task."[5] Cortez continues, saying that "without question, the two central issues of theological anthropology traditionally have been understanding the *imago Dei* and sin."[6] For humans to image God means that they reflect an important truth or truths about God's nature. But something needs to be said about the way in which sin has affected the image. There are a number of different ways that theologians have approached humans' being created in the image of God. Cortez contrasts four different general approaches:

> The most prevalent way of understanding the image of God throughout history has been in terms of some capacity or set of capacities constitutive of being human that reflects the divine being in some way ... A second approach argues that the imago Dei is something that human persons do, rather than something that human persons are. The image is a function of the human person (or the human community) and not a structure of the human person's being ... [A third approach holds that] human persons are fundamentally relational beings—related to God, to other humans, and to creation—and it is this relationality that truly images a God who is himself a relational being ... [A] last approach to understanding the imago Dei has been developed by thinkers who contend that the image of God is a multifaceted concept that cannot be restricted to one set of categories. These scholars argue that the important criticisms leveled against the other three approaches suggest that none of them is sufficient to serve as an adequate explanation of the imago. Instead, we should appeal to all three in developing a robust view of the imago."[7]

Given that the topic of our focus is free will, we will tend to focus on structural capacities that are involved in free will; however, it is not our intention here to claim that the only relevant factors involved in the *imago* are structural capacities that humans share with God. That is, we don't mean for our discussion to deny the importance of function or relationality to a full understanding of the *imago*. Our view is thus consistent with what Cortez calls the "multifaceted approach."

Even with respect to this fourth approach, Cortez differentiates between a broad and a narrow aspect of the image: "The image of God has a broad, structural sense that refers to any and all of humanity's capacities that have an analogical parallel to the divine being (e.g., capacities of rationality, will, love). In the narrower sense, however, the image of God is properly displayed when these capacities are rightly used to reflect the glory of God."[8] We will argue that it is in the *status gloriae* that this narrower sense of the *imago* is perfectly realized.

---

[4]   The philosophical arguments we have in mind here are the traditional arguments for libertarianism and compatibilism. Theologically, some argue that libertarianism is required for a satisfactory response to the logical problem of evil, while others think that compatibilism is necessary for a satisfactory account of divine meticulous providence, omniscience, or divine decrees.

[5]   Marc Cortez, *Theological Anthropology: A Guide for the Perplexed* (London: Bloomsbury, 2010), 5.

[6]   Cortez (2010), 10.

[7]   Cortez (2010), 18, 21, 24, and 28.

[8]   Cortez (2010), 28.

We've already mentioned the basic stages of theological anthropology that we will explore regarding free will below. Before turning toward free will, however, it will be helpful to characterize these stages in a bit more detail. While there are other aspects of these stages that are worth exploring in other contexts (e.g., how the stages are related to grace), our focus will be on what human agents are able to do *vis-à-vis* their free will. As we will focus on the issues, what primarily differs between the stages is not what humans do in fact do, but rather what they are capable and incapable of doing. That is, we will focus primarily on modal facts about persons in the various stages, even though there will also be non-modal facts which differ as well.

The pattern in understanding the stages of theological anthropology that we follow is one which parallels the *exitus reditus* pattern. Speaking of this pattern, Rudi Te Velde says that it is "a double—in fact a circular—movement: the coming forth (*exitus*) of all things from God, and the return (*reditus*) of all things, particularly man, to God as the ultimate goal … It is, so to speak, a metaphysical scheme, derived from the order of reality itself (*ordo rerum*), providing the Christian theologian with a conceptual framework which allows for a systematic treatment of the whole of Christian religion."[9] This pattern traces the overarching relationship of humankind with God from its initial state of creation, through sin and the fall, then returning to God in the eschaton. We think that this pattern, with respect to human freedom, is no accident, but is instead woven into the Christian narrative regarding human nature and its relationship to God. It is, in other words, an attempt to illustrate the contour of the Christian theology that it assumes.

In following this pattern, we will treat human freedom as it is in three different stages: *status integritatis*, *status corruptionis*, and *status gloriae*. In brief, we understand the traditional view of the stages as follows:

> *status integritatis*—the pre-fall state in which humans are freely able to sin and freely able not to sin;
>
> *status corruptionis*—a post-fall state in which fallen humans are freely able to sin but, because of the effects of sin, not able not to sin;[10]
>
> *status gloriae*—the post-glorification state in which redeemed and perfected humans are able not to sin but not able to sin.[11]

We do not, however, mean to suggest that all human agents will, in fact, achieve the *status gloriae*. Insofar as we think both (a) that all humans can, given God's grace, achieve it and (b) that it represents the *telos* of humanity, we will focus on it rather than other potential eschatological realities for humans.[12]

---

9   Rudi te Velde, *Aquinas on God: The "Divine Science" of the* Summa Theologiae (Burlington, VT: Ashgate, 2006), 10f. Te Velde is skeptical of the traditional understanding of Aquinas' *Summa Theologiae* as being structured around the *exitus reditus* movement.

10   This is sometimes also referred to as the *status naturae lapsae*; ibid.

11   Ott refers to this as "*The state of restored nature* (status naturae glorificatae), that is, the condition of those who have achieved their supernatural destiny, i.e., the *Immediate Vision of God*. The state includes in its perfection the sanctifying grace. After their resurrection, the bodies of those in this state will also be endowed with the preternatural gifts of integrity (*non posse peccare, mori, pati*)" (Ott, 1955 105f).

12   See Chapter 5 of Timpe (2013) for a discussion of another potential eschatological reality for humanity, damnation.

Two Approaches to Free Will

As seen in the previous section, the various stages of theological anthropology contain different claims about what human agents can and cannot freely choose to do. We will understand free will to be the capacity or set of capacities which make possible free choices and whose possession serves as a necessary condition for moral responsibility.[13] Before exploring these stages, in the present section we first contrast two different approaches to the nature of human free will: compatibilist accounts and libertarian accounts. In the remaining sections, we will then show how each of these general approaches can account for the claims about human abilities in the various stages as described in the previous section.

At its heart, compatibilism is simply the claim that it is possible that an agent be both fully determined and yet have free will. In other words, it is possible for an agent to be fully determined in all of her choices and yet still freely make at least some of her choices. It is important to note that compatibilism *per se* makes no claim about whether or not determinism is true. Given that there are at least two kinds of determinism—causal determinism and theological determinism—we also need to differentiate between what we might call causal compatibilists and theological compatibilists.[14] Let the thesis of causal determinism be the thesis that the future is necessitated by the conjunction of the non-relational past and the laws of nature. A causal compatibilist thinks that the existence of free will is compatible with the truth of causal determinism. Most causal contemporary compatibilists, who John Martin Fischer calls "free way either way theorists,"[15] want their view of free will to be compatible not only with the truth of causal determinism, but also with its falsity. Indeed, if such a view were true, the existence of free will would not depend on either the truth or falsity of determinism. This fact is a strong motivation for many contemporary compatibilists as it protects human free will regardless of the discoveries of physics regarding the laws of nature. It should be noted that while compatibilism *per se* doesn't commit one to belief in the existence of free will, the vast majority of compatibilists do think that humans are free in the sense at issue.[16]

In the theological realm, compatibilism is the view that an agent's choice may be free even if God has determined the person to make that choice. Consider, for example, Lynne Rudder Baker's compatibilist account of free will:

(CFW) A person S has compatibilist free will for a choice or action if:
  i. S wills X,
  ii. S wants to will X,
  iii. S wills X because she wants to will X, and
  iv. S would still have willed X even if she (herself) had known the provenance of her wanting to will X.[17]

---

[13] We do not think that free will is sufficient for moral responsibility. See Timpe (2013), Chapter 1.

[14] There is an important distinction between causal and theological determinism. Although the debate about free will and causal determinism parallels the debate about free will and theological determinism, the two are orthogonal to each other.

[15] See John Martin Fischer, "Excerpts from John Martin Fischer's Discussion with Members of the Audience," *The Journal of Ethics* 4.4 (2000): 413.

[16] The most striking counterexample is Neil Levy, *Hard Luck: How Luck Undermines Free Will and Moral Responsibility* (Oxford: Oxford University Press, 2011), which argues for free will skepticism.

[17] Lynne Rudder Baker, "Why Christians should not be libertarians: an Augustinian challenge," *Faith and Philosophy* (2003), 467. In Lynne Rudder Baker, "Moral responsibility without libertarianism," *Noûs* 40.2 (2006), 307–33, she contends that a similar account, with only the added stipulation that each piece of the account be attributed to an agent with a first-person perspective, is also sufficient for moral

According to this account, "a person freely wills what is good—to love God, say—if (i) she wills to love God; (ii) she wants to will to love God; (iii) she wills to love God because she wants to will to love God; and (iv) even if she know the provenance of her wanting to will to love God—namely, that wanting to will to love God was caused by God Himself—she would want to will to love God."[18] Under this compatibilist account there is no conflict between God being the ultimate cause of a person's willing of X and that person having free will with regard to X.

Incompatibilists think that the central claim of compatibilist accounts of free will is false; that is, according to incompatibilism, the existence of free will and the truth of determinism are logically incompatible. Insofar as we differentiated causal and theological determinism above, we can also differentiate causal and theological incompatibilists. It is possible for a person to be a compatibilist about one kind of determinism and an incompatibilist about the other.[19] However, in what follows we will simplify our discussion by assuming that the two kinds of incompatibilism go together.

Like compatibilism, incompatibilism is a claim about the modal relationship between the existence of free will and determinism. It, in and of itself, takes no stand on either the existence of free will or the truth of determinism. There are thus a variety of directions incompatibilism can be developed, depending on the stand one takes about these other two issues. Some incompatibilists think that determinism is true and thus that no agent in the actual world possesses free will. Such incompatibilists are often called "hard determinists." Other incompatibilists think that we lack free will for some other reason than the truth of determinism.[20] Those incompatibilists who think that humans do, in fact, have free will (and thus that determinism is false) are referred to as "libertarians." (Libertarianism as a position regarding the nature of free will should not be confused with the political view which goes by the same name. There is no intrinsic connection between these two views.) In what follows, given our focus on human freedom in the various stages of theological anthropology, we will primarily contrast libertarians with those compatibilists who do believe in free will.

The *Status Integritatis*

The first stage of theological anthropology that we will examine is the *status integritatis*, the state of humans (and, by extension, other created moral-agents) prior to their first sin. Insofar as they are created in God's image and are thus morally responsible agents, these agents have free will. Traditionally, Christianity has understood such agents' free will to be capable of choosing either to sin or to refrain from sinning. That is, it is understood

---

responsibility. She calls this the Reflective-Endorsement view and the added stipulation only makes explicit what is implied in the fourth condition of CFW. Here, she defends a challenge to her account by claiming that manipulation that cannot create first-person perspective, such as hypnotism, does not fit within the bounds of her account of free will and moral responsibility.

[18]   Baker (2003), 467–8.

[19]   For a paper on the difference between "soft compatibilism" (according to which freedom is compatible only with natural determinism, but not determinism by another agent) and "hard compatibilism" (according to which freedom is compatible with being determined by another agent), see C.P. Ragland, "Softening Fischer's hard compatibilism," *Modern Schoolman*, 88.1/2 (2011), 51–71.

[20]   See, for example, Derk Pereboom, *Living Without Free Will* (Cambridge: Cambridge University Press, 2001) for a defense of hard incompatibilism. Pereboom argues that free will is incompatible with determinism. Free will would require agent-causation, which he thinks there is good reason to think doesn't exist. As a result, he thinks we're not free (or responsible).

that agents in this stage have a two-way power which can be exercised either in alignment with God's will or against it. Insofar as these creatures are created good, nothing about their agential structure prevents them from choosing to will the good. However, insofar as Christian theology holds that they did in fact freely choose to sin, it must have been possible for them to freely choose to sin.

Reflecting on the human choice to sin brings us to one of the primary motivations for theists to endorse incompatibilism, namely the problem of evil.[21] The free will defense to the logical problem of evil holds that the existence of moral evils does not contradict God's essential goodness because it is possible that the existence of free will, as well as those other goods made possible by free will, are such great goods that they justify the existence of evil, which free will also makes possible.[22] Alvin Plantinga, for instance, writes that "the heart of the Free Will Defense is the claim that it is possible that God could not have created a universe containing moral good (or as much moral good as this world contains) without creating one that also contained moral evil. And if so, then it is possible that God has a good reason for creating a world containing evil."[23] If, as the incompatibilist holds, God cannot determine how creatures use their free will, then his giving them free will explains how it is possible for them to sin. However, insofar as they have not lost original righteousness—that is, they had not yet been contaminated with original sin—it is still going to be possible for them not to sin.

However, it is hard to see how the free will defense will provide the same explanation for moral evil if compatibilism is true. If human's having free will is compatible with God determining them to choose as they do, then God could actualize the good of free will, as well as those additional goods which presuppose free will, without the possibility of moral evil by determining all free creatures never to do evil.[24]

In an article on theistic compatibilism, Paul Helm defends the claim that "in the matter of God's responsibility for evil, 'standard libertarian theodicies' are in no better a position than are compatibilist theodicies." He does acknowledge that there are significant differences between the two theodicies, but since God creates and sustains all of his creatures with perfect foreknowledge of their actions, both good and evil, he's not convinced that there is "much of a moral difference."[25] He suggests that if "for the libertarian God knowingly and hypothetically necessarily permits evil that good may come, for the compatibilist He knowingly and hypothetically necessarily ordains evil that good may come."[26]

However, the compatibilist must still be able to answer the following question: "Why the fall, given that God could have determined humans never to sin?" The compatibilist could argue for a different version of the greater good defense, one in which sin is necessary

---

[21] We have in mind here the logical problem of evil, not the evidential problem of evil. Furthermore, we're not suggesting that the free will defense completely solves even the logical problem of evil, for there might be kinds of evil that it doesn't explain.

[22] The free will defense is thus a species of the greater goods defense according to which the greater good which justifies the existence of moral evil is either free will or some other good for which free will is a necessary component.

[23] Alvin Plantinga, *God, Freedom, and Evil* (Grand Rapids, MI: Eerdmans, 1977), 31.

[24] Though a compatibilist, Cowan agrees: "the FWD works only if creatures have the libertarian freedom that makes it possible for them to sin" (Steven Cowan, "Compatibilism and the sinlessness of the redeemed in heaven," *Faith and Philosophy* 28.4 (2011), 418). For recent arguments that compatibilists can also make use of the free will defense, see John Bishop, "Compatibilism and the Free Will Defense," *Australasian Journal of Philosophy* 71.2 (1993), 104–20 and Jason Turner, "Compatibilism and the Free Will Defense," *Faith and Philosophy* 30.2 (2013), 125–37.

[25] Paul Helm, "God, compatibilism, and the authorship of sin," *Religious Studies* 46.1 (2010), 121.

[26] Helm (2010), 122.

for some other greater good, rather than it being the result of the greater good, namely free will. Despite being an incompatibilist, Plantinga offers a contemporary theodicy along these lines. In a discussion on possible worlds, he suggests the "splendid and gracious marvel of incarnation and atonement" as a greater good that requires the presence of sin. According to him, "no matter how much evil, how much sin and suffering a world contains, the aggregated badness would be outweighed by the goodness of incarnation and atonement, outweighed in such a way that the world in question is very good."[27]

The *Status Corruptionis*

On, then, to the second stage, the *status corruptionis*. In this stage, like the prior, humans are capable of choosing to sin. However, the primary difference between the *status integritatis* and the *status corruptionis* is the loss of original justice (sometimes also referred to as original righteousness). A central element of the loss of original justice is that the individual created will is no longer oriented toward the good of alignment with God. However, as a result of the loss of original justice, Christian orthodoxy maintains that humans are not able to save themselves, that is, that humans are not able to be the efficient cause of their own saving faith in Christ.[28] They are instead saved by divine grace. For example, Augustine writes that "unless this [sinful] will, then, is freed by the grace of God from the servitude by which it has been made a 'servant of sin,' and unless it is aided to overcome its vices, mortal men cannot live rightly and devoutly."[29] Aquinas echoes this sentiment: "a man cannot perform meritorious deeds without grace."[30] And the Council of Trent declares that "the efficient cause [of our justification is] the God of mercy who, of his own free will, washes and sanctifies, placing his seal and anointing with the promised Holy Spirit who is the guarantee of our inheritance."[31]

Here we encounter the theological debate tracing back to Augustine and Pelagius (as well as his disciple Caelestius). The present venue doesn't afford a full discussion of the issues here.[32] Nevertheless, a clarification of what Pelagius was (and wasn't) claiming is necessary for present purposes. Pelagius' view is sometimes described as one according to which grace is not needed for even a fallen human to will the good. This, however, is incorrect. Pelagius consistently maintained that the giving of human nature is itself a grace, and thus grace is needed for an individual to will the good. This grace is sometimes referred to as "enabling grace" or "the grace of creation." Augustine understands Pelagius' view of the grace of creation as "reduce[ing] to the natural capacity for free choice and to the gift of

---

[27] Alvin Plantinga, "Supralapsarianism, or 'O Felix Culpa,'" in *Christian Faith and the Problem of Evil*, ed. Peter van Inwagen (Grand Rapids, MI: Eerdmans, 2004), 10.

[28] Here, we have in mind the act of coming to faith in Christ, and not the theological virtue of faith. The act of coming to faith is sometimes also refers to as the act of justification, "whereby someone from being unjust becomes just, from being an enemy becomes a friend, so that he is an heir *in hope of eternal life*" (Council of Trent, Sixth Session, Chapter VII, in Norman Tanner, ed., *Decrees of the Ecumenical Councils* (Washington, DC: Georgetown University Press, 1990), 673).

[29] Augustine, "Grace and free will" in *The Fathers of the Church*, trans. Robert P. Russell (Washington, DC: Catholic University Press, 1968), 35.

[30] Thomas Aquinas, *Truth*, trans. S.J. Robert Schmidt (Chicago, IL: Henry Regnery Co, 1954), 139.

[31] Council of Trent, Sixth Session, Chapter VII, in Norman Tanner (1990), 673. Also note that efficient causation is the only kind of causation that we are concerned with in the present chapter.

[32] For a further treatment see Chapter 4, "Realigning a Fallen Will," of Timpe (2013).

knowledge of the law."[33] Elsewhere, Augustine notes that according to Pelagius "power God placed in our nature, but will and action are ours by His will; accordingly He does not help us to will, He does not help us to act, He only helps us to be able to will and act."[34] In holding that each individual has the ability to choose the good in the *status corruptionis* on the basis of only the grace of creation, Pelagius was effectively denouncing the doctrine of original sin.[35] Pelagius also thought that each individual is born as free as Adam was before the fall, and thus is able to choose the good through her own will. On this view, then, there is no difference with respect to free will between the *status integritatis* and the *status corruptionis*.[36]

In writing against Pelagius and Caelestius, Augustine—and ultimately Christian orthodoxy—emphasizes that, due to the loss of original righteousness in the fall, all humans in the *status corruptionis* are in bondage to sin and death, unable to will the good (and thus refrain from sinning) apart from a further grace than the grace of nature. Freedom from the bondage of sin can come only through a further grace of Christ, made possible by his atoning life, death, and resurrection. According to Augustine, through Adam's sin "the entire mass of our nature was ruined and fell into the possession of its destroyer. And from him no one—no, not one—had been delivered, or ever will be delivered, except by the grace of our Redeemer."[37] This additional grace is sometimes called "cooperative grace" or what Augustine calls "a unique grace."[38] For Augustine, "this grace is not nature, but that which supports a weak and corrupted nature."[39] For this reason, Augustine asks, "Would it not be the height of absurdity for us to maintain that there was some antecedent good merit in any man's good will to bring about the removal of his stony heart when, in fact, this stony heart simply signifies a will that is obstinate and absolutely unbending in its opposition to God? For where a good will precedes, there is, to be sure, no longer a heart of stone."[40]

Pelagius was excommunicated, largely because of his teachings on grace, by Pope Zosimus in 418. His view was further condemned by the Council of Ephesus in 431 for holding that humans could do good apart from the grace of God. The Council of Orange in

---

[33] William Collinge, "Introduction" to *On the Proceedings of Pelagius* in Augustine (1992), 105. In contrast, Augustine writes that "unless we are assisted by grace, the law will only be a power of sin. Unless we have the spirit of grace to assist us, concupiscence is increased and strengthened by the law and its prohibitions" (Augustine 1992, 260).

[34] *De Gratia Christi et de Peccato Orinali contra Pelagium* 1.5.6, as quoted in Christopher Kirwan, *Augustine* (London: Routledge, 1989), 109. According to Gregory Ganssle, "The development of Augustine's view of the freedom of the will (386–97)," *Modern Schoolman* 74 (1996): 1–18, Augustine himself held this position when writing book I of *On Free Choice of the Will*.

[35] A similar position seems to have been held by Pelagius' disciple Caelestius. Augustine quotes Caelestius as having written that "the grace and assistance of God is not given for individual acts, but consists in the freedom of the will, or in the law and doctrine" (Augustine, *Saint Augustine: Four Anti-Pelagian Writings*, trans. John Mourant and William Collinge (Washington, DC: Catholic University Press, 1992), 141). The Council of Trent condemned the denial of original sin as heretical: "All [have] lost their innocence in the sin of Adam ... as is set out in the decree on original sin. ... [None are] freed from or rise above it by the force of nature ... though their free will, for all that it had been weakened and sapped in strength, was in no way extinct" (Council of Trent, Sixth Session, Chapter I, in Norman Tanner 1990, 671).

[36] Augustine agrees with Pelagius that had it not been for the effects of the fall on human nature, a human would be able to refrain from sinning: "What he [i.e., Pelagius] says is true: God, being as good as he is just, created man with sufficient ability to be without the evil of sin, if only man had been willing" (Augustine 1992, 60). Pelagius' error, then, is holding that humans have this same ability post-fall.

[37] As quoted in Kenneth Latourette, *A History of Christianity*, vol. 1 (New York, NY: Harper, 1975), 178.

[38] Augustine (1992), 69.

[39] Augustine (1992), 131.

[40] Augustine (1992), 282.

529 furthered this condemnation.[41] Among the pronouncements of the Council of Orange are the following:

> If anyone … believes … that the freedom of the soul remains unimpaired …, he is deceived by the error of Pelagius and contradicts the scripture.[42]
>
> If anyone affirms that we can form any right opinion or make any right choice which relates to the salvation of the eternal life, as is expedient for us, or that we can be saved, that is, assent to the preaching of the gospel through our natural powers without the illumination and inspiration of the Holy Spirit, … he is led astray by a heretical spirit.[43]
>
> He [who] denies that the free will of all men has been weakened through the sins of the first man … has no place in the true faith.[44]

The Council concluded that original sin has so weakened free will that "no one thereafter can either love God as he ought or believe in God or do good for God's sake"[45] apart from a unique divine grace which alone makes these good actions possible. Furthermore, the Council declared that "in every good work it is not we who take the initiative and are then assisted through the mercy of God, but God himself first inspires in us both faith in him and love for him without any previous good works of our own."[46]

It is relatively easy to see how the theological compatibilist could account for the abilities attributed to the *status corruptionis*. Insofar as they are fallen, humans are unable to freely choose a good, including the good of coming to faith apart from a unique grace. However, given that they are still free and responsible agents, they still possess free will; that is, they are free to sin. Given compatibilism, God could determine individuals to freely choose any good (including the good of coming to faith) by bestowing upon them a unique but determining grace.

On a libertarian understanding of free will, there's nothing that prevents both of the modal claims (i.e., that it is possible to choose to sin, and that apart from a unique grace it is not possible not to sin) from being true. (The specifics here will, of course, will depend on the specifics of the libertarian in question.) The first ability is the same as found above in the *status integritatis*. If a non-fallen human agent is capable of choosing to sin, then so will be a fallen human agent. And among the effects of sin will be the loss of the ability not to sin apart from a unique grace, either via the damaging effects of original sin on the agential faculties, or the loss of original justice (or both). Because of this impact of sin upon the individual, a unique grace will be needed for the agent to will the good.[47]

---

[41] While the Council of Orange was not an ecumenical council, Pope Boniface II ratified the teaching authority of the council in 531. Thanks to Tim Pawl for this historical information.

[42] *The Canons of the Council of Orange*, Canon 1, http://www.reformed.org/documents/canons_of_orange.html.

[43] *The Canons of the Council of Orange*, Canon 7, http://www.reformed.org/documents/canons_of_orange.html.

[44] *The Canons of the Council of Orange*, Canon 8, http://www.reformed.org/documents/canons_of_orange.html.

[45] *The Canons of the Council of Orange*, Conclusion, http://www.reformed.org/documents/canons_of_orange.html.

[46] *The Canons of the Council of Orange*, Conclusion, http://www.reformed.org/documents/canons_of_orange.html.

[47] For libertarian accounts of how an individual's will can cooperate with a unique grace, see Eleonore Stump, *Aquinas* (New York, NY: Routledge, 2003); C.P. Ragland, "The trouble with quiescence: Stump on grace and freedom," *Philosophia Christi* 8.2 (2006), 343–62; and Kevin Timpe, "Grace and controlling what we do not cause," *Faith and Philosophy* 24.3 (2007), 284–99.

The *Status Gloriae*

In the previous sections, we've outlined how both compatibilists and libertarians can account for the traditional perspectives on what humans can and cannot will in the *status integritatis* and the *status corruptionis*. In this final section, we will show how both views regarding the nature of free will can also account for the inability of the redeemed to sin in the *status gloriae*. Consider, for example, the following passage from Augustine:

> *Neither are we to suppose that because sin shall have no power to delight them [i.e., the redeemed], free will must be withdrawn. It will, on the contrary, be all the more truly free, because set free from delight in sinning to take unfailing delight in not sinning. For the first freedom of will which man received when he was created upright consisted in an ability not to sin, but also in an ability to sin; whereas this last freedom of will shall be superior, inasmuch as it shall not be able to sin.*[48]

Reflecting on this line of thought, Simon Francis Gaine writes, "That impeccability belongs to the orthodox Christian concept of heaven is ... beyond any doubt."[49]

The truth of compatibilism would allow a relatively easy defense of this aspect of the *status gloriae*. For if compatibilism were true, then an agent's being free is consistent with that agent's being determined by God to will as she does in fact will. And if God can determine how agents use their free will, then, by determining them never to sin, He can ensure that the redeemed in heaven do not sin without taking away their free will. If we adopt, for example, Baker's particular compatibilist account of free will outlined above, if a person wills never to sin; she wants to will never to sin; she wills never to sin because she wants to will never to sin; and she would still have willed never to sin even if she had known the provenance of her wanting to never sin (i.e., God's determining that she never sin), then that person could have free will as understood by the compatibilist.[50]

We turn then to libertarian understandings of the *status gloriae*. Here it might seem that the libertarian will have a difficult time accounting for the inability of the redeemed to sin. For how can an agent be free in the way understood by the libertarian and yet be incapable of sinning? If the redeemed are kept from sinning, how they freely use their wills must be reined in in some way. But if the exercise of their free will is reined in, it looks like the central commitment of incompatibilist understandings of freedom is violated.

One might think that the way for the libertarian to respond is to give up one of these claims by which we are understanding the *status gloriae*. Some scholars reject that the

---

[48]   Augustine, *City of God*, trans. Marcus Dods, ed. Philip Schaff (Grand Rapids, MI: Christian Ethereal Library, 2010), XXII.30. Retrieved www.ccel.org/schaff/npnf102.html. For other affirmations of heavenly freedom see Anselm, *On Free Will* and *De Concordia*, section I, chapter 6. Both of these latter works can be found in Anselm, *Anselm of Canterbury: the Major Works*, eds Brian Davies and Gill Evans (Oxford: Oxford University Press, 1998).

[49]   Simon Francis Gaine, *Will there be Free Will in Heaven? Freedom, Impeccability, and Beatitude* (New York: Continuum, 2003), 11. Gaine's book is a wonderful historical discussion of this issue. See also Brian E. Daley, *The Hope of the Early Church: A Handbook of Patristic Eschatology* (Cambridge: Cambridge University Press, 1991). Jerry Walls too writes that "there is ... broad agreement among all Christian traditions that heaven is a place of perfect holiness and nothing sinful or impure can enter here" (Jerry Walls, *Purgatory* (New York, NY: Oxford University Press, 2011), 37).

[50]   Baker (2003), 467.

redeemed are free, while other reject that they will be unable to sin.[51] In our view, to go either of these routes would be to reject one of the two modal claims that have historically been at the heart of the *status gloriae*. It would be better to not reject either of these claims if it's not necessary. And, on our view, the libertarian need not reject either. There are a number of ways that the libertarian could develop her view here, again depending on the details of the view of agency the libertarian adopts. Elsewhere, one of us has argued (with a different co-author) that an agent's moral character puts constraints on those actions that she is capable of choosing.[52] So long as the agent's moral character is freely formed and thus an internal, rather than an external, constraint, it need not count against her being free. Or one might argue that a person is capable of freely choosing X only if she sees a reason for choosing X, and hold that the redeemed see no reason for doing any sinful action.[53] The redeemed in heaven may be such that their moral character prohibits them from choosing any sinful action insofar as they see no good reason for doing so. Both of these approaches can be seen in the following example:

> *A person has the ability to form a moral character which later precludes that person from willing certain things. For instance, neither author of this paper can will to torture an innocent child for a nickel. Our characters are such that we cannot will that; we simply cannot see a good reason for engaging in such behavior. But it doesn't follow that we aren't free, particularly given that our evaluative conclusions are not necessitated products of causally external forces. We are free in that we can choose to perform morally good actions, but our freely formed characters preclude us from doing morally bad actions insofar as those characters lead us to evaluate reasons for acting, or not acting, in certain ways. … One might wonder how it is that one's character could preclude certain actions. We think that one's character directs decisions by both influencing what one sees as reasons for actions and influencing how one weighs reasons for and against those actions. To put this point a slightly different way, in making free decisions, one's character not only affects the weights; it also affects the scales. Both of these aspects can be seen as follows. First, as stated above, given our present moral characters we can see no good reason to torture a child for a nickel (i.e., the nickel is not a good reason). Furthermore, we weigh the good of having a nickel against the goods of the child's bodily and psychological integrity and find that the child's welfare wins. Our characters are involved insofar as if we were more avaricious, we may find monetary gain, even small monetary gain, a good reason to inflict bodily harm on another. Similarly, if we were less empathetic, we may weigh the good of monetary gain more heavily than we do against the good of an innocent child's welfare.*[54]

The libertarian can argue that the redeemed have perfected their character so that they perfectly understand the reasons for acting (and not acting) in various ways, weigh these reasons perfectly, and never act contrary to this proper weighing. For such a person

---

[51]   Stewart Goetz appears to deny the first claim in his (2009), 196 note 40; and John Donnelly clearly rejects the latter claim in John Donnelly, "Eschatological enquiry," *Sophia* 24 (1985), 16–31 and John Donnelly, "Heavenly eviction," *Philosophy Now* 56 (2006), 27–8.

[52]   See Timothy Pawl and Kevin Timpe, "Incompatibilism, Sin, and Free Will in Heaven," *Faith and Philosophy* 26.4 (2009), 396–417; and Timothy Pawl and Kevin Timpe, "Heavenly Freedom: A Reply to Cowan," *Faith and Philosophy* 30.2 (2013), 188–97.

[53]   See Timpe (2013), particularly Chapters 2 and 6.

[54]   Pawl and Timpe (2009), 407.

every sinful choice is in conflict with her character. Given the character that the agent has developed prior to entering the *status gloriae*, every sinful action is for her what Ludwig Ott calls a "moral impossibility."[55] Such people would be what Susan Wolf refers to in a different context as "moral saints."[56]

While the *status gloriae* is the most difficult of the states dealt with here to explain for the libertarian, as we've shown above the libertarian is able to maintain that the redeemed are both free and not able to sin. The desire to preserve tradition regarding the impossibility of sinning in the *status gloriae* need not lead the Christian theist to endorse compatibilism for the sake of eschatological anthropology. While there may well be reasons to prefer a compatibilist account of freedom to an incompatibilist one, both views are able to explain the various states that we've examined above.

Conclusion

Above, we have outlined three stages of theological anthropology with an eye toward what kinds of actions a human agent *is* and *is not* capable of freely choosing at each of those stages. We've also outlined how both compatibilists and libertarians could give an account of the abilities involved at each stage. We have not here argued that one of these approaches to human freedom is superior to the other. That judgment depends not just on issues in theological anthropology, but theology and philosophy more broadly.[57]

---

[55]   Ott (1955), 169. For a further treatment of this issue, see Timpe (2013), particularly Chapters 5 and 6.

[56]   Susan Wolf, "Moral Saints," *The Journal of Philosophy* 79 (1982), 419. In particular, we have in mind here what Wolf refers to as Loving Saints.

[57]   This chapter borrows from Timpe (2007) and (2013). We would like to thank Joshua Farris, Charles Taliaferro, Paul Manata, and a number of anonymous referees for helpful comments on earlier versions of the chapter.

Human Beings, Compatibilist Freedom, and Salvation

Paul Helm

Compatibilism

I shall take it that compatibilism is the view that all human actions for which an agent is responsible are consistent with causal determinism, the belief that an account of all the facts at a time, together with a full account of the laws of nature, entails all that is true at that time.[1] This statement is wide enough to leave us with a variety of possible compatibilistic theories. Suppose that one takes a materialistic view of the human person. Then the beliefs or desires of a person will be understood in exhaustively physical, or materialist, or even mechanical terms. If on the other hand one thinks that a human person is a mental-physical duality, then the beliefs and desires will be no more than partly physical, partly or wholly mental. Then the question is how one understands the relation of "being a cause" for the action. Is a sufficient reason a cause? And what is it to be a cause?

Libertarians or indeterminists deny this thesis, requiring for responsibility that human actions be not determined. It may be that they hold that human beings have the power of alternative choice, or that the self is an autonomous agent of choice. On compatibilism human responsibility is grounded in freedom from coercion, and this in turn may be understood as the exercise of a certain kind of control that the agent has over his actions.[2] I shall assume a version of compatibilism understood in such ways.

In focusing on the relations between compatibilism and theology, it must be remembered that compatibilism is a term employed much later than is the formative Christian theology. Using it generally in theology therefore risks the charge of anachronism. We must be sensitive to this, and not unwittingly impute to classical doctrinal formulations a modern outlook. We must also remember that although our focus is on a philosophical issue, the religious outlooks that a person's theology may represent do not typically arise from the impact of such ideas alone. At least, it is likely that there are few, if any, whose religion arises from compatibilism alone, or from compatibilism in concert with other philosophical doctrines alone. It is much more usual that philosophical concepts enter when people attempt to understand, or understand further the religious and theological ideas they hold.

By understanding here is meant coming to appreciate the logical consistency of one theological position with others that they hold, and the nature of their connectedness, and

---

[1]   I have adapted this from John Martin Fischer (ed.), "Introduction" to *Moral Responsibility* (Ithaca: Cornell University Press, 1986), p. 33.

[2]   John Martin and Mark Ravizza, SJ, *Responsibility and Control: A Theory of Moral Responsibility* (Cambridge: Cambridge University Press, 1998).

that requires an understanding of what crucial terms in their theology mean or may mean. It may be that a person has a strong prior disposition to accept compatibilism because of its place in his or her overall philosophical outlook. If so, it is likely to be attractive to them, in that it is intellectually advantageous to take up a compatibilist outlook in relevant parts of their theology. For where their theology is concerned with human action, it would seem to require the same theory of human action that they hold more generally. It is likely they will wish to integrate their theology with other areas of intellectual enquiry, or *vice versa*. We shall assume the consistency of all truths in what follows. If they are libertarians there will be no incentive to adopt compatibilism in their theological anthropology.

What these remarks suggest is that adopting a philosophical view as one's own may be partly a matter of the intrinsic clarity, coherence, and plausibility of that view itself; the manner in which it does justice to Christian revelation; and partly the result of a trade-off between the merits of that view and other views, which may include positions held as part of a person's scientific outlook, for example, or be philosophical options.

In what follows we shall frame the wisdom of having compatibilism as part of one's theological anthropology in terms of the costs and benefits of such a combination. We shall look at some theological outlooks in which compatibilism looks to be an attractive position to hold, as well as consider the advantages and the costs of integrating compatibilism into one's theological outlook. I hope these discussions will be sufficiently precise as to be interesting, but not so precise as to rule out of court outlooks that have the same general character. And we shall look at different theological positions, in which compatibilism may be consistent with some theological view but not be as compelling. Whether or not this chapter decisively favors compatibilism for a particular person will depend upon the weight that he or she gives to the respective costs and benefits.

Some Assumptions and Cautions

I shall assume an Augustinian or Calvinist (I shall use these adjectives more or less interchangeably) anthropology, and consider it from a philosophical point of view, using philosophical categories and attending to philosophical issues that arise when doing so. But there are compatibilists who are non-Augustinians, and libertarian Calvinists.[3] This implies that compatibilism is not an intrinsic part of Augustinian theology nor is libertarianism a part of Arminianism, which in turn suggests we had better proceed cautiously with compatibilism, on pain of serious misclassification. We shall find other reasons for being cautious.

A second caution is that there is a need to make a distinction between the nature of human action, and the nature of divine action. Talk of the "divine controller," which sometimes occurs in the philosophical literature in connection with Calvinism,[4] as well as the phrase "theological determinism," suggest otherwise. These suggest (to me, at least) that on this view of God He is a determiner or the determiner of human action, using creaturely desires and beliefs as His tools, or as means to His end. The idea is that God's determining power is routed through the agent's beliefs and desires, making these beliefs and desires not

---

[3]   John Locke seems to have been an Arminian compatibilist. For claims that Calvinism is hospitable to a libertarian-style outlook, the "liberty of indifference," see, for example, *Reformed Thought on Freedom: The Concept of Free Choice in Early Modern Reformed Theology*, eds Willem J. van Asselt, J, Martin Bac, and Roelf T. te Velde (Grand Rapids, Mich.: Baker, 2010).

[4]   For example, see Katherin A. Rogers, "The Divine Controller Argument for Incompatibilism" (*Faith and Philosophy*, July 2012), and the literature she refers to.

only Joe's, the human agent's, but God's as well. So that in "God determines human action" and "Smith's beliefs and desires determine his action," "determines" is used univocally. I shall not make that assumption, but leave the exact mode of God's determination an open question.

A third caution is provided by the nature of compatibilism. Some theists, even Christian theists, are materialists. Such a view would or could deliver a kind of compatibilism that is open to different objections, and perhaps has different strengths, than a compatibilism conducted under a metaphysical dualism characteristic of the mainstream Christian anthropology. So that the compatibilism that is in view in what follows, whatever its costs, is not open to the charge that it is literally "mechanistic," since the relevant causal antecedents of responsible action are assumed to be purely or substantially mental in character.

Earlier we left the question, "What is a cause?" hanging in the air. Jonathan Edwards, the eighteenth-century theologian and philosopher, defended a thoroughly compatibilist view of action. Unlike many contemporary compatibilists he regarded indeterminism not as false but as logically incoherent. Yet when he came to state what the causal connection is between the mind and action he was deliberately vague.

> *Therefore I sometimes use the word "cause," in this inquiry, to signify any antecedent, either natural or moral, positive or negative, on which an event, either a thing, or the manner and circumstance of a thing, so depends, that it is the ground or reason, either in whole, or in part, why it is, rather than not; of why it is as it is, rather than otherwise; or in other words, any antecedent with which a consequent event is so connected, that it truly belongs to the reason why the proposition which affirms that event, is true; whether it has any positive influence, or not.*[5]

Notice that there is no mention of efficient causality. Edwards leaves plenty of scope for his readers to fill in their own preferred account of causation. In what follows I shall be Edwardsean to the extent of adopting a version of compatibilism that is consistent with dualism, and think of the antecedents of an action as providing a cause of action, without specifying further the nature of that cause. The cause grounds an action, accounting for it being, in a given set of circumstances, the choice of A or of not A, or A and not B. Such a sufficient condition, of one sort or another, may provide the conditions for God to ensure[6] the action.

The phenomenology of the experience of choice that some indeterminists appeal to is by no means decisively in favor of that view, for compatibilism can encompass the same process. Compatibilism may be consistent with an account of the mental contortions we go through before deciding to act and while acting that the libertarian believes is evidence of libertarian freedom. So I'm going to assume that any account that a libertarian may give of the phenomenology of action is consistent with some version of compatibilism.

I deploy and defend compatibilism in what follows not because I believe it to be a revealed truth. I make no such claim, though others may.[7] I shall assume that it is no more a revealed

---

[5]   *Freedom of the Will*, Pt.I. S. 3. This can be found on page 181 of the Yale University Press Edition, 1957, ed. Paul Ramsey.

[6]   In what follows, for reasons that will I hope become clear, I shall use the antique verb "to ensure," "The action or a means of ensuring or making certain" (*Oxford Shorter Dictionary*, "Insurance") as the verb for God's relation to the actions and events of creation. I dust off this expression to use it to make the point that for all we know God's controlling an outcome, making the occurrence of an action certain, may take various forms, not only that of efficient causality.

[7]   See, for example, Bruce Ware, *God's Greater Glory* (Wheaton, Ill.: Crossway Books, 2004), 78f.

truth than is "Jesus is a divine person with two natures" or "God is timelessly eternal" are revealed truths. Like "person" or "nature" used in connection with understanding God made flesh, and "timelessness." In understanding God and time, "compatibilism" is employed in an endeavor to understand one strand of the data of revelation, that of humankind's actions. How God then ensures that the occurrence of such actions is in accordance with His will may be left open. So "ensure" is used to connote a degree of agnosticism about the how of God's ordination.

In general the motivations for compatibilism have to do with divine sovereignty in creation and in redemption, the unconditional character of the divine operations, and the strength of the divine grace.

Affirmations about God: Costs and Benefits

Here are some affirmations about God of an Augustinian flavor. God creates and ordains the destinies of all creatures and all their actions in a meticulous manner. That is, divine power is exercised in not only creating human beings, but also sustaining and governing them until such time as He brings their earthly lives to an end. So God's relation to human action includes the idea that God ordains whatever comes to pass. He does this *ab initio*, from eternity and not by decreeing something because He foresees it as future, much less because God takes action in time in the light of his human creatures' actions or in the light of some unanticipated condition. But it need not follow from this, in my view, that God's relation to each human action is a uniform one. It isn't necessary that He governs the actions of the wicked, for example, including their base and deplorable motives and intentions and the like, in precisely the same fashion as He governs the good motives and intentions and actions of the righteous. I suppose that when, by the "determinate plan and foreknowledge of God" God delivered up Jesus of Nazareth to be "crucified and killed by the hands of lawless men" (Acts 2.23–4 ESV) his relation to the wicked crucifiers was somewhat different than his relation to those faithful followers of Jesus who watched what they did.

What is sufficient for God ordaining whatever comes to pass is that in one way or another He ensures that it comes to pass. The Eternal Spirit who spoke the universe into being and upholds His creatures and all their actions is likely to have unimaginable resources at His disposal in executing His sovereign decree. The variety of expressions used in scripture to describe His actions, as well as the doxological language prompted by God's ways, in my view warrant caution, as galling as it is to the philosopher. For example, among the expressions used in scripture to describe God's actions are "leads," "guarantees," "covenants," "promises," "opens," "works according to His good pleasure," "chooses," "brings to pass," "withholds," and "forsakes." When Paul says that God's ways are "inscrutable" (Rom. 11.33) I assume that this inscrutability extends to both *what* His purposes are and *how* He accomplishes them. One obvious way in which this distinctness may be made apparent is in the difference between God causing an action and God permitting one. In any case, given that there isn't agreement among philosophers over what it means for a creature to cause something to happen, talking of Almighty God ensuring that a free human action comes to pass leaves plenty of scope for alternative accounts at such points.[8]

Alternatively, eschewing such restraint, a compatibilist might argue or allow that God's relation to a compatibilistic universe that He has created is straightforwardly a case

---

[8]   For more on this see Paul Helm "Discrimination—Aspects of God's causal activity" in *Calvinism and Evil*, edited by David Alexander and Daniel Johnson (Wipf and Stock), forthcoming.

of causation. That God ordains A, where A is any action or event, would entail that God causes A.

Like all philosophically literate theses, the thesis of compatibilism incurs costs, as we are beginning to see, as well as providing benefits. But among the further benefits is liberation from the demands of having to tailor the metaphysical side of one's theology to the constraints of indeterministic free will.

Recent years have seen a willingness on the part of some to accept a view of God's omniscience and omnipotence of a strongly counter-intuitive kind, in order for the character of the *most* Perfect Being to fit the requirements of human indeterministic freedom. So since such freedom, in the eyes of some of those who regard themselves as Openness Theists, requires that all future free actions are presently without a truth-value, not even God can know them. Such say that God is nevertheless omniscient, provided that we understand such omniscience as the knowledge of all that is knowable.

It is generally held by those who take such an outlook that God is in time as we are, and ordains only some of what comes to pass, and that He is constantly having to adjust His beliefs and expectations in the light of what His indeterministically free creatures decide to do. So His power and His knowledge must have a more restricted scope than that of a timeless God who works all things after the counsel of His own will. It is a consequence of a compatibilistic account of human action that God knows whatever grounds and is a sufficient reason for any action, including actions as yet future to us.

Besides being readily able to accept a divine omniscience that is maximal, of the traditional theistic kind, and a knowledge worthy of a worshipful being, there are other gains to holding compatibilism. If there is no creaturely libertarian freedom, then there is no need to attempt to construct a divine middle-knowledge. And while the appeal to libertarian freedom could provide a defense, of the charge that the presence of evil contradicts God's nature, there are other such defenses, and a free will defense cannot amount to a plausible theodicy.[9]

If such a defense is required it can take the form of another kind of greater good defense than that which requires indeterministic free choices. Especially in the area of soteriology, there is no need to tolerate an account of God's grace that meshes seamlessly with the human will's ability to effectively resist and dismiss His gracious endeavors.

These features, in my view, are among the chief benefits of employing compatibilism in theology. Some are theological, and others are philosophical. So what of the liabilities that have to be incurred by adopting it? It is popularly held that one of the chief of these has to do with God's relation to sinful actions. For isn't the sort of relation between God and His creation that has been sketched obviously one that entails that God is "the author of sin," as has been alleged times without number?[10] Those who allege this seem to know what it means to be the author of sin. But what does it mean? Is the author of sin a sinner? And is a sinner one who has a sinful motive or intention in doing what he does, or is culpably careless in omitting to do what he ought to have done? If so, then surely God cannot be the author of sin. When the wicked crucifiers were at work, was God among them? Clearly not. When Joe tells a lie is God his co-liar, or does God lie for Joe? That does not seem very plausible, either. He may on occasion be the author of evil, since pain is an evil and He may be the author of pain. If we could get clearer on what is implied by being the author of sin—perhaps God permits Joe to have the selfishness that brought about his telling a lie—then this would certainly be a liability, the liability of being close to the springs of human agency that is evil. But is there any reason to think this?

---

[9]   See Steven B. Cowan, "Compatibilism and the Sinlessness of the Redeemed in Heaven" (*Faith and Philosophy* 28.4. October, 2011).

[10]   For example, Anthony Kenny, *The God of the Philosophers* (Oxford: Clarendon Press, 1978), Ch. 6.

But suppose that given compatibilism God is the author of sin. Where does a libertarian stand on the question of God's responsibility for moral evil? In standard libertarian theodicy, God knowingly created and sustained the person of Adolf Hitler, infallibly knowing that Auschwitz would follow, while retaining the power to cut short his devilish regime at any time. On this view, God has from all eternity been planning and purposing states of affairs with the infallible knowledge that horrendous evils will result from certain exercises of human free agency, and chooses to do nothing about it.[11]

In the case of Openness Theism, God does not know what will happen, either because He chooses not to know future libertarianly-free actions—itself a remarkable feat—or He cannot know. But it is not difficult to see that, even under Openness auspices, as their Creator, God upholds men and women, possesses remarkable insight, knows men's hearts, and the like. Might He not have delayed things a little in order that youthful Adolf could enjoy his fantasies, but, knowing what such fantasies could lead to, God in this instance provided for Adolf's early demise when painting at the top of a long ladder while in a slightly intoxicated state? The idea that only the compatibilist's God could be arraigned for crimes against humanity is stretching things somewhat, is it not? There are of course important differences between libertarian and compatibilist theodicies. But is it clear that the libertarians have the moral high ground?

Perhaps the case for compatibilism being a liability to the Christian theologian is seen at its sharpest in the biblical account of the Fall.[12] In a world pronounced "good" and "very good" by its Creator, the first human pair, Adam and Eve, defiantly sin in taking the forbidden fruit which was explicitly forbidden by their Lord.[13] There are two features of the event that may seem to be perplexing for the compatibilist. The first is that he could consistently endorse the claim of J.L. Mackie that:

> *If God has made men such that in their free choices they sometimes prefer what is good and sometimes what is evil, why could He not have made men such that they always freely choose the good? If there is no logical impossibility in a man's freely choosing the good on one, or on several occasions, there cannot be a logical impossibility in his freely choosing the good on every occasion.*[14]

The libertarian reply to Mackie, by Alvin Plantinga along with countless others, is that God cannot bring it about that a person always freely does what is right; indeed God cannot intentionally bring it about that a person with libertarian freedom does what is right on any one occasion. Such a reply is not open to the compatibilist.[15]

---

[11]   Paul Helm, "God, compatibilism, and the authorship of sin," *Religious Studies* (2010) 46, 121. For more on this, see William J. Wainwright, "Theological Determinism and the Problem of Evil: Are Arminians any better off?" (*International Journal for the Philosophy of Religion*, 50, 1–3, 2001, 81–96), and Steven R. Cowan, "Compatibilism and the Sinlessness of the Redeemed in Heaven."

[12]   Note in passing that it is possible to discuss Christian theological anthropology without referring to the significance of the Fall. See for example Kelly M. Kapic, "Anthropology" in *Mapping Modern Theology*, ed. Kelly M. Kapic and Bruce L. McCormack (Grand Rapids, Mich.: Baker, 2012). Has modern theology neglected to map it, or airbrushed it away, or simply forgotten that it is there?

[13]   In what follows I shall continue to refer to the first pair, Adam and Eve, as those who "brought death into the world and all our woe" despite the difficulties, the amusement and even ridicule this may cause to some. Here at least there are clear theological contours. What other account could command theological interest of a similar kind? And it is hard to see how, without a fall from initial goodness or innocence, the Christian faith could retain its shape.

[14]   J.L. Mackie, "Evil and Omnipotence," *Mind*, LXIV (1955), 209.

[15]   Alvin Plantinga, *God, and Other Minds* (Ithaca: Cornell University Press, 1967), Ch. 6.

For given compatibilism, God could ensure that a person always freely does what is right, in the sense of "ensure" outlined above. And so in a world created good by God, as it was according to Genesis 1–3, God could have brought it about that the original pair freely did only what was right. Why did He not do so, then? The answer must be, because He had a good reason or reasons not to. Perhaps we can go no further than the judgment of Augustine:

> *I no longer wished individual things to be better, because I considered the totality.*
> *Superior things are self-evidently better than inferior. Yet with a sounder judgement*
> *I held that all things taken together are better than superior things in themselves.*[16]

What Augustine asserts here is rather vague. It can be filled out in the following way. Alvin Plantinga has claimed that "any world with incarnation and atonement is a better world than anything without it—or at any rate better than any world in which God does nothing comparable to incarnation and atonement."[17] Atonement and incarnation are superior things, sin and evil inferior things, but these superior things require some of the inferior things. Plantinga is an indeterminist, and so the possible world that God actualized He could only "weakly actualize." But it is not difficult to transpose his thought into a compatibilist anthropology.

There remains another perplexing feature, the problem of the first entrance of evil. For granted that God did not ensure that the first pair (or any of the rest of us) lived lives of unsullied goodness, the following question arises: How could a person, created good in a world pronounced good by God, actually have chosen the wrong path, the path of disobedience to God our Creator? How could a morally bad choice have arisen in the world made good by God, a choice made by human beings who possess God's image? How could a person, made in the image of God, come to have beliefs and desires that were morally bad? At one level, the narrative of the early chapters of Genesis seems to be highly congruent with compatibilism. Being tempted by the serpent, the woman looked at the tree whose fruit had been forbidden to her and to Adam, and the narrative continues, "So when the woman saw that the tree was good for food, and that it was a delight to the eyes, and that the tree was to be desired to makes one wise, she took of the fruit and ate ..." (Gen. 3.6). But how could it happen? Her entertaining of and being motivated by these beliefs and desires seems at one level entirely natural, but at another level it is defiance of God. How did such defiance come about in one who bore the image of God, and how did it prevail on that occasion?

However such difficulties are approached it must be allowed that the wills of the pair were created "mutable." That is, harking back to Mackie, theologians who subscribe to compatibilism hold that the pair could have been created immutable in goodness, but in the wisdom of God (for a reason that may or may not be evident to us) they were created with the possibility of deviating from God's command.[18] For example, writing of human nature John Calvin says,

> *In this upright state, man possessed freedom of will, by which, if he chose, he was*
> *able to obtain eternal life. It were here unseasonal to introduce the question of the*

---

[16] Augustine, *Confessions*, VII, xiii (19), trans Henry Chadwick (Oxford: Oxford University Press, 1992), 125.

[17] Alvin Plantinga, "'Supralapsarianism, or "O Felix Culpa'" in *Christian Faith and the Problem of Evil*, ed. Peter van Inwagen (Grand Rapids, Mich.: Wm B. Eermans Publishing Company, 2004), p. 10.

[18] It is not altogether clear how we ought to understand such mutability. Not simply bare logical possibility, I presume, but something stronger. There had to be a real chance of a Fall. But we cannot easily assign a probability to the occurrence of an act of defiance in a situation that is without parallel.

> *secret predestination of God, because we are not considering what might or might not happen, but what the nature of man truly was. Adam, therefore, might have stood if he chose, since it was only by his own will that he fell; but it was because his will was pliable in either direction and he had not received constancy to persevere, that he so easily fell. Still he had a free choice of good and evil; and not only so, but in the mind and will there was the highest rectitude, and all the organic parts were duly framed to obedience, until man corrupted his good properties, and destroyed himself. ... [I]t is necessary only to remember, that man, at his first creation, was very different from all his posterity; who, deriving their origin from him after he was corrupted, received a hereditary taint. At first every part of the soul was formed to rectitude. There was soundness of mind and freedom of will to choose the good ... Why he [God] did not sustain him by the virtue of perseverance is hidden in his counsel; it is ours to keep within the bounds of soberness. Man had received the power, if he had the will, but he had not the will which would have given the power; for this will would have been followed by perseverance.*[19]

We might say man was created good and "every part of the soul was formed to rectitude," but that he was not created as good as could be, and certainly not in a state which Calvin refers to as "more excellent." Calvin here followed the distinctions Augustine made, and which became fairly standard.

> *... [W]e must consider with diligence and attention in what respect those differ from one another—to be able not to sin, and not to be able to sin; to be able not to die, and not to be able to die; to be able not to forsake good, and not to be able to forsake good. For the first man was able not to sin, was able not to die, was able not to forsake good ... Therefore the first liberty of the will was to be able not to sin, the last will be much greater, not to be able to sin.*[20]

When Calvin asserts that "in this upright state, man possessed freedom of will," he does not have the freedom of indifference (libertarianism), or even the freedom of spontaneity (compatibilism) in mind. He was not making a metaphysical remark, but offering a moral thesis to do with motivation. Man unfallen was motivated by charity (caritas), by love of God and neighbor. But in his primitive state such motivation was unstable. It was only enjoyed so long as he kept it. He "might have stood if he chose." In this upright state, man possessed freedom of will. He was free to prefer to be motivated by selfishness (cupiditas), or to continue in charity (caritas). It was a state of *posse peccare*, in Augustine's phrase. Once chosen, however, he no longer "stood," and he underwent a ratchet-like "fall." He lost his freedom understood in this moral sense and could not recover it by himself. It was now a case of *non posse non peccare*. He could thereafter only be motivated by selfishness, unless and until God in His grace renewed him. We shall look at the relationship of compatibilism and the effective or efficient grace of God shortly.

---

[19]   John Calvin, *Institutes of the Christian Religion* I. xv. 8, trans. Henry Beveridge (repub. Peabody, Mass.: Hendrickson Publishers, 2008), 111–12. The way in which Calvin writes implies there is a contingent connection between the nature of humankind and the divine decree respecting the race suggests that the problem of anachronism if Calvin's views are discussed in compatibilistic terms is not great.

[20]   Augustine, *On Rebuke and Grace*, Ch. 33 {12}, *A Select Library of the Nicene and Post-Nicene Fathers of the Christian Church* ed. Philip Schaff (Grand Rapids, Mich.: Eerdmans, 1971), vol. V, 483.

We could amplify the account by speculatively introducing the presence of intermediary factors. Perhaps sin enters through the working of self-deception. Or perhaps it is due to a failure of trust that God was not taken at His word. Or perhaps this was the first time on which the pair had experienced a conflict of authorities, and they were overwhelmed by the prospect. Or perhaps their sensuous nature clouded and overwhelmed the judgment of their intellects. Or perhaps we could say, in the spirit of Descartes,[21] that the will extended itself beyond the intellect. Or perhaps we could with Calvin simply appeal to the mutability of the original condition of the first pair.

But in terms of the metaphysics of action, when the first sinful action occurred, nothing changed. If we suppose that Calvin was a compatibilist—he does not tell us in so many words that he was—then in his view, after the Fall human action remained compatibilistic. How this plight was psychologically possible in a man created upright Calvin does not say, nor does he venture to speculate. It seems to me that this failure in explanation is a liability for compatibilism. But it is a liability that recurs, for example, in the incarnation. How can the impeccable God-man be genuinely tempted to sin?[22]

There is also the question of what was decreed. Note that in the passage above Calvin insists there are two distinct questions. The nature of man, free and then fallen in bondage to sin, is one question. The other, not to be conflated with the first question, according to Calvin, is what God secretly decreed with respect to Adam and Eve.

At this point we may briefly consider another problem raised by what Calvinists may say about God: that He has a secret and a revealed will. While there is a revealed will that God has commanded and declared, some of what God has decreed will occur is a secret. God in His secret will may will what in His revealed will He forbids. This is by one commentator to be "deep and thorough deceit."[23] Maybe, but it is not as thorough as Rogers supposes, for it is not the case that the will of God is necessarily or even uniformly secret.[24] And His secret will is also a source of blessing. But quite apart from the ontological and moral distinction between Creator and creature,[25] any system of thought about God and humankind in which God permits sin requires a similar distinction, unless it is held that each of our sins is news to God. Anselm's own solution to the entrance of the first sin, according to Rogers, that unfallen man "drove out the will to persevere by actively choosing something in conflict with it,"[26] leaves us with the conundrum: how could such an action arise in one who was in the condition of being made very good by God?

Jonathan Edwards was much more avowed in his compatibilism than was Calvin, if indeed it is fair to call Calvin a compatibilist. This is clear from his work *The Freedom of the Will*. He is confident that on this point reason can support revelation. But even he is unusually guarded and silent when it comes to providing an account of how the fall of the original pair can be understood in accordance with the compatibilism that was both in accordance with commonsense, and offered an emphatic philosophical rebuttal of Arminianism.

---

[21] René Descartes, *Meditations*, VI.

[22] See Oliver D. Crisp, *God Incarnate: Explorations in Christology* (London: T. & T. Clark, 2009), Ch. 6.

[23] Katherine Rogers, *Anselm on Freedom* (Oxford: Oxford University Press, 2008), p. 89.

[24] In any case the distinction is closely related to the well-known medieval distinction between God's "will of good pleasure" (*voluntas beneplaciti*) and "will of the sign" or "significative will" (*voluntas signi*), which was given prominence in Peter Lombard's *Sentences*.

[25] On this, see e.g. Hugh McCann, "Divine Sovereignty and the Freedom of the Will," *Faith and Philosophy* 12 (1995), 582–98.

[26] Rogers, *Anselm on Freedom*, p. 94. Italics in original.

Basically, Edwards' approach to the issue of "sin's first entrance into the world" was to show that the indeterminists' doctrine does not offer a satisfactory explanation of that entrance. "Nothing that the Arminians say, about the contingence or self-determining power of man's will, can serve to explain with less difficulty, how the first sinful volition of mankind could take place, and man be justly charged with the blame of it."[27] Neither appeal to self-determination, the first sin's being preceded by a sinful volition, or that the first such volition produced itself, or happened accidentally, are of any help. So while the appeal to determining causes is no worse an explanation for the entrance of human evil ("no additional difficulty is incurred by it"), Edwards seems to concede that it is no better. On any outlook the first entrance of sin into the world is inexplicable.

Each of the suggestions is interesting, but the inserting of what may seem to be a plausible psychological mechanism or condition into the narrative cannot take us to the heart of the problem, which is, How could sinful desires or volitions occur in a person created very good by God? How could good nature, though mutable, mutate so as to sin and rebel?[28] It seems that on any account, then, compatibilist or indeterminist, the event is inexplicable. Each account bears a similarly serious cost.

For the Augustinian, as a result of being bound in sin, personal restoration can only come about by God's efficacious grace, which gives life to a spiritually dead soul and restores it to life. A merely or partly human restoration cannot effect this. Although we noted earlier that there are Augustinians who also hold to the liberty of indifference, it is hard to see how they can take up both positions consistently.

Effective Grace

In an early letter, before he became engaged in controversy with the Pelagians, Augustine wrote:

> If God wills to have mercy on men, he can call them in a way that is suited to them, so that they will be moved to understand and to follow. It is true, therefore, that many are called but few chosen. These are those that are effectually [congruenter] called. Those who are not effectually called and do not obey their calling are not chosen, for although they were called they did not follow.[29]

Augustine here distinguished between a call of God, which is an expression of the good will of God, and an action of God that will move the one called "to understand and to follow." He refers to a change in a person's condition that is brought about effectually by the action of God, that is, the change is due solely to God's determination to make the change, as God's call or choice. Sometimes he uses the term "call" to denote this, and sometimes the term "chosen." (Jesus referred to many who are called, and to the comparative few of those who are called as "chosen," and Augustine appropriates this usage). He also uses the phrase

---

[27] Jonathan Edwards, *The Freedom of the Will*, Part IV.11.

[28] Those familiar with Christian theology will see parallel difficulties appearing elsewhere. The Messiah is held by many to be a divine person with two natures. What is it like to be such a person? The New Testament does not say.

[29] "Augustine, "'To Simplician—on Various Questions. Book I.'" in *Augustine: Earlier Writings*, Selected and translated with an Introduction by John H.S. Burleigh (London: SCM Press, 1953), 395. This letter was written in AD 397.

"called according to the purpose of grace."[30] Sometimes he uses other terms: God is said to work in men and women "to will and to do of his good pleasure."

So care is needed, because sometimes the same term, "call," is used to refer to an ineffectual call, one which falls short of producing a permanent spiritual change. So, on the one hand, as Augustine shows, "for whoever are elected are without doubt also called; but not whosoever are called are as a consequence elected."[31] "There is a certain sure calling of those who are called according to God's purpose ... Therefore he said 'But of him that calleth,'—not with any sort of calling whatever but that calling wherewith a man is made a believer."[32] Here he follows Paul who refers to God having called him by His grace, and refers to the Corinthian Christians, who were chosen even though there were not wise etc. Augustine understands these as references to those who are called effectually.

Such an approach to divine grace, found in many Christian theologians and writers, and notably in the magisterial Protestant Reformers such as Luther and Calvin, is clearly consistent with compatibilism. It obviously requires compatibilism. Earlier it was stressed that God ensures that His will is done in a variety of ways. But here in Augustine's idea of effective grace, God's action is clearly efficiently (or effectively) causal. As God's creating the universe is causal, so His new creation of sinners by His grace is causal also. Incompatibilist accounts of efficacious do not seem promising, because incompatibism being an intrinsic feature of human nature, it is always open to humans to reject it, or by a free choice to accept. Augustinians will judge that this does not do justice to the monergism of effective grace.[33]

Such a view is subject to now standard charges that in such an effectual call the recipient is manipulated, and comparisons are drawn with brainwashing, or the application of mechanical force, or (more recently) with being "programmed," being a puppet,[34] or undergoing other types of coercion. Those who think of divine–human relations in the exclusively "conversational" pattern typical of much modern theology think they cannot consistently find a place for effectual calling in this Augustinian sense.[35] Were these claims true, then they would be costs that weighed heavily against the benefits.

But to this sort of objection to effectual call the following reply can be made. We may think of Augustine's and Calvin's "effectual call" as a successful "kiss of life," as akin to successful mouth-to-mouth resuscitation, or heart massage, though unlike the human cases, every such case of divine resuscitation succeeds. It is the kiss or the massage that itself brings a response. True, the one resuscitated was not physical dying or dead, but nevertheless he couldn't help himself. He is a "patient" in the full etymological sense of the word.

---

[30]   On Rebuke and Grace, Ch. 13, 477. Quotations and references from On Rebuke and Grace, On the Predestination of the Saints, and On the Gift of Perseverance are taken from A Select Library of the Nicene and Post-Nicene Fathers, ed. Philip Schaff (Grand Rapids, Mich.: Eerdmans 1971), vol. V, Saint Augustine: Anti-Pelagian Writings.

[31]   On Rebuke and Grace, Ch. 14, 477.

[32]   On the Predestination of the Saints, Ch. 32, 513 Cf. "They are acted upon that they may act." (On Rebuke and Grace, Ch. 4, 473).

[33]   For an example of an indeterminist account of divine grace, see Kevin Timpe, "Grace and Controlling What We Do Not Cause," Faith and Philosophy, 24.3 (July 2007).

[34]   "If God causes the agent to will some moral good, then we might attribute some moral goodness to God in consequence, but why would we attribute moral goodness to the agent, who is nothing but a puppet of God's will?" (Eleonore Stump, "Sanctification, Hardening of the Heart, and Frankfurt's Concept of Free Will," Journal of Philosophy, LXXXV 8, 1988, 412). For other similar references, see William Alston, Divine Nature and Human Language (Ithaca: Cornell University Press, 1989), 148, and Richard Gale, On the Nature and Existence of God (Cambridge: Cambridge University Press, 1991), 121.

[35]   See for example the remarks of Kevin Vanhoozer, Remythologizing Theology (Cambridge: Cambridge University Press, 2010), 370–75.

It is surely a plausible principle of such cases that "attempted resuscitations are often in the patients" best interests. It is true that there are occasionally cases where resuscitation takes place despite the patient's previously-expressed wish not to be resuscitated. So what about "Resuscitations undertaken by someone who is all knowing, wise and loving are always in the patients' best interests?" This seems plausible, and if so then "God's effectual call is always in the patients' best interests" is equally plausible.

We may think of the divine activity as tailored to fit the uniqueness of the total life-situation of each recipient. (In the quotation from Augustine's "Ad Simplicianus" given earlier he appears to be "congruist" in this sense. There may be a tension here between congruence, the matching of grace with the traits and circumstances of character on the one hand, and a direct "supernatural" nature of the divine calling and regeneration on the other. One theological danger lies in "naturalizing" effectual calling, of thinking of it as the mere rearrangement or reordering or strengthening of the patient's already-present powers. But this is not an insuperable difficulty.

It is best not to think of the Spirit's work in regeneration as an operation of a general kind working in a blanket fashion in all those who receive it. It need not be thought of as "one size fits all" but as the one work of regeneration, essentially the same, operating as it is "tailored" to the personality and history and prospects of each particular recipient of the call by grace. Whether or not such a relation is "personal," in the sense employed in much modern theology, we cannot imagine that the relation of God to His human "patient" to be less personal in His relations with those who are given His grace than are relations between one human person and another, but more so.

But what if the Fall were not total in its moral effects in this way? Let's call anything less than this total Fall a "weak Fall." On this view the man's initial sinful choice left him morally wounded, not morally dead. The habit that this first choice formed was ambivalent, that of sometimes choosing morally well and sometimes choosing morally ill. Man lost some moral freedom, but not total moral freedom. (This may correspond to historic Pelagianism or to semi-Pelagianism.) Would such a view be consistent with compatibilism? I can see no reason why not. A person would then be capable of being in a charitable "mood" for some of the time, and sometimes in a selfish "mood"; sometimes motivated to honor God, and have a sufficient reason to do so, at other times motivated to satisfy himself at the expense of honoring God, and have a sufficient reason to act in a way that honors God. I think that it is usually assumed that Augustinianism and Pelagianism are at odds metaphysically as well as salvifically, that a Pelagian must be a libertarian, an Augustinian a compatibilist. Earlier we saw that there have been some who have been both Calvinists and libertarians, upholders of the freedom of indifference. Or at least some have argued this. Perhaps there have been some who are Pelagian or semi-Pelagian who are compatibilists. Maybe John Locke was one.

Summing Up

We have been discussing the contribution that compatibilism makes or may make to Christian anthropology. It has been argued that it has many benefits, particularly a robust account of divine sovereignty, a traditional understanding of the Fall and salvation by God's efficacious grace, what I have called Augustinianism. Further, it can provide reasons for a doctrine of God of classical-theistic proportions, and dispense with an appeal to Middle Knowledge and to the Free Will Defense as a theodicy. It can provide a defense against the charge that evil is at logical odds with an all-powerful, all-good God. All these I judge to be benefits. One cost is not being able to give a clear account of the various ways that God may ensure evil. Regarding the charge that on compatibilism God is the author of sin, this is an area in which other views each have their difficulties. The chief cost is over giving accounting for the entrance of sin into a world that God himself judged to be "very good." But entrance of sin is also a problem borne out in libertarianism.

Compatibilism is consistent with a weaker account of the effects of the Fall than Augustinianism holds to, but then since on such an account a doctrine of efficacious grace is not required, a compatibilistic account, though possible, is not necessary. I am aware that theological positions themselves have costs and benefits, and that the criteria in terms of which theological proposals themselves are to be weighed and tested are not the purely rational criteria of philosophy, but this is not the occasion even to begin to rehearse these.

PART VI
Human Beings in Sin and Salvation

Created Corruptible, Raised Incorruptible: The Importance of Hylomorphic Creationism to the Free Will Defense

Nathan A. Jacobs

In a previous article, I argued that the Eastern Church fathers hold in common the view that all creatures, including "immaterial" spirits, are hylomorphic, or matter-form composites, and I went on to defend this position.[1] In this chapter, I expand this insight to address two rather thorny issues surrounding the problem of evil. The first issue centers on the most common staple of Christian replies to the problem, namely, the free will defense. According to this defense, because free choice entails moral self-determination, not even God can unilaterally determine a will that is free.[2] One significant challenge to the free will defense, however, is the commitment in historical Christian orthodoxy to the twin claims that God is free but God is also incorruptible (i.e., void of the very possibility of decay, both ontological and moral). This theological commitment seems to contradict the equally common commitment that free choice necessitates the possibility of evil. For, if God is free but morally determined, why is it not possible for creatures to be free but morally determined?

The second difficulty is closely related to the first. If an answer can be provided for why creatures cannot be morally determined and yet free, we must ask how this answer affects the Christian hope that believers are no longer capable of sin after the resurrection. Granting that those raised to life are still free in the world to come, we once again face a challenge to the free will defense. To wit, if God can remake man confirmed in righteousness and yet free,

---

[1] Nathan A. Jacobs, "Are Created Spirits Composed of Matter and Form? A Defense of Pneumatic Hylomorphism," *Philosophia Christi* 14:1 (2012): 79–108.

[2] Perhaps the most famous of the contemporary versions of the free will defense is that of Alvin Plantinga, *The Nature of Necessity* (Oxford: Oxford University Press, 1974); and *God, Freedom, and Evil* (New York: Harper and Row, 1974). The appeal to free choice as the cause of evil has been standard since the patristic era. See, e.g., Justin Martyr, *Apologia Prima pro Christianis*, 43–4 (PG 6: 391c–396c); Irenaeus, *Adversus Haereses*, 4.37.1–2 (PG 7:1099b–1101a); Athanasius, *Oratio contra Gentes*, 1.2–5 (PG 25:5c–12d); Basil of Caesarea, *Homilia in Hexaemeron*, 2.4–5, 6.7 (PG 29:35b–42c; 131b–134d); Gregory of Nyssa, *De Virginitate*, 12 (PG 46:369b–376d); Gregory of Nazianzen, *Oratio*, 45.5, 45.8 (PG 36:629a–630b, 631c–634b); John Chrysostom, *Homilia de Imbecillitate Diaboli* (PG 49:241–76); Cyril of Alexandria, *Commentarius in Lucam*, 2 vers. 28, 15 vers. 11 (PG 72:503b–506a, 801b–808d); John of Damascus, *De fide orthodoxa*, 2.4, 2.11–12, 2.27, 4.18–19 (PG 94:873c–878c, 909d–930b, 959b–962b, 1181a–1194c). All patristic citations reference the standard book, chapter, or section divisions, followed by the volume and column number(s) in which the given reference can be found in *Patrologiae cursus completes*, ed. Jacques-Paul Migne (Paris, 1844–66). PL indicates *Patrologiae Latina*; PG indicates *Patrologiae Graeca*.

why can God not make man so from the start? One could, of course, abandon the Christian commitments to either divine incorruptibility or hope of an incorruptible future world, but if one retains both commitments alongside the free will defense, an answer must be given for how such commitments are compatible with one another.

In this chapter, I look at how the Eastern patristic view that all creatures are, of metaphysical necessity, hylomorphic (henceforth "Hylomorphic Creationism," or HC)[3] provides a solution to the first of the above difficulties. I begin by laying bare the rationale for HC among the Eastern fathers, and then show that the hylomorphic nature of creatures, as contrasted with the immateriality of God, clarifies how divine freedom with moral determination is compatible with creaturely freedom that excludes moral determination (section 1). The solution HC supplies only heightens the second of the difficulties noted above, however. That is, how is it that creatures can hope to be confirmed in righteousness, given the metaphysical necessities of their composition? For, the solution to the first difficulty gives reason to think that creatures must remain forever corruptible. Here we will transition from the Eastern patristic understanding of creaturely composition to their soteriology. In specific, we will examine the doctrine of deification, or the view that creatures can participate in the operative powers (*energeiai*) of God through union with Christ and the indwelling Holy Spirit. We will see how this feature of Eastern patristic soteriology supplies the centerpiece of their hope that the believer can put off corruption and put on incorruption (section 2).

Created Corruptible

I do not provide here a complete exposition of the Eastern patristic advocacy of HC, since I do this elsewhere.[4] Instead, I simply highlight a couple of places in their writings where their advocacy of this view becomes apparent.

Common among the Eastern fathers is the insistence that even "immaterial" creatures are material or corporeal. Early fathers take the parable of the Rich Man and Lazarus as scriptural proof that the soul, even without the flesh, has a definite shape, including fingers and tongue;[5] and later fathers clearly affirm body-soul dualism, holding that the body has one nature (a fleshly one) and the soul has its own discrete nature (a spiritual one), even though both natures are held together in the one species (*ousia* or *eidos*), human.[6] In other words, these later writers, though accepting the basics of Aristotle's hylomorphic metaphysic, reject Aristotle's view that the soul is the immanent form of man and the body is the material substratum.[7] Instead, they argue that the body is one hylomorphic entity, having its own nature and material substratum,

---

[3]   In "Are Created Spirits Composed of Matter and Form?," I refer to this position as "Pneumatic Hylomorphism," since the focus of that essay was the hylomorphic nature of spirits. Here, however, the claim is global: to be created is to be hylomorphic. Hence, I have chosen the term "Hylomorphic Creationism."

[4]   For a brief history of Eastern patristic HC, see Jacobs, "Are Created Spirits Composed of Matter and Form?," §1, pp. 81–90.

[5]   E.g., Irenaeus, *Adversus haereses*, 2.34.1 (PG 7:834–5); and Tertullian, *Liber de anima*, 7 (PL 2:656b–657b).

[6]   E.g. John of Damascus, *De Natura Composita contra Acephalos*, 7 (PG 95:119d–121b).

[7]   E.g., Aristotle, *De anima*, 2.1.412a11–21. See also n. 1 above. For hints that Aristotle may have been open to the materiality of the soul, contrary to the popular reading of him, see Michael B. Sullivan, "The Debate over Spiritual Matter in the Late Thirteenth Century: Gonsalvus Hispanus and the Franciscan Tradition from Bonaventure to Scotus" (Ph.D. diss., The Catholic University of America, 2010), 3–9.

while the soul is a second hylomorphic entity, having its own nature and material substratum. And this, they argue, is proved by the intermediate state in which the soul and the body are separated but both endure, indicating that soul and body are two substances, not one.[8] In reference to angels, though the Eastern fathers state that compared with the unrefined nature of "gross matter" (*pachu hylikon*), angels have a "bodiless nature" (*physis asōmatos*) and are "immaterial fire" (*pyr aulos*), they are clear that this is only a relative immateriality. To quote John of Damascus, "in comparison with God, who alone is incorporeal, everything proves to be gross [*pachu*] and material [*hylikon*]."[9] In such statements, we find the global claim of HC that God alone is truly immaterial, while all creatures, even the most ethereal, are material in comparison.[10]

To understand the rationale behind the Eastern patristic view, we must grasp two aspects of their thought: (a) their commitment to moderate realism,[11] and (b) their understanding of matter. Beginning with the former, the discussion of realism centers on universals, or singular terms predicated of multiple particulars and identified by a general noun (e.g., *red, biped, rational, human*), and the question of whether these general nouns have any reality outside of the generic category in the mind.[12] To quote the *locus classicus*, the issue is "(i) Whether genera or species exist in themselves or reside in mere concepts alone, (ii) whether, if they [genera/species] exist, they are corporeal or incorporeal, (iii) whether they [genera/species] exist apart or in sense objects and in dependence on them."[13]

For the extreme realist, the general nouns we use refer to Ideas or Forms that always exist independently from the particulars of which they are predicated, such as in Plato's account.[14] By contrast, the Eastern fathers, as moderate realists, tend more towards the account of Aristotle, according to which universals never exist independently from the

---

[8]   E.g., John of Damascus, *De fide orthodoxa*, 2.12 (PG 94:917d–930b); and Gregory of Nazianzen, *Orationes*, 7.21–24 (PG 35:781c–784b).

[9]   John of Damascus, *De fide orthodoxa*, 2.3 (PG 94:868b).

[10]   See also Tatian, *Oratio adversus Graecos*, 4 (PG 6:811b–814b); *Athenagoras, Legatio pro Christianis*, 24 (PG 6:945a–948b); Irenaeus of Lyons, *On the Demonstration of Apostolic Preaching*, trans. Armitage Robinson (New York: Macmillan Co., 1920), 85–6 [18]; Tertullian, *De carne Christi*, 6 (PL 2:762c–766a); Lactantius, *Divinae institutions* 2.10 (PL 6:927d–929d); Jerome, *Epistolae* 124 (PL 22:1059–72); Origen, *De principiis*, 2.2.2 (PG 11:187); Evagrius Ponticus, Scholion 2 to Ps. 134.6; Scholion 275 to Prov. 24.22; Athanasius, *Vita et conversation* S. Antonii, 31 (PG 26:889–92); Basil of Caesarea, Epistolae 8.2 (PG 32:249); Gregory of Nyssa, *Contra Eunomium*, 1; 8; 9 (PG 45:368a; 793c; 812d); Macarius the Great, *Homilia spirituals* 4.9 (PG 34:479–480); St. Symeon the New Theologian, Ethical Discourse 1.5.2.

[11]   Christophe Erismann, "From Byzantium to the Latin West: Nature and Person in the Thought of Hugh of Honau" in *Knotenpunkt Byzanz: Wissensformen und kulturelle Wechselbeziehungen*, eds A. Speer and D. Wirmer (Berlin: W. de Gruyter, 2012), 232–45; Scott R. Fennema, "Patristic Metaphysics: Is the Divine Essence for John Damascene and Augustine of Hippo an Ontological Universal?" *Glossolalia* 6, no. 1 (2013): 1–21.

[12]   For general studies on universals/particulars and (extreme) realism/nominalism, see, Frederick Copleston, "The Problem of Universals," in *History of Philosophy Vol. II Augustine-Scotus*, 9 vols. (Mahwah: Paulist Press, 1950), 136–55, vol. 2; Jorge J.E. Gracia, *Individuality: An Essay on the Foundations of Metaphysics* (Albany, NY: State University of New York Press, 1988), *passim*, esp. 27–134; Meyrick H. Carré, *Realists and Nominalists* (London: Oxford University Press, 1946); Paul Gould, "The Problem of Universals, Realism, and God," *Metaphysica* 13 (2012): 183–94.

[13]   Porphyry, *Isagoge* (CAG 4.1: p. 1), trans. Edward W. Warren (Toronto: Pontifical Institute of Mediaeval Studies, 1975), 27–8.

[14]   Plato's theory of the Forms is most famously espoused in *The Republic*, 506d–521b. See also James I. Conway, "The Meaning of Moderate Realism," *New Scholasticism* 36 (1962): 141–79; Larry Lee Blackman, "Why Every Realist Should be a Platonist," *Auslegung* 7 (1980): 144–62.

particulars of which they are predicated but are only ever actual within particulars.[15] We might think of the moderate realist position as analogous to the relationship between a computer and a computer program. The computer programmer (representative of God) has in his mind the abstract idea of a game, *Adventure to Mars* (*AM*), which is nowhere actual outside his mind. The programmer then programs *AM* (substantial form) into three different computers (matter), and *AM* is now actual (or immanent) in these three computers. On the level of raw programming data (the essential properties of *AM*), the game is identical on all three computers. But the three instances of *AM* are not identical, all things considered. For these essential properties are now in three distinct machines, combined with various material accidents: Each computer occupies a different location; each game performs different functions; the respective screens yield color variations, and so on. This is akin to how the moderate realist understands the matter–form relationship in creatures. Peter, James, and John are three distinct subjects (*hypostases*) that share a common form, nature, or essence (*ousia*), *human*, and on the level of the essential properties of the species they are identical. Yet, Peter, James, and John are not identical, all things considered. Not only are they distinct subjects, but their common form, *human*, is combined with distinct material accidents in the respective subjects: Peter, James, and John occupy different locations, are different sizes, vary in color, and so on.[16]

This brings us to how the Eastern fathers use the term "matter" (*hylē*). When speaking of matter, these writers do not mean an object that has mass and includes atoms and other particles. Instead, they more often than not mean what Aristotle calls prime matter (*hē prōte hylē/materia prima*).[17] Matter in this sense is nothing more than a substratum of pure potentiality that receives various properties.

An exploration of the phenomenon of change may help clarify the concept. Let us say that Bob's skin is white, but following a long day at the beach, his skin turns red. Bob then retreats indoors for the next week, and his skin again turns white. Such changes in Bob indicate that he has the potential to be red and to cease to be red. But where is this potential located? Presumably *redness* itself did not come to exist for the first time when Bob became red, since there are many things other than Bob that are red; nor did the definition of *red* fluctuate as Bob became more or less red. Thus, despite the changes in Bob's redness, the generic universal, *red*, is not what suffers change. Rather, Bob came to participate in the unchanging universal and then ceased to participate in it. Might the locus of change, then, be Bob himself? The difficulty

---

[15]   Aristotle, *On the Soul*, 412a1–414a28; *Physics*, 192b8–193b21; 194b26–9; *Metaphysics*, 1013a26–8; 1017b14–6; 1017b21–3; 1028b33–1029a33. See also Darrel D. Colson, "Aristotle's Doctrine of 'Universalia in Rebus,'" *Apeiron* 17 (1983): 113–24; Theodore Scaltsas, *Substances and Universals in Aristotle's Metaphysics* (Ithaca: Cornell University Press, 1994), esp. 28–35.

[16]   Moderate realists dispute whether immanent form becomes "particularized" when immanent in the subject (what contemporary metaphysicians call tropes), or whether it remains one and wholly generic even when immanent. Though some Westerners, following Aquinas, advocate a tropes view (e.g., Brian Leftow, "Anti-Social Trinitarianism," in *The Trinity: An Interdisciplinary Symposium on the Trinity*, eds. Stephen T. Davis, Daniel Kendall, and Gerald O'Collins (New York: Oxford University Press, 2004), p. 232), the Eastern fathers reject the divisibility of universals, arguing that the nature is always one, even when in multiple subjects. See, e.g., Gregory of Nyssa, *Quod non Sint tres Dii ad Ablabium* (PG 45:115a–124c); Basil of Caesarea, *Epistulae*, 38 and 236 (PG 32:325a–340c, 875b–886a); and Gregory Nazianzen, *Orationes*, 29, 13 (PG 36:89d–92b. Their rejection of tropes becomes additional evident in their dealings with, and ultimately condemnation of, John Philoponus, who advocates a tropes model. See John of Damascus, *De haeresibus*, 83 (PG 94:741a–754d), where John preserves John Philoponus, *The Arbiter*, chap. 7. See also Jacobs, "Are Created Spirits Composed of Matter and Form?," 99–100; Christophe Erismann, "The Trinity, Universals, and Particular Substances: Philoponus and Roscelin," *Traditio* 63 (2008): 278–305.

[17]   Aristotle, *Physica*, 190 a31–190b15; *Metaphysica*, 1042b9–1042b11. See also H.M. Robinson, "Prime Matter in Aristotle," *Phronesis* 19, no. 2 (1974): 168–88.

here is that if we presume, as the Eastern fathers do, that every changing object also has an identity that endures throughout changes, then the subject (or *hypostasis*) is the locus of this enduring identity, not the locus of change.[18] In other words, Bob remains Bob both before becoming red and after ceasing to be red. The subject somehow suffers change, but the subject is what endures despite change, not what changes. So, if neither Bob (the enduring subject) nor redness (the property received or lost) is the locus of change, then there must be some third component of Bob that is the locus of Bob's potential to receive or lose various properties. This potential is what is meant by the term *prime matter*. Prime matter is nothing but a substratum of pure potentiality. In other words, it has no innate properties of its own, but is a blank slate of potentiality that may receive (and again lose) any number of properties, analogous to the way a shapeless bit of fabric may receive any number of shapes from objects it is draped around. Therefore, when we speak of Bob's potential for change, we are speaking neither of the potential for Bob to cease to be Bob (change in *hypostasis*) nor the potential for red to cease to be red (change in the universal *qua* universal), but of the potential (prime matter) in Bob to manifest properties currently lacking and to lose properties currently had.

Now, the Eastern patristic rationale for why all creatures necessarily have prime matter becomes apparent in the Arian dispute. Amid this dispute, one of the central differences between God and creatures that Athanasius highlights is that God is immutable, but all creatures are mutable.[19] Gross matter, such as flesh, perpetually changes in size, color, position, and so on, and rational creatures, including angels, are at least subject to moral mutations.[20] The implication for Arius' Christology is that if the Son of God is created, he is mutable and is of a nature very unlike that of the immutable God.[21] Amid the dispute, it becomes apparent that Athanasius is not suggesting that all creatures happen to be mutable; rather, he thinks it is metaphysically necessary that every creature *qua* creature is mutable. The rationale he offers is simply this: If the Son of God came to be by moving from nonbeing into being, then this first movement of existence is a mutation.[22]

This rationale reveals Athanasius' commitment to the Aristotelian view that ontology is not binary but consists of a spectrum of becoming, stretching from pure potentiality to pure actuality.[23] The view contrasts with the Eleatic strong disjunctive *either existence or nonexistence*. Working in this disjunctive, change seems to require an absurdity, namely, if a thing comes into being, then *it* (a noun indicating something, not nothing) *moves* (an act of things, not non-things) from *being* (a term denoting existence) *nothing* (a term denoting nonexistence and non-things) to being something. In short, we must speak of things that were not as though they were, which is precisely why the Eleatics were baffled by the phenomena of change.[24] Yet, *potentiality* (or prime matter) breaks the strong disjunctive, allowing us to

---

[18]   Cf. Anna Zhrykova, "Hypostasis—The Principle of Individual Existence in John of Damascus," *The Journal of Eastern Christian Studies* 61, no. 1–2 (2009): 103–10, 125.

[19]   Athanasius, *De incarnation Domini nostri Jesu Christi contra Apollinarium*, 1.3 (PG 26:1097a); *Epistula ad Serapionem* (PG 26:592b); *Oratio de Incarnatione Verbi*, 3 (PG 25:99d–102d); *Orationes tres adversus Arianos*, 1.18 (PG 26:49b).

[20]   Athanasius, *Oratio de Incarnatione Verbi*, 3–4 (PG 25:99d–104c); *Oratio contra gentes* 1.35 (PG 25:69a–72a).

[21]   Athanasius, *De decretis Nicaenae synodi*, 20.2 (PG 25:452a); *Epistula ad Afros episcopos*, 5 (PG 26:1037b); *Orationes tres adversus Arianos*, 1.5, 1.9, 1.22, 1.28, 1.35–6, 1.48, 2.34, 4.12 (PG 26:21c, 29b, 57c, 72a, 84a–88a, 112c, 220a, 481d).

[22]   See nn. 20 and 22.

[23]   Aristotle, *Metaphysica*, 1019a15–1019b15, 1048a25–1048b9, 1048b35–1049b2.

[24]   Parmenides, "Fragments (DK28b2, DK28b6, DK28b8 [Diels/Kranz])," in *The First Philosophers: The PreSocratics and the Sophists*, trans. Robert Waterfield (New York: Oxford University Press, 2000), 58–61; Aristotle, *Metaphysica*, 986b10–987a2, 1046b29–1047b3.

speak of the potential to receive a property and of the varying degrees of reception that occur amid becoming.[25]

Athanasius' sympathies for this metaphysic is reflected in the fact that he speaks of man being created out of nothing (*ouch ontes*), but when speaking of his mutative movement into being, he speaks of man's natural state of nonbeing (*mē einai*) from which he first moved into being and to which he may retreat in corruption.[26] In other words, Athanasius distinguishes creation *ex nihilo*, to borrow the Latin phrase, from becoming. The former affirms that all things, including prime matter, are created by God out of nothing, as opposed to being created out of pre-existent material; yet, the latter affirms that all creatures also receive once-foreign properties when being created and this reception involves mutation.

This metaphysic is the basis for Athanasius' objection to Arius that if the Son is created, then he must be mutable. For, if the Son of God comes into being, then he moves from nonbeing (pure potentiality) into being (actuality). In other words, his existence begins with a mutation or becoming as properties are made actual in matter. Lest we think this objection was lost on the Arians, Arius himself feels compelled to state in his defense that he does not believe that the Son derives subsistence from matter, indicating a clear understanding of Athanasius' point.[27] Moreover, Athanasius' objection to Arianism was not unique. It echoed in other opponents of Arianism in his day; it is reflected in the 325 Nicene Creed, which anathematizes all talk of mutability (*treptos/alloiōtos*) in reference to the Son;[28] and it persists among the fathers in the semi-Arian disputes to follow, reflected specifically, though not exclusively, in the writings of the Cappadocians.[29]

The Eastern patristic rationale for HC is thus rather simple. Prime matter is the locus of becoming. Creatures are that which come into being. Therefore, creatures necessarily have prime matter. The strength of the rationale rests on both its simplicity and its relatively uncontroversial claim that creatures are that which come into being. Once this claim is granted, the moderate realist has few choices but to grant that all creatures bear a substratum of potential that receives those properties that come to be—that is, all creatures are hylomorphic.[30]

---

[25]   Cf. Aristotle, *Physica*, 189a30–192b5.

[26]   Athanasius, *Oratio de Incarnatione Verbi*, 4 (PG 25:104c).

[27]   Arius, *Epistula ad Eusebium Nicomediensem* (PG 42:212b).

[28]   Alexander of Alexandria, *Epistula ad Alexandrum Constantinopolitanum*, 11–13 (PG 18:552b–552c); *Epistula encyclica*, 7ff. (PG 18:573bff.); *Symbolum synodi Nicaenae anno 325* (PG 20:1540c).

[29]   Basil of Caesarea, *Epistula*, 8.2 (PG 32:249); Gregory of Nazianzen, *Orationes*, 2.14; 2.17; 2.28; 29.7; 34.13; 45.4–7 (PG 35: 423a–424b; 36:81c–84a, 253a–254b, 627b–632b); Gregory of Nyssa, *Contra Eunomium*, 1, 2, 8, 9 (PG 45:368a, 459, 793c, 812d).

[30]   Contemporary metaphysicians have developed views of substance, such as bundle theory or relational ontologies, that could be and sometime are used to account for change without appeal to a substratum of potentiality. While all explicit relational ontologies (see Peter van Inwagen, "Relational vs. Constituent Ontologies," *Philosophical Perspectives*, 25, *Metaphysics* (2011): pp. 390–405) utilize universals, bundle theorists typically appeal to tropes (or particularized properties). For a programmatic paper developing a trope bundle theory, see Peter Simons, "Particulars in Particular Clothing," *Philosophy and Phenomenological Research* 54:3 (Sep., 1994): pp. 553–75. For a critique of Simons, see Robert K. Garcia, "Tropes and Dependency Profiles," *American Philosophical Quarterly* (forthcoming). John Hawthorne has a series of papers defending bundle theory with universals (1995, 1998, 2002), but, in his most recent paper with Theodore Sider on the subject, he seems to abandon this model, since they conclude: "Bundle theorist and temporal relationalist alike purchase the modal differences we want with unfamiliar irreducible locutions. The cost is an unsightly ideology, and a holism unworthy of the name metaphysics." John Hawthrone/Theodore Sider, "Locations," *Philosophical Topics* 30 (2002): p. 28. The centrality of tropes to these alternatives is relevant for the purposes of this paper because the Eastern fathers explicitly reject the view that universals are in anyway divided, particularized, or individuated within hypostases. See n. 17 above. Hence, even if realist versions of such contemporary alternatives work (and I am unconvinced they do), they would not be live options for the Eastern fathers.

Perhaps, though, one could argue that there is a sleight of hand in the seemingly uncontroversial claim that creatures are that which came into being. The superficial reading of the claim is that creatures are beings that were not and now are. When we recognize, however, that Athanasius (et al.) has in mind something much more metaphysical—namely, that creation involves the immanentizing of form in prime matter—the claim may not be as *prime facie* as it appears on first blush. Might one, for example, affirm that all creatures are beings that were not but now are while rejecting the claim that this "coming into being" requires mutative generation? If so, the rationale may be evaded by suggesting that God can create out of nothing a fully formed and immutable creature, one that simply bursts into existence in full perfection. This is, in fact, precisely what Arius sought to argue in reference to the Son of God in later stages of the dispute.[31]

Three things are evident about the pro-Nicene reaction to the suggestion that God can create an immutable creature. (1) The pro-Nicenes evidently thought that Arius was attributing to God a metaphysical impossibility when suggesting that he can make an immutable creature. (2) The pro-Nicenes considered an *immutable creature* to be impossible because they took *creation* to be synonymous with *becoming*; that is to say, the term is a contradictory coupling of *immutable* and *mutable*.[32] (3) The pro-Nicenes evidently had realist commitments that led them to conclude that such contradictions fall beyond the bounds of even omnipotence, much like later medieval realists.[33] Unfortunately, point (2), which is the central point of contention, is taken to be so self-evident by the Eastern fathers that the reasons behind it are more difficult to unearth. I do, however, think the case for it can be made on their behalf.

Let us entertain Arius' suggestion that God could create an immutable creature, one wholly devoid of prime matter. The alternative to the pro-Nicene position would be that God could create *ex nihilo* a fully formed entity. Rather than a creature undergoing a generative process by which it comes to have various properties, progressively moving from potential to actual, the entity bursts onto the scene fully formed at its first moment of existence. Yet, keep in mind that the creature is immutable. So, it is insufficient that the creature merely comes to be without mutation; it must be of such a kind that it cannot mutate after its creation. In other words, it must have all properties it will ever have and be incapable of losing the properties it bears. The implication would be that all of its properties are essential to it, since it has no properties that are subject to change. Now, this raises a question of whether properties such as position, location, situation, and so on are accidental. If so, then the creature could not be temporal—lest its relation to time change—or spatial—lest its relation to other objects change. The former point is especially problematic, since the being had a definite origin point, which requires a temporal relation—*before and after its origin*. But, let us say, for argument's sake, that this difficulty could be avoided by denying that such "external" relational changes (or changes in "passive potential") would constitute a mutation.[34] A second difficulty is this. I am unsure how to avoid the conclusion that this "immutable creature" is modally necessary. For, if the creature cannot be deprived of any of its attributes, then it bears these attributes necessarily. I do not see how one could say that a being has no potential for deprivation of its attributes without concluding that it cannot be

---

[31]   Arius, *Epistola ad Alexandrum papum* (PG 26.708c–709a).

[32]   E.P. Meijering, "En Pote Hote Ouk En Ho Hyios: A Discussion on Time and Eternity," *Vigiliae Christianae* 28 (1974): 161–8; Tim Pawl, "Divine Immutability," *IEP* §1b. For a contemporary exponent of the view that there is no contradiction between the terms "created" and "eternal," see, Ilia Delio, "Is Creation Eternal?," *Theological Studies* 66 (2005): 279–303.

[33]   Regarding points (1)–(3), see nn. 20–22. Regarding medieval realism, see, e.g., Aquinas, *Summa Theologiae* Ia q.25 a.4.

[34]   Cf. John Duns Scotus, *Lectura* I.39.5.65, 75, and 84, in his *Opera Omnia*, 26 vols. (Paris, 1891–95).

destroyed. Moreover, once we have said that it necessarily bears its attributes and cannot be deprived of them, I am unsure how to then conceptually deprive the creature of these attributes at an earlier time, namely, prior to its being created. In short, I do not know how to avoid concluding that such a creature cannot be a creature.

Although the above thought experiment is not found amongst the Eastern fathers, I do believe it is true to their rationale.[35] As moderate realists, they maintain that there is always a distinction between the universals had by particulars and the particulars themselves. Singular properties thus subsist in multiple particulars but are not identifiable with any of the particulars having them.[36] If there was a time when the particular did not exist and thus did not have the properties it now bears, then the particular does not have these properties necessarily; at some point this particular came to have them (becoming); and it thus bears the substratum of potential that receives properties.[37] It is irrelevant how quickly this reception took to occur—in a flash of the eye or over a nine month gestation; the being must have received these properties, and we are thus right back to the necessity that this being have prime matter. In short, we arrive at HC.[38]

Once we understand the rationale behind HC, we are in a position to understand how HC aids the free will defense. The problem noted above for this defense is that the theist is, at least historically speaking, committed to the claims that God is free and that God is incorruptible.[39] Such commitments cast a shadow of suspicion over the theist's claim in reference to evil that God cannot create free beings that are determined toward the good. For, if moral necessity and freedom are compatible in God, why are they not in creatures? On this question, HC provides significant help.

We must keep in mind that the pro-Nicenes were realists who placed contradictions beyond the purview of omnipotence. And the Eastern fathers include amongst the logical contradictions that not even God can bring about the creation of non-hylomorphic, immutable beings. If we follow them on this point, HC affords a clear reply to why moral determination is necessary to God but incompatible with creaturely freedom. Recall that prime matter is a substratum of potentiality; it has no properties of its own. That is to say, no property that takes up residence in matter is essential to it. This, of course, is not to say that hylomorphic creatures do not have essential properties. But it is to say that, though various properties are essential to us, it is not essential to matter that it bears our nature. All properties are foreign properties to prime matter. For this reason, matter always retains the potential to lose the properties it receives, for no property belongs to matter *qua* matter. The implication is that every hylomorphic being is, of metaphysical necessity, corruptible. For the terms "generation" and "corruption" refer to the processes of becoming (generation) and ceasing to be (corruption), respectively. And if generate beings are inevitably material beings, as per HC, then they are also corruptible beings.

---

[35]   Cf. John of Damascus, *De fide orthodoxa*, 1.3 (PG 94:793b–797a). This chapter of *De fide orthodoxa* fleshes out more than most patristic writings the rationale behind HC, and in doing so, presses in directions akin to the above argument.

[36]   See nn. 17 and 19 above.

[37]   See nn. 27 and 30 above.

[38]   For additional considerations in defense of HC, see my "Are Created Spirits Matter and Form?," pp. 90–107.

[39]   On divine incorruptibility, see Athanasius, *Orationes tres adversus Arianos*, 1.5, 1.9, 1.22, 1.28, 1.35–6, 1.48, 2.34, 4.12 (PG 26:21c, 29b, 57c, 72a, 84a–88a, 112c, 220a, 481d); Alexander of Alexandria, *Epistula ad Alexandrum Constantinopolitanum*, 11–13 (PG 18:552b–c); Cyril of Alexandria, *Thesaurus de sancta et consubstantiali Trinitate*, 13 (PG 75:205d–234a). On divine freedom, see Irenaeus, *Contra haereses*, 2.1.1, 2.5.4 (PG 7a:709c–710a, 723c–724a); John of Damascus, *De fide orthodoxa.*, 1.14 (PG 94:860a–862a).

This is precisely why the Eastern fathers (and, in the West, Augustine as well)[40] suggest that anything that comes from non-being can return to non-being. The very substratum that supplies the necessary potential for properties to come into being also retains the potential to lose these very same properties, since no property which the substratum takes on is necessary to the substratum. The substratum itself (prime matter) is pure potential. And, according to the Eastern fathers, because our moral properties are subject to change—this being true of humans and angels—these must be included amongst the properties that prime matter receives and can again lose.[41] Hence, our material composition entails the possibilities of moral generation and corruption as well.

Contrast this with God. The Eastern fathers grant many of the basic distinctions between God and creatures found in Aristotle's unmoved mover argument in *Metaphysics* XII. Creatures that are moved from non-being into being must be moved by something that is unmoved. And, of course, by *unmoved* they do not mean inactive but a perfect being having no potential for mutation. The implication is that if prime matter is the locus for potential and mutation, and God has no potential for change, then God has no prime matter. Hence, like Aristotle, the fathers grant the implications that God, being truly immaterial, is immutable (since matter is the locus mutation), atemporal (since they associate time with sequences of mutation), and infinite or aspatial (since circumscription and accidents of finitude are material in nature). Yet, more important for our purposes is that God, having no substratum of potential, cannot know the potential for either increase or decrease in goodness. Hence, whatever he was is what he is and always will be. In short, God is necessarily incorruptible. For, because God does not come into being or receive once-foreign properties, the divine attributes are inherent to God and thus not subject to either increase or loss. In short, God is necessarily incorruptible.[42]

The rudimentary metaphysical distinctions between God and creatures that HC highlights thus necessitate that God is incorruptible, while creatures are corruptible. Divine freedom can only ever express or demonstrate the divine goodness; it cannot increase it or diminish it, since divinity is void of potential for change and thus incompatible with such mutations.[43] Yet, creatures, as entities that acquire properties and may lose properties, are always subject to mutations. Our size, color, position, and even moral disposition are all subject to change.[44] This metaphysical divide between God and creatures thus makes plain why divine freedom is necessarily coupled with moral determination and incorruptibility, while creaturely freedom is necessarily coupled with moral indetermination (we must be morally formed) and corruptibility (we may be morally unformed or malformed).

---

[40]   Augustine, *civitas Dei* 14.13; *Conf.* 12.1.8; *nat. b.* 1; 10; 42.

[41]   See Jacobs, "Are Created Spirits Composed of Matter and Form?," pp. 81–90, 95–8, 100–101.

[42]   See, e.g., John of Damascus, *De fide orthodoxa*, 1.1–7 (PG 94:789a–808b). For a complete study of the Eastern patristic reception (and varied rejections) of Aristotelian theology, see Bradshaw, *Aristotle East and West, passim*, esp. chs. 2 and 6–8.

[43]   On divine freedom in the Eastern fathers, see David Bradshaw, "Divine Freedom in the Greek Patristic Tradition," *Quaestiones Disputatae* 2 (2011), 56–69.

[44]   Athanasius, *Oratio de Incarnatione Verbi*, 1.3–4 (PG 25:99d–104d); Basil of Caesarea, *Epistul*, 8.2 (PG 32:247b–250b); Gregory of Nyssa, *Contra Eunomium*, 2 (PG 45:459); Gregory of Nazianzen, *Oratione*, 29.7 (PG 36:81c–4a)

Raised Incorruptible

Do the metaphysics of HC require that all hylomorphic beings are corrupted at some point? Certainly not. We do find that the Eastern fathers presume all creatures perpetually mutate. However, because they presume an unbridgeable ontological divide between creatures and God, they take it to be possible for a creature to mutate toward the good in perpetuity without hitting an ontic ceiling, as it were.[45] In other words, it is possible for a hylomorphic entity to be and continue to move from glory to glory, as in the case of the elect angels. Yet, there is a rather unsavory implication of HC. If the materiality of creatures is what necessitates the corruptibility of creatures, so long as the materiality of creatures remains, so does creaturely corruptibility. In this light, what becomes of the Christian hope of an incorruptible future world?

We find both the recognition of the problem and the Eastern fathers' preferred solution again in the context of the Arian dispute. Amid the pro-Nicene objections to Arianism that if the Son is created then he is mutable, it becomes apparent that these fathers understand *mutable* to entail *morally turnable* in rational creatures—that is, we can turn either toward or from the good. Hence, the concern is not simply the juxtaposition between mutable (*alloiōtos*) creatures and the immutable (*analloiōtos*) God, but between morally turnable (*treptos*) creatures and the unturnable (*atreptos*) God. This difference between corruptible creatures and the incorruptible God was a central concern among Arius' opponents and the later pro-Nicenes.[46] The concern is soteriological in nature, and is indeed the very concern raised at the opening of this chapter: namely, if *being treptos* is entailed by *being created*, how can we be delivered from the threat of corruption? For readers unfamiliar with the Eastern patristic notion of *theōsis*, or deification, the solution will likely seem peculiar. But Athanasius is clear that the only hope a creature has of being made incorruptible is to partake of the only nature that is essentially good and *atreptos*, namely, God's own.[47] The incarnation, submits Athanasius, supplies this lifeline. Yet, the incarnation is a lifeline only if the Son of God is of the same nature (*homoousia*) as the Father. For, only then is the Son essentially good and *atreptos*.[48] Arius' Christ can offer no such thing. As a creature, the Arian Christ bears accidental goodness; he is metaphysically mutable; and he is therefore morally turnable.[49]

This soteriological concern was not unique to Athanasius, but reflects a common understanding among the Eastern fathers of one of the central soteriological effects of the incarnation. Thus, Gregory of Nyssa likewise, after identifying one of Apollinaris' errors as ascribing mutability to Christ's divinity, reiterates that we can only hope to become *atreptos* if he who united himself with us in the incarnation is *atreptos*.[50]

---

[45]   See Hans Urs von Balthasar, *Presence and Thought: Essay on the Religious Philosophy of Gregory of Nyssa*, trans. Mark Sebanc (San Francisco, CA: Ignatius Press, 1995), 34–5.

[46]   Athanasius, *Orationes tres adversus Arianos*, 1.5, 1.9, 1.22, 1.28, 1.35–6, 1.48, 2.34, 4.12 (PG 26:21c, 29b, 57c, 72a, 84a–88a, 112c, 220a, 481d); *De decretis Nicaenae synodi*, 20.2 (PG 25:452a); *Epistula ad Afros episcopos*, 5 (PG 26:1037b); Alexander of Alexandria, *Epistula ad Alexandrum Constantinopolitanum*, 11–13 (PG 18:552b–c); *Epistula encyclica*, 7ff. (PG 18:573bff.); Basil of Caesarea, *Epistula*, 8.2 (PG 32:249); Cyril of Alexandria, *Thesaurus de sancta et consubstantiali Trinitate*, 13 (PG 75:205d–234a); *Symbolum synodi Nicaenae anno*, 325 (PG 20:1540c).

[47]   Athanasius, *Orationes contra Arianos*, 1.51 (PG 26:117b–120a).

[48]   Athanasius, *Orationes contra Arianos*, 1.43 (PG 26:99c–102b).

[49]   See, e.g., Alexander of Alexandria, *Epistula ad Alexandrum Constantinopolitanum*, 13 (PG 18:552c).

[50]   Gregory of Nyssa, *Adversus Apollinarem* (PG 45:1124–1269, esp. 1128a). See also Maximus the Confessor's comments on the Monothelite heresy in the seventh century: Maximus the Confessor, *Ambiguorum liber* (PG 91:1057c).

The soteriology that pervades this reply, and indeed the writings of the Eastern fathers generally, is much less judicial in orientation than many Western models. The Eastern fathers are less concerned with a future predicament that sinners face at the hands of a divine judge, and are more concerned with life and death. For these writers, the centerpiece of the human condition is that death entered the world through Adam.[51] To the Eastern mind, the wages of sin is death,[52] but not in the sense of a penalty issued by judicial exactitude. Rather, sin brings death by metaphysical necessity, since to retreat from God, the source of life, is to retreat back toward the non-being whence we came. To quote Basil of Caesarea:

> And immediately he [Adam] was outside paradise and outside the blessed way of life, becoming evil not from necessity but from thoughtlessness. Because of this he also sinned through wicked free choice, and he died through the sin. "For the wages of sin is death." For to the extent that he withdrew from life, he likewise drew near to death. For God is life, and the privation of life is death. Therefore Adam prepared death for himself through his withdrawal from God ... Thus God did not create death, but we brought it upon ourselves by a wicked intention.[53]

For this reason, Eastern patristic soteriology focuses less on how we might atone for sin or appease our future judge and much more on the question of how one can be reconnected with the immortal life of God from which we retreated and have been cut off. Forgiveness or cleansing may be a necessary condition for such a reconnection, but the search for the medicine of immortality is the primary concern of their soteriology. The Eastern fathers turn to the incarnation as that point at which the immortal life of God returned to humanity, and the aim of the Christian life is to imbibe this medicine.

To grasp the view and how it affords a reply to the problem of future corruption, we must look at the concept of divine *energeia*.[54] The term *energeia* first comes out of Aristotle. In his early usage, it simply refers to "the exercise of a capacity in contrast to its mere possession."[55] This would correspond to the basic category distinction between having a power, such as sight, and using that power. As Aristotle develops the concept, however, he juxtaposes *energeiai* with mutative motions from potency to actuality. Unlike potency-actuality mutations, *energeiai* are fully actual at any moment.[56] The contrast is thus between acts that are inherently mutative and operations that proceed from a perfection that is already fully actual.[57] By way of analogy, there is a difference between one who plays piano in order to develop that skill (moving this potency into actuality) and one who has this skill already (actuality) and simply demonstrates this perfection by playing piano (operation).

The distinct status of *energeiai* became crucial in early Christian thought for at least two reasons. First, it enabled Christians, with Aristotle, to affirm that God is eternally complete or perfect (*teleia*), and is thus void of movements (i.e., mutations from potency

---

[51] Romans 5:12.

[52] Romans 6:23.

[53] Basil of Caesarea, *Hom. quod Deus non est auctor malorum*, 7 (PG 30:345a).

[54] For a comprehensive survey of the term *energeia*, and its reception in Eastern theology see David Bradshaw, *Aristotle East and West* (New York: Cambridge University Press, 2004).

[55] Bradshaw, *Aristotle East and West*, 3. E.g., Aristotle, *Topics*, 1.15 106b19–20.

[56] Bradshaw, *Aristotle East and West*, 7–12, esp. 12.

[57] Bradshaw, *Aristotle East and West*, 19–23, esp. 22.

to actuality), but still say that God is operative in the world.[58] Second, it became apparent that one had to make a distinction between the nature of a thing (*ousia*) and its operative powers (*energeiai*) because the operative powers of fire, for example, include heating and lighting, but these *energeiai* can be communicated to metal without changing the *ousia* of metal—the metal remains metal but participates in foreign operative powers—namely, those of fire. This *ousia-energeia* distinction provided Christians with a way of speaking about creaturely participation in the divine via *energeia* without collapsing God and world into a common *ousia* (i.e., nature or essence).[59] This insight is traceable to St Paul who utilizes *energeia* to explain how he can do things that humans should not be able to do, such as heal the sick or raise the dead: *It is not me that does it, but God who energizes me.*[60] In other words, it is the operative power of the divine nature that has been communicated to Paul that works through him; it is not the operative power of Paul's human nature. And, in more ominous passages, Paul also speaks of the children of wrath being energized by the Devil.[61]

Following these Pauline cues, *energeia* came to have overt spiritual connotations in its Christian usage. The Eastern fathers used the concept to explain how the human nature of Christ, though distinct from and unmingled with his divine nature, nonetheless displays divine operative powers.[62] For we see in the incarnation that the very body of Christ is infused with the operative power of God, healing those who touch it or are touched by it, and is even transfigured to shine like the sun.[63] Though the Church fathers reject the notion that Christ's two natures mingle into one nature (*contra* monophysitism)—a mingling of *ousiai*—they also reject the notion that there is an impermeable wall between Christ's divine nature and human nature. Rather, the divine and human natures are distinct and unmingled in the one person of Christ, but the operative power of the divine nature is nonetheless communicated to the human nature, resulting in the transfiguration and ultimately deification of his flesh[64]—a transformation manifest in miracles, the transfiguration, and very unusual post-resurrection phenomena. The basic claim is that things that are not God by nature may nonetheless participate in, or be energized by, God by partaking of divine *energeiai*.

If divine *energeiai* can transform we who are bound by death, we must ask how we might access this life. For the Eastern writers, the union language of scripture affords the answer. We are baptized into Christ; we are raised with him through baptism; if we are to have the life of God in us, we must eat his flesh and drink his blood; and, being reconciled with God

58   Aristotle, *Metaphysics*, 12.6 1071b20–22; cf. John of Damascus, *De fide orthodoxa*, 1.1–7 (PG 94:789a–808b). In Basil's *Epistula*, 234, it also becomes apparent that the distinction between *ousia* and *energeia* enabled the Eastern Church fathers to explain how the former is simple and the latter many (see PG 32:869b–870c).

59   E.g., Basil of Caesarea, *De Spiritu Sancto*, 9.23 (PG 32:109a–110c); *Epistula*, 236 (PG 32:876b–886b); Maximus the Confessor, *Ambigua* (PG 91.1088, 1076); Pseudo-Macarius, *Homilia*, 15.38 (PG 34:602b–c).

60   E.g., Colossians 1:29; 2.12; Ephesians 1:19; 3.7; David Bradshaw, "The Divine Energies in the New Testament," *St. Vladimir's Theological Quarterly* 50 (2006): pp. 189–223.

61   E.g., Ephesians 2:2.

62   E.g., John of Damascus, *De fide orthodoxa*, 3.15, 17, 19 (PG 94:1045c–1064a, 1067b–1072b, 1076a–1082a).

63   John 9:1–9, 32; Luke 4:40; 5:12–13; 7:12–15; 8:49–55; 13:10–13; 20:50–51; Mark 1:30–11, 40–42; 3:10; 5:41–2; 6:5; 7:32–5; 8:22–5; Matthew 8:2–3, 14–15; 9:23–30; 20:30–34; Luke 9:28–36; Mark 9:2–9; Matthew 17:1–9; 2 Peter 1:16–18.

64   See, e.g., Gregory of Nyssa, *Ad Theophilum contra Apollinarium*, 124.21–125.10; Cyril of Alexandria, *Commentarium in Evangelium Joannis*, 13:31–2 PG 74:151a–156a); Maximus the Confessor, *Ad Thalassium*, 42 (*Corpus Christianorum Series Graeca* 7:285–9); John of Damascus, *De fide orthodoxa*, 3.17 (PG 94: 1067b–1072b).

through Christ, we receive the gift of the indwelling Holy Spirit.[65] In short, all such things the Eastern fathers understood to be the very means by which believers partake of the divine nature, to use Peter's words.[66] The Eastern fathers understand this partaking to deify the believer, and thus they speak boldly about believers "being made God."[67] Yet, they make equally clear that deification does not make the partaker a fourth, fifth, et cetera, members of the Trinity, for we do not partake of the divine *ousia* but of the *energeiai* that issue from it.[68] In this participation is the locus of life and the hope of immortality.

Participation in the divine is how these writers understand St Paul's insistence that flesh and blood cannot inherit the kingdom of heaven; it must be transformed, putting off corruption and the putting on incorruption.[69] Though matter may inevitably bear certain natural characteristics, the notion of *energeia* indicates that material objects can take on properties that are foreign to them. With regard to incorruptibility, the claim is that God's moral unturnability is communicated to rational creatures in their deification. Matter is not obliterated, as argued by the Origenists,[70] but it is transformed by communion with God.[71] In this light, the very juxtaposition between God and creatures that raised the first problem addressed in this chapter provides the solution to the second.

Now, this solution could be deemed problematic if we understand corruptibility to be an essential property of humanity, and thus incorruptibility is a contrary property, incompatible with our nature. However, corruptibility is not a positive property, but a privative one. In other words, corruptibility is metaphysically necessary to material objects because matter lacks any essential properties of its own. Therefore, we must not deem the corruptibility of matter to be a positive property, as though this lack of properties is a property. The unturnable nature of God, by contrast, is a positive property. Just as life is essential to the divine nature—God does not participate in life but has it in himself[72]—so it is with divine goodness.[73] And if the *atreptos* nature of the divine is a positive property that may be grasped by participation in divine *energeiai*, as the Eastern fathers suggest, then incorruption is something that creatures may come to participate in through deification. It is for this reason that these fathers link not only the future holiness of Saints with the work of the Holy Spirit, but even the holiness of the elect angels. To quote Basil of Caesarea:

> But there is no sanctification without the Spirit. The powers of the heavens are not holy by nature; were it so there would in this respect be no difference between them and the Holy Spirit. It is in proportion to their relative excellence that they have their

[65] E.g., Basil of Caesarea, *De Spiritu Sancto*, 9.23 (PG 32:109a–110c); John of Damascus, *De Haeresibus*, 80 (PG 94:727b–738c); *De fide orthodoxa*, 4.9, 4.13 (PG 94:1117b–1126b, 1135b–1154c).

[66] 2 Peter 1:4.

[67] E.g., Basil of Caesarea, *De Spiritu Sancto*, 9.23 (PG 32:109a–110c); Athanasius, *Oratio de Incarnatione Verbi*, 54 (PG 25.192b).

[68] Basil of Caesarea, *De Spiritu Sancto*, 9.23 (PG 32:109a–110c); Cyril of Alexandria, *Quod unus sit Christus* (PG 75:1269); Maximus the Confessor, *Ambigua*, 7 (PG 91:1076); Pseudo-Macarius, *Homilia*, 15.38 (PG 34:602b–c).

[69] E.g., John of Damascus, *De fide orthodoxa*, 3.28, 4.27 (PG 94:1219a–1228a).

[70] See Constantinople II, anathema 14 in *Decrees of the Ecumenical Councils Vol. I (Nicea I–Lateran V)*, ed. Norman P. Tanner (London: Sheed & Ward/Georgetown University Press, 1990).

[71] Gregory of Nyssa, *Ad Theophilum contra Apollinarium*, 124.21–125.10; Cyril of Alexandria, *Commentarium in Evangelium Joannis*, 13:31–2 PG 74:151a–156a); Maximus the Confessor, *Ad Thalassium*, 42 (Corpus Christianorum Series Graeca 7:285–9); John of Damascus, *De fide orthodoxa*, 3.17 (PG 94:1067b–1072b). Cf. 1 Cor 15:37–50.

[72] John 5:26.

[73] Mark 10:18.

> *need of holiness from the Spirit. The branding-iron is conceived together with the fire; and yet the material and the fire are distinct. Thus too in the case of the heavenly powers; their substance is, peradventure, an aerial spirit, or immaterial fire … But their sanctification, being external to their substance, superinduces their perfection through the communion of the Spirit. They keep their rank by their abiding in the good and true, and while they retain their freedom of will, never fall away from their patient attendance on Him who is truly good.*[74]

The role of divine *energeia* in holiness does raise a question, though, namely, why does God not bestow this property upon creatures from the start? The answer is located in the Eastern father's synergistic view of creaturely holiness. Because creatures move from unformed (non-being) to formed (being) in all respects, including moral ones, it is important to consider the proximate cause of our moral formation. On this point, the Eastern fathers insist that moral formation is incompatible with constraint and necessity; it requires volitional movement toward the good. In short, the will is the proximate cause of virtue. Basil indicates this in the above quotation, and he is quite clear on this point throughout his writings:

> *God does not love what is constrained but what is accomplished out of virtue. And virtue comes into being out of free choice and not out of constraint. But free choice depends on what is up to us. And what is up to us is self-determined. Accordingly, the one who finds fault with the Creator for not fashioning us by nature sinless is no different from one who prefers the nonrational nature to the rational, and what lacks motion and impulse to what has free choice and activity.*[75]

For this reason, deification is necessarily synergistic, not monergistic. The creature, being brought from non-being into being, cannot begin formed in virtue if the will is the proximate cause of moral formation. Thus, the creature must freely move toward virtue as opposed to vice in order to become morally formed. However, because goodness and indeed incorruptibility is located in God, this movement, if to arrive at incorruptibility, must be a movement toward participation in God. For this reason, God must make available to rational creatures his operative power if they are to have hope of putting off corruption and putting on incorruption. This synergy therefore requires both creaturely volition in a movement toward God and divine condescension toward creatures if creatures are to be made (or in our case, remade) incorruptible, putting off corruption and partaking of the only nature that is essentially *atreptos*.

Conclusion

What we have seen is that HC provides an explanation for why not even God can create a being that is immutable or, in the case of rational entities, morally unturnable. HC thus bolsters the central claim of the free will defense that moral evil is an entailment of freedom in creatures that not even God can prevent. Yet, HC also provides a clear explanation for the basic metaphysical differences between God and creatures that explains why divine freedom is accompanied by moral unturnability while creaturely freedom cannot be. Despite the aid

---

[74]   Basil of Caesarea, *De Spiritu Sancto*, 16.38 (PG 32:135a–140b).

[75]   Basil of Caesarea, *Hom. quod Deus non est auctor malorum*, 7 (PG 30:345b). See also Basil of Caesarea, *De Spiritu Sancto*, 18.46 (PG 32:151b–154a).

HC provides in these areas, we found that the view also gives good reason to think that creatures should remain ever turnable. Thus, there is reason to doubt the Christian hope that, following the resurrection unto life, Saints prove to be incorruptible. Here, however, we found that the very difference between God and creatures at the heart of the first problem provides the solution to the second. By looking to their doctrine of deification and the doctrine of divine *energeiai*, we saw that the Eastern fathers locate the hope of future incorruptibility in the believer's partaking of the only nature that is essentially *atreptos*; for in so doing, we too might hope to put off corruption and put on incorruption in the life to come.[76]

---

[76] I would like to extend my thanks to my research assistant, Scott Fennema, for his assistance in preparing this piece for publication.

Redemption of the Human Body

Adam G. Cooper

The Body in Christian Tradition

Christian reflection on redemption has always featured the body front and centre in one way or another. On the one hand, it is the direct handiwork of the creator, the sacred abode of his Spirit, the hinge on which salvation turns, and, through the hypostatic union, intrinsically enfolded within the life of the Trinity as pledge of our true destiny.[1] By the middle of the fourth century Cyril of Jerusalem can speak of an established Christian 'doctrine of the body', insisting that no one deny the body's community with God, nor make it a scapegoat for moral failure.[2] It may be true that the devil has used the body as a weapon against humanity. But Christ has made of his own body, in all its characteristic weaknesses, a counter-weapon to overturn the devil's schemes.[3] Indeed, in his human life a theandric mode of existence has been inaugurated, generating a new level of freedom by which everything that is proper to bodily life is actualised by way of transcendent modalities. Moreover, as Maximus the Confessor teaches, Christ has returned this body with its passions to us as a gift available to all.[4] Transformed by the cooperative activity of the divine and human spirits, the human body is destined with the whole person to be utterly deified, penetrated and overwhelmed with divine glory.[5]

On the other hand, the body both symbolised and brought home the limits hindering many of the aspirations of the spiritual enterprise. Bodily existence confronts the conscious self with a mystery provoking perplexity. 'What is this mystery surrounding me?' is a question asked repeatedly of the body and physical existence.[6] Ascetic writers often bemoan

---

[1]   See Cypriano Vagaggini, *The Flesh Instrument of Salvation: A Theology of the Human Body* (Staten Island, NY: Society of St Paul, 1969); Hannah Hunt, *Clothed in the Body: Asceticism, the Body and the Spiritual in the Late Antique Era* (London: Ashgate, 2012).

[2]   Cyril of Jerusalem, *Catechesis* 4.22, in Edward Yarnold (tr.), *Cyril of Jerusalem* (London: Routledge, 2000), 105.

[3]   Cyril of Jerusalem, *Catechesis* 12.15, in Yarnold, ibid., 146. On this theme in the history of the theology of redemption, see the dated but still classic study by Gustav Aulen, *Christus Victor: An Historical Study of the Three Main Types of the Idea of the Atonement*, tr. A.G. Herbert (London: SPCK, 1950).

[4]   Maximus the Confessor, *Ambiguum* 5, in Joshua Lollar (tr.), *Maximus the Confessor: Ambigua to Thomas and Second Letter to Thomas* (Turnhout: Brepols, 2009), 68–70.

[5]   See Norman Russell, *The Doctrine of Deification in the Greek Patristic Tradition* (Oxford: Oxford University Press, 2004); Adam G. Cooper, *The Body in St Maximus the Confessor: Holy Flesh, Wholly Deified* (Oxford: Oxford University Press, 2005); David Vincent Meconi, *The One Christ: St Augustine's Theology of Deification* (Washington, DC: Catholic University of America Press, 2013).

[6]   See Gregory Nazianzen, *Oration* 14, in J.-P. Migne (ed.), *Patrologia Graeca*, vol. 35 (Paris, 1886), columns 865A–D; John Climacus, *Ladder of Divine Ascent* 15, in Colm Luibheid and Norman Russell (trs.), *John Climacus: Ladder of Divine Ascent* (New York: Paulist, 1982), 186.

the body as paradoxically friend and enemy, an untrustworthy but necessary partner that must be severely disciplined and restrained if it is not to exceed its office of service. Baffled by the paradox of human sublimity and humility, Christian ascetics wonder why we human beings were given a body, if it is true that we are essentially spiritual beings created for a heavenly life of union with God. Their answer is that the body keeps us humble, guarding us from the pride and presumption to which we are vulnerable on account of our spiritual kinship with the divine. None of this prevented them from believing that 'they could sweep the body into a desperate venture', namely, transfiguration with Christ, enlisting its service as 'the discreet mentor of the proud soul'. Peter Brown has argued that we wrongly construe the ascetic ambivalence towards the body if we interpret it as contempt:

> Seldom, in ancient thought has the body been seen as more deeply implicated in the transformation of the soul; and never was it made to bear so heavy a burden. For the Desert Fathers, the body was not an irrelevant part of the human person, that could, as it were, be 'put in brackets'. … It was, rather, grippingly present to the monk: he was to speak of it as 'this body, that God has afforded me, as a field to cultivate, where I might work and become rich'.[7]

Initially this inclusion of the body as crucial target of – and partner in – divine redemption laboured under a metaphysical matrix in which matter sat rather uneasily on the ontological fringes. The tension between the two approaches summarised above consisted in a tension between two worldviews: the Jewish-Christian, in which redemption is conceived in bodily terms and as taking place through the medium of history, and the Hellenistic-Gnostic, in which redemption is conceived as non-somatic, non-terrestrial, and non-historical. These two worldviews represented two distinct cosmologies, two different maps of reality, which should not be thought of as standing in sharp contrast so much as constantly overlapping and in tension. Nonetheless, their relative and respective influence produced differing accounts of redemption and differing conceptions of the way the body and history feature in those accounts.[8]

The Aristotelian revival of the twelfth and thirteenth centuries provided new conceptual resources by which to undergird and strengthen the organically Christian affirmation that human and cosmic physicality constitute an integral ontological good. The hylomorphic integrality of the human being, the origin of knowledge in the senses, the physical character of sacramental mediation: these become commonplace tenets and provide controlling parameters in the orthodox articulation of redemption, despite the continued propagation in folk piety of less refined philosophies of the body somewhat parallel, in the judgement of Caroline Walker Bynum, to 'modern cryonics'.[9]

But it would be incorrect to think of these elements as just philosophical norms imposed on theology from without. Despite the fact that he had been schooled in both, Martin Luther was the friend of neither Aristotle nor Medieval Scholasticism, yet his notion of 'the bodily word of the gospel' (*das leiblich Wort des Evangelii*) – developed partly as a fruit of the late

---

[7]   Peter Brown, *Body and Society* (London: Faber, 1988), 222, 237, 236.

[8]   See further Paula Frederiksen, 'Vile Bodies: Paul and Augustine on the Resurrection of the Flesh', in Mark S. Burrow and Paul Rorem (eds), *Biblical Hermeneutics in Historical Perspective: Studies in Honor of Karlfried Froehlich on His Sixtieth Birthday* (Grand Rapids: Eerdmans, 1991), 75–87.

[9]   Carolyn Walker Bynum, 'Material Continuity: Personal Survival and the Resurrection of the Body: A Scholastic Discussion in its Medieval and Modern Contexts', in id., *Fragmentation and Redemption: Essays on Gender and the Human Body in Medieval Religion* (New York: Zone Books, 1992), 239–97 at 266.

medieval renaissance in biblical and liturgical theology – embraces and magnifies these same somato-centric parameters. No one who has studied Luther's vast *oeuvre* can fail to notice his robust insistence on objectivity and externality in matters of faith and religion, his commitment to seeking God nowhere except in the flesh of Christ, his conviction that 'God will not deal with us except through his external word and sacrament'. In the flesh of Christ and the word-acts that embody and proclaim him God has permanently instituted the exclusive means of creaturely participation in his divine life. Luther knows that God, being God, is indeed present everywhere, yet 'he does not wish that you grope for him everywhere. Grope rather where the word is, and there you will lay hold of him in the right way. Otherwise you are tempting God and committing idolatry.'[10] The communication of properties in the hypostatic union holds true when it comes to the Christ sacramentally present on the altar and in holy communion: 'God is in this flesh. It is God's flesh, a Spirit-flesh. It is in God, and God is in it.' For this reason 'it lives and gives life to all who eat it, both to their bodies and to their souls'.[11] When Jesus requires his followers to eat his flesh and drink his blood, he is basically saying, 'If you touch my flesh, you are not touching simple flesh and blood; you are eating and drinking flesh and blood which makes you divine.'[12] Luther found support for these teachings not in philosophy but in biblical theology and the sacramental realism of liturgical tradition. It is not just scripture, but the whole rich complex of the Church's performative and divinely ordained verbal, sacramental and ritual enactments that together constitute 'the bodily word of the gospel'. This pregnant phrase, apparently coined by Luther and enshrined in the fifth article of the *Augsburg Confession* (1530), dogmatically unites objective redemption and its subjective appropriation in an ecclesial, liturgically constituted kerygmatic modality, a divine modality permeated with human physicality.[13] The Lutheran position here, at least in principle, concurs seamlessly with the Catholic sacramental sense that, normally speaking, no truly redemptive encounter takes place merely through the air, discarnately, but only by 'giving body' to Christ through the Spirit-filled ecclesial, proclamatory and sacramental economies.[14] This body, the same born of Mary, crucified and risen, and now seated at the Father's right hand in glory, 'is a body of grace; it is a grace embodied, the corporeal source of all grace and sanctification'.[15]

Against the backdrop of this much-compressed account of Christian theologising on the body, then, the contemporary turn to the body can be read as both retrieval and development. Attending to the body and the questions it raises for a theology of redemption forces us out of the world of the ideal and abstract and into the world of the actual and concrete. But here we are confronted by our first problem.

---

[10]   *The Sacrament of the Body and Blood of Christ – Against the Fanatics* (1526), in Helmut T. Lehmann et al. (eds), *Luther's Works* [herewith LW], vol. 36 (Philadelphia: Muhlenberg Press, 1959), 342. See also Luther's *Lectures on Genesis: Chapters 15–20* (1539), LW, vol. 3, 272–7.

[11]   *That these Words of Christ, 'This is My Body', etc., Still Stand Firm Against the Fanatics* (1527), LW, vol. 37, 124–5.

[12]   *Sermons on the Gospel of St. John: Chapters 6–8* (1530–32), LW, vol. 23, 122.

[13]   Article 5 of the *Augsburg Confession* (German text), in *Die Bekenntnisschriften der evangelisch-lutherischen Kirche* (1963), 58. See further Oswald Bayer, *Leibliches Wort: Reformation und Neuzeit im Kinflikt* (Tübingen: Mohr Siebeck, 1992).

[14]   See Colman E. O'Neill, *Meeting Christ in the Sacraments* (New York: Alba House, 1991, rev. ed.), 36–42. See further Adam G. Cooper, *Mystic Marriage: A Liturgical Theology of the Body* (New York: Angelico Press, 2014, forthcoming).

[15]   Jean Borella, *The Sense of the Supernatural*, tr. G. John Champoux (Edinburgh: T. and T. Clark, 1998), 82.

The Body as Object of Redemption

Why do we speak of the 'redemption of the body' as though the body were some discrete object? Is not the body something I am rather than something I possess? Does my 'I' designate only a psychic entity, without also emanating from within an organism and somehow including it as intentional and speaking subject? Or is it the case that 'of this body I can neither say that it is I, nor that it is not I'?[16]

The possibility of speaking of the body as the object of redemption has in the first instance to do with the physical conditions that necessarily qualify all human life and action. The experience of redemption is, like the experience of faith, dramatically 'born in the body', to borrow the phrase of Henri Bourgeois. 'To be sure, it is born in the heart, as biblical language has it. But even more it is constituted in the body. God is the God of bodies … It is to bodies that he gives his Spirit and communicates the power of resurrection.'[17] The body is the object of redemption in as much as it is the 'place' and dramatic personal medium in which divine action is experienced and known.

It also has to do with the meaning of the word 'redemption' (Gr. ἀπόλυσις). Read in the light of both biblical and non-biblical semantics of the λύειν word-group, the phrase 'redemption of the body' connotes the idea of the body as the object of a ransom paid or a transaction resulting in its liberation from some sort of slavery and its transfer to new ownership and title.[18] The legal aspects of this image have their background in Israelite family law. On the basis of certain ties of kinship or blood relation, the gō'ēl (Heb. גאל) or kinsman redeemer is obliged to redeem family lives or goods that have fallen into slavery or captivity to some foreign power. The Old Testament often depicts God himself adopting this patriarchal role towards his people, committing himself to the duty of redemption on the basis of kinship relations established by creation, gratuitous election, and, above all, the original promissory covenant with Abraham.[19] Against this theological background, it makes sense to understand the 'body' in the phrase 'redemption of the body' as the special object of saving divine action, laden as it is with a value grounded most universally in the relationship of creature to creator. Whatever we make of the human body, for God it remains his precious handiwork, the bearer of his image, and the permanent sign of his self-appointed obligation to redeem.

Sometimes however the gō'ēl imagery in the Old Testament is additionally expressed in nuptial and filial terms, so that the divine redeemer is envisaged also as husband and father:

> For the creator is your husband, / The Lord of hosts is his name;
> The holy one of Israel is your redeemer, / The God of the whole earth he is called.[20]

The redemption of the body can therefore be construed as signifying more than the restoration of a physical object from whatever kind of harm it may have fallen into. In a unique way the body indicates the relational and social dimensions of the human person, the 'being from', 'being to' and 'being for' aspects of personhood. The body is a precondition

---

[16]   Gabriel Marcel, *Being and Having: An Existentialist Diary*, tr. K. Farrer (New York: Harper and Row, 1965), 12.

[17]   Henri Bourgeois, 'La Foi naît dans le corps', *La Maison-Dieu* 146 (1981), 39–67 at 41.

[18]   See Gerhard Kittel (ed.), *Theological Dictionary of the New Testament*, vol. 4, tr. Geoffrey W. Bromiley (Grand Rapids: Eerdmans, 1967), 328–56.

[19]   Ibid., 330. See also Helmer Ringgren, 'Ga'al' in G. Johannes Botterweck and Helmer Ringgren (eds), *Theological Dictionary of the Old Testament*, vol. 2 (Grand Rapids: Eerdmans, 1975), 351–2.

[20]   Isaiah 54:5. Cf. Is 63:16.

for interpersonal communion. The confrontation of one body with another amounts to a collision of freedoms and the revelation of difference, without which no intersubjective community, which is always mediated by bodies, can arise. Only through another's body does the 'one who sees' become 'one who is seen', opening the space for the emergence of the person in an 'I–Thou' relation.[21] In this connection John Paul II has spoken of the intrinsically 'filial' and 'nuptial' meanings of the body. The human being before God exists first of all as a gift given to himself. His body, his life, his consciousness are all fruits of an infinite divine generosity that precedes and supports him. Something analogous obtains with man and woman before each other. The nuptial meaning of the body has to do with the way the body, particularly in its masculinity and femininity, provides us with 'the basic conditions that *make it possible for us to exist in a relation of reciprocal gift*'.[22]

This more semiotic reflection on the topic leads us to affirm that the body is not only the *object* of redemption, nor does 'body' signify a discrete physical entity without personal and interpersonal reference. If redemption in the full Christian sense issues from the embodied, paternal action of the incarnate God in Christ, and if it really reconciles human beings to God in some kind of liberation and transfer of status, so that they become bound together with him in salvific solidarity and intimate fellowship, then 'the redemption of the body' must be understood as bearing much wider, symbolic scope in terms of subject, object, means, and effects. For the human body to be redeemed is for matter to become fully personal, filial and nuptial, for the whole world to enter into communion with God.

A cursory exegetical exploration of the New Testament data confirms these preliminary considerations. The phrase 'redemption of our body' occurs in the New Testament just once (Rom. 8:23), but does so in striking fashion. Paul uses it to explain what he means by 'adoption' (Gr. υἱοθεσία): the new state of Spirit-wrought filial incorporation in the inner household of God the Father that makes human beings 'heirs of God and co-heirs with Christ'. What is it about this adoption that connects it with bodily redemption?

Attention to the wider context reveals a number of crucial Pauline contrasts at work: spirit and flesh, slavery and sonship, death and life. All of these contrasts stand under the more embracing teleocentric tension between the present and the future, the partial and complete, with each polarity marked by various conditions: suffering, weakness and corruption on the one hand, and glory, freedom and immortality on the other. The force that binds the present to the future is 'hope' expressed in filial petition to God as 'Abba! Father!', as well as in the form of a threefold yearning or 'groaning' by creation (8:22), Christians (8:23) and the Holy Spirit (8:26). The foundation for such hope is twofold: the promissory pattern proleptically fulfilled in the resurrection of God's Son Jesus Christ from the dead, and the inward personal possession of his Holy Spirit as the guarantee and effective agent of our own full salvation from death and damnation.

How does Paul's definition of sonship or adoption as 'the redemption of our body' make sense within these wider polarities and dynamics? The Pauline contrast between spirit (*pneuma*) and flesh (*sarx*) does not equate with a dualistic contrast between soul (*psychê*) and body (*sôma*). The New Testament terms instead commonly designate the whole person according to certain personal determinations relative to God and sin. They signify contesting powers at work within the human person as a whole being, making him or her either a fleshly or spiritual kind of person. 'Fleshly' here does not in the first instance mean

---

[21] See Hans Urs von Balthasar, *Epilogue* (San Francisco: Ignatius, 1991), 141. See also Antoine Vergote, 'The Other as the Foundation of the Ego and Intersubjectivity', in Antoine Vergote, *In Search of a Philosophical Anthropology*, tr. M.S. Muldoon (Leuven: Leuven University Press, 1996), 123–33.

[22] John Paul II, *Man and Woman He Created Them: A Theology of the Body*, tr. Michael Waldstein (Boston: Pauline Books, 2006), 181.

sensual or visceral: the 'sins of the flesh' include ambition, envy and discord as much as drunkenness, greed and fornication (Gal. 5:19–21).

Yet the semantic proximity of the term 'flesh' to 'body' is surely not accidental, for in certain Pauline passages the body is discovered to be deeply implicated in this existential contest. In Romans 1:21–32 for example the failure to offer right worship to God, a fault of the mind and heart, is profoundly linked to the propensity for perverse sexual activity and its defiling degradation of the body. In Romans 10:13 we find a parallelism contrasting living 'according to the flesh', which leads to death, and mortifying 'the deeds of the body', which leads to life. Here 'flesh' and 'body' stand in virtual symmetry. In Romans 7:24 Paul expresses his exasperation with the continual contradiction between wanting good yet doing evil by asking, 'Who will rescue me from this body of death?', or to translate more poignantly, 'this death-dealing body'. The sense in these and similar passages is that the 'mind of flesh', a rebellious spiritual force in league with adversarial cosmic powers fundamentally hostile to God (Rom. 8:7; 8:38; 1 Cor. 15:24; Gal. 4:3–9), makes itself felt most keenly in the conditions of bodily life: liability to suffering and weakness, predilection towards sensual pleasures and temporal satisfactions, perverse uses of sexuality, tendency to self-justification in or over against the community. When later interpreters like Augustine proposed a close connection between sin, the body, and sexual relations, it was not due to Platonic dualism or some pathological phobia but because they discovered in such passages a logic whose phenomenological contours they personally witnessed in the form of an 'outbreak of anarchy' precisely in the sexual, bodily and inter-personal sphere.[23]

It is therefore especially here in this dimension of the 'flesh' and the body, where the personal and human are so easily deposed and displaced, that the human constitution urgently requires healing. Having been dominated so profoundly or for so long by 'the law of sin', even the baptised can find themselves overwhelmed by competing impulses which threaten to break up the integral unification of their physical and spiritual faculties under the gentle rule of the Holy Spirit. The entire experience is one of interior disharmony and disintegration, so that 'what I want to do, I do not do, and what I hate, I do' (Rom. 7:15). It is not the case that sin originates in the body, or that the body is intrinsically inclined to evil. Jesus' teaching on the priority of interior over exterior righteousness makes it clear that all culpable acts have their origin rather in the will or heart (cf. Mt. 5:8; 5:28; 15:8–20; 23:25–8). Yet such inner acts take on a new and critical level of gravity and influence once they (inevitably) emerge at the horizon of the external and bodily, for here they manifestly intersect with the interpersonal and social.

All of this suggests that sin, the state of filial estrangement from the Father and enslavement to idolatrous and self-destructive forces, is not just a mental or spiritual crisis, a dispositional failure to fear, love, and trust God as one ought, but also involves some kind of bodily rupture, a displacement of the embodied self in two dimensions: externally – with respect to God, human society and the created ecosystem, and internally – with respect to one's own psychosomatic integrity. Filial adoption in Christ, actuated by baptismal regeneration, amounts then not just to a spiritual rebirth but to a 'redemption of the body' because it effects a rescue of the body-self from slavery to disorderly and disordering powers, the kind of powers operative and manifest in the 'threefold concupiscence' (1 John 2:16), or in 'the desires of the mortal body' (Rom. 6:12), or in 'the deeds of the body' (Rom. 6:12) arising from 'indwelling sin' (Rom. 7:17). This is why Paul exhorts the baptised, in harmony with their Spirit-given identity as adopted sons in the Son of the Father, to offer the various parts of their body to God as instruments for the accomplishment of righteousness (Rom. 6:12) and

---

[23]   Paul Ramsey, 'Human Sexuality in the History of Redemption', *The Journal of Religious Ethics* 16/1 (1988), 56–86 at 62.

indeed, to make of their entire body a 'living sacrifice, holy and pleasing to God', for herein – and not first of all in one's mental activities – lies one's 'rational' or 'spiritual act of worship' (Rom. 12:1–3). The Fathers of the Church emphasised the pedagogical dynamism of this process, the way the unruly and conflicting elements in our affective and psychosomatic constitution need to be domesticated, educated, refined, and how such vocational institutions as marriage and monasticism serve in realising this redemptive ethics. In the fidelity of chaste marriage and the undivided devotion of consecrated virginity, 'fallen sexuality has a foretaste or token of its final liberation'.[24]

The Ecclesial Body

But this is only half the picture. The term 'body' in Pauline theology very often carries a communal and ecclesial connotation.[25] As Origen of Alexandria long ago noted, the phrase 'the redemption of the body' indicates not just the reunion of the body and the soul at the resurrection, but 'points to the body of the Church as a whole'.[26] In fact the context forces us to think cosmically: the entire creation 'waits with eager expectation for the sons of God to be revealed' (Rom. 8:19), because only at this consummating moment will 'creation itself be liberated from its bondage to decay into the glorious freedom of the children of God' (Rom. 8:21). The 'frustration' that we experience through our moral and physical vulnerabilities, and which inescapably marks the transition from the present age towards the fullness for which we hope, is one that characterises the whole creation under the old Adam.[27] In this way anthropology and cosmology are bound together, the fate of the world being 'decided in the human sphere'.[28]

It must also be recalled that according to the inscrutable economy of gratuitous divine election, divine filiation is a privilege extended first to the covenant people of Israel: 'theirs is the adoption' (Rom. 9:4).[29] The letter to the Ephesians envisions the sinful state of alienation from God in decisively covenantal terms: prior to baptismal incorporation into Christ we were 'excluded from citizenship in Israel, foreigners to the covenants of the promise, without hope and without God in the world' (Eph 2:12). The personal, ecclesial and cosmic salvation realised in the one body of Christ thus is properly said to come 'from the Jews', and all its participants – regardless of ethnicity, social status, or sex – are made children of Abraham in common (Jn. 4:22; Rom. 1:16; Gal. 3:15–29).

This traditional vision of the corporate, covenantal and cosmic nature of corporeal redemption, obscured in more individualistic soteriologies, was masterfully recovered and restated in the first half of the twentieth century by such thinkers as Emile Mersch and

---

[24]   Ramsey, 'Human Sexuality', 80.

[25]   See J.A.T. Robinson, *The Body: A Study in Pauline Theology* (London: SCM Press, 1961); Robert H. Gundry, *Sōma in Biblical Theology with an Emphasis on Pauline Anthropology* (Cambridge: Cambridge University Press, 1976).

[26]   Origen, *Commentary on Romans* 7.5.10, in Thomas P. Scheck (tr.), *Origen: Commentary on the Epistle to the Romans*, vol. 2 (Fathers of the Church 104, Washington, DC: Catholic University of America Press, 2002), 77.

[27]   See Douglas Moo, *The Epistle to the Romans* (New International Commentary on the New Testament, Grand Rapids: Eerdmans, 1996), 519–21.

[28]   Käsemann, *Perspectives on Paul*, 23.

[29]   Brendan Byrne, *Romans* (Sacra Pagina 6, Collegeville: Liturgical Press, 1996), 263.

Henri de Lubac.[30] Humanity has been created as a corporate unity, consisting as it were as a single body. Only as a single body is it redeemed. The fragmentation of humanity into innumerable isolated units, far from being natural, is a consequence of sin. The gratuitous redemption of humanity must consequently take the form of a re-unification. Herein lies the deep connection between creation, Christology and ecclesiology. The eternal Son takes his body from the one, corporate body that is creaturely humanity: According to Athanasius of Alexandria, from our fickle and unstable humanity the Word appropriates for himself what is not his own, renews and transforms it through its reception of divine life, and returns it to us in this stable, deified form as a gift.[31] This is what the scriptures mean when they ascribe 'receiving' to Christ. 'For the Word was not impaired in receiving a body … but rather he deified that which he put on, and more than that, gave it graciously to the race of man.'[32] The humanity of the Word is more than just a representative image or exemplar of our own human nature. Christ's bodily resurrection from the dead is not just a sign of what will happen to us, but is already our resurrection in the making. We do not simply rise after him, in a simple imitation of him, but 'from him and because of him' by our concrete incorporation into his body.[33] The Church in all its various dimensions – spiritual, sacramental, liturgical, hierarchical – is essentially a kind of vast, living extension of this divine humanity. According to this way of seeing, all human beings – believers and unbelievers, Jews and Gentiles, past, present and future – have therefore been implicated and touched by the incarnation, whose reality and effects are irreversible. Only if these propositions are true can the Church consequently be the dynamic social and historical 'body' in which humanity's redemptive, unifying and finally deifying drama unfolds.[34]

Mary's Redeemed Body

It has long been recognised that the role played by Mary the Mother of God in the drama of human redemption is more than simply instrumental. From the time of Justin and Irenaeus in the second century a Mariology has been developed that discerns how the redemption of all humanity is bound to the typological life histories of Adam and Eve, Christ and Mary, and their respective intra-nuptial, sexually specific responses to the saving divine will. Not only does the Virgin of Nazareth embody the personal link between the Old and New Covenants, creation and redemption, nature and grace. Her own reception of redemption – formally expressed in the dogmas of her immaculate conception and bodily assumption – exemplifies its profoundly bodily character, the way it transfigures the sphere of the humanly biological and physical, drawing it up into the realm of Spirit and divinity, without in any way negating or diminishing it.

---

[30]   Emile Mersch, *La corps mystique du Christ* (1936), ET: *The Whole Christ*, tr. John R. Kelly (Milwaukee: Bruce, 1938); Henri de Lubac, *Catholicisme: les aspects sociaux du dogme* (1938), ET: *Catholicism: Christ and the Common Destiny of Man*, tr. L. Sheppard (London: Burns and Oates, 1950).

[31]   Athanasius, *Contra Arianos* I, 12, 1–37, in *Athanasius Werke, Erste Band, Erster Teil: Die Dogmatischen Schriften: 2. Lieferung: Orationes I et II Contra Arianos*, eds. Karin Metzler and Kyriakos Savvidis (Berlin and New York: Walter de Gruyter, 1998), 121–2; *Contra Arianos* I, 16, 1–29 (Metzler and Savvidis 1998, 125–6).

[32]   *Contra Arianos* I, 42, 6–8 (Metzler and Savvidis 1998, 152).

[33]   *Contra Arianos* II, 61, 24–5 (Metzler and Savvidis 1998, 238). See further Adam G. Cooper, 'The Gift of Receptivity: Athanasius on the Security of Salvation', *Phronema* 28/2 (2013), 1–20; John R. Meyer, 'Athanasius' Use of Paul in His Doctrine of Salvation', *Vigiliae Christianae* 52/2 (1998), 146–71.

[34]   See John Paul II, *Encyclical Letter Redemptor hominis* (Boston: Pauline Books, 1979), §§8–14.

In guaranteeing the creaturely and material integrity of Christ's humanity, Mary guarantees the material world's salvation. 'For if he did not receive the substance of flesh from a human being, he neither was made man nor the Son of man'.[35] In contrast to Eve, whose disobedience set in motion the punitive cycle of procreation and death, Mary's word of faith and virginal conception initiates a process through which the bond that binds procreation to death is dissolved, making her the true 'mother of the living'.[36] By her *fiat* and divine motherhood, she co-operated in effecting the world's redemption, and so may rightly be called co-redemptrix and venerated accordingly. The doctrine of Mary's perpetual virginity, like the doctrines of her Immaculate Conception, lifelong sinlessness, and bodily assumption into heaven, implies no contempt for the married state but rather indicates its relative and limited character when compared to the kind of fruitful generativity and transfigured bodiliness of heaven heralded by virginity for the sake of the kingdom. Mary realises in her bodily life the redemptive predestination in Christ of all people in a preeminent and comprehensive way. Her sinlessness and bodily virginity do not simply function as 'background' for the drama of redemption, but are simultaneously co-constitutive and effective fruit of its action. By fulfilling her vocation to divine maternity as a virgin, in keeping with the measure of redemptive grace extended to her, she embodies a certain personal transcendence over the biological sphere, rendering it subordinate to the divine plan being realized within her. In this way Mary transcends biology, without negating biology. Joseph Ratzinger has commented on the relevance this dual vocation of Mary as virgin and mother holds for the contemporary quest for the 'liberation' (redemption!) of sexuality and the body:

> The "biological" and the human are inseparable in the figure of Mary, just as are the human and the "theological". This insight is deeply akin to the dominant movements of our time, yet it also contradicts them at the very core. For while today's anthropological program hinges more radically than ever before on "emancipation", the kind of freedom it seeks is one whose goal is to "be like God" (Gn 3:5). But the idea that we can be like God implies a detachment of man from his biological conditionedness, from the "male and female he created them". This sexual difference is something that man, as a biological being, can never get rid of, something that marks man in the deepest center of his being ... When man reduces this fundamental determination of his being to a despicable trifle that can be treated as a thing, he himself becomes a trifle and a thing, and his "liberation" turns out to be his degradation to an object of production. Whenever biology is subtracted from humanity, humanity itself is negated.[37]

Does this doctrine of Mary's freedom from sin detract from the fullness of Christ's redemptive work? Does it mean she is less redeemed? Karl Rahner has argued to the contrary:

> [T]he freedom from sin of a human being in this world ... is more grace, more redemption, than when a human being is taken up out of the darkness he has loved, into God's light. To be preserved from sin is a more splendid, radiant redemption, but still redemption pure and simple.[38]

---

[35] Irenaeus, *Against Heresies* III.22.1.
[36] Irenaeus, *Against Heresies* III.22.4.
[37] Joseph Ratzinger, 'Thoughts on the Place of Marian Doctrine and Piety in Faith and Theology as a Whole', *Communio* 30/1 (2003), 147–60 at 157.
[38] Karl Rahner, *Mary Mother of the Lord: Theological Meditations*, tr. W.J. O'Hara (Freiburg: Herder, 1963), 75.

In this light it can be said that no one has been so profoundly incorporated into the mystery of Christ's redemption as Mary. And thus, according to John Paul II, no one else can bring us into the divine and human dimensions of this mystery as she can.[39] Here the great theologian of the body touches on the connection between Mariology and ecclesiology. In and with Mary, the Church, being the communion of the redeemed, is able to bear witness to the victorious fruits of Christ's redemption in a hidden yet actual and tangible manner. She effectively embodies this redemption in all her members, those triumphant as well as those militant who are simultaneously fallen and redeemed (*simul lapsus et redemptus*).[40] In this way her holiness is not just an article of faith but a victorious and living power.[41]

This insight becomes one of the most prominent features in John Paul's *Theology of the Body* catecheses. Over and again he repeats the claim that the redemption which Christ enacted and embodied in his sacrificial death 'definitively realises' the great mystery which God planned before the world was made. Redemption is not just a distant hope but 'a truth, a reality, in the name of which man must feel himself called, and called with effectiveness'.[42] Christ's redemptive action results in an 'effective' new form of human life and activity, effective, because it actually is capable of changing a person from the inside. In this way the 'fullness of righteousness' demanded by Christian discipleship (cf. Mt 3:15; 5:17–20; 5:48) is shown to be not simply an impossible ideal but a concrete reality made present and available to those who trust in him. 'Christ's words are *realistic* ... They point out to [man] *the path toward a purity of heart* that is *possible and accessible* for him even in the state of hereditary sinfulness'. These comments express a vital aspect of a Christian theology of bodily redemption: the human person is essentially redeemable, historically and tangibly transformable, such that the domination of sin can be overcome and vanquished not only in principle but also in practice. In many ways it simply echoes the old Augustinian axiom regarding the person touched by redemptive grace: *posse non peccare*.

The Wounded Body

If the mystery of redemption really reaches into the physical sphere and touches the body, what manifest features should we expect it to exhibit? We have already affirmed that holiness and deification, although only perfected in the eschatological fullness of filial adoption and nuptial union, already unfold proleptically within the communion of ecclesial incorporation into Christ. But in keeping with the contrary logic of the cross, by which divine power and wisdom are simultaneously manifest and concealed under the forms of human weakness and folly, it is also the case that the glorious redemption of the body, already anticipated in hope and with inexpressible joy, makes itself most palpably present in the agony of suffering with and on behalf of the crucified Christ. The comprehensive Marian surrender to redemptive grace may have spared her from the pangs of labour pain (cf. Gen. 3:16), but it did not spare her from her vocation to be *mater dolorosa*, sharing the agony and scandal of her

---

[39] John Paul II, *Redemptor hominis* §22.

[40] John Paul II, *Man and Woman He Created Them*, 546.

[41] Rahner, *Mary Mother of the Lord*, 76–7.

[42] John Paul II, *Man and Woman He Created Them*, 312, cf. ibid., 508–10.

Son's contradictory and opprobrious mission (Lk. 2:34–5).[43] For the Apostle Paul, 'always bearing the death of Jesus in his body' and 'always being given over to death for Jesus' sake' constituted the humbling but crucial corollaries to his and his colleagues' apostolic ministry (2 Cor. 4:10–11). Whether his 'thorn in the flesh' indicated a physical, psychological or some other handicap (2 Cor. 12:7), the bodily and Christoform *stigmata* in which he boasted (Gal. 6:17) were welcomed in faith as certain signs of redemptive triumph in which the Lord's gracious power was being made complete in him (2 Cor. 12:9–10).

One crucial question these comments provoke is whether this attribution of some kind of redemptive quality to personal suffering amounts to yet another dubious theodicy. I am speaking of the kind so poignantly criticised by Emmanuel Levinas, for example as a scandalous attempt to acquit God and make sense of an experience which in its essence is an unjustifiable and absurd monstrosity. To the extent that such theodicies have in common 'the justification of the neighbour's pain', and now especially in the shadow of the Holocaust and the murderous horrors of the twentieth century, they function as 'the source of all immorality'.[44]

But Levinas touches on a profound truth in also recognising that bodily human suffering, intrinsically 'useless' and 'sense-less' and 'condemned to itself without exit', opens up a space for 'the inter-human' and, in the midst of this inter-human, a space for the 'beyond' and the entry of the salvific.

> Is not the evil of suffering – extreme passivity, impotence, abandonment and solitude – also the unassumable and thus the possibility of a half-opening, and, more precisely, the possibility that wherever a moan, a cry, a groan or a sigh happen there is the original call for aid, for curative help, for help from the other ego whose alterity, whose exteriority promises salvation?[45]

In this perspective, it is not the case that the suffering of others becomes pardonable or meaningful. Rather their suffering can solicit from me a response within which 'my own adventure of suffering', marked by a 'constitutional or congenital uselessness', can nonetheless 'take on a meaning, the only meaning to which suffering is susceptible, in becoming a suffering for the suffering – be it inexorable – of someone else'.[46]

Nowhere do we find the Apostle Paul offering a systematic and logically watertight justification of suffering or the presence of evil in the world. Even when confronted by the enigma of Israel's unbelief, which he explains in part by appeal to God's inscrutable purposes and his will eventually to have mercy on all, he ends not on a note of apologetic triumph but of humble doxology (Rom. 11:33–6). If we can speak of a Pauline theodicy, it can only be in terms of his conviction that God, in fidelity to his promises, will vindicate the righteous by raising them from death (Rom. 4:17–25). Like Levinas, Paul holds that the apparent withdrawal of God's saving presence compels one all the more to pledge oneself to the truth and perpetuity of sacred history in dutiful opposition to every diabolical project.[47]

---

[43] See Raymond E. Brown, *Birth of the Messiah: A Commentary on the Infancy Narrative in the Gospels of Matthew and Luke* (London: Geoffrey Chapman, 1993), 460–66. Although Brown rejects the *mater dolorosa* tradition as extraneous to Lucan theology, its prominence in traditional Marian piety grants it a fittingness transcending the strict limits of critical exegesis.

[44] Emmanuel Levinas, 'Useless Suffering' in R. Bernasconi and D. Woods (eds), *The Provocation of Levinas* (London: Routledge, 1988), 156–67.

[45] Levinas, 'Useless Suffering', 158.

[46] Levinas, 'Useless Suffering', 159.

[47] Levinas, 'Useless Suffering', 164.

It is only on the basis of his own existential immersion in the redemptive suffering of Christ, his readiness to suffer damnation for the salvation of his own kin (Rom. 9:3), that Paul exhorts his hearers to adopt a similar hermeneutic with respect to their own afflictions. Suffering on Christ's behalf (*hyper Christou*) should be regarded as no less a grace than believing in him (Phil. 1:29), nor of less redemptive import! It is as though physical suffering functions as a privileged mode of actualising Christ's redemptive work in history. When in Philippians 3:10 Paul refers to the Christian's 'fellowship [*koinônian*] in the sufferings of Christ', *koinônia* here is to be understood in the very concrete sense of shared goods or common possessions. Baptism establishes such a profound bond or communion between Christ and the baptised that there can be no complete morphological sharing in Christ's bodily glory without a complete morphological sharing in his bodily suffering and death (Phil. 3:10; 3:21). In fact Paul can go so far as to identify his physical afflictions as filling up what is 'still lacking' (*ta hysterêmata*) in Christ's own sufferings (Col. 1:24). In this curious remark is intimated the mystery that the Church, extending the incarnate Christ into the sphere of temporal history, has her own dramatic role to play in the universally redemptive pathos of God.[48]

There are many in our time especially who judge the theological account offered here with repugnance. Echoing Nietzsche's disgust with the Christian morality of weakness and sacrifice, feminist theology has rendered almost ubiquitous in academia a disdain for the traditional Christian motif of redemptive suffering inasmuch as it has sanctioned an ethics of violence, especially of male violence towards women. Rosemary Radford Ruether rejects the notion of redemptive suffering, whether Christ's or our own. 'What is redemptive is action to extricate ourselves from unjust suffering and changing the conditions that cause it. It is not Jesus' suffering and death that are redemptive, but his life as a praxis of protest against injustice and solidarity in defense of life'.[49] Suffering is a risk belonging to the process of liberation, not a means of redemption.

Girardian scapegoat theory, non-sacrificial theologies of the atonement, and various Protestant emphases on the absolute singularity of Christ's redemptive work to the exclusion of any efficacious human or ecclesial participation in it (let alone fulfilment of it), all represent admirable attempts to answer to the acerbic feminist critique.[50] All three, however, seem to overlook the actual ecstatic or quasi-violent character of love, even in its most life-affirming and edifying modes. According to the Christian mystical tradition, a tradition formed by both men and women and based on intimate personal experience and astute phenomenological observation, authentic love involves the lovers concerned in a 'liquefaction', that is, in a kind of self-dissolution. This is true not only of human lovers. In the language of many mystical treatises and homilies, even God is liquefied, bound, conquered, wounded by his love for sinners. To love is to suffer a kind of life-creating violence.[51]

---

[48]   See John Paul II, *Encyclical Letter Salvifici doloris* (Boston: Pauline Books, 1984); José Granados, 'Toward a Theology of the Suffering Body', *Communio* 33/4 (2006), 540–63.

[49]   Rosemary Radford Ruether, *Women and Redemption: A Theological History* (Minneapolis: Fortress Press, 1998), 279.

[50]   See respectively René Girard, *Violence and the Sacred*, tr. Patrick Gregory (Baltimore: Johns Hopkins University Press, 1977); J. Denny Weaver, *The Nonviolent Atonement* (Grand Rapids: Eerdmans, 2001); John R.W. Stott, *The Cross of Christ* (Leicester: IVP, 1986). A critique of these approaches is developed by John Dunnill, *Sacrifice and the Body: Biblical Anthropology and Christian Self-Understanding* (London: Ashgate, 2013), though in a direction somewhat different from the one taken here.

[51]   See further Bernard McGinn, 'The Abyss of Love', in *The Joy of Learning and the Love of God: Essays in Honor of Jean Leclercq* (Cistercian Studies 160, Kalamazoo: Cistercian Publications, 1995), 95–120; Juan de Dios Larru, 'The Original Source of Love: The Pierced Heart', in Livio Melina and Carl A. Anderson (eds), *The Way of Love: Reflections on Pope Benedict XVI's Encyclical* Deus Caritas Est (San Francisco: Ignatius, 2006), 199–211.

Of course we must take account of the overtly rhetorical style in which such expressions are embedded. They are aimed not at expressing a systematic theology but at arousing an emotional, affective response in their hearers, at heightening their sense of the greatness of divine love and mercy at work in their redemption, their wonder at the sheer power of love, such that it conquers even the erotic God. They parallel the kind of poetic creativity embodied in George Herbert's immortal lines:

> *Love is that liquor sweet and most divine,*
> *Which my God feels as blood; but I as wine.*[52]

But there are systematic and ethical implications to which this mystical theme gives witness, most apposite to the concerns of this chapter. The case has been contended with compelling force by G.J. McAleer in his monograph *Ecstatic Morality and Sexual Politics*.[53] Both feminism and the traditional Christian theology of redemption agree that 'sensuality is a place of metaphysical violence', with the historical body a zone of conflicting forces and sexual difference a fulcrum of division between men and women.[54] Without the liquefaction of the self through ecstatic love, any attempt to liberate the bodily and sensual – my own or another's – can only result in individuation, objectification, and violence. 'With the liquefaction of the body, however', that is, with the lesion or wound opened up in the self through ecstatic love for the beloved, 'the other literally lives in the wound, the space opened up in the lover's flesh for the one loved'.[55] McAleer appeals to the Dionysian and Thomistic doctrine of ecstatic love and John Paul II's *Theology of the Body* to argue that far from doing bodily human nature violence, this wounding corresponds to the deeply inscribed logic of mutual donation which, as a kind of metaphysical 'incision' abiding within our masculinity and femininity, 'decides the nuptial meaning of the human body'.[56]

On this basis it is not only possible but necessary to speak of the redemptive power of human love which, since we are bodily beings, will inevitably manifest itself in the physical and 'inter-human' spheres and occasion a redemptively generative pathos. Ironically, it is the loss or denial of this ecstatic, liquefying, and self-giving bodily dynamic in liberal ideologies – Marxist, Fascist or Kantian – that inexorably leads them to endorse political violence.[57] This is why John Paul II could at once affirm 'the Gospel of Suffering' and condemn 'the Culture of Death'. Bodily acts arising from the liquefaction of ecstatic love and ordered towards the diffusion and deposition of the self, acts such as the Church's Eucharistic communion or the married couple's procreative conjugality, embody and cultivate the redemptive politics of the cross, which the Baptist expressed in his 'I must decrease', Paul in his 'no longer I but Christ', and John in his visionary account of the wedding feast of the slaughtered Lamb. The redeemed body will bear signs of its wounds, even in glory, or else its redemption is an illusion and Christians are of all people the most to be pitied.

---

[52] 'The Agony', in George Herbert, *The Country Parson, The Temple*, ed. John N. Wall (New York: Paulist, 1981), 151.

[53] G.J. McAleer, *Ecstatic Morality and Sexual Politics: A Catholic and Antitotalitarian Theory of the Body* (New York: Fordham University Press, 2005).

[54] McAleer, *Ecstatic Morality*, 95.

[55] McAleer, *Ecstatic Morality*, 75.

[56] McAleer, *Ecstatic Morality*, 81.

[57] See further E. Michael Jones, *Libido Dominandi: Sexual Liberation and Political Control* (South Bend, Indiana: St Augustine's Press, 2005).

Incarnation or the Cross?

On the basis of our explorations we may now offer some concluding remarks concerning the old question whether the conditions for human redemption are best understood as accomplished at Christmas or Easter, in the incarnation or the cross. These two approaches are often said to imply two distinct doctrines of redemption. As Joseph Ratzinger has explained, the first holds the redemptive ontology of Christ to be the vital fact in the face of which all Christ's individual actions are secondary: 'the interlocking of God and man appears as the truly decisive, redemptive factor, as the real future of man, on which all lines eventually converge'.[58] The theology of the cross, by contrast, emphasises the event-character of Christ's sacrificial and victorious death, with the 'exodus' of his passion atoning for the world's sin and pioneering the pathway to its transfiguring resurrection.[59] Granted that these two approaches 'reveal polarities that cannot be surmounted and combined in a neat synthesis',[60] is it possible nonetheless to bring what we have said specifically about the body and its redemption to bear on the question of the relation of these approaches in such a way as to highlight their inseparable unity?

In fact the question of the body played a determinative role in the great Christological controversies of the fourth and fifth centuries, which in turn were not simply terminological wars but urgent contests to preserve the soteriological foundation of the Church's living faith in God. In the heretical diminution of either Christ's true divinity or true humanity the Church discerned doubt over the certainty of salvation. 'How can they be saved unless it was God who worked their salvation upon earth? How shall we pass into God, if God has not first passed into us?'[61] And in the reduction of Christ's bodily humanity to purely instrumental status in the hands of the Logos, the Church discerned a negation not only of God's real solidarity with us in our actual human condition, but also of the truly redemptive quality of Christ's human acts *as human* and therefore of any subsequent possibility of our participation or fellowship in them *as humans*. According to Monophysite versions of the Redeemer 'the flesh is incapable of making either any response to divine leading, or any resistance to temptation; it is forcibly saved under the iron hand of the divine spirit ... '.[62]

On the other hand, the Church has always regarded Pascha especially 'the feast of redemption', and in liturgical tradition it has always been at this time that neophytes are incorporated into the body of Christ through the sacrament of baptism, whose effects include the redemptive removal of all sins, original and personal.[63] While maintaining the over-riding motif of the deifying effect of the Son's incarnation, the towering Christologians of the patristic era – Athanasius, Gregory Nazianzen and, above all, Cyril of Alexandria – did not overlook, 'or in any way underestimate, the peculiar saving efficacy attaching to the Lord's death'.[64] Cyril could even speak of Christ's death as 'the root of life', without which the incarnation would have given us only an exemplary moral teacher.[65] In our own era the forthright Congregationalist preacher of the cross P.T. Forsythe was therefore surely

---

[58] Joseph Cardinal Ratzinger, *Introduction to Christianity*, tr. J.R. Foster (San Francisco: Ignatius, 2004), 229.

[59] Ibid., 229–30.

[60] Ibid., 230.

[61] Irenaeus, *Against Heresies* IV.33.4.

[62] G.L. Prestige, *Fathers and Heretics* (London: SPCK, 1958), 112.

[63] *Catechism of the Catholic Church* (London: Geoffrey Chapman, 1999 rev. edn.), §1263.

[64] J.N.D. Kelly, *Early Christian Doctrines* (London: Adam and Charles Black, 1977, 5th rev. edn.), 397.

[65] Quoted in ibid.

correct when he argued that the Church's recognition of Christ as the incarnate divine Son was itself a fruit of faith-filled apprehension of the world-changing events of Holy Week. 'We know the Incarnation only as the foundation of the cross … For the question of the Christ is the question of the Saviour.'[66] If what we have said above about ecstatic love and the wounding of the lover is true also of the immanent love of the Trinity, then even if the whole of creation was from the beginning ordered towards the incarnation, the incarnation was from its beginning ordered towards the passion. 'Christ is to us just what His cross is … You do not understand Christ till you understand His cross.'[67]

But in the perspective we have outlined in this chapter, it is the twin-affirmation of both these approaches and the exclusion of neither that characterise the fully Christian doctrine of redemption. And we can say this because it is precisely the body of Christ which unites the incarnation and the cross, just as it is our body which gathers into tangible unity all of the disparate 'moments' in our personal progression from conception to death. And so Christianity proclaims neither the incarnate Christ alone, nor the cross alone, but 'Christ crucified' (1 Cor. 1:23), who only through the history of his own 'becoming' is now 'our righteousness, holiness, and redemption' (1 Cor. 1:30).

It is by virtue of the body that a human being lives and dies. It is thus by virtue of the body that a human being may, 'with his life and death, draw near to Christ' and 'enter into Him with all his own self'. No wonder, again, that the nuptial paradigm predominates in classic Christian accounts of bodily redemption and its sacramental and ethical actualisation. Just as the body is ordered 'to the Lord, and the Lord to the body' (1 Cor. 6:13), so a Christian theology of redemption understands that, in a way most closely akin to erotic experience, life in Christ unfolds within a framework of intense nuptial and affective dialectics: presence and absence, anticipation and fulfilment, possession and separation, longing and consummation, yearning and rest, now and not yet. Keeping redemption concrete, the body witnesses to our non-origination in ourselves, to our being-from and being-for another, and finally, through its ritual washing and cruciform signification in baptismal regeneration, to our utter dependence on a gratuitous paternal mercy that pledges our pardon and awaits us as our ultimate hope.

---

[66] P.T. Forsythe, *The Cruciality of the Cross* (Blackwood, South Australia: New Creation Publications, 1984), 30, 25. See further Hans Urs von Balthasar, *Mysterium Paschale: The Mystery of Easter*, tr. Aidan Nichols (San Francisco: Ignatius, 2000).

[67] Forsythe, *The Cruciality of the Cross*, 44–5.

Redemption, the Resurrected Body, and Human Nature[1]

Stephen T. Davis

What are human beings that you are mindful of them, mortals that you care for them?
(Psalms 8:4)

I

What is human nature?[2] Let us assume that the term *human being* refers to a natural kind, where a natural kind is a type of concrete thing that we find naturally occurring in the world and that has various members, like *rock* or *tree* or *cow*. Just as individual things have essences, so do kinds. The essence (or nature) of a kind is simply a list of the properties that all the members of that kind have essentially. So human nature is a list of the properties that all human beings have essentially.

Properties can be had in two different ways, accidentally and essentially. For a thing X to have a property p essentially means that X has p in all possible worlds in which X exists. That is, it is not possible for X to lose p and still exist as the thing that it is. Triangles have the property of having three sides in all possible worlds in which triangles exist. If a given triangle were somehow to become four sided, it would no longer be a triangle. But some properties are had accidentally. For example, I have the property of being a philosophy professor. But that is clearly an accidental property of mine because I could remain who I am even if I took up a new profession or retired.

So, again, human nature is simply the list of all the properties that human beings have essentially. But which properties are they, exactly? Well, certainly not properties like *being six feet tall* or *speaking Swahili*. It is eminently possible to be a human being and fail to possess either or both of those properties. We might be tempted to suggest as a candidate the property of *being born on earth*. That is certainly a property had by all human beings who have ever existed, but it does not appear to be an essential property. It seems quite possible for a human being to be born on the moon or in a space station, and there may well be such

---

[1]   Some of the present chapter is partially based on other things that I have written, e.g., Chapters 5 and 7 of *Risen Indeed: Making Sense of the Resurrection* (Grand Rapids, MI: Eerdmans, 1993) and "Bodily Redemption: A Reformed Perspective," *Salvation in Christ: Comparative Christian Views*, ed. Roger R. Keller and Robert L. Millet (Provo, UT: Brigham Young University, 2005).

[2]   Obviously, people have been debating about this question for centuries. In recent years, some have even vociferously argued against the very idea that there is such a thing as human nature; to suppose so, they say, is to be guilty of the sin of Essentialism. But I am going to assume that there is such a thing as human nature. Some sins are not worth worrying about.

people some day. This then appears to be a common property of all human beings who have existed thus far, but not an essential property.

But what then are some essential properties of the members of the natural kind *human being*? That is unfortunately not easy to say. With abstract objects like triangles, numbers, and sets, distinguishing between accidental and essential properties is sometimes fairly easy. But with concrete objects like human beings, it can be difficult. And this is one of those places where religious people and secular people will part company. Almost everybody, religious or secular, will surely agree that an essential property of being a human being is being a member of the species *homo sapiens*, which entails having the human genotype. A member of another species is not a human being. Most would agree that *having evolved from lower organisms* is also an essential property of human beings, although of course those who reject evolution and accept as literally true the story of the creation of Adam and Eve in Genesis 1 and 2 would demur. No doubt there are other properties of human beings that everybody, or almost everybody, would agree are essential. Possibly the property of *having the capacity to do moral right and wrong* would also count, although perhaps severely disabled people or people in a coma do not have it.

But religious people would doubtless add other properties to the list of essential properties that secular people would dispute. Some such properties might be *being created by God* or *being loved by God* or *having the potential to know God* or *having a soul*. It is impossible to be a human being—so some religious folk would say—without having these properties (and surely others as well) essentially.

Christians also believe in "original sin." What precisely this term means, how original sin works, and how far it reaches, have been much debated in the history of theology. I do not wish to enter into those debates. I will only point out that the notion is taken by virtually all Christians as entailing that every human being is, in some degree or other, self-centered, disobedient, and guilty before God. As Paul says, "All have sinned and fall short of the glory of God" (Romans 3:23). So the idea is that we are all sinners, where a sinner is simply someone who misses the moral standard that God has put before us, as expressed preeminently in the Ten Commandments and the teachings of Jesus.

Is *being a sinner*, then, an essential property of human beings? Christians might be comfortable with the idea that being a sinner is a common property of human beings, but they cannot allow that it is an essential property of human beings. This is true, first of all, because Christians hold that Christ was both a human being in the fullest sense and was sinless (Hebrews 4:15). But there is still a problem here, even if we change the idea slightly to account for the case of Christ. That is, even if we say something like, *all human beings who are not also the Son of God* are sinners essentially, there is (and this is a second point) the common Christian assumption that in the Kingdom of God, after our redemption, we too will be sinless but still human beings.

II

One obvious property of human beings is that we are embodied; we have (or are) physical bodies. Is *being embodied* an essential property of human beings? Again, how you answer this question will depend. It could depend on your metaphysics, especially on whether you are a dualist or physicalist in your understanding of human beings. Those who believe that human beings are, without remainder, physical objects might well affirm that being embodied is an essential property of human beings. When you lack a body (e.g., after death) you no longer exist and accordingly are no longer the human being that you were. But your views on this question could also depend on your religious opinions. Christians, or at least those Christians who believe that after death there will be an interim period of existence apart from the body (which we will discuss below), will say no. Having a body, they claim, is not an essential property of human beings.

What exactly does it mean to be a physical object or, for humans, to be embodied? Well, it appears to mean many things. To be a physical object is to be located in space and time, unlike, say, the number six, which so far as I can tell has no physical (or perhaps temporal) location. To be a physical object is to have a certain velocity in moving through space, unlike the set of all cows which (unlike cows) does not move from place to place at all. To be a physical object is to deflect light rays and to be in principle detectable by ordinary perception, radar, x-rays, ultrasound, etc. This is quite unlike my idea of my grandmother or the slight pain I sometimes feel in my left foot, which so far as I can tell are not detectable in those sorts of ways (unless some version of physicalism is true, i.e., unless ideas and pains just are nothing but states of the brain). To be a physical object is to be subject to the laws of nature (e.g., gravity, entropy), unlike God, who is not a physical object (John 4:24) and transcends the laws of physics.

Being embodied has many advantages. Our bodies allow us to do things, to take action, to initiate causal chains in the spatial and temporal world that we inhabit. Our bodies allow us to move about, to learn, to speak, to work, to play, to reproduce. Sets and numbers cannot do any of those things. Our bodies enable us to enjoy great pleasures, but also to endure great pains. Our bodies make it possible for us to perform virtuous acts, but also to commit egregious sins.

But we need to consider a theory—one that can be either secular or religious—that denies that human beings are essentially embodied. This is a theory known as dualism. Both Plato and Descartes (with some differences) were dualists, as well as many other philosophers and theologians. Dualism says essentially three things[3]: (1) human beings consist of two parts, physical bodies and immaterial souls (or minds); (2) the soul is the essence of the human person (that is, the real Stephen Davis is Stephen Davis' soul, not his body); (3) the soul, although united with a body in this life, can exist quite apart from the body.[4] Let's call this theory "minimal dualism."

Also frequently added to dualism is the idea that at bodily death the soul, and thus the person, quite naturally goes right on existing (this is called the immortality of the soul). Also, some dualists (e.g., Plato) combine dualism with the further idea that the body is inherently evil, while the soul, or spirit, is inherently good. Accordingly, our task as human beings is to escape from the body into the realm of pure spirit or intellect. We can call this theory "expanded dualism."

Is the idea of non-bodily human life even coherent? Many philosophers have thought not.[5] But in 1953, the eminent British philosopher H.H. Price (best known for his work in epistemology) wrote a notable essay that challenged such views.[6] Price was in effect

---

[3]   I will not deal with Aquinas' version of dualism on this occasion. It is variously construed in the secondary literature, and I do not want to get into issues of Thomistic exegesis.

[4]   In the present chapter, I will assume but not argue for the truth of dualism. Despite the rejection of dualism by the majority of contemporary philosophers, I have never been convinced that items like qualia, consciousness, and libertarian freedom (all of which I accept) can be properly accounted for on physicalism, See Richard Swinburne, *The Evolution of the Soul*, rev. ed. (Oxford: Oxford University Press, 1997) and *Mind, Brain, and Free Will* (Oxford: Oxford University Press, 2013).

[5]   See, famously, Antony Flew, "Can a Man Witness His Own Funeral?," *The Hibbert Journal*, 54 (1956).

[6]   H.H. Price, "Survival and the Idea of 'Another World,'" *Proceedings of the Society for Psychical Research*, 50 (1953), pp. 1–25.

defending the coherence (i.e., the logical possibility) of the immortality of the soul, although he himself was agnostic on whether the theory is true. Price posited a world consisting purely of mental images (visual, auditory, telepathic) in which souls are aware of each other's presence, live in a real world that consists of mental images rather than physical objects, communicate with each other telepathically, and have dreamlike (as opposed to bodily) perceptions of their world. Such a world, Price suggested, may have different causal laws than our present world does (e.g., wish-fulfillment may be powerfully efficacious), but it will seem to its denizens just as real and even "solid" a world as our world does to us.

Price's theory has been criticized. John Hick, for example, argued that it is hard to combine Price's theme of the public, non-solipsistic nature of the world he described with the theme that the character of the world will be at least in part a function of the wishes of its inhabitants.[7] If it is a public world, sustained by telepathic contact between different individuals, how can wish-fulfillment be as potent a force in shaping it as Price suggested? Hick is surely correct in detecting a tension in Price's account, but the problem seems solvable. And if there turns out to be no way to reconcile the two themes, the wish-fulfillment one can be jettisoned without damaging the core of Price's argument. In any case, it seems to me that Price's essay goes a long way toward establishing the coherence (although not, as he admits, the truth) of disembodied survival of death.

However, the point that must be made here is that the expanded dualist picture of human beings differs, at important points, from the Christian picture. Of course, Christians can be dualists, and even that part of dualism that amounts to immortality of the soul has had a complicated relationship with resurrection, as we will see below. Still, Christianity, as I understand it, on this topic says four things: (1) human beings are, in their most complete and perfect form, embodied persons. Accordingly, while disembodied human life is in some sense possible, it is an attenuated form of life, and is not at all what God intends for us. (2) Matter and thus human bodies were created by God as parts of a world that was originally "very good" (see Genesis 1:31). Therefore, matter is not inherently evil. (3) Embodied human beings fall into sin and corrupt both themselves and the whole of creation; accordingly, human beings need redemption and the physical world needs restoration (Romans 8:19–22). (4) God is effectively at work in the world; one day the needed work of redemption and restoration will be accomplished.

III

So human beings are fallen and need redemption. We must note an important fact that is relevant to redemption. Human beings face two over-arching problems, guilt and death. Christianity says that they are connected.

Most humans experience at least some degree of guilt. (Indeed, we use the term "sociopath" for people who experience no feelings of guilt or whose behavior is not influenced by the guilt that they do experience.) We want to be admired and respected by others, and especially by ourselves. But we are acutely aware of our own moral failings and do not excel at obeying even the precepts of our own (usually flawed and self-serving) moral standards. And when we compare our behavior with the ethical standards prescribed by the Ten Commandments and the teachings of Jesus, we clearly see our shortcomings. Thus we

---

[7]   John Hick, *Death and Eternal Life* (New York: Harper and Row, 1976), pp. 265–77.

feel guilty and, according to Christian teachings, *are* guilty. So the first great human problem is what to do about our guilt.

Most humans want to live forever. Death ends our lives, careers, and projects, bringing hopes for future accomplishments to naught. We do not know with certainty what, if anything, awaits us after death, and many are frightened at the prospect. We do not want to deprive our loved ones of our presence and support, nor do we want to be deprived of theirs. The thought of no longer existing—of literally not being—frightens most people. Thus the second great human problem is what to do about death and our fear of death.

Redemption occurs, according to Christians, through Jesus Christ. Salvation is not a matter of our own doing. We are forgiven and reconciled to God through Christ's work, not through anything we do or earn. Indeed, we do not deserve redemption. That God loves us and works for our salvation is a sheer fact of grace. Grace (unmerited favor) means that God loves us even though we are unlovable, accepts us even though we are unacceptable, forgives us even though we are unforgivable. God does not have to redeem us. That God freely chooses to redeem us despite our inability to merit redemption is what is mean by grace.

Redemption occurs through the life, death, and resurrection of Christ. Paul placed great emphasis on the cross. Thus he wrote, "For Christ did not send me to baptize but to proclaim the gospel, and not with eloquent wisdom, so that the cross of Christ might not be emptied of its power. For the message about the cross is foolishness to those who are perishing, but to us who are being saved it is the power of God" (I Corinthians 1:17–18; cf. Colossians 1:20). Although incarnation is not the central topic of this chapter, we should note that on the cross and in the resurrection we see most fully who Christ is. He is God himself, condescending to the point of death on our behalf.

The life and teachings of Jesus. The redemptive power of Jesus' life and teachings operates by showing us what God is like and how we are to live in such a way as to honor God. In Jesus, we see that God loves us unconditionally and loves us enough to send his son to live with us in the midst of the fears, contradictions, and perils of human life. Jesus Christ is the supreme example of how human life should be lived. In perfect obedience Jesus fulfilled all the requirements of the law of God; accordingly, in his death he became a perfect sacrifice for our sins.

The death of Christ. As Anselm of Canterbury argued,[8] the death of Christ on the cross is redemptive, because Jesus, "the lamb of God who takes away the sin of the world" (John 1:29), paid the full penalty for our sins. For God had said to Adam and Eve in the Garden of Eden, "of the tree of the knowledge of good and evil you shall not eat, for in the day that you eat of it you shall die" (Genesis 2:17). But they did eat of its fruit and the penalty had to be paid. Jesus died on our behalf, paying with his blood the penalty for our sins (Romans 5:9; Hebrews 9:21–3). Thus we can be forgiven and a right relationship with God restored.

The resurrection of Jesus. God redeemed us through the resurrection by defeating death and promising us eternal life. Since death, along with all God's other enemies, has been defeated, we too can be raised from the dead. Christians take the resurrection of Jesus from the dead as both the model and promise of our resurrection (Romans 8:11; I Corinthians 15:20, 23; Philippians 3:20–21; I Thessalonians 4:14; I John 3:2), which takes place in the eschaton.

Through faith we are united with Christ; Christ dwells in us and we are incorporated into his risen life. Thus we are transformed. We are born again (John 3:3). We become new creations (II Corinthians 5:17). We are justified (Romans 3:24). We are sanctified (I Corinthians 6:11). The person of faith is part of God's people.

---

[8] Anselm, *Cur Deus Homo* in *St Anselm: Basic Writings*, trans. S.N. Dean (LaSalle, IL: Open Court, 1962).

IV

Let us return to the fact of our embodiment. The basic Christian claim about the general resurrection (i.e., the resurrection of all people as opposed to the resurrection of Christ) is this: on some future day all the dead will be bodily raised, both the righteous and the unrighteous, to be judged by God, and the guarantee and model of the general resurrection is the already accomplished resurrection of Christ. But from that point, Christian tradition diverges. There are two main ways of understanding the general resurrection, and especially the "intermediate state," i.e., the state of the person after death and before the general resurrection in the eschaton. I will call the theories "temporary nonexistence" and "temporary disembodiment."

Temporary nonexistence (sometimes in its non-dualistic versions misleadingly called "soul sleep"[9]) is by a wide margin the minority report, so to speak, of Christian theology. On this theory (which is neutral vis-à-vis dualism or physicalism), a given person (we can call him Smith) is born and then dies; after Smith's death, Smith simply does not exist until the eschaton, when God raises Smith's body from the ground and reconstitutes Smith as a living person.[10]

But the majority of Christian theologians who speak of the intermediate state defend temporary disembodiment. The theory, which is based on dualism, says this: a given human being Jones is born, lives as a soul incarnate in a body, and dies; when the body dies the soul goes on existing in an incomplete, disembodied state with God until the general resurrection in the eschaton; at that point Jones' body is resurrected and permanently reunited with Jones' soul.

This theory is based on dualism, but it need not assume that souls naturally, so to speak, survive death, which is a criticism that theologians often raise against immortality of the soul.[11] Defenders of temporary disembodiment can hold that the soul survives the death of the body only because God miraculously causes it to do so. The theory does require that personal identity, along with certain "mental" abilities (to be discussed below), be retained during the interim period.

The theory has several strong points, which is doubtless the reason that most theologians have embraced it, as indeed I do. (1) There is in the theory no temporal gap in the existence of the person; there is no moment in time between Jones' birth and the general resurrection when Jones does not exist. This certainly makes the problem of personal identity easier to solve. (2) If the incorporeal Jones during the interim period is Jones, then Jones' resurrected body does not have to be constructed by God out of the very particles that Jones' body consisted of at his death. (That God had to do so was an assumption made by Patristic and medieval defenders of resurrection, and it led them to have to deal with various conundrums.[12]) As long as the particles of the resurrected body are configured in the right way, the resurrected Jones-like person will be Jones; the presence of Jones' soul will ensure that. (3) Defenders of

---

⁹   The term is misleading because (1) the soul does not actually sleep during the interim period; it simply does not exist; and (2) sleeping is essentially a bodily activity, and during the interim period the body is incapable of any activity (except perhaps rotting away, if that is an activity).

¹⁰   I briefly explored this notion in Chapter 6 of *Risen Indeed: Making Sense of the Resurrection* (Grand Rapids, MI: Eerdmans, 1993).

¹¹   See Oscar Cullmann, "Immortality of the Soul or Resurrection of the Dead?," reprinted (among many other places) in *Immortality*, ed. by Terence Penelhum (Belmont, CA: Wadsworth, 1973).

¹²   For example, how can God resurrect a Christian who drowns at sea and whose body is eaten by various fishes who then scatter to the seven seas? Or what if a Christian's body is eaten by cannibals so that the molecules of his body are now parts of their bodies? In the general resurrection, who gets which parts?

temporary disembodiment see a close fit between their theory and biblical—and especially Pauline—notions of the afterlife. The apostle seems to hold that human beings consist of both material bodies and immaterial souls, that the body is not merely an adornment or drape for the soul, but that it is indeed good, since it can be the temple of the Holy Spirit (I Corinthians 3:15–17; 6:19–20), and that the soul is in some sense separable from the body (II Corinthians 5:6–8; 12:2–3; see also Philippians 1:23). (4) Temporary disembodiment solves an otherwise tricky problem in biblical theology: how can it be true both that the general resurrection will not occur until the eschaton (which seems to be Paul's view; see I Thessalonians 4:13–18) and that Jesus said to the good thief on the cross, "Today you will be with me in paradise" (Luke 23:43). The solution is that the thief was and is with Jesus in paradise in the form of a disembodied soul; his body will be raised later.

The state of being without a body is an abnormal state of the human person. This is one of the clear differences between temporary disembodiment and the immortality of the soul. The second doctrine (at least in versions of it influenced by Plato or Gnosticism) entails that disembodiment is the true or proper or best state of human persons. On the theory we are considering, however, the claim is that a disembodied soul lacks many of the properties and abilities that are normal for and proper to human persons. Disembodied existence is a kind of minimal existence.

But which properties common to embodied human persons will disembodied souls have and which will they lack? Clearly they will lack those properties that essentially involve corporeality. They will possess no spatial location, for example, at least not in the space-time manifold with which we are familiar. They will not be able to perceive their "surroundings" (using that spatial word in a stretched sense)—not at least in the ways in which we perceive our surroundings (that is, through the eyes, ears, and so on). They will not be able to experience bodily pains and pleasures. They will not be able to engage in bodily activities. Taking a walk, getting dressed, playing catch—these sorts of activities will be impossible.

But if by the word "soul" we mean to include the constellation of those human activities that would typically be classified as "mental," then the claim that our souls survive death entails the claim that our mental abilities and properties survive death. Accordingly, human persons in the interim state can be spoken of as still having experiences, beliefs, wishes, knowledge, memory, inner (rather than bodily) feelings, thoughts, language (assuming memory of bodily existence)—in short, just about everything that makes up what we call personality. As noted, Price convincingly argues that disembodied souls can be aware of each other's existence, can communicate with each other telepathically, and can have dreamlike (rather than bodily) perceptions of their worlds.

But Aquinas argued that the disembodied existence of the person during the interim period is so deficient that attainment of ultimate happiness is impossible. No one who lacks some perfection can be perfectly happy, for in such a state there will always be unfulfilled desires. It is contrary to the nature of the soul to be without a body, Aquinas said. He took this to mean both that the disembodied state must be temporary, and that the true bliss of the human person is only attained after re-embodiment, that is, in the general resurrection. Thus he said, "Man cannot achieve his ultimate happiness unless the soul be once again united to the body."[13]

---

[13] Thomas Aquinas, *Summa Contra Gentiles*, trans. Charles J. O'Neill (Notre Dame, IN: Notre Dame University Press, 1979), IV, 79. Joshua Ryan Farris has pointed out to me that in his commentary on II Corinthians 5, Aquinas says that the soul experiences the beatific vision during the interim period. I frankly do not know how to reconcile this point with the opinion expressed in the *Summa Contra Gentiles*, IV, 79.

V

Since redemption must involve the whole person, one crucial aspect of redemption is bodily redemption (the soul, I would say, is a kind of minimal person but not the whole person). We will receive new or glorified bodies that will apparently have certain quite new properties. This claim rests primarily on Paul's discussion of the resurrection in I Corinthians 15, and secondarily on the unusual properties the risen Jesus is depicted as having in some of the accounts of the resurrection appearances in Matthew, Luke, and John. This would include the apparent ability of the risen Jesus in John 20 to appear in a room despite the doors being locked or his apparent ability in Luke 24 to disappear. In I Corinthians, Paul notes that some ask, "How are the dead raised? With what sort of body do they come?" His answer is an argument to the effect that the new "glorified" or "spiritual" body (*soma pneumatikon*) is a transformation of the old body rather than a *de novo* creation, much as a stalk of grain is a transformation of a seed of grain; that is, it exists because of changes that have occurred in the seed and can be considered a new state of the seed. Further, Paul argues, while the old or natural body is physical, perishable, immortal, and sewn in weakness and dishonor, the glorified body is spiritual, imperishable, immortal, and sown in strength and honor. The first body is in the image of the man of dust; the second body is in the image of the man of heaven.

The term "spiritual body" might be misleading; it should not be taken as a denial of corporeality or as a last-minute capitulation to some version of the immortality of the soul as opposed to bodily resurrection. By this term Paul means not a body whose stuff or matter is spiritual (whatever that might mean) or an immaterial existence of some sort; rather, he means a body that is fully obedient to and dominated by the Holy Spirit. Paul says, "Flesh and blood cannot inherit the kingdom of God" (I Corinthians 15:50). What enters the kingdom of heaven, then, is not this present weak and mortal body of flesh and blood, but the new glorified body. This new body is a physical body (Paul's use of the word *soma* implies as much).[14] And if we take seriously Paul's simile of the seed, it is materially related to the old body, at least in the sense of being organically derived from it. But it is a body transformed in such ways as to make it fit for life in God's presence. If by the term "physical object," we mean, as before, an entity that has location in space and time and is capable of being empirically measured, tested, or observed in some sense, then my argument is that the new body of which Paul speaks is a physical object.

In the kingdom of God, there will be no tears (Revelation 21:4), no pain, apparently no entropic ageing. But in detail what will life be like in the "New Jerusalem" (Revelation 21:2)? Will we all be as smart as Einstein? Will we be as musically gifted as Mozart? Will we be able to play soccer like Messi? Will there be challenges, competition, and things to be overcome? Naturally we do not know and cannot even imagine what it will be like. But there is one thing that Christians can confidently assert: we will see God. Thus John the seer wrote, "the throne of God and of the Lamb will be in it [i.e., in the city], and his servants will worship him; they will see his face" (Revelation 22:3–4).

Indeed, virtually the whole of the Christian tradition unites in seeing the end or goal of redemption as our eternal presence with God in paradise. And one concrete way of conceptualizing the experience of the redeemed in paradise is the tradition of the "beatific vision." That is, in paradise, redeemed humanity will see God's face. But is it possible to see God? Well, if God desires a loving relationship between himself and human beings, and if

---

[14] See Robert H. Gundry, *Soma in Biblical Theology* (Cambridge: Cambridge University Press, 1976), pp. 164ff. See also C.F.D. Moule, "St. Paul and Dualism: The Pauline Conception of Resurrection," *New Testament Studies*, 12(2) (1966).

the incarnation of the Second Person of the Trinity is permanent (as the tradition holds), and if resurrected human beings are embodied beings, then it should be possible in some sense for the redeemed to see God. This despite the fact that, apart from the incarnation, God is not an embodied being (John 4:24).

The Bible takes us on a long journey on this issue of seeing God. First, several texts insist that seeing God, or seeing God's face, is forbidden. For example, there is the curious passage in Exodus 33 where Moses wants to see the glory of God. Eventually, God does pass by, while Moses is hidden in the cleft of a rock, and (speaking anthropomorphically) he only gets to see God's back. But the key phrase of the text is clearly Exodus 33:20: "You cannot see my face; for no one shall see me and live."

Second, several biblical passages emphasize the point that it is because of our sinfulness that we are forbidden to see God's face. These scriptures declare that people who are upright, holy, and pure in heart do get to see God. Psalm 11:7 says that "the upright shall behold his [the Lord's] face." The sixth beatitude says, "Blessed are the pure in heart, for they will see God" (Matthew 5:8). And Hebrews 12:14 says, "Pursue peace with everyone, and the holiness without which no one will see the Lord." These are wonderful thoughts, but if our aim is to see God, to achieve the beatific vision, these passages amount to bad news. Which of us can truly claim to be upright, pure, or holy?

Still, the hope of seeing God persists. In Psalm 27:7–8, the poet pleads for the sight of God: "Hear, O Lord, when I cry aloud, be gracious to me and answer me! 'Come,' my heart says, 'seek his face!' Your face, O Lord, do I seek, do not hide your face from me." And although there are thorny textual and lexical problems connected with this passage, the NRSV translates Job 19:25–7 as follows: "For I know that my redeemer lives, and that at the last he will stand upon the earth; and after my skin has thus been destroyed, then in my flesh I shall see God, whom I shall see upon my side, and my eyes shall behold, and not another."

Third, this hope that we shall see God is surely eschatological. In I John 3:2, it says, "Beloved, we are God's children now; what we will be has not yet been revealed. What we do know is this: when he is revealed, we will be like him, for we will see him as he is." And in the text just noted about the New Jerusalem in Revelation, it says, "… his servants shall worship him; they will see his face" (Revelation 22:4).

The expression "seeing God" can be used in two different senses. The first is the sense in which believers do and nonbelievers do not, here and now, see God. This is clearly to use the word *see* in a metaphorical or at least nonliteral sense. It means roughly that believers cannot avoid interpreting their experience, and indeed all of life and reality, in terms of the presence of God; and it means that nonbelievers do not do so. The second is the sense in which no one can now see God, not at least God's face, and that one day the redeemed *will* see God. This, I think, is a literal sense of the word *see*. Believing as I do in both (1) the permanent incarnation of the Son of God, and (2) human bodily redemption (that is, in a general resurrection that is essentially bodily), I have no trouble accepting the idea that the redeemed will one day literally see God.

VI

In conclusion, let us return to human nature. I want to ask what the implications are of the fact that—so Christians believe—God became a human being. As later creeds and theologians affirmed, Christ was "truly human and truly divine." How ought the incarnation affect our understanding of human beings?

301

We noted above that Christians hold that one essential property of human beings is the property of *being loved by God*. Here we see the preeminent reason for that conviction. God loved us enough to condescend to our level, to become one of us, to be (like us) embodied. He left the glorious heavenly realms to enter into our world, with all its perils, fears, pains, ambiguities, and corruption. Jesus got dirt under his fingernails. And Jesus was what human beings are supposed to be. The best model for understanding human nature is Jesus Christ. And we surely learn from him the essential purpose of our existence: we were created in order to know God.[15] We were created for the sake of an intimate, loving relationship with God, the kind of relationship that Jesus had with the Father. Our supreme goal in life is to glorify God (Isaiah 24:15; I Corinthians 10:31) and to enjoy fellowship with God forever.[16]

We noted earlier that human beings face two great problems: guilt and death. Redemption is the solution to both. To those who are troubled by guilt (and virtually all people are), Christianity says that God has freely and graciously provided for our forgiveness. To those who fear death (and nearly everyone does, to some degree or other), Christianity says that God freely and graciously grants us new life after death. Together, forgiveness and resurrection make possible our eternal life in the presence of God.[17]

---

[15] Jesus' presence with human beings on earth is now the Holy Spirit. But in the eucharist, at least for those who believe in the real presence (whether they accept transubstantiation or some other theory), we have an actual encounter with Christ's body.

[16] Will human nature be redeemed? No, only human persons will be redeemed (justified, forgiven, reconciled to God). Human nature, along with the image of God, as well as the earth and the entire creation, will be restored.

[17] I would like to thank Joshua Ryan Farris for his helpful suggestions on an earlier version of this chapter.

Theosis and Theological Anthropology

Ben C. Blackwell and Kris A. Miller

Introduction

As we look to the restoration of humanity in salvation, we see theological anthropology in a holistic framework, with the problems of humanity juxtaposed with the divine intention for humanity. The methodological diversity that marks contemporary scholarship has encouraged a new vigor for addressing these old issues. Our goal here is not to address the topic through a new lens, but rather an old one—theosis. The patristic soteriology of theosis has rightly received increasing attention because of its theologically integrative perspective, bringing together Christology and Pneumatology, protology and eschatology, soteriology and ecclesiology.[1] Our intention in this chapter is to explore how theosis informs the discussion of theological anthropology.[2] Our argument is that theosis reveals the creational intent for humanity to live in a transforming union with the Trinity, which places the emphasis on a relational ontology more than a substance ontology.

The doctrine of theosis was birthed in the Greek patristic tradition and is embodied in Byzantine and modern Orthodox theology. However, a growing number of Protestants have found value in bringing together this ancient doctrine with contemporary conceptions of theology. In our chapter we hope to bring the ancient and modern together. Accordingly, as we explore the importance of theosis for understanding theological anthropology here, we will build from a foundation laid by the patristic and Byzantine tradition as witnessed by Maximus the Confessor, but we will also engage T.F. Torrance who employs this doctrine from a contemporary Protestant perspective. Since all theology is contextual, we highlight their conceptions of theosis according to their respective emphases, Christology and Trinitarianism, because this approach better captures the texture of their arguments. These lenses on the topic, however, are not arbitrary because the discussion of theosis in light of Christology (with Maximus) and the Trinity (with Torrance) follows well-worn paths of theological discussion.[3] These contexts make clear that the study of theological anthropology

---

[1]   Norman Russell's (*The Doctrine of Deification in the Greek Patristic Tradition* [Oxford: Oxford University Press, 2004], 1–2) description of theosis as building upon two pillars *methexis* and *homoiosis*—*participation in* and *likeness to* God in a Trinitarian context—aptly summarizes the key ideas of the wider tradition.

[2]   See also the other essays by Nathan A. Jacobs and Fr. David Vincent Meconi in this collection for other treatments of theosis in the context of theological anthropology.

[3]   Gregory of Palamas, whose Byzantine theology highly influences modern Orthodox theology, importantly speaks of theosis in the context of two other types of union: essential (among the members of the Trinity), hypostatic (between the human and divine natures in Christ), energetic/salvific (between believers and God). See Gregory Palamas, *Against Akindynos* 5.26, *Cod. Coisl. Gr.* Fol 145v. in John Meyendorff, *A Study of Gregory Palamas* 183. Vladimir Lossky (*The Mystical Theology of the Eastern Church*

is not merely about determining the constitution of humans—sorting out the existence and relationship of constitutive parts like soul and body—but should just as much be focused on the divine telos or intention for humans and how humans are constituted through relationship with God. Before treating theosis historically, we first situate the doctrine biblically.

Theosis in Biblical Doctrine

When considering the doctrine of theosis in the context of the Bible,[4] 2 Peter 1.4 is most commonly associated with theosis. The author affirms that believers become "partakers [or sharers] of the divine nature," pointing primarily to the escape from moral corruption.[5] Though the 2 Peter passage is the most famous today, it is Psalm 82.6–7 (cf. John 10.34–6) that led early Christian interpreters to explore the idea of believers as "gods."[6] By the late second century central themes in interpretations of Psalm 82.6–7 became established: *adoption*, becoming a son of God is equivalent to being a god, and *immortality*, with human mortality in direct opposition to divine immortality. Importantly, interpreters considered adoption (or sonship) and mortality/immortality in light of larger biblical themes.

The connection of sin and death highlighted in the passage has direct correlation to the narrative of Genesis 3 and the NT hope of salvation as a restoration of the image of God culminating in resurrection. Accordingly, the doctrine of deification comes to be seen as an overarching account of the biblical theology of creation, fall, and new creation. God's intention for humanity was thwarted through sin, and through the work of Christ and the Spirit God restores believers to that original intention. This restoration is holistic and is experienced as moral, noetic, and somatic incorruption through participation in God's own incorrupt life.

Certain New Testament passages with a confluence of multiple themes—like adoption, immortality, image of God, glory—have played a central role in patristic descriptions of deification: Romans 8, Galatians 4, Philippians 2, 1 Corinthians 15, 2 Corinthians 3–4, and 1 John 3.[7] Other passages that address particular themes are employed variously by the tradition. Still other passages like Colossians 2.9–10 which can easily be read in a theotic direction have received relatively little attention in the tradition of interpretation.[8] Human participation in divine glory is an especially important area of interest. In particular, Christ's own transfiguration in the Gospels often garners much interest as an example of deification.

[Crestwood: St Vladimir's Seminary Press, 1991], 87) writes: "The union to which we are called is neither hypostatic—as in the case of the human nature of Christ—nor substantial, as in that of the three divine Persons: it is union with God in His energies, or union by grace making us participate in the divine nature, without our essence becoming thereby the essence of God."

[4]   Space precludes a full bibliography, for a recent monograph exploring the New Testament background of theosis, see Ben C. Blackwell, *Christosis: Pauline Soteriology in Light of Deification in Irenaeus and Cyril of Alexandria* (WUNT 2/314; Tübingen: Mohr Siebeck, 2011).

[5]   Many Protestants conceive of theosis merely as "sanctification." However, theosis unites protology and eschatology, and salvation holistically as noetic, moral, and somatic transformation. Two particular ways that believers become like God is through sanctification and immortality (or incorruption), so it is not wrong to associate theosis with sanctification, but it is much more than moral transformation.

[6]   Interestingly, the earliest proponents of deification do not make use of this Johannine passage.

[7]   Blackwell, *Christosis*.

[8]   Ben C. Blackwell "You Are Filled in Him: Theosis and Colossians 2–3," *JTI* 8.1 (2014): 103–24.

Thus, while 2 Peter 1.4 stands as a shining marker of the reality of theosis in the Bible, this doctrine arises from a close attention to a variety of biblical texts. Although the language of theosis or deification sounds quite unbiblical, if not downright heretical, the doctrine arose from an attempt to read the Bible holistically, such that the restoration through participation in Christ and the Spirit coheres with and fulfills God's original intention for humanity. This larger biblical-theological perspective on the divine–human relationship is explored more fully in the Greek patristic tradition, of which Maximus the Confessor is our lens for this tradition.

Theosis in Patristic Thought: Maximus the Confessor

Maximus serves as a good test case for seeing how theosis informs an understanding of theological anthropology because he is "at once faithful to the primary lines of tradition in the Greek Fathers as well as their creative interpreter."[9] As a transitional figure who unites mystical and incarnational theologies, Maximus serves as one of the founding pillars of Byzantine theology. He is best known for his vigorous defense of a dyothelite (two will) Christology (later affirmed at Constantinople III in AD 680–81), but his various works address numerous topics, such as promoting spiritual theology, correcting Origenist impulses in the monastic tradition, and tempering the Neoplatonic fervor of Pseudo-Dionysius.

Maximus wholeheartedly accepts the tradition of theosis as the primary description of salvation, and he explores this in relation to his highly developed Christology. For Maximus the perichoretic relationship of the divine and human natures in Christ enables believers to experience a similar perichoretic and participatory union between themselves and God. Like theologians before him, he expresses his doctrine of theosis in the context of correcting and refuting alternate positions. As a monk, Maximus has affinities towards the spirituality of (the Origenist) Evagrius, but he carefully corrects the tradition by refuting the Origenist denigration of the body, not unlike Irenaeus' use of deification in his anti-Gnostic polemic.

Before addressing Maximus' discussion of Christology and theosis, it would be helpful to begin with the concepts of *logos* and *tropos*, which appears in his discussion of the Trinity, Christology, theosis, and anthropology.[10] The *logoi* are metaphysical *principles* defining each specific nature (e.g., human nature), which come from the divine Logos and which create a natural link between creation and the Creator. The *logoi* cannot change because they are the good and perfect creation of God. The variable aspect of creation comes in the context of a being's *tropos*, or *mode* of existence, in which a being actually subsists. The difference between *logos* and *tropos* corresponds to the distinction between nature (*ousia*) and subsistence (*hypostasis*), or the universal and the particular. With this in mind, we can address his theology of Christ and theosis.

---

[9] Adam Cooper, *The Body in St Maximus the Confessor: Holy Flesh, Wholly Deified* (OECS; Oxford: Oxford University Press, 2005), 251.

[10] Lars Thunberg, *Microcosm and Mediator: The Theological Anthropology of Maximus the Confessor* (Lund, Sweden: Gleerup, 1965), 73–93.

Christology and the Hypostatic Union

Maximus was influenced by Neo-Chalcedonian theology (with affinities to Cyril of Alexandria), which emphasized the single subject in Christ. However, Maximus' emphasis on the single acting subject in Christ did not lead him to subscribe to the monenergist or monothelite positions which could reunite the (Cyrillian) monophysites with the Chalcedonians. He adamantly argues for the reality of Christ's human will, as part of his rational human soul, in distinction to his divine will. Accordingly, Maximus defends the reality of two willing activities in Christ in the context of his Neo-Chalcedonian affinities. This concurrent emphasis on the single subject subsisting in two natures enables Maximus to have a robust and nuanced Christology. Following Chalcedon, Maximus affirms the two natures in Christ are joined together in one person "without confusion, without change, without division, without separation." Christ, then, exists as God and as human (two *ousia*) in one person (one *hypostasis*). To share in the human *ousia*, he must share in the *logos* of humanity, which is comprised of a rational soul and a body, a topic to which we will return later.

The result of the hypostatic union of the divine and human natures in Christ is "a new theandric" activity of the God-man, as Pseudo-Dionysius stated. Maximus understands the nature of this theandric activity according to the idea of *perichoresis*, or interpenetration.[11] In *Ambiguum* 5 Maximus writes: "And [Jesus Christ] does human things in a way transcending the human, showing in accordance with the closest union the human energy united without change to the divine power, since the [human] nature, united without confusion to [the divine] nature, is completely interpenetrated (περικεχώρηκε), and in no way annulled, nor separated from the Godhead hypostatically united to it."[12] The communication of properties from this perichoretic union occurs in Christ's mode of existence (*tropos*) and not in the *logos* of humanity because this does not (and cannot) change.

Christ's humanity takes on divine characteristics, and the divine nature assumes human characteristics in the incarnation. In other words, the communication of properties from this intimate union results in the deification of Christ's humanity. Maximus employs the illustration in *Opuscula* 16 of the sword and fire to explain the nature of this hypostatic transformation. The iron sword placed in the fire does not cease to be iron, but it takes on the properties of fire as it emits light and heat. In the same way Christ's humanity remains human, but it also takes on the properties of divinity, such as incorruption, through an unconfused union. This transformation of Christ's own humanity is paradigmatic for the believers who follow him.

Soteriology as Theosis

Drawing directly from his Christology Maximus displays a robust soteriological vision encapsulated in his doctrine of theosis. Sherwood explains: "Deification is the ultimate filling of human nature's capacity for God. The *logos* of our nature remains intact; its powers are renovated, in the Incarnation, that it may attain this end; so then deification is wholly a gift of God and is not attainable by nature's nude powers. In actual historical fact deification

---

[11] See Thunberg, *Microcosm*, 21–37; Verna Harrison, "Perichoresis in the Greek Fathers," *St. Vladimir's Theological Quarterly* 35 (1991): 55–63.

[12] *Ambiguum* 5, translated by Andrew Louth, *Maximus the Confessor* (London: Routledge, 1996), 175.

and salvation are the same."[13] As with his Christology, perichoresis plays an important role for Maximus' soteriology. Describing this deific union, he writes:

> And finally, beyond all these, the human person unites the created nature with the uncreated through love (O the wonder of God's love for us human beings!), showing them to be one and the same through the possession of grace, the whole [person] wholly interpenetrated by God, and become completely whatever God is, save at the level of being, and receiving to itself the whole of God himself.[14]

This passage, which draws upon the doctrine of the *logos* of humanity, describes the intimate union between the believer and God so that the believer participates in God and shares in his likeness. This is not a minor aspect of theology for Maximus—it is the culmination of all theology. In terms of the *logos-tropos* distinction, deification is participation in God's attributes by the grace of God in one's experienced life, or the *tropos*, which is in accordance with our human nature (*logos*). The deific process is a mutual one—involving both God and humans—so believers are actively involved in the process particularly through contemplation and ascesis.

Since deification is an unconfused union of the human and divine, in *Ambiguum 7* Maximus again employs the illustration of the fire and iron (sword).[15] Maximus describes how the believer wholly takes on the characteristics of the one in whom the believer is circumscribed. Consequently, the believer participates in the divine attributes through this union while not ceasing to be human, like the sword is transformed by the fire. The created does not become God in essence but God by grace. According to a taxonomy one of us has previously employed, this is a form of "attributive deification" in that believers experience divine attributes without being assumed into the divine essence as in "essential deification."[16]

Maximus understands deification as the fulfillment of God's creational intent expressed in the language of the "image and likeness of God." Like many that precede him, Maximus sees image and likeness as distinct. The image of God relates to "being and eternal being" and refers to the *logos* of humanity at creation. Likeness regards "well being" and entails sharing divine attributes through the *tropos*.[17] The eschatological culmination of salvation is "eternal well being" where believers participate in God's incorruption noetically and somatically, reintegrating image and likeness.

Theosis and the Human Constitution

Having an understanding of the larger context within which Maximus situates his doctrine of theosis, we can focus more specifically on some key aspects of his theological anthropology. With his concern to correct the Origenist affinities within monastic spirituality, Maximus

---

[13] Polycarp Sherwood, *The Earlier Ambigua of Saint Maximus the Confessor and His Refutation of Origenism* (Rome: Orbis Catholicus Herder, 1955), 71.

[14] *Ambiguum 41*, translated by Andrew Louth, *Maximus the Confessor* (London: Routledge, 1996), 158.

[15] *Ambiguum 7*, translated by Paul Blowers and Robert Louis Wilken, *On the Cosmic Mystery of Jesus Christ* (Crestwood: St Vladimir's Seminary Press, 2003), 51.

[16] Blackwell, *Christosis*, 103–5.

[17] *Four Hundred Texts on Love* 3.25, in *The Philokalia: The Complete Text*, trans. G.E.H. Palmer, Philip Sherrard, and Kallistos Ware (London: Faber and Faber, 1979), 4.86.

clearly specifies how the body and soul, in particular, relate to one another in the context of creation, fall, and salvation.[18] This narrative progression will guide our discussion.

A primary aspect of the Origenist position critiqued by Maximus is the pre-existence of souls and the probationary role of the body for these fallen souls. In contrast, he strongly affirms that bodies are a necessary aspect of being human, even if the soul is closer to God. For instance, he writes: "The human being is composed of soul and body, for soul and body are indissolubly understood to be parts of the whole human being."[19] The body and soul are very distinct but both are necessary to be human because neither is perfect in themselves.[20] Drawing his important *logos-tropos* distinction into the discussion, Maximus argues: "The principle [*logos*] of human nature is to exist in soul and body as one nature constituted of rational soul and a body, but its mode [*tropos*] ... can frequently change and undergo alteration without changing at all the nature along with it."[21] With his focus on the rational soul and the body as constitutive of human nature, Maximus reflects the Greek patristic consensus (cf. the Chalcedonian Definition). Maximus further refines this: To be human is to have a reflexive combination of soul and body, not unlike the interpenetration that characterizes the hypostatic union of the divine and human in Christ.[22]

The variability in the *tropos* is what explains the fall. Though the *logoi* of created beings incline creatures to the Logos from whom they are created, humans turned their contemplation away from God and placed it on the created, sensible world. Humans did not cease to be human according to their *logos*, but they ceased to experience humanity in its fullness since in their *tropoi* (mode) of existence they lived at variance with the *logos*. God through Christ and the Spirit draws humans back to their natural, theocentric state, restoring the *tropos* of existence. Meyendorff summarizes this well: "Man ... possesses an order of nature pre-established by God and common to all men, but his tragedy is that after the fall his mode of existence is in opposition to his nature. The real mode of existence, the perfectly human mode of existence, is restored in Christ."[23] This restoration is none other than the experience of deification.

Since deification is a return to God's creational intention, believers are restored holistically, according to their constitution of body and soul. Deification is, according to Maximus,

> being wholly infused with the fullness of God ... , so that the soul receives changelessness and the body immortality; hence the whole man, as the object of divine action, is divinized by being made god by the grace of God who became man. He remains wholly man in soul and body by nature, and becomes wholly god in body and soul by grace and by the unparalleled divine radiance of blessed glory appropriate to him.[24]

The soul is drawn towards a dispassionate love and the body towards immortality, according to their different roles, but both are necessary for being fully human according to God's creational intention.

Following the Alexandrian and Cappadocian tradition, Maximus distinguishes image from likeness, places the emphasis on the image of God on the soul, and locates likeness to

---

18 See especially *Ambigua* 7 and 42.

19 *Ambiguum* 7, in Blowers and Wilken, *Cosmic Mystery*, 73.

20 Thunberg, *Microcosm*, 99–101.

21 *Ambiguum* 42, in Blowers and Wilken, *Cosmic Mystery*, 90.

22 Cf. *Ambiguum* 7; Cooper, *The Body*, 102–16.

23 John Meyendorff, *Christ in Eastern Christian Thought* (Crestwood: St. Vladimir's Seminary Press, 1975), 145.

24 *Ambiguum* 7, in Blowers and Wilken, *Cosmic Mystery*, 63.

God in the experience of virtue. While this may appear to denigrate the role of the body in his theological anthropology, Maximus argues strongly for the unity between soul and body as part of his anti-Origenist stance.[25] His position might be framed as a substance dualism, but his anthropology is more likely a form of hylomorphism.[26] (Of course, contemporary substance dualist positions are often more nuanced and orthodox than Maximus' Origenist opponents.) For Maximus, the "person" (πρόσοπον, or ὑπόστασις) is not the soul which has a body, but is the soul and body joined together.[27] Can a person live unnaturally, at variance from the *logos* of humanity, say in the intermediate state with the soul separated from the body? Yes, the body and soul are separated but still not independent of one another.[28] The *tropos* can be at variance with the *logos*, but to be truly and fully human, a person must live in a *tropos* in full accordance with God and the *logos* of God's intention, that is, in a deified state.

When considering Maximus' Christology and soteriology together, we see how closely the two correlate. The divine Logos took humanity to himself and deified it through the hypostatic union. Not only that, he deifies all believers who follow him as they experience a perichoretic union with God. But just as Christ's two natures remain distinct, though not separated, so do believers and God in an unconfused union, as they are saved in soul and body.

Theosis in Modern Thought: T.F. Torrance

Moving from the seventh-century Eastern Church, we turn our attention to the twentieth-century Protestant Church to gain insight from the continued discussion of theosis for theological anthropology today. Thomas F. Torrance (1913–2007) was one of the more noteworthy English-speaking, Protestant theologians of the twentieth century for whom the central themes of *theosis* permeated his theology.[29] These themes developed, in part, by his extensive interaction with patristic resources and through his ecumenical dialogues with the Eastern Orthodox Church. One of those central themes that permeated his theology was his notion of participation. We will summarize how his notion of participation is informed by his central theological loci, the Trinity, in order that we might see what implications the notion of theosis has for a constructive theological anthropology today.[30]

---

[25] Blowers and Wilken (*Cosmic Mystery*, 27) write: "Bodies, in their partnership with souls, have been created for ultimate deification. The mystery of *embodiment* is not constrained by a divine 'adjustment' to the fall; rather, *teleologically* speaking, bodies are called into partnership with souls to attain to full communion with God."

[26] Cf. Nathan A. Jabobs, "Are Created Spirits Composed of Matter and Form? A Defense of Pneumatic Hylomorphism," *Philosophia Christi* 14 (2012): 79–108.

[27] Cf. Kyrill and Methody Zinkovskiy, "Hierarchic Anthropology of Saint Maximus the Confessor," IJOT 2.4 (2011): 43–61, at 59.

[28] *Ambiguum 7*, in Blowers and Wilken, *Cosmic Mystery*, 73.

[29] To more generally explore Torrance's notion of theosis, see Myk Habets, *Theosis in the Theology of Thomas Torrance* (Surrey, UK: Ashgate, 2009). For shorter summaries, see Paul D. Molnar, *Thomas F. Torrance* (Surrey, UK: Ashgate, 2009), 157–8, 197–201, 232; Elmer M. Colyer, *How to Read T.F. Torrance: Understanding His Trinitarian and Scientific Theology* (Downers Grove: InterVarsity Press, 2001), 78–9, 92–4, 178–9, 219–20, 252–3.

[30] While Myk Habets has separate chapters on christology and pnuematology to unearth and discuss various themes which contribute to Torrance's mostly implicit doctrine of theosis, this section's much briefer summary utilizes a Trinitarian framework to summarize the singular theme of participation. On christology and pneumatology respectively, see Myk Habets, *Theosis in the Theology of Thomas Torrance*, 49–91, 139–92.

Trinity and Participation

Particularly important in considering Torrance's use of participation language is Calvin's Trinitarian framework in his discussion of theosis.[31] Throughout his career, Torrance recalled a point of Irenaeus that "only God can know himself so it is only through God that God may be known."[32] Similarly, Karl Barth repeatedly emphasized that "God is known through God and through God alone."[33] Yet Barth did not emphasize participation in the Trinity as did Torrance, but instead emphasized the Triune revelation. So if humans are to know God, it is only by somehow sharing or participating in the knowledge which God has of himself. Such sharing is made possible because God and his inner relations are no longer closed to us. God has opened himself as Father, Son, and Holy Spirit to share his love and self-knowledge with humanity through the incarnation. According to Torrance, "God the Father communicates himself to us in his Son and imparts himself to us in his Spirit in such a way as to enable us to receive his revelation and participate in the movement of mutual knowing and loving between the Father and the Son."[34] It is significant that human participation is not by nature but by grace, grace expressed through the Son and the Spirit. First, we note how participation in God is realized through the incarnation for Torrance.

God's self-communication goes beyond a nebulous spiritual, mental, or verbal form of communication, but through Christ God enters into the human situation and assumes it. God takes on an ontological relation with humanity through the hypostatic union in Christ. Such personal and participatory mediation on the part of God with humanity goes further than created intermediations between God and humanity as merely an indirect sharing of himself. as Torrance interpreted Aquinas to maintain.[35] Moreover, God condescends in the incarnation in order to share in humanity, so that humans may share in God's self-knowing and self-loving.[36] Torrance frequently returned to how the Council of Nicea used the term *homoousios* to confess that Jesus is of one and the same Being with God, that is, "God of God and Light of Light." This term "crystallizes the conviction that while the incarnation falls within the structures of our spatio-temporal humanity in this world, it also falls within the Life and Being of God."[37] Hence, Torrance maintained that the *homoousion* was the "linchpin of Christian theology," holding together "that what God is toward us in his saving economic activity in space and time through Christ and in the Holy Spirit, he is antecedently and eternally in himself."[38] Furthermore, the movement of the incarnation is a two-fold movement for Torrance which enables human participation in the life of God.

---

[31]   See especially Carl Mosser, "The Greatest Possible Blessing: Calvin and Deification," *Scottish Journal of Theology* 55 (2002): 36–57.

[32]   Thomas F. Torrance, *The Trinitarian Faith*, 2nd ed. (London: T. & T. Clark, 1997), 54. Hereafter, *TF*. Torrance upheld this point of Irenaeus over fifty years earlier as follows: "It is through God alone that God is known and becomes knowable." "Knowledge of God," *The Auburn Lectures, 1938–39* (The Thomas F. Torrance Manuscript Collection. Special Collections, Princeton Theological Seminary Library), 15.

[33]   Karl Barth, *Church Dogmatics* vol. II, pt. 1 (Peabody, MA: Hendrickson, 2010), 44. Hereafter, *CD* followed by the volume, part and page number: *CD* II/1, 44.

[34]   T.F. Torrance, *The Christian Doctrine of God: One Being Three Persons* (London: T. & T. Clark, 1996), 146. Hereafter, *CDG*.

[35]   T.F. Torrance, *Trinitarian Perspectives: Toward Doctrinal Agreement* (Edinburgh: T. & T. Clark, 1994), 99–100. Hereafter, *TP*.

[36]   T.F. Torrance, *The Ground and Grammar of Theology* (Charlottesville: University Press of Virginia, 1980), 155. Hereafter, *GGT*.

[37]   *GGT*, 160.

[38]   *GGT*, 161.

The incarnation is not only a movement from God to humans as personal Being and Act, but is also a movement from humans to God as we see in Jesus a fully human embodiment of participation in God.[39] The fully human embodiment is part of the "vicarious humanity of Jesus" for Torrance.[40] Jesus not only vicariously died on behalf of humanity, but also lived on behalf of humanity with implications from his entire life for the lives of his followers today.[41] Therefore, the incarnation of Jesus exposits and grounds participation in God within humanity.[42] Torrance wrote, "Into our disobedience and covenant-breaking life, into our disinherited existence, there descends God the Son in order to live out from within it a life of pure obedience, fulfilling the covenant will of God, and bringing humanity back from estrangement to communion with the Father."[43] Through the incarnation, not only does God adapt himself to humanity so that we might know him, but through the incarnation humanity is reconciled and adapted to be in a participatory relationship with God.[44] The adaptation of God to humanity and humanity to God has been actualized in Christ. Thus, participation in God is perfectly and vicariously embodied for humanity within Jesus.[45]

Torrance's conception of theosis was guarded and carefully nuanced through his doctrine of the incarnation, maintaining the ontological distinction between creature and Creator. As Torrance put it in reference to the atoning exchange of the incarnation, "for as he is not less divine in becoming man, so we are not less human in being brought under the immediate presence and power of divine being ... This is a deification, however, which more than recreates our lost humanity, for it lifts us up in Christ to enjoy a new fullness of human life in a blessed communion with divine life."[46] Others can participate in this incarnationally-grounded life through union with Jesus and the enablement of the Spirit to which we now turn.

For Torrance, God enables humans to participate in his life, love, and self-knowledge by the Holy Spirit.[47] The Spirit is an equally important person in the being of God. Yet, the

---

[39]   T.F. Torrance, *Theological Science* (London: Oxford University Press, 1969), 45. Hereafter, *TS*: "These are not two separate movements, each proceeding from its own independent ground to meet the other, but one two-fold movement, for even the movement from the side of man toward God, free and spontaneous as it is, is coordinated with the movement of God toward man, and is part of the divine movement of revelation and reconciliation."

[40]   *The Mediation of Christ* (1983; repr., Colorado Springs: Helmers & Howard, 1992), *passim*; *GR*, 133–64; See also James B. Torrance, "The Vicarious Humanity of Christ" in T.F. Torrance, ed., *The Incarnation: Ecumenical Studies in the Nicene-Constantinopolitan Creed* (Edinburgh: Handsel, 1981), 127–47; Colyer, *How to Read T.F. Torrance*, 97–126.

[41]   See Christian D. Kettler, *The God Who Believes: Faith, Doubt and the Vicarious Humanity of Christ* (Eugene, OR: Cascade, 2005), *passim*.

[42]   *TP*, 99–100.

[43]   T.F. Torrance, *Incarnation: The Person and Life of Christ*, Robert T. Walker, ed. (Milton Keynes, UK: Paternoster; Downers Grove, IL: InterVarsity Press, 2008), 114.

[44]   *TS*, 48.

[45]   *TS*, 50–52. Christian D. Kettler engages T.F. Torrance and develops this theme in chapter 3, "Jesus Knows God For Us and In Our Place," in *The God Who Believes: Faith, Doubt, and the Vicarious Humanity of Christ* (Eugene, OR: Cascade Books, 2005), 58–90.

[46]   *TF*, 188–9.

[47]   Concerning Torrance's pneumatology, see T.F. Torrance, *Theology in Reconciliation: Essays Toward Evangelical and Catholic Unity in East and West* (Grand Rapids, MI: Eerdmans, 1975), 192–258; Hereafter, *TIR*; T.F. Torrance, *God and Rationality* (London: Oxford University Press, 1971), 165–94. Hereafter, *GR*; T.F. Torrance, *Karl Barth: Biblical and Evangelical Theologian* (Edinburgh: T. & T. Clark, 1990), 208–12. Hereafter, *KBBET*; *TF*, 191–251; *CDG*, 59–67, 147–55, 180–94. See also Elmer Colyer, "Thomas F. Torrance on the Holy Spirit," *Word and World* 23 (2003): 160–67; Colyer, *How to Read T.F. Torrance*, 211–41; Gary Deddo, "The Holy Spirit in T.F. Torrance's Theology," in *The Promise of Trinitarian Theology: Theologians*

Holy Spirit does not work independently or provide an independent way of participation apart from the Son and the Father.[48] Instead, Torrance wrote, the Spirit "proceeds from the Father and is sent by the Son, and who as the Spirit of the Father and of the Son imparted to us enables us in communion with himself to participate in God's knowing of himself."[49] Torrance extended this argument by maintaining that the Spirit is the living presence of God and the very Being of God who interacts with creation. He acts upon humans so that the knowing relation is rooted in God's being and action.[50] His activity is eloquent, for God is not a mute being. Thus, it is by the Spirit that God communicates his Word or himself.[51] The Spirit is at work not only in revelation external to humans, but also at work within humans "creating and calling forth from us forms of thought and speech" through which God may disclose Himself to us.[52] The Spirit prepares and opens our minds to receive God's self-communication, creating in us the capacity to know God without suppressing or bypassing our minds. "Hence through the Spirit we are given to participate in God's own rationality, in his own self-knowledge or self-witness."[53] Nevertheless, beyond our rational structures, the Spirit also works to rehabilitate the human person and relationships because the Spirit is at work as "personalizing Spirit." From within the inner relations of the Trinity, the Spirit redeems and reveals God in the context of persons in relationship.[54] "The Holy Spirit is the eternal Communion of the Father and the Son and therefore when He is sent into our hearts by the Father in the Name of the Son we are made *partakers* with the Son in his Communion with the Father and thus of God's own self-knowledge."[55]

To summarize, it is through the movements of the incarnation and of the Spirit that humans are lifted up to share in the life, self-love, and self-knowledge of the Trinity. As Torrance put it, "The Love with which we are loved by God is the Love with which the Father, Son, and Holy Spirit love one another in the Trinity, and the knowledge with which we know him is a sharing in the eternal knowing in which the Father, the Son and the Holy Spirit know one another coeternally."[56] Or most simply, Torrance quoted Paul, that it is "through Jesus we are given access to the Father in one Spirit."[57] Torrance's notion of participation is thoroughly Trinitarian. It is the Triune God who is the source, determines the nature, and actualizes the possibility of participation in God. For Torrance, humans are

---

in *Dialogue with T.F. Torrance*, ed. Elmer Colyer (Lanham, MD: Rowman & Littlefield, 2001), 81–114; Paul D. Molnar, "The Role of the Holy Spirit in knowing the Triune God," in *Trinitarian Theology after Barth*, ed. Myk Habets and Phillip Tolliday (Eugene, OR: Pickwick, 2011), 3–47, esp. 33–45.

[48]   *GR*, 172: "Thus it is through the Son that the Spirit comes, from the Son that He shines forth, to the Son that He bears witness, and in the Spirit that God is known and man is recreated after His Image in Jesus Christ."

[49]   *CDG*, 117; Also 148. *GR*, 173–4: "The Holy Spirit is the eternal Communion of the Father and the Son and therefore when He is sent into our hearts by the Father in the Name of the Son we are made partakers with the Son in His Communion with the Father and thus of God's own self-knowledge."

[50]   *GR*, 176–7. See note 72 on Torrance's agreement with Calvin's doctrine of direct, intuitive knowledge of God.

[51]   *GR*, 179–83.

[52]   *GR*, 183.

[53]   *TIR*, 94–5.

[54]   *GR*, 188–9.

[55]   *GR*, 173–4. Emphasis mine.

[56]   T.F. Torrance, *Reality and Scientific Theology* (1985. Reprint, Eugene, OR: Wipf & Stock, 2001), 183. Hereafter, *RST*. Also, T.F. Torrance, *Reality and Evangelical Theology* (1982. Reprint, Eugene, OR: Wipf & Stock, 2003), 21–4. Hereafter, *RET*; *GGT*, 154–5.

[57]   *TF*, 55, quoting Ephesians 2:18.

adapted for union, communion, and participation in God through Christ and by the Spirit without losing our humanity.

Anthropology and Participation

Torrance introduces the term "onto-relation," which he defined as "the kind of relation subsisting between things which is an essential constituent of their being, and without which they would not be what they are. It is a being-constituting relation."[58] Torrance used the example of particle theory which had moved beyond the "analytical concept of separated particles" and had discovered that particles "interpenetrate and contain one another in such a way that the relations between particles are just as ontologically significant as the particles themselves."[59] The basic notion of an ontologically-constituting relationship was derived from Torrance's doctrine of the Trinity. To further the discussion of Torrance's concept of onto-relations, we note that his primary use for this concept is for the idea of a person.

It was significant for Torrance that the doctrine of *person* emerged from Trinitarian reflection as opposed to emerging from philosophical speculation on individuals or on rational nature.[60] He contended that an onto-relational concept of a person developed as the Church Fathers worked out the doctrines of Christ and the Trinity:[61]

> *It was in connection with this refined conception of* perichoresis *in its employment to speak of the intra-trinitarian relations in God, that Christian theology developed what I have long called its* onto-relational *concept of the divine Persons, or an understanding of the three divine Persons in the one God in which the ontic relations between them belong to what they essentially are in themselves in their distinctive* hypostases.[62]

In describing the being and persons of the Trinity, a new notion of person arose in which the relations connecting the divine persons belong to what the divine persons are.

Torrance's concept of onto-relations meant that the persons of the Trinity are distinct, yet constituted and known by their relationship with one another. He maintained that the term "Father" is used in a two-fold way in the New Testament and in the theology of the early church. First, "Father" is used in reference to the Creator as the "heavenly Father" and secondly, it is used in reference to the relationship which the Father has with the Son, the "Father of our Lord Jesus Christ."[63] It is the second use that Torrance emphasized. Torrance recalled Gregory Nazianzen's reference to "the three divine Persons as relations or *scheseis* eternally and hypostatically subsisting in God."[64] The Son is one with the Father for

---

[58] *RET*, 42–3.

[59] Ibid., 43. Also, *GGT*, 175.

[60] *GGT*, 173–4; *RET*, 43; *RST*, 171–2.

[61] *CDG*, 102–3, 156–7, 159; *TP*, 98–9, 124–5; *RET*, 43; *RST*, 177; T.F. Torrance, *The Christian Frame of Mind* 2nd ed. (Colorado Springs, CO: Helmers and Howard, 1989), 30–31. Hereafter, *CFM*. For resources on the development of the use of "person" for God, see Kärkkäinen, *The Trinity*, 30.

[62] *CDG*, 102. Also, *TP*, 98; *GGT*, 173; *RST*, 174–8.

[63] *CDG*, 137–41. He further notes how "Father" is used to refer to the one Being of God or the Godhead on 140. Torrance reminds us that Gregory Nazianzen pointed out that the term "Father" does not refer to being, but to the relation between Father and Son. *TP*, 27–8.

[64] *TP*, 27.

"everything that God the Father is, the Son is, except his being 'Father.'"[65] The person of the Son is distinct from Father and Spirit, and yet distinctively embodies and communicates the fullness of God in the incarnation for the work of reconciliation and revelation.[66] The Spirit is known in relation to the Father and particularly the Son who is the "informational content of God's self-revelation," yet the distinctive work of the Spirit is to mediate and actualize knowledge of God within us, enabling us to participate in the life and knowledge of God.[67] Torrance summarized,

> Each divine Person retains his unique characteristics as Father, Son, or Holy Spirit, in a union without confusion, for the individual characteristics of each of the three Persons do not separate them, but constitute the deep mutual belonging together. There is no Son apart from the Father and the Holy Spirit, and no Father, apart from the Son and the Holy Spirit, and no Holy Spirit apart from the Father and the Son. Homoousially and hypostatically they interpenetrate each other in such a way that each Person is distinctively who he is in relation to the other two.[68]

In other words, the Trinity consists of three distinct Persons who are in relationship with one another and those relationships define their distinct personhood. The onto-relations within the Trinity constitute the one Being of God for Torrance. Such onto-relations extend outward beyond the inner life of the immanent Trinity to include humanity in the movement of the economic Trinity.

Torrance has reminded us from a Trinitarian center that the idea of a person is to be understood relationally. Consequently, humans are to be understood in light of their relation with the Triune God as their origin and end. This suggests a relational ontology of humans. Thus, we can say that participation in Triune life and love constitutes the horizons of humanity. In the tradition of Athanasius, Torrance reminded us that the relations and movements of the Trinity not only condescend to humanity, but also lift and transform humanity to their true *telos*. Humans are not only created in the image of the Triune God, but through the Son and the Spirit are eschatologically elevated to be participants of divine life, for now in part, and in the future, fully. The created past and eschatological present-future surrounds the identity of humanity, which is both stamped by the image of God and has the pull of future glory and the restoration of that divine image.

Conclusion

By drawing from two figures within different confessional traditions and with different theological contexts, we have gathered a necessarily limited perspective on a diverse and deep doctrine that touches a variety of theological loci. Our focus on Maximus, with his contribution to the dyothelite Christological debates, placed the stress on the incarnation and Christology as a means to explore his employment of theosis. The revival of interest in the Trinity in the twentieth century likewise colored our discussion of theosis in Torrance. While situated differently the perspectives offered by Torrance and Maximus do cohere

---

[65] CDG, 145.

[66] Ibid., 141–7. His extensive discussion on this theme is chap. 4, "God of God, Light of Light," TF, 110–45.

[67] Ibid., 147–55. Also TF, 215–31.

[68] Ibid., 145.

and present a relational lens for viewing theological anthropology. Though many things could be noted, we will focus on three aspects of how theosis shapes a view of theological anthropology. Namely, a theological anthropology informed by the doctrine of theosis is not merely about determining the constitution of humans but must be just as much focused on the divine telos or intention for humans and how humans are constituted through relationship with God in creation and redemption. Accordingly, the doctrine of theosis points to the priority of a relational ontology for understanding theological anthropology.[69]

Creational Telos

Theosis provides a holistic perspective, holding together the biblical narrative of creation and redemption, and thus provides a unifying perspective on the Trinitarian economy. The incarnation, cross and resurrection along with the Holy Spirit's empowering presence have a clear place in the divine economy to bring about the original creational intent.[70] Humans, as the climax of creation and the center of the story of redemption, therefore experience salvation in accordance with God's creational purpose. The *telos* of humanity is captured in their creation as divine image bearers, and salvation is nothing less than the culmination of being re-formed into God's image and likeness through a participatory relationship with Father, Son, and Holy Spirit. The *telos* of humanity is suggestive of the metaphysics of personhood.

Theosis is our anthropological *telos*, giving us a vision of the final transformation toward which the people of God are heading. Moreover, it gives us a vision of the transformation in which we participate now, maintaining continuity from the future into the present. Accordingly, salvation is not a simple three-stage progression (justification, sanctification, glorification), but an integrated process of sharing in the divine life, affecting the whole of the person—morally and noetically now, and somatically in the future—in accordance with God's creational intention. Theosis thus maintains that the framework of spiritual formation is from creation to new creation. To be deified is not to become less human and more divine, but more human by becoming more divine to fulfill the *telos* of that God had intended for humanity through relationship with him.

Redemption as Union and Participation

This theotic relationship with God—as Father, Son, and Spirit—is the basis of human identity as believers are united to him. This is God's original intention, and through the hypostatic union in the incarnation and the empowering presence of the Spirit with his people, God unites humans to himself again. To speak of theosis is to speak about God and God's redemptive work. The fact that the doctrine of theosis flowered most fully in the fourth to seventh centuries means that the doctrine is highly influenced by the Trinitarian and Christological debates. Indeed, the emerging doctrine of theosis both supported and was supported by Trinitarian and Christological developments. The Trinity establishes that God is relational and has created and redeemed humanity to participate in his divine life in

---

[69] Our proposals have affinities to Kathryn Tanner, *Christ the Key* (Cambridge: Cambridge University Press, 2010).

[70] Cf. Andrew Louth, "The Place of Theosis in Orthodox Theology," in *Partakers in the Divine Nature: The History and Development of Deification in the Christian Traditions* (ed. Michael J. Christensen and Jeffery A. Wittung; Grand Rapids: Baker Academic, 2007), 32–46.

union through the Son by the Holy Spirit. The incarnation demonstrates that the divine and human need not be at odds with one another, but can rather exist in a perfect but unconfused unity in one person. Humans are thus created and saved to enjoy an unconfused union of their humanity with the divine, experiencing what we call "attributive deification."[71]

As God's creation, humans always stand in distinction to him and always in a state of dependence. They do not create their own life; rather, they participate (or share) in divine life through the personal presence of God through the Spirit. A similar point can be made about divine character within humans, the virtues. Humans are thus formed and transformed through a participatory relationship with the Triune God. The nature of that participatory relationship is conceived in a variety of ways depending on the spirituality of each tradition, such that one method does not appear to be part of dogmatic necessity.[72] For example, Maximus, following the Greek mystical tradition, sets participation in a sacramental context driven by a monastic spirituality that emphasizes a movement towards a transrational (or mystical) union with God through love. Others would not emphasize the transrational aspect, but a union of finite creatures with an infinite God will surely push beyond human boundaries.

Human Constitution

Just as theosis highlights a holistic soteriology, it relies upon a holistic perspective of humans. Drawing from the Christological councils, the Greek fathers affirmed that humans consist of a rational soul and a body. Therefore, when believers' humanity is fully restored in salvation, they will experience noetic and somatic transformation. However, they do not change to another species or become something more or less human. If Christ became human so that humans could become Gods (literally, by nature), then they would cease to be humans.[73] Rather, believers remain uniquely human by constitution but become gods (metaphorically, by grace) as they experience the life of God. The illustration of the iron (sword) in the fire captures this well. Just as Christ's own humanity did not become less human in the incarnation, neither do believers in their transformation. As Torrance reminded us, humans are constituted relationally with the Triune God.

The specific nature of the body–soul relationship is not part of dogmatic considerations with regard to theosis, but in the Greek tradition the immaterial soul is uniformly seen as closer to God than the material body. However, since the timeless *logos* of humanity (per Maximus) is the combination of soul and body together, any salvation of the human cannot be more or less than the salvation of both aspects. Though not solely a polemical doctrine, we should not miss the fact that deification was part of the polemic against major movements that denigrated the body, namely, Gnosticism and Origenism. (Of course, modern substance dualists do not repeat the problems offered by these ancient forms.) While Maximus' position leads one in the direction of hylomorphism, this area needs more study.

---

[71]   Cf. Blackwell, *Christosis*, 103–5, 262–3.

[72]   Much more could be explored with regard to the metaphysics of participation. This raises important questions that go beyond our discussion here.

[73]   Jonathan D. Jacobs, "An Eastern Orthodox Conception of Theosis and Human Nature," *Faith and Philosophy* 26 (2009): 615–27, at 620–22.

Concluding Remarks

Of course, this discussion of the theological anthropology within the context of theosis is only preliminary and only addresses certain aspects of the various issues, leaving others for further discussions, including spiritual formation, ethics, and the development of virtue. Another particularly important issue that we have not discussed is that of original sin and how that effects conceptions of divine and human agency. The debates about the role and effect of theosis among other doctrines are welcome and necessary. Ultimately, though, the doctrine of theosis draws anthropological discussions back to the theocentric intention for humanity, redemption as union and participation, and a relational ontology of humans.

Glory and Human Nature

Charles Taliaferro

Theological anthropology is broader in scope than mainline philosophy of mind in the twentieth and twenty-first centuries. For over a hundred years, most philosophy of mind in the Anglophone world has been carried out quite independent of taking into account the theological significance of its different theories of mind. For the most part, philosophers have also foregone situating philosophy of mind in relationship to the theory of values. Theological anthropology, on the other hand, includes serious attention to the goodness of human life, offering accounts of the values and disvalues of human living and the powers and liabilities of being embodied persons. It is because of the importance of values in theological anthropology that it is important to consider the charge by some feminists that Christian theism is inseparably linked to patriarchy and illicit forms of domination. Emilie Judge-Becker and I seek to represent this critique and respond to it in the chapter "Feminism and Human Nature." In this chapter, I assume that charge is answered (or answerable) and go on to propose we think about linking our understanding of the meaning of life itself. For Christian theists, this involves a recognizing the goodness of creation, the reality of evil as that which is abhorrent to God, and recognizing opportunities for redemption. For a philosopher who is exploring the theological implications of our understanding of human nature, this exploration requires expertise in both philosophy of mind, the theory of values as well as theology in addition to being able to draw on the sciences and the history of ideas. This is a tall order, and I do not pretend to have expertise on the scale needed for such a systematic inquiry. Tossing caution to the wind, I propose we at least make a start in this chapter on a neglected theme in Christian theological anthropology: glory.

This chapter is dedicated to presenting and assessing a theological anthropology in light of Christian teachings about glory, both the glory of God and the calling of creatures to share in divine glory. While there are explicit Christian elements (the Trinity and incarnation) in the theological anthropology of this chapter, much of it is relevant to Judaism and Islam, both of which also extol, especially the glory of God or Allah. After a brief, further observation about the difference between theological anthropology and philosophy of mind, there are three sections: the first introduces the concept(s) of glory, the second focuses on whether the Christian theology of glory is incompatible with a recognition of human dignity, and the third section considers whether the Christian theological anthropology of glory goes beyond anthropology (beyond *anthropos* or being human). From a Christian point of view, is the glorified follower of Christ led to become trans-human or evolve beyond what we think of as human nature?

Theological Anthropology and Philosophy of Mind

Standard work in philosophy of mind, at least in the analytic tradition, takes up questions about the nature (and existence or non-existence) of consciousness, the mental and physical, the impact of the brain sciences on our ordinary (folk) ways of thinking about ourselves, the reality and unity of the self, and so on. But rarely is the topic *the goodness of being human*. For example, in the debate over Donald Davidson's form of materialism, there is more concern about whether his theory can account for human action theoretically without pausing to think about *the goodness or value of human agency*. One reason for philosophy of mind as a field not taking into account goodness may be that such goodness is obvious and, if one wanted important work on the values and disvalues of human health, you may find that in the sub-field of medical ethics or bio-ethics or in some works in political philosophy. But in theological anthropology there is rarely a separation of the topic of what humans are (in terms of metaphysics) and matters of value. I suggest that the separation one finds in philosophy of mind is regrettable.

I propose that the customary practice of addressing topics in philosophy of mind independent of the theory of values leads to a truncated concept of human persons. It is so narrowed that we lose sight of our shared, common sense understanding of what makes being an embodied human person good. Consider the following depiction of what it is to be human in George Orwell's famous essay "A Hanging." Orwell offers an account of a person walking to his execution with an acute appreciation for what is lost when a person dies. I cite a significant passage both to underscore the way in which such a rich understanding of human embodiment is not, but should be, a datum in mainstream philosophy of mind, but also because I will refer back to this passage when, later, section three addresses glory and human nature. Here is a segment of Orwell's 1931 essay:

> It was about forty yards to the gallows. I watched the bare brown back of the prisoner marching in front of me. He walked clumsily with his bound arms, but quite steadily, with that bobbing gait of the Indian who never straightens his knees. At each step his muscles slid neatly into place, the lock of hair on his scalp danced up and down, his feet printed themselves on the wet gravel. And once, in spite of the men who gripped him by each shoulder, he stepped slightly aside to avoid a puddle on the path.
>
> It is curious, but till that moment I had never realized what it means to destroy a healthy, conscious man. When I saw the prisoner step aside to avoid the puddle, I saw the mystery, the unspeakable wrongness, of cutting a life short when it is in full tide. This man was not dying; he was alive just as we were alive. All the organs of his body were working—bowels digesting food, skin renewing itself, nails growing, tissues forming—all toiling away in solemn foolery. His nails would still be growing when he stood on the drop, when he was falling through the air with a tenth of a second to live. His eyes saw the yellow gravel and the grey walls, and his brain still remembered, foresaw, reasoned—reasoned even about puddles. He and we were a party of men walking together, seeing, hearing, feeling, understanding the same world; and in two minutes, with a sudden snap, one of us would be gone—one mind less, one world less.[1]

In this passage, Orwell brings to the fore what we know (on some level) implicitly: the goodness of seeing, hearing, feeling, and understanding; the goodness of our organs

---

[1]   George Orwell: *A Hanging*, first published 1931, *Adelphi* magazine. London.

functioning so that we might act in coordination with other persons; the goodness of reasoning, and memory, and more.

I suggest that a broader description of human nature in terms of values, such as we find in Orwell's essay, is evident not just in conditions of crisis, but in ordinary contexts. Arguably, one may be thought to have a massively misleading account of being human if one thought it would suffice to understand humans only in light of how we might be analyzed in terms of computational mechanisms or in reference to a theory of reductive or emergent causal powers. This is not to belittle the painstaking, necessary work needed in understanding the way we think, act, feel, reason, and so on in light of contemporary science, but I believe we need a reminder of the richer concept of being human that we find in Orwell's essay as well as the theological anthropology to which I ask you to turn in the next section.

On Glory

"Glory to the Father, and to the Son, and to the Holy Spirit; as it was in the beginning, is now, and will be for ever. Amen." These words appear in *The Book of Common Prayer*, the core text for the Anglican communion, and are widely in use in the liturgies of Roman Catholicism, in multiple Protestant or Reformed denominations, and in Eastern Orthodoxy. The English term "glory" is derived from the Latin *Gloria*, and it is used variously to express and refer to praise, worship, adoration, and awe showed by creatures in response to God's being or in response to particular acts or manifestations of God. To speak of the Glory of God is also to speak of God in terms of majesty, unsurpassable honor, and of such supreme goodness that all worldly glory (the seeking of a good reputation for oneself, the imperial pursuit of powerful authority, and so on) is to be subordinated to God's preeminent excellence and greatness. Traditionally, the call to give God greater glory has been interpreted as the call to be less tethered to temporal goods, as one finds in the motto of St Ignatius to live for the greater glory of God (*ad majoram Dei gloriam*).

"Glory" is the term used to translate the Hebrew words *Hod* (הוד) and *kabod*, a word that may also mean "heaviness" or "weight" in the context of majesty, honor or importance. In the New Testament the word often translated as "glory" is *doxa* (δόξα) which also may be taken to be a matter of praise (as in the term *doxology*) and, in early Christian theology, glory came to be linked with awesome light, brightness or brilliance and praise. Augustine proposed that glory is *clara notitia cum laude* or brilliant celebrity with praise. The meaning and shape of the concept of glory in Christian tradition may be highlighted by contrasting it with the concept of glory in pre-Christian Ancient Greece.

In the Homeric tradition, glory or *kleos* appears in the context of violent struggle; a hero gains glory by triumphing over a warrior of great strength. In the Iliad, there is even a suggestion that the armor of a defeated enemy covered in his blood may count as glory. When a hero wins glory in the Homeric context, he is worthy of praise and fear; a glorious warrior is recognized as dangerous and victorious in a life and death struggle. Speaking in vast generalities, this pre-Christian pagan notion of glory was not eliminated in the Christian era. One can find a pagan notion of glory in the superficially Christian work *The Song of Roland*, and in the days of imperial expansion in the early modern era, the appeal of glory was powerful (think, for example, of Napoleon, especially early in his military career in seeking to win glory in Egypt).

As we look to specifically Christian views of glory, there is a subversion of pagan glory at the heart of orthodox treatments of Jesus. Unlike Achilles who achieves glory by spilling Hector's blood before his city of Troy, Jesus is believed to have achieved glory by having his own blood spilled in order to bring about healing, redemption, and salvation. And, in the Christian tradition, glory is not the exclusive property of God, but all people are called to an end that is a share in the glory of God (II Corinthians 3, for example).

Before turning to the challenges facing a theological anthropology of glory, I note that the form of Christian theism I shall assume here is in the long tradition of Christian Platonism, stretching from the Alexandrians (Clement and Origin) to Boethius, Augustine, Aquinas, the Cambridge Platonists, and in philosophers and theologians in our time such as Hans von Balthasar and John Finnis. In various publications, I have defended the seventeenth-century Cambridge Platonists as exemplifying a philosophy of God and human nature that gives prominence to the ideal unity of the good, the true, and the beautiful. For a twentieth-century statement of the importance of beauty in philosophical theology, consider the following from the work of von Balthasar:

> We no longer dare to believe in beauty and we make of it a mere appearance in order the more easily to dispose of it. Our situation today shows that beauty demands for itself at least as much courage and decision as do truth and goodness, and she will not allow herself to be separated and banned from her two sisters without taking them along with herself in an act of mysterious vengeance. We can be sure that whoever sneers at her name as if she were the ornament of a bourgeois past—whether he admits it or not—can no longer pray and soon will no longer be able to love.[2]

I suggest there is a profound truth here in terms of love, prayer, philosophy of mind and theological anthropology. Theologically, the glory of God may be distinguished from the beauty of God, but for most Christian philosophers the divine attributes are so interwoven that they are inseparable.

A theological anthropology that takes glory seriously faces at least two challenges:

First: Is the practice of glorifying God compatible with dignity? In Jewish, Christian, and Islamic traditions, glorifying God appears to involve a self-abasement, a surrender of one's mind and body as a "living sacrifice" to God. Is such a sacrifice supremely virtuous and ennobling or, rather, is it a kind of self-abnegation or (metaphorically) a self-immolation (lighting oneself on fire) that is contrary to the dignity of what it is to be a mature, free, rational human being?

Second: In the theology of glory, there is a widespread teaching that creatures are called to share in the glory of God (II Corinthians 3). Does this involve human persons being called to transcend their humanity? If so, it seems that, technically, a "theological anthropology" of glory appears to lead us beyond "anthropos" (the Greek term for being human). Is this only a problem with definitions or a more serious matter?

The Glory of Human Dignity

In early modern philosophy, Immanuel Kant stands out as one of the most critical of the practice of worship. Kant offers this succinct verdict:

---

[2]   Hans Urs von Balthasar: *The Glory of the Lord: A Theological Aesthetics: Seeing the Form* (San Francisco: Ignatius Press, 1982).

Kneeling down or groveling on the ground, even to express your reverence for heavenly things, is contrary to human dignity.[3]

James Rachels in the twentieth century advanced a similar critique of worshiping God as incompatible with human dignity.

Rachels is a very clear writer and his argument does not require much paraphrasing. An important premise in Rachels' critique is that in a case of worship, the worshipers assume they are inferior to the object of worship.

Worship presumes the superior status of the one worshiped. This is reflected in the logical point that there can be no such things as mutual or reciprocal worship, unless one or the other of the parties is mistaken as to his own status. We can very well comprehend people loving one another or respecting one another, but not (unless they are misguided) worshiping one another. This is because the worshiper necessarily assumes his own inferiority; and since inferiority is an asymmetrical relation, so is worship.[4]

Rachels does not argue that humans are superior to God, nor does he challenge that humans are (in some important respects) inferior to the divine. There is some hint of the Kantian supposition that worship involves an undignified self-abasement, but his main argument concerns a particular self-abnegation or renunciation. Dignified humans should not surrender their responsibility to think for themselves in matters of values. In worshiping God, according to Rachels, one acknowledges or is committed to acting on the grounds that God, rather than the individual him or herself, is the authority and merits obedience in matters of morality.

On this view, to deliver oneself over to a moral authority for directions about what to do is simply incompatible with being a moral agent. To say "I will follow so-and-so's directions no matter what they are and no matter what my own conscience would otherwise direct me to do" is to opt out of moral thinking altogether; it is to abandon one's role as a moral agent. And it does not matter whether "so-and-so" is the law, the customs of one's society, or Jehovah. This does not, of course, preclude one from seeking advice on moral matters and even on occasion following that advice blindly, trusting in the good judgment, of the adviser. But this is justified by the details of the particular case—for example, that you cannot form any reasonable judgment of your own because of ignorance or inexperience or lack of time. What is precluded is that a person should, while in possession of his wits, adopt this style of decision making (or perhaps we should say this style of abdicating decision making) as a general strategy of living, or abandon his own best judgment when he can form a judgment of which he is reasonably confident.

Is the thesis that God is to be glorified (and thus worshiped) by us incompatible with the belief that we are persons with dignity who should not surrender to another our responsibility to think and act as moral agents?

---

[3]   Immanuel Kant: *The Metaphysics of Morals*. First published 1797. Trans. by Mary J. Gregor (Cambridge: Cambridge University Press, 1991).

[4]   James Rachels: *Can Ethics Provide Answers?: and Other Essays in Moral Philosophy* (Lanham: Rowman and Littlefield, 1996).

Three points should be noted in reply. First, worship and glory does not entail that the worshiper is inferior to the one worshiped. According to a prominent theology of God as Triune, there is an inner glory of God in which the Father glories in the Son and the Holy Spirit, the Son glories in the Father and Holy Spirit, and the Holy Spirit glories in the Father and the Son. There are some technical theological relations of "begetting" and "begotten" and "procession" that may hint at some primacy or eternal structure of an ordered being, but the Athanasius Creed and a great deal of theological tradition affirms equality of Persons in the Godhead. I am not here suggesting that it is acceptable for humans to worship God if and only if they are equal in stature with God. I am instead making the point that the very idea of worship does not necessitate inequality and, even more important, that worship itself need not reflect anything degrading. From the standpoint of Trinitarian theology, worship may be seen as a manifestation of mutual, shared love within the Godhead.

Second, the praise or worship or giving glory to some great, highly valuable (especially an unsurpassably excellent) being can be life-enhancing and elevating. Consider C.S. Lewis' observation about the element of love and delight that is a part of praise.

> But the most obvious fact about praise—whether of God or anything—strangely escaped me. I thought of it in terms of compliment, approval, or the giving of honor. I had never noticed that all enjoyment spontaneously overflows into praise ... The world rings with praise—lovers praising their mistresses, readers their favorite poet, walkers praising the countryside, players praising their game ... I think we delight to praise what we enjoy because the praise not merely expresses but completes the enjoyment; it is appointed consummation.[5]

This portrait of praise or giving glory is radically different from the image of a worshiper as cringing, groveling on the ground, and the like.

Third, in the Christian theology at work in this chapter is in the Platonic tradition of seeing God as essentially good, and thus no arbitrary potentate whose command would make rape, murder, torture, lying, and so on, ethical. Rachels might suppose that this theology falls short of recognizing God as supremely authoritative, but this would be based on confusing worshiping God and worshiping the appearance of God or our picture of God. Platonic Christians may well allow that we need some appearance or picture or idea of God to engage in worship, but these are to be used to worship God, not the pictures, ideas ... So our ideas of God must be scrutinized, but this scrutiny is in the service of proper worship. One reason to think you are not worshiping God (in the Platonic Christian tradition) is if you are worshiping a God who commands you to do what is evidently unjust. This is a matter of epistemology that is essential in any religious practice (engaging in proper prayer rather than praying to some projection of your narcissistic ego).

I conclude that there is no reason to think a theology of divine glory is incompatible with a commitment to human dignity and the responsibility of our thinking and acting as moral agents. But this brings us to a second worry: In Christian theological tradition, humans may come to share in divine glory. Would this ultimately mean human persons ceasing to be human?

---

[5] C.S. Lewis taken from *For the Fame of God's Name: Essays in Honor of John Piper*, eds Sam Storms and Justin Taylor (Wheaton: Crossway, 2010).

Is the Glory of Human Persons Post-Anthropological?

In one of the great texts on glory, "The Weight of Glory," C.S. Lewis describes human beings as *en route* either to a glorious or inglorious state:

> It is a serious thing to live in a society of possible gods and goddesses, to remember that the dullest most uninteresting person you talk to may one day be a creature which, if you saw it now, you would be strongly tempted to worship ... There are no ordinary people. You have never talked to a mere mortal. Nations, cultures, arts, civilizations—these are mortal, and their life is to ours as the life of a gnat. But it is immortals whom we joke with, work with, marry, snub, and exploit—immortal horrors or everlasting splendors.[6]

Would this process of being glorified or being ignoble and inglorious make human persons transcend (or descend from) humanity? Philip Kitcher seems to think so.

Before going directly to Kitcher's claim that if human persons were to live everlastingly or beyond death or be immortal, they would not be humans, consider his general conception of death. In *Secular Humanism*, Kitcher acknowledges that, from his atheistic humanist perspective, there is a sense in which death is more of a calamity than if Christian theism were true. However Kitcher construes the proper fear of death as a fear of losing a relationship with people who matter to you, not as a fear of (eventual) annihilation. Once those whom he cares for have also died, Kitcher finds himself indifferent about his death, and presumably indifferent about whether he is alive or dead.

> As I imagine the world in the years immediately *following my death, I feel a more intense regret about not being part of it than when I project forward a century, or even half a century. Increasing the time interval diminishes my sadness—it fades relatively swiftly to indifference. Not because I'm envious of those who live happily and actively into extreme old age. I don't even yearn for the longevity advances in medicine may some day achieve for future generations. Absence from the period just after my death is poignant because so much of the stuff of my life will be continued in it.* Whenever I die, people about whom I care most deeply will live on, and I should like to be there, sustaining them and being sustained by them. Endeavors to which I have committed my energies will remain unfinished. Loose ends will be left, and I should like to tie them up—while knowing that ends are always beginnings and strands will inevitably dangle. By contrast, the connections with the more distant future are dim, and I cannot even be confident of the large contours of the remote world from which I shall be excluded. Were I to survive into that world, there would be a continuously evolving set of relationships and activities that would give me a stake in it, but, lacking any experience of that development of my life, the concerns I would come to have are not vivid for me. So, as I look forward sufficiently far, regret declines into indifference.[7]

Let us consider this passage first and then turn to the question of glory and anthropology.

Kitcher's perspective, phrased in the first-person, seems as though it is realistic and perhaps even humble. But imagine it is in the second person and you are contemplating the absence or the annihilation of someone whom you deeply love. Imagine someone named

---

6   C.S. Lewis: *The Weight of Glory*. First published in 1941, Theology periodical, London.

7   Phillip Kitcher: *Life After Faith: The Case for Secular Humanism*. Forthcoming Publication, Yale University Press.

Mary, perhaps your daughter, and imagine two alternatives: you may desire that she live in a cosmos in which individual persons, including her, are annihilated or simply cease to be after some specified time, or imagine she lives in a created order sustained by an all good, super-abundant loving God who cares for her and, in relationship with this God and countless other creatures and in such a cosmos there will be a future of open-ended rhythmic, repeated and not repeated moments for vivid love, struggles, redemption and the like. Wouldn't there be something to be said for the second? I believe so, and I think that for someone to hope or choose the first would be hard to reconcile with the claim to love Mary.

Kitcher seeks to challenge (or critique) the urge for us to desire everlasting life on the grounds that this would be for us to desire to no longer be human. Apparently, according to Kitcher, to be an individual human is to be such that the individual will perish into oblivion at biological death. Going to my proposal that loving Mary is incompatible (or at least in tension) with desiring her annihilation, what if the desire for Mary to have everlasting life (or life without end) would entail our desiring that Mary cease to be human? Kitcher writes:

> We cannot, I think, fully imagine what it would be like to be the kind of being for which immortality was a condition of eternal joy. If my diagnosis is correct, distress at the prospect of not being is founded in a confusion. For absence from any part of the future is only terrible because something is felt as having been lost. If extended sufficiently far, however, human lives would not be vulnerable to any real loss through the threat of termination—indeed, cessation would ultimately appear as a blessing. What lies behind the sense of horror at not being is regret at being human. To my humanist sensibility that species of regret appears one we should try to overcome—just as we should seek to accept, even enjoy, the arc of our aging. Our real problem is posed by the prospect of a removal from a web of connections that matter deeply to us.

Is it an essential part of human nature that individual persons cease to be? Or, if not essential, would it be horrifying or regrettable for us to not perish? Is Kitcher correct that we should enjoy "the arc of aging" when it ends in personal oblivion?

In response, let it be granted that the human bodily life of persons could not be endless or everlasting without a radical change in the laws of nature or a miracle. Unless our cellular constitution was to be profoundly self-renewing or renewed through external forces, our bodily life will have a natural, temporal end. But there is a substantial literature that supports the idea that everlasting life or life beyond this life is coherent, not just on a dualist anthropology, but from the standpoint of physicalism.[8] If we bracket physical obstacles to the possibility of life without end and we understand persons as subjects who think, feel, have emotions, sensations, memories, reasoning, powers to act, and so on, is there any reason to believe that there is a fixed, terminal point when persons with such powers (and accompanying liabilities) would find their continuation intolerable or logically or metaphysically impossible? For the life of me, I can't think of any reason whatsoever for such a negative conclusion. I do not doubt that Kitcher himself might lose concern for his non-existence once those people and projects that matter to him die, but what sort of person would desire to be indifferent as to whether those who matter to him or her perish everlastingly? Can you love another person and *enjoy* their decreasing strength, their gradual loss of mental powers that end in the person's oblivion?

---

8   William Hasker, "Afterlife," *The Stanford Encyclopedia of Philosophy* (Spring 2014 Edition), Edward N. Zalta (ed.), URL = http://plato.stanford.edu/archives/spr2014/entries/afterlife/ [accessed on August 18, 2014].

By Kitcher's lights, what makes life meaningful, in part, lies in people mattering to each other. I think this is a misleading way of recognizing the good of persons as the ground for why our concern and love for others (and ourselves) is important, but let Kitcher's thesis stand in his terms. If there is a glory of God and a call of human creatures to share in the divine glory, wouldn't this be a call to a radically enhanced arena of fulfillment and awe? To reply that this call is horrible because it would be a desire to no longer be human seems to me to reflect a question-begging stipulative definition of "being human." In the past, when people have professed to believe that some humans have not died (Malchizadech, Elijah, King Arthur ...) were they involved in a conceptual or grammatical confusion? This seems even less likely when Christians for two thousand years have professed that the risen Christ reigns forever as God incarnate, fully human and fully divine. One can, by fiat, define "being human" to rule out such cases, but one can just as easily rule by fiat that such cases are (as they seem) coherent.

There is not space to address here the further implications of what is technically, in theology, termed eschatology and its relationship to anthropology. But it is worth concluding in the spirit of Winston Churchill: if we human persons are only human at the start, then theological anthropology is a theology of the beginning and it includes a theology of the end of the beginning. But it is not even close to being the beginning of the end.

PART VII
Christological Theological Anthropology

PART VII

The Mortal God:
Materialism and Christology

Glenn Andrew Peoples

"Tis mystery all: the Immortal dies: Who can explore His strange design?'
Charles Wesley

Theological anthropology is at the same time Christology, for in the incarnation the Son of God became human. If we, like a growing number of Evangelicals, adopt a materialist view of human beings, then many of the things that Christians affirm will need to be revisited to see what they look like from within this new outlook (one that, these evangelicals insist, is an old outlook, finding itself at home within a biblical worldview). In particular, we must look again at the old doctrine of the incarnation to see what it looks like through new eyes.

This revisitation raises two main questions: how does a materialist view of humanity make sense of the problem of Christology in general, and in particular how can it accommodate the death of Jesus?

Alvin Plantinga doubtless expresses the view of many when he claims that materialism about human beings[1] is at odds with the doctrine of the incarnation. What happened in the incarnation? Plantinga responds:

> As I understand the scripture and the creeds (Nicene, Athanasian, the Chalcedonian formulation), this involves the second person of the Trinity's actually becoming human. The Logos became a human being, acquiring the property necessary and sufficient for being human. Prior to the incarnation, however, the second person of the Trinity was not a material object, but an immaterial being. If, however, as materialists assert, to be a human being is to be a material object, then the second person of the Trinity must have become a material object. If he has remained a human being, furthermore, he is presently a material object. But then an immaterial being became a material object; and this seems to me to be impossible.[2]

---

[1]   Hereafter, 'materialism' means materialism about human nature, specifically the rejection of a substance dualist account of human beings. It does not name only one view but rather a family of views defined chiefly by what it is not. 'Dualism' here means substance dualism about human beings. Materialism thus construed is not the rejection of property dualism or Aristotle's hylemorphism, which in recent times some philosophers have taken to calling hylemorphic 'dualism'.

[2]   Alvin Plantinga, 'On Heresy, Mind and Truth', *Faith and Philosophy* 16:2 (1999), 186.

In context, Plantinga is dealing with two models of the incarnation: an abstract view (or abstractism) and a concrete view (or concretism), explaining that he holds the former. In brief, the abstract view (Plantinga's view) is that the immaterial entity that is the Logos itself became human, i.e. it took the property of being human (and, since Plantinga does not believe that human beings are material things, this did not require that the Logos be material in the incarnation). A concrete view, by contrast, holds that the Logos entered a relationship with something that was fully human, i.e. it took 'hold of' everything that is included in human nature to itself without becoming human, in the same way that it took a body to itself without becoming a body (assuming for now that the Logos did not become a physical thing).[3] Notably, an abstract view assumes that one can in principle be fully human without having a body. After all, the Logos does not include a body, and yet the Logos, on an abstract view, took on the property of being human. If the Logos itself became human (i.e. if abstractism is correct) and humans are material things, then Plantinga is correct: the Logos would have become material in the incarnation, which Plantinga and doubtless many others take to be a serious problem.

Just how formidable an objection is this? There appear to be two avenues that the materialist can take to get out of the problem. The materialist could simply reject an abstract view of the incarnation altogether, thereby avoiding the need to say that the Logos became anything, let alone material. The Logos instead was combined with a human nature, which involved no non-material substances other than the Logos itself. Alternatively, the materialist would need to offer a defence of the view that the Logos became a human, either showing that the Logos could have become physical without incoherence (or at very least, showing that incoherence has not been proven), or showing that the Logos could have been human, that humans lack any non-material substances and that this does not entail the Logos' becoming physical (surely a formidable task!). Moreover, in order to exonerate materialism as a live option for a Christian, one would also need to show that materialism is compatible with the life and deeds of the historical Jesus of Nazareth, most importantly his death and resurrection. At the least, I hope to persuade some people that a materialist view of human beings presents no more difficulty than a dualistic view does when it comes to the incarnation of God in Christ.

The Problem of Christology and Dualism's Illusion of Ease

The perennial problem of Christology is in maintaining that Jesus is one person while maintaining that he has a complete human nature and divine nature (avoiding Apollinarianism), and maintaining that Jesus has these two natures while being just one person (avoiding Nestorianism). Obviously formulating a Christology that meets these demands is not uniquely a problem for those with a materialist view of human beings. The major Christological heresies, after all, were formulated by dualists.

Some suppose that dualism has a clear advantage when trying to explain the incarnation. William Lane Craig, answering a question on how he could give an account of God becoming

---

3   Brian Leftow, in defending a concrete view of the incarnation, argues that in fact once you say that the Logos took on the property of being human, you are committed to saying that the Logos took on a human body and soul (if humans have souls), for these are necessary conditions of being human. Brian Leftow, 'A Timeless God Incarnate' in Stephen T. Davis, Daniel Kendall SJ, Gerald O'Collins SJ (eds), *The Incarnation: An Interdisciplinary Symposium on the Incarnation of the Son of God* (Oxford: Oxford University Press, 2002). None of what I say in this chapter depends on whether or not this claim is true. As such I will take no stance on its truth.

a human being in the person of Jesus, apparently hoped that dualism about humans in general would be able to provide a swift solution.

> I believe that human beings are units that have immaterial and physical portions. And in essence what the incarnation says is that the mind or the soul of Jesus of Nazareth was the Second Person of the Trinity. And therefore, I don't see any more difficulty in having an incarnation of a divine mind than I do in having an incarnation in our own case of a human finite mind.[4]

Since dualism is unproblematic, the incarnation of God in Christ too is unproblematic since it is essentially the same: a soul or mind (the divine Logos) associated with a body. This, as Craig is aware, is Apollinarianism. Apollinarius noted that if the Logos was added to a human body and soul, namely to a complete human being, then this is not an incarnation, for it would amount to a divine person 'indwelling' a human person, resulting in two people.[5] His solution, Craig observes, was as follows:

> In Jesus, the divine Logos took the place of the human nous and thus became embodied. As a result, in Christ God was constitutionally conjoined with man. Just as the soul and the body are essentially different but in man are combined in one human nature, so also in Christ there exists one nature composed of a part coessential with God and another part coessential with human flesh. The Logos came to experience the world through his flesh and to act through the flesh as his instrument. Having only a single intellect and will belonging properly to the Logos, Christ was without sinful desires and incapable of sin ...
>
> Apollinarianism achieved a genuine Incarnation that, given anthropological dualism, is no more inherently implausible than the soul's union with the body.[6]

Anecdotally, from the pews this is a widely held view of the person of Jesus: the divine part is the part we don't see and the human part is the part we see, so that Jesus is no more than a spiritual divine being walking around in a human body.[7]

It is easy to sympathise with Craig's Christological project, for Apollinarianism certainly has its rationale. As Oliver Crisp points out, 'Normally, possession of a human body and

---

[4]   William Lane Craig and Frank Zindler, *Atheism vs Christianity: Where does the Evidence Point?* (videorecorded debate) (Grand Rapids: Zondervan, 1994).

[5]   William Lane Craig and James Porter Moreland, *Philosophical Foundations for a Christian World-view* (Downers Grove: InterVarsity, 2003), 598.

[6]   Craig and Moreland, *Philosophical Foundations*, 599.

[7]   For example, an evangelistic article called 'Why Christianity' says:

> ... Jesus was not just a teacher, he was and still is a mediator between man and God, because although his body was human, his spirit was divine.

http://www.messageofjesus.co.uk/beliefs/whychristianity.php, accessed 30 November 2013. One might think that, for the Cartesian, this is true of all humans: We are a spirit being walking around in a physical body, as a reviewer pointed out. But the important difference here is that we are not divine, so there is no problem of whether or not we have a complete human nature. We are complete human beings and nothing else. The popular view to which I refer here is the view that the spiritual part of Jesus is the part that is divine and not human, while the physical part is human and not divine. This differs from the Chalcedonian view, wherein there is a physical part that is human and also a 'rational soul' that is human, in addition to the non-material part (the Logos) that is divine.

soul is sufficient for a human person to exist.'[8] If Jesus of Nazareth had a human body and a 'rational soul' (an immaterial human soul) as stipulated by Chalcedon as well as the presence of the second person of the Trinity from all eternity – which is surely a person, then by any standard count Jesus was two persons, which is Nestorianism, a view no less heretical in historical terms than Apollinarianism. Even when writing in full awareness of the need to avoid both Apollinarianism and Nestorianism, Evangelical theologian Millard Erickson, in my view, was unable to avoid the latter. When addressing the question of Christ's impeccability (whether or not Jesus could have sinned), Erickson offers the following suggestion of what might have happened had Christ sinned:

> At the very brink of the decision to sin, where that decision had not yet taken place, but the Father knew it was about to be made, the Second Person of the Trinity would have left the human nature of Jesus, dissolving the incarnation … . Had the Logos departed, Jesus would not have died. That would have been the case only if the person had been merely divine, only the Logos, as various forms of Apollinarianism required. Rather, Jesus would have survived, but would have 'slumped' to mere humanity, and sinful mere humanity at that.[9]

In swerving to avoid Apollinarianism, the proverbial 'overcorrection' results in the opposite heresy: Jesus didn't have just a body with the divine Logos attached, he had a fully functioning human being – body and soul – capable of living a human life without the Logos. Perhaps most evangelicals would not countenance the metaphysical possibility of such a separation, but why not? A dualistic anthropology stipulates either that a person is a soul, or else a body and a soul. Either way, surely all the ingredients of two persons are present in the Chalcedonian formula, and it is only a matter of squeamishness about heresy that stops orthodox Christology from contemplating the possibility of Christ's separation into two persons as described by Erickson. On the face of it, it is hard not to agree with Craig and Moreland in rejecting a concretist view of the incarnation (given dualism, with a human body, a human soul and the Logos) for this very reason: 'if the concept of personhood is bound up with that of a complete human nature, then it seems very difficult, given the rejection of Apollinarianism, to affirm two natures in Christ while avoiding Nestorianism'.[10]

Craig and Moreland call us to reconsider Apollinarianism, suggesting that it may have been regarded as heresy because it was misunderstood.

> Apollinarius may have been misunderstood when his critics charged him with giving Christ a truncated human nature. When Apollinarius argued that the Logos was not only the image of God but also the archetypal man and in this latter sense already possessed human nature in his preexistent form, his opponents like Gregory of Nazianzus understood him to mean that the flesh of Christ was prexistent. Apollinarius may have been more subtle than this; what he may have meant is that the Logos contained perfect human personhood archetypally in his own nature. The result was that in assuming a hominid body the Logos brought to Christ's animal nature just those properties that would serve to make it a complete human nature.
> … God himself is personal, and inasmuch as we are persons we resemble him. Thus God already possesses the properties sufficient for human personhood even

---

[8] Oliver Crisp, *God Incarnate: Explorations in Christology* (London: T. & T. Clark, 2009), 79.
[9] Millard J. Erickson, *The Word Became Flesh: A Contemporary Incarnational Christology* (Grand Rapids: Baker, 1991), 563–4.
[10] Craig and Moreland, *Philosophical Foundations*, 600.

prior to the Incarnation, lacking only corporeality. The Logos already possessed in his preincarnate state all the properties necessary for a human self. In assuming a hominid body, he brought to it all that was necessary for a complete human nature [all emphasis original].[11]

In avoiding the problem of Christ having an incomplete human nature, some curious conclusions follow from this model.

Firstly, on Apollinarianism thus described, God did not become man in the incarnation of Jesus because he was already man in the most important sense. The Logos already possessed 'the properties sufficient for human personhood, says Craig'.[12] It is true, as noted above, that Craig maintains that in taking a body, the Logos assumes a 'complete human nature'. But insofar as Craig effectively bundles the human mind into the Logos itself so that a 'rational soul' (i.e. a human soul) is not required, there has always been a human mind. Indeed, upon the death of Christ, a dualistic model typically assumes that his mind survives. To say that his human nature separated from his human nature is not permitted by orthodoxy, so Craig must surely maintain that after the death of Christ, a being with a human nature survived, namely the Logos: precisely the same Logos that had existed from eternity. Perhaps the gentler way to state this curiosity is that God had always been human, but in the incarnation he became more 'fully human' (a term that mirrors Craig's term 'complete human nature').

But orthodox Christian theology has always maintained that in the incarnation, God in the Son became man, something that he would not have been but for the incarnation. It is a belief reflected in the Nicene Creed: 'For us and for our salvation he came down from heaven: by the power of the Holy Spirit he became incarnate from the Virgin Mary, and was made man.' It is there in the Fathers who expressed the hope of divinisation. Clement of Alexandria expressed this hope, saying that 'the Word of God became man, that thou mayest learn from man how man may become God'.[13] Athanasius reiterated the claim that 'He was made man that we might be made God.'[14] The conviction that in the incarnation God became human is reflected in the title of St Anselm's masterwork *Cur Deus Homo* (why God became man). Whatever the sufficient conditions for being human are, the Logos would not have met them but for the incarnation.

Secondly, if the second person of the Trinity was the 'archetypal man' even without the incarnation, then a curious (although by no means show-stopping) implication seems to be that humanity exists necessarily. Classical Christian theism maintains that God's nature, as well as God's existence, is necessary.[15] It is impossible that God should not have existed, and it is impossible that God should have been different from the way that God actually is in

---

[11] Craig and Moreland, *Philosophical Foundations*, 608–9.

[12] It is true that Craig and Moreland then say that in taking a body, the Logos acquired 'all that was necessary for a complete human nature'. However on the dualism of Craig and Moreland, a human person can exist without a body and so without a 'complete' human nature in this sense (as this is what they maintain happens when a human body dies and the person continues to exist in disembodied form). Thus, human nature already existed in the Logos in the same way that it is exists in a disembodied human soul.

[13] Clement of Alexandria, *Exhortation to the Heathen*, Chapter 1.

[14] Athanasius, *On the Incarnation of the Word*, Chapter 54.

[15] It is true that Craig rejects the doctrine of divine simplicity and, like some others, affirms that God has accidental and essential attributes. Be that as it may, the nature of the Logos from eternity surely cannot be accidental. I am therefore assuming that even denying that God has all of his attributes necessarily, Craig must commit to the view that humanity exists necessarily, and not simply the concept of humanity but an instantiation of it.

his nature, and hence the Logos could not have been any different. If humanity is contained within the Logos, then what follows is that it is impossible that humanity not exist.

Lastly, even this more sympathetic revision of Apollinarius is subject to what looks like a grave objection: That which is not assumed is not saved. Gregory Nazianzen is our main source for the theology of Apollinarius. Craig may have successfully fended off his objections to do with Christ having a human body from all eternity. But Gregory's criticism that Apollinarianism poses a serious problem for human salvation remains:

> If anyone has put his trust in Him as a Man without a human mind, he is really bereft of mind, and quite unworthy of salvation. For that which He has not assumed He has not healed; but that which is united to His Godhead is also saved. If only half Adam fell, then that which Christ assumes and saves may be half also; but if the whole of his nature fell, it must be united to the whole nature of Him that was begotten, and so be saved as a whole. ...
>
> Further let us see what is their account of the assumption of Manhood, or the assumption of Flesh, as they call it. [I]f it was that He might destroy the condemnation by sanctifying like by like, then as He needed flesh for the sake of the flesh which had incurred condemnation, and soul for the sake of our soul, so, too, He needed mind for the sake of mind, which not only fell in Adam, but was the first to be affected, as the doctors say of illnesses. For that which received the command was that which failed to keep the command, and that which failed to keep it was that also which dared to transgress; and that which transgressed was that which stood most in need of salvation; and that which needed salvation was that which also He took upon Him. Therefore, Mind was taken upon Him. [emphasis added][16]

If Christ brought the larger part of human nature with him into the world, assuming only a partial human nature in this world, then only that which Jesus assumed – the human body – is redeemed. The human mind was never assumed, for the Logos, on Apollinarianism, always had the only mind or soul he would ever have. In a strange twist, this model results in a redeemed body but an unredeemed mind.

The point in all of this is not to show that none of the problems of incarnation could ever be solved within a dualistic framework, but just that there are problems, and that they are not small. Consequently, the fact that a materialist who wishes to be faithful to orthodox Christology faces difficulty should be neither surprising nor a reason to abandon materialism.

Possibilities for a Materialist Christology

In a superficial way, any materialist Christology is doomed to unorthodoxy. The Chalcedonian definition stipulates that Jesus Christ is 'at once complete in Godhead and complete in manhood, truly God and truly man, consisting also of a reasonable soul and body'. However, the only reason the Chalcedonian definition required that Christ have a human body and soul was to say that Jesus was truly human, and human beings, so the framers maintained, have a body and a reasonable soul. The goal was not to have a model

---

[16] Gregory Nazianzus, 'To Cledonius the Priest Against Apollinarius', *Nicene and Post Nicene Fathers* part 2, volume 7 (Grand Rapids, MI: Christian Classics Ethereal Library, n.d.), 648.

of Christ that was dualistic, but to have a model of Christ that was really human. That it was also dualistic was incidental.[17]

One of the worries about a Christology that does not include a human soul might be that it is Apollinarianism: A human body and the Logos, without a human soul. This, however, terribly misunderstands materialism. Any respectable materialist view is not just Cartesian dualism with the soul removed, so that what is left is a passive body, a truncated human nature. For the Christian materialist, a complete human being does not require an immaterial soul in the first place. Whatever materialist model one settles on, be it property dualism, emergentism or nonreductive physicalism, all of the mental aspects of a human being are obtained without reference to a soul, so the incarnation does not require a 'reasonable soul' in order for Christ to be fully human any more than a soul is required for any of us to be truly human. As Crisp explains,

> [I]t may be that the Fathers of Chalcedon thought that the only way to rebut Apollinarianism was to fall back upon some version of substance dualism. But the restricted materialist would be right to point out that if this is true, the Fathers of Chalcedon were mistaken. For it turns out that restricted materialism is consistent with Christ having the requisite sort of irreducibly mental life necessary for being fully human, such that Apollinarianism is blocked. Yet restricted materialism postulates no human soul in order to do so. One might construe the Chalcedonian claim that Christ had a 'rational soul', that is, a human nous, to mean the mental part or component of a human being. ... But that, the materialist will point out, is consistent with the tenets of restricted materialism given local property dualism, and is also anti-Apollinarian. Such reasoning does justice to what Chalcedon says about Christ's 'rational soul', without appeal to an immaterial substance.[18]

We may, therefore, affirm the point of Chalcedon without accepting the dualistic framework within which that point was expressed.

But what about the relationship between the Logos and Christ's human nature? Suppose we adopt a concretist view of the Incarnation and say that the Logos acquired or assumed a human nature. If this is true then Plantinga's objection never arises, since now even if human beings are material things, the incarnation can occur without the Logos becoming a material thing.

The possible concern with a concretist view, however, is that it is Nestorianism. Although a reasonable concern, it is not one that uniquely targets either materialism or dualism. Just as a human body and soul (given dualism) when added to the Logos seems like two people, so too a human body configured the right way (given materialism) when added to the Logos seems like two people. Either way we appear to be saying that we have all the ingredients of

---

[17] It is easy to sympathise with Hud Hudson's description of Church Fathers and theologians as (or so I take him to be saying) imperfect and culturally influenced purveyors of timeless truths:

> When we turn to the question of whether dualism is true, we may ask whether [many Church Fathers'] widespread commitment to dualism is one of the truths revealed by God or whether it is rather simply a common feature of his instruments, like the pattern of a grain that appears when a carpenter selects one type of wood over another for the purpose of providing a supporting beam in the construction of a house.

Hud Hudson, *A Materialist Metaphysics of the Human Person* (Ithaca: Cornell University Press, 2001), 173. I am grateful to a reviewer for bringing Hudson's work to my attention.

[18] Crisp, *God Incarnate*, 152.

a human being plus the Second Person of the Trinity. How do we avoid the existence of two people, given a concrete view of the incarnation?

Here I will co-opt an argument from someone who is not a materialist, Brian Leftow. Leftow argues that the combination of a body and soul (supposing, he adds, that humans have souls) may be what humans are made of, but that does not mean that the presence of a body and a soul is necessarily the presence of a human being. Leftow proposes that if we think of a human being as constituted by a particular body and soul, we can go on to think of circumstances under which a human body and soul exist in combination but fail to constitute a human person. One such possible example, he proposes, is the incarnation of the Logos. He explains a possible model as follows:

> [T]he Son assumes Christ's body (henceforth B) and soul (henceforth S) before S and B can on their own constitute a human being or person. ... For if he does not, then either concretism is Nestorian, or the Son's assumption destroys the person to whom S + B previously belonged – turning the incarnation into a bizarre form of human sacrifice. Just when S + B would on their own constitute and compose a person or a human being is a knotty issue. ... [O]ne can assume that the Son 'gets to' S + B before S + B are or constitute persons by holding that Christ assumes S + B as a zygote, at the moment of conception.[19]

The incarnation did not include two people because the Logos prevented the body and the soul from working as they normally would to constitute a person, making it so that they constitute a person in combination with the Logos. Had the Logos not intervened, there would simply have been a human person, but by throwing itself into the process at human conception, as it were, the presence of the Logos caused something else to be there – containing all the elements of a human nature (i.e. a body and a soul), but being a different type of person (e.g., a divine person with a human nature), having a divine nature as well.

If this model is tenable then it can obviously be pressed into the service of a materialist Christology. Perhaps it is true that a human body can constitute a human being by itself, provided it comes to function in a given way (roughly similar to the way that I am functioning now), but this does not mean that the presence of human body is a sufficient condition for the presence of a human being.

Just as, on Leftow's model, the Logos may have 'gotten to' the human body and soul of Jesus (let us say at the moment of conception) to prevent them from functioning as a complete human being all by themselves, it is similarly available to the materialist to claim that the Logos may have 'gotten to' the human body of Jesus before it was able to constitute a human being all by itself. The result is a fully functioning human body whose life (i.e. whose timeline) was the life of the incarnate Son of God rather than whatever life it would otherwise have constituted. It may even turn out that a materialist view of human beings has a marked advantage over substance dualism here. It is easy to think that a human body might fail to be a human being or a person, but it is much more difficult to think of a simple, immaterial human soul that is not a person. What else can a Cartesian soul be but a person?

---

[19]   Brian Leftow, 'A Timeless God Incarnate' in Stephen T. Davis, Daniel Kendall SJ, Gerald O'Collins SJ (eds), *The Incarnation: An Interdisciplinary Symposium on the Incarnation of the Son of God* (Oxford: Oxford University Press, 2002), 280, 281.

If Leftow's proposal is not tenable, however, then it is not materialism that is undercut, but concretism in general, whether dualist or materialist.[20]

The Death of a Physical Christ

The philosopher (like Plantinga) may be more concerned with questions about how the material interacts with the immaterial or whether or not one can become the other (an issue that I do not explore here at all). A question of greater theological importance, however, is what our view of the person of Jesus of Nazareth requires us to make of the cross and our doctrine of God. Might our view of human nature, if we believe that the man Jesus of Nazareth died, undercut the doctrine that God is a Trinity? If, as materialists tend to believe, we do not survive our own death, surely the number of persons in the Trinity is reduced from two to three when Jesus died: The Son and the Spirit. This, at least, is the charge laid by some Evangelicals.[21]

Should the Christian materialist be dissuaded? I think not, and two lines of response suggest themselves.

The Death in Time of the Timeless Logos

Firstly, suppose that the classical doctrine of divine timelessness is true. One of the oddities of thinking about God as timeless but of Jesus of Nazareth as the embodiment of the Second

---

[20] Space prevents me offering in any detail an abstract and materialist view of the sort that Plantinga takes issue with. For a stimulating defence of the view that the Logos did become human and a physical entity, see Trenton Merricks, 'The Word Made Flesh: Dualism, Physicalism and the Incarnation', in Peter Van Inwagen and Dean W. Zimmerman (eds), *Persons: Human and Divine* (Oxford: Clarendon, 2007), 281–300.

Merricks's argument deserves as much space as what I have devoted to Leftow's, so the reader is encouraged to read it in his own words. Very briefly, he argues that the best dualist account of a soul's embodiment (namely that soul S has direct causal control over and has epistemic access to body B) is problematic because it seems to imply that God is embodied in every body. Avoiding this would involve abandoning any familiar conception of embodiment and embracing one that is 'ad hoc or implausible or darkly mysterious' (p. 293). It is comforting to note that I am not alone in one of my concerns about Apollinarianism – and for that matter a concern about any dualist view of the incarnation, and that Merricks too is concerned that given dualism, 'one could conclude that the Son could have become human without ever having a body' (p. 294). The remainder of his argument, so it seems to me, is focused on the objection to the possibility of a non-material Logos becoming material, a proposition rejected on the basis of incredulity rather than argument. What is literally impossible, he asks, about a non-material entity taking on physical properties? Is it any more impossible than (on an abstract view) a divine person taking on the property of being human? After all, 'the difference between God the Son and each of us is staggering. The difference between a non-physical human person and a physical human person is comparatively trivial. If we believe that God the Son became a human being, we have swallowed the camel. To insist that God the Son could not possibly become a physical human is to strain out a gnat' (p. 297).

For a response to Merricks's criticism of a dualist conception of the incarnation, see Luke Van Horn, 'Merricks's Soulless Saviour', *Faith and Philosophy* 27:3 (2010), 340–41.

So my point is not that a concretist view defended via Leftow's argument is the only option for a materialist, but only that there are options, and this is one of them – one that takes for granted a very orthodox way of thinking about the incarnation (namely, concretism), and for what it is worth, one that I find least susceptible to serious objections.

[21] John Cooper raises this objection in *Body, Soul, & Life Everlasting: Biblical Anthropology and the Monism-Dualism Debate* (Grand Rapids: Eerdmans, 1989), 144–5.

Person of the Trinity in time is here: from the beginning of the incarnation there was a sense in which there were two Second Persons of the Trinity: One eternal and timeless and one embodied and walking around in Israel. But that sense should not trouble us if we mean what theologians have traditionally meant when we say that God is timeless. For if – apart from the incarnation – God the Son does not exist in time, then there were never two Sons of God existing at the same time. The only way in which God the Son has ever existed in time is through the person of Jesus Christ, as Paul Helm explains.

> The incarnation is a unique case of God's acting in time. One thing to note is that if God the Son is timelessly eternal and yet incarnate in Jesus Christ, there is no time in his existence when he was not incarnate, though since he became incarnate at a particular time in our history there were times in that history before the incarnation, and times since. …
>
> The incarnation is the 'projection' of the eternal God. There is therefore no sense in talking of the eternal Son of God apart from the incarnation except to make the point that the incarnation was logically contingent. That is, there is no point to it if by this we mean that there was a time when the eternal Son of God existed unincarnated. It is of course possible to think of the eternal Son of God as unincarnated, by an abstraction of thought, but that is a different matter. The point is, as Herbert McCabe says, there is no pre-existent Christ with a life history independent of and prior to the incarnation. There was no time when the eternal God was not Jesus of Nazareth. There is no other life story – story in time – of God than the story of the incarnation. [emphasis added].[22]

Had the incarnation never occurred, it would have been true at any point in time to say 'the Second Person of the Trinity exists', although not that the Second Person of the Trinity has existed in every moment in time. The Son of God would have existed timelessly. At any time during the life of Jesus of Nazareth it was still true that the Son of God exists timelessly, so even if the person Jesus of Nazareth was killed completely without any surviving remnant (for example, the Logos that lives on when the body dies), it would have continued to be the case that the Son of God existed timelessly. If this is so then the Trinitarian Godhead of the Athanasian Creed: 'The Father eternal, the Son eternal, and the Holy Spirit eternal', cannot be affected by the death of Christ in time, because nothing that happens in time can affect any aspect of God's timeless existence.[23]

Of course, it is true that not all Christian theologians and philosophers accept the doctrine of divine timelessness. Some accept that God would be timeless were it not for the creation of the universe but that he is in time as of the first moment of creation, while some

---

[22] Paul Helm, 'Divine Timeless Eternity' in Gregory G. Ganssle (ed.), *God and Time: Four Views* (Downers Grove: InterVarsity, 2001), 54–5.

[23] The doctrine of divine timelessness may also be a resource that materialists who maintain that the Logos became a physical being can use to address the objection noted by Andrew Loke. The objection is that such a view makes it 'metaphysically impossible for [Christ] to possess divine properties such as having the knowledge of all truths, having the power of omnipotence, etc., as there seems to be a metaphysical limit as to how much information and power a physical body can hold.' 'Immaterialist, Materialist, and Substance Dualist accounts of Incarnation' in *Neue Zeitschrift für Systematische Theologie und Religionsphilosophie* 54(4), 2012, 421. The limits that Loke refers to may be irrelevant if Jesus of Nazareth has access to the knowledge of the timeless Logos in the way that a local computer with a small hard drive has access to the content of a large server via the internet. A problem may arise if Christ's omniscience is supposed to be construed propositionally (so that he knows an infinite number of propositions at once), but this is by no means the only way (or in my view the correct way) to construe omniscience.

simply maintain that God is in time full stop, with or without the universe. Nonetheless, the view that God is timeless has a very respectable pedigree, being both explicit and implicit in the work of many of our orthodox forbears. It is therefore significant that a view such as this one, which might be regarded as on the fringes of orthodoxy or perhaps even heretical (namely a view of the incarnation incorporating a materialist view of human beings), can claim an ally in such a historically respectable view of God.

The Biblical Witness

For somebody with Evangelical commitments, the primary source for Christology, as for theology in general, is scripture. Although it is not realistic to expect to find a well-developed Christology in the New Testament, this should not take away from what we find affirmed there. The second response to the objection to materialism from the death of Christ is to note that the biblical writers themselves went out of their way to affirm that which a dualist might have a problem with, namely that Jesus of Nazareth truly and fully died, so that Christology should be done in light of what we find revealed. I must be brief, but here are the kinds of biblical material that are relevant here.

First we are faced with the fact that the biblical writers described Jesus' death just as one would if they wished to convey total demise, without a surviving remnant.[24] Writing on a theme related to the death of Christ, namely the punishment for sin, Edward Fudge offers a helpful summary:

> *The Bible exhausts the vocabulary of dying in speaking of what happened to Jesus. He 'died for our sins' (1 Cor. 15:3). He 'laid down his life [psychē]' (John 10:15). He was destroyed (Matt. 27:20, KJV) or killed (Acts 3:15). Jesus compared his own death to the dissolution of a kernel of wheat in the same passage that mentions losing one's life (psychē) rather than loving it in order to find life eternal (John 12:23–6). 'Jesus poured out his life (psychē) unto death' and was thus 'numbered with the transgressors' (Isa. 53:12). ...*
>
> *Every scriptural implication is that if Jesus had not been raised, he – like those fallen asleep in him – would simply have perished (1 Cor. 15:18).*[25]

Secondly, the theological role of Christ as sin bearer reinforces the view of his death as personal destruction. James Dunn illuminates Paul's discussion of Jesus as the representative of humanity in 2 Corinthians 5:14. In representing us in death, Christ bore and destroyed sin. '[T]here is no other end possible for men – all mankind dies, as he died, as flesh, as the end of sinful flesh, as the destruction of sin.'[26] Unless we think of the human soul as being somehow

---

[24] Naturally, that a person fully dies (i.e. does not survive death) does not entail that they were a material being, for presumable even a dualist allows for the possibility, even if not the actuality, of a soul ceasing to live when its body dies. However, the objection to a materialist Christology that I am now considering is that if Jesus of Nazareth was wholly material then he would have truly died (i.e. not survived death). But if scripture indicates that he fully died in precisely the way we would expect it to if he did not survive, then this objection can be met with the reply that we simply have to bite the bullet. Jesus really did fully die, and any objection to a materialist Christology that assumes otherwise can be dismissed.

[25] Edward Fudge, *The Fire that Consumes: The Biblical Case for Conditional Immortality* (Carlisle: Paternoster, 1994, 2nd ed.), 142–3.

[26] James D.G. Dunn, 'Paul's Understanding of the Death of Jesus' in Robert Banks (ed.), *Reconciliation and Hope: New Testament Essays on Atonement and Eschatology Presented to L.L. Morris on his 60th Birthday* (Carlisle: The Paternoster Press, 1974), 130.

untainted by sin but the flesh being evil, this destruction cannot but befall the whole human Christ, leaving us with either a separation of the human and divine nature (something forbidden by Chalcedon), or else complete death of the person of Jesus in the same way that sin was destroyed through Jesus' death. Driving the point home, Dunn quotes Barth, speaking of Christ's death: 'Man could not be helped other than through his annihilation.'[27]

Thirdly, it was important to the Apostles that Jesus' body was raised rather than re-created. In one of the most unhelpful translations still used by modern readers of scripture, St Peter applies the saying of the psalmist to Jesus after his death as fulfilled in his resurrection: 'thou wilt not leave my soul in hell, neither wilt thou suffer thine Holy One to see corruption' (Acts 2:27, KJV). Visions of a disembodied ghost in the nether regions spring to mind until we recognise firstly the common Hebrew idiom of using 'my nephesh' to simply mean 'me', and hades (translated 'hell' in older translations) commonly referring to the state of all the dead or the grave.[28] This is why the translators of the *New International Reader's Version* correctly give us 'You will not leave me in the grave. You will not let your faithful one rot away.' The two statements form a parallelism to express the same idea in different ways.[29] St Paul makes the same claim in Acts 13:34–7, that King David died and decayed, but Christ did not. The question of importance, however, is why it was so important that Jesus' body remained if his human nature could so easily have survived even though his body died. This is the type of concern that one has if one is convinced that Christ was a physical person so that the loss of his physical integrity would have amounted to the loss of himself.[30]

The bottom line is that unless one simply assumes that words like 'soul' (increasingly rare in modern translations) or 'spirit' necessitate dualistic conclusions, the New Testament portrait of the person, life and death of Jesus of Nazareth offers little or nothing by way of support for a dualistic portrait of the Saviour.

---

[27]   Actually Dunn cites a common source for this quote, G.C. Berkouwer, *The Triumph of Grace in the Theology of Karl Barth* (Grand Rapids, 1956), 135.

[28]   Bible translator William Tyndale complained of the fact that 'hell' was used to translate a number of different words (including the Latin infernus, the equivalent of the Greek hades) and was potentially misleading as a translation:

> *Infernus and Gehenna differ much in signification, though we have none other interpretation for either of them, than this English word, hell. For Gehenna signifieth a place of punishment: but Infernus is taken for any manner of place beneath in the earth, as a grave, sepulchre or cave.*

David Daniell (ed.), *Tyndale's New Testament: Translated from the Greek in 1534* (New Haven and London: Yale University Press, 1989), 429.

[29]   The great Reformed theologian and biblical translator Theodore Beza gave 'Non derelinques cadaver meum in sepulcra', the equivalent of 'You will not abandon my cadaver in the sepulcher.' However as Luckock noted, 'he changed it in a later edition, because he said some persons were offended by the rendering'. Herbert Mortimer Luckock, *The Intermediate State Between Death and Judgment* (New York: Thomas Whittaker, 1891), 130.

[30]   An alternative theory might be that Peter's speech reflected the view that the soul remains near the body for three days and then leaves when the body starts to decay. However this is unlikely to be in Peter's or Paul's mind, for even in that view David's soul was not left in the grave longer than three days, whereas their point was that Jesus was different from David because he was not left in the tomb whereas David was. The tradition is important, however, for it can be used to make the point that Jesus was raised before he would have been considered to be a decaying body, thus God did not allow his holy one to see decay. For details of this tradition, see Midrash Genesis Rabbah 100, 7, cited in Wilhelmus G.B.M. Valkenberg, *Words of the Living God: Place and Function of Holy Scripture in the Theology of St Thomas Aquinas* (Leuven: Peeters, 2000), 86, fn 106.

Closing Thoughts

As Evangelicals become increasingly willing to consider materialism as a live option, more of them will turn to think about how the things that Christians have always affirmed can be formulated and expressed without the dualism that many of our forebears have held. What I hope to have done here is to show that in the case of one of our most important such affirmations – that God in Christ became one of us – there is no cause for despair but much to be encouraged by, and easily as much room to accommodate the essentials of our faith as – and maybe even more than – the dualist framework with which most of us are familiar.

Hylomorphic Christology

Josef Quitterer

Introduction

According to Christian doctrine, Jesus Christ is one person who has two natures—human and divine. It is affirmed that he is "truly divine and truly human in two natures" but at the same time "one person and substance." The Council of Chalcedon declared in 451:

> ... one and the same Christ ... acknowledged in two natures, without mingling, without change, indivisibly, undividedly, the distinction of the natures nowhere removed on account of the union but rather the peculiarity of each nature being kept, and uniting in one person and substance, not divided or separated into two persons, but one and the same Son ...[1]

For centuries theologians and Christian philosophers have tried to develop metaphysical models with which they could take into account this dichotomy between the unity of the person of Jesus Christ and the duality of his divine and human natures. Hylomorphism is perhaps one of the most influential models for a rational reconstruction of this fundamental Christian dogma. Hylomorphism is the view that all living beings are a compound of form and matter. Applied to the human person this means that the soul as the substantial form configures matter in such a way that it becomes a human body [see contribution Hylomorphism]. The main topic of this chapter is the question how the hylomorphic form-matter-distinction can be applied to the person of Christ which is a union of a human and a divine nature. The Hylomorphic model, which is presupposed in this contribution, is the Aristotelian form-matter-distinction in the Thomist understanding of Aristotelianism. Can the person of Christ be reconstructed as a compound of form and matter? A direct application of Hylomorphism to Jesus Christ would imply that the divine nature would be the formal part of the compound Jesus Christ, and the human nature the material part.[2] This solution, though, would be incompatible with Hylomorphism itself. There are two main arguments against such a direct application of the hylomorphic model to the person of Jesus Christ, which can be both derived from Hylomorphism itself:

---

[1]   Denzinger, *The Sources of Catholic Dogma*. Translated by Roy J. Deferarri from the Thirtieth Edition of Henry Denzinger's Enchiridion Symbolorum. B. Herder Book: St. Louis 1957, No. 148.

[2]   According to Thomas Aquinas this was the position held by Arius; Thomas Aquinas, *Summa Contra Gentiles* [S. c. G.], ed. Joseph Kenny, O.P. (New York: Hanover House, 1955–57), IV, 41: "For some thought of this union after the mode of things united into one nature: so Arius and Apollinaris, holding that the Word stood to the body of Christ as soul or as mind ..."; cfr. also S. c. G. IV, 32: "For Arius held that in Christ there was no soul, but that He assumed only flesh, and that divinity stood to this as soul."

    i.   concerning the nature of the human body which Christ adopted at his incarnation;

   ii.   concerning the divine person who became incarnate as a human being.

Hylomorphism and the Two Natures of Christ

I) According to Hylomorphism the material aspect of a human person is something which is determined by its form. However, in the case of Christ, his human nature cannot be regarded as a material aspect of him open for determinations by his divine nature, which in this case would be the formal aspect. According to Christian doctrine, the second person of the Trinity did not adopt any random matter or physical stuff, but he became incarnate specifically in a human body. A human body, according to the hylomorphic account, is already formally determined by a human substantial form (*forma substantialis*) or a human soul. To deny that Christ's human body was determined by a human substantial form would entail the unorthodox view that God did not genuinely assume a human body in the incarnation. The hylomorphic account can also be described as a version of top-down-causation. In a top-down-model, the higher levels causally influence the lower ones in a formal way. Top-down-causation starts on the macro-level with the structure and functioning of entire organisms. It is assumed that these structures and functions causally influence the constituents and processes on the micro-level. Individual micro-level events and phenomena can be explained only as components of larger macro-level functional units. For example, within an organism, which has specific cognitive abilities, like willing and understanding, there is a typical causal role of physical processes which differs from the causal role of similar processes in organisms without these cognitive abilities. Formal causation here means that the fact that basic physical processes take place within a human organism with specific cognitive capacities shapes the very performance of those processes. For this reason, the divine word can only adopt a human body when this body is already fully determined through the substantial form of a human being, which is a rational soul.

The case would be different, given a physicalistic, bottom-up, understanding of the human body. In a physicalistic understanding, there are no specific physical structures which belong exclusively to the human body. The basic physical structures of a human body are of a kind which can also be found in other (non-human) organic bodies. The difference between a human and a non-human body is mainly a matter of complexity. The highly sophisticated processes of human life are the product of basic physical processes which can be found in many different organic entities. Given such a view, the second person of the Trinity would be thought to have adopted a physical body with a specific complexity. This physical body could be informed through the divine, such that it would be the body of Jesus Christ. However, in the hylomorphic understanding, a body is only human if it is already fully determined as human at the moment of its assumption by the second person of the Trinity.[3] Even the most primitive biological process or body part is human only if it

---

[3]   S. c. G. IV, 44: "The body assumed in the moment of conception was a formed body, if the assumption of something not formed was improper for the Word. But the soul demands its proper matter, just as any other natural form does. But the proper matter of the soul is the organized body, for a soul is 'the entelechy of a natural organic body having life potentially.' If, then, the soul from the beginning of the conception was united to the body (this has been shown), the body from the beginning of the conception was of necessity organized and formed."

is formally determined by the substantial form of a human being, a human soul.[4] Therefore God cannot simply assume a body which through incarnation would become a human body; God must also assume a human soul with all its rational, sensory and vegetative capacities because, according to the hylomorphic account, a body is a human body only if the form that determines it is a human soul.

For the same reason, Christ's divine nature could not have assumed the role which in human beings is performed by the intellect. If the divine Word unites with the body, by becoming that body's highest cognitive capacity, then that Word would not in fact be adopting a human nature because it would be incarnate as a body with only sensory and vegetative abilities, since the higher capacities of its human soul would have been replaced by the Word.[5] According to the hylomorphic account there is no human body without a human intellect. This requirement holds in at least the Thomistic version of Hylomorphism, according to which the intellect, as the highest cognitive capacity, is the first entelechy, which is the form for all the other "lower" capacities of the body and makes them human capacities. This implies that Christ's human body must have had a human rational soul at the moment of incarnation.

II) The second argument against a direct application of the hylomorphic form-matter-distinction to the person of Jesus Christ has to do with the second person of the Trinity himself. The divine Word—according to the hylomorphic model—cannot fulfill the role of a substantial form of any body. This is an implication of the non-dualistic conception of the soul in Aristotelian and Thomist Hylomorphism. The notion of the soul as the substantial form of the body has its roots in Aristotle's conceptual and ontological classifications. In the introduction of De Anima Aristotle invokes the lowest common denominator of different conceptions of the notion "soul": soul is the principle of living beings.[6] If "soul" refers to the essential constituent of a living being, the only possible category for it is the category of substance (*ousia*), for the essential principle of a living being cannot be an accident. What does it mean that the soul is an *ousia*? Aristotle distinguishes three different meanings of that word: 1) *ousia* as matter, i.e. the basic substrate of entities; 2) *ousia* as form, i.e. the essential property of an entity; 3) *ousia* as a concrete entity. In this line of argument it is obvious that "soul" refers to *ousia* in the sense of form. This means that the soul is neither the living body as a whole nor the (material) body as such, but rather the essential form or principle which makes the body a living body. Understanding the soul as the essential form and thus the principle of life in an organism is incompatible with the second person of the Trinity being the formal part of Christ's human body: A complete substance like the divine Word cannot be the substantial form of Jesus Christ, since Christ is himself a complete substance. The possibility that a divine nature could be the form of a human body has to be rejected for the same reason as dualistic conceptions of the soul, in which a spiritual substance would be the substantial form of a human body, are rejected:

---

[4] S. c. G. IV, 32: "It is on the soul, furthermore, that not only man's essence, but that of his single parts, depends; and so, with the soul gone, the eye, the flesh, and the bone of a dead man are equivocally named, 'like a painted or a stone eye.' Therefore, if in Christ there was no soul, of necessity there was neither true flesh in Him nor any of the other parts of man ...."

[5] According to Aquinas, Christ would have adopted the nature of an animal if he had become incarnate in a body with only vegetative and sensory capacities (Thomas Aquinas, *Summa Theologica*, ed. Fathers of the English Dominican Province (Benziger Bros. edition, 1947), III, 5, 4). This position is attributed by Aquinas to Apollinarius (see S. c. G. IV, 33).

[6] Aristotle "De Anima" [De an.], in W.D. Ross (ed.), *The Works of Aristotle* (Oxford: Clarendon Press, 1952), vol. 3, 402a6f.

> *For it is not God alone who cannot be the form of a body, neither can any of the supercelestial spirits among whom Arius held the Son of God supreme. Exception might be made for the position of Origen, who held that human souls were of the very same species and nature as the supercelestial spirits. The falsity of this opinion was explained above.*[7]

Being a complete entity, the second person of the Trinity cannot be identical with the essential formal determination of Christ's human body.[8] For this reason, the divine Word cannot be brought into a direct union with a physical body; it can only become incarnate by taking on a specific human soul and a specific human body. The "target" of the incarnation is a complete human body which has as its form a specific human soul. One consequence of this conception of the incarnation is that the divine nature does not add anything to the human nature; each nature, the divine and the human, is complete in itself. The unification of the two natures which happens in the incarnation leaves the two natures unchanged. These natures cannot mix or change in incarnation because this would imply a substantial change. In this case, incarnation would be equivalent to some kind of enlargement of the respective natures; the species of the involved entity would change as well and Christ would not be a human individual any more. But not only would the human nature of Christ cease to be human, also his divine nature would cease to be divine. Christ would be an entity of a new kind—something like a half god:

> *But form is an essential principle. So, every addition of form makes another species and another nature (as we are now speaking of nature). If, then, the divinity of the Word be added to the human nature as a form, it will make another nature. And thus Christ will not be of the human nature but of some other, just as an animated body is of another nature than that which is body only.*[9]

Thus far our analysis has shown that the logic of the hylomorphic model is incompatible with direct application to the person of Jesus Christ. More specifically, it cannot be applied to Christ as a union of a divine and a human nature.[10] The question is whether it can be successfully applied to each of the two natures in a specific way for each one. On this view, the person of Christ, with his two natures, would become a combination of two units with two different substantial forms.

> *It is by its nature that something is called a natural thing. One calls it a natural thing because it has a form .... The form of a natural thing is, then, its nature. But one must say that in Christ there are two forms, even after the union.*[11]

---

[7] S. c. G., IV, 32.

[8] Ibid.: "... God cannot be the form of a body. Since, therefore, the Word of God is God, as was shown, it is impossible that the Word of God be the form of a body, so as to be able to stand as a soul to flesh."

[9] S. c. G., IV, 35; cfr. also ibid., IV, 41.

[10] Eleonore Stump puts this in the following way: "The divine person does not configure the human body and soul as a substantial soul. The divine person is not a form configuring matter; the divine person is a complete thing in its own right, as the substantial form of a material composite is not" (Eleonore Stump, *Aquinas* (London: Routledge, 2003), p. 410).

[11] S. c. G., IV, 35.

Under normal circumstances something which has its own nature and its own substantial form is a substance of its own. There would be two substances in Jesus Christ—a divine and a human one. This, however, would clearly contradict the doctrine of the union between the divine and human nature in incarnation (hypostatic union) and the Christological dogma that Jesus Christ is only one person and one subsisting thing (suppositum/hypostasis). How can two substantial forms be united into one subsisting thing? The answer of Aquinas in the *Summa Theologiae* is that a duality of natures does not necessarily imply a duality of (first) substances.[12] He admits that in normal things ("rebus creatis") a variety of natures implies a numerical variety of subsisting things; this assumption, however, does not follow from the two concepts, "nature" and "substance' (hypostasis or suppositum). As Aquinas points out, a subsisting thing always comprises more than its nature—e.g. it also comprises its accidental properties and its concrete realization. For this reason, there is no conceptual contradiction if it is claimed that in the person of Christ there is one substance in the first sense (or one suppositum, or one hypostasis) and two natures or two substantial forms.

Two Natures—Two Subjects?

A second matter arises, however, in connection with the assumption that the person of Jesus Christ has two natures: each nature has its own mode of operation; there are specific activities connected with each nature, such that it is necessary to ascribe to Christ two different kinds of (cognitive) operations, two kinds of volitions and two modes of reasoning.[13] The hylomorphic account is consistent with the Christian Dogma at this point as well: according to the third Council of Constantinople (681), there are in Christ "two natural wills" and "two natural operations," the human being subject to the divine.[14]

According to Aquinas, Christ has a human and a divine intellect;[15] like every other human intellect, the human mind of Christ needs information which is provided through sense perception [*conversio ad phantasmata*]. Consequently, the human intellect is unable to grasp fully the essence of the divine person of Christ.[16] This creates a very delicate situation when it comes to the self-knowledge of Christ. Does the inability of the person, Jesus Christ, to comprehend with his human intellect his own divine nature imply that Jesus Christ, as a human being, fails to refer to himself as the Son of God? What are the consequences of the assumption of two different kinds of cognitive operations when applied to the problem of the self-reference of Christ? If Jesus Christ in his human nature has a different knowledge about himself than he has in his divine nature, does he refer in these two modes of self-knowledge to two numerically different subjects? To whom is Christ referring to when he says 'I am thirsty'—is it only his human or also his divine nature?

---

[12]   S. Th., III, 2, 3.

[13]   S. c. G., IV, 36: "Every nature, of course, has a proper operation of its own, for the form is the principle of operation, and in accord with its form every nature has the species proper to it. Hence, as of diverse natures there are diverse forms, there must be also diverse actions. If, then, in Christ there be one action, it follows that there is in him but one nature. This last belongs to the Eutychean heresy. We then conclude that it is false to say there is but one operation in Christ."

[14]   Denzinger, *The Sources of Catholic Dogma*, no. 291.

[15]   S. Th., III, 9, 1: "... because, since everything is on account of its operation, ... Christ would have had an intellective soul to no purpose if He had not understood by it; and this pertains to created knowledge."

[16]   S. Th., III, 10, 1: "... it must be said that the soul of Christ nowise comprehends the Divine Essence."

Self-knowledge can be understood in two different ways. In the first way we can have knowledge about ourselves in an informational or empirical way; we can grasp in self-knowledge a variety of subjective information which concerns our physical and psychical existence—information about our character-traits, memorized experiences, knowledge about our psychical and physical constitution etc. This kind of self-knowledge can be more or less adequate and it can be fallible—as studies about the quality of introspective self-reports confirm.[17] Self-knowledge understood in this first (empirical) sense should not pose a serious problem for the unity of the person Jesus Christ, having self-knowledge in both his natures. Even if the self-knowledge, based on the human intellect of Christ, cannot fully comprehend the essence of the divine person, it could still refer to the same subject—the person of Jesus Christ—which is also the target of divine self-knowledge.[18]

The case is different with the second kind of self-knowledge. This form of self-knowledge is called by Lynne Rudder Baker "first-person perspective." It can also be described as the ability to "conceive of oneself as oneself" or as having "a perspective from which one thinks of oneself as an individual facing a world, as a subject distinct from everything else."[19] It means the ability to know that specific, physical, or psychical, properties, experiences, are my properties and not the properties of somebody else. Unlike the first kind of self-knowledge, it provides no further information concerning my properties but it provides a kind of "extra truth" about the person who has these properties.[20] In this sense, first-person-access to oneself is immune to referential errors: according to Baker, "I am never mistaken about who is picked out by my competent uses of 'I.'"[21] For this reason, the sameness of first-person perspective provides a solid justification for personal identity, because it excludes indeterminacy in identity-statements. Departing from the first-person perspective there is always a determinate answer to the question, with whom I am identical. If two persons, P_1 and P_2, have the same first-person perspective, they are the same person.[22] Consequently, the existence of different first-person perspectives implies the existence of different persons.

If the difference between the divine and human self-knowledge of Christ is understood in this way, as a difference in first-person perspective, there would be a problem for the unity of the person of Christ. Let us assume that Christ's human and divine self-knowledge each had their own different first-person perspectives. In this case Christ would refer to himself as a divine subject in his divine intellect[23] and a human subject in his human intellect. If sameness of first-person perspective is a necessary condition of personal identity, subjects with different first-person perspectives obviously cannot be identical. Christ would have consisted of two selves or personal subjects, whose identity are connected with their respective capacity for self-reflection. We would have not only two natures in Christ, but also two persons in the Lockean Sense. According to John Locke, a person "is a thinking intelligent being, that has reason and reflection, and can consider itself as itself, the same

---

[17] William E. Lyons, *The Disappearance of Introspection* (Cambridge, Mass.: MIT Press, 1986).

[18] Karl Rahner seems to have this in mind, when he explains that Jesus in his human intellect had to develop his knowledge about himself as the son of God, but never arrived at a full understanding of his divine nature. Rahner calls this the "asymptotic recovery ['asymptotisches Einholen'] of what and who oneself already is" (Karl Rahner, *Sämtliche Werke Band 12—Menschsein und Menschwerdung Gottes. Studien zur Grundlegung der Dogmatik, zur Christologie, Theologischen Anthropologie und Eschatologie, Bearbeitet von Herbert Vorgrimmler* (Freiburg: Herder 2005), p. 340).

[19] Lynne Rudder Baker, *Persons and Bodies: A Constitution View* (Cambridge: Cambridge University Press, 2000), p. 66.

[20] Richard Swinburne, "Substance Dualism," *Faith and Philosophy*, 26 (2009), pp. 501–13, p. 506.

[21] Baker, *Persons and Bodies*, p. 65.

[22] Baker, *Persons and Bodies*, p. 132.

[23] It is not clear whether it is even possible to speak about a divine intellect.

thinking being in different times and places."[24] Based on this definition, the identity of the divine person would be connected with its divine capacity of self-reflection or self-consciousness and the identity of the human person with its own, different, human form of self-consciousness.

Since the nineteenth century there have been different attempts in Christian philosophy and theology to reconcile the Chalcedonian definition with a modern understanding of personhood, in which personal identity is intrinsically connected with the capacity for self-consciousness and self-reflection.[25] Contemporary authors of analytic philosophy of religion, like Richard Swinburne and Thomas V. Morris, which link the personhood of Jesus Christ to his self-reflective activities try to describe the difference between the human and the divine ways of self-understanding in Jesus Christ through analogies derived from psychological disorders like split mind or multiple personality disorder.[26] The two modes of cognitive operations would correspond to two operating subjects, each with its own distinct identity and with its own enduring pattern of perceiving, relating to, and thinking about its environment and self. At least two of these identities or personality states recurrently take control of the person's behavior. These different selves or personalities have different volitions, beliefs, etc. and are also ignorant of each other's volitions, intentions, and beliefs. Thomas V. Morris, for example, discusses the split mind-analogy as a possible explanation of the different cognitive activities connected with the divine and human nature of Christ.[27] Richard Swinburne seems to assume a similar model, when he speaks about the Freudian account of the divided mind which "helps us to see the logical possibility of an individual for good reason with conscious intention keeping a lesser belief system separate from his main belief system, and simultaneously doing different actions guided by different sets of belief of which he is consciously aware."[28]

Morris and Swinburne are far from identifying multiple personalities or divided minds with multiple persons.[29] Their psychological analogies, however, end up as versions of the two-persons-view, if split mind or multiple personality is interpreted as the existence of different selves or personality-centres to which the different self-referential activities refer. This stronger interpretation of the split mind analogy, i.e. two separate selves, subjects or persons, one human and one divine, can hardly be avoided if the human soul of Christ is understood in a dualistic sense. If the soul of Christ is a mental substance, and a mental substance is, as Swinburne defines it, a "substance to whose existence that substance necessarily has privileged access,"[30] then the two modes of self-knowledge in Jesus Christ imply two numerically different subjects. In this case we would have a human mental substance, the soul, toward which only the human being, Jesus Christ, has infallible access and a divine mental substance toward which only the second person of the Trinity has his own privileged access. There would be two different persons, as implied by two different first-person perspectives. Swinburne himself avoids this unorthodox conclusion by assuming

---

[24]   John Locke, *An Essay Concerning Human Understanding*, ed. Alexander C. Fraser (2 vols, New York: Dover, 1959), vol. 1, Book II, ch. 27, §9.

[25]   See Georg Essen, *Die Freiheit Jesu. Der neuchalkedonische Enhypostasiebegriff im Horizont neuzeitlicher Subjekt- und Personphilosophie* (Regensburg: Verlag Friedrich Pustet, 2001).

[26]   While the notion of "multiple personality disorder" is used in DSM-III, DSM-IV classified these diseases under the notion of "dissociative identity disorder (DID)"; American Psychiatric Association (ed.), *Diagnostic and Statistical Manual of Mental Disorders, Fourth Edition* (Washington, 1994).

[27]   Thomas V. Morris, *The Logic of God Incarnate* (Ithaca: Cornell University Press, 1986), p. 105.

[28]   Richard Swinburne, *The Christian God* (Oxford: Clarendon Press, 1994), p. 201

[29]   Morris, *God Incarnate*, p. 106.

[30]   Swinburne, "Substance Dualism," p. 503.

that the soul of the person Jesus Christ does not belong to his human nature. He argues against Aquinas' thesis that the second person of the Trinity adopted an individual human nature together with an individual substantial form or soul. According to Swinburne, it is the individual divine soul of Christ which adopts a universal human nature at the incarnation. Swinburne's solution is a consequence of his dualist conception of the soul. For him the soul of Christ, like any other soul, is a mental substance which is the essential part of a person. As a mental substance the soul cannot be a part of the human nature which would be united with the divine Word. Since a mental substance is defined by its specific privileged access or first-person perspective, a human soul understood as a human mental substance would have its own first-person perspective which is different from the self-referential activities of the second person of the Trinity. There would be two separate substances. The only solution to this problem is to assume a soul for the second person of the Trinity which is united with the universal human nature of Jesus Christ at the incarnation.[31]

Aquinas, however, explicitly maintains that the divine Word adopted no universal, but an individual human nature.[32] But if there are different kinds of self-knowledge connected with the two individual natures, how can we avoid concluding that Christ referred in these two modes of self-knowledge to two numerically different subjects? Hylomorphism can provide a solution to this problem. As we have seen above, the two-persons-problem is essentially connected with a dualistic understanding of the soul as a mental substance toward which the subject has privileged access. If the soul is both the subject and object of the first-person perspective, which the subject has toward itself, then the incarnation either has to be interpreted as a divine soul adopting a universal human nature (Swinburne) or as the union of a divine and a human subject or person. By assuming a non-dualistic understanding of the soul as substantial form of a body, we can avoid being forced to posit two subjects. In Hylomorphism the soul is not a complete substance, but a substance only in the sense of a formal principle, the substantial principle in virtue of which a body is a living body. "Soul" is the principle of living beings.[33] As a substantial form the soul cannot be identical with the thing whose form it is and therefore it cannot be a complete mental substance.

Moreover the reality of the soul is classified in Hylomorphism as a dispositional, not a manifest, form of reality. In *De Anima*, 412a 24f., Aristotle makes it clear that the soul is actuality (entelecheia) "in the first sense, viz. that of knowledge as possessed ... but not employed ... ." The soul, as a basic capacity, is the form of the human organism and as such it causes the body to be the kind of living substance it is.[34] The soul is a basic disposition for specific cognitive and non-cognitive activities. By saying that the soul is a dispositional entity, I do not claim that the soul is mere potency. This would be a complete misunderstanding, and it would contradict the hylomorophic view that the soul is actuality. The dispositional nature of the soul is better described as the power to perform specific acts. Being a capacity or a power, the soul cannot be the kind of substance which is presupposed in substance-dualism. We can further assume that the human soul comprises the capacity for

---

[31] Swinburne, *Christian God*, pp. 212–15.

[32] S.Th., III, 2, 2: "The Word of God 'did not assume human nature in general, but in atomo' — that is, in an individual ... otherwise every man would be the Word of God, even as Christ was. ... Therefore, although this human nature is a kind of individual in the genus of substance, it has not its own personality, because it does not exist separately, but in something more perfect, viz. in the Person of the Word. Therefore the union took place in the person."

[33] De an., 402a6f.

[34] De an., 412a7ff.

self-knowledge; it can be seen as the capacity to have a first-person perspective.[35] As a basic capacity the soul satisfies a necessary condition for referring to ourselves as subjects, but it is not identical with the subject itself. If the rational soul provides for the subject the power to have privileged access toward itself—the capacity to have a first-person perspective—it is not identical with the subject, to whom it gives that power. If we abandon the assumption that the soul as the basic capacity for a first-person perspective is identical with a self-referring subject, it is metaphysically possible that there are two basic powers for one subject.

This application of Hylomorphism to Christology comes very close to Michael Rea's proposal. Rea also resolves the two-persons-problem by assuming two fundamental powers—the divine and human nature—in the person of Christ.[36] Concerning human nature, there is, however, a difference between our thesis that the soul is a basic power and Rea's proposal. For Rea human nature is already the fundamental power which unites other human powers. In our conception it is the human soul which is the fundamental power; human nature can be regarded as powerful only insofar as the soul is an essential part of it.[37] The reason why the human nature alone cannot be identified with a fundamental power lies in the definition of the concept "nature." The nature of things, like humans, does not comprise form alone but form and matter.[38] As any other human nature, Christ's human nature is composed of a material body and a rational soul. Even if nature plays—as Rea maintains—the role of form, it contains also matter in its formal characterization. "Humanity" means the form of an entity which consists of a rational soul and a human body. Therefore, nature fulfills only partly the role of a power; it also contains aspects which are not powerful but determined by powers. The only thing which can be identified with a form or a basic power (substantial form) is the soul. But the soul can perform this role as a basic capacity, not as an immaterial substance but only as the form of a living body. Therefore, in our view, the only reason why the human nature of Christ can be called a fundamental power consists in the soul being the substantial form of a living human body.

Conclusion: The Legitimate Use of Hylomorphism in Christology

In Hylomorphism the soul of Jesus is not identical with the subject or self of Jesus Christ, which constitutes his being a person.[39] The soul is a fundamental power for the human cognitive and non-cognitive operations performed by the person of Christ. In this dispositional understanding of the soul, Christ's human self-knowledge which is different from his divine self-understanding, does not imply the existence of a human subject which is numerically different from the divine subject. The difference between the two forms of self-knowledge must not be interpreted in the sense of two different first-person perspectives; it matters only for the type of information acquired: self-knowledge based upon the human nature of Jesus, unlike that based on the divine, does not attain a full comprehension of the person of Christ.

---

[35]   Josef Quitterer, "Hylomorphism and the Constitution View," in G. Gasser (ed.), *Personal Identity and Resurrection. How Do We Survive Our Death?* (Farnham: Ashgate, 2010), pp. 177–90, p. 185f.

[36]   Michael C. Rea, "Hylomorphism and the incarnation," in A. Marmodoro and J. Hill (eds), *The Metaphysics of the Incarnation* (Oxford: Oxford University Press, 2011), pp. 134–52, p. 139ff.

[37]   Part is here understood as a metaphysical constituent which is neither a mereological part nor a set theoretical element.

[38]   S.Th., I, 75, 4.

[39]   Thomas Aquinas, *Ad Corinthios lectura, Caput.* 15, lectio 2: " ... anima autem cum sit pars corporis hominis, non est totus homo, et anima mea non est ego; ..."

The existence of a specific human and a divine form of self-knowledge in one and the same subject can be compared with the existence of different operations, which are executed on the basis of numerically different natural principles in one and the same human being: hearing, smelling, and knowing are numerically different operations not because they belong to different subjects but because they are executed on the basis of numerically different principles (or powers) in one and the same subject. In a similar way, the cognitive operations, which are executed on the basis of Christ's divine nature, on the one hand, and those belonging to the human nature, on the other, do not require two subjects, but are performed by one and the same person with the help of different fundamental powers.

> Again, in one who is pure man, although he is one in supposit there are many appetites
> and operations according to the diversity of natural principles. For in his rational part
> there is will; in his sensitive, the irascible and concupiscible appetites; and, further,
> the natural appetite following on natural powers. In the same way he sees with the eye,
> bears with the ear, steps with the foot, speaks with the tongue, and understands with
> the mind, and these are diverse operations. The case is such because the operations
> are not multiplied according to diverse subjects operating only, but as well according
> to diverse principles by which one and the same subject operates, and from which
> the operations take their species. But the divine nature is much more removed from
> human nature than the principles of human nature are from one another. Therefore,
> the will and operation of the divine and the human nature in Christ are distinguished
> from one another, although Christ Himself is one in each of the natures.[40]

As has been shown above, there is no direct application of the hylomorphic account to the divine-human combination, Jesus Christ; the divine nature cannot be the substantial form of the human nature in the same way as the soul is the substantial form of the body. Nevertheless there is the possibility of an indirect application: the relationship between the different powers of the soul in Hylomorphism—intellectual, sensory, and others—can be used for reconstructing the relationship between the divine and the human nature in one and the same person. Even if the intellectual and sensory operations are performed with the help of different powers of the soul, they do not presuppose different acting subjects. If we apply this model to the specific difference between divine and human self-knowledge, the following picture appears. Human self-knowledge, which is performed by the human intellect, refers to the same subject—the person of Jesus Christ—as does the divine self-knowledge. Different kinds of (self-)knowledge or volition which are executed on the basis of numerically different fundamental basic powers do not imply different subjects. In a similar way as information gained through the sensory powers differs from knowledge acquired through the intellect, there can be a qualitative difference in the way Jesus Christ has knowledge about himself through his divine and human self-knowledge. By his human way of referring to himself he is unable fully to grasp the essence of his being the Son of God, the full self-knowledge being possible only by his divine intellect. Nevertheless he has also by his human self-understanding the same first-person perspective toward himself as he has in his divine intellect; in this sense he has privileged access toward himself as the Son of God, even though he is unable to grasp the divine essence of himself in human cognition.[41]

---

40 Contra Gentiles, lib. 4 cap. 36 n. 7.

41 This explains—according to Rahner—why Jesus Christ, in his human mind, can gradually develop an ever more adequate understanding of what he in his divine nature is.

A Cartesian Approach to the Incarnation

J.H.W. Chan

Introduction

The incarnation is the central Christian doctrine that states that the Word (the second person of the Trinity) assumed a human nature in addition to his divine nature. Cartesian dualism (CD), roughly speaking, is the view that human persons are essentially immaterial souls, contingently attached to the parcels of matter known as bodies. In this chapter we examine whether the doctrine of the incarnation can be explicated in terms of CD.

We begin by outlining CD and its relation to human nature. This is followed by a discussion of the various ways human nature, in terms of CD, can be construed in the incarnation. In the remaining sections we navigate through the various heresies that must be avoided in an orthodox account of the incarnation. CD *per se* is not defended here, nor is it argued that CD is the only way to articulate human nature in the incarnation. Rather the aim here is a modest one: to explore the possibility of an orthodox doctrine of the incarnation with the presupposition of CD. Presumably, a creedally orthodox theory of human persons must be coherent with the incarnation; thus the doctrine can be seen to be operating here as an 'acid test' for the viability of CD as a theological anthropology.

Cartesian Dualism and Human Nature

A Cartesian interpretation of the human nature assumed in the incarnation is not entirely uncontroversial. Although the Christian tradition has undisputedly been on the side of the substance dualist in terms of understanding human nature, this does not necessarily mean that the brand of substance dualism was of a Cartesian variety.[1] However, the early church Fathers did use the term 'soul' in a Platonic as well as an Aristotelian sense. In particular the Alexandrians appear to have held to something very similar to a Cartesian view. J.N.D. Kelly writes:

> We have seen how frequently the union of the body and soul, two disparate substances, was quoted by the Alexandrian teachers as an illustration of the union of divinity and humanity in Christ … each individual soul was created independently by God at the moment of its infusion to the body.[2]

---

[1]   See John Cooper, *Body, Soul and Life Everlasting* (Grand Rapids, MI: Eerdmans, 1989), pp. 7–17.

[2]   J.N.D. Kelly, *Early Christian Doctrines* (London: A. and C. Black Limited, 1958), pp. 344–5. This is a Cartesian rather than a hylomorphic interpretation because the soul is said to be created independently of the body. Speaking of the latter, Eleonore Stump writes, 'when material components are combined

Though it is not clear whether something like CD was a widely held view in the Christian tradition, it is at least a view that was held by some. John Calvin was a substance dualist in the Platonic/Cartesian tradition[3] and Aquinas recognizes a position he associates with Platonism which is very similar to CD.[4] One might object that using the term CD to refer to a generally Platonic theory of souls is in a sense anachronistic since the latter predates the philosopher René Descartes. However, CD simply refers to the view of human nature that is most commonly associated with Descartes – the view that a person is identical to her soul and not her body. Such use is common in the contemporary literature. Let us examine this view further.

According to CD, embodiment is a contingent state of affairs – the minimum requirement for personhood is being identical to a soul; being 'attached' to a particular hunk of matter is not necessary. To clarify: a soul need not be attached to a human body to exist, nor is it necessary for a soul to be attached to a human body to belong to the category 'person'. To introduce a distinction, human nature could be understood to either be the property of a soul *simpliciter* or a property possessed by a soul in virtue of being in certain causal relations with a human body. Let us distinguish between these two views more clearly. Taking human nature to be a property of a particular kind of soul *simpliciter* is to say that a soul of a particular kind just is a human person.[5] Call this the *simpliciter* view. On this view there are kinds of souls, some of which are specifically human. Alternatively, we might take human nature to be a relational property. Such a view would entail that there are no distinguishable 'types' of souls. Rather, there are souls (that have the property of personhood) but whose 'humanhood' is derived from being 'attached' to a particular biological organism that belongs to the species *homo sapiens*. Call this the relational view of souls. The relational view has the unintuitive implication that humanhood is not an essential property of a person. If souls are generic and derive humanhood from being in specific causal relations with particular parcels of matter, then humanhood is contingent on such a relation. Therefore at somatic death, when the connection between the body and the soul is severed, one ceases to be human.[6] Moreover, if humanhood is derived from being in the right causal relations with a human body, then it seems that 'froghood' could be gained by a soul being in the right causal relations with the body of a frog.[7] Thus there is the strange consequence for the relational view that I could lose my humanhood and gain froghood, thereby becoming a frog. This is strange because the

---

into something higher level [sic] with a particular configuration, a substance will come into being … . In general, then, a substantial material form is the configurational state of a material object that makes that object a member of the kind or species to which it belongs and gives it the causal powers characteristic of that kind', *Aquinas* (London: Routledge, 2003), pp. 196–7. On a hylomorphic interpretation, the soul is said to emerge from a material configuration and cannot be created independently of the material body on this account of persons.

[3] '… Calvin is a substance dualist. He thought that among the philosophers only Plato had the right idea, linking the soul to the image of God and affirming its immortality', Paul Helm, *John Calvin's Ideas* (Oxford: Oxford University Press, 2004), p. 129. See also John Calvin, *Institutes of the Christian Religion* 1.15.6.

[4] *Aquinas*, p. 19. Although Aquinas repudiates such a view it is the observation that Cartesian dualism is a view that has been associated with the Christian tradition that we are interested in here. See also *Summa Contra Gentiles* II. 57, ST Ia89.1.

[5] We say 'of a particular kind' just in case there are other immaterial souls that do not belong to the natural kind 'human souls', i.e. angels. If there are souls of animals or higher mammalians species, they too would not belong to the same natural kind as human souls. We neither assert nor deny the existence of other types of souls in this chapter.

[6] Although one does not cease to be a person.

[7] Oliver Crisp, *Divinity and Humanity: The Incarnation Reconsidered* (Cambridge: Cambridge University Press, 2007), pp. 56–7.

property of being human is one that seems *prima facie* to be an essential property of mine, i.e. a property that I could not lose without ceasing to be me. In addition to this, the relational view appears to have some unwelcome consequences when applied to the incarnation. In becoming incarnate, the Word takes on a human nature. But if human nature is dependent on causal relations with a human body, then the human nature that Christ assumes is not only contingent, but also temporary. At death, there is a separation between Christ's soul and his body. Therefore (on the relational view), Christ relinquishes his human nature at death. But it is the traditional view that once the Word assumes human nature, he does not abdicate it.[8] Perhaps this problem can be resolved by arguing that 'ceasing to be human' or that the 'temporary loss of humanhood' is a metaphysical consequence of this particular Cartesian view (i.e. all human persons at some stage in their existence are temporarily disembodied souls and lack the property of 'humanhood' between death and resurrection). If this is the case then the human nature that Christ assumes also lacks 'humanhood' for a short duration of time on the relational view of souls. It could be argued that the lack of humanhood between death and resurrection just is a metaphysical consequence of this view – 'human nature' entails the lack of humanhood for a temporary duration of time for any entity that possesses humanhood and this includes Christ. While this addresses the temporary lack of human nature, the denial that humanhood is an essential property still remains on the relational view.

This may be good reason to prefer the alternative, *simpliciter* view. However, with respect to the incarnation, it is not without problems of its own. Trenton Merricks has argued that the embodiment of the Word should be entailed by the incarnation. He argues that if it is not, then the Word can assume a human nature without assuming a body, which seems strange.[9] The *simpliciter* view is open to this charge because the assumption of human nature in the incarnation does not require the assumption of a physical body on this view – a human soul alone is sufficient for humanhood. This does not apply to the relational view since a human person on this view is a soul with the right causal connections to a human body. According to the relational view of souls, the assumption of human nature in the incarnation requires that the Word become embodied. This is not the case for the *simpliciter* view. The following are some responses to Merricks's objection.

First, it might be argued that embodiment *per se* is not a necessary requirement of being human, even on a materialist view of human nature. Take Merricks's metaphysical view of persons – animalism. According to such a view, a person is identical to his/her body and/ or brain/brain-plus-central nervous system and mental states. On the animalist's conception of human nature, persons are minimally brains that persist with the right psychological/ memory links from one time to the next. Consider the following: mild mannered Jason Becker is captured by the evil scientist Professor Govan, who removes Jason's brain and places it in a vat. The brain is kept alive and conscious and lives for a year on Govan's mantelpiece. Eventually, Govan decides to put the brain back in Jason's body (which has been preserved in cryogenic freeze) and Jason is released from Govan's lair. For all intents and purposes, he is no worse for wear than the day he was captured. Does Jason survive

---

[8]   See *Summa Theologiae* Q.50, Article 4, Objection 1: 'It would seem that Christ was a man during the three days of His death, because Augustine says (De Trin. ii.) "Such was assuming [of nature] as to make God to be man, and man to be God". But this assuming [of nature] did not cease at Christ's death. Therefore it seems that He did not cease to be a man in consequence of death.' Reply to objection 1: 'The Word of God assumed a united soul and body: and the result of this assumption was that God is man, and man is God. But this assumption did not cease by the separation of the Word from the soul or from the flesh; yet the union of soul and flesh ceased.'

[9]   Trenton Merricks, 'The Word Made Flesh' in Peter van Inwagen and Dean Zimmerman (eds), *Persons: Human and Divine* (Oxford: Oxford University Press, 2008), pp. 281–301.

this bizarre and traumatic series of events? If no, then the removal of his brain resulted in the end of his existence. If yes, Jason either survives fully, or he survives partially. But the survival of a person in degrees or in part does not make any sense. So if we believe that Jason survives the experiment, then it appears that he survives fully and non-intermittently as a brain. In materialist or animalist terms, it seems that Jason is identical to his brain (or brain plus central nervous system).[10] Since identity is a necessary relation, if Jason is identical to his brain while his brain is out of his body, it follows that even when his brain is returned to his body and he is embodied, he is still identical to his brain.[11] Therefore, if we accept that Jason is the same person before and after his brush with Govan, it would appear that the bare minimum requirement for being a human person according to the animalist is being identical to a brain (or a brain plus central nervous system). Given this, the Word could have assumed human nature by simply becoming a brain.[12] Therefore embodiment is not a necessary feature of a materialist incarnation either. Merricks might reply that this objection misses the point – it isn't just the case that on the *simpliciter* view the incarnation would not necessarily require a body, but rather that the incarnation could take place without the Word needing to assume any physicality at all. Some minimal notion of being physical or 'enfleshed' in the incarnation is required by the materialist but not by the *simpliciter* version of CD. Even if the brain is not a complete human body, it is an important part of it, and a part that is physical. What Merricks purports to show with this argument is the 'weirdness' of an incarnation that appears to be incomplete. However there is equal weirdness on the materialist side of the coin even if a materialist incarnation entails the Word being at least partially 'enfleshed'.

Second, a proponent of the *simpliciter* view can claim that embodiment is an important part of human nature, even if it is not necessarily entailed by human personhood. Augustine writes that 'a man's body is no mere adornment, or external convenience; it belongs to his very nature as a man' and so one might claim that the fullness of humanity is not attained without a body.[13] Just because one can be a human person without being embodied, it does not follow that being disembodied is the natural state for a human person.[14] The life spent on this earth is embodied. Therefore the *simpliciter* view Cartesian can borrow a page from the hylomorphist's book on personhood even though they do not share the same metaphysical convictions on the nature of the body. On Aquinas's view, 'disembodied existence is not natural to the soul … the soul's existence in a disembodied state is an impermanent as well as an unnatural condition. It is contrary to the nature of the soul to be without the body.'[15] The proponent of the *simpliciter* view of the soul can differentiate between the necessary and sufficient conditions for being a human person, i.e. being identical to a human soul, and the necessary conditions for possessing a full humanity.

Third, if being a soul is sufficient for being minimally human, but being embodied is necessary for full humanity, it could be argued that in the incarnation, the assumption of the properties of a soul without embodiment would be insufficient to bring about the reconciliation of human beings to God. Although becoming embodied in the incarnation

---

[10]   Or if not identical, then 'constituted' by his brain.

[11]   *Mutatis mutandis* for a constitutional view, i.e. if Jason was constituted by his brain before the incident he continues to be constituted by his brain after.

[12]   Or *per impossibile* by coming to be constituted by a brain.

[13]   Augustine of Hippo, *The City of God* (New York: Penguin, 1984), Book I, Chapter 13, p. 22.

[14]   Eleonore Stump, *Aquinas*, p. 211. Also 'The disembodied soul which persists is not the complete human being who was the composite but only a part of that being', ibid. See also footnote 90, 'Aquinas would therefore not accept the claim that anything which is embodied is necessarily embodied', ibid.

[15]   Ibid.

(according to the *simpliciter* view) is not necessary for assuming a human nature, it might be argued that it is necessary for the atonement since we are embodied creatures – following Gregory of Nazianzus, 'what Christ has not assumed, he has not healed; but what has been united with God is saved'.[16] Although incarnation and becoming embodied are ontologically distinct, *contra* Merricks, the incarnation nonetheless requires embodiment to fulfil the purpose of the incarnation.[17]

Relational Souls and the Bicentennial Man Argument

Merricks's objection that the incarnation can take place *sans* embodiment does not apply to the relational view of souls. On this view, humanhood is derived from a soul being in the correct causal relations with a human body. The incarnation on this account entails the Word taking on the appropriate set of relations to a human body. But a potential problem for the relational view is that Christ's human body has different causal origins to every other human person in history. Given the unique and distinctive biological origins of the incarnate Son it can be argued that it provides only the appearance and not the reality of full humanity, which is the heresy of Docetism.

In this section we address the biological facts that may entail the heresy of Docetism and preclude the possibility of an orthodox incarnation on the relational view. A novel argument based on differentiating the causal origin of certain cells combined with the observation of cell turnover in a biological organism is offered in response.[18] We take Oliver Crisp's construal of the conception of Christ as our point of departure.[19]

Crisp takes the same position as a number of classical theologians in assuming that, like us, Christ shares a biological kinship with all humans through the common process of fertilization of an ovum by the requisite genetic material. Crisp writes:

> The Virginal Conception of Christ refers to the miraculous asexual action of the Holy Spirit in generating the human nature of Christ in the womb of the Virgin Mary, using an ovum from the womb of the Virgin Mary and supplying the missing genetic material (specifically the Y chromosomes) necessary for the production of a human male.[20]

Christ's physical body was formed from the ovum of a female and the miraculously created genetic material from the Holy Spirit that would normally have come from a spermatozoon. However, the fact that the genetic material necessary for conception was not generated by a human male might be seen as a problem for Christ's humanity; one might claim that he is not fully human because of this difference in causal origin. Crisp points out:

---

[16] Gregory Nazianzus, *Epistle 51*, to Cledonius, from http://www.newadvent.org/fathers/3103a. htm.

[17] Assuming there really is an objective external world and that human persons are physically embodied. If it there is no mind-independent world *à la* Berkeley, then the incarnation would not require embodiment in a strictly physical sense.

[18] The argument is named after the 1999 movie, *The Bicentennial Man*. The movie is based on an Isaac Asimov short story about a robot that becomes human by gradually replacing all of his material robotic parts with human parts.

[19] Oliver Crisp, *God Incarnate: Explorations in Christology* (London: T. & T. Clark, 2009), p. 79.

[20] Ibid.

> *If a miraculously generated part of that genetic heritage is introduced into a kind, it might be thought this is like the introduction of an alien body into a living organism that is able to mimic, or simulate, the characteristics of the living organism, passing itself off as part of that living organism.*[21]

Given this reasoning, it is not surprising that some have suggested that the biological facts of Christ's origin imply Docetism.[22] If the traditional view entails that Christ only appeared to be fully human then the traditional view is heretical. Crisp argues that one way to block this line of argument is to suggest that there is a certain material criterion that must be obtained in order for an organism to belong to the natural kind 'human person'. He states that it is possible that a threshold exists for belonging to this natural kind. On this view, 'Christ is a human being because he shares with the rest of humanity a certain amount of genetic material which is sufficient for Christ's humanity to be the same as the humanity of Mary.'[23] If one assumes that this threshold amount of genetic material can be found in an unfertilized human ovum, then Christ has this minimum amount of genetic material required at conception. If however it is the case that kind-membership is an all-or-nothing-affair then the human genetic material found in Mary's ovum is insufficient for membership of the natural kind human. Thus it might be worth considering whether or not the biologically-docetic-type arguments can be blocked if this is the case.

A presupposition of the Bicentennial Man argument is the assumption that the gradual and complete replacement of the genetic material of a particular human person leads to, first, discontinuity with that natural kind 'human' (i.e. that person ceases to be human)[24] and second results at some later point, in membership of a new natural kind. For example, if the genetic material had by a human person were gradually replaced by Martian genetic material, at a certain point in time, he would no longer be human, and at some point he would be considered a Martian. These points do not necessarily need to be simultaneous. It may be that at some time t1 after gradual replacement with Martian genetic material, Bob ceases to be human, but does not have sufficient Martian genetic material to be considered part of the natural kind 'Martian' yet. I take it that the converse is also true, i.e. if a Martian body were to be gradually replaced by human genetic material, the Martian would eventually become human.

As mentioned previously, the genetic material that would normally be supplied by a human male in the case of Christ is supplied by the Holy Spirit. Although it is indistinguishable from that which would normally be provided by a human male, it is a divine creation of the required human genetic material, supplied by the miraculous working of the Holy Spirit. Hence the only relevant metaphysical difference between Christ's conception and typical human conception lies in the causal origin of the 'male' genetic material. However, in some cases, causal origin marks the difference between the genuine article and a counterfeit. A British ten pound note has a certain appearance, certain physical properties. If someone were to produce an identical replica of a banknote, even if it was indistinguishable from the real thing it would be a counterfeit. The fake note would always be fake because of its

---

[21]   Ibid., p. 83.

[22]   Arthur Peacocke claims that the biological considerations to do with whether Christ has sufficient human genetic material to be counted a human being has docetic implications. Arthur Peacocke 'DNA of our DNA' in George J. Brooke (ed.), *The Birth of Jesus, Biblical and Theological Reflections* (Edinburgh: T. & T. Clark, 2000), pp. 64–5.

[23]   Oliver Crisp, *God Incarnate: Explorations in Christology*, p. 81.

[24]   This is in line with the relational view of souls since humanhood is taken to be a non-essential property of souls.

illegitimate causal origin, regardless of how much it looked, felt and smelt like the original. Thus, a second presupposition of the Bicentennial Man argument is that causal origin is a factor in determining legitimacy. Therefore, the genetic material provided by the Holy Spirit in the womb of Mary is non-human, not by virtue of its biological structure but because of its causal origin.

However, mitosis, the process by which cells replicate and organisms grow and replace old cells, is a human process.[25] As mitosis takes place in the fused gametes in the womb of Mary, the new genetic material produced has a human origin; eventually the non-human genetic material of the first cell is phased out completely (as the non-human cells are sloughed off and replaced over time), and the zygote that forms is produced entirely by this process.

Consider the following clarification: female cells contain two X chromosomes whereas human males have one X and one Y chromosome. The conception of a human male comprises two gametes: the X from the female ovum and the Y from the male spermatozoon. The following is a simplistic representation of what occurs in the conception of Christ; asterisk indicates non-human genetic material.[26]

(X) Chromosome strand from Mary's ovum
(Y*) Chromosome strand from spermatozoon/genetic material provided by Holy Spirit.

At conception, chromosomes fuse and implant in womb of Mary:[27]

The very first cell after conception is constituted by: (XY*) made from half human, half non-human genetic material.

After first cell division via mitosis we now have two cells: (XY*) + (XY)

The amount of non-human material has reduced from 50 per cent to 25 per cent after first split because the new cell has a human causal origin.

Each cell continues to undergo the process of mitosis. So after second split: (XY*) + (XY) + (XY) + (XY)

The amount of non-human material has now reduced from 25 per cent to 12.5 per cent.

After third split: (XY*) + (XY) + (XY) + (XY) + (XY) + (XY) + (XY) + (XY)

The amount of non-human material is now 6.25 per cent.

---

[25] Mitosis is not an exclusively human process – cells in any living organism divide in this fashion. However with respect to the causal origin of cells in a human body, it is a fully human process in that it is the normal way in which new cells are formed.

[26] I.e. (X*Y*) = non-human X chromosome, non-human Y chromosome. (XY*) = human X chromosome, non-human Y chromosome.

[27] Precisely where the human and non-human genetic material is distributed in the cells is simplified in this argument. First, the mitochondrial DNA is only inherited from the maternal parent, so presumably, the percentage would not quite be 50–50; the slight majority going in favour of the human material. Second, it would be more complicated in actuality because in mitosis a chromosome which is made from two strands of DNA, splits, and from the two halves, two new chromosomes are formed; so the 'new' chromosomes each have half the original genetic material in them. Although the percentages as shown in the overall organism are broadly speaking 'correct', the distribution would look slightly different.

So each split, of which many more must occur before an embryo is formed, reduces the amount of non-human material exponentially. To clarify, because the process of mitosis is a human biological act, any cell or cells generated by mitosis subsequent to the act of syngamy will be counted as 'human' cells because they will have been generated through a normal biological process. Hence, for every cell-split, the newly generated cell will be 'human' and, as a consequence only the amount of 'human' biological material will increase with mitosis. The resulting human nature of Christ is 'human' (or at least, mostly human for the first period of development *in utero*) because the cells generated after syngamy will count as human.[28] Therefore, the human nature that the Word assumes according to the relational view is fully human once the non-human cells are replaced and sloughed off via the process of mitosis and cell turnover.[29]

Having addressed some of the problems unique to the *simpliciter* and relational views of the soul, we will now examine various models of the incarnation available to the proponent of CD.

A Cartesian Incarnation

In the relevant philosophical-theological literature regarding the incarnation, the human nature that is assumed by the Word is usually said to be either 'abstract' or 'concrete'.[30] To say that human nature is abstract is to say that it is fundamentally a property or a set of properties.[31] For the Word to become incarnate according to this view is for the second person of the Trinity to assume a property or a set of properties. Alternatively, to say human nature is concrete is to take it to be a concrete particular. For the Word to become incarnate on this view is for him to begin to bear a certain relation to a concrete particular (e.g. a soul or a body, or a soul/body-plus-soul composite), in virtue of which he becomes human. Whether one thinks that human nature is a concrete particular or an abstract property determines how a model of the incarnation is explicated.

---

[28]   It should be pointed out that this is a metaphysical rather than a biological argument.

[29]   The Bicentennial Man argument is a metaphysical 'just-so' story set up to address the potential problem of docetism for the relational view of souls. We are not claiming here that this is the only way to block docetism, or that the biological facts necessarily imply this heresy. It may be the case that the biological facts do not entail the heresy of docetism – one might deny that causal origin determines whether one belongs to the human race, that human nature is an intrinsic rather than a relational property.

[30]   For some examples of abstract nature views see William Lane Craig and J.P. Moreland, *Philosophical Foundations for a Christian Worldview* (Downers Grove: IVP, 2003); Trenton Merricks, 'The Word Made Flesh: Physicalism, Dualism and the Incarnation' in van Inwagen and Dean Zimmerman (eds), *Persons: Divine and Human* (Oxford: Oxford University Press, 2008); Thomas Morris, *The Logic of God Incarnate* (Ithaca, NY: Cornell University Press, 1986); Alvin Plantinga, 'On Heresy Mind and Truth', *Faith and Philosophy* 16 (1999): 182–93 and Richard Swinburne, *The Christian God* (Oxford: Clarendon Press, 1994). For some examples of concrete nature views see Oliver Crisp, *Divinity and Humanity: The Incarnation Reconsidered* (Cambridge: Cambridge University Press, 2007); Richard Cross, *The Metaphysics of the Incarnation* (Oxford: Clarendon Press, 2002); Brian Leftow, 'A Timeless God Incarnate' in Stephen Davis, S.D Kendall, and Gerard O'Collins (eds), *The Incarnation* (Oxford: Clarendon Press, 2002) and Eleonore Stump, *Aquinas* (London: Routledge, 2003).

[31]   Abstract entities are taken to be objects which are causally inert, see Gideon Rosen, 'Abstract Objects', *The Stanford Encyclopedia of Philosophy* (Fall 2009 Edition), Edward N. Zalta (ed.), URL: http://plato.stanford.edu/archives/fall2009/entries/abstract-objects/ for a brief introduction to some of the issues regarding abstract objects and the difficulty in their definition.

Concrete Nature Models

Concrete nature models espoused by the Cartesian can be described as mereological – they involve the Word gaining concrete parts consisting of a human soul and a human body. In the incarnation there is a composite whose mereological sum consists of the divine Word (W) + body (B) + soul (S). The sum total of these parts is Jesus Christ. But there are different ways we might construe this model of a compositional Christ and in the relevant literature there have been two distinguishable versions of the compositional model: either the Word is taken to be identical with Jesus Christ, or the Word is taken simply to be a proper part of Jesus Christ.

If we take the former view, it is said that in assuming human nature in the incarnation, the Son combines his original divine substance with the body and soul that he assumes in the incarnation.[32] Call this the Whole version of the concrete model since the Word is taken to be equivalent to the sum total of the mereological parts on this interpretation.[33] Another way of understanding a compositional incarnation has been explicated by Brian Leftow.[34] In the incarnation, the Word gains proper parts in the form of a body and soul, but is not numerically identical to the composite unity that is formed by this assumption – the Son remains a simple entity, but is said to be a proper part of a larger composite entity that is formed; the second person of the Trinity is not identical to Jesus Christ. The Word is just a proper part of the mereological sum, Jesus Christ. Call this the Parts version of the concrete model since the Word is only seen as one part of the mereological sum that is Christ.

In order for concretism to remain orthodox, it needs to offer an account of the incarnation whereby it is reasonable to deny the personhood of the human nature assumed. But on a Cartesian view of human nature, it is difficult at best and impossible at worst to do this because both the relational and the *simpliciter* view hold that a Cartesian soul is a person. If human nature is a concrete particular then in the incarnation, the Word assumes a Cartesian soul. But if this is the case then the result is two distinct persons in Christ.

Thomas Senor writes of a compositional account of the incarnation:

> Recall that JC [Jesus Christ], is a composite consisting of GS [God the Son, the Word], and the human body and mind [or human soul] assumed in the Incarnation. So if GS is but a proper part of the individual who is Jesus Christ, then the friend of the CA [compositional account of the Incarnation] is committed to saying that GS and JC are not identical. Their non-identity brings with it one or the other of two unwelcome consequences: either there are two persons in the Incarnation or the composite Christ is not a person.[35]

---

[32] See Thomas P. Flint, 'Should Concretists Part with Mereological Models of the Incarnation', in Anna Marmodoro and Jonathan Hill (eds), *The Metaphysics of the Incarnation* (Oxford: Oxford University Press, 2011), pp. 67–87. This is the view that Thomas Aquinas held: 'to be made man is to be made simply, in all those in whom human nature begins to be in a newly created *suppositum*. But God is said to have been made, inasmuch as the human nature began to be in an eternally pre-existing *suppositum* of the Divine nature.' *Summa Theologiae* III, 16, 6, reply to objection 1.

[33] Strictly speaking if the Word is essentially immaterial then it makes no sense to say that he is equivalent to a mereological sum consisting of parts both material and immaterial. However, we can understand this in the same way that if Cartesian dualism is true, then I am equal to my soul plus body even though I am essentially an immaterial soul and my body is only a contingent part of me.

[34] Brian Leftow, 'A Timeless God Incarnate' in Stephen T. Davis, Daniel Kendall and Gerald O'Collins (eds), *The Incarnation: An Interdisciplinary Symposium on the Incarnation of the Son of God* (Oxford: Oxford University Press, 2002), pp. 273–99.

[35] Thomas Senor, 'The Compositional Account of the Incarnation', *Faith and Philosophy* 24/1 (January 2007), 52–71, p. 55.

The Parts version embraces the non-identity of the Word and Christ, which brings about or entails, according to Senor, Nestorianism. Senor writes of Leftow, who defends the Parts version, '[Leftow] thinks that GS is not identical with JC because the former is simple and the latter a complex whole composed of the Son, and the human body plus soul.'[36] Senor argues that either it is the case that Nestorianism obtains here or that Christ does not assume a complete human nature. If we take a Cartesian view of human nature in addition to the Parts version, Nestorianism appears to obtain, no matter what.

This is true also for the Whole version. Eleonore Stump writes that in the incarnation, the body and soul assumed fails to be a person distinct from the Word 'in virtue of being subsumed into the larger whole'; the human body and soul are 'part of a larger composite'.[37] Stump, however is referring to a hylomorphic account of persons, in which God the Son assumes the human body and soul before the pair has a chance to compose a distinct human, that is, the assumption takes place at conception. So, she argues, even if the particular body and soul that the Son assumes would have composed a distinct human person had they existed on their own, it does not follow that they do when they are taken on by God the Son at the moment they come into existence. It is not entirely clear whether this is sufficient to block Nestorianism for the hylomorphist but in any case, it does not work for CD. This is because there does not appear to be any time at which the Word can assume a Cartesian soul without it already being a person. In the incarnation the Word acquires a human nature, but on the Cartesian account of things a human nature is either identical to a human soul (for the *simpliciter* view) or alternatively, identical to a soul with the correct causal relations to a human body (according to the relational view). But a Cartesian soul is simple and always has the property of personhood essentially. For the hylomorphist the soul is the form of the body and at conception there isn't necessarily a human person present.[38] But at what point could the Word assume a Cartesian soul in order to prevent it being a person in its own right? There is no such time, because as soon as you have a Cartesian soul present you have a person present.

Given this presupposition of CD, a concrete view of the incarnation results in two separate persons in the body of Christ (a Cartesian soul, in addition to the Word), which is unacceptable as far as orthodoxy is concerned.

Christ is a divine person with a human nature, not a human person with a divine nature, nor a human person and a divine person subsisting. Although the Word possesses a complete human nature, this human nature does not form a human person independent of the Word. Rather, the Word 'assumes' this human nature into his person at the incarnation. (Christ's human nature is 'enhypostatic'.)[39]

But it seems for all intents and purposes, there is no Cartesian human nature (in the concrete sense) that can be enhypostatic. There is no 'space' for the Word to 'personalize' a particular human nature in order to make it his own. This problem of Nestorianism results from the Cartesian understanding of soul. As Richard Swinburne (who takes a similar view of the soul) recognizes, if a soul is sufficient for personhood, we are going to have this Christological problem. He writes,

---

[36] Ibid., p. 56.

[37] Eleonore Stump, *Aquinas*, p. 211.

[38] This is true on Leftow's interpretation of Aquinas, 'Thomas in an emergentist. As he sees it, just by coming to be in a new state, matter can constitute a new substance, distinct from any that has gone before' see 'Souls Dipped in Dust', in *Soul, Body and Survival* (Ithaca, NY: Cornell University Press, 2001), pp. 120–21. On such a view, a human person would not yet be present at conception.

[39] Oliver Crisp, *God Incarnate*, p. 79.

> *Even if what individuates other humans is an individual human soul, in the sense of a restriction in the form of humanity, a divine individual cannot acquire such a soul. For such a soul would already be the individuating principle of a human. He can only take on a human soul in the sense of a human way of thinking and acting; and a soul in this sense (even with a body) is not enough to individuate a human.*[40]

A human soul in the Cartesian sense is enough to 'individuate' a human, thus the result is two distinct persons in Christ, which is the heresy of Nestorianism. The concrete view itself may not entail Nestorianism, but when taken in conjunction with CD, Nestorianism obtains – the Word is said to assume a human soul, which in no possible world fails to be a human person.

Abstract Nature Model

In the previous section we argued that given CD, it is not possible to outline a concrete nature incarnation without falling into Nestorianism. In this section, we outline a Cartesian abstract nature incarnation in an attempt to show that the Cartesian abstract model has the metaphysical resources to avoid Nestorianism and Apollinarianism. Swinburne describes an abstract nature account of the incarnation that avoids the latter heresy,

Certainly a divine individual can become human. He would do this by acquiring a human body (joining his Soul to an unowned human body), acting, acquiring beliefs, sensations, and desires through it. Remaining divine, he would have become human by acquiring an extension to his normal modes of operation. A divine individual who became incarnate in Christ in this way would, I suggest, have satisfied the Chalcedonian definition of being one individual with both a divine and a human nature, on a not unreasonable interpretation of the latter.[41]

Recall that Apollinarianism is the heresy that Christ has an incomplete human nature, the place of the 'reasonable soul' usurped by the Word. However, this abstract nature version of the incarnation implies that Christ has the requisite mental life to facilitate being 'fully human' despite the absence of a distinct human soul.[42] We can gain some insight into the abstract nature model from the observations of John McGuckin. On McGuckin's reading of Apollinaris, the Word does not need to assume a human soul in addition to a human body at the incarnation (in order to become fully human) because the Word of God is the archetype of the image of God. The 'nous' or rational soul ennobles the human being, giving him or her the quality of being made God's image.[43]

The Apollinarian heresy comes from the assumption that if Christ does not have a rational soul, then he is not complete in his humanity. But on McGuckin's interpretation of the incarnation, a human soul distinct from the Word is not necessary for Christ's full

---

[40] Richard Swinburne, *The Christian God*, p. 215.

[41] Richard Swinburne, *The Christian God*, p. 196.

[42] Chalcedon also declared that Christ had a 'reasonable soul' and by this it seems to have meant an acquired 'human soul'. But the Council could not have meant by this that there were in Christ both a divine and a human soul … . For that would have been to say that Christ was two individuals, a doctrine to which Chalcedon was greatly opposed. Rather in the affirmation that Christ had a 'reasonable soul', 'soul' is to be understood as saying that Christ had a human way of thinking and acting, as well as his divine way. Richard Swinburne, *The Christian God*, pp. 196–7.

[43] John Anthony McGuckin, *St. Cyril of Alexandria: The Christological Controversy: Its History, Theology and Texts* (New York: St. Vladimir's Seminary Press 2004), p. 180.

humanity since the pre-incarnate Word already possesses all the properties required to be a human person. Therefore, in the incarnation, there is no deficiency in Christ's humanity. Since Word is the archetype of all souls, all that the Word required to become incarnate was a human body.[44] We can flesh out the abstract nature view with the relational version of Cartesianism. On such an account the Word assumes a human nature by becoming embodied – the Word assumes the necessary and sufficient causal relations to a human body and assumes human nature without falling into Apollinarianism. Nestorianism is also avoided since no soul or distinct person is assumed in the incarnation.

There is however, one theological heresy that remains on the abstract CD incarnation. It seems that there is only space for one will on the abstract nature view. The orthodox view known as dyothelitism is that Christ had two wills, one human and one divine.[45] In an abstract nature incarnation, the Word becomes human by assuming the property of a human soul in addition to its pre-existing properties of being a divine soul. The Word already has all the properties necessary for being a human soul since he is the prototype of all human souls and to become incarnate all that is required is that he becomes embodied. This model does not appear to have the 'space' for another will. But in order for Christ to be fully human, he needs a human will.

In a bid to avoid monothelitism, Alvin Plantinga predicates two distinct properties of the Word, which are 'having the nature of a human will' and 'having the nature of a divine will'.[46] Crisp has objected to this move arguing that it simply means that the Word has a divine will *qua* his divine nature and a human will *qua* his human nature – this, according to Crisp is insufficient as there are not two distinct wills. It is similar to attributing two wills to Clark Kent, one that belongs to Kent *qua* Kent and another belonging to Superman *qua* Superman.[47]

An alternate analogy has been provided by Thomas Morris who explains the two-wills doctrine without the need to posit an entity separate from the Word in Christ. Morris uses the analogy of a computer program that exhibits an asymmetrical relationship between the two spheres of operation. Morris writes:

> Think, for example, of two computer programs or informational systems, one containing but not contained by the other. The divine mind had full and direct access to the earthly, human experience resulting from the Incarnation, but the earthly consciousness did not have such full and direct access to the content of the overarching

---

[44] William Lane Craig and J.P. Moreland also defend this view of the incarnation. 'In assuming a hominid body, he brought to it all that was necessary for a *complete* human nature. Christ the one self-conscious subject who is the Logos possessed divine and human natures that were both complete [my emphasis].' William Lane Craig and J.P. Moreland, *Philosophical Foundations for a Christian Worldview* (Downers Grove, IL.: IVP, 2003), p. 609. The Word eternally possesses the properties of being human since 'Human beings do not bear God's image in virtue of their animal bodies [because of the Imago Dei] … Rather in being persons they uniquely reflect God's nature … Thus God already possesses the properties sufficient for human personhood even prior to the Incarnation.' Ibid., p. 609.

[45] The third Council of Constantinople refuted the heresy of monothelitism which held that Christ only had a single, divine will. See Henry R. Percival (ed.), *The Seven Ecumenical Councils of the Undivided Church* (Oxford: James Parker and Company, 1899), pp. 325–53. Due to considerations of space, we do not address the viability of monotheism but for a compelling treatment of the issue see Jordan Wessling, 'Christology and Conciliar Authority: On the Viability of Monothelitism for Protestant Theology' in Oliver Crisp and Fred Sanders (eds), *Christology, Ancient and Modern: Explorations in Constructive Dogmatics* (Michigan: Zondervan, 2013), pp. 151–70.

[46] Alvin Plantinga, 'On Heresy, Mind and Truth', *Faith and Philosophy*, 16/2 (1999): 268–76.

[47] Oliver Crisp, *Divinity and Humanity*, p. 60.

omniscience proper to the Logos, but only such access, on occasion, as the divine mind allowed it to have.[48]

Therefore, on an abstract view of the incarnation, we can say that the Word takes on a human will in virtue of taking on the properties of becoming a human soul. The relation between the human will and divine will are attributed to the human mind and divine mind of Christ, respectively.[49]

Perhaps the additional human will can be thought of as his divine mind dividing, as in the case of commissurotomy.[50] In commissurotomy cases, there is a sense in which a single person apparently possesses two distinct streams of consciousness.[51]

If Christ's human mind is a subsystem of his divine mind and the result is two separate spheres of consciousness which entails two distinct wills, then one could make the case that we do have dyothelitism in an abstract nature incarnation. As in the case of commissurotomy, the left and right hemispheres belong to the same person, but there appear to be two spheres of comprehension and action.

Parting Thoughts

In this chapter it was argued that if one holds a Cartesian view of human nature, a concrete nature incarnation entails Nestorianism. This is because a Cartesian soul is a person *simpliciter* and in a concrete nature incarnation, the Word assumes a human nature in virtue of a Cartesian soul.[52] In doing so he takes on a distinct person on both *simpliciter* and the relational versions of CD. This problem can be avoided if we take the human nature assumed in the incarnation to be abstract – in doing so it was also argued that it is possible to sidestep Apollinarianism. Therefore the abstract nature view of human nature is preferable with respect to Cartesian construals of the incarnation. Although more work is needed to explain how the Word might be able to divide his consciousness in order to avoid monothelitism for a Cartesian abstract nature incarnation, we hope to have shown that CD is a promising candidate for an orthodox theological anthropology.[53]

---

[48]   Thomas Morris, *The Logic of God Incarnate*, p. 103.

[49]   Similarly, Swinburne writes, 'his divine knowledge system will inevitably include the knowledge that his human system contains the beliefs that it does; and it will include those among the latter which are true. The separation of belief systems would be a voluntary act, knowledge of which was part of the divine-knowledge system but not of the human-knowledge system. We thus get a picture of a divine consciousness and a human consciousness of God incarnate, the former including the latter but not conversely.' Richard Swinburne, *The Christian God*, p. 202.

[50]   In neurosurgery this is the procedure that separates the hemispheres of the brain and prevents them from communicating with one another.

[51]   Thomas Morris, *The Logic of God Incarnate*, p. 158.

[52]   Even if a soul is not necessarily a *human* person on the relational view, a soul is still a person *simpliciter*.

[53]   My thanks to Oliver Crisp, Joshua Farris, Stewart Goetz, Stuart Judge, Rebekah Yeoh, and especially Jonathan Loose for invaluable feedback, comments and criticisms on earlier drafts of this chapter. Any errors that may remain are my own, due to my merely human nature.

Index

The Abolition of Man (Lewis) 126
Abraham, William J. 2
Acacius 202
Adam
　the Fall 200, 209, 223, 240, 250, 271, 297
　hylomorphism 192, 194–5
　imago Dei 196, 223 *see also imago Dei*
　incompleteness 196–7, 200–201
　link to animals 54
　mikros kosmos 192, 194–5
adoption, divine 281, 282–3, 304
Against Celsus (Origen) 187–8
Alexandrians 193–4, 308–9, 322, 355
　Clement of Alexandria 186–7, 193–4, 197,
　　199, 335
　Origen 187–8, 195, 196–7, 200, 211, 283, 348
Alston, William P. 82–3, 87
analytic theology 2–3
Analytic Theology (Rea and Crisp, eds.) 2
Anderson, Pamela Sue 81, 84, 86, 87–8
Anderson, Ray 15, 19
angels 221, 263, 265, 269, 270
animalism 357–8
animals *see* non-humans
Anselm of Canterbury 253, 297, 335
Anselmian revival 86
Apollinarianism 333–4, 334–6, 337, 365–6, 367
Aquinas, Thomas
　Arian dispute 345
　bodily resurrection 122, 123, 124
　body–soul relation 36, 119
　death 113
　dualism 153
　embodiment 358
　grace 239
　human souls 117–18, 119
　imago Dei 170
　the Incarnation 348, 349, 352, 354, 357, 363
　intellect of Christ 349
　interim existence 122, 123, 299
　knowledge of God 70
　Platonism 356
　substantial forms 115, 116
　virtues 63

Arian dispute 265–6, 267, 270
Aristotle
　energeia 271
　form and matter 36, 114, 117, 264
　life 113
　souls 185, 262, 347, 352
　universals and particulars 263–4
　unmoved mover 269
Arminianism 253–4
art 52–3
artificial intelligence 58, 61, 64
Asimov, Isaac 179
Athanasian Creed 324, 340
Athanasius 193, 199–200, 218, 265–6, 267, 270,
　284, 335
Atran, Scott 70
attachment styles 100–101
Augustine
　ADAM 195
　Adam and Eve's incompleteness 200
　called and chosen 254–5
　embodiment 358
　free will 242, 251, 252
　glory, defining 321
　grace 239, 239–40, 240, 254–5
　imago Dei 26, 165, 166, 198, 199, 208, 215
　original sin 202, 239, 240
　salvation 208
　self-knowledge 66
　souls 132–3, 165
　traducianism 152
　women 26

Baar, Bernard 66
Baker, Lynne Rudder 67, 109, 110, 120, 236–7, 350
baptism 194, 211, 212, 216, 272, 282, 288
Barnes, Gordon 116
Barnett, David 126, 132
Barrett, Justin 70, 71
Barth, Karl
　Christological anthropology 18–19
　　interdisciplinary dialogue 23–4
　　issues of concern 24–6
　　methodology 21–2

"moments" 20–21
    theological explanation 19–20
Christ's death 342
doctrine of election 19, 24–5
imago Dei 26
influence on von Balthasar 213
knowing God 310
Basil of Caesarea 199, 271, 273–4
Bavinck, Herman 220
beauty 204, 322
Bering, Jesse 70, 125
Bicentennial Man argument 360–62
Big Bang cosmology 38
Blackwell, Ben 173
Bloom, Paul 70, 126
bodily resurrection
    in Aquinas 122
    in Aristotelian hylomorphism 122–4
    biblical emphasis 29, 34, 121
    constitution account 109–12
    identity 135–6, 160
    in Lewis 136–7
    in Paul's letters 300
    physicalism approach 103–9, 112
    properties 300–301
    through Christ's 284
body, human
    in Christian tradition 277–9
    as object of redemption 280–83
    patristic views 308
    suffering 286–9
    see also bodily resurrection; body–soul
        relation; embodiment
Body of Christ 177–8, 207, 209, 212, 213, 214,
    283–4
body–soul relation
    in Adam 194–5
    dualism *see* dualism; monism–dualism
        debate
    in Edwards 144–7
    in Gnosticism 195–6
    in Greek philosophy 195, 196, 316
    history of thought 127
    hylomorphism *see* hylomorphism,
        Aristotelian; hylomorphism,
        Christological; hylomorphism, patristic
    in Maximus 308, 309
    monism *see* monism; monism–dualism
        debate
    relational view 356–7
    in scripture 29–35
    simpliciter view 356, 357–9
    spatial relationship 177
    theosis 316
The Book of Common Prayer 321

bounded rationality 62
Bourgeois, Henri 280
Boyer, Pascal 69–70
brain damage 154
brain sciences
    human nature 75
    human uniqueness 75
    imago Dei 75–6
    mental causation 74
    monism–dualism debate 91–2
    and religious experience 73, 76–9 *see also*
        cognitive sciences; Complex Emergent
        Developmental Linguistic Relational
        Neurophysiologicalism (CEDLRN)
brains
    animalism 357
    creationism 153, 153–4, 155
    emergent dualism 127
    emergentism 152, 155–61
    humanization 119
    monism 40
    reductionism 151–2
    and souls 146
    see also brain sciences; cognitive
        sciences; Complex Emergent
        Developmental Linguistic Relational
        Neurophysiologicalism (CEDLRN)
Broks, Paul 126
Brown, Peter 278
Brown, Warren 68
Buller, David 60–61
Buss, David 60

Calvin, John
    free will 251–2, 253
    imago Dei 170, 218, 219, 220
    knowledge of God 70
    souls 183, 186
    substance dualism 356
Cambridge Platonists 86, 322
Cappadocians 199, 266
Cassian, John 201
Catechism of the Catholic Church 74, 219, 223
causal closure, doctrine of 156, 157–8
causation 122, 153, 156, 157–8, 236, 239, 247,
    248–9, 346
Chalcedonian Christology 39, 306, 308, 334, 336,
    337, 345, 365
Chalmers, David 59, 65
character development 63–4
Christ *see* Jesus Christ
Christological anthropology 15
    Barth's 18–19
        interdisciplinary dialogue 23–4
        issues of concern 24–6

methodology 21–2
  "moments" 20–21
  theological explanation 19–20
  criticisms 16–18
  imago Dei 223–9
Clark, Andy 59
Clarke, Norris 195
Clement of Alexandria 186–7, 193–4, 197, 199, 335
Climacus, John 202
cognitive neuroscience 60
cognitive science of religion (CSR) 69–71
cognitive sciences 57
  cognitive neuroscience 60
  cognitive science of religion (CSR) 69–71
  computationalism 58–9
  connectionism 59
  consciousness 58–9, 65–8
  evolutionary psychology 60–61
  extended cognition 59–60
  as field of research 57–61
  functional decomposition 58–9
  mental representations 58
  the self 65
  soul, rejection of 65
  and theological anthropology 61–4
  see also brain sciences
compatibilism 256–7
  assumptions and cautions 246–8
  causation 40
  costs and benefits 248–54
  grace 254–6
  overview 236–7, 245–6
  status corruptionis 238–9, 241
  status gloriae 242
Complex Emergent Developmental Linguistic
    Relational Neurophysiologicalism
    (CEDLRN) 92, 101
  complexity 93–4
  development 96–7
  emergence 94–5
  linguistics 97–8
  neurophysiologicalism 92–3
  relationality 99–101
compounds 113, 114–15, 116
computationalism 58–9
connectionism 59
consciousness
  in animals 46, 75
  consciousness studies 58–9, 65–8
  created minds 144
  creationism 153, 154
  defining 65
  in Edwards 141–2, 143, 144
  emergentism 157, 159

functionalist theories 66
human uniqueness 51
material existence in 141–2, 143
representational theories 65–6
vs the self 66
constitution account 109–12
Conway, Anne 86
Corcoran, Kevin 2, 68
corruptibility 268, 269, 273
Cortez, Marc 166–7, 234
Council of Orange 240–41
Council of Trent 211–12, 216, 239, 240
Craig, William Lane 332–3, 334–5, 366
Cranefield, Paul 186
creation
  Aristotelian hylomorphism 119–20
  and evolution 45–6
  of humans 29–30, 54, 119–20, 180–83, 191,
      194–5, 200 *see also imago Dei*
  souls 152, 180–83
creationism 152, 153–5, 156, 160, 161, 262–9
Crisp, Oliver 2, 143–4, 147, 150, 333–4, 337,
    359–60, 366
Critchley, H.D. 78
the cross 286–7, 290–91, 297
Cunningham, David 53–4
Cur Deus Homo (Anselm) 335
Curtis, Susan 97
Cyril of Alexandria 290
Cyril of Jerusalem 194, 277

Damasio, Antonio 62, 66
Darwin, Charles 47
Davidson, Donald 320
De Anima (Aristotle) 113, 114, 347, 352
De Trinitate (Augustine) 198
Deacon, Terrence 98
Deane-Drummond, Celia 53
death
  Christ's 34, 286, 288, 290–91, 297, 339–42, 357
  fear of 297, 325–6
  Kitcher's view 325–6
  scriptural teaching 32–5, 341
  wages of sin 271
  see also bodily resurrection; body–soul
      relation; interim existence; resurrection
      of the dead
Dediu, Dan 52
deification *see* theosis/deification
Deism 37
Descartes, René 36, 127, 133–4, 153, 154, 295,
    356 *see also* the Incarnation, Cartesian
    approach
determinism 39, 40, 236, 237, 242, 245, 246
development, human 96–7

Dionysius the Areopagite 199
diversity-in-unity 31
"divine summons" 20
Docetism 359–60, 362
Dorotheus of Gaza 203–4
dualism
    and brain sciences 91
    Cartesian 127, 133–4, 153, 355–9
    Chalcedonian Christology 39
    and cognitive sciences 65, 68
    as common belief 125–6, 129–30, 135
    compound substance dualism 169
    creationism 153–5
    defining 125, 295
    diversity-in-unity 31–2, 39–40
    dual natures of Jesus 332–6
    ecumenical position 35–6, 39–40, 91, 135
    emergent 36, 41, 127
    expanded 295, 296
    general beliefs 27
    history of thought 127
    Homeric tradition 130
    and hylomorphism 121
    implications 135–7
    interim existence 298
    philosophical 132–5
    and scripture 128–32
    Thomistic 153
    see also monism–dualism debate
Dunn, James 341, 342
dynamic systems theory 94–5
dyothelitism 366, 367
dysnarrativia 98

Ecstatic Morality and Sexual Politics (McAleer) 289
Edwards, Jonathan
    body–soul relation 144–5
        communication between 146–7
        differences between 145
        union of 146
    compatibilism 247, 253–4
    ontology 139–40
        applications 148–9
        concerns 149–50
        human person 148
        immaterial world 143–4
        material world 141–3
        theocentrism 140–41
Eleatics 265
election 19, 20, 24–5, 54–6, 283
embodiment 59, 93, 294–6 *see also* dualism;
    monism; monism–dualism debate; the
    Incarnation
emergence 91, 94–5, 111
emergent dualism 36, 41, 127

emergent material persons (EMPs) theory
    158–9
emergentism 38, 40, 152, 155–61
emotions 62–3
energeiai 271–4
Enns, Peter 225
epiphenomenalism 157
Ereshefsky, Marc 48
Erickson, Millard 334
eschatology, biblical 32–5
Eve 200, 250, 251, 297
evolutionary biology 45, 56
    biological essentialism 48–9
    and Christological *imago Dei* 227–8
    and creationism 154–5
    and emergentism 155–6
    evolutionary continuity 46–8
    "human nature" problem 49
    human uniqueness 50–53
    humans and animals 46–8
    scientific acceptance 46
    "species," defining 47–9
    theological acceptance 45–6
evolutionary psychology 60–61
extended cognition 59–60
"The extended mind" (Chalmers and Clark) 59

the Fall 200, 209–10, 216, 223, 250–54, 271, 297,
    308
Farris, Joshua 222
feminism 81–2
    critiques of traditional theological
        anthropology 82–4, 85–8, 319
    feminist theological anthropology 85
    redemptive suffering 288, 289
Fergusson, David 220–21
first-person perspective 110, 111–12, 350, 352,
    353
Fischer, John Martin 236
Flew, Antony 87
form 36, 113–14, 115–16 *see also* hylomorphism,
    Aristotelian; hylomorphism,
    Christological; hylomorphism, patristic
Forsythe, P.T. 290–91
Frankenberry, Nancy 82–4, 86
free will 244
    challenges to 261–2
    cognitive sciences 64
    compatibilism 236–7
    defining 236
    dualism 39
    Hylomorphic Creationism (HC) 262–9,
        274–5
    libertarianism 237
    monism 40

patristic views
    created corruptible 262–9
    raised incorruptible 270–74
reductionism 151–2
stages 235
in *status corruptionis* stage 239–41
in *status gloriae* stage 242–4
in *status integritatis* stage 237–9
The Freedom of the Will (Edwards) 253
Freeman, Walter 95
"From Image to Likeness" (Young) 202
frontier beings 195
Fudge, Edward 341

Gaine, Simon Francis 242
Gassendi, Pierre 186
Gasser, Georg 2
Gaudium et Spes 211, 212, 213, 216
Gell, Alfred 126
gender bias 82–3
ghosts 129–30, 132
glory
    and being human 325–7
    Christian tradition 321–2
    defining 321
    of God 22, 145, 321, 322
    of human dignity 322–4
    humans as reflectors 171, 234
    pagan tradition 321
Gnosticism 195–6
God
    all life through 30–31, 119
    aspatiality 269
    atemporality 269
    compatibilist affirmations 248–54
    creation in 140
    glory 22, 145, 321, 322
    goodness 238, 324
    grace *see* grace
    holistic pairing with world 85
    image of *see* imago Dei
    immateriality 39, 263, 269, 301
    immutability 269
    incarnation in Jesus *see* the Incarnation
    incorruptibility 261, 269
    knowledge of 70
    love 34, 85, 209, 214–15, 297, 302, 307
    as male 83
    omniscience 249
    only true substance 140–41
    oppositional pairing with world 83–4
    ordination of the universe 248
    seeing 300–301
    self-determination 19, 22
    and sin 249–51

timelessness 339–41
    will 253
God–human relationship
    Augustine's view 208
    election 55
    human uniqueness *see* imago Dei
    Irenaeus' view 209–10
    Luther's view 210–11
    purpose of existence 302
    repairing 271 *see also* redemption; salvation
    Second Vatican Council 211–13
    true humanity 24
    von Balthasar's view 213–15
    see also theosis/deification
God Incarnate (Crisp) 2
goodness
    of being human 320, 320–21
    of God 238, 324
grace
    co-operation with 216, 239–41
    compatibilist understanding 254–6
    deification 307, 308, 310
    love of God 297
    perfection of nature 170
    salvation through 209, 210, 215, 239, 240–41
Gregory of Nazianzus 194–5, 199, 336, 359
Gregory of Nyssa 25, 270
Gregory of Palamas 303
guilt 151, 296–7, 302

"A Hanging" (Orwell) 320–21
Harrison, Victoria 81
Hartmann, Heidi 83
Heidegger, Martin 47
Helm, Paul 238, 340
Herbert, George 289
Hick, John 296
Hobbes, Thomas 37–8
Hoekema, Anthony 217, 220
Holy Spirit
    anointment 239
    conception of Christ 359, 360, 361
    deification 310
    God–human relationship 282, 315, 316
    indwelling 262, 273, 281
    leading the church 35
    restoring humans 171, 176, 219, 223, 225, 226,
        273–4
    Trinity 310, 311–12, 314
Homer 130, 321
hominins, non-human 52–3
homoousion 310
Hudson, Hud 337
human behavior 58, 62
human constitution 316

human dignity 322–4
human properties 293–4, 299, 356–7
human uniqueness
    and brain sciences 75
    and cognitive sciences 62, 68
    as doctrine 74
    election 54–6
    extending/rejecting *imago Dei* 52–4
    as *imago Dei* 50–52, 173, 179, 184, 221–2 *see also imago Dei*
    souls 179
humanization 119–20
Hume, David 37, 63, 153
Humphrey, Nicholas 126
Hylomorphic Creationism (HC) 262–9, 274–5
hylomorphism, Aristotelian 113
    applications
        creation and humanization 119–20
        moral responsibility and moral status 120–21
        resurrection of the dead 121–4
    compounds 114–15
    disputed issues
        human souls 116–18
        number of substantial forms 115–16
    form 113–14
    human souls 347, 352–3
    matter 114
hylomorphism, Christological 345–6, 353–4
    two natures of Christ 346–9
    two subjects 349–53
hylomorphism, patristic 262–3
    Arian dispute 265
    energeiai 271–4
    free will 268–9
    incorruptible future world 270–74
    matter 264–6
    mutation 265–6
    rationale 266–8
    realism 263–4
hypostatic union 224–5, 228, 277, 279, 303, 306, 309, 310, 315

I, Robot (Asimov) 179
idealism 32, 37
identity
    Christocentric 207, 210–11, 213, 214
    diachronic 123–4, 149–50
    first-person perspective 350–51
    pre-/post-resurrection 67
        in constitution account 111–12
        in dualism 135–7, 298
        in emergent dualism 160–61
        in hylomorphism 121–4
        in monism 40–41

    spatiotemporal gaps 108–9
    relationship with God 315–16
imago Christi 176–7
imago Dei
    approaches to 234
    and brain sciences 75–6
    characteristics 166–7
    Christ-participatory view 165, 167–8, 178
        historic situation 169
        illustration 170, 171–2
        scripture references 172–5
        stronger image 176
        weaker image 175–6
    Christological model 217–18, 228–9
        argument for 223–6
        objections to 226–8
    as doctrine 74
    dual-functionality 191–2, 204–5
    dualism 39
    ecclesial–narrative model 207, 215–16
        Augustine 208
        Balthasar 213–15
        Irenaeus of Lyons 209–10
        Luther 210–11
        Second Vatican Council 211–13
    election 54–6
    fulfillment 199–201
    heaven and earth function 193–7
    and human nature 49–50
    and human souls 179–80
    human uniqueness 50–52, 52–4, 184
    humans as gods 199–201
    and likeness of God 196–7, 200–201, 209, 217, 307, 308–9
    location 193–4
    maturation of humans 200–201
    monism 40
    multifaceted approach 234
    Near Eastern background 54–5, 225
    and non-humans 53
    patristic views 202–4
        Athanasius 193, 199–200
        Augustine 198, 200, 202, 208
        Basil the Great 199
        Cappadocians 199
        Clement of Alexandria 193–4, 199
        Cyril of Jerusalem 194
        desert fathers 202–4
        Dionysis the Areopagite 199
        Gnosticism 195–6
        Gregory of Nazianzus 194–5
        Irenaeus of Lyons 196, 200–201, 209–10
        Origen 195, 196–7
        Philo of Alexandria 193
        Platonism 195–6

post-Vatican II views 213–15
Reformation views 210–11
relational approach 220–23
relationality 197–9
scripture references 55, 191–2
Second Vatican Council 211–13
and souls 185–90
substantive soul model 165–6, 168–9, 178,
   218–19
  Christology 177–8
  historic situation 169–70
  illustration 171–2
  imago Christi 176–7
  problems with 219–20
  scripture references 172–5
  teology 177
immortality 304
  of the soul 33, 185, 194, 295–6, 299, 308
the Incarnation
  abstract view 332, 362, 365–7
  Alexandrian approach 355
  Apollinarianism 333–4, 334–6, 365–6, 367
  archetypal human being 209, 225–6
  Bicentennial Man argument 360–62
  Cartesian approach 355, 362, 367
    abstract nature model 365–7
    concrete nature models 363–5
    human nature 355–9
    relational souls 359–62
  Chalcedonian definition 336–7, 345
  concrete view 332, 337–8, 362, 363–5
  dualist views 135, 332–3
  Edwards, lack of discussion in 149
  hylomorphic approach 345–6, 353–4
    two natures of Christ 346–9
    two subjects 349–53
  materialist approach 331–2, 336–9, 343
    death of Christ 339–42
    two natures of Christ 332–6
  Nestorianism 334, 366, 367
  participation in God 310–11, 312, 315–16
  perfection 205
  permanent 301–2
  redemptive power *see* redemption
  relational view 356–7
  salvation through 270, 271, 290–91, 297
  simpliciter view 356, 357–9
  timelessness 340
  two natures 272, 332–6, 346–9
  uniqueness 18–19
  wills 366–7
incompatibilism 237, 238
incorruptibility
  future hope of 270–74, 275
  of God 261, 268, 269

indeterminism 245, 247, 249
injustice 85–6
Institutes (Cassian) 201
intellect 62, 64, 347, 349–50, 354
interdisciplinary dialogue 23–4
interim existence
  Aquinas' view 123
  Cartesian approach 357
  constitution account 110–11
  dualism 32, 36, 39, 295–6
  emergent dualism 160
  human properties 299
  hylomorphism 263
  mental abilities 299
  monism 32, 37–8, 40–41
  New Testament references 33–5
  Old Testament references 33
  Second Temple Judaism 33
  temporary disembodiment theory 298–9
  temporary nonexistence theory 298
Irenaeus of Lyons 25, 196, 200–201, 209–10, 214,
   216, 217–18, 310

James, William 73, 193
Jaworski, William 124
Jenson, Robert 62, 221–2
Jesus Christ
  Arian dispute 265–6, 270
  Chalcedonian Christology 39
  Crucifixion 286–7
  death 34, 297, 339–42, 357
  descent into underworld 214
  dual nature 15, 306, 310, 332–6 *see also*
    hylomorphism, Christological
  God-for-us 19
  humanity *see* Christological anthropology
  as *imago Dei* 167, 168, 197, 212, 217–18, 222–9
  immutability 265–6
  incarnation of God *see* the Incarnation
  redemption through *see* redemption
  Resurrection 34, 39, 40, 110, 129, 284, 297,
    300
  salvation through *see* salvation
  as Second Adam 223
  self-knowledge 349–50, 353–4
  as sin bearer 341
  sinlessness 17, 19–20, 223, 225, 294, 333
  soul 351–2, 353
  substantial form 115–16
  suffering 287–8
  timelessness 339–41
  virginal conception 359–62
John of Damascus 263
John Paul II 46, 281, 286, 289
Johnson, Elizabeth 83

Johnson, Samuel 180
Johnston, Mark 104–7
Judge-Becker, Emilie 319

Kant, Immanuel 63, 322–3
Kelemen, Deborah 70
Kelly, J.N.D. 355
Kevin of Glendalough 202–3
Kim, Jaegwon 157
Kitcher, Philip 325–7

language-use 49, 52, 53, 58, 97–8, 110
Lee, Sang Hyun 143, 148
Leftow, Brian 332, 338, 363, 364
Leibniz, Gottfried Wilhelm 159
Levinas, Emmanuel 287
Levinson, Stephen C. 52
Lewis, C.S.
    bodily resurrection 136, 136–7
    common sense 126
    dualism 127
    ghosts 129
    human glory 325
    the Incarnation 135
    praise 324
    A Preface to Paradise Lost 128
    scripture 128–9
    souls 126, 137
libertarianism 237, 242–3, 245, 252, 257
Libet, Benjamin 64
life everlasting 34–5, 36, 42, 251, 297, 302, 326
likeness of God 54, 55, 56, 192, 217, 307, 308–9
    growing towards 196–7, 200–201, 208, 209,
        212
Locke, John 37, 246, 350–51
Logos 168, 173, 176, 197 see also Jesus Christ; the
    Incarnation
logos 305, 306, 307, 308, 309, 316
Loke, Andrew 340
love 288–9
    God's 34, 85, 209, 214–15, 297, 302, 307, 312
    humans' 31, 192, 198, 222, 322, 324, 326–7
Lubac, Henri de 284
Lumen Gentium 211, 212, 212–13, 216
Luther, Martin 210–11, 216, 278–9

Machen, Greshen 220
Mackie, J.L. 250
Marr, David 58
Mary, Mother of God 284–6, 359
materialism
    and Christology
        Christ's death 339–42
        the Incarnation 331–2, 336–9
    Edwards' view 139

eliminative 157
history 37–8
vs immaterialism 27–8
see also physicalism
matter
    in Aquinas 36, 122
    in Aristotelian philosophy 114
    continuity 122–3
    in Edwards 141–3
    explanations from 118
    patristic understanding 264–5
    quantum mechanics 153
    and sensation 136–7
    see also hylomorphism, Aristotelian;
        hylomorphism, Christological;
        hylomorphism, patristic
Maximus the Confessor 25, 277, 305–9, 314–15,
    316
McAleer, G.J. 289
McClymond, Michael 141
McDermott, Gerald 141
McFague, Sallie 85
McGuckin, John 196, 365–6
McLeod Harrison, Mark 224
meaning making 96–7
Meditations (Descartes) 133–4
Mele, Alfred 64
Melzoff, Andrew 99
Merricks, Trenton 339, 357, 358
Mersch, Emile 283–4
Metaphysics XII (Aristotle) 269
Metzinger, Thomas 67
Meyendorff, John 308
Miller, Christian 64
Minimal Counterintuitiveness theory 69–70
mitosis 361–2
Miyakawa, Teihei 77–8
monism
    biblical 41–2
    Christology 40
    defining 27
    diversity-in-unity 31–2
    eschatologies 40–41
    free will 40
    and holism 32
    image of God 40
    immaterialism vs materialism 27
    psychophysical 37–8, 40
    scriptural understanding 30
    and theistic naturalism 40–41
    see also monism–dualism debate
monism–dualism debate
    current positions 42
        Biblical monism 41–2
        historic dualism-in-unity 39–40

theistic naturalism and monism 40–41
historical development 38–9
   historical ecumenical position 35–6
   idealism 37
   materialism 37–8
   modern Christianity 37–8
   naturalism 37
   realism 37
overview 27–8
scripture, use of 28–9, 35
   eschatology 32–5
   God's composition of human beings
      29–30
   unity of body and soul 30–32
see also dualism; monism
monophysitism 272, 290
moral agency 120, 323
moral cognition 63
moral responsibility 64, 67, 120, 149, 236
moral status 120–21
Moreland, J.P. 155, 169, 222, 334–5, 366
Moritz, Joshua 54–6
Morris, Thomas V. 351, 366–7
mortification 212
Murphy, Nancey 67–8

Nagel, Thomas 58, 65
narrative 98, 100–101
Neanderthals 52–3
Nelson, Kevin 73
Neoplatonism 203, 204
nephesh 29, 31, 33, 129, 180, 182–3, 184, 185, 342
nervous system 152, 155, 160, 357 *see also*
   brain sciences; Complex Emergent
   Developmental Linguistic Relational
   Neurophysiologicalism (CEDLRN)
neshama 29–30
Nestorianism 334, 337, 364–5, 366, 367
neurophysiologicalism 92–3 *see also* Complex
   Emergent Developmental Linguistic
   Relational Neurophysiologicalism
   (CEDLRN)
neuroscience 51, 59, 91 *see also* brain sciences;
   cognitive sciences; Complex Emergent
   Developmental Linguistic Relational
   Neurophysiologicalism (CEDLRN)
A New Climate for Theology (McFague) 85
Nicene Creed 266, 335
non-humans
   consciousness 46, 75, 154
   creation 181–2, 183, 184, 191
   evolutionary link to humans 47–8
   hominins 52–3
   imago Dei 53
   interaction with God 29, 221

language-use 97–8
souls 154–5, 186, 356

O'Connor, Timothy 158
The Odyssey (Homer) 130
Ogata, Akira 77–8
"On Atoms" (Edwards) 141
"On Being" (Edwards) 140, 144
On the Creation of the World (Philo) 188–9
On the Soul (Tertullian) 187
onto-relations 313–14
Openness Theism 250
Origen 187–8, 195, 196–7, 200, 211, 283, 348
original justice 239
original sin 63, 144–5, 152, 202, 208, 240, 241, 294
Orwell, George 320–21

paleoanthropology 51–2, 53
panentheism 139–40, 148
Pannenberg, Wolfhart 46, 50, 50–51, 62, 219, 226
patriarchy 81, 82, 83–4, 85, 86, 319
Pelagianism 215, 239–41, 256
Pelikan, Jaroslov 199
Personal Identity and the Resurrection (Gasser,
      ed.) 2
personhood
   in Aristotelian hylomorphism 121
   Cartesian approach 356
   CEDLRN model *see* Complex Emergent
      Developmental Linguistic Relational
      Neurophysiologicalism (CEDLRN)
   of Christ 334–5, 351
   as communicative event 148
   human beings–human persons dualism
      120–21
   human body 280
   Locke's definition 350–51
   of Trinity 313–14
   women's 83
   see also identity
Persons (van Inwagen and Zimmerman, eds.) 2
Peterson, Gregory 53, 63
Philo of Alexandria 33, 188–9, 193
philosophy of biology 48
philosophy of mind 59, 319, 320–21
physicalism
   bodily resurrection 112
      constitution account 109–12
      mainstream physicalism 103–9
   body–soul relation 41
   defining 111
   mental properties 157
   personhood 67–8, 92
   souls 38
Pinker, Steven 60

Plantinga, Alvin
    evolutionary biology 155
    free will 238, 250
    good and evil 239
    the Incarnation 331–2, 366
    incarnation and atonement 251
    materialism 109
    patriarchy 82–3
Plato/Platonism
    the body 187
    Cambridge Platonists 86, 322
    dualism 36, 129–32, 295, 356
    imago Dei 196, 199
    immortality of the soul 33, 185
    Neoplatonism 203, 204
    souls 187, 187–8, 189, 191
    two worlds 195, 203
Plotinus 195, 203
positive psychology 63–4
praise 321, 324
prayer 221–2, 322
A Preface to Paradise Lost (Lewis) 128
Price, H.H. 295–6, 299
projectivism 86

quantum mechanics 153, 157

Rabin, John 76–7
Rachels, James 323
Radford Ruether, Rosemary 288
Rahner, Karl 50, 62, 285–6, 350
Rashi 183
rationalism, Christian 37
rationality 51, 62, 87, 88, 121, 188, 219–20
Ratzinger, Joseph 285, 290
Rauser, Randall 2
Rea, Michael 2, 353
realism 263–4
reason 62
The Recalcitrant Imago Dei (Moreland) 169
redemption
    defining 280
    doctrine of deification 304
    of human body
        body as object of redemption 280–83
        Christian tradition 277–9
        Mary's role 284–6
        suffering 286–9
    human need 296
    the Incarnation 311
    incarnation vs cross 290–91
    resurrection of the dead 34, 300–301
    seeing God 300–301
    as union and participation 315–16
    see also salvation

reductionism 151–2, 156, 157
Reformation 210, 216
relationality 99–101, 192, 197–9, 215, 221, 222, 234
"Religion and Neurology" (James) 73
religious belief/experience 69–71, 73, 76–9
respect 74, 82, 212, 213
Resurrection of Christ 34, 39, 40, 110, 129, 284, 297, 300, 342
resurrection of the dead 298
    in Aristotelian hylomorphism 121–4
    in emergent dualism 160–61
    identity 135–6
    monism 32, 38, 40–41
    nature of 34
    New Testament references 33–5
    Old Testament references 29
    scriptural teaching 33–5, 297
    Second Temple Judaism 33
    soul, requirement for 135–7
    timing of 34
    see also bodily resurrection; interim existence
Rogers, Katherine 253
ruach 29–30, 31, 33

salvation
    in Augustine 208
    Christ's work 21
    by grace 239, 297
    from the Jews 283
    in Luther 210, 211
    in patristic hylomorphism 270–74
    theosis 303, 306–7, 315, 316
    see also redemption
Saver, Jeffrey 76–7
scientific worldview 37, 38, 40–41
scripture 28–9, 35–6, 37, 128–9 *see also* Index of Scripture References
Searle, John 58, 65
Second Vatican Council 211–13, 216
Secular Humanism (Kitcher) 325
Seebass, H. 182
self-consciousness 46, 65–8, 75, 110, 351
self-knowledge 74, 311, 312, 349–50, 353–4
Senor, Thomas 363–4
Shea, John 52
Sheol 30, 32, 33, 129
Sherwood, Polycarp 306–7
Shults, LeRon 184
Simeon Stylites 202
sin
    and the body 282
    and death 271, 304
    destruction through the cross 341–2
    entrance into world 251–4
    God's relationship to 249–51

and *imago Dei* 167, 199, 225, 234
   see also free will; original sin
Sober, Elliot 47
Socrates 191
Soskice, Janet 81
soteriology *see* salvation
Soul, Body and Survival (Corcoran, ed.) 2
Soul Dust (Humphrey) 126
souls
   in Aquinas 117–18, 119
   in Aristotle 185, 262, 347, 352
   in Augustine 132–3, 165
   and brains 146
   in Calvin 183, 186
   Christ's 351–2, 353
   in cognitive sciences 65
   at creation 152, 180–83
   in creationism 152, 153–5
   defining 126, 151, 180
   in emergentism 152, 155–6
   human uniqueness 179
   in hylomorphism 113–14, 116–18, 347, 352–3
   and *imago Dei see imago Dei*, substantive soul
      model
   immortality 33, 185, 194, 295–6, 299, 308
   in Lewis 126, 137
   Near Eastern background 185
   of non-humans 154–5, 186
   non-humans 154–5
   in physicalism 38
   Plato/Platonism 187, 187–8, 189, 191
   in reductionism 151–2
   relational 185–90, 359–62
   relationship to space 132–4
   and resurrection 135–7
   simpliciter view 356, 357–9
   simplicity and complexity 126–7
   see also body–soul relation; interim existence
spatiotemporal gaps 108–9
"species," defining 47–9
Spinoza, Baruch 38
stages of theological anthropology 233–5
Stanford Encyclopedia of Philosophy 82–4
"stern-mindedness" 201–2
Stone, Lawson 183, 185
story-telling 98
Stump, Eleonore 201–2, 348, 358, 364
suffering, human 287
Summa Contra Gentiles (Aquinas) 348, 354
Summa Theologiae (Aquinas) 349
Swinburne, Richard 82–3, 87, 177, 351–2, 364–5, 367

Tanner, Kathryn 165, 167–8
Te Velde, Rudi 235

telos 173, 194, 235, 314, 315
Temmet, Dainel 78
temporary disembodiment theory 298–9
temporary nonexistence theory 298
Tertullian 187
theistic naturalism 37, 38, 40–41, 71
Thelen, Esther 59
Theology as Epistemology (Rauser) 2
Theology of the Body (John Paul II) 286
theosis/deification 314–15, 317
   in Biblical doctrine 304–5
   creational *telos* 315
   human constitution 316
   in modern thought 309
      anthropology and participation
         313–14
      Trinity and participation 310–13
   overview 303–4
   in patristic thought 305–6
      energeia 273, 274
      and human constitution 307–9
      imago Dei 199
      soteriology as 306–7
   redemption 315–16
Third Council of Constantinople 349, 366
timelessness 339–41
Torrance, T.F. 18, 309–15
traducianism 152
trichotomy 31, 32
Trinity 198, 310–14, 315–16, 340
trinity within humans 198
tropos 305, 306, 307, 308, 309
twinning 119–20

uniformity of nature 37
unity of form doctrine 115–16
unity-of-consciousness argument 159
universalism 211

Valentinus 196
values 319, 320, 321
van Huyssteen, J. Wentzel 50, 51–2, 68, 70–71
van Inwagen, Peter 2, 103, 104, 107–8
Virgin Mary 284–6, 359
virtue 63–4
visual agnosia 154
von Balthasar, Hans Urs 213–15, 216, 322

Walker Bynum, Caroline 278
Wegner, Daniel 64
"The Weight of Glory" (Lewis) 325
Wesley, Charles 331
Westermann, Claus 54
Wildman, Esley 71

Willis, Thomas 186
The Works of Jonathan Edwards (Edwards) 140,
    141, 142, 143, 144, 145, 146, 147
worship 322–4
Wright, N.T. 128, 131–2

Young, Frances 202

Zimmerman, Dean 2, 108–9
Zizioulas, John 46
Zosimus 240

Index of
Scripture References

Genesis
  1-2 187, 188–90
  1 and 2 54
  1:12 182
  1:21 182, 183
  1:22 184
  1:24 182, 183
  1:26 192, 196, 198
  1:26-27 55, 172, 217, 220, 221
  1:26-28 184, 191–2
  1:27 179, 196
  1:28 55
  1:30 182, 183, 184
  1:31 200, 296
  2:5 285
  2:7 29, 30, 151, 180–83, 184
  2:15-16 55
  2:17 297
  2:19 181, 183
  3 220
  3:5 200
  3:6 251
  3:16 286
  3:19 181
  5:3 197
  6:17 181
  7:15 181–2
  7:21-22 182
  9:6 172, 197
  9:10 182
  37:35 33

Exodus, 33:20 301

Leviticus
  2:1 182
  4:2 182
  7:20 182
  26:13 195

Deuteronomy, 6:5 31

1 Samuel, 28 33

Job
  7 184
  19:25-27 301
  19:26 33
  32:8 181
  33:4 181

Psalms
  8 30
  8:4 293
  8:144 184
  11:7 301
  16:10 33
  19 45
  23:6 33
  27:7-8 301
  49:15 33
  82:6-7 304
  84:2 31
  90:3 181
  103:14 181
  104:29 181
  104:29-30 29
  146:4 181

Ecclesiastes
  3:18-21 181
  3:19-20 30
  9:1-10 30
  12:7 30, 33, 181

Isaiah
  14 33
  24:15 302
  26:19 33
  53:12 341
  54:5 280
  63:16 280

Ezekiel
  37 33
  37:1-10 29, 30

Daniel, 12:2 33

Matthew
 3:15 286
 5:8 282, 301
 5:17-20 286
 5:28 282
 5:48 286
 8:2-3 272
 8:14-15 272
 9:23-30 272
 10:28 34
 14:2 131
 14:26 34, 129
 15:8-20 282
 16:13-14 130–31
 17:1-9 272
 20:30-34 272
 23:25-28 282
 27:20 341

Mark
 1:27 131
 1:30 272
 1:40-42 272
 3:10 272
 5:41-42 272
 6:5 272
 6:49 34
 7:32-35 272
 8:22-25 272
 9:2-9 272
 10:18 273
 12:30 31

Luke
 1:46-47 31
 2:34-35 287
 4:40 272
 5:12-13 272
 7:12-15 272
 8:49-55 272
 9:28-36 272
 13:10-13 272
 20:50-51 272
 23:43 34, 130, 299
 24 300
 24:37 129
 24:37-39 34
 24:39-40 110

John
 1:29 297
 3:3 297
 4:22 283
 4:24 295, 301
 5:26 273

 6:54 34
 8:58 227
 9:1-9 272
 9:32 272
 10:15 341
 11:24 34
 11:25-26 34
 12:23-26 341
 20 300

Acts
 2:23-24 248
 2:27 342
 3:15 341
 12:15 129
 13:34-37 342
 23:6-8 33
 23:8 34
 27:37 188

Romans
 1:16 283
 1:21-32 282
 3:23 294
 3:24 297
 4:17-25 287
 5:9 297
 5:12 271
 5:12-19 223
 5:14 192, 197
 6:12 282
 6:23 271
 7:15 282
 7:17 282
 7:24 282
 8 304
 8:7 282
 8:11 297
 8:18-23 34
 8:19 283
 8:19-22 296
 8:21 283
 8:22 281
 8:23 281
 8:26 281
 8:29 197, 217
 8:29-30 167, 168
 8:38 282
 8:38-39 34
 9:3 288
 9:4 283
 10:13 282
 11:33 248
 11:33-36 287
 12:1-3 283

1 Corinthians
    1:17-18 297
    1:23 291
    1:30 291
    3:15-17 299
    6:11 297
    6:13 291
    6:19-20 299
    10:31 302
    11:1 16
    11:1-7 173
    11:7 172–3
    15 304
    15:3 341
    15:18 341
    15:20 34, 297
    15:22 107
    15:23 297
    15:24 282
    15:28 204
    15:35–54 34
    15:37-50 273
    15:42-44 121
    15:42-55 110
    15:50 300
    15:52 33

2 Corinthians
    3-4 304
    4:4 167, 168, 197, 212, 217
    4:10-11 287
    5:1-9 130
    5:6-8 33, 299
    5:6-10 130
    5:14 341
    5:17 297
    12:2-3 299
    12:2-4 33–4, 130
    12:7 287
    12:9-10 287

Galatians
    3:15-29 283
    4 304
    4:3-9 282
    5:19-21 282
    6:17 287

Ephesians
    1:10 209
    1:19 272
    2:2 272
    2:10 226
    2:12 283

2:18 312
3:7 272
4:24 226

Philippians
    1:20-22 33
    1:23 299
    1:29 288
    2 304
    3:10 288
    3:20-21 297
    3:21 288

Colossians
    1:12-16 197
    1:15 168, 174, 192, 197, 212, 217
    1:15-21 172
    1:16 174
    1:19 174
    1:20 297
    1:24 288
    1:29 272
    2:9-10 304
    2:12 272
    3:10 226

1 Thessalonians
    4:13-18 299
    4:14 297
    4:16 33
    5:23 31

Hebrews
    1:3 197, 217
    2:6-9 184
    4:15 223, 225, 294
    9:21-23 297
    12:14 301
    12:26 34

James, 3:9 173

1 Peter
    2:21 16
    3:19 34

2 Peter
    1:4 199, 273, 304
    1:16-18 272

1 John
    2:16 282
    3 304
    3:2 297, 301

Revelation
  6:9-11 34
  7 34
  20 34

21:2 300
21:4 300
22:3-4 300
22:4 301

#0142 - 251018 - C0 - 244/170/22 - PB - 9781138051560